THE PRELUDE
1799, 1805, 1850

AUTHORITATIVE TEXTS
CONTEXT AND RECEPTION
RECENT CRITICAL ESSAYS

WILLIAM WORDSWORTH

THE PRELUDE
1799, 1805, 1850

AUTHORITATIVE TEXTS
CONTEXT AND RECEPTION
RECENT CRITICAL ESSAYS

⇒⇒⇒⇐⇐⇐

JONATHAN WORDSWORTH
EXETER COLLEGE, OXFORD

M. H. ABRAMS
CORNELL UNIVERSITY

STEPHEN GILL
LINCOLN COLLEGE, OXFORD

W · W · NORTON & COMPANY
New York • *London*

ACKNOWLEDGMENTS

"The Idea of *The Prelude*" (revised) and "The Design of *The Prelude*: Wordsworth's Long Journey Home" (revised) from *Natural Supernaturalism*, by M. H. Abrams. Reprinted by permission of W. W. Norton & Company, Inc., New York, and Oxford University Press, London. Copyright © 1971 by W. W. Norton & Company, Inc.

From *Collected Letters of Samuel Taylor Coleridge*, edited by E. L. Griggs (1956), vol. 1, p. 538, and vol. 2, p. 1104. Reprinted by permission of Oxford University Press, Oxford.

From *The Notebooks of Samuel Taylor Coleridge*, edited by Kathleen Coburn (New York and London, 1957), volume I, entry nr. 1801. Reprinted by permission of Routledge & Kegan Paul, Ltd., and Pantheon Books, Inc .

"Sense in *The Prelude*" from William Empson, *The Structure of Complex Words*. All rights reserved. Reprinted by permission of the author, New Directions Publishing Corporation, New York, and Chatto & Windus, Ltd.

W. B. Gallie, "Is *The Prelude* a Philosophical Poem?" from *Philosophy*, XXII (1947), pp. 124–38. Reprinted by permission of the author and The Royal Institute of Philosophy.

Geoffrey H. Hartman, "A Poet's Progress and the *Via Naturaliter Negativa*," from *Modern Philology*, LIX, 1962, pp. 214–24. Copyright 1962 by the University of Chicago. Reprinted by permission of the author and The University of Chicago Press.

From Herbert Lindenberger, *On Wordsworth's Prelude* (copyright © 1963 by Princeton University Press), pp. 69–98. Reprinted by permission of Princeton University Press.

"Metaphors of Beginning and Where They Lead," in Richard J. Onorato, *The Character of the Poet: Wordsworth in The Prelude* (copyright © 1971 by Princeton University Press), pp. 100–15. Reprinted by permission of Princeton University Press.

Jonathan Wordsworth, "The Growth of a Poet's Mind," from the *Cornell Library Journal*, no. 11 (Spring 1970), pp. 3–24. Reprinted by permission of the publisher.

From *The Letters of William and Dorothy Wordsworth: The Later Years*, edited by Ernest de Selincourt, 1st ed. (6 vols. 1935–1939), vol. 1, p. 28; vol. II, p. 969; vol. III, pp. 1386–87. Reprinted by permission of Oxford University Press, Oxford.

From *The Letters of William and Dorothy Wordsworth: The Early Years*, edited by Ernest de Selincourt, 2nd ed., revised by Chester L. Shaver (1967), pp. 459, 436, 440, 447, 448–51, 454, 458–59, 470, 477, 517–18, 576, 586–87, 650, 664. Reprinted by permission of Oxford University Press, Oxford.

From *Wordsworth: The Prelude*, edited by Ernest de Selincourt, 2nd ed., revised by Helen Darbishire (1959), p. xxiii. Reprinted by permission of Oxford University Press, Oxford.

Copyright © 1979 by W. W. Norton & Company, Inc.

Library of Congress Cataloging in Publication Data
Wordsworth, William, 1770–1850.
   The prelude, 1799, 1805, 1850.
   (A Norton critical edition)
   Bibliography: p.
   1. Wordsworth, William, 1770–1850. The Prelude—Addresses, essays, lectures. I. Wordsworth, Jonathan.
II. Abrams, Meyer Howard. III. Gill, Stephen Charles.
IV. Title.
PR5864.A2W6 1979   821'.7   79–13933
ISBN 0–393–04496–3
ISBN 0–393–09071–X pbk.

Published simultaneously in Canada by George J. McLeod Limited, Toronto. Printed in the United States of America.

FIRST EDITION

1 2 3 4 5 6 7 8 9 0

Contents

Preface

This is the first edition of *The Prelude* to offer Wordsworth's greatest poem in three separate forms. For fifty years now it has been possible to read the manuscript version of 1805 alongside the much revised work that was published after the poet's death in 1850. In addition to newly edited texts of these two established *Preludes*, we now include the two-Part version of the poem, composed in 1798–99, which contains within its small compass much of Wordsworth's most famous and most impressive poetry. Each of the three poems has its distinctive character and poetic qualities; to read them in sequence provides an incomparable opportunity to observe a great poet composing and recomposing, through a long life, his major work.

In its subject matter and colloquial blank verse *The Prelude* owes a great deal to Cowper, whose long reflective poem *The Task* was published in 1785, and to the Conversation Poems of Coleridge. Wordsworth, however, thought of his work as in a direct line from Spenser and Milton, the two poets who exemplified for him the "enthusiastic and meditative imagination." Above all, it was Milton against whom he matched himself; and of the major long poems in English only *The Prelude* stands comparison with *Paradise Lost*. Wordsworth adapted Milton's Christian epic to the spiritual autobiography of a poet. The result is the first example of what has since become a major genre: the account of the growth of an individual mind to artistic maturity, and of the sources of its creative powers.

No literary masterpiece has a more complicated textual history than *The Prelude*. Wordsworth worked on the poem at intervals for more than forty years. His first drafts are 1798, the last full-scale revision is 1839, and there may well have been later corrections. Aside from notebooks that contain isolated drafts, seventeen major *Prelude* manuscripts survive in the Wordsworth Library at Grasmere, and many of these contain several stages of revision. The *Preludes* of 1799 and 1805 are each preserved in duplicate faircopies, showing that in both cases Wordsworth for a time regarded his task as being complete. For the text of 1850 he himself prepared the printer's copy, which his executors published with unwarranted editorial changes soon after his death. It is interesting that even at this final stage Wordsworth did not give *The Prelude* a name. He thought of it always as "the poem to Coleridge," and as a part—first a tailpiece, then a "preparatory poem"—in his scheme for *The Recluse*, the never-completed magnum opus that preoccupied him for much of his adult life. The title of *The Prelude* was suggested by the poet's widow.

1. The Two-Part *Prelude* of 1799

What became *The Prelude* began as a series of questions that Wordsworth put to himself at Goslar in Germany in October–November 1798. He was twenty-eight years old, and had come with his sister, Dorothy, to learn German, and to get on with writing the philosophical *Recluse*, which he and Coleridge had planned in the spring. *The Recluse*, however, was not getting written, and he asked himself why: "Was it for this / That one, the fairest of all rivers, loved / To blend his murmurs with my nurse's song?" Could he be wrong in his sense of vocation, his feeling that his childhood among the lakes and mountains of Cumberland had been that of "a favored being"? This last question took him back into reminiscences, and he wrote very quickly the famous episodes that were later included in Book I of the 1805 and 1850 *Preludes*: the account of birds-nesting, of snaring woodcock on the fells, and of furtively borrowing a shepherd's boat in Patterdale. Then two months later, as his poem grew, he asked himself another question. What was the link between such experiences and his adult creativity? It is the glory of the 1799 poem that it alone goes straight on to provide an answer, in the celebrated "spots of time" sequence which in later versions of *The Prelude* is relegated, to suit an altered structural design, almost to the end (1805, XI, 258–389; 1850, XII, 208–335).

Part I of 1799 discussed the formative implications of childhood: Part II, written a year later, when Wordsworth was back in England, takes the poem on through adolescence. Together the two Parts make a compact and rounded whole, concluding in a valediction to Coleridge, whose presence has throughout been implied. The work in this form consists of 978 lines, and was transcribed at the beginning of December 1799, the month in which Wordsworth and Dorothy went to live at Dove Cottage, Grasmere. It was first published by Jonathan Wordsworth and Stephen Gill in *The Norton Anthology of English Literature* (third edition, 1974); the chronology of its composition had been established by the editors the previous year in "The Two-Part *Prelude* of 1798–99," *JEGP*, LXXII. The poem has more recently been presented, with photographic reproductions of the manuscripts, by Stephen Parrish in the Cornell Wordsworth series, 1977.

2. The *Prelude* of 1805

Two years after the 1799 *Prelude* was transcribed Wordsworth made a brief attempt to extend it, but not till the beginning of 1804 did work on *The Prelude* begin again in earnest. Wishing then to do something for Coleridge, who was leaving for the Mediterranean in search of better health, Wordsworth decided to make a new version of *The Prelude* in five Books. This impressive poem, which cannot be printed here because too little survives in faircopy, may well have been completed when in early March Wordsworth again decided to reorganize and extend his material. In May of the following year he finished the thirteen-Book *Prelude* of 1805. Though the five-Book poem had contained already the concluding epiphany on Mount Snowdon, and had to some extent anticipated the development-crisis-recovery pattern of the longer work, it had taken the poet's life no further than his attendance at Cambridge University. The 1805 version presents for the first time the narrative of Wordsworth's experiences in France, his commitment to the French Revolution, and subsequent allegiance to Godwinian rationalism, his spiritual breakdown in the spring of 1796, and his recovery through the influence of Dorothy and the healing powers of Nature.

On completing his work in 1805 Wordsworth as before had two copies made, and then laid the poem aside. On this occasion, however, he did so with the conscious determination that it would not be published during his lifetime unless it could take its intended place as a part of *The Recluse*. He felt that it was "unprecedented in literary history that a man should talk so much about himself." Only completion of *The Recluse* could, he thought, justify the claims that he had made in challenging the supremacy of Milton's Christian epic:

> Of genius, power,
> Creation, and divinity itself,
> I have been speaking, for my theme has been
> What passed within me . . .
> This is in truth heroic argument . . .
> (1805, III, 171–74, 182)

In the event, the poem as finished by Wordsworth in 1805 remained in manuscript until printed by Ernest de Selincourt in 1926. The text presented below is more accurate than de Selincourt's, but has profited throughout from his remarkable scholarly achievement.

3. The *Prelude* of 1850

The 1850 *Prelude* is the result of three full-scale reworkings of the poem, and numerous minor revisions. In 1816/19, 1832, and 1839, new faircopies were made, and from the last of these *The Prelude* was finally printed just ten weeks after Wordsworth's death. The only major structural changes between 1805 and 1850 are the omission of the episode of Vaudracour and Julia (published separately in 1820) and the division of Book X, which increased the number of Books in 1850 to fourteen. In stylistic quality and tone, however, 1850 is very different from 1805. In successive revisions Wordsworth had smoothed out what had come to seem rough spots, clarified the syntax, elaborated the detail, and most conspicuously, had toned down, by touches of Christian piety, the poem's more radical statements of the divine sufficiency of the human mind in its interchange with Nature. We present below, for the first time, the 1850 *Prelude* as Wordsworth left it, freed from the alterations and intrusions of his executors.

Our wish in this volume is to make the poetry readily accessible to the student as well as the specialist. We therefore present, after a minimum of preliminary matter, reading texts of the 1799, 1805, and 1850 *Preludes*, the last two on facing pages for convenience of comparison. The three complete versions are followed by "MS. Drafts and Fragments," which contains an edited text of Wordsworth's first drafts for the *Prelude, MS. JJ* of October–November 1798, together with the most important draft passages of 1799–1804 that were not included in the three major versions of the poem. We have tried to present all our texts in a way that will make them entirely accessible and self-sufficient, even to readers who come to *The Prelude* for the first time. The footnotes, accordingly, point out important differences between versions of the poem, gloss unfamiliar terms and idiosyncrasies of Wordsworth's usage, offer guidance when the sense or syntax is obscure, explain allusions, and quote important parallels in other poems by Wordsworth as well as passages from writers whom Wordsworth echoes or alludes to. Footnotes that apply equally to the 1799 and 1805 *Preludes* have been duplicated for convenience; those that apply equally to 1805 and 1850 have been furnished with numbers in both texts. Wordsworth's poems, as quoted in the footnotes, are either from manuscript or from the early printed volumes, and styled in the same manner as 1799 and 1805. In the text of 1799, bracketed entries in the left-hand margin identify the equivalent passage in 1805. In the text of 1805, the bracketed entries identify the equivalent passage in 1850.

A preliminary table, "Events of Wordsworth's Life," enables the reader to put into context biographical allusions in the texts and footnotes. Following the texts of *The Prelude*, there is a brief description of all the manuscripts from which these texts have been transcribed. The overall principles governing these transcriptions are described in the section "General Editorial Procedures"; the details and circumstances of composition of each of the three versions are described in the section "Composition and Texts."

To make it possible to study at first hand Wordsworth's changing
intentions, including the evolving relation of *The Prelude* to *The
Recluse*, we include, under "References to *The Prelude* in Process,"
the most significant allusions to the poem by Wordsworth and his
circle between 1799 and 1850. Another section, "Early Reception,"
reprints important comments on the poem and major reviews of the
published version of 1850. A final section reprints seven recent essays,
chosen to represent the diversity of critical views that have been
brought to bear on *The Prelude*.

This book was planned jointly, and the completed parts have been
viewed by the three editors. The texts, introductions, footnotes, and
appendices ("MS Drafts and Fragments, 1798–1804"), as well as
the section of "References to *The Prelude* in Process," are the work
of Jonathan Wordsworth, with collaboration, chiefly in the earlier
stages, from Stephen Gill; the sections on "The Early Reception"
and "Recent Critical Essays" were contributed by M. H. Abrams.
We gratefully acknowledge the work of Ernest de Selincourt, Helen
Darbishire, and other scholars in the field; our debts to them far
exceed those identified in the footnotes. At the cost of a great deal
of valuable time, Beth Darlington has read the proofs—"a laborious
work," but one that has added very much to the accuracy of the
book as a whole. We wish also to pay tribute to the extraordinarily
skilled and sensitive editorial assistance of John Benedict, of W. W.
Norton & Company. The Trustees of Dove Cottage, Grasmere,
have generously provided access to the manuscripts in the Wordsworth Library and authorized their publication in this volume.

JONATHAN WORDSWORTH
M. H. ABRAMS
STEPHEN GILL

Events of Wordsworth's Life

1770	Born, April 7.
1771	Birth of Dorothy Wordsworth, December 25.
1772	Birth of Samuel Taylor Coleridge, October 21.
1778	Death of Wordsworth's mother.
1779	Sent to Hawkshead Grammar School.
1783	Death of Wordsworth's father.
1787	Enters St. John's College, Cambridge (1805, III).
1789	French Revolution begins with storming of the Bastille, July 14; for three years, until the king was deposed in August 1792, its course was largely peaceful, as the republicans attempted to work within a constitutional framework.
1790	Walking tour with Robert Jones through France and Alps in Summer (1805, VI).
1791	B.A., January. Climbs Mount Snowdon (1805, XIII). Returns to France, November.
1792	Love affair with Annette Vallon and important friendship with French republican Michel Beaupuy (1805, IX). Returns to England late autumn. Illegitimate daughter baptized as Anne Caroline Wordsworth in Orleans Cathedral, December 15.
1793	Execution of King Louis XVI, January. War with France and publication of Godwin's *Political Justice*, February. Writes but does not publish republican *Letter to the Bishop of Llandaff*, ca. March. Publication of *Evening Walk, Descriptive Sketches* July–August; first version of *Salisbury Plain* composed. Crosses Salisbury Plain on foot (1805, XII). Visits Tintern Abbey for the first time.
1794	British political situation worsening: repressive government measures, treason trials. Robespierre's execution, August (1805, X), brings to an end the Reign of Terror in France.
1795	Receives legacy from Raisley Calvert (1805, XIII). Frequent meetings in London with Godwin (1805, X), and first meeting with Coleridge. Goes with Dorothy to live at Racedown in Dorset. Writes *Adventures on Salisbury Plain*. Coleridge marries Sara Fricker, October.
1796	Wordsworth's crisis of moral confidence in spring (1805, X). *The Borderers* begun, autumn.
1797	*Borderers* completed, first version of *Ruined Cottage* composed. Moves with Dorothy to be near Coleridge at Al-

foxden, July. Coleridge writes *Kubla Khan* and first version of *Ancient Mariner*.

1798   *Discharged Soldier* composed (1805, IV); *Pedlar* written, as central section of *Ruined Cottage*. Scheme for *Recluse* drawn up. Moves with Dorothy to Goslar, Germany (October). 1799 *Prelude* begun; most of Lucy Poems, *Nutting*, *There was a boy* (1805, V), composed. Publication of *Lyrical Ballads*.

1799   Completion of 1799, I, before Wordsworths leave Goslar, February. Summer–autumn with Hutchinsons (family of poet's future wife) at Sockburn. 1799, II written October–December, and poem transcribed. Walking tour in Lake District with Coleridge, November; "Glad Preamble" composed (1805, I, 1–54). Moves with Dorothy to Dove Cottage, Grasmere, December 20.

1800   *Hart Leap Well*, *Brothers*, and bulk of *Home at Grasmere* (including Prospectus to *The Recluse*) composed, January–March. Coleridge moves to Greta Hall, Keswick, fourteen miles from Grasmere. Preface to *Lyrical Ballads* and *Michael* composed, autumn.

1801   Two-volume *Lyrical Ballads* published, January.

1802   *Intimations*, stanzas 1–4, and *Leech Gatherer* composed, spring. Visit with Dorothy to Annette and Caroline during Peace of Amiens (first truce in nine years of war with France). Many sonnets. Marriage to Mary Hutchinson, October 4.

1803   Fears of French invasion; little composition; Scottish walking tour with Dorothy; Coleridge's health worsening fast.

1804   *Intimations Ode* completed, *Ode to Duty* and *Daffodils* written, *Prelude* at least nearly completed in version of five Books (not corresponding to 1805, I–V), January–early March. Coleridge leaves for Malta. *Prelude* material rearranged and start made on longer, different version. 1805, VI, IX and first half of X probably composed spring–early summer, followed in autumn by VIII, VII, and second half of X.

1805   Death at sea (February 5) of poet's brother John. 1805 completed May 19. *Solitary Reaper* composed, November. Dorothy copying 1805 (MS. A).

1806   *Waggoner* and *Peele Castle* composed, *Home at Grasmere* completed. Coleridge returns. Wordsworth and growing family move to Sir George Beaumont's house, Coleorton, in December, for four months. First extensive revisions of 1805.

1807   Coleridge writes *To William Wordsworth* after listening to 1805. Collection of Wordsworth's lyric poems published in two volumes. *White Doe of Rylstone* begun.

1808   Wordsworths leave Dove Cottage, though remaining in Grasmere. Work on *Tuft of Primroses*, intended for *Recluse*, and *Convention of Cintra* (protest about British handling of Peninsular War).

1809   *Convention* published. Wordsworths at Allan Bank, Grasmere; Coleridge staying with them, and producing his periodical, *The Friend*, almost consistently, June–March 1810.

1810   *Guide to Lakes* published (as anonymous preface to Wilkinson, *Select Views*). Quarrel with Coleridge, after certain not very charitable Wordsworth comments get back to him. Work on *Excursion*.

1812   Deaths of two Wordsworth children, Catharine and Thomas, aged three and six respectively.

1813   Wordsworth becomes civil servant (Distributor of Stamps for Westmorland). Family leaves Grasmere for Rydal Mount (in next valley). *Excursion* completed.

1814   *Excursion* published.

1815   Publication of *Poems* (first Collected Edition with important critical Preface) and *White Doe of Rylstone*.

1816–19 Major *Prelude* revision (resulting in MS. C). Coleridge publishes *Biographia Literaria* and *Sybilline Leaves* (1817). Wordsworth publishes *Peter Bell* and *Waggoner* (1819).

1820   *Miscellaneous Poems* issued. *Duddon Sonnets* and *Vaudracour and Julia* (1805, IX) published.

1822   *Ecclesiastical Sketches* published.

1824   First American Collected Edition of Wordsworth published in Boston.

1827   *Poetical Works*; further collected editions, augmented in each case by new poems, 1832, 1836, 1846.

1831–32 Extensive *Prelude* revision (MS. D).

1835   *Yarrow Revisited and Other Poems*.

1838–39 Last major *Prelude* revision (MS. E).

1842   *Poems Chiefly of Early and Late Years*, first publication of *Salisbury Plain* (1795) and *The Borderers* (1796–97).

1843   Wordsworth becomes poet laureate.

1847   Death of poet's daughter, Dora, aged forty-two.

1849   *Poetical Works* with the poet's final revisions.

1850   Death of Wordsworth, April 23. Publication of *Prelude* (so named by Mary), July.

Abbreviations

Bicentenary Studies	Bicentenary Wordsworth Studies, ed. Jonathan Wordsworth (Ithaca and London, 1970)
Biographia	Coleridge, Samuel Taylor, Biographia Literaria, ed. George Watson, Everyman (corrected ed., London and New York, 1965)
B.L.	The British Library
BNYPL	Bulletin of the New York Public Library
CC	The Collected Works of Samuel Taylor Coleridge; General Editor, Kathleen Coburn (Princeton and London, 1971–). IV: The Friend, ed. by Barbara Rooke (2 vols., 1969).
CW	The Cornell Wordsworth; General Editor, Stephen Parrish (Ithaca, 1975–). I: The Salisbury Plain Poems, ed. Stephen Gill (1975); II: The Prelude, ed. Stephen Parrish (1977); III: Home at Grasmere, ed. Beth Darlington (1977)
DC	Dove Cottage, The Wordsworth Library
EY	The Letters of William and Dorothy Wordsworth, ed. E. de Selincourt, The Early Years, 1787–1805, revised Chester L. Shaver (Oxford, 1967)
Greig	The Farington Diary, ed. James Greig (8 vols., London, 1922–28)
Griggs	Collected Letters of Samuel Taylor Coleridge, ed. E. L. Griggs (6 vols., Oxford, 1956–71)
Havens	Havens, Raymond Dexter, The Mind of a Poet: A Study of Wordsworth's Thought (2 vols., Baltimore, 1941)
Howe	Hazlitt, William, Works, ed. P. P. Howe (21 vols., London, 1930–34)
JEGP	Journal of English and Germanic Philology
Johnson's Dictionary	A Dictionary of the English Language, compiled Samuel Johnson (revised ed., 2 vols., London, 1786)
Journals	The Journals of Dorothy Wordsworth, ed. E. de Selincourt (2 vols., London, 1941)
Ketcham	The Letters of John Wordsworth, ed. Carl H. Ketcham (Ithaca, 1969)

Legouis   Emile Legouis, *The Early Life of William Wordsworth, 1770–1798*, trans. J. W. Matthews (London, 1897)

LY   *The Letters of William and Dorothy Wordsworth*, ed. E. de Selincourt, *The Later Years, 1821–50* (3 vols., Oxford, 1939)

Maxwell   William Wordsworth, *The Prelude*, ed. James Maxwell, Penguin (London, 1971)

Memoirs   Christopher Wordsworth, *Memoirs of William Wordsworth* (2 vols., London, 1851)

Moorman   Moorman, Mary, *William Wordsworth: A Biography. The Early Years* (Oxford, 1957); *The Later Years* (Oxford, 1965)

Morley   Henry Crabb Robinson: *On Books and Their Writers*, ed. E. J. Morley (3 vols., London, 1938)

Music of Humanity   Wordsworth, Jonathan, *The Music of Humanity* (London and New York, 1969)

MY   *The Letters of William and Dorothy Wordsworth*, ed. E. de Selincourt. *The Middle Years, 1806–11*, revised Mary Moorman (Oxford, 1969); *The Middle Years, 1812–20*, revised Mary Moorman and Alan Hill (Oxford, 1970)

NED   *A New English Dictionary*, corrected reissue (13 vols., Oxford, 1933)

Notebooks   *The Notebooks of Samuel Taylor Coleridge*, ed. Kathleen Coburn (New York, 1957–)

NQ   *Notes and Queries*

Oxford "Prelude"   *William Wordsworth: The Prelude*, ed. Ernest de Selincourt (Oxford, 1926); 2nd ed., revised Helen Darbishire (Oxford, 1959)

Oxford Wordsworth   *The Poetical Works of William Wordsworth*, ed. E. de Selincourt and Helen Darbishire (5 vols., Oxford, 1940–49)

PMLA   *Publications of the Modern Language Association of America*

Prose Works   *The Prose Works of William Wordsworth*, ed. W. J. B. Owen and Jane Worthington Smyser (3 vols., Oxford, 1974)

Reed   Reed, Mark L., *Wordsworth: The Chronology of the Early Years, 1770–1799* (Cambridge, Mass., 1967); *Wordsworth: The Chronology of the Middle Years, 1800–1815* (Cambridge, Mass., 1975)

Schneider   Schneider, Ben Ross, Jr., *Wordsworth's Cambridge Education* (Cambridge, 1957)
Thompson   T. W. Thompson, *Wordsworth's Hawkshead,* ed. Robert Woof (Oxford, 1970)
TLS   *The Times* (London) *Literary Supplement*
Vincent   *Letters of Dora Wordsworth,* ed. Howard P. Vincent (Chicago, 1944)

In memory of
　　Joanna Hutchinson, 1892–1966
　　Dorothy Wordsworth Hutchinson, 1883–1972
　　Thomas Hutchinson, 1890–1975
"last of all their race."

The Prelude
1799, 1805, 1850

The Two-Part *Prelude*
of 1799 [†]

[First Part]

[271]   Was it for this
That one, the fairest of all rivers, loved
To blend his murmurs with my nurse's song,
And from his alder shades and rocky falls,
[275] And from his fords and shallows, sent a voice   5
That flowed along my dreams? For this didst thou,
O Derwent, travelling over the green plains
Near my 'sweet birthplace',[1] didst thou, beauteous stream,
Make ceaseless music through the night and day,
[280] Which with its steady cadence tempering   10
Our human waywardness, composed my thoughts
To more than infant softness, giving me
Among the fretful dwellings of mankind
A knowledge, a dim earnest, of the calm
[285] Which Nature breathes among the fields and groves?   15
Beloved Derwent, fairest of all streams,
Was it for this[2] that I, a four years' child,
A naked boy, among thy silent pools
Made one long bathing of a summer's day,
[295] Basked in the sun, or plunged into thy streams,   20
Alternate, all a summer's day, or coursed
Over the sandy fields, and dashed the flowers
Of yellow grunsel;[3] or, when crag and hill,
The woods, and distant Skiddaw's[4] lofty height,
[300] Were bronzed with a deep radiance, stood alone   25
A naked savage in the thunder-shower?

---

† Bracketed marginal entries identify the equivalent passage in *1805*.
1. Wordsworth's quotation marks draw attention to a borrowing from Coleridge's *Frost at Midnight*, 27–28: "already had I dreamt / Of my sweet birth-place." There is a special appropriateness in the reference, as *1799* was from the first written with Coleridge in mind, and at a later stage addressed to him. The river Derwent flows along the far side of the garden wall of the house where Wordsworth was born in Cockermouth.
2. At no stage in his work on *1799* did Wordsworth provide an antecedent for the reiterated "this" of lines 1, 6, and 17.

In general terms, he is referring to failure to begin work on the main philosophical section of *The Recluse* (see Composition and Texts: *1799*, Introduction, below); but correspondence in *TLS* in April–September 1975 showed that these opening lines reproduce an established rhetorical pattern, going back to Thomson, Pope, Milton, Ariosto, and Virgil.
3. The plant is ragwort—i.e., ragweed—(as in the *1850* text) not the modern groundsel.
4. Skiddaw, nine miles due east of Cockermouth, is the fourth highest peak in the Lake District (3,053 feet).

And afterwards ('twas in a later day,
[311] Though early), when upon the mountain slope
The frost and breath of frosty wind had snapped
The last autumnal crocus, 'twas my joy   30
To wander half the night among the cliffs
[315] And the smooth hollows where the woodcocks ran
Along the moonlight turf. In thought and wish
That time, my shoulder all with springes hung,[5]
I was a fell destroyer. Gentle powers,   35
Who give us happiness and call it peace,
When scudding on from snare to snare I plied
[320] My anxious visitation, hurrying on,
Still hurrying, hurrying onward, how my heart
Panted; among the scattered yew-trees and the crags   40
That looked upon me, how my bosom beat
[325] With expectation! Sometimes strong desire
Resistless overpowered me, and the bird
Which was the captive of another's toils[6]
Became my prey; and when the deed was done   45
I heard among the solitary hills
[330] Low breathings coming after me, and sounds
Of undistinguishable motion, steps
Almost as silent as the turf they trod.

Nor less in springtime, when on southern banks   50
The shining sun had from his knot of leaves
[335] Decoyed the primrose flower, and when the vales
And woods were warm, was I a rover then
In the high places, on the lonesome peaks,
Among the mountains and the winds. Though mean   55
[340] And though inglorious were my views, the end[7]
Was not ignoble. Oh, when I have hung
Above the raven's nest, by knots of grass
Or half-inch fissures in the slipp'ry rock
But ill sustained, and almost, as it seemed,   60
[345] Suspended by the blast which blew amain,
Shouldering the naked crag, oh, at that time,
While on the perilous ridge I hung alone,
With what strange utterance did the loud dry wind
Blow through my ears; the sky seemed not a sky   65
[350] Of earth, and with what motion moved the clouds!

---

5. Compare Thomas Pennant's *Tour of Scotland in 1772,* p. 32: "Saw on the plain part of these hills numbers of springes for woodcocks, laid between tufts of heath, with avenues of small stones on each side, to direct these foolish birds into the snares, for they will not hop over the pebbles. Multitudes are taken in this manner in the open weather; and sold on the spot for sixteen pence or twenty pence a couple * * * and sent to the all-devouring capital, by the *Kendal* stage."
6. "Toils" can mean snares ("springes"), as well as labors.
7. Result, as opposed to aim ("views"), which was to steal ravens' eggs.

The mind of man is fashioned and built up
Even as a strain of music. I believe
That there are spirits which, when they would form
A favored being, from his very dawn   70
[365] Of infancy do open out the clouds
As at the touch of lightning, seeking him
With gentle visitation—quiet powers,
Retired, and seldom recognized, yet kind,
And to the very meanest not unknown—   75
With me, though rarely, in my boyish days
They communed. Others too there are, who use,
Yet haply aiming at the self-same end,
[370] Severer interventions, ministry
More palpable—and of their school was I.   80

They guided me: one evening led by them
I went alone into a shepherd's boat,
A skiff, that to a willow-tree was tied
[375] Within a rocky cave, its usual home.
The moon was up, the lake was shining clear   85
Among the hoary mountains; from the shore
[385] I pushed, and struck the oars, and struck again
In cadence, and my little boat moved on
Just like a man who walks with stately step
Though bent on speed.[8] It was an act of stealth   90
And troubled pleasure. Not without the voice
[390] Of mountain echoes did my boat move on,
Leaving behind her still on either side
Small circles glittering idly in the moon,
Until they melted all into one track   95
Of sparkling light.[9] A rocky steep uprose
[395] Above the cavern of the willow-tree,
And now, as suited one who proudly rowed
With his best skill, I fixed a steady view
Upon the top of that same craggy ridge,   100
The bound of the horizon—for behind
[400] Was nothing but the stars and the grey sky.
She was an elfin pinnace;[1] twenty times
I dipped my oars into the silent lake,
And as I rose upon the stroke my boat   105
Went heaving through the water like a swan—
[405] When from behind that rocky steep, till then
The bound of the horizon, a huge cliff,
As if with voluntary power instinct,

8. Lines 89–90 recall *Paradise Lost*, XII, 1–2: "As one who in his journey bates at noon, / Though bent on speed." The lake was Ullswater.
9. Probably, as J. C. Maxwell suggests, a recollection of the "tracks of shining white," made by the water-snakes, in Coleridge's *Ancient Mariner* (1798), 265–66.
1. An archaic word for a small boat.

Upreared its head.[2] I struck, and struck again,   110
And, growing still in stature, the huge cliff
[410] Rose up between me and the stars, and still,
With measured motion, like a living thing
Strode after me. With trembling hands I turned,
And through the silent water stole my way   115
Back to the cavern of the willow-tree.
[415] There in her mooring-place I left my bark,
And through the meadows homeward went with grave
And serious thoughts; and after I had seen
That spectacle, for many days my brain   120
Worked with a dim and undetermined sense
[420] Of unknown modes of being. In my thoughts
There was a darkness—call it solitude,
Or blank desertion—no familiar shapes
Of hourly objects, images of trees,   125
Of sea or sky, no colours of green fields,
But huge and mighty forms that do not live
[425] Like living men moved slowly through my mind
By day, and were the trouble of my dreams.

     Ah, not in vain ye beings of the hills,   130
And ye that walk the woods and open heaths
By moon or star-light, thus, from my first dawn
Of childhood, did ye love to intertwine
The passions that build up our human soul
[435] Not with the mean and vulgar works of man,   135
But with high objects, with eternal things,[3]
With life and Nature, purifying thus
The elements of feeling and of thought,
And sanctifying by such discipline
[440] Both pain and fear, until we recognise   140
A grandeur in the beatings of the heart.
Nor was this fellowship vouchsafed to me
With stinted kindness. In November days,
When vapours rolling down the valleys made
[445] A lonely scene more lonesome, among woods   145
At noon, and 'mid the calm of summer nights
When by the margin of the trembling lake
Beneath the gloomy hills I homeward went
In solitude, such intercourse was mine.

2. The "huge cliff" is probably Black
Crag (2,232 feet, and west of Ullswater),
which would appear suddenly behind the
nearer ridge, Stybarrow Crag, as the child
rowed out from the shore. "Instinct":
imbued.
3. The major stylistic influence on *1799*,
I, was Mark Akenside (1721–70), who
was highly thought of by both Coleridge
and Wordsworth. With the tones, rhythms
and diction of lines 130–36 compare, for

instance: "Nor will I e'er forget you; nor
shall e'er / The graver tasks of manhood,
or the advice / Of vulgar wisdom, move
me to disclaim / Those studies which
possessed me in the dawn / Of life, and
fixed the colour of my mind / For every
future year * * *" *Pleasures of the Imagination* [1757], IV, 46–51)
    "Vulgar" (line 135): ordinary, com-
monplace.

And in the frosty season, when the sun 150
Was set, and visible for many a mile
The cottage windows through the twilight blazed,
[455] I heeded not the summons. Clear and loud
The village clock tolled six; I wheeled about
Proud and exulting, like an untired horse 155
[460] That cares not for its home. All shod with steel
We hissed along the polished ice in games
Confederate, imitative of the chace
And woodland pleasures, the resounding horn,
The pack loud bellowing, and the hunted hare. 160
[465] So through the darkness and the cold we flew,
And not a voice was idle. With the din,
Meanwhile, the precipices rang aloud;
The leafless trees and every icy crag
Tinkled like iron; while the distant hills 165
[470] Into the tumult sent an alien sound
Of melancholy, not unnoticed; while the stars,
Eastward, were sparkling clear, and in the west
The orange sky of evening died away.

Not seldom from the uproar I retired 170
[475] Into a silent bay, or sportively
Glanced sideway, leaving the tumultuous throng,
To cut across the shadow[4] of a star
That gleamed upon the ice. And oftentimes
When we had given our bodies to the wind, 175
[480] And all the shadowy banks on either side
Came sweeping through the darkness, spinning still
The rapid line of motion, then at once
Have I, reclining back upon my heels
Stopped short—yet still the solitary cliffs 180
[485] Wheeled by me, even as if the earth had rolled
With visible motion her diurnal round.[5]
Behind me did they stretch in solemn train,[6]
Feebler and feebler, and I stood and watched
Till all was tranquil as a summer sea.[7] 185

[490] Ye powers of earth, ye genii of the springs,
And ye that have your voices in the clouds,
And ye that are familiars of the lakes

---

4. Reflection, as at line 240 below.
5. "Diurnal": daily. Compare *A slumber did my spirit seal*, 5–8, also written at Goslar, November–December 1798: "No motion has she now, no force, / She neither hears nor sees, / Rolled round in earth's diurnal course / With rocks and stones and trees."

6. Sequence, succession.
7. Though belonging to the same period as the previous episodes, the Skating lines (150–85) do not occur in *MS. JJ* (1798). They were incorporated in Part I as an afterthought during the transcription of *MS. V*, early December 1799.

And of the standing pools,[8] I may not think
A vulgar hope was yours when ye employed   190
Such ministry—when ye through many a year
[495] Thus, by the agency of boyish sports,
On caves and trees, upon the woods and hills,
Impressed upon all forms the characters[9]
Of danger or desire, and thus did make   195
The surface of the universal earth
[500] With meanings of delight, of hope and fear,
Work[1] like a sea.[2]

             Not uselessly employed,
I might pursue this theme through every change
Of exercise and sport to which the year   200
Did summon us in its delightful round.
[505] We were a noisy crew; the sun in heaven
Beheld not vales more beautiful than ours,
Nor saw a race in happiness and joy
More worthy of the fields where they were sown.   205
I would record with no reluctant voice
[535] Our home amusements by the warm peat fire
At evening, when with pencil and with slate,
In square divisions parcelled out, and all
With crosses and with cyphers scribbled o'er,[3]   210
We schemed and puzzled, head opposed to head,
[540] In strife too humble to be named in verse;
Or round the naked table, snow-white deal,
Cherry, or maple, sate in close array,
And to the combat—lu or whist—led on   215
A thick-ribbed army, not as in the world
[545] Discarded and ungratefully thrown by
Even for the very service they had wrought,
But husbanded through many a long campaign.[4]
Oh, with what echoes on the board they fell—   220
Ironic diamonds, hearts of sable hue,
[560] Queens gleaming through their splendour's last decay,

8. Lines 186–89 contain a verbal echo of Shakespeare's *Tempest*, V, i, 33, "Ye elves of hills, brooks, standing lakes, and groves," but attendant spirits ("genii," "familiars") were a commonplace of eighteenth-century poetry.
9. Marks, signs; "impressed": stamped, imprinted, as at line 240 below.
1. "Work" seethe, move restlessly.
2. As W. J. B. Owen points out ("Annotating Wordsworth," p. 65) Wordsworth thinks, "whether instinctively or from literary training," in terms of the eighteenth-century aesthetic categories of the sublime and the beautiful. The beautiful in nature was small and orderly, evoking a quiet pleasure; the sublime was vast,

disordered, evoking fear. Compare lines 432–35 below, and *1805*, I, 305–6: "Fair seed-time had my soul, and I grew up / Fostered alike by beauty and by fear."
3. Tick-tack-toe (noughts and crosses), described by a mock-heroic rendering of Milton's line, "With centric and eccentric scribbled o'er" (*Paradise Lost*, VIII, 83).
4. "Lu" (line 215) is the card game, loo; "thick-ribbed" (line 216) refers probably to the thickening of cards' edges through use. In lines 216–19 Wordsworth has in mind his own account of a Discharged Soldier, which was written January–February 1798, and finally became *1805*, IV, 363–504.

Knaves wrapt in one assimilating gloom,
And kings indignant at the shame incurred
By royal visages.[5] Meanwhile abroad   225
The heavy rain was falling, or the frost
Raged bitterly with keen and silent tooth,
[565] And, interrupting the impassioned game,
Oft from the neighbouring lake the splitting ice,
While it sank down towards the water, sent   230
Among the meadows and the hills its long
And frequent yellings, imitative some
[570] Of wolves that howl along the Bothnic main.[6]

    Nor with less willing heart would I rehearse
[510] The woods of autumn, and their hidden bowers   235
With milk-white clusters hung;[7] the rod and line—
True symbol of the foolishness of hope—
Which with its strong enchantment led me on
By rocks and pools, where never summer star
[515] Impressed its shadow, to forlorn cascades   240
Among the windings of the mountain-brooks;
The kite in sultry calms from some high hill
Sent up, ascending thence till it was lost
Among the fleecy clouds—in gusty days
Launched from the lower grounds, and suddenly   245
[524] Dashed headlong and rejected by the storm.
All these, and more, with rival claims demand
Grateful acknowledgement. It were a song
Venial, and such as—if I rightly judge—
I might protract unblamed, but I perceive   250
That much is overlooked, and we should ill
Attain our object if, from delicate fears
Of breaking in upon the unity
Of this my argument,[8] I should omit
To speak of such effects as cannot here   255
Be regularly classed, yet tend no less
To the same point, the growth of mental power
And love of Nature's works.

                    Ere I had seen
[V, 450] Eight summers—and 'twas in the very week
When I was first transplanted to thy vale,   260

5. Taken as a whole, the card game is a playful imitation of Pope's mock-heroic game of ombre, *Rape of the Lock*, III, 37–100, but lines 221–22 echo "The Winter Evening" (1785) of William Cowper, who is a dominant influence on satirical parts of *The Prelude*: "Ensanguin'd hearts, clubs typical of strife, / And spades, the emblem of untimely graves" (*The Task*, IV, 218–19).

6. The northern Baltic.
7. Lines 234–36 are seemingly a reference to *Nutting* (October–December 1798), which Wordsworth later claimed had been written for *The Prelude*. "Rehearse": relate, describe; already a poeticism in Wordsworth's day.
8. Theme, as in *Paradise Lost*, I, 24: "the highth of this great argument."

Beloved Hawkshead;[9] when thy paths, thy shores
And brooks, were like a dream of novelty
[V, 454] To my half-infant mind—I chanced to cross
One of those open fields which, shaped like ears,
Make green peninsulas on Esthwaite's lake.   265
Twilight was coming on, yet through the gloom
[V, 460] I saw distinctly on the opposite shore,
Beneath a tree and close by the lake side,
A heap of garments, as if left by one
Who there was bathing. Half an hour I watched   270
And no one owned them; meanwhile the calm lake
Grew dark with all the shadows on its breast,
[V, 465] And now and then a leaping fish disturbed
The breathless stillness. The succeeding day
There came a company, and in their boat   275
Sounded with iron hooks and with long poles.
[V, 470] At length the dead man, 'mid that beauteous scene
Of trees and hills and water, bolt upright
Rose with his ghastly face.[1] I might advert
To numerous accidents in flood or field,[2]   280
Quarry or moor, or 'mid the winter snows,
Distresses and disasters, tragic facts
Of rural history, that impressed my mind
With images to which in following years
Far other feelings were attached—with forms   285
That yet exist with independent life,
And, like their archetypes, know no decay.[3]

There are in our existence spots of time
Which with distinct preeminence retain
[XI, 259] A fructifying virtue,[4] whence, depressed   290
By trivial occupations and the round
Of ordinary intercourse, our minds—
Especially the imaginative power—
[XI, 264] Are nourished and invisibly repaired;[5]

9. Wordsworth was in fact nine when he went to Hawkshead Grammar School, ca. May 15, 1779. In an expanded form the episode of the Drowned Man (lines 258–79) became part of Book IV of the short-lived five-Book *Prelude* of January–early March 1804 (see Composition and Texts: *1805/1850*, Introduction, below); it was then transferred to *1805*, V, 450–73.
1. James Jackson, schoolmaster at the neighboring village of Sawrey, was drowned on June 18, 1779, while bathing in Esthwaite Water.
2. An echo of Shakespeare's *Othello*, I, iii, 134–35: "Wherein I spake of most disastrous chances, / Of moving accidents by flood and field."

3. The link passage lines 279–87 has no counterpart in later versions of *The Prelude*, but is of considerable importance. Visual impressions are stored in the memory, and assume new significance with the passage of time. Theirs is an independent life of the imagination, and within the mind they attain the permanence of the natural scenes from which they derive (their "archetypes").
4. The power to make fruitful; "renovating" (substituted in *1805* and *1850*), loses the implication that the mind becomes creative.
5. As in *Tintern Abbey*, written six months before, Wordsworth is concerned with moods "In which the heavy and the weary weight / Of all this unintelligible

Such moments chiefly seem to have their date   295
XI, 275] In our first childhood. I remember well
('Tis of an early season that I speak,
The twilight of rememberable life),
While I was yet an urchin, one who scarce
XI, 280] Could hold a bridle, with ambitious hopes   300
I mounted, and we rode towards the hills.
We were a pair of horsemen: honest James
Was with me, my encourager and guide.[6]
We had not travelled long ere some mischance
XI, 285] Disjoined me from my comrade, and, through fear   305
Dismounting, down the rough and stony moor
I led my horse, and stumbling on, at length
Came to a bottom[7] where in former times
A man, the murderer of his wife, was hung
[XI, 290] In irons.[8] Mouldered was the gibbet-mast;   310
The bones were gone, the iron and the wood;
Only a long green ridge of turf remained
[XI, 301] Whose shape was like a grave. I left the spot,
And reascending the bare slope I saw
A naked pool that lay beneath the hills,   315
The beacon on the summit,[9] and more near
[XI, 305] A girl who bore a pitcher on her head
And seemed with difficult steps to force her way
Against the blowing wind. It was in truth
An ordinary sight, but I should need   320
Colours and words that are unknown to man
[XI, 310] To paint the visionary dreariness
Which, while I looked all round for my lost guide,
Did at that time invest the naked pool,
The beacon on the lonely eminence,   325
The woman and her garments vexed and tossed
XI, 315] By the strong wind.

Nor less I recollect—
Long after, though my childhood had not ceased—
Another scene which left a kindred power
Implanted in my mind. One Christmas-time,   330

---

world / Is lightened * * *" (lines 40–
42) by imaginative recreation of past experience. The pantheist claims of *Tintern
Abbey* have gone, however; the poet is no
longer enabled to "see into the life of
things."
6. Wordsworth, probably aged five, was
staying with his grandparents at Penrith.
"Honest James" was presumably their
servant.
7. Valley bottom.
8. Wordsworth is conflating two murder
stories. Thomas Nicholson had murdered

a local butcher near Penrith and been
hanged there in 1767, eight years before
the probable date of the *Prelude* incident.
A hundred years earlier, in 1672, Thomas
Lancaster had poisoned his wife (and
others) and been hung in irons on a gibbet in the water-meadows near the home
of Ann Tyson, Wordsworth's landlady at
Hawkshead; *Prose Works*, II, pp. 445–56.
9. The impressive stone signal-beacon,
built in 1719 on the hill (737 feet) above
Penrith. Nicholson was hanged a mile or
so to the east, near the Edenhall road.

[XI, 345] The day before the holidays began,
Feverish, and tired, and restless, I went forth
Into the fields, impatient for the sight
Of those three horses which should bear us home,
My brothers and myself.[1] There was a crag,   335
[XI, 350] An eminence, which from the meeting-point
Of two highways ascending overlooked
At least a long half-mile of those two roads,
By each of which the expected steeds might come—
The choice uncertain. Thither I repaired   340
[XI, 355] Up to the highest summit.[2] 'Twas a day
Stormy, and rough, and wild, and on the grass
I sate half sheltered by a naked wall.
Upon my right hand was a single sheep,
A whistling hawthorn on my left, and there,   345
[XI, 360] Those two companions at my side, I watched
With eyes intensely straining, as the mist
Gave intermitting prospects of the wood
And plain beneath. Ere I to school returned
That dreary time, ere I had been ten days   350
[XI, 365] A dweller in my father's house, he died,
And I and my two brothers, orphans then,
Followed his body to the grave.[3] The event,
With all the sorrow which it brought, appeared
A chastisement; and when I called to mind   355
[XI, 370] That day so lately passed, when from the crag
I looked in such anxiety of hope,
With trite reflections of morality,
Yet with the deepest passion, I bowed low
To God who thus corrected my desires.   360
[XI, 375] And afterwards the wind and sleety rain,
And all the business of the elements,
The single sheep, and the one blasted tree,
And the bleak music of that old stone wall,
The noise of wood and water, and the mist   365
[XI, 380] Which on the line of each of those two roads
Advanced in such indisputable shapes[4]—
All these were spectacles and sounds to which
I often would repair, and thence would drink
As at a fountain. And I do not doubt   370
[XI, 385] That in this later time, when storm and rain
Beat on my roof at midnight, or by day

1. The date was almost certainly December 19, 1783; Wordsworth was thirteen. Two of his three brothers, Richard (born 1768) and John (born 1772), were also at Hawkshead Grammar School at this time.
2. Wordsworth was waiting on the ridge north of Borwick Lodge, a mile and a half from the school.
3. John Wordsworth, Sr., died on December 30, 1783. Wordsworth's mother had died five years before.
4. Scansion: "indísputáblĕ shápes."

When I am in the woods, unknown to me
The workings of my spirit thence are brought.[5]

Nor, sedulous as I have been to trace   375
How Nature by collateral[6] interest,
And by extrinsic passion, peopled first
My mind with forms or beautiful or grand
And made me love them,[7] may I well forget
[575] How other pleasures have been mine, and joys   380
Of subtler origin—how I have felt
Not seldom, even in that tempestuous time,
Those hallowed and pure motions of the sense[8]
Which seem in their simplicity to own
[580] An intellectual charm, that calm delight   385
Which, if I err not, surely must belong
To those first-born affinities[9] that fit
Our new existence to existing things,
And, in our dawn of being, constitute
[585] The bond of union betwixt life and joy.[1]   390

Yes, I remember when the changeful earth
And twice five seasons on my mind had stamped
The faces of the moving year, even then,
A child, I held unconscious intercourse
[590] With the eternal beauty, drinking in   395
A pure organic pleasure from the lines
Of curling mist,[2] or from the level plain
Of waters coloured by the steady clouds.
The sands of Westmoreland, the creeks and bays
[595] Of Cumbria's[3] rocky limits, they can tell   400
How when the sea threw off his evening shade
And to the shepherd's hut beneath the crags
Did send sweet notice of the rising moon,

5. In April 1805 an extended version of lines 288–374, the "spots of time" sequence, became *1805*, XI, 257–388.. At an intervening stage in early March 1804 this extended sequence had had very briefly formed the climax of a five-book *Prelude*; see Composition and Texts: *1805/ 1850*, Introduction, below.
6. Indirect; "sedulous": diligent, active.
7. Wordsworth's stress is on the child's unconsciousness of Nature's working: her forms "people" his memory not because he wishes them to do so, but as a result of emotions that are "extrinsic"—not directly relevant—experienced during his "boyish sports." The uneasy transition in line 375 is an afterthought drawn from *Paradise Lost*, IX, 27: "Not sedulous by nature to indite."
8. J.C. Maxwell points out that Wordsworth is "recalling, and reversing" Shakespeare's *Measure for Measure*, I, iv, 59: "The wanton stings and motions of the sense."
9. "Intellectual" (line 385): in *The Prelude* consistently synonymous with "spiritual." "First-born affinities" (line 387): those with which the child is born; compare "those first affections," *Intimations Ode*, 151.
1. Lines 381–90 affirm Wordsworth's view that in the spontaneous sensuousness of childhood there is a quality of mind (akin to Blake's Innocence) vital to the development of the child's sense of belonging in the physical world.
2. *MS. JJ* provides support for a Platonic interpretation of "the eternal beauty" (line 395) as God (MS Drafts and Fragments, 1[a], 102–15, below). "Organic": sensual, bodily.
3. Cumberland's.

How I have stood, to images like these
[601] A stranger, linking with the spectacle   405
No body of associated forms,
And bringing with me no peculiar sense
Of quietness or peace⁴—yet I have stood
[605] Even while my eye has moved o'er three long leagues
Of shining water, gathering, as it seemed,   410
Through the wide surface of that field of light
New pleasure, like a bee among the flowers.

     Thus often in those fits of vulgar joy⁵
[610] Which through all seasons on a child's pursuits
Are prompt attendants, 'mid that giddy bliss   415
Which like a tempest works along the blood
And is forgotten, even then I felt
Gleams like the flashing of a shield. The earth
[615] And common face of Nature spake to me
Rememberable things—sometimes, 'tis true,   420
By quaint associations, yet not vain
[620] Nor profitless, if haply they impressed
Collateral objects and appearances,⁶
Albeit lifeless then, and doomed to sleep
Until maturer seasons called them forth   425
To impregnate and to elevate the mind.
[625] And if the vulgar joy by its own weight
Wearied itself out of the memory,
The scenes which were a witness of that joy
Remained, in their substantial lineaments   430
Depicted on the brain, and to the eye
[630] Were visible, a daily sight. And thus
By the impressive agency of fear,
By pleasure and repeated happiness—
So frequently repeated—and by force   435
Of obscure feelings representative
[635] Of joys that were forgotten, these same scenes,
So beauteous and majestic in themselves,
Though yet the day was distant, did at length

---

4. Wordsworth is looking back to a period at which the beautiful scenes of Nature could be admired in and for themselves, neither conjuring up other scenes within the mind, nor setting up a response determined by previous experience. For the educated contemporary reader, lines 406–7, "linking * * * associated forms" would suggest David Hartley's theory of the "association of ideas" in his *Observations on Man* (1749). According to Hartley, ideas (replicas of sense perception), which have occurred together or successively in sensation, recall one another in thought or imagination; from this basic principle of association he derives all the operations of man's mind. Hartley dominated Coleridge's thinking in the mid-1790s, and to a lesser extent influenced Wordsworth as well.
5. Ordinary pleasures (as opposed to the heightened joy of communion).
6. Lines 420–23 are easily misread. The "associations," or juxtapositions, are quaint at times, but not vain or profitless if indirectly, "collaterally," they impress natural objects and appearances on the mind.

Become habitually dear, and all 440
Their hues and forms were by invisible links
[640] Allied to the affections.[7]

I began
My story early, feeling, as I fear,
The weakness of a human love for days
Disowned by memory—ere the birth of spring 445
Planting my snowdrops among winter snows.[8]
[645] Nor will it seem to thee, my friend, so prompt
In sympathy, that I have lengthened out
With fond and feeble tongue a tedious tale.[9]
Meanwhile my hope has been that I might fetch 450
Reproaches from my former years, whose power
May spur me on, in manhood now mature,
To honourable toil.[1] Yet should it be
That this is but an impotent desire—
That I by such inquiry am not taught 455
[655] To understand myself, nor thou to know
With better knowledge how the heart was framed
Of him thou lovest—need I dread from thee
Harsh judgements if I am so loth to quit
Those recollected hours that have the charm 460
[660] Of visionary things,[2] and lovely forms
And sweet sensations, that throw back our life
And make our infancy a visible scene
On which the sun is shining?[3]

Second Part

Thus far, my friend, have we retraced the way
Through which I travelled when I first began
[5] To love the woods and fields;[1] the passion yet

7. "Affections": feelings. Wordsworth
seems uncertain how far the "Rememberable things" spoken by Nature were
consciously experienced at the time.
"Gleams like the flashing of a shield"
are positively "felt" in lines 417–18; but
natural "objects and appearances" in
lines 424–25 are "lifeless," and "doomed
to sleep / Until maturer seasons [call]
them forth."
8. I.e., attributing snowdrops—a full
flowering of memory—to a period when
there would have been only snow.
9. The banal alliteration is a joke for
Coleridge (the "friend" of line 447)
about poetic craftsmanship.
1. Especially writing the main philosophical section of *The Recluse*; see
Composition and Texts: *1799*, Introduc-
1850, below.
tion, and Composition and Texts, *1805*/

2. Things seen in the imagination, with
the inward eye.
3. Beneath the concluding line in *MS.
18A* Wordsworth has written, "Here we
pause / Doubtful; or lingering with a
truant heart, / Slow and of stationary
character, / Rarely adventurous, studious more of peace / And soothing quiet
which we here have found." See II, 3*n*,
below for an attempted opening of the
Second Part that belongs probably to the
same moment, ca. May 1799.
1. Overleaf from the draft conclusion of
Part I *MS. 18A* (quoted I, 464*n*, above),
Wordsworth made a brief attempt to
begin Part II: "Friend of my heart and
genius, we had reached / A small green
island which I was well pleased / To pass
not lightly by, for though I felt / Strength
unabated, yet I seemed to need / Thy
chearing voice or ere I could pursue /

Was in its birth, sustained, as might befal,
By nourishment that came unsought—for still   5
From week to week, from month to month, we lived
A round of tumult. Duly² were our games
[10] Prolonged in summer till the daylight failed:
No chair remained before the doors, the bench
And threshold steps were empty, fast asleep   10
The labourer and the old man who had sate
A later lingerer, yet the revelry
[15] Continued and the loud uproar. At last,
When all the ground was dark and the huge clouds
Were edged with twinkling stars, to bed we went   15
With weary joints and with a beating mind.
Ah, is there one who ever has been young
[20] And needs a monitory voice to tame
The pride of virtue and of intellect?³
And is there one, the wisest and the best   20
Of all mankind, who does not sometimes wish
For things which cannot be, who would not give,
[25] If so he might, to duty and to truth
The eagerness of infantine desire?
A tranquillizing spirit presses now   25
On my corporeal frame,⁴ so wide appears
The vacancy between me and those days,
[30] Which yet have such self-presence⁵ in my heart
That sometimes when I think of them I seem
Two consciousnesses—conscious of myself,   30
And of some other being.
                                    A grey stone
Of native rock, left midway in the square
[35] Of our small market-village, was the home
And centre of these joys; and when, returned
After long absence thither I repaired,   35
I found that it was split and gone to build
A smart assembly-room that perked and flared
[40] With wash and rough-cast, elbowing the ground
Which had been ours.⁶ But let the fiddle scream,
And be ye happy! Yet I know, my friends,   40
That more than one of you will think with me

My voyage, resting else for ever there."
The lines date from ca. May 1799, and
illustrate the dependence Wordsworth
placed on Coleridge's encouragement and
approval.
2. Appropriately.
3. I.e., can anyone who remembers the
vitality of youth need to be warned not
to overrate the qualities of age?
4. A recollection of *Tintern Abbey*, 44–
46, "the breath of this corporeal frame /
And even the motion of our human

blood / Almost suspended. * * *" In
each case the corporeality of the body
is stressed to show the dominance of
mind.
5. Actuality. Compare, among many other
Wordsworth compounds, "self-transmuted," "under-presence" (*1805*, IV, 141;
XIII, 71, below).
6. The resented "assembly-room" is the
Hawkshead Town Hall, built in 1790.
"Wash" is whitewash, "roughcast" a
facing of mortar and gravel.

Of those soft starry nights, and that old dame
[45] From whom the stone was named, who there had sate
And watched her table with its huckster's wares,
Assiduous, for the length of sixty years.[7]   45

We ran a boisterous race, the year span round
With giddy motion; but the time approached
[50] That brought with it a regular desire
For calmer pleasures—when the beauteous scenes
Of Nature were collaterally attached   50
To every scheme of holiday delight,
And every boyish sport, less grateful else
[55] And languidly pursued.[8] When summer came
It was the pastime of our afternoons
To beat along the plain of Windermere   55
With rival oars; and the selected bourn[9]
Was now an island musical with birds
[60] That sang for ever, now a sister isle
Beneath the oak's umbrageous[1] covert, sown
With lilies-of-the-valley like a field,   60
And now a third small island where remained
An old stone table and one mouldered cave—
[65] A hermit's history.[2] In such a race,
So ended, disappointment could be none,
Uneasiness, or pain, or jealousy;   65
We rested in the shade, all pleased alike,
Conquered or conqueror. Thus our selfishness
Was mellowed down, and thus the pride of strength
[70] And the vainglory of superior skill
Were interfused with objects which subdued   70
And tempered them, and gradually produced
A quiet independence of the heart.
And to my friend who knows me I may add,
[75] Unapprehensive of reproof, that hence
Ensued a diffidence and modesty,   75
And I was taught to feel—perhaps too much—
The self-sufficing power of solitude.
No delicate viands sapped our bodily strength:
[80] More than we wished we knew the blessing then
Of vigorous hunger, for our daily meals   80
Were frugal, Sabine fare—and then, exclude

---

7. Lines 6–45 were inserted by Wordsworth after November 26, 1799, as a result of a visit to Hawkshead with his
brother John and Coleridge on November 2.
8. Nature is still not sought for herself,
but her "collateral" pleasures are now
valued, where at the stage represented
by I, 424–25 they had been not merely
incidental, but "lifeless * * * Until maturer seasons called them forth." "Grateful": pleasing.
9. Goal, destination.
1. Shady.
2. The island is Lady Holm, traditionally
the site of a chapel dedicated to the Virgin Mary.

A little weekly stipend,[3] and we lived
Through three divisions of the quartered year
[85] In pennyless poverty. But now, to school
Returned from the half-yearly holidays,   85
We came with purses more profusely filled,[4]
Allowance which abundantly sufficed
To gratify the palate with repasts
[90] More costly than the dame of whom I spake,
That ancient woman, and her board, supplied.   90
Hence inroads into distant vales, and long
Excursions far away among the hills,
Hence rustic dinners on the cool green ground—
[95] Or in the woods, or by a river-side
Or fountain[5]—festive banquets, that provoked   95
The languid action of a natural scene
By pleasure of corporeal appetite.[6]
    Nor is my aim neglected if I tell
[100] How twice in the long length of those half-years
We from our funds perhaps with bolder hand   100
Drew largely, anxious for one day at least
To feel the motion of the galloping steed;
And with the good old innkeeper, in truth
[105] I needs must say, that sometimes we have used
Sly subterfuge, for the intended bound   105
Of the day's journey was too distant far
For any cautious man: a structure famed
Beyond its neighbourhood, the antique walls
[110] Of a large abbey,[7] with its fractured arch,
Belfry, and images, and living trees—   110
A holy scene. Along the smooth green turf
[115] Our horses grazed. In more than inland peace,
Left by the winds that overpass the vale,
In that sequestered ruin trees and towers—
[119] Both silent and both motionless alike—   115
Hear all day long the murmuring sea that beats
Incessantly upon a craggy shore.
    Our steeds remounted, and the summons given,
With whip and spur we by the chantry[8] flew
In uncouth race, and left the cross-legged knight   120
[125] And the stone abbot,[9] and that single wren

3. "Exclude": overlook. In 1787, his last year at school, Wordsworth had sixpence a week pocket money, and his youngest brother Christopher threepence. "Sabine fare" (line 81): a reference to the frugality of Horace on his Sabine farm.
4. In January 1787 Wordsworth returned to school with a guinea, Christopher with 10s. 6d.
5. Spring, stream.
6. As R. D. Havens puts it, "These pompously expressed lines mean that the enjoyment of food stimulated the enjoyment of scenery." "Action": effect.
7. Furness Abbey, roughly twenty miles south of Hawkshead.
8. A chapel endowed for the singing of masses for the dead.
9. The cross-legged knight has been moved, but may still be seen at Furness; it is less easy to identify the stone abbot.

Which one day sang so sweetly in the nave
Of the old church that, though from recent showers
The earth was comfortless, and, touched by faint
[130] Internal breezes, from the roofless walls   125
The shuddering ivy dripped large drops, yet still
So sweetly 'mid the gloom the invisible bird
Sang to itself that there I could have made
My dwelling-place, and lived for ever there,
[135] To hear such music. Through the walls we flew   130
And down the valley, and, a circuit made
In wantonness of heart, through rough and smooth
We scampered homeward. O, ye rocks and streams,
And that still spirit of the evening air,
[140] Even in this joyous time I sometimes felt   135
Your presence, when, with slackened step, we breathed[1]
Along the sides of the steep hills, or when,
Lightened by gleams of moonlight from the sea,
[144] We beat with thundering hoofs the level sand.[2]   140
    There was a row of ancient trees, since fallen,
That on the margin of a jutting land
Stood near the lake of Coniston, and made,
With its long boughs above the water stretched,
A gloom through which a boat might sail along
As in a cloister. An old hall[3] was near,   145
Grotesque and beautiful, its gavel-end[4]
And huge round chimneys to the top o'ergrown
With fields of ivy. Thither we repaired—
'Twas even a custom with us—to the shore,
And to that cool piazza. They who dwelt   150
In the neglected mansion-house supplied
Fresh buttter, tea-kettle and earthernware,
And chafing-dish with smoking coals; and so
Beneath the trees we sate in our small boat,
And in the covert eat our delicate meal   155
Upon the calm smooth lake.[5] It was a joy
Worthy the heart of one who is full grown
To rest beneath those horizontal boughs
And mark the radiance of the setting sun,
Himself unseen, reposing on the top   160
Of the high eastern hills.[6] And there I said,
That beauteous sight before me, there I said

1. Let our horses get their breath back.
2. Their direct route to Hawkshead would have been along the Dalton road to Ulverston, but the "circuit" referred to at line 131 took them twelve miles along Levens Sands from Rampside, opposite Piel Castle, to Greenodd.
3. Coniston Hall dates from 1580.
4. "Gavel" is a northern variant of "gable."
5. This was no doubt a fishing expedition, and the delicious meal would be of Coniston trout, cooked in the chafing dish. "Eat": ate.
6. As frequently in the Lake District, the sun ("himself" in line 160) setting in the west is causing a pink glow above the eastern fells.

(Then first beginning in my thoughts to mark
That sense of dim similitude which links
Our moral feelings with external forms)   165
That in whatever region I should close
My mortal life I would remember you,
Fair scenes—that dying I would think on you,
My soul would send a longing look to you,
Even as that setting sun, while all the vale   170
Could nowhere catch one faint memorial gleam,
Yet with the last remains of his last light
Still lingered, and a farewell lustre threw
On the dear mountain-tops where first he rose.[7]
'Twas then my fourteenth summer, and these words   175
Were uttered in a casual access
Of sentiment, a momentary trance
That far outran the habit of my mind.[8]
[145]   Upon the eastern shore of Windermere
Above the crescent of a pleasant bay   180
There was an inn, no homely-featured shed,
Brother of the surrounding cottages,
But 'twas a splendid place, the door beset
[150] With chaises, grooms, and liveries, and within
Decanters, glasses and the blood-red wine.   185
In ancient times, or ere the hall was built
On the large island, had the dwelling been
More worthy of a poet's love, a hut
[155] Proud of its one bright fire and sycamore shade;[9]
But though the rhymes were gone which once inscribed   190
The threshold, and large golden characters
On the blue-frosted signboard had usurped
The place of the old lion, in contempt
[160] And mockery of the rustic painter's hand,
Yet to this hour the spot to me is dear   195
With all its foolish pomp. The garden lay
Upon a slope surmounted by the plain
Of a small bowling-green; beneath us stood
[165] A grove, with gleams of water through the trees
And over the tree-tops—nor did we want   200
Refreshment, strawberries and mellow cream—
And there through half an afternoon we played
On the smooth platform, and the shouts we sent

7. Wordsworth's reflections may or may not have occurred to him on the spot, but are to be found in his *Vale of Esthwaite* of 1785–87, on which *1799* draws heavily at lines 161–62, 166–74. See *The Vale of Esthwaite* (*Oxford Wordsworth*, I, p. 281).
8. This important episode (lines 140–78) is omitted in *1805*, but partially restored in *1850*, VIII, 458–75. "Trance" (line 177): here no more than a moment of abstraction.
9. The hall of Belle Isle on Windermere was completed in the early 1780s, and had the effect of bringing custom to the neighborhood. The inn was the old White Lion at Bowness.

[170] Made all the mountains ring. But ere the fall
Of night, when in our pinnace we returned   205
Over the dusky lake, and to the beach
Of some small island steered our course, with one,
The minstrel of our troop,[1] and left him there,
[175] And rowed off gently, while he blew his flute
Alone upon the rock, oh, then the calm   210
And dead still water lay upon my mind
Even with a weight of pleasure, and the sky,
Never before so beautiful, sank down
[180] Into my heart and held me like a dream.

    Thus day by day my sympathies increased,   215
And thus the common range of visible things
Grew dear to me: already I began
To love the sun, a boy I loved the sun
[185] Not as I since have loved him—as a pledge
And surety of my earthly life, a light   220
Which while I view I feel I am alive—
But for this cause, that I had seen him lay
His beauty on the morning hills, had seen
[190] The western mountain touch his setting orb
In many a thoughtless hour, when from excess   225
Of happiness my blood appeared to flow
With its own pleasure, and I breathed with joy.
And from like feelings, humble though intense,
[195] To patriotic and domestic love
Analogous, the moon to me was dear: 230
For I would dream away my purposes
Standing to look upon her, while she hung
Midway between the hills as if she knew
[200] No other region but belonged to thee,
Yea, appertained by a peculiar right   235
To thee and thy grey huts,[2] my native vale.

    Those incidental charms which first attached
My heart to rural objects, day by day
[205] Grew weaker, and I hasten on to tell
How Nature, intervenient[3] till this time   240
And secondary, now at length was sought
For her own sake. But who shall parcel out
His intellect by geometric rules,
[210] Split like a province into round and square?
Who knows the individual hour in which   245

1. Robert Greenwood, later Senior Fellow of Trinity College, Cambridge, but
remembered by Wordsworth's landlady
Ann Tyson as "t'lad wi't' flute" (Thompson, pp. 78–79, 147).

2. Cottages built of gray local stone.
3. Literally, "coming between"; Nature
had asserted herself *amid* other preoccupations.

His habits were first sown even as a seed?
Who that shall[4] point as with a wand, and say
'This portion of the river of my mind
[215] Came from yon fountain'?[5] Thou, my friend, art one   250
More deeply read in thy own thoughts, no slave
[221] Of that false secondary power by which
In weakness we create distinctions, then
Believe our puny boundaries are things
Which we perceive, and not which we have made.
[225] To thee, unblinded by these outward shews,   255
The unity of all has been revealed;
And thou wilt doubt with me, less aptly skilled
Than many are to class the cabinet
Of their sensations,[6] and in voluble phrase
[230] Run through the history and birth of each   260
As of a single independent thing.
Hard task to analyse a soul,[7] in which
Not only general habits and desires,
But each most obvious and particular thought—
Not in a mystical and idle sense,   265
[235] But in the words of reason deeply weighed—
Hath no beginning.

                    Blessed the infant babe—
For my best conjectures I would trace
The progress of our being—blest the babe
[240] Nursed in his mother's arms, the babe who sleeps   270
Upon his mother's breast, who, when his soul
Claims manifest kindred with an earthly soul,[8]
Doth gather passion from his mother's eye.
Such feelings pass into his torpid life
[245] Like an awakening breeze, and hence his mind,   275
Even in the first trial of its powers,
Is prompt and watchful, eager to combine
In one appearance all the elements
And parts of the same object, else detached
[250] And loth to coalesce.[9] Thus day by day   280
Subjected to the discipline of love,
His organs and recipient faculties

4. "Who is there that would be able to?"
5. For the importance of the river as an image of the mind in *1805*, see e.g. III, 10–12, IV, 39–55, XIII, 172–84.
6. To classify their feelings, as if they were exhibits in a display-case. "Doubt" in line 257 refers back to the possibility of "parcelling out" the intellect (lines 242–49).
7. See *Paradise Lost*, V, 564, where Raphael speaks of relating the war in heaven as "Sad task and hard." As J. C.

Maxwell suggests, this is "one of Wordsworth's implied claims for epic, or more than epic, status for his poem." "Phrase" (line 259): phraseology, style.
8. When his soul forms an evident relationship with the soul of another human being.
9. Emotion acts as a unifying factor because it awakens and alerts the mind, enabling it to make the basic imaginative step of forming parts into wholes; see line 305n, below.

Are quickened, are more vigorous; his mind spreads,
Tenacious of the forms which it receives.[1]
[255] In one beloved presence—nay and more,   285
In that most apprehensive habitude[2]
And those sensations which have been derived
From this beloved presence—there exists
A virtue which irradiates and exalts
[260] All objects through all intercourse of sense.[3]   290
No outcast he, bewildered and depressed;
Along his infant veins are interfused
The gravitation and the filial bond
Of Nature that connect him with the world.[4]
[265] Emphatically such a being lives,   295
An inmate of this *active* universe.
From Nature largely he receives, nor so
Is satisfied, but largely gives again;
For feeling has to him imparted strength,
[270] And—powerful in all sentiments of grief,   300
Of exultation, fear and joy—his mind,
Even as an agent of the one great mind,
Creates, creator and receiver both,
Working but in alliance with the works
[275] Which it beholds.[5] Such, verily, is the first   305
Poetic spirit of our human life—
By uniform control of after years
In most abated and suppressed, in some
Through every change of growth or of decay
[280] Preeminent till death.   310

             From early days,
Beginning not long after that first time
In which, a babe, by intercourse of touch
I held mute dialogues with my mother's heart,
I have endeavoured to display the means
[285] Whereby this infant sensibility,   315
Great birthright of our being, was in me
Augmented and sustained. Yet is a path

1. Retentive of visual images.
2. In that relationship ("habitude") best suited to learning ("most apprehensive").
3. As F. R. Leavis pointed out (*Revaluation*, p. 160), there is a clear and interesting connection with *Tintern Abbey*, 101–2, "A motion and a spirit, that impels / All thinking things, all objects of all thought.* * *" For the child, objects are irradiated and exalted by the "beloved presence" (line 288) of the mother, just as for the adult, consciousness of a disturbing transcendental "presence" (*Tintern Abbey*, 95) shows them to be impelled by "a motion and a spirit."

4. Innate in the child is a force pulling him towards the world ("gravitation"). In 1799 Wordsworth sees this in terms of the "filial bond" of child and mother, which establishes the larger bond of man and Nature; for a very different position five years later, see *Intimations Ode*, 67–84.
5. Strengthened by the mother's love, and working in harmony with external Nature, the child's mind shows itself to be creative as well as receptive. It is thus not merely an agent, but in its creativity a reflection, of the mind of God.

More difficult before me, and I fear
That in its broken windings we shall need
[290] The chamois' sinews and the eagle's wing.   320
For now a trouble came into my mind
From obscure causes:[6] I was left alone
Seeking this visible world, nor knowing why.
The props of my affections were removed,
[295] And yet the building stood, as if sustained   325
By its own spirit. All that I beheld
Was dear to me, and from this cause it came
That now to Nature's finer influxes[7]
My mind lay open—to that more exact
[300] And intimate communion which our hearts   330
Maintain with the minuter properties
Of objects which already are beloved,
And of those only.

                    Many are the joys
Of youth, but oh, what happiness to live
[305] When every hour brings palpable access   335
Of knowledge, when all knowledge is delight,
And sorrow is not there. The seasons came,
And every season brought a countless store
Of modes and temporary qualities
[310] Which but for this most watchful power of love   340
Had been neglected, left a register
Of permanent relations else unknown.[8]
Hence life, and change, and beauty, solitude
More active even than 'best society',[9]
[315] Society made sweet as solitude   345
By silent inobtrusive sympathies,
And gentle agitations of the mind
From manifold distinctions,[1] difference
Perceived in things where to the common eye
[320] No difference is, and hence, from the same source,   350
Sublimer joy. For I would walk alone
In storm and tempest,[2] or in starlight nights
Beneath the quiet heavens, and at that time
Would feel whate'er there is of power in sound

6. Nature herself was the disturbing force. The chamois (line 320) is a mountain antelope of great agility, hunted in the Alps.
7. Influences.
8. Love of Nature makes the child responsive to whatever the seasons bring, creating from passing experience permanent relationships—permanent presumably in their effect upon the mind—that are recorded in the memory, and so known to have existed.

9. Wordsworth's quotation marks draw attention to *Paradise Lost*, IX, 249, "For solitude sometimes is best society."
1. The "gentle agitations" do not depend on "by" in the previous line; they are the last item in the list that follows "Hence" in line 343.
2. Lines 352–71 were written, in the third person, in January–February 1798, probably to describe the narrator of *The Ruined Cottage*.

[325] To breathe an elevated mood, by form   355
   Or image unprofaned; and I would stand
   Beneath some rock, listening to sounds that are
   The ghostly[3] language of the ancient earth,
   Or make their dim abode in distant winds.[4]
[330] Thence did I drink the visionary power.   360
   I deem not profitless these fleeting moods
   Of shadowy exaltation; not for this,
   That they are kindred to our purer mind
   And intellectual[5] life, but that the soul—
[335] Remembering how she felt, but what she felt   365
   Remembering not—retains an obscure sense[6]
   Of possible sublimity, to which
   With growing faculties she doth aspire,
   With faculties still growing, feeling still
[340] That whatsoever point they gain they still   370
   Have something to pursue.

                And not alone
   In grandeur and in tumult, but no less
   In tranquil scenes, that universal power
   And fitness in the latent qualities
[345] And essences of things, by which the mind   375
   Is moved with feelings of delight, to me
   Came strengthened with a superadded soul,
   A virtue not its own.[7] My morning walks
   Were early: oft before the hours of school
[350] I travelled round our little lake, five miles   380
   Of pleasant wandering—happy time, more dear
   For this, that one was by my side, a friend
   Then passionately loved.[8] With heart how full
   Will he peruse these lines, this page—perhaps
[355] A blank to other men—for many years   385
   Have since flowed in between us, and, our minds
   Both silent to each other, at this time
   We live as if those hours had never been.
   Nor seldom did I lift our cottage latch
[360] Far earlier, and before the vernal thrush   390

---

3. Spiritual; also, disembodied.

4. Compare *Intimations Ode*, 28, "The winds come to me from the fields of sleep." For the inspiring and visionary power that winds had for Wordsworth, see M. H. Abrams, "The Correspondent Breeze," in *English Romantic Poets: Modern Essays in Criticism*, ed. Abrams (2nd ed., 1975).

5. In effect, spiritual.

6. Scansion: an óbscŭre sénse; Milton too sometimes stresses the first syllable.

7. To the power to please that natural objects have in and for themselves is added a virtue not their own—and not at all clearly defined. The "soul" is "superadded" to the inherent qualities of landscape, and yet "comes" to Wordsworth, rather than being, as one would expect, projected by him in a mood of "shadowy exaltation" (lines 361–2).

8. School began at six or six-thirty in the summer months at Hawkshead, and an hour later in the winter. The lake was Esthwaite Water; the friend, John Fleming, is enthusiastically referred to in *The Vale of Esthwaite* (1785–87).

Was audible, among the hills I sate
Alone upon some jutting eminence[9]
At the first hour of morning, when the vale
Lay quiet in an utter solitude.
[365] How shall I trace the history, where seek   395
The origin of what I then have felt?
Oft in those moments such a holy calm
Did overspread my soul that I forgot
The agency of sight, and what I saw
[370] Appeared like something in myself, a dream,   400
A prospect[1] in my mind.

                              'Twere long to tell
What spring and autumn, what the winter snows,
And what the summer shade, what day and night,
The evening and the morning, what my dreams
[375] And what my waking thoughts, supplied to nurse   405
That spirit of religious love in which
I walked with Nature. But let this at least
Be not forgotten, that I still retained
My first creative sensibility,
[380] That by the regular action of the world   410
My soul was unsubdued. A plastic[2] power

Abode with me, a forming hand, at times
Rebellious, acting in a devious mood,
A local spirit of its own, at war
[385] With general tendency, but for the most   415
Subservient strictly to the external things
With which it communed.[3] An auxiliar light
Came from my mind, which on the setting sun
Bestowed new splendour; the melodious birds,
[390] The gentle breezes, fountains that ran on   420
Murmuring so sweetly in themselves, obeyed
A like dominion, and the midnight storm
Grew darker in the presence of my eye.
Hence my obeisance, my devotion hence,
[395] And *hence* my transport.[4]   425

                              Nor should this, perchance,
Pass unrecorded, that I still[5] had loved
The exercise and produce of a toil

---

9. Compare Thomson's *Seasons*, II, 1042:
"Sad on the jutting eminence he sits."
1. View, landscape.
2. Formative, creative.
3. Wordsworth is saying that his creativity, though at times capricious in its refusal to conform, was for the most part stabilized by subordination to Nature.

4. Wordsworth's submission and devotion to Nature, and the joy that he derives from her, are paradoxically based on the fact that she is herself subordinate to his creative sensibility. "Transport": exaltation, extreme emotion.
5. Always.

Than analytic industry to me
More pleasing, and whose character I deem
[400] Is more poetic, as resembling more   430
Creative agency—I mean to speak
Of that interminable building reared
By observation of affinities
In objects where no brotherhood exists
[405] To common minds. My seventeenth year was come,   435
And, whether from this habit rooted now
So deeply in my mind, or from excess
Of the great social principle of life
Coercing all things into sympathy,
[410] To unorganic natures I transferred   440
My own enjoyments, or, the power of truth
Coming in revelation, I conversed
With things that really are, I at this time
Saw blessings spread around me like a sea.[6]
[415] Thus did my days pass on, and now at length   445
From Nature and her overflowing soul
I had received so much that all my thoughts
Were steeped in feeling. I was only then
Contented when with bliss ineffable
[420] I felt the sentiment of being spread   450
O'er all that moves, and all that seemeth still,
O'er all that, lost beyond the reach of thought
And human knowledge, to the human eye
Invisible, yet liveth to the heart
[425] O'er all that leaps, and runs, and shouts, and sings,   455
Or beats the gladsome air, o'er all that glides
Beneath the wave, yea, in the wave itself
And mighty depth of waters. Wonder not
If such my transports were, for in all things
[430] I saw one life, and felt that it was joy;   460
One song they sang and it was audible—
Most audible then when the fleshly ear,
O'ercome by grosser prelude of that strain,
Forgot its functions and slept undisturbed.[7]
[435]   If this be error, and another faith   465
Find easier access to the pious mind,
Yet were I grossly destitute of all

6. Wordsworth appears in lines 435–44 to be offering three alternatives when in fact he offers two, of which the first is subdivided. The boy either transfers his own enjoyments to inanimate ("unorganic") Nature—through excess of fellow feeling—or he rightly perceives the existence of a shared life-force.
7. Lines 446–64 were written as third-person narrative for *The Ruined Cottage* in February–March 1798. Hearing the song of the One Life (line 461), like seeing into the "life of things" in *Tintern Abbey*, 50, is a metaphor that should not be taken too literally. The "grosser prelude" (line 463) can stand for any external stimulus. *MS. RV* incorporates at this point a version of the remarkable pantheist fragment of summer 1799, printed in MS. Drafts and Fragments, 2(d), below.

Those human sentiments which make this earth
So dear if I should fail with grateful voice
[440] To speak of you, ye mountains, and ye lakes   470
And sounding cataracts, ye mists and winds
That dwell among the hills where I was born.
If in my youth I have been pure in heart,
If, mingling with the world, I am content
[445] With my own modest pleasures, and have lived   475
With God and Nature communing, removed
From little enmities and low desires,
The gift is yours; if in these times of fear,
This melancholy waste[8] of hopes o'erthrown,
[450] If, 'mid indifference and apathy   480
And wicked exultation, when good men
On every side fall off we know not how
To selfishness, disguised in gentle names
Of peace and quiet and domestic love[9]—
[455] Yet mingled, not unwillingly, with sneers   485
On visionary minds[1]—if, in this time
Of dereliction and dismay, I yet
Despair not of our nature, but retain
A more than Roman confidence, a faith
[460] That fails not, in all sorrow my support,   490
The blessing of my life, the gift is yours
Ye mountains, thine O Nature. Thou hast fed
My lofty speculations, and in thee
For this uneasy heart of ours I find
[465] A never-failing principle of joy   495
And purest passion.

                Thou, my friend, wast reared
In the great city, 'mid far other scenes,[2]
But we by different roads at length have gained
The self-same bourne. And from this cause to thee
[470] I speak unapprehensive of contempt,   500
The insinuated scoff of coward tongues,

8. Desert.
9. The sudden entrance into the poem of a concern with "hopes o'erthrown" derives from a Coleridge letter of ca. September 1799: "I wish you would write a poem, in blank verse, addressed to those, who, in consequence of the complete failure of the French Revolution, have thrown up all hopes of the amelioration of mankind, and are sinking into an almost epicurean selfishness, disguising the same under the soft titles of domestic attachment and contempt for visionary *philosophes*. It would do great good, and might form a part of 'the Recluse' * * *" (Griggs, I, p. 527). When he was finishing the thirteen-book *Prelude* in May 1805, Wordsworth's thoughts interestingly reverted to this earlier conclusion; compare *1805*, XIII, 431–52.

1. See, e.g., Hazlitt's description in *The Spirit of the Age* (1825) of the notorious lectures of 1799 in which Sir James Mackintosh, one-time apologist for the French Revolution (*Vindiciae Gallicae*, 1791), abjured earlier friends and opinions (Howe, XI, pp. 98–100).

2. Coleridge is very much in Wordsworth's mind as he rounds off Part II. Although he does not use quotation marks as at I, 8, he again quotes verbatim from *Frost at Midnight*, lines 51–52: "For I was reared / In the great city, pent 'mid cloisters dim."

And all that silent language which so oft
In conversation betwixt man and man
Blots from the human countenance all trace
[475] Of beauty and of love.[3] For thou hast sought   505
The truth in solitude, and thou art one
The most intense of Nature's worshippers,
In many things my brother, chiefly here
In this my deep devotion.[4] Fare thee well:
[480] Health and the quiet of a healthful mind   510
Attend thee, seeking oft the haunts of men—
But yet more often living with thyself,
And for thyself—so haply shall thy days
Be many, and a blessing to mankind.[5]

End of the second Part

3. Wordsworth's great earlier declaration of faith lies behind much of this concluding section: lines 473–78 should be compared with *Tintern Abbey*, 108–12, and lines 489–96, 501–5, with *Tintern Abbey*, 122–35.

4. Compare the concluding lines of *1805*, where despite his changing views Coleridge is still classed with Wordsworth himself as a "prophet of Nature" (XIII, 442).

5. In November 1799 Coleridge had gone south to become a journalist in London— "seeking oft the haunts of men." Wordsworth's farewell has thus an immediate reference in addition to its obvious structural implications.

The Prelude of 1805, in Thirteen Books†

Book First

Introduction: Childhood and School-time

Oh there is blessing in this gentle breeze,
That blows from the green fields and from the clouds
And from the sky; it beats against my cheek,
And seems half conscious of the joy it gives.
O welcome messenger! O welcome friend!   5
A captive greets thee, coming from a house
Of bondage, from yon city's walls set free,
A prison where he hath been long immured.²
Now I am free, enfranchised and at large,
May fix my habitation where I will.   10
[10] What dwelling shall receive me, in what vale
Shall be my harbour, underneath what grove
Shall I take up my home, and what sweet stream
Shall with its murmurs lull me to my rest?
The earth is all before me—with a heart   15
[15] Joyous, nor scared at its own liberty,
I look about, and should the guide I chuse
Be nothing better than a wandering cloud
I cannot miss my way.³ I breathe again—
Trances of thought and mountings of the mind   20
[20] Come fast upon me. It is shaken off,
As by miraculous gift 'tis shaken off,
That burthen of my own unnatural self,
The heavy weight of many a weary day

---

† Footnotes to *1805* and *1850* are numbered in a single sequence. When the same note applies to both texts, its superscript number is entered in each text. Notes which apply only to *1805*, together with those which apply to both texts, are printed on the left-hand page; notes which apply only to *1850* are printed on the right-hand page. Bracketed marginal entries refer to *1850*.

2. Despite the circumstantial detail of his reference to city walls (see also *1850*, 87–89, and *1805*, VII, 1–4, VIII, 347–53), it is almost certain that Wordsworth was in the Lake District when he wrote these opening lines. The city, characterized by an allusion to Exodus 13:3—"out from Egypt, out of the house of bondage"—is partly London, partly Goslar; it evokes a pent-up state of mind which Wordsworth had doubtless experienced in both, and from which he now suddenly felt free.

3. A reference to the concluding lines of *Paradise Lost*: "The world was all before them, where to choose / Their place of rest, and providence their guide: / They hand in hand with wandering steps and slow, / Through Eden took their solitary way."

The Prelude of 1850, in Fourteen Books[†]

Book First

Introduction—Childhood and School-time

O there is a blessing in this gentle breeze,
A visitant that while he fans my cheek
Doth seem half-conscious of the joy he brings
From the green fields, and from yon azure sky.
Whate'er his mission, the soft breeze can come   5
To none more grateful than to me;[1] escaped
From the vast city, where I long had pined
A discontented sojourner: now free,
Free as a bird to settle where I will.
What dwelling shall receive me? in what vale   10
Shall be my harbour? underneath what grove
Shall I take up my home? and what clear stream
Shall with its murmur lull me into rest?
The earth is all before me. With a heart
Joyous, nor scared at its own liberty,   15
I look about; and should the chosen guide
Be nothing better than a wandering cloud,
I cannot miss my way.[3] I breathe again!
Trances of thought and mountings of the mind
Come fast upon me: it is shaken off,   20
That burthen of my own unnatural self,
The heavy weight of many a weary day

---

1. There is no manuscript authority for the first edition reading "it," "it," "its," for "he," "he," "his," applied to the breeze in lines 2–5. The substitution was made in proof, probably by Christopher Wordsworth, Jr., later Bishop of Lincoln, to remove the characteristic but unorthodox Wordsworthian animism.

Not mine, and such as were not made for me. 25
Long months of peace—if such bold word accord
[25] With any promises of human life—
Long months of ease and undisturbed delight
Are mine in prospect. Whither shall I turn,
By road or pathway, or through open field, 30
Or shall a twig or any floating thing
[30] Upon the river point me out my course?

    Enough that I am free, for months to come
May dedicate myself to chosen tasks,
May quit the tiresome sea and dwell on shore— 35
If not a settler on the soil, at least
To drink wild water, and to pluck green herbs,
And gather fruits fresh from their native bough.
Nay more, if I may trust myself, this hour
Hath brought a gift that consecrates my joy; 40
For I, methought, while the sweet breath of heaven
Was blowing on my body, felt within
[35] A corresponding mild creative breeze,
A vital breeze which travelled gently on
O'er things which it had made, and is become 45
A tempest, a redundant energy,
Vexing its own creation.[4] 'Tis a power
That does not come unrecognised, a storm
[40] Which, breaking up a long-continued frost,
Brings with it vernal promises, the hope 50
Of active days, of dignity and thought,
Of prowess in an honorable field,[5]
Pure passions, virtue, knowledge, and delight,
[45] The holy life of music and of verse.[6]

    Thus far, O friend, did I, not used to make 55
A present joy the matter of my song,
Pour out that day my soul in measured strains,

---

4. *1805*, 43–47 are found (with line 20, above) in *MS. JJ*; see *MS.* Drafts and Fragments, 1(h), i–iii, below. For the relation of winds to inspiration and a revived creativity in the poetry of Wordsworth, see M. H. Abrams, "The Correspondent Breeze." "Redundant" *1805*, 46; *1850*, 37): superabundant, exuberant, superfluous (Johnson's *Dictionary*).
5. Wordsworth has in mind the writing of the central philosophical section of *The Recluse*, planned in March 1798, but consistently deferred; see Composition and Texts: *1799, 1805/1850*, Section iii, below.
6. *1805*, 1–54 (*1850*, 1–45), referred to at VII, 4 as Wordsworth's "glad preamble," draw on material in *MS. JJ* from Octo-

ber–November 1798 (see 47*n*, above); in its present form, however, the passage seems to have been written on or shortly after November 18, 1799 (see John Alban Finch, "Wordsworth's Two-Handed Engine," *Bicentenary Studies*, pp. 1–13). It must originally have been a separate "effusion," and was not incorporated in *The Prelude* until Wordsworth made a start on the five-book poem in January 1804.

    The revisions of *1805*, lines 33–54, sound for the first time in the poem the characteristic voice, or tone, of *1850*; *1805*, lines 33–38 were not cut until the final corrections to *MS. E*, in or after 1839.

Not mine, and such as were not made for me.
Long months of peace (if such bold word accord
With any promises of human life),   25
Long months of ease and undisturbed delight
Are mine in prospect; whither shall I turn
By road or pathway, or through trackless field,
Up hill or down, or shall some floating thing
Upon the river point me out my course?   30

    Dear Liberty! Yet what would it avail
But for a gift that consecrates the joy?
For I, methought, while the sweet breath of heaven
Was blowing on my body, felt within
A corresondent breeze, that gently moved   35
With quickening virtue, but is now become
A tempest, a redundant energy,
Vexing its own creation[4] Thanks to both,
And their congenial powers, that, while they join
In breaking up a long-continued frost,   40
Bring with them vernal promises, the hope
Of active days urged on by flying hours,—
Days of sweet leisure, taxed with patient thought
Abstruse, not wanting punctual service high,
Matins and vespers, of harmonious verse![6]   45

    Thus, O Friend! did I, not used to make
A present joy the matter of a song,
Pour forth that day my soul in measured strains

Even in the very words which I have here
[50] Recorded. To the open fields I told
A prophesy; poetic numbers came   60
Spontaneously, and clothed in priestly robe
My spirit, thus singled out, as it might seem,
For holy services. Great hopes were mine:
[55] My own voice cheared me, and, far more, the mind's
Internal echo of the imperfect sound—   65
To both I listened, drawing from them both
A chearful confidence in things to come.

　　Whereat, being not unwilling now to give
[60] A respite to this passion, I paced on
Gently, with careless steps, and came erelong   70
To a green shady place where down I sate
Beneath a tree, slackening my thoughts by choice
And settling into gentler happiness.
[65] 'Twas autumn, and a calm and placid day
With warmth as much as needed from a sun   75
Two hours declined towards the west, a day
With silver clouds and sunshine on the grass,
And, in the sheltered grove where I was couched,
[70] A perfect stillness. On the ground I lay
Passing through many thoughts, yet mainly such   80
As to myself pertained. I made a choice
Of one sweet vale whither my steps should turn,
And saw, methought, the very house and fields
Present before my eyes;[7] nor did I fail   85
To add meanwhile assurance of some work
Of glory there forthwith to be begun—
[80] Perhaps too there performed. Thus long I lay
Cheared by the genial pillow of the earth
Beneath my head, soothed by a sense of touch
From the warm ground, that balanced me, else lost   90
Entirely, seeing nought, nought hearing, save
When here and there about the grove of oaks
Where was my bed, an acorn from the trees
[85] Fell audibly, and with a startling sound.

　　Thus occupied in mind I lingered here   95
Contented, nor rose up until the sun
Had almost touched the horizon; bidding then
A farewell to the city left behind,[8]

7. The "vale" is Grasmere; Dove Cottage, into which the Wordsworths moved on December 20, 1799, and where they stayed until 1808, was then divided from the lake only by fields.

8. Insofar as Wordsworth had particular city walls in mind, they were those of Goslar, Germany, where he had spent the autumn and winter, 1798–99; see *1805*, VIII, 347–53, below.

That would not be forgotten, and are here
Recorded: to the open fields I told   50
A prophecy: poetic numbers came
Spontaneously to clothe in priestly robe
A renovated spirit singled out,
Such hope was mine, for holy services.
My own voice cheered me, and, far more, the mind's   55
Internal echo of the imperfect sound;
To both I listened, drawing from them both
A cheerful confidence in things to come.

   Content and not unwilling now to give
A respite to this passion, I paced on   60
With brisk and eager steps; and came, at length,
To a green shady place, where down I sate
Beneath a tree, slackening my thoughts by choice,
And settling into gentler happiness.
'Twas autumn, and a clear and placid day,   65
With warmth, as much as needed, from a sun
Two hours declined towards the west; a day
With silver clouds, and sunshine on the grass,
And in the sheltered and the sheltering grove
A perfect stillness. Many were the thoughts   70
Encouraged and dismissed, till choice was made
Of a known Vale,[7] whither my feet should turn,
Nor rest till they had reached the very door
Of the one cottage which methought I saw.
No picture of mere memory ever looked   75
So fair; and while upon the fancied scene
I gazed with growing love, a higher power
Than Fancy gave assurance of some work
Of glory there forthwith to be begun,
Perhaps too there performed. Thus long I mused,   80
Nor e'er lost sight of what I mused upon,
Save when, amid the stately grove of oaks,
Now here, now there, an acorn, from its cup
Dislodged, through sere leaves rustled, or at once
To the bare earth dropped with a startling sound.   85
From that soft couch I rose not, till the sun
Had almost touched the horizon; casting then
A backward glance upon the curling cloud
Of city smoke, by distance ruralised;
Keen as a Truant or a Fugitive,   90

Even with the chance equipment of that hour
I journeyed towards the vale which I had chosen.   100
It was a splendid evening, and my soul
[95] Did once again make trial of the strength
Restored to her afresh; nor did she want
Eolian visitations—but the harp
Was soon defrauded,[9] and the banded host   105
Of harmony dispersed in straggling sounds,
And lastly utter silence. 'Be it so,
It is an injury', said I, 'to this day
[100] To think of any thing but present joy.'
So, like a peasant, I pursued my road   110
Beneath the evening sun, nor had one wish
Again to bend the sabbath of that time
[105] To a servile yoke. What need of many words?—
A pleasant loitering journey, through two days
Continued, brought me to my hermitage.[2]   115

    I spare to speak, my friend, of what ensued—
The admiration and the love, the life
In common things, the endless store of things
[110] Rare, or at least so seeming, every day
Found all about me in one neighbourhood,   120
The self-congratulation,[3] the complete
Composure, and the happiness entire.
But speedily a longing in me rose
[115] To brace myself to some determined aim,
Reading or thinking, either to lay up   125
New stores, or rescue from decay the old
By timely interference. I had hopes
Still higher, that with a frame[4] of outward life
[120] I might endue, might fix in a visible home,
Some portion of those phantoms of conceit,   130
That had been floating loose about so long,
And to such beings temperately deal forth
The many feelings that oppressed my heart.[5]
But I have been discouraged: gleams of light

9. The Aeolian harp, or wind harp—a fashionable toy in the late eighteenth century—became for the Romantics a symbol of poetic creation. It consisted of a set of strings stretched across a rectangular sounding box from which the wind evoked varying tones and harmonies.
2. Wordsworth had spent the night of November 17, 1799, at the foot of Ullswater, only twenty-one miles or so from Grasmere *via* the Kirkstone Pass. The change from "two days" to *1850* "three" is an emendation of 1839, or later; Wordsworth probably noticed that the

1805 reading could imply merely one full day (plus the evening of November 18, on which he set out), and wished to stress that because of the loitering he had taken two.
3. Used (as in *Old Cumberland Beggar*, 117) without the modern pejorative implication, to mean "rejoicing."
4. Anything constructed of various parts or members (Johnson's *Dictionary*).
5. Mental images ("phantoms of conceit") are to be embodied in narrative poetry, and endowed in moderation with the poet's own feelings.

But as a Pilgrim resolute, I took,
Even with the chance equipment of that hour,
The road that pointed toward the chosen Vale.
It was a splendid evening, and my soul
Once more made trial of her strength, nor lacked 95
Æolian visitations; but the harp
Was soon defrauded,⁹ and the banded host
Of harmony dispersed in straggling sounds,
And lastly utter silence! 'Be it so;
Why think of any thing but present good?' 100
So, like a home-bound labourer I pursued
My way beneath the mellowing sun, that shed
Mild influence;¹ nor left in me one wish
Again to bend the Sabbath of that time
To a servile yoke. What need of many words? 105
A pleasant loitering journey, through three days
Continued, brought me to my hermitage.²
I spare to tell of what ensued, the life
In common things—the endless store of things,
Rare, or at least so seeming, every day 110
Found all about me in one neighbourhood—
The self-congratulation,³ and, from morn
To night, unbroken cheerfulness serene.
But speedily an earnest longing rose
To brace myself to some determined aim, 115
Reading or thinking; either to lay up
New stores, or rescue from decay the old
By timely interference: and therewith
Came hopes still higher, that with outward life
I might endue some airy phantasies 120
That had been floating loose about for years,
And to such beings temperately deal forth
The many feelings that oppressed my heart.
That hope hath been discouraged; welcome light

---

1. An allusion to *Paradise Lost*, VII, 375, where the Pleiades dance before the sun, "Shedding sweet influence."

[125] Flash often from the east, then disappear,   135
And mock me with a sky that ripens not
Into a steady morning. If my mind,
Remembering the sweet promise of the past,
Would gladly grapple with some noble theme,
[130] Vain is her wish—where'er she turns she finds   140
Impediments from day to day renewed.

      And now it would content me to yield up
Those lofty hopes awhile for present gifts
Of humbler industry. But, O dear friend,
[135] The poet, gentle creature as he is,   145
Hath like the lover his unruly times—
His fits when he is neither sick nor well,
Though no distress be near him but his own
Unmanageable thoughts. The mind itself,
The meditative mind, best pleased perhaps   150
[140] While she as duteous as the mother dove
Sits brooding,[6] lives not always to that end,
But hath less quiet instincts—goadings on
That drive her as in trouble through the groves.
With me is now such passion, which I blame   155
[145] No otherwise than as it lasts too long.

      When, as becomes a man who would prepare
For such a glorious work, I through myself
Make rigorous inquisition, the report
Is often chearing; for I neither seem   160
[150] To lack that first great gift, the vital soul,
Nor general truths which are themselves a sort
Of elements and agents, under-powers,
Subordinate helpers of the living mind.
Nor am I naked in external things,   165
[155] Forms, images,[7] nor numerous other aids
Of less regard, though won perhaps with toil,
And needful to build up a poet's praise.
Time, place, and manners,[8] these I seek, and these
I find in plenteous store, but nowhere such   170
[160] As may be singled out with steady choice—
No little band of yet remembered names
Whom I, in perfect confidence, might hope
To summon back from lonesome banishment

6. The human mind initiates the creative process by brooding, as the Holy Spirit in Milton's Christian epic had brooded over Chaos: "thou from the first / Wast present, and with mighty wings outspread / Dove-like sat'st brooding on the vast abyss / And madest it pregnant . . ." (*Paradise Lost*, I, 19–22).
7. Landscapes as they present themselves to the eye (or are retained within the mind).
8. General way of life; morals; habits (Johnson's *Dictionary*).

Dawns from the east, but dawns to disappear   125
And mock me with a sky that ripens not
Into a steady morning: if my mind,
Remembering the bold promise of the past,
Would gladly grapple with some noble theme,
Vain is her wish; where'er she turns she finds   130
Impediments from day to day renewed.

   And now it would content me to yield up
Those lofty hopes awhile, for present gifts
Of humbler industry. But, oh, dear Friend!
The Poet, gentle creature as he is,   135
Hath, like the Lover, his unruly times;
His fits when he is neither sick nor well,
Though no distress be near him but his own
Unmanageable thoughts: his mind, best pleased
While she as duteous as the mother dove   140
Sits brooding,[6] lives not always to that end,
But like the innocent bird, hath goadings on
That drive her as in trouble through the groves;
With me is now such passion, to be blamed
No otherwise than as it lasts too long.   145

   When, as becomes a man who would prepare
For such an arduous work, I through myself
Make rigorous inquisition, the report
Is often cheering; for I neither seem
To lack that first great gift, the vital soul,   150
Nor general Truths, which are themselves a sort
Of Elements and Agents, Under-powers,
Subordinate helpers of the living mind:
Nor am I naked of external things,
Forms, images,[7] nor numerous other aids   155
Of less regard, though won perhaps with toil
And needful to build up a Poet's praise.
Time, place, and manners[8] do I seek, and these
Are found in plenteous store, but nowhere such
As may be singled out with steady choice;   160
No little band of yet remembered names
Whom I, in perfect confidence, might hope
To summon back from lonesome banishment,

And make them inmates in the hearts of men 175
[165] Now living, or to live in times to come.
Sometimes, mistaking vainly, as I fear,
Proud spring-tide swellings for a regular sea,
I settle on some British theme, some old
Romantic tale by Milton left unsung;[9] 180
[170] More often resting at some gentle place
Within the groves of chivalry I pipe
Among the shepherds, with reposing knights
Sit by a fountain-side and hear their tales.
Sometimes, more sternly moved, I would relate 185
How vanquished Mithridates northward passed
And, hidden in the cloud of years, became
That Odin, father of a race by whom
[190] Perished the Roman Empire;[2] how the friends
And followers of Sertorius, out of Spain 190
Flying, found shelter in the Fortunate Isles,
And left their usages, their arts and laws,
To disappear by a slow gradual death,
[195] To dwindle and to perish one by one,
Starved in those narrow bounds—but not the soul 195
Of liberty, which fifteen hundred years
Survived, and, when the European came
With skill and power that could not be withstood,
[200] Did like a pestilence maintain its hold,
And wasted down by glorious death that race 200
Of natural heroes.[3] Or I would record
How in tyrannic times, some unknown man,
Unheard of in the chronicles of kings,
[205] Suffered in silence for the love of truth;
How that one Frenchman, through continued force 205

9. Milton's decision not to write a romance about knights in battles and
tournaments is recorded in *Paradise Lost*,
IX, 25–41, a passage that seems frequently to have been in Wordsworth's
mind as he attempted to define his own
position as a poet (see especially, *1805*,
III, 183*n*, below).
2. Mithridates the Great, King of Pontus,
was defeated by Pompey in 66 B.C. and
died two years later; Odin, in one tradition, was a barbarian who led his tribe
north from the sea of Asov to Sweden in
the hope that one day their descendants
might carry out his revenge upon the
Romans. Gibbon, *Decline and Fall of
the Roman Empire*, I (1776), p. 246, associates the two figures, and suggests that
Odin's expedition would make a subject
for an epic poem.
3. The Roman general Sertorius, contemporary and ally of Mithridates, gained
control of most of Spain, but was unsuccessful in his attempt to master Rome
from the provinces; he was assassinated
in 72 B.C. According to legend, his followers emigrated to the Canary Islands
after his death, and there founded a race
that flourished until the arrival of the
Spanish at the end of the fifteenth century.

And make them dwellers in the hearts of men
Now living, or to live in future years.   165
Sometimes the ambitious Power of choice, mistaking
Proud spring-tide swellings for a regular sea,
Will settle on some British theme, some old
Romantic tale by Milton left unsung;[9]
More often turning to some gentle place   170
Within the groves of Chivalry, I pipe
To shepherd swains, or seated harp in hand,
Amid reposing knights by a river side
Or fountain, listen to the grave reports
Of dire enchantments faced and overcome   175
By the strong mind, and tales of warlike feats,
Where spear encountered spear, and sword with sword
Fought, as if conscious of the blazonry
That the shield bore, so glorious was the strife;
Whence inspiration for a song that winds   180
Through ever changing scenes of votive quest
Wrongs to redress, harmonious tribute paid
To patient courage and unblemished truth,
To firm devotion, zeal unquenchable,
And Christian meekness hallowing faithful loves.[1]   185
Sometimes, more sternly moved, I would relate
How vanquished Mithridates northward passed,
And, hidden in the cloud of years, became
Odin, the Father of a race by whom
Perished the Roman Empire:[2] how the friends   190
And followers of Sertorius, out of Spain
Flying, found shelter in the Fortunate Isles,
And left their usages, their arts and laws,
To disappear by a slow gradual death,
To dwindle and to perish one by one,   195
Starved in those narrow bounds: but not the soul
Of Liberty, which fifteen hundred years
Survived, and, when the European came
With skill and power that might not be withstood,
Did, like a pestilence, maintain its hold   200
And wasted down by glorious death that race
Of natural heroes:[3] or I would record
How, in tyrannic times, some high-souled man,
Unnamed among the chronicles of kings,
Suffered in silence for Truth's sake: or tell,   205
How that one Frenchman, through continued force

---

1. In this greatly extended evocation of Edmund Spenser, Wordsworth gives the poetry a moral turn of which, in de Selincourt's words, it had been "quite innocent" in the *1805* version. "Faithful loves" in line 185 echoes the opening stanza of *The Faerie Queene*, "Fierce warres and faithful loves shall moralize my song."

Of meditation on the inhuman deeds
Of the first conquerors of the Indian Isles,
Went single in his ministry across
[210] The ocean, not to comfort the oppressed,
But like a thirsty wind to roam about   210
Withering the oppressor;[4] how Gustavus found
Help at his need in Dalecarlia's mines;[5]
How Wallace fought for Scotland, left the name
Of Wallace to be found like a wild flower
All over his dear country, left the deeds   215
[215] Of Wallace like a family of ghosts
To people the steep rocks and river-banks,
Her natural sanctuaries, with a local soul
[220] Of independence and stern liberty.[6]
Sometimes it suits me better to shape out   220
Some tale from my own heart, more near akin
To my own passions and habitual thoughts,
Some variegated story, in the main
[225] Lofty, with interchange of gentler things.
But deadening admonitions will succeed,   225
And the whole beauteous fabric seems to lack
Foundation, and withal appears throughout
Shadowy and unsubstantial.

            Then, last wish—
My last and favorite aspiration—then
I yearn towards some philosophic song   230
[230] Of truth that cherishes our daily life,
With meditations passionate from deep
Recesses in man's heart, immortal verse
Thoughtfully fitted to the Orphean lyre;
But from this awful burthen I full soon   235
[235] Take refuge, and beguile myself with trust
That mellower years will bring a riper mind
And clearer insight.[7] Thus from day to day
I live a mockery of the brotherhood
Of vice and virtue, with no skill to part   240
Vague longing that is bred by want of power,
[240] From paramount impulse not to be withstood;

4. "Dominique de Gourges, a French gentleman who went in 1568 to Florida to avenge the massacre of the French by the Spaniards there" (*Prelude* note, 1850).
5. Gustavus Vasa of Sweden raised support among peasants in the mining district of Dalecarlia, and freed his country from Danish rule in 1521–23.
6. William Wallace, hero of Scottish nationalism, was captured and executed by Edward I in 1305. Wordsworth's interest had been stirred during his tour of Scot-

land with Dorothy in August–September 1803.
7. Another reference to *The Recluse*; *Home at Grasmere* (largely 1800, completed 1806), which was to be the first Book of the main philosophical section of the poem, does precisely cherish the daily life (*1805*, 231; *1850*, 230) of the Wordsworths, holding it up as a type for general future happiness. Later tradition represented Orpheus (*1805*, *1850*, 232–34) as a philosopher rather than a musician.

Of meditation on the inhuman deeds
Of those who conquered first the Indian Isles,
Went single in his ministry across
The Ocean; not to comfort the oppressed,   210
But, like a thirsty wind, to roam about
Withering the Oppressor:[4] how Gustavus sought
Help at his need in Dalecarlia's mines;[5]
How Wallace fought for Scotland; left the name
Of Wallace to be found, like a wild flower,   215
All over his dear Country; left the deeds
Of Wallace, like a family of Ghosts,
To people the steep rocks and river banks,
Her natural sanctuaries, with a local soul
Of independence and stern liberty.[6]   220
Sometimes it suits me better to invent
A tale from my own heart, more near akin
To my own passions and habitual thoughts;
Some variegated story, in the main
Lofty, but the unsubstantial structure melts   225
Before the very sun that brightens it,
Mist into air dissolving! Then a wish,
My best and favourite aspiration, mounts
With yearning toward some philosophic song
Of Truth that cherishes our daily life;   230
With meditations passionate from deep
Recesses in man's heart, immortal verse
Thoughtfully fitted to the Orphean lyre;
But from this awful burthen I full soon
Take refuge and beguile myself with trust   235
That mellower years will bring a riper mind
And clearer insight.[7] Thus my days are past
In contradiction; with no skill to part
Vague longing, haply bred by want of power,
From paramount impulse not to be withstood,   240

A timorous capacity, from prudence;
From circumspection, infinite delay.[8]
Humility and modest awe themselves   245
Betray me, serving often for a cloak
[245] To a more subtle selfishness, that now
Doth lock my functions up in blank reserve,[9]
Now dupes me by an over-anxious eye
That with a false activity beats off   250
Simplicity and self-presented truth.
[250] Ah, better far than this to stray about
Voluptuously through fields and rural walks
And ask no record of the hours given up
To vacant musing, unreproved neglect   255
Of all things, and deliberate holiday.
[255] Far better never to have heard the name
Of zeal and just ambition than to live
Thus baffled by a mind that every hour
Turns recreant to her task, takes heart again,   260
Then feels immediately some hollow thought
[260] Hang like an interdict[1] upon her hopes.
This is my lot; for either still I find
Some imperfection in the chosen theme,
Or see of absolute accomplishment   265
Much wanting—so much wanting—in myself
[265] That I recoil and droop, and seek repose
In indolence from vain perplexity,
Unprofitably travelling towards the grave,
Like a false steward who hath much received   270
And renders nothing back.[2]

                    Was it for this
[270] That one, the fairest of all rivers, loved
To blend his murmurs with my nurse's song,
And from his alder shades and rocky falls,
And from his fords and shallows, sent a voice   275
That flowed along my dreams?[3] For this didst thou,
[275] O Derwent, travelling over the green plains
Near my 'sweet birthplace',[5] didst thou, beauteous stream,

8. Wordsworth, in the mood he describes
in *1805*, 238–44 (*1850*, 237–42), is not
decisive enough to be either vicious or
virtuous; he cannot distinguish between
vague but feeble longings to write *The
Recluse*, and an overwhelming impulse
to do so, between timorousness and prudence, between mere delay and circum-
pection.
9. Total inaction.
1. Prohibition; pronounced "interdite."
2. See the parable of the false steward,
Matthew 25:14–30.
3. This question had of course been the
opening of the two-Part *Prelude*, expressing already in October–November 1798
the poet's discontent at failure to make
progress with *The Recluse*. The river is
the Derwent, which flows along the far
side of the garden wall of the house
where Wordsworth was born at Cockermouth.
5. Wordsworth's quotation marks draw
attention to a borrowing from Coleridge's
Frost at Midnight, 28. There is a special appropriateness in the reference, as
The Prelude was in all its versions the
"Poem to Coleridge."

A timorous capacity from prudence,
From circumspection, infinite delay.[8]
Humility and modest awe themselves
Betray me, serving often for a cloak
To a more subtle selfishness; that now   245
Locks every function up in blank reserve,[9]
Now dupes me, trusting to an anxious eye
That with intrusive restlessness beats off
Simplicity and self-presented truth.
Ah! better far than this, to stray about   250
Voluptuously through fields and rural walks,
And ask no record of the hours, resigned
To vacant musing, unreproved neglect
Of all things, and deliberate holiday.
Far better never to have heard the name   255
Of zeal and just ambition, than to live
Baffled and plagued by a mind that every hour
Turns recreant to her task; takes heart again,
Then feels immediately some hollow thought
Hang like an interdict[1] upon her hopes.   260
This is my lot; for either still I find
Some imperfection in the chosen theme,
Or see of absolute accomplishment
Much wanting, so much wanting, in myself,
That I recoil and droop, and seek repose   265
In listlessness from vain perplexity,
Unprofitably travelling toward the grave,
Like a false steward who hath much received
And renders nothing back.[2]

                  Was it for this
That one, the fairest of all rivers, loved   270
To blend his murmurs with my nurse's song,
And, from his alder shades and rocky falls,
And from his fords and shallows, sent a voice
That flowed along my dreams?[3] For this, didst thou,
O Derwent! winding among grassy holms[4]   275
Where I was looking on, a babe in arms,

4. Islands.

Make ceaseless music through the night and day,
Which with its steady cadence tempering   280
Our human waywardness, composed my thoughts
To more than infant softness, giving me
Among the fretful dwellings of mankind,
[280] A knowledge, a dim earnest, of the calm
Which Nature breathes among the hills and groves?   285
When, having left his mountains, to the towers
Of Cockermouth that beauteous river came,
Behind my father's house he passed, close by,
[286] Along the margin of our terrace walk.
He was a playmate whom we dearly loved: 290
Oh, many a time have I, a five years' child,
A naked boy, in one delightful rill,
A little mill-race severed from his stream,
[290] Made one long bathing of a summer's day,
Basked in the sun, and plunged, and basked again,   295
Alternate, all a summer's day, or coursed
Over the sandy fields, leaping through groves
Of yellow grunsel; or, when crag and hill,
[295] The woods, and distant Skiddaw's lofty height,[7]
Were bronzed with a deep radiance, stood alone   300
Beneath the sky, as if I had been born
On Indian plains,[8] and from my mother's hut
Had run abroad in wantonness to sport,
[300] A naked savage, in the thunder-shower.

        Fair seed-time had my soul, and I grew up   305
Fostered alike by beauty and by fear,
Much favored in my birthplace, and no less
In that beloved vale to which erelong
[305] I was transplanted.[9] Well I call to mind—

        'Twas at an early age, ere I had seen   310
Nine summers —when upon the mountain slope
The frost and breath of frosty wind had snapped
The last autumnal crocus, 'twas my joy
To wander half the night among the cliffs
And the smooth hollows where the woodcocks ran   315
Along the open turf. In thought and wish
[310] That time, my shoulder all with springes[2] hung,
I was a fell destroyer. On the heights

7. Skiddaw, nine miles due east of Cockermouth, is the fourth highest peak in the Lake District (3,053 feet). "Grunsel" (*1805*, 298): ragwort—i.e., ragweed —(as in *1850*), not the modern groundsel.
8. Wordsworth's reference is to the American Indian.
9. The experiences that follow take place after Wordsworth has been "transplanted" to Hawkshead Grammar School, thirty-five miles from Cockermouth, in May 1779.
2. Snares.

Make ceaseless music that composed my thoughts
To more than infant softness, giving me
Amid the fretful dwellings of mankind
A foretaste, a dim earnest, of the calm   280
That Nature breathes among the hills and groves.
When he had left the mountains and received
On his smooth breast the shadow of those towers
That yet survive, a shattered monument
Of feudal sway,[6] the bright blue river passed   285
Along the margin of our terrace walk;
A tempting playmate whom we dearly loved.
Oh, many a time have I, a five years' child,
In a small mill-race severed from his stream,
Made one long bathing of a summer's day;   290
Basked in the sun, and plunged and basked again
Alternate, all a summer's day, or scoured
The sandy fields, leaping through flowery groves
Of yellow ragwort; or when rock and hill,
The woods, and distant Skiddaw's lofty height,[7]   295
Were bronzed with deepest radiance, stood alone
Beneath the sky, as if I had been born
On Indian plains,[8] and from my mother's hut
Had run abroad in wantonness, to sport
A naked savage, in the thunder shower.   300

    Fair seed-time had my soul, and I grew up
Fostered alike by beauty and by fear:
Much favoured in my birth-place, and no less
In that beloved Vale to which erelong
We were transplanted[9]—there were we let loose   305
For sports of wider range. Ere I had told
Ten birth-days,[1] when among the mountain slopes
Frost, and the breath of frosty wind, had snapped
The last autumnal crocus, 'twas my joy
With store of springes[2] o'er my shoulder hung   310
To range the open heights where woodcocks ran
Along the smooth green turf. Through half the night,
Scudding away from snare to snare, I plied
That anxious visitation;—moon and stars

---

6. Cockermouth Castle.

1. The right number (Wordsworth was nine years old), as against that in *1805*.

Scudding away from snare to snare, I plied
My anxious visitation, hurrying on,   320
Still hurrying, hurrying onward. Moon and stars
[315] Were shining o'er my head; I was alone,
And seemed to be a trouble to the peace
That was among them. Sometimes it befel
In these night-wanderings, that a strong desire   325
O'erpowered my better reason, and the bird
[320] Which was the captive of another's toils[3]
Became my prey; and when the deed was done
I heard among the solitary hills
Low breathings coming after me, and sounds   330
Of undistinguishable motion, steps
[325] Almost as silent as the turf they trod.

    Nor less in springtime, when on southern banks
The shining sun had from her knot of leaves
Decoyed the primrose flower, and when the vales   335
And woods were warm, was I a plunderer then
In the high places, on the lonesome peaks,
Where'er among the mountains and the winds
The mother-bird had built her lodge. Though mean
My object and inglorious, yet the end[5]   340
[330] Was not ignoble. Oh, when I have hung
Above the raven's nest, by knots of grass
And half-inch fissures in the slippery rock
But ill sustained, and almost, as it seemed,
Suspended by the blast which blew amain,   345
[335] Shouldering the naked crag, oh, at that time
While on the perilous ridge I hung alone,
With what strange utterance did the loud dry wind
Blow through my ears; the sky seemed not a sky
Of earth, and with what motion moved the clouds!   350

    The mind of man is framed even like the breath
[341] And harmony of music. There is a dark
Invisible workmanship that reconciles
Discordant elements, and makes them move
In one society. Ah me, that all   355
[345] The terrors, all the early miseries,
Regrets, vexations, lassitudes, that all
The thoughts and feelings which have been infused
Into my mind, should ever have made up
The calm existence that is mine when I   360
[350] Am worthy of myself. Praise to the end,

3. "Toils" can mean snares, as well as labors. Pennant's contemporary account of woodcock snaring on the fells is quoted in *1799*, I, 49*n*, above.
5. Result, as opposed to aim.

Were shining o'er my head. I was alone,   315
And seemed to be a trouble to the peace
That dwelt among them. Sometimes it befel
In these night wanderings, that a strong desire
O'erpowered my better reason, and the bird
Which was the captive of another's toil[3]   320
Became my prey; and when the deed was done
I heard among the solitary hills
Low breathings coming after me, and sounds
Of undistinguishable motion, steps
Almost as silent as the turf they trod.   325

    Nor less when spring had warmed the cultured Vale,[4]
Roved we as plunderers where the mother-bird
Had in high places built her lodge; though mean
Our object and inglorious, yet the end[5]
Was not ignoble. Oh! when I have hung   330
Above the raven's nest, by knots of grass
And half-inch fissures in the slippery rock
But ill-sustained, and almost (so it seemed)
Suspended by the blast that blew amain,
Shouldering the naked crag, oh, at that time   335
While on the perilous ridge I hung alone,
With what strange utterance did the loud dry wind
Blow through my ear! the sky seemed not a sky
Of earth—and with what motion moved the clouds!

    Dust as we are, the immortal spirit grows[6]   340
Like harmony in music; there is a dark
Inscrutable workmanship that reconciles
Discordant elements, makes them cling together
In one society. How strange that all
The terrors, pains, and early miseries,   345
Regrets, vexations, lassitudes interfused
Within my mind, should e'er have borne a part,
And that a needful part, in making up
The calm existence that is mine when I
Am worthy of myself! Praise to the end!   350

---

4. The part of the valley that was under cultivation.

6. A pietistic line that appears first in *MS. D* (1832).

Thanks likewise for the means! But I believe
That Nature, oftentimes, when she would frame
A favored being, from his earliest dawn
Of infancy doth open out the clouds   365
As at the touch of lightning, seeking him
With gentlest visitation; not the less,
Though haply aiming at the self-same end,
Does it delight her sometimes to employ
[355] Severer interventions, ministry   370
More palpable—and so she dealt with me.

    One evening—surely I was led by her[7]—
I went alone into a shepherd's boat,
A skiff that to a willow-tree was tied
Within a rocky cave, its usual home.   375
'Twas by the shores of Patterdale, a vale
Wherein I was a stranger, thither come
A schoolboy traveller at the holidays.
Forth rambled from the village inn alone,
No sooner had I sight of this small skiff,   380
Discovered thus by unexpected chance,
[360] Than I unloosed her tether and embarked.
The moon was up, the lake was shining clear
Among the hoary mountains; from the shore
I pushed, and struck the oars, and struck again   385
In cadence, and my little boat moved on
Even like a man who moves with stately step
[361] Though bent on speed.[8] It was an act of stealth
And troubled pleasure. Nor without the voice
Of mountain-echoes did my boat move on,   390
Leaving behind her still on either side
[365] Small circles glittering idly in the moon,
Until they melted all into one track
Of sparkling light.[9] A rocky steep uprose
Above the cavern of the willow-tree,   395
And now, as suited one who proudly rowed
With his best skill, I fixed a steady view
[370] Upon the top of that same craggy ridge,
The bound of the horizon—for behind
Was nothing but the stars and the grey sky.   400
She was an elfin pinnace;[1] lustily
I dipped my oars into the silent lake,

7. In 351–72 (composed January 1804)
"Nature" replaces the sub-classical spirits of *1799*, I, 67–81.
8. Lines 387–88 recall *Paradise Lost*,
XII, 1–2: "As one who in his journey
bates at noon, / Though bent on speed."
The lake was Ullswater.

9. Probably, as J. C. Maxwell suggests,
a recollection of the "tracks of shining
white," made by the water snakes, in
Coleridge's *Ancient Mariner* (1798), 265–
66.
1. Small boat.

Thanks to the means which Nature deigned to employ;
Whether her fearless visitings, or those
That came with soft alarm, like hurtless light
Opening the peaceful clouds; or she may use
Severer interventions, ministry   355
More palpable, as best might suit her aim.

   One summer evening (led by her)⁷ I found
A little boat tied to a willow tree
Within a rocky cave, its usual home.
Straight I unloosed her chain, and stepping in   360
Pushed from the shore. It was an act of stealth
And troubled pleasure, nor without the voice
Of mountain-echoes did my boat move on;
Leaving behind her still, on either side,
Small circles glittering idly in the moon,   365
Until they melted all into one track
Of sparkling light.⁹ But now, like one who rows,
Proud of his skill, to reach a chosen point
With an unswerving line, I fixed my view
Upon the summit of a craggy ridge,   370
The horizon's utmost boundary; for above
Was nothing but the stars and the grey sky.
She was an elfin pinnace;¹ lustily
I dipped my oars into the silent lake,

[375] And as I rose upon the stroke my boat
Went heaving through the water like a swan—
When from behind that craggy steep, till then   405
The bound of the horizon, a huge cliff,
As if with voluntary power instinct,
[380] Upreared its head.[2] I struck, and struck again,
And, growing still in stature, the huge cliff
Rose up between me and the stars, and still   410
With measured motion, like a living thing
[385] Strode after me. With trembling hands I turned
And through the silent water stole my way
Back to the cavern of the willow-tree.
There, in her mooring-place, I left my bark   415
And through the meadows homeward went with grave
[390] And serious thoughts; and after I had seen
That spectacle, for many days my brain
Worked with a dim and undetermined sense
Of unknown modes of being. In my thoughts   420
There was a darkness—call it solitude
[395] Or blank desertion—no familiar shapes
Of hourly objects, images of trees,
Of sea or sky, no colours of green fields,[3]
But huge and mighty forms that do not live
Like living men moved slowly through my mind   425
[400] By day, and were the trouble of my dreams.

    Wisdom and spirit of the universe,
Thou soul that art the eternity of thought,
That giv'st to forms and images a breath   430
And everlasting motion —not in vain,
[405] By day or star-light, thus from my first dawn
Of childhood didst thou intertwine for me
The passions that build up our human soul,
Not with the mean and vulgar[4] works of man,   435
But with high objects, with enduring things,
[410] With life and Nature, purifying thus
The elements of feeling and of thought,
And sanctifying by such discipline
Both pain and fear, until we recognise   440
A grandeur in the beatings of the heart.
[415] Nor was this fellowship vouchsafed to me
With stinted kindness. In November days,
When vapours rolling down the valleys made

---

2. The "huge cliff" is probably Black Crag (2,232 feet, and west of Ullswater), which would appear suddenly behind the nearer ridge, Stybarrow Crag, because the child was rowing out from the shore. "Instinct": imbued.

3. The child is deserted by *visual* reassurance, the power to conjure up pictures, "images," of familiar objects in the natural world.
4. Ordinary, commonplace.

And, as I rose upon the stroke, my boat 375
Went heaving through the water like a swan;
When, from behind that craggy steep till then
The horizon's bound, a huge peak, black and huge,
As if with voluntary power instinct
Upreared its head.[2] I struck and struck again, 380
And growing still in stature the grim shape
Towered up between me and the stars, and still,
For so it seemed, with purpose of its own
And measured motion like a living thing,
Strode after me. With trembling oars I turned, 385
And through the silent water stole my way
Back to the covert of the willow tree;
There in her mooring-place I left my bark,—
And through the meadows homeward went, in grave
And serious mood; but after I had seen 390
That spectacle, for many days, my brain
Worked with a dim and undetermined sense
Of unknown modes of being; o'er my thoughts
There hung a darkness, call it solitude
Or blank desertion. No familiar shapes 395
Remained, no pleasant images of trees,
Of sea or sky, no colours of green fields;[3]
But huge and mighty forms, that do not live
Like living men, moved slowly through the mind
By day, and were a trouble to my dreams. 400

    Wisdom and Spirit of the universe!
Thou Soul that art the eternity of thought,
That givest to forms and images a breath
And everlasting motion, not in vain
By day or star-light thus from my first dawn 405
Of childhood didst thou intwine for me
The passions that build up our human soul;
Not with the mean and vulgar[4] works of man,
But with high objects, with enduring things—
With life and nature, purifying thus 410
The elements of feeling and of thought,
And sanctifying, by such discipline,
Both pain and fear, until we recognise
A grandeur in the beatings of the heart.
Nor was this fellowship vouchsafed to me 415
With stinted kindness. In November days,
When vapours rolling down the valley made

A lonely scene more lonesome, among woods   445
At noon, and 'mid the calm of summer nights
[420] When by the margin of the trembling lake
Beneath the gloomy hills I homeward went
In solitude, such intercourse was mine—
'Twas mine among the fields both day and night,   450
And by the waters all the summer long.

[425]   And in the frosty season, when the sun
Was set, and visible for many a mile
The cottage windows through the twilight blazed,
I heeded not the summons; happy time   455
It was indeed for all of us, to me
[430] It was a time of rapture. Clear and loud
The village clock tolled six; I wheeled about
Proud and exulting, like an untired horse
That cares not for its home. All shod with steel   460
We hissed along the polished ice in games
[435] Confederate, imitative of the chace
And woodland pleasures, the resounding horn,
The pack loud bellowing, and the hunted hare.
So through the darkness and the cold we flew,   465
And not a voice was idle. With the din,
[440] Meanwhile, the precipices rang aloud;
The leafless trees and every icy crag
Tinkled like iron; while the distant hills
Into the tumult sent an alien sound   470
Of melancholy, not unnoticed; while the stars,[5]
[445] Eastward, were sparkling clear, and in the west
The orange sky of evening died away.

    Not seldom from the uproar I retired
Into a silent bay, or sportively   475
Glanced sideway, leaving the tumultuous throng,
[450] To cut across the image of a star
That gleamed upon the ice. And oftentimes
When we had given our bodies to the wind,
And all the shadowy banks on either side   480
[455] Came sweeping through the darkness, spinning still
The rapid line of motion, then at once
Have I, reclining back upon my heels,
Stopped short—yet still the solitary cliffs
Wheeled by me, even as if the earth had rolled   485
[460] With visible motion her diurnal round.[7]

5. An alexandrine, or six-foot line, which was probably not intended in the first place, but which persists through all versions of The Prelude.
7. Diurnal: daily. Compare A slumber did my spirit seal, 7–8, written at Goslar, November–December 1798: "Rolled round in earth's diurnal course / With rocks and stones and trees."

A lonely scene more lonesome, among woods
At noon, and 'mid the calm of summer nights,
When, by the margin of the trembling lake,   420
Beneath the gloomy hills homeward I went
In solitude, such intercourse was mine;
Mine was it in the fields both day and night,
And by the waters, all the summer long.

    And in the frosty season, when the sun   425
Was set, and visible for many a mile
The cottage windows blazed through twilight gloom,
I heeded not their summons: happy time
It was indeed for all of us—for me
It was a time of rapture! Clear and loud   430
The village clock tolled six,—I wheeled about,
Proud and exulting like an untired horse
That cares not for his home. All shod with steel,
We hissed along the polished ice in games
Confederate, imitative of the chase   435
And woodland pleasures,—the resounding horn,
The pack loud chiming, and the hunted hare.
So through the darkness and the cold we flew,
And not a voice was idle; with the din
Smitten, the precipices rang aloud;   440
The leafless trees and every icy crag
Tinkled like iron; while far distant hills
Into the tumult sent an alien sound
Of melancholy not unnoticed, while the stars[5]
Eastward were sparkling clear, and in the west   445
The orange sky of evening died away.
Not seldom from the uproar I retired
Into a silent bay, or sportively
Glanced sideway, leaving the tumultuous throng,
To cut across the reflex[6] of a star   450
That fled, and, flying still before me, gleamed
Upon the glassy plain; and oftentimes,
When we had given our bodies to the wind,
And all the shadowy banks on either side
Came sweeping through the darkness, spinning still   455
The rapid line of motion, then at once
Have I, reclining back upon my heels,
Stopped short; yet still the solitary cliffs
Wheeled by me—even as if the earth had rolled
With visible motion her diurnal round![7]   460

6. "Shadow" (*1799*), "image" (*1805*),   but Wordsworth's final choice has an in-
"reflex" (*1850*), all mean "reflection,"   definable rightness.

Behind me did they stretch in solemn train,[8]
Feebler and feebler, and I stood and watched
Till all was tranquil as a dreamless sleep.

     Ye presences of Nature, in the sky   490
[465] Or on the earth, ye visions of the hills
And souls of lonely places, can I think
A vulgar hope was yours when ye employed
Such ministry—when ye through many a year
Haunting me thus among my boyish sports,   495
[470] On caves and trees, upon the woods and hills,
Impressed upon all forms the characters[9]
Of danger or desire, and thus did make
The surface of the universal earth
With triumph, and delight, and hope, and fear,[1]   500
[475] Work like a sea?

          Not uselessly employed,
I might pursue this theme through every change
Of exercise and play to which the year
Did summon us in its delightful round.
We were a noisy crew; the sun in heaven   505
[480] Beheld not vales more beautiful than ours,
Nor saw a race in happiness and joy
More worthy of the fields where they were sown.
I would record with no reluctant voice
The woods of autumn, and their hazel bowers   510
[485] With milk-white clusters hung,[2] the rod and line—
True symbol of the foolishness of hope—
Which with its strong enchantment led us on
By rocks and pools, shut out from every star
All the green summer, to forlorn cascades   515
[490] Among the windings of the mountain brooks.
Unfading recollections—at this hour
The heart is almost mine with which I felt
From some hill-top on sunny afternoons
The kite, high up among the fleecy clouds,   520
[495] Pull at its rein like an impatient courser,

8. Sequence, succession.
9. Marks, signs; as at VI, 570, below.
"Impressed": stamped, imprinted.
1. As W.J.B. Owen points out ("An-notating Wordsworth," p. 65) Words-worth thinks, "whether instinctively or from literary training," in terms of the eighteenth-century distinction between the beautiful (the small and orderly) and the sublime (the vast and terrify-ing). Compare lines 305–6, above: "Fair seed-time had my soul, and I grew up / Fostered alike by beauty and by fear
* * *"
    "Work" (line 501): seethe, move rest-lessly.
2. *1805*, 509–11 (*1850*, 484–85) are seemingly a reference to *Nutting* (Octo-ber–December 1798), which Wordsworth later claimed had been written for *The Prelude*, though there is no manuscript evidence to suggest that it was at any time incorporated in *1799*.

Behind me did they stretch in solemn train,[8]
Feebler and feebler, and I stood and watched
Till all was tranquil as a dreamless sleep.

   Ye Presences of Nature in the sky
And on the earth! Ye Visions of the hills!   465
And Souls of lonely places! can I think
A vulgar hope was yours when ye employed
Such ministry, when ye through many a year
Haunting me thus among my boyish sports,
On caves and trees, upon the woods and hills,   470
Impressed upon all forms the characters[9]
Of danger or desire; and thus did make
The surface of the universal earth
With triumph and delight, with hope and fear,
Work like a sea?[1]   475

               Not uselessly employed,
Might I pursue this theme through every change
Of exercise and play, to which the year
Did summon us in his delightful round.

   We were a noisy crew; the sun in heaven
Beheld not vales more beautiful than ours;   480
Nor saw a band in happiness and joy
Richer, or worthier of the ground they trod.
I could record with no reluctant voice
The woods of autumn, and their hazel bowers
With milk-white clusters hung;[2] the rod and line,   485
True symbol of hope's foolishness, whose strong
And unreproved enchantment led us on
By rocks and pools shut out from every star,
All the green summer, to forlorn cascades
Among the windings hid of mountain brooks   490
—Unfading recollections! at this hour
The heart is almost mine with which I felt,
From some hill-top on sunny afternoons,
The paper kite high among fleecy clouds
Pull at her rein like an impetuous courser;   495

Or, from the meadows sent on gusty days,
Beheld her breast the wind, then suddenly
Dashed headlong and rejected by the storm.[3]

Ye lowly cottages in which we dwelt, 525
[500] A ministration of your own was yours,
A sanctity, a safeguard, and a love.
Can I forget you, being as ye were
So beautiful among the pleasant fields
In which ye stood? Or can I here forget 530
The plain and seemly countenance with which
[505] Ye dealt out your plain comforts? Yet had ye
Delights and exultations of your own:
Eager and never weary we pursued
Our home amusements by the warm peat fire 535
At evening, when with pencil and with slate,
[510] In square divisions parcelled out, and all
With crosses and with cyphers scribbled o'er,[4]
We schemed and puzzled, head opposed to head,
In strife too humble to be named in verse; 540
Or round the naked table, snow-white deal,
[515] Cherry, or maple, sate in close array,
And to the combat—lu or whist—led on
A thick-ribbed army, not as in the world
Neglected and ungratefully thrown by 545
Even for the very service they had wrought,
[520] But husbanded through many a long campaign.[5]
Uncouth assemblage was it, where no few
Had changed their functions—some, plebean cards
Which fate beyond the promise of their birth 550
Had glorified, and called to represent
[525] The persons of departed potentates.
Oh, with what echoes on the board they fell!
Ironic diamonds—clubs, hearts, diamonds, spades,
A congregation piteously akin. 555
Cheap matter did they give to boyish wit,
[530] Those sooty knaves, precipitated down
With scoffs and taunts like Vulcan out of heaven;
The paramount ace, a moon in her eclipse;
Queens, gleaming through their splendour's last decay; 560
And monarchs, surly at the wrongs sustained

3. *1805*, 510–24 follow 535–70 in *1799*.
4. Tick-tack-toe (noughts and crosses), described by a mock-heroic rendering of Milton's line, "With centric and eccentric scribbled o'er" (*Paradise Lost*, VIII, 83).
5. "Lu" is the card-game loo; "thick-ribbed" at line 544 refers probably to the thickening of the cards' edges through use. In lines 544–47 Wordsworth has in mind his own account of a Discharged Soldier, which was written January-February 1798, and finally became *1805*, IV, 363–504.

Or, from the meadows sent on gusty days,
Beheld her breast the wind, then suddenly
Dashed headlong, and rejected by the storm.[3]

Ye lowly cottages wherein we dwelt,
A ministration of your own was yours;   500
Can I forget you, being as you were
So beautiful among the pleasant fields
In which ye stood? or can I here forget
The plain and seemly countenance with which
Ye dealt out your plain comforts? Yet had ye   505
Delights and exultations of your own.
Eager and never weary we pursued
Our home-amusements by the warm peat-fire
At evening, when with pencil, and smooth slate
In square divisions parcelled out and all   510
With crosses and with cyphers scribbled o'er,[4]
We schemed and puzzled, head opposed to head
In strife too humble to be named in verse:
Or round the naked table, snow-white deal,
Cherry or maple, sate in close array,   515
And to the combat, Loo or Whist, led on
A thick-ribbed army; not, as in the world,
Neglected and ungratefully thrown by
Even for the very service they had wrought,
But husbanded through many a long campaign.[5]   520
Uncouth assemblage was it, where no few
Had changed their functions; some, plebeian cards
Which Fate, beyond the promise of their birth,
Had dignified, and called to represent
The persons of departed potentates.   525
Oh, with what echoes on the board they fell!
Ironic diamonds,—clubs, hearts, diamonds, spades,
A congregation piteously akin!
Cheap matter offered they to boyish wit,
Those sooty knaves, precipitated down   530
With scoffs and taunts, like Vulcan out of heaven:
The paramount ace, a moon in her eclipse,
Queens gleaming through their splendour's last decay,
And monarchs surly at the wrongs sustained

[535] By royal visages.[6] Meanwhile abroad
The heavy rain was falling, or the frost
Raged bitterly with keen and silent tooth;
And, interrupting the impassioned game,   565
From Esthwaite's neighbouring lake the splitting ice,
While it sank down towards the water, sent
[541] Among the meadows and the hills its long
And dismal yellings, like the noise of wolves
When they are howling round the Bothnic main.[7]   570

        Nor, sedulous as I have been to trace[8]
[545] How Nature by extrinsic passion first
Peopled my mind with beauteous forms or grand
And made me love them,[9] may I well forget
How other pleasures have been mine, and joys   575
Of subtler origin—how I have felt,
[550] Not seldom, even in that tempestuous time,
Those hallowed and pure motions of the sense[1]
Which seem in their simplicity to own
An intellectual charm,[2] that calm delight   580
Which, if I err not, surely must belong
[555] To those first-born affinities[3] that fit
Our new existence to existing things,
And, in our dawn of being, constitute
The bond of union betwixt life and joy.[4]   585

        Yes, I remember when the changeful earth
[560] And twice five seasons on my mind had stamped
The faces of the moving year, even then,
A child, I held unconscious intercourse

6. In Wordsworth's extension here of the description of the card game in *1799*, the influence of Cowper is less apparent, and that of Pope becomes more obvious. See *1799*, I, 225n, above; and with *1805*, 549–51 (*1850*, 522–29), compare Pope's *Rape of the Lock* (1717), III, 54, "Gain'd but one Trump and one *Plebeian* Card."
7. The northern Baltic. In *1799*, lines 510–24 appear at this point, followed by versions of the Drowned Man (*1805*, V, 450–73) and of the "spots of time" sequence (XI, 257–388). At an intervening stage in early March 1804, the Drowned Man had been part of Book IV, and the "spots of time" the climax of Book V, of the short-lived five-Book *Prelude*; see Composition and Texts: *1805/1850*, Introduction, below.
8. This uneasy transition is an afterthought drawn from *Paradise Lost*, IX, 27: "Not sedulous by nature to indite." "Sedulous": diligent, active.

9. Wordsworth's stress is on the child's unconsciousness of Nature's working: her forms "people" his memory not because he wishes them to do so, but as a result of emotions that are "extrinsic"—not directly relevant—experienced during his "boyish sports."
1. Maxwell points out that Wordsworth is "recalling, and reversing" Shakespeare's *Measure for Measure*, I, iv, 59, "The wanton stings and motions of the sense."
2. In *The Prelude*, "intellectual" is consistently synonymous with "spiritual."
3. Affinities with which the child is born; compare "those first affections," *Intimations Ode*, 151.
4. *1805*, 576–85 (*1850*, 549–58) affirm Wordsworth's view that in the spontaneous sensuousness of childhood there is a quality of mind (akin to Blake's Innocence) vital to the development of ontological security.

By royal visages.[6] Meanwhile abroad   535
Incessant rain was falling, or the frost
Raged bitterly, with keen and silent tooth;
And, interrupting oft that eager game,
From under Esthwaite's splitting fields of ice
The pent-up air, struggling to free itself,   540
Gave out to meadow grounds and hills a loud
Protracted yelling, like the noise of wolves
Howling in troops along the Bothnic Main.[7]

Nor, sedulous as I have been to trace[8]
How Nature by extrinsic passion first   545
Peopled the mind with forms sublime or fair,
And made me love them,[9] may I here omit
How other pleasures have been mine, and joys
Of subtler origin; how I have felt,
Not seldom even in that tempestuous time,   550
Those hallowed and pure motions of the sense[1]
Which seem, in their simplicity, to own
An intellectual charm;[2] that calm delight
Which, if I err not, surely must belong
To those first-born affinities[3] that fit   555
Our new existence to existing things,
And, in our dawn of being, constitute
The bond of union between life and joy.[4]

Yes, I remember when the changeful earth,
And twice five summers on my mind had stamped   560
The faces of the moving year, even then
I held unconscious intercourse with beauty

With the eternal beauty, drinking in 590
A pure organic[6] pleasure from the lines
[565] Of curling mist, or from the level plain
Of waters coloured by the steady clouds.
The sands of Westmoreland, the creeks and bays
Of Cumbria's[7] rocky limits, they can tell 595
How when the sea threw off his evening shade
[570] And to the shepherd's huts beneath the crags
Did send sweet notice of the rising moon,
How I have stood, to fancies such as these,
Engrafted in the tenderness of thought, 600
A stranger, linking with the spectacle
No conscious memory of a kindred sight,
[575] And bringing with me no peculiar sense
Of quietness or peace[8]—yet I have stood
Even while mine eye has moved o'er three long leagues 605
Of shining water, gathering, as it seemed,
Through every hair-breadth of that field of light
[580] New pleasure, like a bee among the flowers.

Thus often in those fits of vulgar joy[9]
Which through all seasons on a child's pursuits 610
Are prompt attendants, 'mid that giddy bliss
Which like a tempest works along the blood
[585] And is forgotten, even then I felt
Gleams like the flashing of a shield. The earth
And common face of Nature spake to me 615
Rememberable things; sometimes, 'tis true,
By chance collisions and quaint accidents—
[590] Like those ill-sorted unions, work supposed
Of evil-minded fairies[1]—yet not vain
Nor profitless, if haply they impressed 620
Collateral[2] objects and appearances,
Albeit lifeless then, and doomed to sleep
[595] Until maturer seasons called them forth
To impregnate and to elevate the mind.
And if the vulgar joy by its own weight 625
Wearied itself out of the memory,

6. Sensual, bodily.
7. Cumberland's.
8. Wordsworth is looking back to a period at which the beautiful scenes of Nature could be admired in and for themselves, neither conjuring up other scenes within the mind, nor setting up a response determined by previous experience. For the contemporary reader there would be a tacit reference—explicit in 1799, I, 406—to the theory of the mind's "association of ideas" derived from sense-experience, as formulated by David Hartley (1705–57), who dominated Coleridge's thinking in the mid-1790s, and was to a lesser extent an influence on Wordsworth himself.
9. Ordinary pleasures, as opposed to the heightened joy of communion.
1. Fairies were supposed to cause ill-assorted couples to fall in love, as in Shakespeare's *Midsummer Night's Dream*.
2. Indirect.

Old as creation,[5] drinking in a pure
Organic[6] pleasure from the silver wreaths
Of curling mist, or from the level plain   565
Of waters coloured by impending clouds.

    The sands of Westmoreland, the creeks and bays
Of Cumbria's[7] rocky limits, they can tell
How, when the Sea threw off his evening shade,
And to the shepherd's hut on distant hills   570
Sent welcome notice of the rising moon,
How I have stood, to fancies such as these
A stranger, linking with the spectacle
No conscious memory of a kindred sight,
And bringing with me no peculiar sense   575
Of quietness or peace;[8] yet have I stood,
Even while mine eye hath moved o'er many a league
Of shining water, gathering as it seemed
Through every hair-breadth in that field of light
New pleasure like a bee among the flowers.   580

    Thus oft amid those fits of vulgar joy[9]
Which, through all seasons, on a child's pursuits
Are prompt attendants, 'mid that giddy bliss
Which, like a tempest, works along the blood
And is forgotten; even then I felt   585
Gleams like the flashing of a shield;—the earth
And common face of Nature spake to me
Rememberable things; sometimes, 'tis true,
By chance collisions and quaint accidents
(Like those ill-sorted unions, work supposed   590
Of evil-minded fairies),[1] yet not vain
Nor profitless, if haply they impressed
Collateral[2] objects and appearances,
Albeit lifeless then, and doomed to sleep
Until maturer seasons called them forth   595
To impregnate and to elevate the mind.
—And if the vulgar joy by its own weight
Wearied itself out of the memory,

5. Wordsworth's original phrase, "the eternal beauty" (*1799* and *1805*), has been modified to remove the possibility of transcendental interpretation; see *1799*, I, 397*n*, above.

The scenes which were a witness of that joy
[600] Remained, in their substantial lineaments
Depicted on the brain, and to the eye
Were visible, a daily sight. And thus   630
By the impressive discipline of fear,
By pleasure and repeated happiness—
[605] So frequently repeated—and by force
Of obscure feelings representative
Of joys that were forgotten, these same scenes,   635
So beauteous and majestic in themselves,
Though yet the day was distant, did at length
[610] Become habitually dear, and all
Their hues and forms were by invisible links
Allied to the affections.³   640

                    I began
My story early, feeling, as I fear,
The weakness of a human love for days
[615] Disowned by memory—ere the birth of spring
Planting my snowdrops among winter snows.⁴
Nor will it seem to thee, my friend, so prompt   645
In sympathy, that I have lengthened out
[620] With fond and feeble tongue a tedious tale.⁶
Meanwhile my hope has been that I might fetch
Invigorating thoughts from former years,
Might fix the wavering balance of my mind,   650
And haply meet reproaches too, whose power
[625] May spur me on, in manhood now mature,
To honorable toil.⁷ Yet should these hopes
Be vain, and thus should neither I be taught
To understand myself, nor thou to know   655
With better knowledge how the heart was framed
[630] Of him thou lovest, need I dread from thee
Harsh judgments if I am so loth to quit
Those recollected hours that have the charm
Of visionary things,⁸ and lovely forms   660
And sweet sensations, that throw back our life

---

3. Feelings. As Havens points out, *1805*, 609–40 (*1850*, 581–612) are to some extent contradictory. Wordsworth seems uncertain how far the "Rememberable things" spoken by Nature were consciously experienced at the time. "Gleams like the flashing of a shield" are positively "felt" in *1805*, 613–14 (*1850*, 585–86) but natural "objects and appearances" in *1805*, 621–23 (*1850*, 593–95) are "lifeless," and "doomed to sleep / Until maturer seasons [call] them forth." 4. Attributing snowdrops—a full flower-ing of memory—to a period when there would have been only snow.
6. The banal alliteration is a joke for Coleridge (the "friend" of line 645) about poetic craftsmanship.
7. Especially the writing of the main section of *The Recluse*, a concern as vital to Wordsworth in 1804 as it had been when these lines were written for *1799*; see *1805*, 674n, below.
8. Things seen in the imagination, with the inward eye.

The scenes which were a witness of that joy
Remained in their substantial lineaments   600
Depicted on the brain, and to the eye
Were visible, a daily sight; and thus
By the impressive discipline of fear,
By pleasure and repeated happiness,
So frequently repeated, and by force   605
Of obscure feelings representative
Of things forgotten, these same scenes so bright,
So beautiful, so majestic in themselves,
Though yet the day was distant, did become
Habitually dear, and all their forms   610
And changeful colours by invisible links
Were fastened to the affections.[3]

                    I began
My story early—not misled, I trust,
By an infirmity of love for days
Disowned by memory—fancying flowers where none,   615
Not even the sweetest, do or can survive,
For him at least whose dawning day they cheered.[5]
Nor will it seem to thee, O Friend! so prompt
In sympathy, that I have lengthened out
With fond and feeble tongue a tedious tale.[6]   620
Meanwhile, my hope has been, that I might fetch
Invigorating thoughts from former years;
Might fix the wavering balance of my mind,
And haply meet reproaches too, whose power
May spur me on, in manhood now mature,   625
To honourable toil.[7] Yet should these hopes
Prove vain, and thus should neither I be taught
To understand myself, nor thou to know
With better knowledge how the heart was framed
Of him thou lovest; need I dread from thee   630
Harsh judgements, if the song be loth to quit
Those recollected hours that have the charm
Of visionary things,[8] those lovely forms
And sweet sensations that throw back our life,

5. Lines 615–17 are a late correction by Wordsworth which his executors chose to ignore. The first edition, without author-ity from the poet, reads as *1805*, 640–44, but with "breath" for "birth" in line 643.

[635] And almost make our infancy itself
A visible scene on which the sun is shining?

One end hereby at least hath been attained—
My mind hath been revived—and if this mood   665
Desert me not, I will forthwith bring down
[640] Through later years the story of my life.
The road lies plain before me. 'Tis a theme
Single and of determined bounds, and hence
I chuse it rather at this time than work   670
Of ampler or more varied argument,
[645] Where I might be discomfited and lost,
And certain hopes are with me that to thee
This labour will be welcome, honoured friend.[9]

9. Wordsworth's concluding verse-paragraph was written in January 1804, and states plainly to Coleridge why it is that he chooses to shelve the philosophical section of *The Recluse* in order to write an extended autobiography (at that time, of course, the five-Book *Prelude*).

And almost make remotest infancy   635
A visible scene, on which the sun is shining?

  One end at least hath been attained; my mind
Hath been revived, and if this genial mood
Desert me not, forthwith shall be brought down
Through later years the story of my life.   640
The road lies plain before me;—'tis a theme
Single and of determined bounds; and hence
I choose it rather at this time, than work
Of ampler or more varied argument,
Where I might be discomfited and lost: 645
And certain hopes are with me, that to thee
This labour will be welcome, honoured Friend![9]

Book Second

School-time (Continued)

Thus far, O friend, have we, though leaving much
Unvisited, endeavoured to retrace
My life through its first years, and measured back
The way I travelled when I first began
[5] To love the woods and fields. The passion yet   5
Was in its birth, sustained, as might befal,
By nourishment that came unsought—for still
From week to week, from month to month, we lived
A round of tumult. Duly[1] were our games
[10] Prolonged in summer till the daylight failed: 10
No chair remained before the doors, the bench
And threshold steps were empty, fast asleep
The labourer and the old man who had sate
A later lingerer, yet the revelry
[15] Continued and the loud uproar. At last,   15
When all the ground was dark and the huge clouds
Were edged with twinkling stars, to bed we went
With weary joints and with a beating mind.
Ah, is there one who ever has been young
[20] And needs a monitory voice to tame   20
The pride of virtue and of intellect?[2]
And is there one, the wisest and the best
Of all mankind, who does not sometimes wish
For things which cannot be, who would not give,
[25] If so he might, to duty and to truth   25
The eagerness of infantine desire?
A tranquillizing spirit presses now
On my corporeal frame,[3] so wide appears
The vacancy between me and those days,
[30] Which yet have such self-presence[4] in my mind   30
That sometimes when I think of them I seem
Two consciousnesses—conscious of myself,
And of some other being. A grey stone
Of native rock, left midway in the square
[35] Of our small market-village, was the home   35
And centre of these joys; and when, returned
After long absence, thither I repaired,
I found that it was split and gone to build

---

1. Appropriately.
2. Wordworth's syntax is cryptic, but his meaning is clear: "Can anyone who remembers the vitality of youth need to be warned not to overrate the qualities of age?"
3. A recollection of *Tintern Abbey*, 44–46: "the breath of this corporeal frame / And even the motion of our human blood / Almost suspended * * *" In each case the corporeality of the body is stressed to show the dominance of mind.
4. Actuality; compare, among many other Wordsworth compounds, "self-transmuted," "under-presence" (*1805*, IV, 141; XIII, 71, below).

Book Second

School-time (Continued)

Thus far, O Friend! have we, though leaving much
Unvisited, endeavoured to retrace
The simple ways in which my childhood walked;
Those chiefly that first led me to the love
Of rivers, woods, and fields. The passion yet   5
Was in its birth, sustained as might befal
By nourishment that came unsought; for still
From week to week, from month to month, we lived
A round of tumult. Duly[1] were our games
Prolonged in summer till the day-light failed: 10
No chair remained before the doors; the bench
And threshold steps were empty; fast asleep
The labourer, and the old man who had sate
A later lingerer; yet the revelry
Continued and the loud uproar: at last,   15
When all the ground was dark, and twinkling stars
Edged the black clouds, home and to bed we went,
Feverish with weary joints and beating minds.
Ah! is there one who ever has been young,
Nor needs a warning voice to tame the pride   20
Of intellect and virtue's self-esteem?[2]
One is there, though the wisest and the best
Of all mankind, who covets not at times
Union that cannot be;—who would not give,
If so he might, to duty and to truth   25
The eagerness of infantine desire?
A tranquillising spirit presses now
On my corporeal frame,[3] so wide appears
The vacancy between me and those days
Which yet have such self-presence[4] in my mind,   30
That musing on them, often do I seem
Two consciousnesses, conscious of myself
And of some other Being. A rude mass
Of native rock, left midway in the square
Of our small market village, was the goal   35
Or centre of these sports; and when, returned
After long absence, thither I repaired,
Gone was the old grey stone, and in its place

A smart assembly-room that perked and flared
With wash and rough-cast, elbowing the ground   40
[40] Which had been ours.[5] But let the fiddle scream,
And be ye happy! Yet, my friends, I know
That more than one of you will think with me
Of those soft starry nights, and that old dame
From whom the stone was named, who there had sate   45
[45] And watched her table with its huxter's wares,
Assiduous through the length of sixty years.[6]

We ran a boisterous race, the year span round
With giddy motion; but the time approached
That brought with it a regular desire   50
[50] For calmer pleasures—when the beauteous forms
Of Nature were collaterally attached
To every scheme of holiday delight,
And every boyish sport, less grateful élse
And languidly pursued.[7] When summer came   55
[55] It was the pastime of our afternoons
To beat along the plain of Windermere
With rival oars; and the selected bourne[8]
Was now an island musical with birds
That sang for ever, now a sister isle   60
[60] Beneath the oak's umbrageous[9] covert, sown
With lilies-of-the-valley like a field,
And now a third small island where remained
An old stone table and a mouldered cave—
[65] A hermit's history.[1] In such a race,   65
So ended, disappointment could be none,
Uneasiness, or pain, or jealousy;
We rested in the shade, all pleased alike,
Conquered and conqueror. Thus the pride of strength
[70] And the vainglory of superior skill   70
Were interfused with objects which subdued
And tempered them, and gradually produced
A quiet independence of the heart.
And to my friend who knows me I may add,
Unapprehensive of reproof, that hence   75
[75] Ensued a diffidence and modesty,

5. The resented "assembly-room" is the Hawkshead Town Hall, built in 1790. "Wash" in 1805 is whitewash, "rough-cast" a facing of mortar and gravel.
6. Wordsworth and his brother John returned to Hawkshead, the scene of their schooldays, with Coleridge on November 2, 1799.
7. Nature is still not sought for herself, but her "collateral" pleasures are now valued, where at the stage represented by 1805, 622–23 they had been not merely incidental, but "lifeless * * * / Until maturer seasons called them forth." "Grateful": pleasing.
8. Goal, destination.
9. Shady.
1. The 1850 reference to "Our Lady" identifies the island as Lady Holm, traditionally the site of a chapel dedicated to the Virgin Mary.

A smart Assembly-room usurped the ground
That had been ours.[5] There let the fiddle scream,   40
And be ye happy! Yet, my Friends! I know
That more than one of you will think with me
Of those soft starry nights, and that old Dame
From whom the stone was named, who there had sate,
And watched her table with its huckster's wares   45
Assiduous, through the length of sixty years.[6]

    We ran a boisterous course; the year span round
With giddy motion. But the time approached
That brought with it a regular desire
For calmer pleasures, when the winning forms   50
Of Nature were collaterally attached
To every scheme of holiday delight
And every boyish sport, less grateful else
And languidly pursued.[7]

                  When summer came,
Our pastime was, on bright half-holidays,   55
To sweep along the plain of Windermere
With rival oars; and the selected bourne[8]
Was now an Island musical with birds
That sang and ceased not; now a Sister Isle
Beneath the oak's umbrageous[9] covert, sown   60
With lilies of the valley like a field;
And now a third small Island, where survived
In solitude the ruins of a shrine
Once to Our Lady dedicate, and served
Daily with chaunted rites.[1] In such a race   65
So ended, disappointment could be none,
Uneasiness, or pain, or jealousy:
We rested in the shade, all pleased alike,
Conquered and conqueror. Thus the pride of strength,
And the vain-glory of superior skill,   70
Were tempered; thus was gradually produced
A quiet independence of the heart;
And to my Friend who knows me I may add,
Fearless of blame, that hence for future days
Ensued a diffidence and modesty,   75

And I was taught to feel—perhaps too much—
The self-sufficing power of solitude.

    No delicate viands sapped our bodily strength:
More than we wished we knew the blessing then   80
[80] Of vigorous hunger, for our daily meals
Were frugal, Sabine fare—and then, exclude
A little weekly stipend,[2] and we lived
Through three divisions of the quartered year
In pennyless poverty. But now, to school   85
[85] Returned from the half-yearly holidays,
We came with purses more profusely filled,[3]
Allowance which abundantly sufficed
To gratify the palate with repasts
More costly than the dame of whom I spake,   90
That ancient woman, and her board, supplied.
Hence inroads into distant vales, and long
Excursions far away among the hills,
Hence rustic dinners on the cool green ground—
[90] Or in the woods, or near a river-side,   95
Or by some shady fountain[4]—while soft airs
Among the leaves were stirring, and the sun,
Unfelt, shone sweetly round us in our joy.

    Nor is my aim neglected if I tell
[95] How twice in the long length of those half-years   100
We from our funds perhaps with bolder hand
Drew largely, anxious for one day at least
To feel the motion of the galloping steed.
And with the good old innkeeper, in truth,
On such occasion sometimes we employed   105
[100] Sly subterfuge, for the intended bound
Of the day's journey was too distant far
For any cautious man: a structure famed
Beyond its neighbourhood, the antique walls
Of that large abbey which within the Vale   110
Of Nightshade, to St Mary's honour built,
[105] Stands yet,[6] a mouldering pile with fractured arch,
Belfry, and images, and living trees—
A holy scene. Along the smooth green turf
Our horses grazed. To more than inland peace   115
Left by the sea-wind passing overhead
[110] (Though wind of roughest temper) trees and towers

2. In 1787, his last year at school, Wordsworth had sixpence a week pocket money,
and his youngest brother Christopher,
threepence. "Sabine fare" (*1805*, 82): a
reference to the frugality of the Roman
poet Horace on his Sabine farm.

3. In January 1787 Wordsworth returned
to school with a guinea, Christopher with
10s. 6d.
4. Spring or stream.
6. Furness Abbey, roughly twenty miles
south of Hawkshead.

And I was taught to feel, perhaps too much,
The self-sufficing power of Solitude.

    Our daily meals were frugal, Sabine fare!
More than we wished we knew the blessing then
Of vigorous hunger—hence corporeal strength   80
Unsapped by delicate viands; for, exclude
A little weekly stipend,[2] and we lived
Through three divisions of the quartered year
In penniless poverty. But now to school
From the half-yearly holidays returned,   85
We came with weightier purses,[3] that sufficed
To furnish treats more costly than the Dame
Of the old grey stone, from her scant board, supplied.
Hence rustic dinners on the cool green ground,
Or in the woods, or by a river side   90
Or shady fountains,[4] while among the leaves
Soft airs were stirring, and the mid-day sun
Unfelt shone brightly round us in our joy.
Nor is my aim neglected if I tell
How sometimes, in the length of those half-years,   95
We from our funds drew largely;—proud to curb,
And eager to spur on, the galloping steed;
And with the cautious inn-keeper, whose stud
Supplied our want, we haply might employ
Sly subterfuges, if the adventure's bound   100
Were distant: some framed temple where of yore
The Druids worshipped,[5] or the antique walls
Of that large abbey, where within the Vale
Of Nightshade, to St. Mary's honour built,
Stands yet[6] a mouldering pile with fractured arch,   105
Belfry, and images, and living trees,
A holy scene! Along the smooth green turf
Our horses grazed. To more than inland peace
Left by the west wind sweeping overhead
From a tumultuous ocean, trees and towers   110

5. Wordsworth has in mind the stone circle at Swinside, west of Duddon Bridge, to which in 1793 he had drawn attention in a note to *Evening Walk*, 171. The mistaken association of stone circles with the druids was widespread at the time.

May in that valley oftentimes be seen
Both silent and both motionless alike,
Such is the shelter that is there, and such   120
The safeguard for repose and quietness.

[115]   Our steeds remounted, and the summons given,
With whip and spur we by the chauntry[7] flew
In uncouth race, and left the cross-legged knight,
And the stone abbot,[8] and that single wren   125
Which one day sang so sweetly in the nave
[120] Of the old church that, though from recent showers
The earth was comfortless, and, touched by faint
Internal breezes—sobbings of the place
And respirations—from the roofless walls   130
The shuddering ivy dripped large drops, yet still
[125] So sweetly 'mid the gloom the invisible bird
Sang to itself that there I could have made
My dwelling-place, and lived for ever there
To hear such music. Through the walls we flew   135
And down the valley, and, a circuit made
[130] In wantonness of heart, through rough and smooth
We scampered homeward. Oh, ye rocks and streams,
And that still spirit of the evening air,
Even in this joyous time I sometimes felt   140
Your presence, when, with slackened step, we breathed[9]
[135] Along the sides of the steep hills, or when,
Lighted by gleams of moonlight from the sea,
We beat with thundering hoofs the level sand.[1]

        Upon the eastern shore of Windermere   145
Above the crescent of a pleasant bay
[140] There was an inn, no homely-featured shed,
Brother of the surrounding cottages,
But 'twas a splendid place, the door beset
With chaises, grooms, and liveries, and within   150
Decanters, glasses, and the blood-red wine.
[145] In ancient times, or ere the hall was built
On the large island, had this dwelling been
More worthy of a poet's love, a hut
Proud of its one bright fire and sycamore shade;[2]   155

7. A chapel endowed for the singing of masses for the dead.
8. The cross-legged knight has been moved, but may still be seen at Furness; it is less easy to identify the stone abbot.
9. Let our horses get their breath back.
1. Their direct route to Hawkshead would have been along the Dalton road to Ulverston, but the "circuit" referred to at *1805*, 136 (*1850*, 129) took them twelve miles along Levens Sands from Ramp-side, opposite Piel Castle, to Greenodd. Compare *1805*, 559–66, below, where the lines are recollected. *1799*, II, 140–78 are omitted at this point; the sequence is re-introduced in part at *1850*, VIII, 458–75.
2. The hall of Belle Isle on Windermere was completed in the early 1780s, and had the effect of bringing custom to the neighborhood. The inn was the old White Lion at Bowness.

In that sequestered valley may be seen,
Both silent and both motionless alike;
Such the deep shelter that is there, and such
The safeguard for repose and quietness.

   Our steeds remounted and the summons given,   115
With whip and spur we through the chauntry[7] flew
In uncouth race, and left the cross-legged knight,
And the stone-abbot,[8] and that single wren
Which one day sang so sweetly in the nave
Of the old church, that—though from recent showers   120
The earth was comfortless, and touched by faint
Internal breezes, sobbings of the place
And respirations from the roofless walls
The shuddering ivy dripped large drops—yet still
So sweetly 'mid the gloom the invisible bird   125
Sang to herself, that there I could have made
My dwelling-place, and lived for ever there
To hear such music. Through the walls we flew
And down the valley, and, a circuit made
In wantonness of heart, through rough and smooth   130
We scampered homewards. Oh, ye rocks and streams,
And that still spirit shed from evening air!
Even in this joyous time I sometimes felt
Your presence, when with slackened step we breathed[9]
Along the sides of the steep hills, or when   135
Lighted by gleams of moonlight from the sea
We beat with thundering hoofs the level sand.[1]

   Midway on long Winander's eastern shore,
Within the crescent of a pleasant bay,
A tavern stood; no homely-featured house,   140
Primeval like its neighbouring cottages,
But 'twas a splendid place, the door beset
With chaises, grooms, and liveries, and within
Decanters, glasses, and the blood-red wine.
In ancient times, or ere the Hall was built   145
On the large island, had this dwelling been
More worthy of a poet's love, a hut
Proud of its one bright fire and sycamore shade.[2]

But though the rhymes were gone which once inscribed
[150] The threshold, and large golden characters
On the blue-frosted signboard had usurped
The place of the old lion, in contempt
And mockery of the rustic painter's hand,   160
Yet to this hour the spot to me is dear
[155] With all its foolish pomp. The garden lay
Upon a slope surmounted by the plain
Of a small bowling-green; beneath us stood
A grove, with gleams of water through the trees   165
And over the tree-tops—nor did we want
[160] Refreshment, strawberries and mellow cream—
And there through half an afternoon we played
On the smooth platform, and the shouts we sent
Made all the mountains ring. But ere the fall   170
[165] Of night, when in our pinnace we returned
Over the dusky lake, and to the beach
Of some small island steered our course, with one,
The minstrel of our troop,[3] and left him there,
And rowed off gently, while he blew his flute   175
[170] Alone upon the rock, oh, then the calm
And dead still water lay upon my mind
Even with a weight of pleasure, and the sky,
Never before so beautiful, sank down
Into my heart and held me like a dream.   180
[175] Thus daily were my sympathies enlarged,
And thus the common range of visible things
Grew dear to me: already I began
To love the sun, a boy I loved the sun
Not as I since have loved him—as a pledge   185
[180] And surety of our earthly life, a light
Which while we view we feel we are alive—
But for this cause, that I had seen him lay
His beauty on the morning hills, had seen
[185] The western mountain touch his setting orb   190
In many a thoughtless hour, when from excess
Of happiness my blood appeared to flow
With its own pleasure, and I breathed with joy.
And from like feelings, humble though intense,
[190] To patriotic and domestic love   195
Analogous, the moon to me was dear;
For I would dream away my purposes
Standing to look upon her, while she hung
Midway between the hills as if she knew
[195] No other region but belonged to thee,   200

3. Robert Greenwood, later Senior Fellow of Trinity, Cambridge, but remembered by Wordsworth's landlady Ann Tyson as "t' lad wi' t' flute" (Thompson, pp. 78–79, 147).

But—though the rhymes were gone that once inscribed
The threshold, and large golden characters,   150
Spread o'er the spangled sign-board, had dislodged
The old Lion and usurped his place, in slight
And mockery of the rustic painter's hand—
Yet, to this hour, the spot to me is dear
With all its foolish pomp. The garden lay   155
Upon a slope surmounted by the plain
Of a small bowling-green; beneath us stood
A grove, with gleams of water through the trees
And over the tree-tops; nor did we want   160
Refreshment, strawberries and mellow cream.
There, while through half an afternoon we played
On the smooth platform, whether skill prevailed
Or happy blunder triumphed, bursts of glee
Made all the mountains ring. But, ere night-fall,   165
When in our pinnace we returned at leisure
Over the shadowy lake, and to the beach
Of some small island steered our course with one,
The Minstrel of the Troop,[3] and left him there,
And rowed off gently, while he blew his flute   170
Alone upon the rock—oh, then, the calm
And dead still water lay upon my mind
Even with a weight of pleasure, and the sky,
Never before so beautiful, sank down
Into my heart, and held me like a dream!   175
Thus were my sympathies enlarged, and thus
Daily the common range of visible things
Grew dear to me: already I began
To love the sun; a boy I loved the sun,
Not as I since have loved him, as a pledge   180
And surety of our earthly life, a light
Which we behold and feel we are alive;
Nor for his bounty to so many worlds—
But for this cause, that I had seen him lay
His beauty on the morning hills, had seen   185
The western mountains touch his setting orb,
In many a thoughtless hour, when, from excess
Of happiness, my blood appeared to flow
For its own pleasure, and I breathed with joy.
And, from like feelings, humble though intense,   190
To patriotic and domestic love
Analogous, the moon to me was dear;
For I would dream away my purposes,
Standing to gaze upon her while she hung
Midway between the hills, as if she knew   195
No other region, but belonged to thee,

Yea, appertained by a peculiar right
To thee and thy grey huts,[4] my darling vale.

    Those incidental charms which first attached
My heart to rural objects, day by day
[200] Grew weaker, and I hasten on to tell   205
How Nature, intervenient[5] till this time
And secondary, now at length was sought
For her own sake. But who shall parcel out
His intellect by geometric rules,
[205] Split like a province into round and square?   210
Who knows the individual hour in which
His habits were first sown even as a seed,
Who that shall[6] point as with a wand, and say
'This portion of the river of my mind
[210] Came from yon fountain'?[7] Thou, my friend, art one   215
More deeply read in thy own thoughts; to thee
Science appears but what in truth she is,
Not as our glory and our absolute boast,
But as a succedaneum, and a prop
[215] To our infirmity.[8] Thou art no slave   220
Of that false secondary power by which
In weakness we create distinctions, then
Deem that our puny boundaries are things
Which we perceive, and not which we have made.
[220] To thee, unblinded by these outward shows,   225
The unity of all has been revealed;
And thou wilt doubt with me, less aptly skilled
Than many are to class the cabinet
[225] Of their sensations,[9] and in voluble phrase[1]
Run through the history and birth of each   230
As of a single independent thing.
Hard task to analyse a soul,[2] in which
Not only general habits and desires,
But each most obvious and particular thought—
[230] Not in a mystical and idle sense,
But in the words of reason deeply weighed—   235
Hath no beginning.

4. Cottages built of gray local stone.
5. Literally, "coming between"; Nature had asserted herself amid other preoccupations.
6. "Who is there that would be able to?"
7. For the importance of the river as an image of the mind see, e.g., *1805*, III, 10–12, IV, 39–55, XIII, 172–84, below.
8. *1805*, 216–20 (*1850*, 211–15), belonging probably to January 1804, define the attitude of Wordsworth—though surely not of Coleridge, to whom they are addressed—towards learning (Latin "*scientia*," not modern "science"). "Succedaneum": remedy (*NED*; in fact this is a misuse of the word).
9. To classify their feelings, as if they were exhibits in a display case. "Doubt" in *1805*, 227 (*1850*, 222) refers back to the possibility of "parcelling out" the intellect, *1805*, 208–15 (*1850*, 203–10).
1. Phraseology, style.
2. See *Paradise Lost*, V, 564, where Raphael speaks of relating the war in heaven as "Sad task and hard." As Maxwell suggests, this is "one of Wordsworth's implied claims for epic, or more than epic, status for his poem."

Yea, appertained by a peculiar right
To thee and thy grey huts,[4] thou one dear Vale!

Those incidental charms which first attached
My heart to rural objects, day by day
Grew weaker, and I hasten on to tell   200
How Nature, intervenient[5] till this time
And secondary, now at length was sought
For her own sake. But who shall parcel out
His intellect by geometric rules,
Split like a province into round and square?   205
Who knows the individual hour in which
His habits were first sown, even as a seed?
Who that shall[6] point as with a wand and say
'This portion of the river of my mind
Came from yon fountain?'[7] Thou, my Friend! art one   210
More deeply read in thy own thoughts; to thee
Science appears but what in truth she is,
Not as our glory and our absolute boast,
But as a succedaneum, and a prop
To our infirmity.[8] No officious slave   215
Art thou of that false secondary power
By which we multiply distinctions, then
Deem that our puny boundaries are things
That we perceive, and not that we have made.
To thee, unblinded by these formal arts,   220
The unity of all hath been revealed,
And thou wilt doubt with me, less aptly skilled
Than many are to range the faculties
In scale and order, class the cabinet
Of their sensations,[9] and in voluble phrase[1]   225
Run through the history and birth of each
As of a single independent thing.
Hard task, vain hope, to analyse the mind,[2]
If each most obvious and particular thought,
Not in a mystical and idle sense,   230
But in the words of Reason deeply weighed,
Hath no beginning.

Blessed the infant babe—
For with my best conjectures I would trace
The progress of our being—blest the babe
[235] Nursed in his mother's arms, the babe who sleeps   240
Upon his mother's breast, who, when his soul
Claims manifest kindred with an earthly soul,[3]
Doth gather passion from his mother's eye.
Such feelings pass into his torpid life
Like an awakening breeze, and hence his mind,   245
Even in the first trial of its powers,
Is prompt and watchful, eager to combine
In one appearance all the elements
And parts of the same object, else detached
And loth to coalesce.[4] Thus day by day   250
Subjected to the discipline of love,
His organs and recipient faculties
Are quickened, are more vigorous; his mind spreads,
Tenacious of the forms which it receives[5]
In one beloved presence—nay and more,   255
In that most apprehensive habitude[6]
And those sensations which have been derived
From this beloved presence—there exists
A virtue which irradiates and exalts
[240] All objects through all intercourse of sense.[7]   260
No outcast he, bewildered and depressed;
Along his infant veins are interfused
The gravitation and the filial bond
[244] Of Nature that connect him with the world.[8]
Emphatically such a being lives,   265
An inmate of this *active* universe.
From Nature largely he receives, nor so
Is satisfied, but largely gives again;
[255] For feeling has to him imparted strength,
And—powerful in all sentiments of grief,   270
Of exultation, fear and joy—his mind,
Even as an agent of the one great mind,

3. When his soul forms an evident relationship with the soul of another human being.
4. Emotion acts as a unifying factor because it awakens and alerts the mind, enabling it to make the basic imaginative step of forming parts into wholes; see line 275n, below.
5. Retentive of visual images.
6. In that relationship ("habitude") best suited to learning ("most apprehensive").
7. As F. R. Leavis pointed out (*Revaluation*, p. 160), there is a clear and interesting connection with *Tintern Abbey*, 101–2: "A motion and a spirit, that impels / All thinking things, all objects of all thought * * *" For the child objects are irradiated and exalted by the "beloved presence" (*1805*, 255) of the mother, just as for the adult, consciousness of a disturbing transcendental "presence" (*Tintern Abbey*, 95) shows them to be impelled by "a motion and a spirit."
8. Innate in the child is a force pulling him towards the world ("gravitation"). In 1799, when these lines were written, Wordsworth sees this force as the "filial bond" of child and mother, which establishes the larger bond of man and Nature; for a very different position, see *Intimations Ode*, 67–84, of spring 1804.

Blest the infant Babe
(For with my best conjecture I would trace
Our Being's earthly progress), blest the Babe,
Nursed in his Mother's arms, who sinks to sleep   235
Rocked on his Mother's breast; who with his soul
Drinks in the feelings of his Mother's eye!
For him, in one dear Presence, there exists
A virtue which irradiates and exalts
Objects through widest intercourse of sense.[7]   240
No outcast he, bewildered and depressed:
Along his infant veins are interfused
The gravitation and the filial bond
Of nature that connect him with the world.[8]
Is there a flower, to which he points with hand   245
Too weak to gather it, already love
Drawn from love's purest earthly fount for him
Hath beautified that flower; already shades
Of pity cast from inward tenderness
Do fall around him upon aught that bears   250
Unsightly marks of violence or harm.
Emphatically such a Being lives,
Frail creature as he is, helpless as frail,
An inmate of this active universe.
For feeling has to him imparted power   255
That through the growing faculties of sense
Doth like an agent of the one great Mind

Creates, creator and receiver both,
Working but in alliance with the works
[260] Which it beholds.[9] Such, verily, is the first   275
Poetic spirit of our human life—
By uniform controul of after years
In most abated and suppressed, in some
Through every change of growth or of decay
[265] Preeminent till death.[1]   180

                From early days,
Beginning not long after that first time
In which, a babe, by intercourse of touch
I held mute dialogues with my mother's heart,
I have endeavoured to display the means
[270] Whereby the infant sensibility,   265
Great birthright of our being, was in me
Augmented and sustained. Yet is a path
More difficult before me, and I fear
That in its broken windings we shall need
[275] The chamois' sinews and the eagle's wing.   290
For now a trouble came into my mind
From unknown causes:[3] I was left alone
Seeking the visible world, nor knowing why.
The props of my affections were removed,
[280] And yet the building stood, as if sustained   295
By its own spirit. All that I beheld
Was dear to me, and from this cause it came
That now to Nature's finer influxes[4]
My mind lay open—to that more exact
And intimate communion which our hearts   300
Maintain with the minuter properties
Of objects which already are beloved,
And of those only.

                Many are the joys
[285] Of youth, but, oh, what happiness to live
When every hour brings palpable access   305
Of knowledge, when all knowledge is delight,
And sorrow is not there. The seasons came,
And every season to my notice brought
[290] A store of transitory qualities

9. Strengthened by the mother's love, and working in harmony with external Nature, the child's mind shows itself to be creative as well as receptive. It is thus not merely an agent, but in its creativity a reflection, of the mind of God.
1. Wordsworth's lines imply a confidence that was not, of course, sustained; compare *1805*, XI, 337–38, below, written in April 1805, "I see by glimpses now, when age comes on / May scarcely see at all."
3. Nature herself was the disturbing force, or "trouble." The chamois (*1805*, 290; *1850*, 275) is a mountain antelope of great agility, hunted in the Alps; see *Descriptive Sketches* (1793), 366–413.
4. Influences.

Create, creator and receiver both,
Working but in alliance with the works
Which it beholds.[9]—Such, verily, is the first   260
Poetic spirit of our human life,
By uniform control of after years,
In most, abated or suppressed; in some,
Through every change of growth and of decay,
Pre-eminent till death.[1,2]   265

                   From early days,
Beginning not long after that first time
In which, a Babe, by intercourse of touch
I held mute dialogues with my Mother's heart,
I have endeavoured to display the means
Whereby this infant sensibility,   270
Great birthright of our being, was in me
Augmented and sustained. Yet is a path
More difficult before me; and I fear
That in its broken windings we shall need
The chamois' sinews, and the eagle's wing: 275
For now a trouble came into my mind
From unknown causes.[3] I was left alone
Seeking the visible world, nor knowing why.
The props of my affections were removed,
And yet the building stood, as if sustained   280
By its own spirit! All that I beheld
Was dear, and hence to finer influxes[4]
The mind lay open, to a more exact
And close communication. Many are our joys
In youth, but oh! what happiness to live   285
When every hour brings palpable access
Of knowledge, when all knowledge is delight,
And sorrow is not there! The seasons came,
And every season wheresoe'er I moved
Unfolded transitory qualities,   290

---

2. Wordsworth's revisions of the passage on the Infant Babe (*1805*, 237–80) are found chiefly in *MS. D* (1832 and 1838/ 39). *1805*, 244–57, 267–68, 270–71 are cut, and *1850*, 245–51 and 53 inserted. The child's power and creativity are thus reduced—he now works "like," where before he worked "*as* an agent of the one great mind"—and his responses have been sentimentalized. The result is a more credible baby, but a weakened statement of Wordsworth's intuition of strength drawn from the child-mother relationship.

Which but for this most watchful power of love   310
Had been neglected, left a register
Of permanent relations else unknown.[5]
Hence, life, and change, and beauty, solitude
[295] More active even than 'best society',[6]
Society made sweet as solitude   315
By silent inobtrusive sympathies,
And gentle agitations of the mind
From manifold distinctions,[7] difference
[300] Perceived in things where to the common eye
No difference is, and hence, from the same source,   320
Sublimer joy. For I would walk alone
In storm and tempest,[8] or in starlight nights
Beneath the quiet heavens, and at that time
Have felt whate'er there is of power in sound
[305] To breathe an elevated mood, by form   325
Or image unprofaned; and I would stand
Beneath some rock, listening to sounds that are
The ghostly language of the ancient earth,
[310] Or make their dim abode in distant winds.[9]
Thence did I drink the visionary power.   330
I deem not profitless those fleeting moods
Of shadowy exultation; not for this,
That they are kindred to our purer mind
[315] And intellectual[1] life, but that the soul—
Remembering how she felt, but what she felt   335
Remembering not—retains an obscure sense[2]
Of possible sublimity, to which
With growing faculties she doth aspire,
[320] With faculties still growing, feeling still
That whatsoever point they gain they still   340
Have something to pursue.

                    And not alone
In grandeur and in tumult, but no less
In tranquil scenes, that universal power
[325] And fitness in the latent qualities
And essences of things, by which the mind   345

---

5. Love of Nature makes the child responsive to whatever the seasons bring, creating from passing experience permanent relationships—permanent presumably in their effect upon the mind—that are recorded in the memory, and so known to have existed.
6. Wordsworth's quotation marks draw attention to *Paradise Lost*, IX, 249, "For solitude sometimes is best society."
7. The "gentle agitations" do not depend on "by" in the previous line; they are the last item in the list that follows

"Hence," in *1805*, 313 (*1850*, 294).
8. *1805*, 322–41 (*1850*, 303–22) were written, in the third person, in January–February 1798, probably to describe the narrator of *The Ruined Cottage*.
9. Compare *Intimations Ode*, 28: "The winds come to me from the fields of sleep." "Ghostly": spiritual; but also "disembodied."
1. In effect, "spiritual."
2. Scansion: an óbscure seńse; Milton too sometimes stresses the first syllable.

Which, but for this most watchful power of love,
Had been neglected; left a register
Of permanent relations, else unknown.[5]
Hence life, and change, and beauty, solitude
More active even than 'best society'[6]—   295
Society made sweet as solitude
By inward concords, silent, inobtrusive
And gentle agitations of the mind
From manifold distinctions,[7] difference
Perceived in things, where, to the unwatchful eye,   300
No difference is, and hence, from the same source,
Sublimer joy; for I would walk alone,
Under the quiet stars,[8] and at that time
Have felt whate'er there is of power in sound
To breathe an elevated mood, by form   305
Or image unprofaned; and I would stand,
If the night blackened with a coming storm,
Beneath some rock, listening to notes that are
The ghostly language of the ancient earth,
Or make their dim abode in distant winds.[9]   310
Thence did I drink the visionary power;
And deem not profitless those fleeting moods
Of shadowy exultation: not for this,
That they are kindred to our purer mind
And intellectual[1] life; but that the soul,   315
Remembering how she felt, but what she felt
Remembering not, retains an obscure sense[2]
Of possible sublimity, whereto
With growing faculties she doth aspire,
With faculties still growing, feeling still   320
That whatsoever point they gain, they yet
Have something to pursue.

            And not alone
'Mid gloom and tumult, but no less 'mid fair
And tranquil scenes, that universal power
And fitness in the latent qualities   325
And essences of things, by which the mind

Is moved by feelings of delight, to me
Came strengthened with a superadded soul,
A virtue not its own.³ My morning walks
[330] Were early: oft before the hours of school   350
I travelled round our little lake, five miles
Of pleasant wandering—happy time, more dear
For this, that one was by my side, a friend
Then passionately loved.⁴ With heart how full
[335] Will he peruse these lines, this page—perhaps   355
A blank to other men—for many years
Have since flowed in between us, and, our minds
Both silent to each other, at this time
We live as if those hours had never been.
Nor seldom did I lift our cottage latch
[340] Far earlier, and before the vernal thrush   360
Was audible, among the hills I sate
Alone upon some jutting eminence⁶
At the first hour of morning, when the vale
[345] Lay quiet in an utter solitude.
How shall I trace the history, where seek   365
The origin of what I then have felt?
Oft in those moments such a holy calm
Did overspread my soul that I forgot
[350] That I had bodily eyes, and what I saw
Appeared like something in myself, a dream,   370
A prospect⁷ in my mind.

           'Twere long to tell
What spring and autumn, what the winter snows,
And what the summer shade, what day and night,
[355] The evening and the morning, what my dreams
And what my waking thoughts, supplied to nurse   375
That spirit of religious love in which
I walked with Nature. But let this at least
Be not forgotten, that I still retained
[360] My first creative sensibility,
That by the regular action of the world   380
My soul was unsubdued. A plastic⁸ power
Abode with me, a forming hand, at times
Rebellious, acting in a devious mood,

---

3. To the power to please that natural objects have in and for themselves is added a virtue not their own—and not at all clearly defined. The "soul" is "superadded" to the inherent qualities of landscape, and yet "comes" to Wordsworth, rather than being, as one would expect, projected by him in a mood of "shadowy exultation" (*1805*, 331–32; *1850*, 312–13).

4. School began at six or six-thirty in the summer months at Hawkshead and an hour later in the winter. The lake was Esthwaite Water; the friend, John Fleming, is enthusiastically referred to in *The Vale of Esthwaite* (1785–87).
6. Compare Thomson's *Seasons*, II, 1042, "Sad on the jutting eminence he sits."
7. View, landscape.
8. Formative, creative.

Is moved with feelings of delight, to me
Came strengthened with a superadded soul,
A virtue not its own.[3] My morning walks
Were early;—oft before the hours of school 330
I travelled round our little lake, five miles
Of pleasant wandering. Happy time! more dear
For this, that one was by my side, a Friend
Then passionately loved;[4] with heart how full
Would he peruse these lines! For many years 335
Have since flowed in between us, and, our minds
Both silent to each other, at this time
We live as if those hours had never been.
Nor seldom did I lift our cottage latch
Far earlier, and ere one smoke-wreath had risen 340
From human dwelling, or the thrush, high perched,
Piped to the woods his shrill *reveillé*,[5] sate
Alone upon some jutting eminence,[6]
At the first gleam of dawn-light, when the Vale,
Yet slumbering, lay in utter solitude. 345
How shall I seek the origin? where find
Faith in the marvellous things which then I felt?
Oft in these moments such a holy calm
Would overspread my soul, that bodily eyes
Were utterly forgotten, and what I saw 350
Appeared like something in myself, a dream,
A prospect[7] in the mind.

        'Twere long to tell
What spring and autumn, what the winter snows,
And what the summer shade, what day and night,
Evening and morning, sleep and waking thought, 355
From sources inexhaustible, poured forth
To feed the spirit of religious love
In which I walked with Nature. But let this
Be not forgotten, that I still retained
My first creative sensibility; 360
That by the regular action of the world
My soul was unsubdued. A plastic[8] power
Abode with me; a forming hand, at times
Rebellious, acting in a devious mood;

---

5. Lines 341–42 belong to 1838/39 and were omitted by the poet's executors. The reading of the first edition—"or the vernal thrush / Was audible; and sate among the woods"—seems to have been invented by them on the basis of *MS. C.*

[365] A local spirit of its own, at war
　　With general tendency, but for the most　　　　　385
　　Subservient strictly to the external things
　　With which it communed.[9] An auxiliar light
　　Came from my mind, which on the setting sun
[370] Bestowed new splendor; the melodious birds,
　　The gentle breezes, fountains that ran on　　　　390
　　Murmuring so sweetly in themselves, obeyed
　　A like dominion, and the midnight storm
　　Grew darker in the presence of my eye.
[375] Hence my obeisance, my devotion hence,
　　And hence my transport.[1]　　　　　　　　　　395

　　　　　　　　　　Nor should this, perchance,
　　Pass unrecorded, that I still[2] had loved
　　The exercise and produce of a toil
　　Than analytic industry to me
[380] More pleasing, and whose character I deem
　　Is more poetic, as resembling more　　　　　　400
　　Creative agency—I mean to speak
　　Of that interminable building reared
　　By observation of affinities
[385] In objects where no brotherhood exists
　　To common minds. My seventeenth year was come,　405
　　And, whether from this habit rooted now
　　So deeply in my mind, or from excess
　　Of the great social principle of life
[390] Coercing all things into sympathy,
　　To unorganic natures I transferred　　　　　　410
　　My own enjoyments, or, the power of truth
　　Coming in revelation, I conversed
　　With things that really are, I at this time
[395] Saw blessings spread around me like a sea.[3]
　　Thus did my days pass on, and now at length　　415
　　From Nature and her overflowing soul
　　I had received so much that all my thoughts
　　Were steeped in feeling. I was only then
[400] Contented when with bliss ineffable
　　I felt the sentiment of being spread　　　　　420
　　O'er all that moves, and all that seemeth still,

---

9. Wordsworth is saying that his creativity, though at times capricious in its refusal to conform, was for the most part stabilized by subordination to Nature.
1. Wordsworth's submission and devotion to Nature, and the joy that he derives from her, are paradoxically based on the fact that she is herself subordinate to his creative sensibility. "Transport": exaltation, extreme emotion.

2. Always.
3. Wordsworth appears in *1805*, 405–14 (*1850*, 386–95) to be offering three alternatives, when in fact he offers two, of which the first is subdivided. The boy either transfers his own enjoyments to inanimate ("unorganic") Nature—through excess of fellow feeling—or he rightly perceives the existence of a shared life-force.

A local spirit of his own, at war 365
With general tendency, but, for the most,
Subservient strictly to external things
With which it communed.[9] An auxiliar light
Came from my mind, which on the setting sun
Bestowed new splendour; the melodious birds, 370
The fluttering breezes, fountains that ran on
Murmuring so sweetly in themselves, obeyed
A like dominion, and the midnight storm
Grew darker in the presence of my eye:
Hence my obeisance, my devotion hence, 375
And hence my transport.[1]

                 Nor should this, perchance,
Pass unrecorded, that I still[2] had loved
The exercise and produce of a toil,
Than analytic industry to me
More pleasing, and whose character I deem 380
Is more poetic as resembling more
Creative agency. The song would speak
Of that interminable building reared
By observation of affinities
In objects where no brotherhood exists 385
To passive minds. My seventeenth year was come;
And, whether from this habit rooted now
So deeply in my mind, or from excess
In the great social principle of life
Coercing all things into sympathy, 390
To unorganic natures were transferred
My own enjoyments; or the power of truth
Coming in revelation, did converse
With things that really are; I, at this time,
Saw blessings spread around me like a sea.[3] 395
Thus while the days flew by, and years passed on,
From Nature overflowing on my soul,
I had received so much, that every thought
Was steeped in feeling; I was only then
Contented, when with bliss ineffable 400
I felt the sentiment of Being spread
O'er all that moves and all that seemeth still;

O'er all that, lost beyond the reach of thought
And human knowledge, to the human eye
[405] Invisible, yet liveth to the heart,
O'er all that leaps, and runs, and shouts, and sings,   425
Or beats the gladsome air, o'er all that glides
Beneath the wave, yea, in the wave itself
And mighty depth of waters. Wonder not
[410] If such my transports were, for in all things
I saw one life, and felt that it was joy;   430
[415] One song they sang, and it was audible—
Most audible then when the fleshly ear,
O'ercome by grosser prelude of that strain,
Forgot its functions and slept undisturbed.[5]

     If this be error, and another faith   435
[420] Find easier access to the pious mind,
Yet were I grossly destitute of all
Those human sentiments which make this earth
So dear if I should fail with grateful voice
To speak of you, ye mountains, and ye lakes   440
[425] And sounding cataracts, ye mists and winds
That dwell among the hills where I was born.
If in my youth I have been pure in heart,
If, mingling with the world, I am content
With my own modest pleasures, and have lived   445
[430] With God and Nature communing, removed
From little enmities and low desires,
The gift is yours; if in these times of fear,
This melancholy waste of hopes o'erthrown,[6]
If, 'mid indifference and apathy   450
[435] And wicked exultation, when good men
On every side fall off we know not how
To selfishness, disguised in gentle names
Of peace and quiet and domestic love—
Yet mingled, not unwillingly, with sneers   455
[440] On visionary minds[7]—if, in this time
Of dereliction and dismay, I yet
Despair not of our nature, but retain
A more than Roman confidence, a faith

---

5. *1805*, 416–34 (*1850*, 396–418) were
written as third-person narrative for *The
Ruined Cottage* in February–March 1798.
Hearing the song of the One Life (*1805*,
431), like seeing into the "life of things"
in *Tintern Abbey*, 50, is a metaphor that
should not be taken too literally. The
"grosser prelude" (line 433) can stand
for any external stimulus.
6. The sudden entrance into the poem of
a concern with the destruction of hopes

aroused in the early days of the French
Revolution derives from a Coleridge letter of ca. September 1799, quoted in
1799, II, 484n, above. "Waste": desert.
7. See, e.g., Hazlitt's description in *The
Spirit of the Age* (1825) of the notorious
lectures of 1799 in which Sir James Mackintosh, one-time apologist for the French
Revolution (*Vindiciae Gallicae*, 1791),
abjured earlier friends and opinions;
Howe, XI, pp. 98–100.

O'er all that, lost beyond the reach of thought
And human knowledge, to the human eye
Invisible, yet liveth to the heart;   405
O'er all that leaps and runs, and shouts and sings,
Or beats the gladsome air; o'er all that glides
Beneath the wave, yea, in the wave itself,
And mighty depth of waters. Wonder not
If high the transport, great the joy I felt,   410
Communing in this sort through earth and heaven
With every form of creature, as it looked
Towards the Uncreated with a countenance
Of adoration, with an eye of love.[4]
One song they sang, and it was audible,   415
Most audible, then, when the fleshly ear,
O'ercome by humblest prelude of that strain,
Forgot her functions, and slept undisturbed.[5]

    If this be error, and another faith
Find easier access to the pious mind,   420
Yet were I grossly destitute of all
Those human sentiments that make this earth
So dear, if I should fail with grateful voice
To speak of you, ye mountains, and ye lakes
And sounding cataracts, ye mists and winds   425
That dwell among the hills where I was born.
If in my youth I have been pure in heart,
If, mingling with the world, I am content
With my own modest pleasures, and have lived
With God and Nature communing, removed   430
From little enmities and low desires,
The gift is yours; if in these times of fear,
This melancholy waste of hopes o'erthrown,[6]
If, 'mid indifference and apathy
And wicked exultation, when good men   435
On every side fall off we know not how,
To selfishness, disguised in gentle names
Of peace and quiet and domestic love,
Yet mingled not unwillingly with sneers
On visionary minds;[7] if, in this time   440
Of dereliction and dismay, I yet
Despair not of our nature, but retain
A more than Roman confidence, a faith

---

4. Wordsworth preserved the pantheist assertion of *1805*, lines 429–30, written at Alfoxden in 1798, until his final revision of *The Prelude* in, or after, 1839; but he then replaced it with lines designed precisely to emphasize the difference between God, "the Uncreated," and His Creation.

That fails not, in all sorrow my support,   460
[445] The blessing of my life, the gift is yours
Ye mountains, thine, O Nature. Thou hast fed
My lofty speculations, and in thee
For this uneasy heart of ours I find
[450] A never-failing principle of joy   465
And purest passion.

         Thou, my friend, wert reared
In the great city, 'mid far other scenes,[8]
But we by different roads at length have gained
The self-same bourne. And for this cause to thee
[455] I speak unapprehensive of contempt,   470
The insinuated scoff of coward tongues,
And all that silent language which so oft
In conversation betwixt man and man
Blots from the human countenance all trace
[460] Of beauty and of love. For thou hast sought   475
The truth in solitude, and thou art one
The most intense of Nature's worshippers,
[465] In many things my brother, chiefly here
In this my deep devotion. Fare thee well.
Health and the quiet of a healthful mind   480
Attend thee, seeking oft the haunts of men—
And yet more often living with thyself,
[470] And for thyself—so haply shall thy days
Be many, and a blessing to mankind.[1]

8. A verbatim quotation from Coleridge's *Frost at Midnight*, 51–52; see *1799*, II, 497*n*, above.

1. For the original circumstances of this farewell, see *1799*, II, 514*n*, above.

That fails not, in all sorrow my support,
The blessing of my life; the gift is yours,   445
Ye winds and sounding cataracts! 'tis yours,
Ye mountains! thine, O Nature! Thou hast fed
My lofty speculations; and in thee,
For this uneasy heart of ours, I find
A never-failing principle of joy   450
And purest passion.

        Thou, my Friend! wert reared
In the great city, 'mid far other scenes;[8]
But we, by different roads, at length have gained
The self-same bourne. And for this cause to thee
I speak, unapprehensive of contempt,   455
The insinuated scoff of coward tongues,
And all that silent language which so oft
In conversation between man and man
Blots from the human countenance all trace
Of beauty and of love. For thou hast sought   460
The truth in solitude, and, since the days
That gave thee liberty, full long desired,
To serve in Nature's temple, thou hast been
The most assiduous of her ministers;[9]
In many things my brother, chiefly here   465
In this our deep devotion.

        Fare thee well!
Health and the quiet of a healthful mind
Attend thee! seeking oft the haunts of men,
And yet more often living with thyself,
And for thyself, so haply shall thy days   470
Be many, and a blessing to mankind.[1]

9. Lines 461–64 are among Wordsworth's final revisions, made at least five years after
Coleridge's death in 1834.

Book Third

Residence at Cambridge

It was a dreary morning when the chaise
Rolled over the flat plains of Huntingdon
And through the open windows first I saw
The long-backed chapel of King's College rear
[5] His pinnacles above the dusky groves.[1]　　　　　　　5
Soon afterwards we espied upon the road
A student clothed in gown and tasselled cap;
[11] He passed—nor was I master of my eyes
Till he was left a hundred yards behind.
The place as we approached seemed more and more　　10
To have an eddy's force, and sucked us in
More eagerly at every step we took.[2]
[15] Onward we drove beneath the castle, down
By Magdalene Bridge we went and crossed the Cam,
And at the Hoop we landed, famous inn.　　　　　　15

　　My spirit was up, my thoughts were full of hope;
Some friends I had—acquaintances who there
[20] Seemed friends—poor simple schoolboys now hung round
With honour and importance. In a world
Of welcome faces up and down I roved—　　　　　　20
Questions, directions, counsel and advice
Flowed in upon me from all sides. Fresh day
[25] Of pride and pleasure: to myself I seemed
A man of business and expense, and went
From shop to shop about my own affairs,　　　　　　25
To tutors or to tailors as befel,
From street to street with loose and careless heart.
[30] I was the dreamer, they the dream; I roamed
Delighted through the motley spectacle:
Gowns grave or gaudy, doctors, students, streets,　　30
Lamps, gateways, flocks of churches, courts and towers—
Strange transformation for a mountain youth,
[35] A northern villager. As if by word

1. Wordsworth reached Cambridge on
October 30, 1787, and took his B.A. on
January 21, 1791.
2. Cambridge is an eddy in the river of

Wordsworth's development. The image
originates in *1799*, II, 247–49, and is applied specifically to university life at
1805, IV, 39–55.

Book Third

Residence at Cambridge

It was a dreary morning when the wheels
Rolled over a wide plain o'erhung with clouds,
And nothing cheered our way till first we saw
The long-roofed chapel of King's College lift
Turrets and pinnacles in answering files,   5
Extended high above a dusky grove.[1]

   Advancing, we espied upon the road
A student clothed in gown and tasselled cap,
Striding along as if o'ertasked by Time,
Or covetous of exercise and air;   10
He passed—nor was I master of my eyes
Till he was left an arrow's flight behind.
As near and nearer to the spot we drew,
It seemed to suck us in with an eddy's force.[2]
Onward we drove beneath the Castle; caught,   15
While crossing Magdalene Bridge, a glimpse of Cam;
And at the *Hoop* alighted, famous Inn.[3]

   My spirit was up, my thoughts were full of hope;
Some friends I had, acquaintances who there
Seemed friends, poor simple school-boys, now hung round   20
With honour and importance: in a world
Of welcome faces up and down I roved;
Questions, directions, warnings and advice,
Flowed in upon me, from all sides; fresh day
Of pride and pleasure! to myself I seemed   25
A man of business and expense, and went
From shop to shop about my own affairs,
To Tutor or to Tailor, as befel,
From street to street with loose and careless mind.

   I was the Dreamer, they the Dream; I roamed   30
Delighted through the motley spectacle;
Gowns grave, or gaudy, doctors, students, streets,
Courts, cloisters, flocks of churches, gateways, towers:
Migration strange for a stripling of the hills,
A northern villager.   35

---

3. Singled out by Matthew Arnold (*On Translating Homer*, 1861) because it "shows excellently how a poet may sink with his subject by resolving not to sink with it" (*Complete Prose Works*, I, p. 187); but de Selincourt is surely right that Wordsworth is being playful, not pompous, and treats his early Cambridge days "in something of the mock-heroic manner."

Of magic or some fairy's power, at once
Behold me rich in monies and attired   35
In splendid clothes, with hose of silk, and hair
Glittering like rimy trees when frost is keen[4]—
[40] My lordly dressing-gown, I pass it by,
With other signs of manhood which supplied
The lack of beard. The weeks went roundly on,   40
With invitations, suppers, wine, and fruit,
Smooth housekeeping within, and all without
[45] Liberal and suiting gentleman's array.

The Evangelist St John my patron was;
Three gloomy courts are his, and in the first   45
Was my abiding-place, a nook obscure.
Right underneath, the college kitchens made
[50] A humming sound, less tuneable than bees
But hardly less industrious; with shrill notes
Of sharp command and scolding intermixed.   50
Near me was Trinity's loquacious clock
Who never let the quarters, night or day,
[55] Slip by him unproclaimed, and told the hours
Twice over with a male and female voice.
Her pealing organ was my neighbour too;   55
And from my bedroom I in moonlight nights
Could see right opposite, a few yards off,
[60] The antechapel, where the statue stood
Of Newton with his prism and silent face.

Of college labours, of the lecturer's room   60
[65] All studded round, as thick as chairs could stand,
With loyal students faithful to their books,
Half-and-half idlers, hardy recusants,[6]
And honest dunces; of important days,
Examinations, when the man was weighed   65
[70] As in the balance;[7] of excessive hopes,
Tremblings withal and commendable fears,
Small jealousies and triumphs good or bad—
I make short mention. Things they were which then
I did not love, nor do I love them now: 70
Such glory was but little sought by me,
[75] And little won. But it is right to say
That even so early, from the first crude days
Of settling-time in this my new abode,

---

4. Wordsworth at this stage wore his
hair powdered, in the fashion of the time.
"Rimey": covered with rime, hoar-frost.
6. Originally, those who refused to attend
Church of England services; here, those
who refused to do academic work.
7. A pun, as Maxwell points out, on
Latin *examen*, "a balance."

As if the change
Had waited on some Fairy's wand, at once
Behold me rich in monies, and attired
In splendid garb, with hose of silk, and hair
Powdered like rimy trees, when frost is keen.[4]
My lordly dressing-gown, I pass it by,   40
With other signs of manhood that supplied
The lack of beard.—The weeks went roundly on,
With invitations, suppers, wine and fruit,
Smooth housekeeping within, and all without
Liberal, and suiting gentleman's array.   45

The Evangelist St. John my patron was:
Three Gothic courts are his, and in the first
Was my abiding-place, a nook obscure;
Right underneath, the College kitchens made
A humming sound, less tuneable than bees,   50
But hardly less industrious; with shrill notes
Of sharp command and scolding intermixed.
Near me hung Trinity's loquacious clock,
Who never let the quarters, night or day,
Slip by him unproclaimed, and told the hours   55
Twice over with a male and female voice.
Her pealing organ was my neighbour too;
And from my pillow, looking forth by light
Of moon or favouring stars, I could behold
The antechapel where the statue stood   60
Of Newton with his prism and silent face,
The marble index of a mind for ever
Voyaging through strange seas of Thought, alone.[5]

Of College labours, of the Lecturer's room
All studded round, as thick as chairs could stand,   65
With loyal students faithful to their books
Half-and-half idlers, hardy recusants,[6]
And honest dunces—of important days,
Examinations, when the man was weighed
As in a balance![7] of excessive hopes,   70
Tremblings withal and commendable fears,
Small jealousies, and triumphs good or bad,
Let others that know more speak as they know.
Such glory was but little sought by me,
And little won. Yet from the first crude days   75
Of settling time in this untried abode,

5. These famous lines were introduced in 1838/39, and draw on lines 125–28 of Thomson's elegy on Newton: "The noiseless tide of time, all bearing down / To vast eternity's unbounded sea, / Where the green islands of the happy shine, / He stemmed alone * * *."

Not seldom I had melancholy thoughts   75
From personal and family regards,
Wishing to hope without a hope—⁸ some fears
About my future worldly maintenance,
[80] And, more than all, a strangeness in my mind,
A feeling that I was not for that hour   80
Nor for that place. But wherefore be cast down,
Why should I grieve?—I was a chosen son.⁹
For hither I had come with holy powers
[89] And faculties, whether to work or feel:
To apprehend all passions and all moods   85
Which time, and place, and season do impress
Upon the visible universe, and work
Like changes there by force of my own mind.
I was a freeman, in the purest sense
Was free, and to majestic ends was strong—   90
I do not speak of learning, moral truth,
Or understanding—'twas enough for me
To know that I was otherwise endowed.
When the first glitter of the show was passed,
And the first dazzle of the taper-light,   95
As if with a rebound my mind returned
Into its former self. Oft did I leave
[92] My comrades, and the crowd, buildings and groves,
And walked along the fields, the level fields,
With heaven's blue concave reared above my head.   100
And now it was that through such change entire,
And this first absence from those shapes sublime
[95] Wherewith I had been conversant, my mind
Seemed busier in itself than heretofore—
At least I more directly recognised   105
My powers and habits. Let me dare to speak
[100] A higher language, say that now I felt
The strength and consolation which were mine.
As if awakened, summoned, rouzed, constrained,
I looked for universal things, perused   110
[110] The common countenance of earth and heaven,
And, turning the mind in upon itself,
Pored, watched, expected, listened, spread my thoughts,
And spread them with a wider creeping, felt
Incumbences more awful,¹ visitings   115
[120] Of the upholder, of the tranquil soul,
Which underneath all passion lives secure

8. Wordsworth was burdened by the assumption of his family that he would obtain a Fellowship at St. John's (see Schneider, pp. 7–9).
9. Wordsworth's unequivocal claim to be chosen son of Nature was allowed to stand until the revisions of 1838/39. Compare the pious alteration in *1850*, lines 83–88.
1. "Incumbences": spiritual brooding or overshadowing (*NED*). "Awful": awe-inspiring.

I was disturbed at times by prudent thoughts,
Wishing to hope without a hope,[8] some fears
About my future worldly maintenance,
And, more than all, a strangeness in the mind,   80
A feeling that I was not for that hour,
Nor for that place. But wherefore be cast down?
For (not to speak of Reason and her pure
Reflective acts to fix the moral law
Deep in the conscience nor of Christian Hope,   85
Bowing her head before her sister Faith
As one far mightier), hither I had come,
Bear witness Truth, endowed with holy powers
And faculties, whether to work or feel.
Oft when the dazzling show no longer new   90
Had ceased to dazzle, ofttimes did I quit
My comrades, leave the crowd, buildings and groves,
And as I paced alone the level fields
Far from those lovely sights and sounds sublime
With which I had been conversant, the mind   95
Drooped not; but there into herself returning,
With prompt rebound seemed fresh as heretofore.
At least I more distinctly recognized
Her native instincts: let me dare to speak
A higher language, say that now I felt   100
What independent solaces were mine,
To mitigate the injurious sway of place
Or circumstance, how far soever changed
In youth, or *to* be changed in manhood's prime;
Or for the few who shall be called to look   105
On the long shadows in our evening years,
Ordained precursors to the night of death.
As if awakened, summoned, roused, constrained,
I looked for universal things; perused
The common countenance of earth and sky: 110
Earth, nowhere unembellished by some trace
Of that first Paradise whence man was driven;
And sky, whose beauty and bounty are expressed
By the proud name she bears—the name of Heaven.
I called on both to teach me what they might;   115
Or turning the mind in upon herself
Pored, watched, expected, listened, spread my thoughts
And spread them with a wider creeping; felt
Incumbencies more awful,[1] visitings
Of the Upholder, of the tranquil soul,   120
That tolerates the indignities of Time,
And, from the centre of Eternity
All finite motions overruling, lives

A steadfast life. But peace, it is enough
[125] To notice that I was ascending now
To such community with highest truth.   120
A track pursuing not untrod before,
From deep analogies by thought supplied,
Or consciousnesses not to be subdued,
[130] To every natural form, rock, fruit or flower,
Even the loose stones that cover the highway,   125
I gave a moral life—I saw them feel,
Or linked them to some feeling. The great mass
Lay bedded in a quickening soul,[2] and all
[135] That I beheld respired with inward meaning.
Thus much for the one presence, and the life   130
Of the great whole; suffice it here to add
That whatsoe'er of terror, or of love,
Or beauty, Nature's daily face put on
From transitory passion, unto this
I was as wakeful even as waters are   135
[140] To the sky's motion, in a kindred sense
Of passion was obedient as a lute
That waits upon the touches of the wind.
So was it with me in my solitude:
So often among multitudes of men.   140
Unknown, unthought of, yet I was most rich,
I had a world about me—'twas my own,
[145] I made it; for it only lived to me,
And to the God who looked into my mind.
Such sympathies would sometimes shew themselves   145
By outward gestures and by visible looks—
Some called it madness; such indeed it was,
[150] If childlike fruitfulness in passing joy,
If steady moods of thoughtfulness matured
To inspiration, sort with such a name;   150
If prophesy be madness; if things viewed
By poets of old time, and higher up
[155] By the first men, earth's first inhabitants,
May in these tutored days no more be seen
With undisordered sight. But leaving this,   155
It was no madness; for I had an eye
Which in my strongest workings evermore
[160] Was looking for the shades of difference
As they lie hid in all exterior forms,
Near or remote, minute or vast—an eye   160
Which from a stone, a tree, a withered leaf,
To the broad ocean and the azure heavens

2. I.e., the material world draws its life and nourishment like a plant from an underlying spirit. "Quickening": life-giving.

In glory immutable. But peace! enough
Here to record I had ascended now   125
To such community with highest truth.

　　A track pursuing, not untrod before,
From strict analogies by thought supplied
Or consciousnesses not to be subdued,
To every natural form, rock, fruit or flower,   130
Even the loose stones that cover the high-way,
I gave a moral life: I saw them feel,
Or linked them to some feeling: the great mass
Lay bedded in a quickening soul,[2] and all
That I beheld respired with inward meaning.   135
Add that whate'er of Terror or of Love
Or Beauty, Nature's daily face put on
From transitory passion, unto this
I was as sensitive as waters are
To the sky's influence: in a kindred mood   140
Of passion, was obedient as a lute
That waits upon the touches of the wind
Unknown, unthought of, yet I was most rich—
I had a world about me—'twas my own;
I made it, for it only lived to me,   145
And to the God who sees into the heart.
Such sympathies, though rarely, were betrayed
By outward gestures and by visible looks:
Some called it madness—so indeed it was,
If child-like fruitfulness in passing joy,   150
If steady moods of thoughtfulness matured
To inspiration, sort with such a name;
If prophecy be madness; if things viewed
By poets in old time, and higher up
By the first men, earth's first inhabitants,   155
May in these tutored days no more be seen
With undisordered sight. But leaving this,
It was no madness, for the bodily eye
Amid my strongest workings evermore
Was searching out the lines of difference   160
As they lie hid in all external forms,
Near or remote, minute or vast, an eye
Which from a tree, a stone, a withered leaf,
To the broad ocean and the azure heavens

[165] Spangled with kindred multitudes of stars,
Could find no surface where its power might sleep,
Which spake perpetual logic to my soul,   165
And by an unrelenting agency
Did bind my feelings even as in a chain.[3]

[170]   And here, O friend, have I retraced my life
Up to an eminence, and told a tale
Of matters which not falsely I may call   170
The glory of my youth. Of genius, power,
Creation, and divinity itself,
[175] I have been speaking, for my theme has been
What passed within me. Not of outward things
Done visibly for other minds—words, signs,   175
Symbols or actions—but of my own heart
Have I been speaking, and my youthful mind.
[180] O heavens, how awful is the might of souls,
And what they do within themselves while yet
The yoke of earth is new to them, the world   180
Nothing but a wild field where they were sown.
This is in truth heroic argument,
[185] And genuine prowess[4]—which I wished to touch,
With hand however weak—but in the main
It lies far hidden from the reach of words.   185
Points have we all of us within our souls
Where all stand single; this I feel, and make
[190] Breathings for incommunicable powers.[5]
Yet each man is a memory to himself,
And, therefore, now that I must quit this theme,   190
I am not heartless;[6] for there's not a man
That lives who hath not had his god-like hours,
[195] And knows not what majestic sway we have
As natural beings in the strength of Nature.

       Enough, for now into a populous plain   195
We must descend. A traveller I am,
And all my tale is of myself—even so—
[200] So be it, if the pure in heart delight
To follow me, and thou, O honored friend,
Who in my thoughts art ever at my side,   200
Uphold as heretofore my fainting steps.

---

3. *1805*, 82, 122–27, 141–47 and 156–67
were originally written as third-person
narrative for *The Ruined Cottage* in February–March 1798.
4. *1805*, 171–83 (*1850*, 173–85) define a
new theme ("argument") for epic poetry;
in justifying his treatment of the Fall,
Milton had claimed to be replacing the
battle poetry of Homer and Virgil—
"Wars, hitherto the only argument / He

roic deemed * * * " (*Paradise Lost*, IX,
28–29). Now Wordsworth takes the further step and asserts that Christian epic
too is out of date, dealing merely with
"outward things / Done visibly."
5. A baffling statement that persists
through *1850*. "Breathings" are perhaps
the poet's own inadequate attempts to
communicate the incommunicable.
6. Discouraged.

Spangled with kindred multitudes of stars,   165
Could find no surface where its power might sleep;
Which spake perpetual logic to my soul,
And by an unrelenting agency
Did bind my feelings even as in a chain.

   And here, O Friend! have I retraced my life   170
Up to an eminence, and told a tale
Of matters which not falsely may be called
The glory of my youth. Of genius, power,
Creation and divinity itself
I have been speaking, for my theme has been   175
What passed within me. Not of outward things
Done visibly for other minds, words, signs,
Symbols or actions, but of my own heart
Have I been speaking, and my youthful mind.
O Heavens! how awful is the might of souls,   180
And what they do within themselves while yet
The yoke of earth is new to them, the world
Nothing but a wild field where they were sown.
This is, in truth, heroic argument,
This genuine prowess,[4] which I wished to touch   185
With hand however weak, but in the main
It lies far hidden from the reach of words.
Points have we all of us within our souls
Where all stand single; this I feel, and make
Breathings for incommunicable powers;[5]   190
But is not each a memory to himself?
And, therefore, now that we must quit this theme,
I am not heartless,[6] for there's not a man
That lives who hath not known his godlike hours,
And feels not what an empire we inherit   195
As natural beings in the strength of Nature.

   No more: for now into a populous plain
We must descend. A Traveller I am,
Whose tale is only of himself; even so,
So be it, if the pure of heart be prompt   200
To follow, and if thou, my honoured Friend!
Who in these thoughts art ever at my side,
Support, as heretofore, my fainting steps.

It hath been told already how my sight
[205] Was dazzled by the novel show, and how
Erelong I did into myself return.
So did it seem, and so in truth it was—   205
Yet this was but short-lived. Thereafter came
Observance less devout: I had made a change
In climate, and my nature's outward coat
Changed also, slowly and insensibly.
[210] To the deep quiet and majestic thoughts   210
Of loneliness succeeded empty noise
And superficial pastimes, now and then
Forced labour, and more frequently forced hopes,
And, worse than all, a treasonable growth
[215] Of indecisive judgements that impaired   215
And shook the mind's simplicity. And yet
This was a gladsome time. Could I behold—
Who less insensible than sodden clay
On a sea-river's bed at ebb of tide
[220] Could have beheld—with undelighted heart   220
So many happy youths, so wide and fair
A congregation in its budding-time
Of health, and hope, and beauty, all at once
So many divers samples of the growth
[225] Of life's sweet season, could have seen unmoved   225
That miscellaneous garland of wild flowers
Upon the matron temples of a place
So famous through the world?[7] To me at least
It was a goodly prospect; for, through youth,
[230] Though I had been trained up to stand unpropped,   230
And independent musings pleased me so
That spells seemed on me when I was alone,
Yet could I only cleave to solitude
In lonesome places—if a throng was near
[235] That way I leaned by nature, for my heart   235
Was social and loved idleness and joy.[8]

Not seeking those who might participate
My deeper pleasures—nay, I had not once,
Though not unused to mutter lonesome songs,
[240] Even with myself divided such delight,   240
Or looked that way for aught that might be cloathed
In human language—easily I passed
From the remembrances of better things,

---

7. Undergraduates are seen as flowers
that Cambridge, Wordsworth's *alma
mater*, wears on her brow.
8. Not the usual view of Wordsworth,
but supported by a letter of November
1794: "I begin to wish much to be in
town; cataracts and mountains, are good
occasional society, but they will not do
for constant companions" (*EY*, p. 136).

It hath been told, that when the first delight
That flashed upon me from this novel show   205
Had failed, the mind returned into herself;
Yet true it is, that I had made a change
In climate, and my nature's outward coat
Changed also slowly and insensibly.
Full oft the quiet and exalted thoughts   210
Of loneliness gave way to empty noise
And superficial pastimes; now and then
Forced labour, and more frequently forced hopes;
And, worst of all, a treasonable growth
Of indecisive judgments, that impaired   215
And shook the mind's simplicity.—And yet
This was a gladsome time. Could I behold—
Who, less insensible than sodden clay
In a sea-river's bed at ebb of tide,
Could have beheld,—with undelighted heart,   220
So many happy youths, so wide and fair
A congregation in its budding-time
Of health, and hope, and beauty, all at once
So many divers samples from the growth
Of life's sweet season—could have seen unmoved   225
That miscellaneous garland of wild flowers
Decking the matron temples of a place
So famous through the world?[7] To me, at least,
It was a goodly prospect: for, in sooth,
Though I had learnt betimes to stand unpropped,   230
And independent musings pleased me so
That spells seemed on me when I was alone,
Yet could I only cleave to solitude
In lonely places; if a throng was near
That way I leaned by nature; for my heart   235
Was social, and loved idleness and joy.[8]

Not seeking those who might participate
My deeper pleasures (nay, I had not once,
Though not unused to mutter lonesome songs,
Even with myself divided such delight,   240
Or looked that way for aught that might be clothed
In human language), easily I passed
From the remembrances of better things,

And slipped into the weekday works of youth,
[245] Unburthened, unalarmed, and unprofaned.[9]   245
Caverns there were within my mind which sun
Could never penetrate, yet did there not
Want store of leafy arbours where the light
Might enter in at will. Companionships,
[250] Friendships, acquaintances, were welcome all;   250
We sauntered, played, we rioted, we talked
Unprofitable talk at morning hours,
Drifted about along the streets and walks,
Read lazily in lazy books, went forth
[255] To gallop through the country in blind zeal   255
Of senseless horsemanship, or on the breast
Of Cam sailed boisterously, and let the stars
Come out, perhaps without one quiet thought.

       Such was the tenor of the opening act
[260] In this new life. Imagination slept,   260
And yet not utterly: I could not print
Ground where the grass had yielded to the steps
Of generations of illustrious men,
Unmoved; I could not always lightly pass
[265] Through the same gateways, sleep where they had slept,   265
Wake where they waked, range that enclosure old,
That garden of great intellects, undisturbed.
Place also by the side of this dark sense
Of nobler feeling, that those spiritual men,
[270] Even the great Newton's own etherial self,   270
Seemed humbled in these precincts, thence to be
The more beloved, invested here with tasks
Of life's plain business, as a daily garb—
Dictators at the plough[3]—a change that left
[277] All genuine admiration unimpaired.   275

       Beside the pleasant mills of Trompington
I laughed with Chaucer; in the hawthorn shade
[280] Heard him, while birds were warbling, tell his tales
Of amorous passion.[4] And that gentle bard
Chosen by the Muses for their Page of State,
Sweet Spencer, moving through his clouded heaven   280
With the moon's beauty and the moon's soft pace—

---

9. Compare "Unbodied, unsoul'd, un-heard, unseene" (*Faerie Queene*, VII, vii, 46) and "Unshaken, unseduced, unterri-fied" (*Paradise Lost*, VI, 899).
3. A reference to Cincinnatus, tradition-ally said to have been ploughing when summoned to be dictator of Rome in 458 B.C.
4. Chaucer's *Reeve's Tale* is set at Trompington, and concerns the wenching of two students from Cambridge.

And slipped into the ordinary works
Of careless youth, unburthened, unalarmed.   245
Caverns there were within my mind which sun
Could never penetrate, yet did there not
Want store of leafy *arbours* where the light
Might enter in at will. Companionships,
Friendships, acquaintances, were welcome all.   250
We sauntered, played, or rioted; we talked
Unprofitable talk at morning hours;
Drifted about along the streets and walks,
Read lazily in trivial books, went forth
To gallop through the country in blind zeal   255
Of senseless horsemanship, or on the breast
Of Cam sailed boisterously, and let the stars
Come forth, perhaps without one quiet thought.

   Such was the tenor of the second act[1]
In this new life. Imagination slept,   260
And yet not utterly. I could not print
Ground where the grass had yielded to your steps
Ye generations of illustrious men,
Unmoved. I could not always lightly pass
Through the same gateways, sleep where ye had slept,   265
Wake where ye waked, range that inclosure old,
That garden of great intellects, undisturbed.
Place also by the side of this dark sense
Of nobler feeling, that those spiritual men,
Even the great Newton's own ethereal self,   270
Seemed humbled in these precincts, thence to be
The more endeared. Their several memories here
(Even like their persons in their portraits clothed
With the accustomed garb of daily life)[2]
Put on a lowly and a touching grace   275
Of more distinct humanity, that left
All genuine admiration unimpaired.

   Beside the pleasant Mill of Trompington
I laughed with Chaucer; in the hawthorn shade
Heard him, while birds were warbling, tell his tales   280
Of amorous passion. And that gentle Bard,
Chosen by the Muses for their Page of State—
Sweet Spenser, moving through his clouded heaven
With the moon's beauty and the moon's soft pace,

1. Wordsworth's correction of *1805* "opening act" to *1850* "*second* act" is a reminder that "the ordinary works / Of careless youth" (lines 244–45) had followed an earlier phase of his life in which the effect of Cambridge had been to turn the poet's mind in upon itself.
2. Academic dress had changed very little, so that in their portraits great Cambridge men of the past wore the same clothes as undergraduates of Wordsworth's own time.

[285] I called him brother, Englishman, and friend.
    Yea, our blind poet, who, in his later day
    Stood almost single, uttering odious truth,   285
    Darkness before, and danger's voice behind[5]—
    Soul awful, if the earth hath ever lodged
[290] An awful soul—I seemed to see him here
    Familiarly, and in his scholar's dress
    Bounding before me, yet a stripling youth,   290
    A boy, no better, with his rosy cheeks
    Angelical, keen eye, courageous look,
[295] And conscious step of purity and pride.

    Among the band of my compeers was one,   295
    My class-fellow at school, whose chance it was
    To lodge in the apartments which had been
    Time out of mind honored by Milton's name—
    The very shell reputed of the abode
    Which he had tenanted. O temperate bard!
    One afternoon, the first time I set foot   300
[300] In this thy innocent nest and oratory,
    Seated with others in a festive ring
    Of commonplace convention,[6] I to thee
    Poured out libations, to thy memory drank
    Within my private thoughts, till my brain reeled,   305
    Never so clouded by the fumes of wine
[305] Before that hour, or since. Thence, forth I ran
    From that assembly, through a length of streets
    Ran ostrich-like to reach our chapel door
    In not a desperate or opprobrious time,   310
    Albeit long after the importunate bell
[310] Had stopped, with wearisome Cassandra voice
    No longer haunting the dark winter night.[7]
    Call back, O friend, a moment to thy mind
    The place itself and fashion of the rites.   315
    Upshouldering in a dislocated lump
    With shallow ostentatious carelessness
    My surplice, gloried in and yet despised,
[315] I clove in pride through the inferior throng
    Of the plain burghers, who in audience stood   320

5. Abdiel in *Paradise Lost* traditionally represents Milton's own position, and is twice referred to as "single" in his loyalty (V, 903; VI, 30). Henry Crabb Robinson records that "Wordsworth, when he resolved to be a poet, feared competition only with Chaucer, Spenser, Shakespeare, and Milton" (*Books and Their Writers*, ed. E. J. Morley, II, p. 776). Spenser and Milton had both been at Cambridge—Spenser at Pembroke Hall, Milton at Christ's.

6. Meeting, gathering.
7. Attendance at chapel was compulsory; see *1805*, 415–27, below. Wordsworth runs "ostrich-like" (*1805*, 309; *1850*, 307) because his academic gown has been hitched up for greater speed. "Opprobrious" (*1805*, 310; *1850*, 308): disgraceful (Johnson's *Dictionary*). "Cassandra voice" (*1805*, 312; *1850*, 310): Priam's daughter Cassandra foretold the fall of Troy.

I called him Brother, Englishman, and Friend! 285
Yea, our blind Poet, who in his later day,
Stood almost single; uttering odious truth—
Darkness before, and danger's voice behind,[5]
Soul awful—if the earth hath ever lodged
An awful soul—I seemed to see him here 290
Familiarly, and in his scholar's dress
Bounding before me, yet a stripling youth—
A boy, no better, with his rosy cheeks
Angelical, keen eye, courageous look,
And conscious step of purity and pride. 295
Among the band of my compeers was one
Whom chance had stationed in the very room
Honoured by Milton's name. O temperate Bard!
Be it confest that, for the first time, seated
Within thy innocent lodge and oratory, 300
One of a festive circle, I poured out
Libations, to thy memory drank, till pride
And gratitude grew dizzy in a brain
Never excited by the fumes of wine
Before that hour, or since. Forth I ran 305
From the assembly; through a length of streets,
Ran, ostrich-like, to reach our chapel door
In not a desperate or opprobrious time,
Albeit long after the importunate bell
Had stopped, with wearisome Cassandra voice 310
No longer haunting the dark winter night.[7]
Call back, O Friend! a moment to thy mind
The place itself, and fashion of the rites.
With careless ostentation shouldering up
My surplice, through the inferior throng I clove 315
Of the plain Burghers, who in audience stood

On the last skirts of their permitted ground,
Beneath the pealing organ.[8] Empty thoughts,
I am ashamed of them; and that great bard,
[320] And thou, O friend, who in thy ample mind   325
Hast stationed me for reverence and love,
Ye will forgive the weakness of that hour,
In some of its unworthy vanities
Brother of many more.

                    In this mixed sort
[325] The months passed on, remissly, not giving up   330
To wilful alienation from the right,
Or walks of open scandal, but in vague
And loose indifference, easy likings, aims
Of a low pitch—duty and zeal dismissed,
[330] Yet Nature, or a happy course of things,
Not doing in their stead the needful work.   335
The memory languidly revolved, the heart
Reposed in noontide rest, the inner pulse
[334] Of contemplation almost failed to beat.
Rotted as by a charm, my life became
A floating island, an amphibious thing,   340
Unsound, of spungy texture, yet withal
Not wanting a fair face of water-weeds
And pleasant flowers.[9] The thirst of living praise,
[340] A reverence for the glorious dead, the sight
Of those long vistos,[10] catacombs in which   345
Perennial minds lie visibly entombed,
Have often stirred the heart of youth, and bred
A fervent love of rigorous discipline.
[345] Alas, such high commotion touched not me;
No look was in these walls to put to shame   350
My easy spirits, and discountenance
Their light composure—far less to instil
A calm resolve of mind, firmly addressed
[350] To puissant[1] efforts. Nor was this the blame
Of others, but my own; I should in truth,   355
As far as doth concern my single self,

---

8. Townspeople would be confined to limited areas in the College Chapel. "Surplice" (*1805*, 318; *1850*, 315): a white linen robe that members of the College were required to wear during services, although Wordsworth seems to have entered the chapel with his bunched over his shoulder.
9. An image that was vivid for Wordsworth himself because he had a specific picture in mind: "there occasionally ap-

pears above the surface of Derwent-water, and always in the same place, a considerable tract of spongy ground covered with aquatic plants, which is called the Floating * * * Island" (Wordsworth, *Guide to the Lakes*; *Prose Works*, II, p. 184).
10. Common eighteenth-century spelling of "vistas."
1. Powerful.

On the last skirts of their permitted ground,[8]
Under the pealing organ. Empty thoughts!
I am ashamed of them: and that great Bard,
And thou, O Friend! who in thy ample mind   320
Hast placed me high above my best deserts,
Ye will forgive the weakness of that hour,
In some of its unworthy vanities,
Brother to many more.

                In this mixed sort
The months passed on, remissly, not given up   325
To wilful alienation from the right,
Or walks of open scandal, but in vague
And loose indifference, easy likings, aims
Of a low pitch—duty and zeal dismissed,
Yet Nature, or a happy course of things,   330
Not doing in their stead the needful work,
The memory languidly revolved, the heart
Reposed in noontide rest, the inner pulse
Of contemplation almost failed to beat.
Such life might not inaptly be compared   335
To a floating island, an amphibious spot
Unsound, of spongy texture, yet withal
Not wanting a fair face of water weeds
And pleasant flowers.[9] The thirst of living praise,
Fit reverence for the glorious Dead, the sight   340
Of those long vistas, sacred catacombs,
Where mighty *minds* lie visibly entombed,
Have often stirred the heart of youth, and bred
A fervent love of rigorous discipline.—
Alas! such high emotion touched not me.   345
Look was there none within these walls to shame
My easy spirits, and discountenance
Their light composure, far less to instil
A calm resolve of mind, firmly addressed
To puissant[1] efforts. Nor was this the blame   350
Of others, but my own; I should, in truth,
As far as doth concern my single self,

'Misdeem most widely, lodging it elsewhere.²
For I, bred up in Nature's lap, was even
[355] As a spoiled child; and, rambling like the wind
As I had done in daily intercourse   360
With those delicious rivers, solemn heights,
And mountains, ranging like a fowl of the air,
I was ill-tutored for captivity—
[360] To quit my pleasure, and from month to month
Take up a station calmly on the perch   365
Of sedentary peace. Those lovely forms
Had also left less space within my mind,
Which, wrought upon instinctively, had found
[365] A freshness in those objects of its love,
A winning power beyond all other power.   370
Not that I slighted books—that were to lack
All sense—but other passions had been mine,
More fervent, making me less prompt perhaps
[370] To indoor study than was wise or well,
Or suited to my years. Yet I could shape   375
The image of a place which—soothed and lulled
As I had been, trained up in paradise
Among sweet garlands and delightful sounds,
Accustomed in my loneliness to walk
With Nature magisterially³—yet I   380
Methinks could shape the image of a place
[376] Which with its aspect should have bent me down
To instantaneous service, should at once
Have made me pay to science and to arts
And written lore, acknowledged my liege lord,   385
[380] A homage frankly offered up like that
Which I had paid to Nature. Toil and pains
In this recess which I have bodied forth⁵
Should spread from heart to heart; and stately groves,
Majestic edifices, should not want   390
[385] A corresponding dignity within.
The congregating temper⁶ which pervades
Our unripe years, not wasted, should be made
To minister to works of high attempt,
Which the enthusiast would perform with love.   395
[390] Youth should be awed, possessed, as with a sense

2. Dorothy ascribed her brother's failure
to achieve a fellowship to his dislike of
mathematics, the dominant subject at
Cambridge, and at this period the only
one in which academic distinction could
be achieved: "William you may have
heard lost the chance, indeed the certainty, of a fellowship by not combat-
ing his inclinations * * * He reads Italian, Spanish, French, Greek and Latin,
and English, but never opens a mathematical book" (*EY*, p. 52).
3. I.e., as if I had been Nature's master.
5. I.e., academic work, carried out in
this secluded place to which my thoughts
have given substance. Wordsworth is describing what he might have done in an
ideal academic environment.
6. Gregariousness.

Misdeem most widely, lodging it elsewhere:[2]
For I, bred up 'mid Nature's luxuries,
Was a spoiled child, and rambling like the wind,   355
As I had done in daily intercourse
With those crystalline rivers, solemn heights,
And mountains; ranging like a fowl of the air,
I was ill-tutored for captivity,
To quit my pleasure, and, from month to month,   360
Take up a station calmly on the perch
Of sedentary peace. Those lovely forms
Had also left less space within my mind,
Which, wrought upon instinctively, had found
A freshness in those objects of her love,   365
A winning power, beyond all other power.
Not that I slighted books,—that were to lack
All sense,—but other passions in me ruled,
Passions more fervent, making me less prompt
To in-door study than was wise or well,   370
Or suited to those years. Yet I, though used
In magisterial[4] liberty to rove,
Culling such flowers of learning as might tempt
A random choice, could shadow forth a place
(If now I yield not to a flattering dream)   375
Whose studious aspect should have bent me down
To instantaneous service; should at once
Have made me pay to science and to arts
And written lore, acknowledged my liege lord,
A homage frankly offered up, like that   380
Which I had paid to Nature. Toil and pains
In this recess, by thoughtful Fancy built,
Should spread from heart to heart; and stately groves,
Majestic edifices, should not want
A corresponding dignity within.   385
The congregating temper[6] that pervades
Our unripe years, not wasted, should be taught
To minister to works of high attempt—
Works which the enthusiast would perform with love.
Youth should be awed, religiously possessed   390

4. Masterful.

Religious, of what holy joy there is
In knowledge if it be sincerely sought
For its own sake—in glory, and in praise,
If but by labour won, and to endure.   400
[395] The passing day should learn to put aside
Her trappings here, should strip them off abashed
Before antiquity and stedfast truth,
And strong book-mindedness; and over all
Should be a healthy sound simplicity,   405
[400] A seemly plainness—name it as you will,
Republican or pious.[7]

                        If these thoughts
Be a gratuitous emblazonry
That does but mock this recreant age, at least
Let Folly and False-seeming (we might say)   410
[405] Be free to affect whatever formal gait
Of moral or scholastic discipline
Shall raise them highest in their own esteem;
Let them parade among the schools at will,
But spare the house of God. Was ever known   415
[409] The witless shepherd who would drive his flock
With serious repetition to a pool
Of which 'tis plain to sight they never taste?
A weight must surely hang on days begun
And ended with worst mockery. Be wise,   420
Ye Presidents and Deans, and to your bells
[416] Give seasonable rest, for 'tis a sound
Hollow as ever vexed the tranquil air,
And your officious doings bring disgrace
On the plain steeples of our English Church,   425
[420] Whose worship, 'mid remotest village trees,
Suffers for this. Even science[9] too, at hand
In daily sight of such irreverence,
Is smitten thence with an unnatural taint,
Loses her just authority, falls beneath   430
[425] Collateral suspicion, else unknown.
This obvious truth did not escape me then,
Unthinking as I was, and I confess
That—having in my native hills given loose
To a schoolboy's dreaming—I had raised a pile   435
[429] Upon the basis of the coming time
Which now before me melted fast away,
Which could not live, scarcely had life enough

---

7. The plainness described is that of the
early Roman Republic, but Wordsworth
leaves it open to those who dislike the
current associations of republicanism
with the French Revolution to think of it
in terms of primitive Christianity.
9. Knowledge, learning in general (though
at line 384 above "science" seems to
have its modern sense).

With a conviction of the power that waits
On knowledge, when sincerely sought and prized
For its own sake, on glory and on praise
If but by labour won, and fit to endure.
The passing day should learn to put aside   395
Her trappings here, should strip them off abashed
Before antiquity and stedfast truth
And strong book-mindedness; and over all
A healthy sound simplicity should reign,
A seemly plainness, name it what you will,   400
Republican or pious.[7]

       If these thoughts
Are a gratuitous emblazonry
That mocks the recreant age *we* live in, then
Be Folly and False-seeming free to affect
Whatever formal gait of discipline   405
Shall raise them highest in their own esteem—
Let them parade among the Schools at will,
But spare the House of God. Was ever known
The witless shepherd who persists to drive
A flock that thirsts not to a pool disliked?   410
A weight must surely hang on days begun
And ended with such mockery. Be wise,
Ye Presidents and Deans, and, till the spirit
Of ancient times revive, and youth be trained
At home in pious service,[8] to your bells   415
Give seasonable rest, for 'tis a sound
Hollow as ever vexed the tranquil air;
And your officious doings bring disgrace
On the plain steeples of our English Church,
Whose worship, 'mid remotest village trees,   420
Suffers for this. Even Science,[9] too, at hand
In daily sight of this irreverence,
Is smitten thence with an unnatural taint,
Loses her just authority, falls beneath
Collateral suspicion, else unknown.   425
This truth escaped me not, and I confess,
That having 'mid my native hills given loose
To a schoolboy's vision, I had raised a pile

---

8. Wordsworth, whose brother Christopher was Master of Trinity, Cambridge, and unpopular for enforcement of chapel attendance, shows his continuing independence of mind in not toning down substantially the advice given in *1805*.

To mock the builder. Oh, what joy it were
[431] To see a sanctuary for our country's youth   440
With such a spirit in it as might be
Protection for itself, a virgin grove,
Primaeval in its purity and depth—
Where, though the shades were filled with chearfulness,
[435] Nor indigent of songs warbled from crowds   445
In under-coverts, yet the countenance
Of the whole place should wear a stamp of awe—
A habitation sober and demure
For ruminating creatures,[1] a domain
[440] For quiet things to wander in, a haunt   450
In which the heron might delight to feed
By the shy rivers, and the pelican
Upon the cypress-spire in lonely thought
Might sit and sun himself.[2] Alas, alas,
[445] In vain for such solemnity we look;   455
Our eyes are crossed by butterflies, our ears
Hear chattering popinjays—the inner heart
Is trivial, and the impresses without
Are of a gaudy region.[3]

                    Different sight
[450] Those venerable doctors saw of old   460
When all who dwelt within these famous walls
Led in abstemiousness a studious life,
When, in forlorn and naked chambers cooped
And crowded, o'er their ponderous books they sate
[455] Like caterpillars eating out their way   465
In silence, or with keen devouring noise
Not to be tracked or fathered.[4] Princes then
At matins froze, and couched at curfew-time,[5]
Trained up through piety and zeal to prize
[460] Spare diet, patient labour, and plain weeds.[6]   470
O seat of Arts, renowned throughout the world,
Far different service in those homely days
The nurslings of the Muses underwent
From their first childhood. In that glorious time
[465] When Learning, like a stranger come from far,   475
Sounding through Christian lands her trumpet, rouzed
The peasant and the king; when boys and youths,

---

1. Literally, animals that chew the cud.
2. Wordsworth draws the image of the pelican from William Bartram's *Travels Through North and South Carolina* (1791), more famous as a source for the "deep, romantic chasm" of Coleridge's *Kubla Khan*.
3. I.e., the impressions made by the external world are of gaudiness.
4. Attributed to a source; compare imagination as the "unfathered vapour," at VI, 527, below.
5. "Matins": Morning prayer. "Curfew-time": time of the evening bell.
6. Garments.

Upon the basis of the coming time,
That fell in ruins round me. Oh, what joy   430
To see a sanctuary for our country's youth
Informed with such a spirit as might be
Its own protection; a primeval grove,
Where, though the shades with cheerfulness were filled,
Nor indigent of songs warbled from crowds   435
In under-coverts, yet the countenance
Of the whole place should bear a stamp of awe;
A habitation sober and demure
For ruminating creatures;[1] a domain
For quiet things to wander in; a haunt   440
In which the heron should delight to feed
By the shy rivers, and the pelican
Upon the cypress spire in lonely thought
Might sit and sun himself.[2]—Alas! Alas!
In vain for such solemnity I looked;   445
Mine eyes were crossed by butterflies, ears vexed
By chattering popinjays; the inner heart
Seemed trivial, and the impresses without
Of a too gaudy region.[3]

               Different sight
Those venerable Doctors saw of old,   450
When all who dwelt within these famous walls
Led in abstemiousness a studious life;
When, in forlorn and naked chambers cooped
And crowded, o'er the ponderous books they hung
Like caterpillars eating out their way   455
In silence, or with keen devouring noise
Not to be tracked or fathered.[4] Princes then
At matins froze, and couched at curfew-time,[5]
Trained up through piety and zeal to prize
Spare diet, patient labour, and plain weeds.[6]   460
O seat of Arts! renowned throughout the world!
Far different service in those homely days
The Muses' modest nurslings underwent
From their first childhood: in that glorious time
When Learning, like a stranger come from far,   465
Sounding through Christian lands her trumpet, roused
Peasant and king; when boys and youths, the growth

The growth of ragged villages and huts,
Forsook their homes and—errant in the quest
[470] Of patron, famous school or friendly nook,   480
Where, pensioned, they in shelter might sit down—
From town to town and through wide scattered realms
Journeyed with their huge folios in their hands,
And often, starting from some covert place,
[475] Saluted the chance comer on the road,   485
Crying, 'An obolus, a penny give
To a poor scholar'; when illustrious men,
Lovers of truth, by penury constrained,
Bucer, Erasmus, or Melancthon, read
[480] Before the doors or windows of their cells
By moonshine through mere lack of taper light.[7]   490

        But peace to vain regrets. We see but darkly
Even when we look behind us; and best things
Are not so pure by nature that they needs
[485] Must keep to all—as fondly all believe—   495
Their highest promise. If the mariner,
When at reluctant distance he hath passed
Some fair enticing island, did but know
What fate might have been his, could he have brought
[490] His bark to land upon the wished-for spot,   500
Good cause full often would he have to bless
The belt of churlish surf that scared him thence,
Or haste of the inexorable wind.
For me, I grieve not; happy is the man
[495] Who only misses what I missed, who falls   505
No lower than I fell. I did not love,
As hath been noticed heretofore, the guise
Of our scholastic studies—could have wished
The river to have had an ampler range
[500] And freer pace. But this I tax[8] not; far,   510
Far more I grieved to see among the band
Of those who in the field of contest stood
As combatants, passions that did to me
Seem low and mean—from ignorance of mine,
In part, and want of just forbearance; yet
My wiser mind grieves now for what I saw.   515
Willingly did I part from these, and turn
Out of their track to travel with the shoal
[507] Of more unthinking natures, easy minds

---

7. *1805*, 484–87 (*1850*, 474–77) allude to the disgraced Byzantine general, Belisarius, traditionally said to have been blinded, and to have begged in Constantinople with the words, "*Date obolum Belisario*" ("Give a penny to Belisarius"). Bucer, Erasmus and Melancthon (*1805*, 489; *1850*, 479) were three of the most distinguished early sixteenth-century scholars, the first two working at Cambridge and Oxford respectively.
8. Blame.

Of ragged villages and crazy huts,
Forsook their homes, and, errant in the quest
Of Patron, famous school or friendly nook, 470
Where, pensioned, they in shelter might sit down,
From town to town and through wide scattered realms
Journeyed with ponderous folios in their hands;
And often, starting from some covert place,
Saluted the chance comer on the road, 475
Crying 'An obolus, a penny give
To a poor scholar!'—when illustrious men,
Lovers of truth, by penury constrained,
Bucer, Erasmus, or Melancthon, read
Before the doors or windows of their cells 480
By moonshine through mere lack of taper light.[7]

But peace to vain regrets! We see but darkly
Even when we look behind us, and best things
Are not so pure by nature that they needs
Must keep to all, as fondly all believe, 485
Their highest promise. If the mariner
When at reluctant distance he hath passed
Some tempting island, could but know the ills
That must have fallen upon him had he brought
His bark to land upon the wished-for shore, 490
Good cause would oft be his to thank the surf
Whose white belt scared him thence, or wind that blew
Inexorably adverse: for myself
I grieve not; happy is the gownèd youth,
Who only misses what I missed, who falls 495
No lower than I fell.

I did not love,
Judging not ill perhaps, the timid course
Of our scholastic studies; could have wished
To see the river flow with ampler range
And freer pace; but more, far more, I grieved 500
To see displayed among an eager few,
Who in the field of contest persevered,
Passions unworthy of youth's generous heart
And mounting spirit, pitiably repaid,
When so disturbed, whatever palms are won. 505
From these I turned to travel with the shoal
Of more unthinking natures, easy minds

And pillowy, and not wanting love that makes   520
The day pass lightly on,[9] when foresight sleeps,
[510] And wisdom and the pledges interchanged
With our own inner being, are forgot.

To books, our daily fare prescribed, I turned
With sickly appetite; and when I went,   525
At other times, in quest of my own food,
I chaced not steadily the manly deer,
But laid me down to any casual feast
Of wild wood-honey; or, with truant eyes
Unruly, peeped about for vagrant fruit.   530
And as for what pertains to human life,
The deeper passions working round me here—
Whether of envy, jealousy, pride, shame,
Ambition, emulation, fear, or hope,
Or those of dissolute pleasure—were by me   535
Unshared, and only now and then observed,
So little was their hold upon my being,
As outward things that might administer
To knowledge or instruction. Hushed meanwhile
Was the under-soul, locked up in such a calm,   540
That not a leaf of the great nature stirred.[1]
Yet was this deep vacation not given up
To utter waste.[2] Hitherto I had stood
In my own mind remote from human life,
[515] At least from what we commonly so name,   545
Even as a shepherd on a promontory,
Who, lacking occupation, looks far forth
Into the endlesss sea, and rather makes
Than finds what he beholds.[3] And sure it is,
[520] That this first transit from the smooth delights 550
And wild outlandish walks of simple youth
To something that resembled an approach
Towards mortal business, to a privileged world
Within a world, a midway residence
[525] With all its intervenient imagery,   555
Did better suit my visionary mind—
Far better, than to have been bolted forth,[4]

9. The love which these unthinking men do not lack (are "not wanting") is a superficial kind, and merely serves to pass the time agreeably. "Shoal" (*1805*, 518; *1850*, 506): crowd, throng (Johnson's *Dictionary*).
1. Lines 524-41 were cut in 1816/19. The impression given both of Cambridge, and of Wordsworth's own behavior, can be filled out by comparison with a letter of March 6, 1804, to De Quincey, who had just gone up to Oxford (*EY*, p. 454).

2. It is the supposedly active part of the university year that Wordsworth refers to as vacation.
3. Wordsworth has in mind the literary "shepherd of the Hebrid Isles" who in Thomson's *Castle of Indolence* (1748), Book I, stanza xxx, sees, or thinks he sees, "A vast assembly" as Phoebus dips his wain into the ocean.
4. Forced out of the protected world of childhood as an animal is forced to bolt from cover.

And pillowy; yet not wanting love that makes
The day pass lightly on,[9] when foresight sleeps,
And wisdom and the pledges interchanged   510
With our own inner being are forgot.

    Yet was this deep vacation not given up
To utter waste.[2] Hitherto I had stood
In my own mind remote from social life
(At least from what we commonly so name),   515
Like a lone shepherd on a promontory
Who lacking occupation looks far forth
Into the boundless sea, and rather makes
Than finds what he beholds.[3] And sure it is,
That this first transit from the smooth delights   520
And wild outlandish walks of simple youth
To something that resembled an approach
Towards human business, to a privileged world
Within a world, a midway residence
With all its intervenient imagery,   525
Did better suit my visionary mind,
Far better, than to have been bolted forth,[4]

Thrust out abruptly into fortune's way
Among the conflicts of substantial life—
[530] By a more just gradation did lead on   560
To higher things, more naturally matured
For permanent possession, better fruits,
Whether of truth or virtue, to ensue.[5]

[535]   In playful zest of fancy did we note—   565
How could we less?—the manners and the ways
Of those who in the livery were arrayed
Of good or evil fame, of those with whom
By frame of academic discipline
[540] Perforce we were connected, men whose sway,
And whose authority of office, served   570
To set our minds on edge,[6] and did no more.
Nor wanted we rich pastime of this kind—
Found everywhere, but chiefly in the ring
[545] Of the grave elders, men unscoured, grotesque
In character, tricked out like aged trees   575
Which through the lapse of their infirmity
Give ready place to any random seed
That chuses to be reared upon their trunks.
[550] Here on my view, confronting as it were
Those shepherd swains whom I had lately left,   580
Did flash a different image of old age—
How different—yet both withal alike
A book of rudiments for the unpractised sight,
[554] Objects embossed, and which with sedulous[7] care
Nature holds up before the eye of youth   585
In her great school—with further view, perhaps,
To enter early on her tender scheme
[560] Of teaching comprehension with delight
And mingling playful with pathetic thoughts.

    The surfaces of artificial life   590
And manners finely spun, the delicate race
Of colours, lurking, gleaming up and down
[565] Through that state arras woven with silk and gold—
This wily interchange of snaky hues,
Willingly and unwillingly revealed,[8]   595

---

5. Wordsworth's syntax in *1805*, 560–63
(*1850*, 530–33) is uncommonly cryptic.
The halfway stage ("just gradation") of
university life leads on to "higher things,
more naturally matured," with the result
that better fruits may follow.
6. In the context, presumably "to irri-
tate"—by analogy with setting teeth
on edge—rather than to stimulate, or
sharpen.

7. Diligent, as at I, 571, above.
8. In evoking the artificial surface of
life Wordsworth draws on Spenser, the
"gentle bard" of *1805*, 279–83; see especially *Faerie Queene*, III, stanza 28,
which describes an "arras," or tapestry,
"Woven with gold and silk," in which
the "rich metal lurked privily," yet here
and there "shewd itself and shone unwillingly."

Thrust out abruptly into Fortune's way
Among the conflicts of substantial life;
By a more just gradation did lead on   530
To higher things; more naturally matured,
For permanent possession, better fruits,
Whether of truth or virtue, to ensue.[5]
In serious mood, but oftener, I confess,
With playful zest of fancy did we note   535
(How could we less?) the manners and the ways
Of those who lived distinguished by the badge
Of good or ill report; or those with whom
By frame of Academic discipline
We were perforce connected, men whose sway   540
And known authority of office served
To set our minds on edge,[6] and did no more.
Nor wanted we rich pastime of this kind,
Found everywhere, but chiefly in the ring
Of the grave Elders, men unscoured, grotesque   545
In character, tricked out like aged trees
Which through the lapse of their infirmity
Give ready place to any random seed
That chooses to be reared upon their trunks.

    Here on my view, confronting vividly   550
Those shepherd swains whom I had lately left,
Appeared a different aspect of old age;
How different! yet both distinctly marked,
Objects embossed to catch the general eye,
Or portraitures for special use designed,   555
As some might seem, so aptly do they serve
To illustrate Nature's book of rudiments—
That book upheld as with maternal care
When she would enter on her tender scheme
Of teaching comprehension with delight,   560
And mingling playful with pathetic thoughts.

    The surfaces of artificial life
And manners finely wrought, the delicate race
Of colours, lurking, gleaming up and down
Through that state arras woven with silk and gold: 565
This wily interchange of snaky hues,
Willingly or unwillingly revealed,[8]

I had not learned to watch, and at this time
Perhaps, had such been in my daily sight,
I might have been indifferent thereto
As hermits are to tales of distant things.
Hence, for these rarities elaborate   600
Having no relish yet, I was content
With the more homely produce rudely piled
[570] In this our coarser warehouse. At this day
I smile in many a mountain solitude
At passages and fragments that remain   605
Of that inferior exhibition, played
By wooden images, a theatre
[576] For wake or fair. And oftentimes do flit
Remembrances before me of old men,
Old humourists,[9] who have been long in their graves,   610
And, having almost in my mind put off
[580] Their human names, have into phantoms passed
Of texture midway betwixt life and books.

    I play the loiterer, 'tis enough to note   615
That here in dwarf proportions were expressed
The limbs of the great world—its goings-on
[585] Collaterally pourtrayed as in mock fight,
A tournament of blows, some hardly[1] dealt
Though short of mortal combat—and whate'er
Might of this pageant be supposed to hit   620
A simple rustic's notice, this way less,
[590] More that way, was not wasted upon me.
And yet this spectacle may well demand
A more substantial name, no mimic show,
Itself a living part of a live whole,   625
A creek of the vast sea. For, all degrees
[595] And shapes of spurious fame and short-lived praise
Here sate in state, and, fed with daily alms,
Retainers won away from solid good.
And here was Labour, his own Bond-slave; Hope   630
That never set the pains against the prize;
[600] Idleness, halting with his weary clog;
And poor misguided Shame, and witless Fear,
And simple Pleasure, foraging for Death;
Honour misplaced, and Dignity astray;   635
Feuds, factions, flatteries, Enmity and Guile,
[605] Murmuring Submission and bald Government
(The idol weak as the idolator)
And Decency and Custom starving Truth,
And blind Authority beating with his staff   640

9. In the old sense: eccentric or fan-   1. Hard, severely.
tastic men.

I neither knew nor cared for; and as such
Were wanting here, I took what might be found
Of less elaborate fabric. At this day   570
I smile, in many a mountain solitude
Conjuring up scenes as obsolete in freaks
Of character, in points of wit as broad,
As aught by wooden images performed
For entertainment of the gaping crowd   575
At wake or fair. And oftentimes do flit
Remembrances before me of old men—
Old humourists,[9] who have been long in their graves,
And having almost in my mind put off
Their human names, have into phantoms passed   580
Of texture midway between life and books.

    I play the loiterer: 'tis enough to note
That here in dwarf proportions were expressed
The limbs of the great world; its eager strifes
Collaterally pourtrayed, as in mock fight,   585
A tournament of blows, some hardly[1] dealt
Though short of mortal combat; and whate'er
Might in this pageant be supposed to hit
An artless rustic's notice, this way less,
More that way, was not wasted upon me—   590
And yet the spectacle may well demand
A more substantial name, no mimic show,
Itself a living part of a live whole,
A creek in the vast sea; for, all degrees
And shapes of spurious fame and short-lived praise   595
Here sate in state, and fed with daily alms
Retainers won away from solid good;
And here was Labour, his own bond-slave; Hope,
That never set the pains against the prize;
Idleness halting with his weary clog,   600
And poor misguided Shame, and witless Fear,
And simple Pleasure foraging for Death;
Honour misplaced, and Dignity astray;
Feuds, factions, flatteries, enmity, and guile;
Murmuring submission, and bald government,   605
(The idol weak as the idolator),
And Decency and Custom starving Truth,
And blind Authority beating with his staff

The child that might have led him; Emptiness
[610] Followed as of good omen, and meek Worth
Left to itself unheard of and unknown.[2]

    Of these and other kindred notices
I cannot say what portion is in truth   645
The naked recollection of that time,
[615] And what may rather have been called to life
By after-meditation. But delight,
That, in an easy temper lulled asleep,
Is still with innocence its own reward,   650
This surely was not wanting. Carelessly
I gazed, roving as through a cabinet[3]
[620] Or wide museum, thronged with fishes, gems,
Birds, crocodiles, shells, where little can be seen,
Well understood, or naturally endeared,   655
Yet still does every step bring something forth
That quickens, pleases, stings—and here and there
A casual rarity is singled out
And has its brief perusal, then gives way
To others, all supplanted in their turn.   660
Meanwhile, amid this gaudy congress framed
[625] Of things by nature most unneighbourly,
The head turns round, and cannot right itself;
And, though an aching and a barren sense
Of gay confusion still be uppermost,   665
With few wise longings and but little love,
[630] Yet something to the memory sticks at last
Whence profit may be drawn in times to come.

    Thus in submissive idleness, my friend,
The labouring time of autumn, winter, spring—   670
Nine months—rolled pleasingly away, the tenth
[635] Returned me to my native hills again.

---

2. A passage which shows how well Wordsworth could, when he chose, manage the personifications that he had rejected in the Preface to *Lyrical Ballads.*
3. Display case.

The child that might have led him; Emptiness
Followed as of good omen, and meek Worth
Left to herself unheard of and unknown.[2]

    Of these and other kindred notices
I cannot say what portion is in truth
The naked recollection of that time,
And what may rather have been called to life
By after-meditation. But delight
That, in an easy temper lulled asleep,
Is still with innocence its own reward,
This was not wanting. Carelessly I roamed
As through a wide museum from whose stores
A casual rarity is singled out
And has its brief perusal, then gives way
To others, all supplanted in their turn;
Till 'mid this crowded neighbourhood of things
That are by nature most unneighbourly,
The head turns round and cannot right itself;
And though an aching and a barren sense
Of gay confusion still be uppermost,
With few wise longings and but little love,
Yet to the memory something cleaves at last,
Whence profit may be drawn in times to come.

    Thus in submissive idleness, my Friend!
The labouring time of autumn, winter, spring,
Eight months! rolled pleasingly away; the ninth
Came and returned me to my native hills.

Book Fourth

Summer Vacation

A pleasant sight it was when, having clomb
The Heights of Kendal, and that dreary moor
Was crossed, at length as from a rampart's edge
[5] I overlooked the bed of Windermere.[1]
  I bounded down the hill, shouting amain   5
A lusty summons to the farther shore
For the old ferryman; and when he came
[16] I did not step into the well-known boat
Without a cordial welcome. Thence right forth
I took my way, now drawing towards home,   10
To that sweet valley where I had been reared;
[20] 'Twas but a short hour's walk ere, veering round,
I saw the snow-white church upon its hill
Sit like a thronèd lady, sending out
A gracious look all over its domain.[3]   15
[27] Glad greetings had I, and some tears perhaps,
From my old dame, so motherly and good,
While she perused me with a parent's pride.
[30] The thoughts of gratitude shall fall like dew
Upon thy grave, good creature:[4] while my heart   20
Can beat I never will forget thy name.
Heaven's blessing be upon thee where thou liest
After thy innocent and busy stir
[35] In narrow cares, thy little daily growth
Of calm enjoyments, after eighty years,   25
And more than eighty, of untroubled life—
Childless, yet by the strangers to thy blood
Honoured with little less than filial love.
[40] Great joy was mine to see thee once again,
Thee and thy dwelling, and a throng of things   30

1. Wordsworth was standing on the ridge by Cleabarrow, five or six hundred feet above the lake. "Clomb" (line 1): climbed.
3. Hawkshead, where the poet had been at school. As one approaches it—like Wordsworth—along Esthwaite Water, the church does seem to sit above the roofs of the village.
4. Ann Tyson, Wordsworth's landlady, died in 1796, aged eighty-three.

Book Fourth

Summer Vacation

BRIGHT was the summer's noon when quickening steps
Followed each other till a dreary moor
Was crossed, and a bare ridge clomb, upon whose top
Standing alone, as from a rampart's edge,
I overlooked the bed of Windermere,[1]   5
Like a vast river, stretching in the sun.
With exultation, at my feet I saw
Lake, islands, promontories, gleaming bays,
A universe of Nature's fairest forms
Proudly revealed with instantaneous burst,   10
Magnificent, and beautiful, and gay.
I bounded down the hill shouting amain
For the old Ferryman; to the shout the rocks
Replied, and when the Charon of the flood
Had staid his oars, and touched the jutting pier,   15
I did not step into the well-known boat
Without a cordial greeting.[2] Thence with speed
Up the familiar hill I took my way
Towards that sweet Valley where I had been reared;
'Twas but a short hour's walk, ere veering round   20
I saw the snow-white church upon her hill
Sit like a thronèd Lady, sending out
A gracious look all over her domain.[3]
Yon azure smoke betrays the lurking town;
With eager footsteps I advance and reach   25
The cottage threshold where my journey closed.
Glad welcome had I, with some tears, perhaps,
From my old Dame, so kind and motherly,
While she perused me with a parent's pride.
The thoughts of gratitude shall fall like dew   30
Upon thy grave, good creature![4] While my heart
Can beat never will I forget thy name.
Heaven's blessing be upon thee where thou liest
After thy innocent and busy stir
In narrow cares, thy little daily growth   35
Of calm enjoyments, after eighty years,
And more than eighty, of untroubled life,
Childless, yet by the strangers to thy blood
Honoured with little less than filial love.
What joy was mine to see thee once again,   40
Thee and thy dwelling, and a crowd of things

2. As de Selincourt comments, an "in-
apt allusion"; Charon ferried the souls
of the dead across the rivers Styx and
Acheron of the Greek underworld, and
exchanged no cordial greetings with his
passengers.

127

About its narrow precincts, all beloved
And many of them seeming yet my own.

    Why should I speak of what a thousand hearts
[45] Have felt, and every man alive can guess?
The rooms, the court, the garden were not left   35
Long unsaluted, and the spreading pine
And broad stone table underneath its boughs—
Our summer seat in many a festive hour—
[50] And that unruly child of mountain birth,
The froward brook, which, soon as he was boxed   40
Within our garden, found himself at once
As if by trick insidious and unkind,
Stripped of his voice, and left to dimple down
[55] Without an effort and without a will
A channel paved by the hand of man.   45
I looked at him and smiled, and smiled again,
And in the press of twenty thousand thoughts,
[59] 'Ha', quoth I, 'pretty prisoner, are you there!'
—And now, reviewing soberly that hour,
I marvel that a fancy did not flash   50
Upon me, and a strong desire, straitway,
At sight of such an emblem that shewed forth
So aptly my late course of even days
And all their smooth enthralment, to pen down
A satire on myself. My aged dame   55
[65] Was with me, at my side; she guided me,
I willing, nay—nay, wishing to be led.
The face of every neighbour whom I met
Was as a volume to me; some I hailed
Far off, upon the road, or at their work—   60
[70] Unceremonious greetings, interchanged
With half the length of a long field between.
Among my schoolfellows I scattered round
A salutation that was more constrained
Though earnest—doubtless with a little pride,   65
[75] But with more shame, for my habiliments,
The transformation and the gay attire.

    Delighted did I take my place again
At our domestic table; and, dear friend,
Relating simply as my wish hath been   70
[80] A poet's history, can I leave untold
The joy with which I laid me down at night
In my accustomed bed, more welcome now
Perhaps than if it had been more desired,
Or been more often thought of with regret—   75
[85] That bed whence I had heard the roaring wind
And clamorous rain, that bed where I so oft

About its narrow precincts all beloved,
And many of them seeming yet my own!
Why should I speak of what a thousand hearts
Have felt, and every man alive can guess? 45
The rooms, the court, the garden were not left
Long unsaluted, nor the sunny seat
Round the stone table under the dark pine,
Friendly to studious or to festive hours;
Nor that unruly child of mountain birth, 50
The froward brook, who, soon as he was boxed
Within our garden, found himself at once,
As if by trick insidious and unkind,
Stripped of his voice and left to dimple down
(Without an effort and without a will) 55
A channel paved by man's officious care.
I looked at him and smiled, and smiled again,
And in the press of twenty thousand thoughts,
'Ha', quoth I, 'pretty prisoner, are you there!'
Well might sarcastic Fancy then have whispered, 60
'An emblem here behold of thy own life;
In its late course of even days with all
Their smooth enthralment'; but the heart was full,
Too full for that reproach. My aged Dame
Walked proudly at my side: she guided me; 65
I willing, nay—nay, wishing to be led.
—The face of every neighbour whom I met
Was like a volume to me: some were hailed
Upon the road, some busy at their work,
Unceremonious greetings interchanged 70
With half the length of a long field between.
Among my schoolfellows I scattered round
Like recognitions, but with some constraint
Attended, doubtless, with a little pride,
But with more shame, for my habiliments, 75
The transformation wrought by gay attire.
Not less delighted did I take my place
At our domestic table: and, dear Friend!
In this endeavour simply to relate
A Poet's history, may I leave untold 80
The thankfulness with which I laid me down
In my accustomed bed, more welcome now
Perhaps than if it had been more desired
Or been more often thought of with regret;
That lowly bed whence I had heard the wind 85
Roar and the rain beat hard, where I so oft

Had lain awake on breezy nights to watch
The moon in splendour couched among the leaves
Of a tall ash that near our cottage stood,   80
[90] Had watched her with fixed eyes, while to and fro
In the dark summit of the moving tree
She rocked with every impulse of the wind.

    Among the faces which it pleased me well
To see again was one by ancient right   85
[95] Our inmate, a rough terrier of the hills,
By birth and call of nature preordained
To hunt the badger and unearth the fox
Among the impervious crags. But having been
From youth our own adopted, he had passed   90
[100] Into a gentler service; and when first
The boyish spirit flagged, and day by day
Along my veins I kindled with the stir,
The fermentation and the vernal heat
Of poesy, affecting private shades   95
[105] Like a sick lover, then his dog was used
To watch me, an attendant and a friend,
Obsequious to my steps early and late,
Though often of such dilatory walk
Tired, and uneasy at the halts I made.   100
[110] A hundred times when in these wanderings
I have been busy with the toil of verse—
Great pains and little progress—and at once
Some fair enchanting image in my mind
Rose up, full-formed like Venus from the sea,   105
[115] Have I sprung forth towards him and let loose
My hand upon his back with stormy joy,
Caressing him again and yet again.[5]
And when in the public roads at eventide
I sauntered, like a river murmuring   110
[120] And talking to itself, at such a season
It was his custom to jog on before;
But, duly whensoever he had met
A passenger[6] approaching, would he turn
To give me timely notice, and straitway,   115
[125] Punctual to such admonishment, I hushed
My voice, composed my gait, and shaped myself
To give and take a greeting that might save
My name from piteous rumours, such as wait
[130] On men suspected to be crazed in brain.   120

5. Lines 101–8 are a playful rewriting of lines from *The Dog: An Idyllium*, composed by Wordsworth in 1786–87—the period to which the passage refers: "If while I gazed, to Nature blind, / In the calm ocean of my mind / Some new-created image rose / In full-grown beauty at its birth, / Lovely as Venus from the sea, / Then, while my glad hand sprung to thee, / We were the happiest pair on earth" (*Oxford Wordsworth*, I, p. 264).
6. Passerby.

Had lain awake on summer nights to watch
The moon in splendour couched among the leaves
Of a tall ash, that near our cottage stood;
Had watched her with fixed eyes while to and fro   90
In the dark summit of the waving tree
She rocked with every impulse of the breeze.

    Among the favourites whom it pleased me well
To see again, was one by ancient right
Our inmate, a rough terrier of the hills;   95
By birth and call of nature pre-ordained
To hunt the badger and unearth the fox
Among the impervious crags, but having been
From youth our own adopted, he had passed
Into a gentler service. And when first   100
The boyish spirit flagged, and day by day
Among my veins I kindled with the stir,
The fermentation, and the vernal heat
Of poesy, affecting private shades
Like a sick Lover, then this dog was used   105
To watch me, an attendant and a friend,
Obsequious to my steps early and late,
Though often of such dilatory walk
Tired, and uneasy at the halts I made.
A hundred times when, roving high and low,   110
I have been harassed with the toil of verse,
Much pains and little progress, and at once
Some lovely Image in the song rose up
Full-formed, like Venus rising from the sea;
Then have I darted forwards to let loose   115
My hand upon his back with stormy joy,
Caressing him again and yet again.
And when at evening on the public way
I sauntered, like a river murmuring
And talking to itself when all things else   120
Are still, the creature trotted on before;
Such was his custom; but whene'er he met
A passenger[6] approaching, he would turn
To give me timely notice, and straightway,
Grateful for that admonishment, I hushed   125
My voice, composed my gait, and, with the air
And mien of one whose thoughts are free, advanced
To give and take a greeting that might save
My name from piteous rumours, such as wait
On men suspected to be crazed in brain.   130

Those walks, well worthy to be prized and loved—
Regretted, that word too was on my tongue,
But they were richly laden with all good,
And cannot be remembered but with thanks
[135] And gratitude and perfect joy of heart—   125
Those walks did now like a returning spring
Come back on me again. When first I made
Once more the circuit of our little lake
If ever happiness hath lodged with man
[140] That day consummate⁷ happiness was mine—   130
Wide-spreading, steady, calm, contemplative.
The sun was set, or setting, when I left
Our cottage door, and evening soon brought on
A sober hour, not winning or serene,
[145] For cold and raw the air was, and untuned;   135
But as a face we love is sweetest then
When sorrow damps it, or, whatever look
It chance to wear, is sweetest if the heart
Have fulness in itself, even so with me
[150] It fared that evening. Gently did my soul   140
Put off her veil, and, self-transmuted, stood
Naked as in the presence of her God.⁸
As on I walked, a comfort seemed to touch
A heart that had not been disconsolate,
[155] Strength came where weakness was not known to be,   145
At least not felt; and restoration came
Like an intruder knocking at the door
Of unacknowledged weariness. I took
The balance in my hand and weighed myself:
[161] I saw but little, and thereat was pleased;   150
Little did I remember, and even this
Still pleased me more—but I had hopes and peace
And swellings of the spirits, was rapt and soothed,
Conversed with promises, had glimmering views
[165] How life pervades the undecaying mind,   155
How the immortal soul with godlike power
Informs, creates, and thaws the deepest sleep
That time can lay upon her, how on earth
Man if he do but live within the light
[170] Of high endeavours, daily spreads abroad   160
His being with a strength that cannot fail.
Nor was there want of milder thoughts, of love,
Of innocence, and holiday repose,
And more than pastoral quiet in the heart
[175] Of amplest projects, and a peaceful end   165

7. Complete; pronounced "consummit."
8. When Moses in Exodus 34:33–34,
came down from Mount Sinai, his face
shone so brightly that he covered it with
a veil, but he took the veil off when talking to God.

Those walks well worthy to be prized and loved—
Regretted!—that word, too, was on my tongue,
But they were richly laden with all good,
And cannot be remembered but with thanks
And gratitude, and perfect joy of heart—   135
Those walks in all their freshness now came back
Like a returning Spring. When first I made
Once more the circuit of our little lake,
If ever happiness hath lodged with man,
That day consummate[7] happiness was mine,   140
Wide-spreading, steady, calm, contemplative.
The sun was set, or setting, when I left
Our cottage door, and evening soon brought on
A sober hour, not winning or serene,
For cold and raw the air was, and untuned;   145
But as a face we love is sweetest then
When sorrow damps it, or, whatever look
It chance to wear is sweetest if the heart
Have fulness in herself; even so with me
It fared that evening. Gently did my soul   150
Put off her veil, and, self-transmuted, stood
Naked, as in the presence of her God.[8]
While on I walked, a comfort seemed to touch
A heart that had not been disconsolate:
Strength came where weakness was not known to be,   155
At least not felt; and restoration came
Like an intruder knocking at the door
Of unacknowledged weariness. I took
The balance, and with firm hand weighed myself.
—Of that external scene which round me lay,   160
Little, in this abstraction, did I see;
Remembered less; but I had inward hopes
And swellings of the spirit, was rapt and soothed,
Conversed with promises, had glimmering views
How life pervades the undecaying mind;   165
How the immortal soul with God-like power
Informs, creates, and thaws the deepest sleep
That time can lay upon her; how on earth,
Man, if he do but live within the light
Of high endeavours, daily spreads abroad   170
His being armed with strength that cannot fail.
Nor was there want of milder thoughts, of love,
Of innocence, and holiday repose;
And more than pastoral quiet, 'mid the stir
Of boldest projects, and a peaceful end   175

At last, or glorious, by endurance won.
Thus musing, in a wood I sate me down
Alone, continuing there to muse. Meanwhile
The mountain heights were slowly overspread
[180] With darkness, and before a rippling breeze   170
The long lake lengthened out its hoary line,
And in the sheltered coppice⁹ where I sate,
Around me, from among the hazel leaves—
Now here, now there, stirred by the straggling wind—
[185] Came intermittingly a breath-like sound,   175
A respiration short and quick, which oft,
Yea, might I say, again and yet again,
Mistaking for the panting of my dog,
The off-and-on companion of my walk,
[189] I turned my head to look if he were there.   180

    A freshness also found I at this time
In human life, the life I mean of those
Whose occupations really I loved.
The prospect often touched me with surprize:
Crowded and full, and changed, as seemed to me,   185
[195] Even as a garden in the heat of spring
After an eight-days' absence. For—to omit
The things which were the same and yet appeared
So different—amid this solitude,
The little vale where was my chief abode,   190
[200] 'Twas not indifferent to a youthful mind
To note, perhaps, some sheltered seat in which
An old man had been used to sun himself,
Now empty; pale-faced babes whom I had left
In arms, known children of the neighbourhood,   195
[205] Now rosy prattlers, tottering up and down;
And growing girls whose beauty, filched away
With all its pleasant promises, was gone
To deck some slighted playmate's homely cheek.¹

    Yes, I had something of another eye,   200
[210] And often looking round was moved to smiles
Such as a delicate work of humour breeds.
I read, without design, the opinions, thoughts,
Of those plain-living people, in a sense
Of love and knowledge: with another eye   205
[215] I saw the quiet woodman in the woods,
The shepherd on the hills. With new delight,
This chiefly, did I view my grey-haired dame,
Saw her go forth to church, or other work

---

9. Copse: a small wood typically composed of hazel-bushes.

1. An echo of *Lycidas*, 65, "To tend the
homely slighted shepherd's trade."

At last, or glorious, by endurance won.
Thus musing, in a wood I sate me down
Alone, continuing there to muse: the slopes
And heights meanwhile were slowly overspread
With darkness, and before a rippling breeze   180
The long lake lengthened out its hoary line,
And in the sheltered coppice[9] where I sate,
Around me from among the hazel leaves,
Now here, now there, moved by the straggling wind,
Came ever and anon a breath-like sound,   185
Quick as the pantings of the faithful dog,
The off and on companion of my walk;
And such, at times, believing them to be,
I turned my head to look if he were there;
Then into solemn thought I passed once more.   190

      A freshness also found I at this time
In human Life, the daily life of those
Whose occupations really I loved;
The peaceful scene oft filled me with surprise
Changed like a garden in the heat of spring   195
After an eight-days' absence. For (to omit
The things which were the same and yet appeared
Far otherwise) amid this rural solitude,
A narrow Vale where each was known to all,
'Twas not indifferent to a youthful mind   200
To mark some sheltering bower or sunny nook,
Where an old man had used to sit alone,
Now vacant; pale-faced babes whom I had left
In arms, now rosy prattlers at the feet
Of a pleased grandame tottering up and down;   205
And growing girls whose beauty, filched away
With all its pleasant promises, was gone
To deck some slighted playmate's homely cheek.[1]

      Yes, I had something of a subtler sense,
And often looking round was moved to smiles   210
Such as a delicate work of humour breeds;
I read, without design, the opinions, thoughts,
Of those plain-living people now observed
With clearer knowledge; with another eye
I saw the quiet woodman in the woods,   215
The shepherd roam the hills. With new delight,
This chiefly, did I note my grey-haired Dame;
Saw her go forth to church or other work

Of state, equipped in monumental trim—   210
[220] Short velvet cloak, her bonnet of the like,
A mantle such as Spanish cavaliers
Wore in old time. Her smooth domestic life—
Affectionate without uneasiness—
Her talk, her business, pleased me; and no less   215
[225] Her clear though shallow stream of piety,
That ran on sabbath days a fresher course.
With thoughts unfelt till now I saw her read
Her bible on the Sunday afternoons,
And loved the book when she had dropped asleep   220
[230] And made of it a pillow for her head.

   Nor less do I remember to have felt
Distinctly manifested at this time,
A dawning, even as of another sense,
A human-heartedness about my love   225
For objects hitherto the gladsome air
[235] Of my own private being, and no more[2]—
Which I had loved, even as a blessèd spirit
Or angel, if he were to dwell on earth,
Might love in individual happiness.   230
But now there opened on me other thoughts,
[240] Of change, congratulation and regret,
A new-born feeling. It spread far and wide:
The trees, the mountains shared it, and the brooks,
The stars of heaven, now seen in their old haunts—   235
White Sirius glittering o'er the southern crags,
[245] Orion with his belt, and those fair Seven,
Acquaintances of every little child,
And Jupiter, my own belovèd star.[3]
Whatever shadings of mortality   240
[250] Had fallen upon these objects heretofore
Were different in kind: not tender—strong,
Deep, gloomy were they, and severe, the scatterings
Of childhood, and moreover, had given way
In later youth to beauty and to love   245
[255] Enthusiastic, to delight and joy.

   As one who hangs down-bending from the side
Of a slow-moving boat upon the breast
Of a still water, solacing himself

2. Looking back, Wordsworth dates the stages of his development differently at different times. The dawning of "human-heartedness" in his love for Nature is here recorded as occurring in 1788. In *Tintern Abbey* (1798), however, Nature is said to have been "all in all" as late as 1793, and Wordsworth by implication has come only quite recently to hear "the still, sad music of humanity" (lines 73–76, 89–94).

3. Wordsworth was born on April 7, and thus under the planet Jupiter. "Those fair Seven" are the Seven Sisters, or Pleiades.

Of state, equipped in monumental trim;
Short velvet cloak (her bonnet of the like),   220
A mantle such as Spanish Cavaliers
Wore in old time. Her smooth domestic life,
Affectionate without disquietude,
Her talk, her business, pleased me; and no less
Her clear though shallow stream of piety   225
That ran on Sabbath days a fresher course;
With thoughts unfelt till now I saw her read
Her Bible on hot Sunday afternoons,
And loved the book, when she had dropped asleep
And made of it a pillow for her head.   230

    Nor less do I remember to have felt,
Distinctly manifested at this time,
A human-heartedness about my love
For objects hitherto the absolute wealth
Of my own private being and no more:[2]   235
Which I had loved, even as a blessed spirit
Or Angel, if he were to dwell on earth,
Might love in individual happiness.
But now there opened on me other thoughts
Of change, congratulation or regret,   240
A pensive feeling! It spread far and wide;
The trees, the mountains shared it, and the brooks,
The stars of Heaven, now seen in their old haunts—
White Sirius glittering o'er the southern crags,
Orion with his belt, and those fair Seven,   245
Acquaintances of every little child,
And Jupiter, my own beloved star![3]
Whatever shadings of mortality,
Whatever imports from the world of death
Had come among these objects heretofore,   250
Were, in the main, of mood less tender: strong,
Deep, gloomy were they, and severe; the scatterings
Of awe or tremulous dread, that had given way
In later youth to yearnings of a love
Enthusiastic, to delight and hope.   255

    As one who hangs down-bending from the side
Of a slow-moving boat, upon the breast
Of a still water, solacing himself

With such discoveries as his eye can make   250
[260] Beneath him in the bottom of the deeps,
Sees many beauteous sights—weeds, fishes, flowers,
Grots, pebbles, roots of trees—and fancies more,
Yet often is perplexed, and cannot part
The shadow from the substance, rocks and sky,   255
[265] Mountains and clouds, from that which is indeed
The region, and the things which there abide
In their true dwelling; now is crossed by gleam
Of his own image, by a sunbeam now,
And motions that are sent he knows not whence,   260
[270] Impediments that make his task more sweet;
Such pleasant office have we long pursued
Incumbent o'er the surface of past time—
With like success. Nor have we often looked
On more alluring shows—to me at least—   265
More soft, or less ambiguously descried,
[275] Than those which now we have been passing by,
And where we still are lingering. Yet in spite
Of all these new employments of the mind
There was an inner falling off. I loved,[4]   270
Loved deeply, all that I had loved before,
[280] More deeply even than ever; but a swarm
Of heady thoughts jostling each other, gawds
And feast and dance and public revelry
And sports and games—less pleasing in themselves   275
[285] Than as they were a badge, glossy and fresh,
Of manliness and freedom—these did now
Seduce me from the firm habitual quest
Of feeding pleasures,[5] from that eager zeal,
Those yearnings which had every day been mine,   280
[290] A wild, unworldly-minded youth, given up
To Nature and to books, or, at the most,
From time to time by inclination shipped
One among many, in societies
That were, or seemed, as simple as myself.   285
But now was come a change—it would demand
Some skill, and longer time than may be spared,
To paint even to myself these vanities,
And how they wrought—but sure it is that now
Contagious air did oft environ me,   290

4. The mutilated faircopy of Book IV of the five-Book *Prelude* that is preserved in *MS. W* opens at this point with five important lines not present in *1805*: "Auspicious was this outset, and the days / That followed marched in flattering symphony / With such a fair presage; but 'twas not long / Ere fallings-off and indirect desires / Told of an inner weakness. Much I loved * * *" Book IV in this original version seems to have been a shorter form of *1805*, IV and V, into which it was very quickly expanded.
5. I.e., pleasures that supplied nutrition to the mind. "Gawds" (*1805*, 273; *1850*, 281): gaieties (*NED*).

With such discoveries as his eye can make
Beneath him in the bottom of the deep,   260
Sees many beauteous sights—weeds, fishes, flowers,
Grots, pebbles, roots of trees, and fancies more,
Yet often is perplexed and cannot part
The shadow from the substance, rocks and sky,
Mountains and clouds, reflected in the depth   265
Of the clear flood, from things which there abide
In their true dwelling; now is crossed by gleam
Of his own image, by a sun-beam now,
And wavering motions sent he knows not whence,
Impediments that make his task more sweet;   270
Such pleasant office have we long pursued
Incumbent o'er the surface of past time
With like success, nor often have appeared
Shapes fairer or less doubtfully discerned
Than these to which the Tale, indulgent Friend!   275
Would now direct thy notice. Yet in spite
Of pleasure won, and knowledge not withheld,
There was an inner falling off—I loved,
Loved deeply all that had been loved before,
More deeply even than ever: but a swarm   280
Of heady schemes jostling each other, gawds,
And feast and dance, and public revelry,
And sports and games (too grateful in themselves,
Yet in themselves less grateful, I believe,
Than as they were a badge glossy and fresh   285
Of manliness and freedom) all conspired
To lure my mind from firm habitual quest
Of feeding pleasures,[5] to depress the zeal
And damp those daily yearnings which had once been mine—
A wild, unworldly-minded youth, given up   290
To his own eager thoughts. It would demand
Some skill, and longer time than may be spared,
To paint these vanities, and how they wrought

Unknown," among these haunts in former days.
[295] The very garments that I wore appeared
To prey upon my strength, and stopped the course
And quiet stream of self-forgetfulness.
Something there was about me that perplexed   295
Th' authentic sight of reason,[6] pressed too closely
On that religious dignity of mind
That is the very faculty of truth,
Which wanting—either, from the very first
A function never lighted up, or else   300
Extinguished—man, a creature great and good,
Seems but a pageant plaything with vile claws,[7]
And this great frame of breathing elements
A senseless idol.

            This vague heartless[8] chace
Of trivial pleasures was a poor exchange   305
For books and Nature at that early age.
[300] 'Tis true, some casual knowledge might be gained
Of character or life; but at that time,
Of manners put to school[9] I took small note,
And all my deeper passions lay elsewhere—   310
Far better had it been to exalt the mind
[305] By solitary study, to uphold
Intense desire by thought and quietness.
And yet, in chastisement of these regrets,
The memory of one particular hour   315
Doth here rise up against me. In a throng,
[310] A festal company of maids and youths,
Old men and matrons, staid, promiscuous rout,[2]
A medley of all tempers,[3] I had passed
The night in dancing, gaiety and mirth—   320
With din of instruments, and shuffling feet,
And glancing forms, and tapers glittering,
[315] And unaimed prattle flying up and down,
Spirits upon the stretch, and here and there
Slight shocks of young love-liking interspersed   325
That mounted up like joy into the head,
And tingled through the veins. Ere we retired
[320] The cock had crowed, the sky was bright with day;

6. De Selincourt draws attention to Coleridge's later definition of reason as "the
mind's eye," "an organ bearing the same
relation to spiritual objects * * * as the
eye bears to material and contingent
phaenomena" (*CC*, IV, i, pp. 155–57).
7. As with the floating island of III,
339–43, Wordsworth's image contains a
specific reference. Owen points out ("Tipu's Tiger," *NQ*, CCXV [1970], pp. 379–
80) that he had in mind a near life-sized
model of a tiger savaging a white man,
captured at the fall of Seringapatam,
India, in 1799, and on show at the East
India Company in London. The tiger is
now in the Victoria and Albert Museum.
8. Discouraging, depressing.
9. I.e., the study of human behavior.
2. "Promiscuous rout": varied company;
both words are used in a Miltonic sense.
3. Temperaments.

In haunts where they, till now, had been unknown.   295
It seemed the very garments that I wore
Preyed on my strength, and stopped the quiet stream
Of self-forgetfulness.

                  Yes, that heartless[8] chase
Of trivial pleasures was a poor exchange
For books and nature at that early age.   300
'Tis true, some casual knowledge might be gained
Of character or life; but at that time,
Of manners put to school[9] I took small note,
And all my deeper passions lay elsewhere.
Far better had it been to exalt the mind
By solitary study, to uphold   305
Intense desire through meditative peace;
And yet, for chastisement of these regrets,
The memory of one particular hour
Doth here rise up against me.[1] 'Mid a throng
Of maids and youths, old men, and matrons staid   310
A medley of all tempers,[3] I had passed
The night in dancing, gaiety, and mirth,
With din of instruments and shuffling feet,
And glancing forms, and tapers glittering,
And unaimed prattle flying up and down;   315
Spirits upon the stretch, and here and there
Slight shocks of young love-liking interspersed,
Whose transient pleasure mounted to the head,
And tingled through the veins. Ere we retired,
The cock had crowed, and now the eastern sky   320

---

1. The omission of *1805*, lines 282–86, 289–90, 285–304, makes for an easier lead into the consecration scene that follows.

Two miles I had to walk along the fields
Before I reached my home. Magnificent   330
The morning was, a memorable pomp,
[325] More glorious than I ever had beheld.
The sea was laughing at a distance; all
The solid mountains were as bright as clouds,
Grain-tinctured, drenched in empyrean light;[4]   335
And in the meadows and the lower grounds
[330] Was all the sweetness of a common dawn—
Dews, vapours, and the melody of birds,[5]
And labourers going forth into the fields.
Ah, need I say, dear friend, that to the brim   340
My heart was full? I made no vows, but vows
[335] Were then made for me: bond unknown to me
Was given, that I should be—else sinning greatly—
A dedicated spirit.[6] On I walked
In blessedness, which even yet remains.   345

   Strange rendezvous my mind was at that time,
[340] A party-coloured shew of grave and gay,
Solid and light, short-sighted and profound,
Of inconsiderate habits and sedate,
Consorting in one mansion unreproved.   350
I knew the worth of that which I possessed,
[345] Though slighted and misused. Besides in truth
That summer, swarming as it did with thoughts
Transient and loose, yet wanted not a store
Of primitive hours,[8] when—by these hindrances   355
Unthwarted—I experienced in myself
[350] Conformity as just as that of old
To the end and written spirit of God's works,
Whether held forth in Nature or in man.   360

   From many wanderings that have left behind
Remembrances not lifeless, I will here
Single out one, then pass to other themes.
A[9] favorite pleasure hath it been with me
From time of earliest youth to walk alone   365
Along the public way, when, for the night

4. Wordsworth, in this deliberately Miltonic line, has in 'mind the description of Raphael's wings as "Sky-tinctured grain" (*Paradise Lost*, V, 285); "grain" literally means "fast-dyed," but was associated in poetic usage with crimson. The "empyrean" is the highest heaven, the sphere of the pure element of fire.
5. Another Miltonic echo: "fruits and flowers, / Walks, and the melody of birds" (*Paradise Lost*, VIII, 527–28).
6. Wordsworth does not say that his dedication was to a life of poetry, but it is a very strong implication.
8. I.e., times at which Wordsworth responded with his original immediacy.
9. The incident of the Discharged Soldier (lines 363–504) was written as an independent poem, a companion piece to *The Old Cumberland Beggar*, in January–February 1798. See Beth Darlington's text in *Bicentenary Studies*, pp. 433–37. In place of lines 363–64 was the half-line "I love to walk."

Was kindling, not unseen, from humble copse
And open field, through which the pathway wound,
And homeward led my steps. Magnificent
The morning rose, in memorable pomp,
Glorious as e'er I had beheld—in front,⁣ 325
The sea lay laughing at a distance; near
The solid mountains shone, bright as the clouds,
Grain-tinctured, drenched in empyrean light;⁴
And in the meadows and the lower grounds
Was all the sweetness of a common dawn— 330
Dews, vapours, and the melody of birds,⁵
And labourers going forth to till the fields.

    Ah! need I say, dear Friend! that to the brim
My heart was full; I made no vows, but vows
Were then made for me; bond unknown to me 335
Was given, that I should be, else sinning greatly,
A dedicated Spirit.⁶ On I walked
In thankful blessedness, which yet survives.

    Strange rendezvous my mind was at that time,⁷
A parti-coloured show of grave and gay, 340
Solid and light, short-sighted and profound;
Of inconsiderate habits and sedate,
Consorting in one mansion unreproved.
The worth I knew of powers that I possessed,
Though slighted and too oft misused. Besides, 345
That summer, swarming as it did with thoughts
Transient and idle, lacked not intervals
When Folly from the frown of fleeting Time
Shrunk, and the mind experienced in herself
Conformity as just as that of old 350
To the end and written spirit of God's works,
Whether held forth in Nature or in Man.

    When from our better selves we have too long
Been parted by the hurrying world, and droop,
Sick of its business, of its pleasures tired, 355
How gracious, how benign, is Solitude;
How potent a mere image of her sway;
Most potent when impressed upon the mind
With an appropriate human centre—hermit,
Deep in the bosom of the wilderness; 360
Votary (in vast cathedral, where no foot
Is treading, where no other face is seen)

---

7. With no support from the manuscripts the first edition reads, "Strange rendezvous!
My mind was at that time * * *."

Deserted, in its silence it assumes
[368] A character of deeper quietness
Than pathless solitudes. At such an hour
Once, ere these summer months were passed away,
I slowly mounted up a steep ascent   370
Where the road's wat'ry surface, to the ridge
[380] Of that sharp rising, glittered in the moon
And seemed before my eyes another stream
Creeping with silent lapse to join the brook
[384] That murmured in the valley.² On I went   375
Tranquil, receiving in my own despite
Amusement, as I slowly passed along,
From such near objects as from time to time
Perforce intruded on the listless sense,
Quiescent and disposed to sympathy,   380
With an exhausted mind worn out by toil
And all unworthy of the deeper joy
Which waits on distant prospect—cliff or sea,
The dark blue vault and universe of stars.
Thus did I steal along that silent road,   385
My body from the stillness drinking in
A restoration like the calm of sleep,
But sweeter far. Above, before, behind,
Around me, all was peace and solitude;
I looked not round, nor did the solitude   390
Speak to my eye, but it was heard and felt,
O happy state! what beauteous pictures now
Rose in harmonious imagery; they rose
As from some distant region of my soul
And came along like dreams—yet such as left   395
Obscurely mingled with their passing forms
A consciousness of animal delight,
A self-possession felt in every pause
And every gentle movement of my frame.

  While thus I wandered, step by step led on,   400
It chanced a sudden turning of the road
Presented to my view an uncouth shape,
[388] So near that, slipping back into the shade
Of a thick hawthorn, I could mark him well,
[390] Myself unseen. He was of stature tall,   405

---

2. Wordsworth has a specific landscape in mind—the "ascent" is Briers Brow, above the Windermere Ferry, and the corner round which the soldier is discovered is just past Far Sawrey, three miles from Hawkshead (see Thompson, pp. 139–41). He is, however, prepared to include a detail noticed by Dorothy at Alfoxden on January 31, 1798, a day or two before he was writing: "The road to the village of Holford glittered like another stream." "Lapse" (*1805, 374; 1850, 382*): gentle flow; see *Paradise Lost*, VIII, 263, "And liquid lapse of murmuring streams."

Kneeling at prayers; or watchman on the top
Of lighthouse, beaten by Atlantic waves;
Or as the soul of that great Power is met   365
Sometimes embodied on a public road,
When, for the night deserted, it assumes
A character of quiet more profound
Than pathless wastes.

        Once, when those summer months
Were flown, and autumn brought its annual show   370
Of oars with oars contending, sails with sails,
Upon Winander's spacious breast, it chanced
That—after I had left a flower-decked room
(Whose in-door pastime, lighted up, survived
To a late hour), and spirits overwrought   375
Were making night do penance for a day
Spent in a round of strenuous idleness[1]—
My homeward course led up a long ascent,
Where the road's watery surface, to the top
Of that sharp rising, glittered to the moon   380
And bore the semblance of another stream
Stealing with silent lapse to join the brook
That murmured in the vale.[2] All else was still;
No living thing appeared in earth or air,
And, save the flowing water's peaceful voice,   385
Sound there was none—but, lo! an uncouth shape,
Shown by a sudden turning of the road,
So near that, slipping back into the shade
Of a thick hawthorn, I could mark him well,
Myself unseen. He was of stature tall,   390

1. As de Selincourt remarks, the addition of this passage "was unnecessary and the rather elaborate style in which it is written contrasts awkwardly with the bare, telling simplicity of the narration that follows." "Strenuous idleness" (line 378): a translation of Horace "*strenua * * * inertia*" (*Epistles*, I, xi, 28); Wordsworth uses the Horatian phrase again in "This lawn, a carpet all alive," written in 1829.

A foot above man's common measure tall,
Stiff in his form, and upright, lank and lean—
A man more meagre, as it seemed to me,
Was never seen abroad by night or day.[3]
His arms were long, and bare his hands; his mouth   410
[395] Shewed ghastly[4] in the moonlight; from behind,
A milestone propped him, and his figure seemed
Half sitting, and half standing. I could mark
That he was clad in military garb,
Though faded yet entire.[5] He was alone,   415
Had no attendant, neither dog, nor staff,
[400] Nor knapsack; in his very dress appeared
A desolation, a simplicity
That seemed akin to solitude. Long time
Did I peruse him with a mingled sense   420
Of fear and sorrow. From his lips meanwhile
There issued murmuring sounds, as if of pain
[405] Or of uneasy thought; yet still his form
Kept the same steadiness, and at his feet
His shadow lay, and moved not. In a glen   425
Hard by, a village stood, whose roofs and doors
Were visible among the scattered trees,
Scarce distant from the spot an arrow's flight.
I wished to see him move, but he remained
Fixed to his place, and still from time to time   430
Sent forth a murmuring voice of dead complaint,
Groans scarcely audible. Without self-blame
I had not thus prolonged my watch; and now,
Subduing my heart's specious cowardice,[7]   435
[410] I left the shady nook where I had stood
And hailed him. Slowly from his resting-place
He rose, and with a lean and wasted arm
In measured gesture lifted to his head
Returned my salutation, then resumed
[415] His station as before. And when erelong   440
I asked his history, he in reply
Was neither slow nor eager, but, unmoved,
And with a quiet uncomplaining voice,
A stately air of mild indifference,

3. Lines 405-9 are a shortened, and much less impressive, form of *Discharged Soldier*, 41-47: "He was in stature tall, / A foot above man's common measure tall, / And lank, and upright. There was in his form / A meagre stiffness. You might almost think / That his bones wounded him. His legs were long, / So long and shapeless that I looked at them / Forgetful of the body they sustained."
4. Ghostly (Johnson's *Dictionary*).
5. Two sentences of the earlier poem have been omitted at this point, describing the soldier's detachment: "His face was turned / Towards the road, yet not as if he sought / For any living thing. He appeared / Forlorn and desolate, a man cut off / From all his kind, and more than half detached / From his own nature" (*Discharged Soldier*, 55-60).
7. I.e., "the cowardice of my specious heart"; Wordsworth had been pretending to himself to have better motives than he really had.

A span above man's common measure tall,
Stiff, lank, and upright; a more meagre man
Was never seen before by night or day.
Long were his arms, pallid his hands; his mouth
Looked ghastly[4] in the moonlight: from behind, 395
A mile-stone propped him; I could also ken
That he was clothed in military garb,
Though faded, yet entire. Companionless,
No dog attending, by no staff sustained,
He stood, and in his very dress appeared 400
A desolation, a simplicity,
To which the trappings of a gaudy world
Make a strange back-ground.[6] From his lips, ere long,
Issued low muttered sounds, as if of pain
Or some uneasy thought; yet still his form 405
Kept the same awful steadiness—at his feet
His shadow lay, and moved not. From self-blame
Not wholly free, I watched him thus; at length
Subduing my heart's specious cowardice,[7]
I left the shady nook where I had stood 410
And hailed him. Slowly from his resting-place
He rose, and with a lean and wasted arm
In measured gesture lifted to his head
Returned my salutation; then resumed
His station as before; and when I asked 415
His history, the veteran, in reply,
Was neither slow nor eager; but, unmoved,
And with a quiet uncomplaining voice,
A stately air of mild indifference,

6. It is odd that Wordsworth could ever have preferred these two empty lines to the beautiful reading of *1805*, "That seemed akin to solitude." On the whole he tended to cut the episode in successive versions; of the 142 lines of *1805*, less than a hundred stand in *1850*, the major cuts taking place in 1832 or 1838/39.

[420] He told in simple words a soldier's tale: 445
That in the tropic islands he had served,
Whence he had landed scarcely ten days past—
That on his landing he had been dismissed,
[424] And now was travelling to his native home.[8]
At this I turned and looked towards the village,   450
But all were gone to rest, the fires all out,
And every silent window to the moon
Shone with a yellow glitter. 'No one there',
Said I, 'is waking; we must measure back
The way which we have come. Behind yon wood   455
A labourer dwells, and, take it on my word,
He will not murmur should we break his rest,
And with a ready heart will give you food
And lodging for the night.' At this he stooped,
And from the ground took up an oaken staff   460
By me yet unobserved, a traveller's staff—
[428] Which I suppose from his slack hand had dropped,
And lain till now neglected in the grass.

  Towards the cottage without more delay
We shaped our course. As it appeared to me   465
[431] He travelled without pain, and I beheld
With ill-suppressed astonishment his tall
And ghastly figure moving at my side;
Nor while we journeyed thus could I forbear
To question him of what he had endured   470
[436] From hardship, battle, or the pestilence.
He all the while was in demeanor calm,
[440] Concise in answer. Solemn and sublime
He might have seemed, but that in all he said
There was a strange half-absence, and a tone   475
Of weakness and indifference, as of one
Remembering the importance of his theme
But feeling it no longer. We advanced
Slowly, and ere we to the wood were come
[445] Discourse had ceased. Together on we passed   480
In silence through the shades, gloomy and dark;
Then, turning up along an open field,
We gained the cottage. At the door I knocked,
Calling aloud, 'My friend, here is a man
By sickness overcome. Beneath your roof   485
This night let him find rest, and give him food
If food he need, for he is faint and tired.'

8. *Discharged Soldier*, 103–4, reads "And with the little strength he yet had left / Was travelling to regain * * *" The soldier had been in the West Indies, which accounts for his wasted condition. It is reckoned that by 1796 the British forces there had lost 40,000 men through yellow fever, and that as many again had been rendered unfit for further service—being no doubt dismissed on their return.

He told in few plain words a soldier's tale— 420
That in the Tropic Islands he had served,
Whence he had landed scarcely three weeks past;
That on his landing he had been dismissed,
And now was travelling towards his native home.[8]
This heard, I said, in pity, 'Come with me.' 425
He stooped, and straightway from the ground took up
An oaken staff by me yet unobserved—
A staff which must have dropt from his slack hand
And lay till now neglected in the grass.
Though weak his step and cautious, he appeared 430
To travel without pain, and I beheld,
With an astonishment but ill suppressed,
His ghostly[9] figure moving at my side;
Nor could I, while we journeyed thus, forbear
To turn from present hardships to the past, 435
And speak of war, battle, and pestilence,
Sprinkling this talk with questions, better spared,
On what he might himself have seen or felt.
He all the while was in demeanour calm,
Concise in answer; solemn and sublime 440
He might have seemed, but that in all he said
There was a strange half-absence, as of one
Knowing too well the importance of his theme,
But feeling it no longer. Our discourse
Soon ended, and together on we passed 445
In silence through a wood gloomy and still.
Up-turning, then, along an open field,
We reached a cottage. At the door I knocked,
And earnestly to charitable care
Commended him as a poor friendless man, 450
Belated and by sickness overcome.

9. Assumed by de Selincourt to be a copyist's error for *1805* "ghastly," but the change is made in the base text of *MS. D* (1832), and not corrected in subsequent revisions. The two words still meant the same, and Wordsworth very probably decided to avoid repetition of "ghastly" in line 395.

Assured that now my comrade would repose
In comfort, I entreated that henceforth
He would not linger in the public ways,   490
[455] But ask for timely furtherance, and help
Such as his state required. At this reproof,[1]
With the same ghastly mildness in his look,
He said, 'My trust is in the God of Heaven,
And in the eye of him that passes me.'   495
[460] The cottage door was speedily unlocked,
And now the soldier touched his hat again
With his lean hand, and in a voice that seemed
To speak with a reviving interest,
Till then unfelt, he thanked me; I returned   500
[465] The blessing of the poor unhappy man,
And so we parted. Back I cast a look,
And lingered near the door a little space,
Then sought with quiet heart my distant home.[3]

---

1. In the early version the poet's reproof had been sharper, more intrusive: "And told him, feeble as he was, 'twere fit / He asked relief or alms" (*Discharged Soldier*, 161–62).

3. The final sentence is not present in *The Discharged Soldier*.

Assured that now the traveller would repose
In comfort, I entreated that henceforth
He would not linger in the public ways,
But ask for timely furtherance and help   455
Such as his state required. At this reproof,
With the same ghastly mildness in his look,
He said, 'My trust is in the God of Heaven,
And in the eye of him who passes me!'

    The cottage door was speedily unbarred,   460
And now the soldier touched his hat once more
With his lean hand, and in a faltering voice,
Whose tone bespake reviving interests
Till then unfelt, he thanked me; I returned
The farewell blessing of the patient man,[2]   465
And so we parted. Back I cast a look,
And lingered near the door a little space,
Then sought with quiet heart my distant home.

    This passed, and he who deigns to mark with care
By what rules governed, with what end in view,   470
This Work proceeds, *he* will not wish for more.[4]

2. A very different emphasis from Words-worth's original reading, "the poor un-happy man" (*Discharged Soldier* and *1805*).

4. Lines 469–71 were omitted in the first edition, but stand in *MSS. D* and *E.* In each case the copyist has entered a query as to whether they should be cut, but there is no evidence to suggest that Wordsworth ever decided against them.

Book Fifth

Books

Even in the steadiest mood of reason,[1] when
All sorrow for thy transitory pains
Goes out, it grieves me for thy state, O man,
Thou paramount creature, and thy race, while ye
Shall sojourn on this planet, not for woes   5
[6] Which thou endur'st—that weight, albeit huge,
I charm away[2]—but for those palms atchieved
[10] Through length of time, by study and hard thought,
The honours of thy high endowments; there
My sadness finds its fuel. Hitherto   10
In progress through this verse my mind hath looked
Upon the speaking face of earth and heaven
As her prime teacher, intercourse with man
[15] Established by the Sovereign Intellect,
Who through that bodily image hath diffused   15
A soul divine which we participate,
A deathless spirit.[3] Thou also, man, hast wrought,
For commerce of thy nature with itself,[4]
[20] Things worthy of unconquerable life;
And yet we feel—we cannot chuse but feel—   20
That these must perish. Tremblings of the heart
It gives, to think that the immortal being
· No more shall need such garments;[5] and yet man,
[25] As long as he shall be the child of earth,
Might almost 'weep to have' what he may lose—   25
Nor be himself extinguished, but survive
Abject, depressed, forlorn, disconsolate.[6]

1. In Book IV of the five-Book *Prelude* there was no break between the Discharged Soldier (*1805*, IV, 360–504) and *1805*, V, 1–48. *MS. W* preserves the transition-piece that carried Wordsworth from the personal sufferings of 'the poor unhappy man', through to more general reflections: "Enough of private sorrow—longest lived / Is transient, severest doth not lack / A mitigation in th'assured trust / Of the grave's quiet comfort and blest home, / Inheritance vouchsafed to man perhaps / Alone of all that suffer on the earth. / Even in the steadiest * * *"
2. I.e., I propose to ignore.
3. I.e., intercourse between man and Nature has been established by "the Sovereign Intellect" (God—called elsewhere "the one great mind"), who has diffused through the physical world a soul, or life force, shared by man. (In line 15, "bodily" means "physical, substantial," and "image" refers back to "the speaking force" of visible Nature, line 12.) This late but unequivocal restatement of the pantheist position of *Tintern Abbey*,

94–103, was modified in the revisions of *MS. D* (1832 or 1838/39) but did not until the poet's final corrections to *MS. E* reach the wording of *1850*, where all reference to the "soul divine" has gone, and the perception even of a "deathless spirit" in Nature becomes a whim of transitory man (*1850*, 17–18).
4. I.e., man (as well as the "Sovereign Intellect") has created works by which to communicate with other men.
5. I.e., to think that man, when he becomes an immortal being, shall no longer need the works described in *1805*, 19 (*1850*, 20).
6. Wordsworth's syntax in *1805*, 23–27 (*1850*, 24–28) is strained, but a key to his meaning is provided by Shakespeare's sonnet 64, to which his quotation marks draw attention: "This thought is as a death, which cannot choose / But weep to have that which it fears to lose." While he is on earth man is in the position almost of grieving to possess those works that may be taken from him while he lives on abject and disconsolate.

Book Fifth

Books

WHEN Contemplation, like the night-calm felt
Through earth and sky, spreads widely, and sends deep
Into the soul its tranquillizing power,
Even then I sometimes grieve for thee, O Man,
Earth's paramount Creature! not so much for woes   5
That thou endurest; heavy though that weight be,
Cloud-like it mounts, or touched with light divine
Doth melt away; but for those palms achieved,
Through length of time, by patient exercise
Of study and hard thought; there, there, it is   10
That sadness finds its fuel. Hitherto,
In progress through this work, my mind hath looked
Upon the speaking face of earth and heaven
As her prime teacher, intercourse with man
Established by the sovereign Intellect,   15
Who through that bodily image hath diffused,
As might appear to the eye of fleeting time,
A deathless spirit. Thou also, man! hast wrought,
For commerce of thy nature with herself,[4]
Things that aspire to unconquerable life;   20
And yet we feel—we cannot choose but feel—
That they must perish. Tremblings of the heart
It gives, to think that our immortal being
No more shall need such garments;[5] and yet man,
As long as he shall be the child of earth,   25
Might almost 'weep to have' what he may lose,
Nor be himself extinguished, but survive,
Abject, depressed, forlorn, disconsolate.[6]

A thought is with me sometimes, and I say,
[30] 'Should earth by inward throes be wrenched throughout,
 Or fire be sent from far to wither all   30
 Her pleasant habitations, and dry up
 Old Ocean in his bed, left singed and bare,
 Yet would the living presence still subsist
[35] Victorious; and composure would ensue,
 And kindlings like the morning—presage sure, 35
 Though slow perhaps, of a returning day.'
 But all the meditations of mankind,
 Yea, all the adamantine holds[7] of truth
[40] By reason built, or passion (which itself
 Is highest reason in a soul sublime),[8]   40
 The consecrated works of bard and sage,
 Sensuous or intellectual, wrought by men,
 Twin labourers and heirs of the same hopes—
[45] Where would they be? Oh, why hath not the mind
 Some element to stamp her image on   45
 In nature somewhat nearer to her own?
 Why, gifted with such powers to send abroad
 Her spirit, must it lodge in shrines so frail?

[50] One day, when in the hearing of a friend
 I had given utterance to thoughts like these,   50
 He answered with a smile that in plain truth
 'Twas going far to seek disquietude—
 But on the front of his reproof confessed
[55] That he at sundry seasons had himself
 Yielded to kindred hauntings, and, forthwith, 55
 Added that once upon a summer's noon
 While he was sitting in a rocky cave
 By the seaside, perusing as it chanced,
[60] The famous history of the errant knight
 Recorded by Cervantes,[9] these same thoughts 60
 Came to him, and to height unusual rose
 While listlessly he sate, and, having closed
 The book, had turned his eyes towards the sea.
[65] On poetry and geometric truth
 (The knowledge that endures) upon these two, 65
 And their high privilege of lasting life
 Exempt from all internal injury,
 He mused—upon these chiefly—and at length,
 His senses yielding to the sultry air,
[70] Sleep seized him and he passed into a dream.   70

7. Indestructible fortresses.
8. Compare *1805*, XIII, 166–70, where imagination comes to be seen as "reason in her most exalted mood."

9. *Don Quixote* (1605), a major influence on eighteenth-century English literature; it had been read by Wordsworth as a child (see *1805*, 179n, below).

A thought is with me sometimes, and I say,—
Should the whole frame of earth by inward throes 30
Be wrenched, or fire come down from far to scorch
Her pleasant habitations, and dry up
Old Ocean, in his bed left singed and bare,
Yet would the living Presence still subsist
Victorious, and composure would ensue, 35
And kindlings like the morning—presage sure
Of day returning and of life revived.
But all the meditations of mankind,
Yea, all the adamantine[7] holds of truth
By reason built, or passion, which itself 40
Is highest reason in a soul sublime;[8]
The consecrated works of Bard and Sage,
Sensuous or intellectual, wrought by men,
Twin labourers and heirs of the same hopes;
Where would they be? Oh! why hath not the Mind 45
Some element to stamp her image on
In nature somewhat nearer to her own?
Why, gifted with such powers to send abroad
Her spirit, must it lodge in shrines so frail?

   One day, when from my lips a like complaint 50
Had fallen in presence of a studious friend,
He with a smile made answer, that in truth
'Twas going far to seek disquietude;
But on the front of his reproof confessed
That he himself had oftentimes given way 55
To kindred hauntings. Whereupon I told,
That once in the stillness of a summer's noon,
While I was seated in a rocky cave
By the sea-side, perusing, so it chanced,
The famous history of the errant knight 60
Recorded by Cervantes,[9] these same thoughts
Beset me, and to height unusual rose,
While listlessly I sate, and, having closed
The book, had turned my eyes toward the wide sea.
On poetry and geometric truth, 65
And their high privilege of lasting life,
From all internal injury exempt,
I mused, upon these chiefly: and at length,
My senses yielding to the sultry air,
Sleep seized me, and I passed into a dream. 70

He saw before him an Arabian waste,
A desart, and he fancied that himself
Was sitting there in the wide wilderness
Alone upon the sands. Distress of mind
Was growing in him when, behold, at once   75
To his great joy a man was at his side,
[76] Upon a dromedary mounted high.
He seemed an arab of the Bedouin tribes;
A lance he bore, and underneath one arm
A stone, and in the opposite hand a shell   80
[80] Of a surpassing brightness. Much rejoiced
The dreaming man that he should have a guide
To lead him through the desart; and he thought,
While questioning himself what this strange freight
[85] Which the newcomer carried through the waste   85
Could mean, the arab told him that the stone—
To give it in the language of the dream—
Was *Euclid's Elements*.[2] 'And this', said he,
'This other', pointing to the shell, 'this book
Is something of more worth.' 'And, at the word,   90
The stranger', said my friend continuing,
[90] 'Stretched forth the shell towards me, with command
That I should hold it to my ear. I did so
And heard that instant in an unknown tongue,
Which yet I understood, articulate sounds,   95
[95] A loud prophetic blast of harmony,
An ode[3] in passion uttered, which foretold
Destruction to the children of the earth
By deluge now at hand. No sooner ceased
The song, but with calm look the arab said   100
[100] That all was true, that it was even so
As had been spoken, and that he himself
Was going then to bury those two books—
The one that held acquaintance with the stars,
And wedded man to man by purest bond   105
[105] Of nature, undisturbed by space or time;
Th' other that was a god, yea many gods,
Had voices more than all the winds, and was
A joy, a consolation, and a hope.'
[110] My friend continued, 'Strange as it may seem   110
I wondered not, although I plainly saw
The one to be a stone, th' other a shell,
Nor doubted once but that they both were books,
Having a perfect faith in all that passed.
A wish was now engendered in my fear   115

2. Euclid was a Greek mathematician of the third century B.C.; his *Elements* established the mathematical science of geometry.

3. A poem written to be sung to music (Johnson's *Dictionary*).

I saw before me stretched a boundless plain
Of sandy wilderness, all black and void,
And as I looked around, distress and fear
Came creeping over me, when at my side,
Close at my side, an uncouth shape appeared[1]   75
Upon a dromedary, mounted high.
He seemed an Arab of the Bedouin tribes:
A lance he bore, and underneath one arm
A stone, and in the opposite hand, a shell
Of a surpassing brightness. At the sight   80
Much I rejoiced, not doubting but a guide
Was present, one who with unerring skill
Would through the desert lead me; and while yet
I looked and looked, self-questioned what this freight
Which the new-comer carried through the waste   85
Could mean, the Arab told me that the stone
(To give it in the language of the dream)
Was 'Euclid's Elements';[2] and 'This', said he,
'Is something of more worth'; and at the word
Stretched forth the shell, so beautiful in shape,   90
In colour so resplendent, with command
That I should hold it to my ear. I did so,
And heard that instant in an unknown tongue,
Which yet I understood, articulate sounds,
A loud prophetic blast of harmony;   95
An Ode,[3] in passion uttered, which foretold
Destruction to the children of the earth
By deluge, now at hand. No sooner ceased
The song, than the Arab with calm look declared
That all would come to pass of which the voice   100
Had given forewarning, and that he himself
Was going then to bury those two books:
The one that held acquaintance with the stars,
And wedded soul to soul in purest bond
Of reason, undisturbed by space or time;   105
The other that was a god, yea many gods,
Had voices more than all the winds, with power
To exhilarate the spirit, and to soothe,
Through every clime, the heart of human kind.
While this was uttering, strange as it may seem,   110
I wondered not, although I plainly saw
The one to be a stone, the other a shell;
Nor doubted once but that they both were books,
Having a perfect faith in all that passed.
Far stronger, now, grew the desire I felt   115

---

1. Wordsworth's final reading associates the Arab with the Discharged Soldier, also "an uncouth shape" when first perceived (*1805*, IV, 402).

[116] To cleave unto this man, and I begged leave
To share his errand with him. On he passed
Not heeding me; I followed, and took note
That he looked often backward with wild look,
[120] Grasping his twofold treasure to his side.   120
Upon a dromedary, lance in rest,
He rode, I keeping pace with him; and now
I fancied that he was the very knight
Whose tale Cervantes tells, yet not the knight,
But was an arab of the desert too,   125
[125] Of these was neither, and was both at once.
His countenance meanwhile grew more disturbed,
And looking backwards when he looked I saw
A glittering light, and asked him whence it came.
[130] "It is", said he, "the waters of the deep   130
Gathering upon us." Quickening then his pace
He left me; I called after him aloud;
He heeded not, but with his twofold charge
[135] Beneath his arm—before me full in view—
I saw him riding o'er the desert sands   135
With the fleet waters of the drowning world
In chace of him; whereat I waked in terror,
And saw the sea before me, and the book
[140] In which I had been reading at my side.'⁴

    Full often, taking from the world of sleep   140
This arab phantom which my friend beheld,
This semi-Quixote, I to him have given
A substance, fancied him a living man—
[145] A gentle dweller in the desert, crazed
By love, and feeling, and internal thought   145
Protracted among endless solitudes—
Have shaped him, in the oppression of his brain,
Wandering upon this quest and thus equipped.
And I have scarcely pitied him, have felt
[150] A reverence for a being thus employed,   150
And thought that in the blind and awful lair
Of such a madness reason did lie couched.
Enow⁵ there are on earth to take in charge
Their wives, their children, and their virgin loves,
[155] Or whatsoever else the heart holds dear—   155
Enow to think of these—yea, will I say,
In sober contemplation of the approach

4. The dream of the Arab and his two "books," ascribed to a friend in *1805* and to Wordsworth himself in *1850*, is in fact a brilliantly imaginative transformation of a dream experienced by the philosopher Descartes in 1619. It had pre- sumably been related to Wordsworth by Coleridge; see Jane Worthington Smyser, "Wordsworth's Dream of Poetry and Science," *PMLA*, LXXI (1956), pp. 269–75.

5. Enough.

To cleave unto this man; but when I prayed
To share his enterprise, he hurried on
Reckless of me: I followed, not unseen,
For oftentimes he cast a backward look,
Grasping his twofold treasure.—Lance in rest,   120
He rode, I keeping pace with him; and now
He, to my fancy, had become the knight
Whose tale Cervantes tells; yet not the knight,
But was an Arab of the desert too;
Of these was neither, and was both at once.   125
His countenance, meanwhile, grew more disturbed;
And, looking backwards when he looked, mine eyes
Saw, over half the wilderness diffused,
A bed of glittering light: I asked the cause:
'It is', said he, 'the waters of the deep   130
Gathering upon us'; quickening then the pace
Of the unwieldly creature he bestrode,
He left me: I called after him aloud;
He heeded not; but, with his twofold charge
Still in his grasp, before me, full in view,   135
Went hurrying o'er the illimitable waste,
With the fleet waters of a drowning world
In chase of him; whereat I waked in terror,
And saw the sea before me, and the book,
In which I had been reading, at my side.[4]   140

Full often, taking from the world of sleep
This Arab phantom, which I thus beheld,
This semi-Quixote, I to him have given
A substance, fancied him a living man,
A gentle dweller in the desert, crazed   145
By love and feeling, and internal thought
Protracted among endless solitudes;
Have shaped him wandering upon this quest!
Nor have I pitied him; but rather felt
Reverence was due to a being thus employed;   150
And thought that, in the blind and awful lair
Of such a madness, reason did lie couched.
Enow[5] there are on earth to take in charge
Their wives, their children, and their virgin loves,
Or whatsoever else the heart holds dear;   155
Enow to stir for these; yea, will I say,
Contemplating in soberness the approach

Of such great overthrow, made manifest
By certain evidence, that I methinks
[160] Could share that maniac's anxiousness, could go   160
Upon like errand. Oftentimes at least
Me hath such deep entrancement half-possessed
When I have held a volume in my hand—
Poor earthly casket of immortal verse—
[165] Shakespeare or Milton, labourers divine.   165

    Mighty, indeed supreme, must be the power
Of living Nature which could thus so long
Detain me from the best of other thoughts.
[170] Even in the lisping time of infancy
And, later down, in prattling childhood—even   170
While I was travelling back among those days—
How could I ever play an ingrate's part?[6]
Once more should I have made those bowers resound,
[175] And intermingled strains of thankfulness
With their own thoughtless melodies. At least   175
It might have well beseemed me to repeat
Some simply fashioned tale, to tell again
In slender accents of sweet verse some tale
[180] That did bewitch me then, and soothes me now.[8]
O friend, O poet, brother of my soul,   180
Think not that I could ever pass along
Untouched by these remembrances; no, no,
But I was hurried forward by a stream
And could not stop. Yet wherefore should I speak,
Why call upon a few weak words to say   185
[185] What is already written in the hearts
Of all that breathe—what in the path of all
Drops daily from the tongue of every child
Wherever man is found? The trickling tear
Upon the cheek of listening infancy   190
Tells it, and the insuperable look
[190] That drinks as if it never could be full.

    That portion of my story I shall leave
There registered. Whatever else there be
Of power or pleasure, sown or fostered thus—   195

6. Behave like an ungrateful person; "ingrate" is applied by God to Adam in *Paradise Lost*, III, 97. "Travelling back" (*1805*, 171; *1850*, 172) refers to Wordsworth's return, in memory, to his childhood in the process of composing *The Prelude*.
8. "Of my earliest days at school," Wordsworth commented in 1847, "I have little to say but that they were very happy ones, chiefly because I was left at lib-
erty * * * to read whatever books I liked. For example, I read all Fielding's works, *Don Quixote*, *Gil Blas*, and any part of Swift that I liked; *Gulliver's Travels*, and the *Tale of the Tub*, being both much to my taste" (*Memoirs*, I, p. 10).
    Still earlier reading can be deduced from the references to fairy-stories in lines 364–69 below, and to the *Arabian Nights*, in 482–500.

Of an event so dire, by signs in earth
Or heaven made manifest, that I could share
That maniac's fond anxiety, and go   160
Upon like errand. Oftentimes at least
Me hath such strong entrancement overcome,
When I had held a volume in my hand,
Poor earthly casket of immortal verse,
Shakespeare, or Milton, labourers divine!   165

  Great and benign, indeed, must be the power
Of living nature, which could thus so long
Detain me from the best of other guides
And dearest helpers, left unthanked, unpraised.
Even in the time of lisping infancy,   170
And later down, in prattling childhood even,
While I was travelling back among those days,
How could I ever play an ingrate's part?[6]
Once more should I have made those bowers resound,
By intermingling strains of thankfulness   175
With their own thoughtless melodies; at least
It might have well beseemed me to repeat
Some simply fashioned tale, to tell again,
In slender[7] accents of sweet verse, some tale
That did bewitch me then, and soothes me now.[8]   180
O Friend! O Poet! brother of my soul,
Think not that I could pass along untouched
By these remembrances. Yet wherefore speak?
Why call upon a few weak words to say
What is already written in the hearts   185
Of all that breathe?—what in the path of all
Drops daily from the tongue of every child,
Wherever man is found? The trickling tear
Upon the cheek of listening Infancy
Proclaims it, and the insuperable look   190
That drinks as if it never could be full.

  That portion of my story I shall leave
There registered: whatever else of power
Or pleasure, sown or fostered thus, may be

7. Graceful.

[195] Peculiar to myself—let that remain
Where it lies hidden in its endless home
Among the depths of time. And yet it seems
That here, in memory of all books which lay
Their sure foundations in the heart of man,   200
[200] Whether by native prose, or numerous verse,[9]
That in the name of all inspirèd souls—
From Homer the great thunderer, from the voice
Which roars along the bed of Jewish song,
And that, more varied and elaborate,   205
[205] Those trumpet-tones of harmony that shake
Our shores in England, from those loftiest notes
Down to the low and wren-like warblings, made
For cottagers and spinners at the wheel
And weary travellers when they rest themselves   210
[210] By the highways and hedges: ballad-tunes,
Food for the hungry ears of little ones,
And of old men who have survived their joy—
It seemeth in behalf of these, the works,
And of the men who framed them, whether known,   215
[215] Or sleeping nameless in their scattered graves,
That I should here assert their rights, attest
Their honours, and should once for all pronounce
Their benediction, speak of them as powers[1]
For ever to be hallowed—only less   220
[220] For what we may become, and what we need,
Than Nature's self which is the breath of God.

　　Rarely and with reluctance would I stoop
To transitory themes,[3] yet I rejoice,
[225] And, by these thoughts admonished, must speak out   225
Thanksgivings from my heart that I was reared
Safe from an evil which these days have laid
Upon the children of the land—a pest
That might have dried me up body and soul.[4]
[230] This verse is dedicate to Nature's self   230
And things that teach as Nature teaches: then,

---

9. A reminiscence of *Paradise Lost*, V, 150. "Native": produced by nature; natural, not artificial (Johnson's *Dictionary*). "Numerous": harmonious; consisting of parts rightly numbered (ibid.).
1. Compare *1805*, XII, 309–12, where the poet records his own ambition to create a work that "might become / A power like one of Nature's."
3. In the central 200 lines of the Book (*1805*, 223–422) Wordsworth's thoughts turn to the "transitory theme" of educational theory.

4. Compare "vain th' attempt / To advertise in verse a public pest" (Cowper, *The Task*, IV, 500–1). The "evil" that Wordsworth refers to was the plague of educational theories that had followed the publication of Rousseau's *Émile* (1762). Among the most recent and influential of these works was *Practical Education*, published by Maria Edgeworth and her father in summer 1798, and read by Coleridge when he and the Wordsworths were at Hamburg in September (Griggs, I, p. 418).

Peculiar to myself, let that remain   195
Where still it works, though hidden from all search
Among the depths of time. Yet is it just
That here, in memory of all books which lay
Their sure foundations in the heart of man,
Whether by native prose, or numerous verse,[9]   200
That in the name of all inspirèd souls,
From Homer the great Thunderer, from the voice
That roars along the bed of Jewish song,
And that more varied and elaborate,
Those trumpet-tones of harmony that shake   205
Our shores in England,—from those loftiest notes
Down to the low and wren-like warblings, made
For cottagers and spinners at the wheel,
And sun-burnt travellers resting their tired limbs,
Stretched under wayside hedge-rows, ballad tunes,   210
Food for the hungry ears of little ones,
And of old men who have survived their joys:
'Tis just that in behalf of these, the works,
And of the men that framed them, whether known,
Or sleeping nameless in their scattered graves,   215
That I should here assert their rights, attest
Their honours, and should, once for all, pronounce
Their benediction; speak of them as Powers
For ever to be hallowed;[1] only less,
For what we are and what we may become,   220
Than Nature's self, which is the breath of God,
Or his pure Word by miracle revealed.[2]

  Rarely and with reluctance would I stoop
To transitory themes;[3] yet I rejoice,
And, by these thoughts admonished, will pour out   225
Thanks with uplifted heart, that I was reared
Safe from an evil which these days have laid
Upon the children of the land, a pest
That might have dried me up, body and soul.[4]
This verse is dedicate to Nature's self,   230
And things that teach as Nature teaches: then,

2. Wordsworth's reference to Christian revelation appears in the revisions to *MS. D* (1832 or 1838/39).

Oh, where had been the man, the poet where—
Where had we been we two, belovèd friend,
[235] If we, in lieu of wandering as we did
Through heights and hollows and bye-spots of tales   235
Rich with indigenous produce, open ground
Of fancy, happy pastures ranged at will,
Had been attended, followed, watched, and noosed,[5]
Each in his several[6] melancholy walk,
[240] Stringed like a poor man's heifer at its feed,   240
Led through the lanes in forlorn servitude;
Or rather like a stallèd ox shut out
From touch of growing grass, that may not taste
A flower till it have yielded up its sweets
[245] A prelibation[7] to the mower's scythe.   245

      Behold the parent hen amid her brood,
Though fledged and feathered, and well pleased to part
And straggle from her presence, still a brood,
And she herself from the maternal bond
[250] Still undischarged. Yet doth she little more   250
Than move with them in tenderness and love,
A centre of the circle which they make;
And now and then—alike from need of theirs
And call of her own natural appetites—
[255] She scratches, ransacks up the earth for food   255
Which they partake at pleasure. Early died
My honoured mother, she who was the heart
And hinge[8] of all our learnings and our loves;
She left us destitute, and as we might
[260] Trooping together. Little suits it me   260
To break upon the sabbath of her rest
With any thought that looks at others' blame,
Nor would I praise her but in perfect love;
Hence am I checked,[9] but I will boldly say
[265] In gratitude, and for the sake of truth,   265
Unheard by her, that she, not falsely taught,
Fetching her goodness rather from times past
Than shaping novelties from those to come,
Had no presumption, no such jealousy—
[270] Nor did by habit of her thoughts mistrust   270
Our nature, but had virtual[1] faith that He

5. Fitted with a halter.
6. Separate.
7. An offering of the first fruits, or of
the first taste. In 1805 and 1850, 238–45,
Wordsworth has in mind the reduction
of literature to edifying tales such as
those of Thomas Day's *Sandford and
Merton* (1783–89) and Maria Edgeworth's
Parents' Assistant (1796–1801).

8. Pivot.
9. Wordsworth, as R. D. Havens has
pointed out, hesitates to praise his mother
by contrasting her sympathy with the
lack of understanding shown by her rela-
tives, the Cooksons, after her death. For
Dorothy's account of the Cooksons' petty
tyrannies, see *EY*, pp. 3–5.
1. Effective, powerful.

Oh! where had been the Man, the Poet where,
Where had we been, we two, beloved Friend!
If in the season of unperilous choice,
In lieu of wandering, as we did, through vales   235
Rich with indigenous produce, open ground
Of Fancy, happy pastures ranged at will,
We had been followed, hourly watched, and noosed,⁵
Each in his several⁶ melancholy walk
Stringed like a poor man's heifer at its feed,   240
Led through the lanes in forlorn servitude;
Or rather like a stallèd ox debarred
From touch of growing grass, that may not taste
A flower till it have yielded up its sweets
A prelibation⁷ to the mower's scythe.   245

Behold the parent hen amid her brood,
Though fledged and feathered, and well pleased to part
And straggle from her presence, still a brood,
And she herself from the maternal bond
Still undischarged; yet doth she little more   250
Than move with them in tenderness and love,
A centre to the circle which they make;
And now and then, alike from need of theirs
And call of her own natural appetites,
She scratches, ransacks up the earth for food,   255
Which they partake at pleasure. Early died
My honoured Mother, she who was the heart
And hinge⁸ of all our learnings and our loves:
She left us destitute, and, as we might,
Trooping together. Little suits it me   260
To break upon the sabbath of her rest
With any thought that looks at others' blame;
Nor would I praise her but in perfect love.
Hence am I checked:⁹ but let me boldly say,
In gratitude, and for the sake of truth,   265
Unheard by her, that she, not falsely taught,
Fetching her goodness rather from times past,
Than shaping novelties for times to come,
Had no presumption, no such jealousy,
Nor did by habit of her thoughts mistrust   270
Our nature, but had virtual¹ faith that He

Who fills the mother's breasts with innocent milk
Doth also for our nobler part provide,
Under His great correction and controul,
[275] As innocent instincts, and as innocent food.   275
This was her creed, and therefore she was pure
[280] From feverish dread of error and mishap
And evil, overweeningly so called,
Was not puffed up by false unnatural hopes,
Nor selfish with unnecessary cares,   280
Nor with impatience from the season asked
[285] More than its timely produce—rather loved
The hours for what they are, than from regards
Glanced on their promises[2] in restless pride.
Such was she: not from faculties more strong   285
Than others have, but from the times, perhaps,
[290] And spot in which she lived, and through a grace
Of modest meekness, simple-mindedness,
A heart that found benignity and hope,
Being itself benign.

         My drift hath scarcely   290
I fear been obvious, for I have recoiled
From showing as it is the monster birth
Engendered by these too industrious times.
Let few words paint it:[3] 'tis a child, no child,
But a dwarf man; in knowledge, virtue, skill,   295
In what he is not, and in what he is,
The noontide shadow of a man complete;
A worshipper of worldly seemliness—
[300] Not quarrelsome, for that were far beneath
His dignity; with gifts he bubbles o'er   300
As generous as a fountain; selfishness
May not come near him, gluttony or pride;
[305] The wandering beggars propagate his name,
Dumb creatures find him tender as a nun.
Yet deem him not for this a naked dish   305
Of goodness merely—he is garnished out.[4]
[310] Arch are his notices, and nice his sense
Of the ridiculous;[5] deceit and guile,
Meanness and falsehood, he detects, can treat
With apt and graceful laughter; nor is blind   310

---

2. Anticipations of the future. "Regards": looks.

3. The description of the Infant Prodigy (lines 294–369) was written in February 1804 as a contrast to the Wordsworthian assimilation of "natural wisdom" in "There was a boy" (lines 389–422, be-low), now first incorporated in *The Prelude*.

4. I.e., the child's (affected) goodness is garnished with elegance.

5. His "notices" (remarks, observations) are witty, and his sense of the ridiculous (in others) is precise.

Who fills the mother's breast with innocent milk,
Doth also for our nobler part provide,
Under His great correction and control,
As innocent instincts, and as innocent food;   275
Or draws for minds that are left free to trust
In the simplicities of opening life
Sweet honey out of spurned or dreaded weeds.
This was her creed, and therefore she was pure
From anxious fear of error or mishap,   280
And evil, overweeningly so called;
Was not puffed up by false unnatural hopes,
Nor selfish with unnecessary cares,
Nor with impatience from the season asked
More than its timely produce; rather loved   285
The hours for what they are, than from regard
Glanced on their promises² in restless pride.
Such was she—not from faculties more strong
Than others have, but from the times, perhaps,
And spot in which she lived, and through a grace   290
Of modest meekness, simple-mindedness,
A heart that found benignity and hope,
Being itself benign.

                    My drift I fear
Is scarcely obvious; but, that common sense
May try this modern system by its fruits,   295
Leave let me take to place before her sight
A specimen pourtrayed with faithful hand.
Full early trained to worship seemliness,
This model of a child is never known
To mix in quarrels; that were far beneath   300
His dignity; with gifts he bubbles o'er
As generous as a fountain; selfishness
May not come near him, nor the little throng
Of flitting pleasures tempt him from his path;
The wandering beggars propagate his name,   305
Dumb creatures find him tender as a nun,
And natural or supernatural fear,
Unless it leap upon him in a dream,
Touches him not. To enhance the wonder, see
How arch his notices, how nice his sense   310
Of the ridiculous;⁵ nor blind is he

To the broad follies of the licensed[6] world;
Though shrewd, yet innocent himself withal,
[314] And can read lectures upon innocence.
He is fenced round, nay armed, for ought we know,
In panoply complete;[7] and fear itself,   315
[307] Natural or supernatural alike,
Unless it leap upon him in a dream,
Touches him not.[8] Briefly, the moral part
Is perfect, and in learning and in books
He is a prodigy. His discourse moves slow,   320
Massy and ponderous as a prison door,
Tremendously embossed with terms of art.[9]
Rank growth of propositions overruns
The stripling's brain; the path in which he treads
Is choked with grammars. Cushion of divine   325
Was never such a type of thought profound
As is the pillow where he rests his head.[1]
The ensigns of the empire which he holds—
The globe and sceptre of his royalties—
Are telescopes, and crucibles, and maps.[2]   330
[316] Ships he can guide across the pathless sea,
And tell you all their cunning;[3] he can read
The inside of the earth, and spell the stars;
He knows the policies of foreign lands,
[320] Can string you names of districts, cities, towns,   335
The whole world over, tight as beads of dew
Upon a gossamer thread. He sifts, he weighs,
Takes nothing upon trust.[4] His teachers stare,
The country people pray for God's good grace,
And tremble at his deep experiments.[5]   340
All things are put to question: he must live
Knowing that he grows wiser every day,

6. I.e., given license to ignore conventional restraints.
7. Full armor.
8. Wordsworth himself had grown up "Fostered alike by beauty and by fear" (*1805*, 306, above). In lines 315–18, accordingly, the child is not being praised for bravery, but is shown to have armed himself against one of the two major beneficial influences of Nature.
9. Technical language.
1. In Wordsworth's rather labored irony, the prodigy's pillow is an even better emblem ("type") of profound thought than the cushion on which the parson's Bible rests in front of a pulpit.
2. Scientific instruments and maps symbolize the intellectual power that he wields, just as the globe and scepter symbolize the sovereignty of a king.

3. Art, skill, knowledge (Johnson's *Dictionary*).
4. "I have known some who have been *rationally* educated, as it is styled," Coleridge wrote in October 1797: "They were marked by a microscopic acuteness; but when they looked at great things, all became a blank and they saw nothing—and denied (very illogically) that any thing could be seen * * * [they] called the want of imagination Judgment, and the never being moved to Rapture Philosophy!" (Griggs, I, pp. 354–55).
5. Ignorant country people are terrified lest his experiments go *too* deep, become a search for forbidden knowledge. Maxwell draws attention to Shakespeare's *Henry IV*, Part I, III, i, 50; where Glendower refers to his practices in magic as "deep experiments."

To the broad follies of the licensed[6] world,
Yet innocent himself withal, though shrewd,
And can read lectures upon innocence;
A miracle of scientific lore,   315
Ships he can guide across the pathless sea,
And tell you all their cunning;[3] he can read
The inside of the earth, and spell the stars;
He knows the policies of foreign lands;
Can string you names of districts, cities, towns,   320
The whole world over, tight as beads of dew
Upon a gossamer thread; he sifts, he weighs;
All things are put to question;[4] he must live
Knowing that he grows wiser every day

[325] Or else not live at all, and seeing too
Each little drop of wisdom as it falls
[327] Into the dimpling cistern of his heart.[6]   345
[337] Meanwhile old Grandame Earth is grieved to find
The playthings which her love designed for him
Unthought of—in their woodland beds the flowers
[340] Weep, and the river-sides are all forlorn.[7]

      Now this is hollow, 'tis a life of lies   350
From the beginning, and in lies must end.
Forth bring him to the air of common sense
And, fresh and shewy as it is, the corps[8]
Slips from us into powder. Vanity,
That is his soul: there lives he, and there moves—   355
It is the soul of every thing he seeks—
That gone, nothing is left which he can love.
Nay, if a thought of purer birth should rise
To carry him towards a better clime,
Some busy helper still is on the watch   356
[335] To drive him back, and pound him like a stray
With the pinfold of his own conceit,[9]
Which is his home, his natural dwelling-place.
Oh, give us once again the wishing-cap
Of Fortunatus, and the invisible coat   365
Of Jack the Giant-killer, Robin Hood,
And Sabra in the forest with St George![1]
[345] The child whose love is here, at least doth reap
One precious gain—that he forgets himself.

      These mighty workmen of our later age   370
Who with a broad highway have overbridged
The froward[3] chaos of futurity,
[350] Tamed to their bidding[4]—they who have the art
To manage books, and things, and make them work

6. Wordsworth's image is of a rain barrel with water dripping into it.
7. Compare lines 346–49 with *Intimations Ode*, 77 ff., also presumably written in February 1804. The phrase "old Grandame Earth" is a conflation of references in Shakespeare's *Henry IV*, Part I, III, i, 32 and 34, to "old beldame earth" and "our grandam earth."
8. The earlier spelling of "corpse" (*NED*).
9. If the child's thoughts should stray beyond himself, the educationalist is always ("still") on the watch to impound ("pound") him like a stray in the enclosure ("pinfold") formed by his own conceit.
1. Fortunatus, owner of the magic purse, had also a hat that would transport him wherever he wanted to go; Jack the Giant-Killer ridded the land of giants by virtue of a coat that made him invisible, shoes that gave him speed, and a magic sword; St. George rescued Sabra from a dragon, and married her.
3. Unruly.
4. Lines 370–422 go back in their original form to winter 1798–99, where they show "There was a boy" being used as part of a discussion of education, *before* being printed without introductory lines in *Lyrical Ballads* (1800). The "mighty" educationalists of line 370 are diminished by implicit comparison with Sin and Death, who in *Paradise Lost*, X, 282–305 built a bridge over Chaos.

Or else not live at all, and seeing too   325
Each little drop of wisdom as it falls
Into the dimpling cistern of his heart:[6]
For this unnatural growth the trainer blame,
Pity the tree.—Poor human vanity,
Wert thou extinguished, little would be left   330
Which he could truly love; but how escape?
For, ever as a thought of purer birth
Rises to lead him toward a better clime,
Some intermeddler still is on the watch
To drive him back, and pound him, like a stray,   335
Within the pinfold of his own conceit.
Meanwhile old grandame earth is grieved to find
The playthings, which her love designed for him,
Unthought of: in their woodland beds the flowers
Weep, and the river sides are all forlorn.[7]   340
Oh! give us once again the wishing cap
Of Fortunatus, and the invisible coat
Of Jack the Giant-killer, Robin Hood,
And Sabra in the forest with St. George![1]
The child, whose love is here, at least, doth reap   345
One precious gain, that he forgets himself.[2]

These mighty workmen of our later age,
Who, with a broad highway, have overbridged
The froward[3] chaos of futurity,
Tamed to their bidding; they who have the skill   350
To manage books, and things, and make them act

2. Alongside the passage on the Infant Prodigy Wordsworth wrote in *MS. B,* "This is heavy and must be much shortened." The final version—reached in 1839—is twenty-six lines shorter than *1805,* thirty-eight having been cut and twelve added.

Gently on infant minds as does the sun   375
Upon a flower—the tutors of our youth,
The guides, the wardens of our faculties
And stewards of our labour, watchful men
And skilful in the usury of time,
[355] Sages, who in their prescience would controul   380
All accidents, and to the very road
Which they have fashioned would confine us down
Like engines[5]—when will they be taught
That in the unreasoning progress of the world
[360] A wiser spirit is at work for us,   385
A better eye than theirs, most prodigal
Of blessings, and most studious of our good,
Even in what seem our most unfruitful hours?

    There was a boy[6]—ye knew him well, ye cliffs
[365] And islands of Winander—many a time   390
At evening, when the stars had just begun
To move along the edges of the hills,
Rising or setting, would he stand alone
Beneath the trees or by the glimmering lake,
[370] And there, with fingers interwoven, both hands   395
Pressed closely palm to palm, and to his mouth
Uplifted, he as through an instrument
Blew mimic hootings to the silent owls
That they might answer him. And they would shout
[375] Across the wat'ry vale, and shout again,   400
Responsive to his call, with quivering peals[7]
And long halloos, and screams, and echoes loud,
Redoubled and redoubled—concourse wild
Of mirth and jocund din. And when it chanced
[380] That pauses of deep silence mocked his skill,   405
Then sometimes in that silence, while he hung
Listening, a gentle shock of mild surprize
Has carried far into his heart the voice
Of mountain torrents;[8] or the visible scene
[385] Would enter unawares into his mind   410
With all its solemn imagery, its rocks,
Its woods, and that uncertain heaven, received
Into the bosom of the steady lake.

5. In confining natural development, tying the child down to a specific course of study, educationalists resemble constricting implements ("engines") of torture.
6. For the original version of "There was a boy" (lines 389–413), written by Wordsworth in the first person, together with drafts of *1799*, I, see *MS. JJ*, MS. Drafts and Fragments, 1(d), below.

7. Used more generally than at present; "a succession of loud sounds" (Johnson's *Dictionary*).
8. "This very expression, 'far'", wrote Thomas De Quincey in 1839, "by which space and its infinities are attributed to the human heart, and to its capacities of re-echoing the sublimities of nature, has always struck me as with a flash of sublime revelation" (*Recollections*, p. 161).

On infant minds as surely as the sun
Deals with a flower; the keepers of our time,
The guides and wardens of our faculties,
Sages who in their prescience would control   355
All accidents, and to the very road
Which they have fashioned would confine us down,
Like engines;[5] when will their presumption learn,
That in the unreasoning progress of the world
A wiser spirit is at work for us,   360
A better eye than theirs, most prodigal
Of blessings, and most studious of our good,
Even in what seem our most unfruitful hours?

  There was a Boy: ye knew him well, ye cliffs
And islands of Winander!—many a time   365
At evening, when the earliest stars began
To move along the edges of the hills,
Rising or setting, would he stand alone
Beneath the trees or by the glimmering lake,
And there, with fingers interwoven, both hands   370
Pressed closely palm to palm, and to his mouth
Uplifted, he, as through an instrument,
Blew mimic hootings to the silent owls,
That they might answer him; and they would shout
Across the watery vale, and shout again,   375
Responsive to his call, with quivering peals,[7]
And long halloos and screams, and echoes loud,
Redoubled and redoubled, concourse wild
Of jocund din; and, when a lengthened pause
Of silence came and baffled his best skill,   380
Then sometimes, in that silence while he hung
Listening, a gentle shock of mild surprise
Has carried far into his heart the voice
Of mountain torrents;[8] or the visible scene
Would enter unawares into his mind,   385
With all its solemn imagery, its rocks,
Its woods, and that uncertain heaven, received
Into the bosom of the steady lake.

This boy was taken from his mates, and died
[390] In childhood ere he was full ten years old.   415
Fair are the woods, and beauteous is the spot,
The vale where he was born; the churchyard hangs
Upon a slope above the village school,
And there, along that bank, when I have passed
[395] At evening, I believe that oftentimes   420
A full half-hour together I have stood
Mute, looking at the grave in which he lies.[1]
Even now methinks I have before my sight
That self-same village church: I see her sit—
[400] The thronèd lady spoken of erewhile—   425
On her green hill, forgetful of this boy
Who slumbers at her feet, forgetful too
Of all her silent neighbourhood of graves,
And listening only to the gladsome sounds
[405] That, from the rural school ascending, play   430
Beneath her and about her. May she long
Behold a race of young ones like to those
With whom I herded—easily, indeed,
We might have fed upon a fatter soil
[410] Of Arts and Letters, but be that forgiven—   435
A race of real children, not too wise,
Too learned, or too good, but wanton, fresh,
And bandied up and down by love and hate;
[415] Fierce, moody, patient, venturous, modest, shy,
Mad at their sports like withered leaves in winds;   440
Though doing wrong and suffering, and full oft
Bending beneath our life's mysterious weight
Of pain and fear,[2] yet still in happiness
[420] Not yielding to the happiest upon earth.
Simplicity in habit, truth in speech,   445
Be these the daily strengtheners of their minds!
May books and Nature be their early joy,
And knowledge, rightly honored with that name—
[425] Knowledge not purchased with the loss of power!

Well do I call to mind the very week   450
When I was first entrusted to the care
Of that sweet valley—when its paths, its shores
And brooks, were like a dream of novelty
[430] To my half-infant thoughts—that very week,
While I was roving up and down alone   455
Seeking I knew not what, I chanced to cross

1. There is little reason to suppose that Wordsworth had in mind the death of a particular Hawkshead school friend.
2. Pain and fear are "mysterious"—be-yond normal human understanding—but may of course be beneficial, as at *1805*, I, 306, above.

This Boy was taken from his mates, and died
In childhood, ere he was full twelve years old.[9]   390
Fair is the spot, most beautiful the vale
Where he was born; the grassy churchyard hangs
Upon a slope above the village school,
And through that churchyard when my way has led
On summer evenings, I believe that there   395
A long half hour together I have stood
Mute, looking at the grave in which he lies![1]
Even now appears before the mind's clear eye
That self-same village church; I see her sit
(The thronèd Lady whom erewhile we hailed)   400
On her green hill, forgetful of this Boy
Who slumbers at her feet,—forgetful, too,
Of all her silent neighbourhood of graves,
And listening only to the gladsome sounds
That, from the rural school ascending, play   405
Beneath her and about her. May she long
Behold a race of young ones like to those
With whom I herded!—(easily, indeed,
We might have fed upon a fatter soil
Of arts and letters—but be that forgiven)—   410
A race of real children; not too wise,
Too learned, or too good; but wanton, fresh,
And bandied up and down by love and hate;
Not unresentful where self-justified;
Fierce, moody, patient, venturous, modest, shy;   415
Mad at their sports like withered leaves in winds;
Though doing wrong and suffering, and full oft
Bending beneath our life's mysterious weight
Of pain, and doubt, and fear,[2] yet yielding not
In happiness to the happiest upon earth.   420
Simplicity in habit, truth in speech,
Be these the daily strengtheners of their minds;
May books and Nature be their early joy!
And knowledge, rightly honoured with that name—
Knowledge not purchased by the loss of power!   425

    Well do I call to mind the very week
When I was first intrusted to the care
Of that sweet Valley; when its paths, its shores,
And brooks were like a dream of novelty
To my half-infant thoughts; that very week,   430
While I was roving up and down alone,
Seeking I knew not what, I chanced to cross

---

9. The child's age is increased from ten to twelve in a correction to *MS. A*, probably of 1816/19.

One of those open fields, which, shaped like ears,
Make green peninsulas on Esthwaite's Lake.
[435] Twilight was coming on, yet through the gloom
I saw distinctly on the opposite shore   460
A heap of garments, left as I supposed
By one who there was bathing. Long I watched,
But no one owned them; meanwhile the calm lake
[440] Grew dark, with all the shadows on its breast,
And now and then a fish up-leaping snapped   465
The breathless stillness. The succeeding day—
[443] Those unclaimed garments telling a plain tale—
Went there a company, and in their boat
[447] Sounded with grappling-irons and long poles:
At length, the dead man, 'mid that beauteous scene   470
Of trees and hills and water, bolt upright
[450] Rose with his ghastly face, a spectre shape—
Of terror even.[4] And yet no vulgar fear,
Young as I was, a child not nine years old,
Possessed me, for my inner eye had seen   475
Such sights before among the shining streams
[455] Of fairyland, the forests of romance—
Thence came a spirit hallowing what I saw
With decoration and ideal grace,
A dignity, a smoothness, like the words   480
Of Grecian art and purest poesy.[5]

[460]   I had a precious treasure at that time,
A little yellow canvass-covered book,
A slender abstract of the *Arabian Tales*;[6]
And when I learned, as now I first did learn   485
From my companions in this new abode,
That this dear prize of mine was but a block
[465] Hewn from a mighty quarry—in a word,
That there were four large volumes, laden all
With kindred matter—'twas in truth to me   490
A promise scarcely earthly. Instantly
I made a league, a covenant with a friend
[470] Of my own age, that we should lay aside
The monies we possessed, and hoard up more,
Till our joint savings had amassed enough   495
To make this book our own. Through several months

4. James Jackson, schoolmaster at the neighbouring village of Sawrey, was drowned on June 18, 1779, while bathing in Esthwaite Water. For the original text of lines 450–73 (*1850*, 426–51), composed ca. January 1799, see *1799*, I, 258–79.
5. Compare Coleridge in the letter of 1797 quoted at 338*n*, above: "from my early reading of Faery Tales, and Genii &c &c—my mind has been habituated *to the Vast*—and I never regarded *my senses* in any way as the criteria of my belief" (Griggs, I, p. 354; Coleridge's italics).
6. *The Arabian Nights*.

One of those open fields, which, shaped like ears,
Make green peninsulas on Esthwaite's Lake:
Twilight was coming on, yet through the gloom   435
Appeared distinctly on the opposite shore
A heap of garments, as if left by one
Who might have there been bathing. Long I watched,
But no one owned them; meanwhile the calm lake
Grew dark with all the shadows on its breast,   440
And, now and then, a fish up-leaping snapped
The breathless stillness. The succeeding day,
Those unclaimed garments telling a plain tale
Drew to the spot an anxious crowd; some looked
In passive expectation from the shore,   445
While from a boat others hung o'er the deep,[3]
Sounding with grappling irons and long poles.
At last, the dead man, 'mid that beauteous scene
Of trees and hills and water, bolt upright
Rose, with his ghastly face, a spectre shape   450
Of terror;[4] yet no soul-debasing fear,
Young as I was, a child not nine years old,
Possessed me, for my inner eye had seen
Such sights before, among the shining streams
Of faëry land, the forests of romance.   455
Their spirit hallowed the sad spectacle
With decoration of ideal grace;
A dignity, a smoothness, like the works
Of Grecian art, and purest poesy.[5]

A precious treasure I had long possessed,   460
A little yellow, canvas-covered book,
A slender abstract of the Arabian tales;[6]
And, from companions in a new abode,
When first I learnt, that this dear prize of mine
Was but a block hewn from a mighty quarry—   465
That there were four large volumes, laden all
With kindred matter, 'twas to me, in truth,
A promise scarcely earthly. Instantly,
With one not richer than myself, I made
A covenant that each should lay aside   470
The moneys he possessed, and hoard up more,
Till our joint savings had amassed enough
To make this book our own. Through several months,

---

3. Lines 444–46 were inserted in 1816/19, and place the solitary experience re- corded in *1799* and *1805* in an untypically social context.

Religiously did we preserve that vow,
And spite of all temptation hoarded up,
[475] And hoarded up; but firmness failed at length,
Nor were we ever masters of our wish.   500

    And afterwards, when, to my father's house
Returning at the holidays, I found
That golden store of books which I had left
Open to my enjoyment once again,
[480] What heart was mine! Full often through the course   505
Of those glad respites in the summertime
When armed with rod and line we went abroad
For a whole day together, I have lain
Down by thy side, O Derwent, murmuring stream,
[485] On the hot stones and in the glaring sun,   510
And there have read, devouring as I read,
Defrauding the day's glory—desperate—
Till with a sudden bound of smart reproach
Such as an idler deals with in his shame,
[490] I to my sport betook myself again.   515

    A gracious spirit o'er this earth presides,
And o'er the heart of man: invisibly
It comes, directing those to works of love
[495] Who care not, know not, think not, what they do.
The tales that charm away the wakeful night   520
In Araby—romances, legends penned
For solace by the light of monkish lamps;
Fictions, for ladies of their love, devised
[500] By youthful squires; adventures endless, spun
By the dismantled warrior[7] in old age   525
Out of the bowels of those very thoughts
In which his youth did first extravagate[8]—
These spread like day, and something in the shape
[505] Of these will live till man shall be no more.
Dumb yearnings, hidden appetites, are ours,   530
And they must have their food. Our childhood sits,
Our simple childhood, sits upon a throne
That hath more power than all the elements.[9]
[510] I guess not what this tells of being past,[1]
Nor what it augurs of the life to come,   535
But so it is;[2] and in that dubious hour,

---

7. Time has dismantled the warrior and
stripped him of his usefulness.
8. Indulge; literally to wander at large,
roam at will.
9. Forces of Nature. Compare Shakespeare's *King Lear*, III, ii, 16: "I tax
not you, you elements, with unkindness."
Wordsworth's context suggests that the
child's "throne," the seat or basis of his
power, consists in undiminished imaginative response.
1. I.e., the past state of being.
2. Wordsworth, who has very probably
just completed the *Intimations Ode*, de-
clines on this occasion to speculate about
preexistence, or an afterlife.

In spite of all temptation, we preserved
Religiously that vow; but firmness failed,   475
Nor were we ever masters of our wish.

   And when thereafter to my father's house
The holidays returned me, there to find
That golden store of books which I had left,
What joy was mine! How often in the course   480
Of those glad respites, though a soft west wind
Ruffled the waters to the angler's wish
For a whole day together, have I lain
Down by thy side, O Derwent! murmuring stream,
On the hot stones, and in the glaring sun,   485
And there have read, devouring as I read,
Defrauding the day's glory, desperate!
Till with a sudden bound of smart reproach,
Such as an idler deals with in his shame,
I to the sport betook myself again.   490

   A gracious spirit o'er this earth presides,
And o'er the heart of man: invisibly
It comes, to works of unreproved delight,
And tendency benign, directing those
Who care not, know not, think not what they do.   495
The tales that charm away the wakeful night
In Araby, romances; legends penned
For solace by dim light of monkish lamps;
Fictions, for ladies of their love, devised
By youthful squires; adventures endless, spun   500
By the dismantled warrior[7] in old age,
Out of the bowels of those very schemes
In which his youth did first extravagate;[8]
These spread like day, and something in the shape
Of these will live till man shall be no more.   505
Dumb yearnings, hidden appetites, are ours,
And *they must* have their food. Our childhood sits,
Our simple childhood, sits upon a throne
That hath more power than all the elements.[9]
I guess not what this tells of Being[1] past,   510
Nor what it augurs of the life to come;
But so it is,[2] and, in that dubious hour,

That twilight when we first begin to see
This dawning earth, to recognise, expect—
[515] And in the long probation that ensues,
The time of trial ere we learn to live   540
In reconcilement with our stinted powers,
To endure this state of meagre vassalage,
Unwilling to forego, confess, submit,
[520] Uneasy and unsettled, yoke-fellows
To custom, mettlesome and not yet tamed   545
And humbled down—oh, then we feel, we feel,
We know, when we have friends.[3] Ye dreamers, then,
Forgers of lawless tales, we bless you then—
[525] Impostors, drivellers, dotards, as the ape
Philosophy will call you[4]—then we feel   550
With what, and how great might ye are in league,
Who make our wish our power, our thought a deed,
An empire, a possession. Ye whom time
[530] And seasons serve—all faculties—to whom
Earth crouches, th' elements[5] are potter's clay,   555
Space like a heaven filled up with northern lights,
Here, nowhere, there, and everywhere at once.

    It might demand a more impassioned strain
To tell of later pleasures linked to these,
[536] A tract of the same isthmus which we cross   560
In progress from our native continent
To earth and human life[6]—I mean to speak
Of that delightful time of growing youth
[540] When cravings for the marvellous relent,
And we begin to love what we have seen;   565
And sober truth, experience, sympathy,
Take stronger hold of us; and words themselves
[545] Move us with conscious pleasure.

                        I am sad
At thought of raptures now for ever flown,
Even unto tears I sometimes could be sad   570
To think of, to read over, many a page—
Poems withal of name—which at that time
[550] Did never fail to entrance me, and are now

3. I.e., writers of imaginative literature.
4. Wordsworth denounces the kind of
analytic and rational philosophy which
condemns works of imaginative fiction as
false and trivial.
5. Here, "the four elements" (earth, air,
water, fire) of which the ancient world
believed matter to be composed; not, as
in *1805*, 533, *1850*, 509, above, the forces
of Nature.

6. The literary pleasures that followed
Wordsworth's childish reading are seen
as part of the same "isthmus," a strip
of land connecting preexistence (the "native continent") to adult participation in
the earth and human life. It is interesting
that his image should derive from Pope:
"Plac'd on this isthmus of a middle
state" (*Essay on Man*, II, 3)—see 594n,
below.

That twilight when we first begin to see
This dawning earth, to recognise, expect,
And in the long probation that ensues,   515
The time of trial, ere we learn to live
In reconcilement with our stinted powers,
To endure this state of meagre vassalage;
Unwilling to forego, confess, submit,
Uneasy and unsettled, yoke-fellows   520
To custom, mettlesome, and not yet tamed
And humbled down; oh! then we feel, we feel,
We know where we have friends.³ Ye dreamers, then,
Forgers of daring tales! we bless you then,
Imposters, drivellers, dotards, as the ape   525
Philosophy will call you:⁴ *then* we feel
With what, and how great might ye are in league,
Who make our wish, our power, our thought a deed,
An empire, a possession,—ye whom time
And seasons serve; all Faculties; to whom   530
Earth crouches, the elements⁵ are potters' clay,
Space like a heaven filled up with northern lights,
Here, nowhere, there, and everywhere at once.

    Relinquishing this lofty eminence
For ground, though humbler, not the less a tract   535
Of the same isthmus, which our spirits cross
In progress from their native continent
To earth and human life,⁶ the Song might dwell
On that delightful time of growing youth,
When craving for the marvellous gives way   540
To strengthening love for things that we have seen;
When sober truth and steady sympathies,
Offered to notice by less daring pens,
Take firmer hold of us, and words themselves
Move us with conscious pleasure.   545

                              I am sad
At thought of raptures now for ever flown;
Almost to tears I sometimes could be sad
To think of, to read over, many a page,
Poems withal of name, which at that time
Did never fail to entrance me, and are now   550

Dead in my eyes as is a theatre
Fresh emptied of spectators. Thirteen years,   575
Or haply less, I might have seen when first
My ears began to open to the charm
[555] Of words in tuneful order, found them sweet
For *their own sakes*—a passion and a power—
And phrases pleased me, chosen for delight,   580
For pomp, or love. Oft in the public roads,
Yet unfrequented, while the morning light
[560] Was yellowing the hilltops, with that dear friend
(The same whom I have mentioned heretofore)[8]
I went abroad, and for the better part   585
Of two delightful hours we strolled along
By the still borders of the misty lake
Repeating favorite verses with one voice,
[565] Or conning[9] more, as happy as the birds
That round us chaunted. Well might we be glad,   590
Lifted above the ground by airy fancies
More bright than madness or the dreams of wine.
And though full oft the objects of our love
[570] Were false and in their splendour overwrought,[1]
Yet surely at such time no vulgar power   595
Was working in us, nothing less in truth
Than that most noble attribute of man—
Though yet untutored and inordinate[2]—
[575] That wish for something loftier, more adorned,
Than is the common aspect, daily garb,   600
Of human life. What wonder then if sounds
Of exultation echoed through the groves—
For images, and sentiments, and words,
[580] And every thing with which we had to do
In that delicious world of poesy,   605
Kept holiday, a never-ending show,
With music, incense, festival, and flowers!

    Here must I pause: this only will I add
[585] From heart-experience, and in humblest sense
Of modesty, that he who in his youth   610
A wanderer among the woods and fields
With living Nature hath been intimate,
Not only in that raw unpractised time

---

8. John Fleming, mentioned at *1805*, II,
352–53 (*1799*, II, 382–83), above.
9. Learning by heart; compare *Intimations Ode*, 102.
1. It is probably James Macpherson, imi-
tated and echoed in Wordsworth's *The
Vale of Esthwaite* (1785–87), yet condemned in the 1815 "Essay Supplementary," whom Wordsworth has in mind.

The works Macpherson published as
translations of the Gaelic poet Ossian
(1760–63) were doubly false—not merely
oversplendid, but a fake.
2. Unordered. For Wordsworth the "most
noble attribute of man" was aspiration,
the reaching out imaginatively, or through
depth of feeling, beyond immediate circumstance.

Dead in my eyes, dead as a theatre
Fresh emptied of spectators. Twice five years[7]
Or less I might have seen, when first my mind
With conscious pleasure opened to the charm
Of words in tuneful order, found them sweet   555
For their own *sakes*, a passion, and a power;
And phrases pleased me chosen for delight,
For pomp, or love. Oft, in the public roads
Yet unfrequented, while the morning light
Was yellowing the hill tops, I went abroad   560
With a dear friend,[8] and for the better part
Of two delightful hours we strolled along
By the still borders of the misty lake,
Repeating favourite verses with one voice,
Or conning[9] more, as happy as the birds   565
That round us chaunted. Well might we be glad,
Lifted above the ground by airy fancies,
More bright than madness or the dreams of wine;
And, though full oft the objects of our love
Were false, and in their splendour overwrought,[1]   570
Yet was there surely then no vulgar power
Working within us,—nothing less, in truth,
Than that most noble attribute of man,
Though yet untutored and inordinate,[2]
That wish for something loftier, more adorned,   575
Than is the common aspect, daily garb,
Of human life. What wonder, then, if sounds
Of exultation echoed through the groves!
For, images, and sentiments, and words,
And everything encountered or pursued   580
In that delicious world of poesy,
Kept holiday, a never-ending show,
With music, incense, festival, and flowers!

   Here must we pause: this only let me add,
From heart-experience, and in humblest sense   585
Of modesty, that he, who in his youth
A daily wanderer among woods and fields
With living Nature hath been intimate,
Not only in that raw unpractised time

---

7. Wordsworth's emendation of *1805*, "thirteen years", has the air of poeticism rather than accuracy. It dates probably from 1816/19.

[590] Is stirred to ecstasy, as others are,
By glittering verse, but he doth furthermore, 615
In measure only dealt out to himself,
Receive enduring touches of deep joy
From the great Nature that exists in works
[595] Of mighty poets.[3] Visionary power
Attends upon the motions of the winds 620
Embodied in the mystery of words;
There darkness makes abode, and all the host
Of shadowy things do work their changes there
[600] As in a mansion like their proper home.
Even forms and substances are circumfused 625
By that transparent veil with light divine,
And through the turnings intricate of verse
Present themselves as objects recognised
[605] In flashes, and with a glory scarce their own.[4]

    Thus far a scanty record is deduced 630
Of what I owed to books in early life;
Their later influence yet remains untold,
But as this work was taking in my thoughts
[610] Proportions that seemed larger than had first
Been meditated, I was indisposed 635
To any further progress at a time
When these acknowledgements were left unpaid.[5]

3. Wordsworth's claim is that a country child will feel a special joy in poetic descriptions of Nature.
4. Wordsworth in *1805*, 622–29 (*1850*, 598–605) is playing on two senses of the word "darkness." At one level the dark is physical, and inhabited by fairies who work their magic transformations; at another, it has the common eighteenth-century meaning of something mysterious, difficult to understand.
5. A version of lines 294–607, 630–37, formed the last half of Book IV of the five-Book *Prelude*.

Is stirred to extasy, as others are, 590
By glittering verse; but further, doth receive,
In measure only dealt out to himself,
Knowledge and increase of enduring joy
From the great Nature that exists in works
Of mighty Poets.[3] Visionary power 595
Attends the motions of the viewless winds,
Embodied in the mystery of words:
There, darkness makes abode, and all the host
Of shadowy things work endless changes there,
As in a mansion like their proper home. 600
Even forms and substances are circumfused
By that transparent veil with light divine,
And, through the turnings intricate of verse,
Present themselves as objects recognised,
In flashes, and with glory not their own.[4] 605

    Thus far a scanty record is deduced
Of what I owed to books in early life;
Their later influence yet remains untold;
But as this work was taking in my mind
Proportions that seemed larger than had first 610
Been meditated, I was indisposed
To any further progress at a time
When these acknowledgements were left unpaid.[6]

6. There is no manuscript support for the omission of lines 606–13 in the first edition.

Book Sixth

Cambridge and the Alps

The leaves were yellow when to Furness Fells,[1]
The haunt of shepherds, and to cottage life
I bade adieu, and, one among the flock
Who by that season are convened, like birds
[5] Trooping together at the fowler's lure,   5
Went back to Granta's cloisters[2]—not so fond
Or eager, though as gay and undepressed
In spirit, as when I thence had taken flight
A few short months before. I turned my face
[10] Without repining from the mountain pomp   10
Of autumn and its beauty (entered in
With calmer lakes and louder streams);[4] and you,
Frank-hearted maids of rocky Cumberland,
[15] You and your not unwelcome days of mirth
I quitted, and your nights of revelry,   15
And in my own unlovely cell sate down
In lightsome mood—such privilege has youth,
That cannot take long leave of pleasant thoughts.

    We need not linger o'er the ensuing time,
But let me add at once that now, the bonds   20
[20] Of indolent and vague society
Relaxing in their hold, I lived henceforth
More to myself, read more, reflected more,
Felt more, and settled daily into habits
More promising. Two winters may be passed   25
Without a separate notice;[5] many books
Were read in process of this time—devoured,
Tasted or skimmed, or studiously perused—
[25] Yet with no settled plan. I was detached
Internally from academic cares,   30
From every hope of prowess and reward,
And wished to be a lodger in that house
Of letters, and no more—and should have been
Even such, but for some personal concerns
That hung about me in my own despite   35
Perpetually, no heavy weight, but still

---

1. The southwestern area of the Lake District, surrounding Coniston, and reaching across to Hawkshead and Windermere. "Fells": hills and mountains.
2. Wordsworth is being deliberately poetic in referring to Cambridge as "Granta," an old name for the River Cam, which flows through the town.

4. Wordsworth's revisions of this passage make it clear that it is the beauty of (late) autumn that has entered in, and that he associated this season with diminishing wind and increasing rain—hence calmer lakes, but louder streams.
5. The winters of 1788–89 and 1789–90.

Book Sixth

Cambridge and the Alps

THE leaves were fading when to Esthwaite's banks
And the simplicities of cottage life
I bade farewell; and, one among the youth
Who, summoned by that season, reunite
As scattered birds troop to the fowler's lure,   5
Went back to Granta's cloisters,[2] not so prompt
Or eager, though as gay and undepressed
In mind, as when I thence had taken flight
A few short months before. I turned my face
Without repining from the coves and heights   10
Clothed in the sunshine of the withering fern;[3]
Quitted, not loth, the mild magnificence
Of calmer lakes and louder streams; and you,
Frank-hearted maids of rocky Cumberland,
You and your not unwelcome days of mirth,   15
Relinquished, and your nights of revelry,
And in my own unlovely cell sate down
In lightsome mood—such privilege has youth
That cannot take long leave of pleasant thoughts.

   The bonds of indolent society   20
Relaxing in their hold, henceforth I lived
More to myself. Two winters may be passed
Without a separate notice:[5] many books
Were skimmed, devoured, or studiously perused,
But with no settled plan. I was detached   25
Internally from academic cares;

3. A magnificent line produced by successive revisions in *MS. D*, in 1832 and
1838/39. Wordsworth's first attempt was
"In the soft sunshine of the golden fern."

A baffling and a hindrance, a controul
Which made the thought of planning for myself
A course of independent study seem
An act of disobedience towards them   40
Who loved me, proud rebellion and unkind.[6]
[30] This bastard virtue—rather let it have
A name it more deserves, this cowardise—
Gave treacherous sanction to that over-love
Of freedom planted in me from the very first,   45
And indolence, by force of which I turned
From regulations even of my own
[35] As from restraints and bonds.[7] And who can tell,
Who knows what thus may have been gained, both then
And at a later season, or preserved—   50
What love of Nature, what original strength
Of contemplation, what intuitive truths,
[40] The deepest and the best, and what research
Unbiassed, unbewildered, and unawed?

        The poet's soul was with me at that time,   55
Sweet meditations, the still overflow
Of happiness and truth. A thousand hopes
[45] Were mine, a thousand tender dreams, of which
No few have since been realized, and some
Do yet remain, hopes for my future life.[8]   60
Four years and thirty, told this very week,
[49] Have I been now a sojourner on earth,
And yet the morning gladness is not gone
Which then was in my mind.[9] Those were the days
Which also first encouraged me to trust   65
With firmness, hitherto but lightly touched
[55] With such a daring thought, that I might leave
Some monument behind me which pure hearts
Should reverence. The instinctive humbleness,
Upheld even by the very name and thought   70
Of printed books and authorship, began
[60] To melt away; and further, the dread awe
Of mighty names was softened down, and seemed

---

6. Wordsworth decided, at least by December 1789, not to read for Honors (*1805*, 29–31; *1850*, 25–29), thus in effect rejecting the Fellowship that his relations intended for him; see *1805*, III, 77*n*, above.
7. I.e., Wordsworth's actual motive for not pursuing an independent course of study is cowardice rather than a sense of letting his relations down.
8. Notably of course the plan to write the main section of *The Recluse*, shelved again in March 1804 on Wordsworth's decision to abandon the five-Book *Prelude* and work towards a longer version; see Composition and Texts: *1805/1850*, Introduction, below.
9. Wordsworth was thirty-four on April 7, 1804. Book VI was under way by March 29, and completed by April 29. The last stanzas of the *Intimations Ode* had recently defined the sense in which "morning gladness" (*1805*, 63) could be said to continue in his mind.

Yet independent study seemed a course
Of hardy disobedience toward friends
And kindred, proud rebellion and unkind.[6]
This spurious virtue, rather let it bear   30
A name it more deserves, this cowardice,
Gave treacherous sanction to that over-love
Of freedom which encouraged me to turn
From regulations even of my own
As from restraints and bonds.[7] Yet who can tell—   35
Who knows what thus may have been gained, both then
And at a later season, or preserved;
What love of nature, what original strength
Of contemplation, what intuitive truths,
The deepest and the best, what keen research,   40
Unbiassed, unbewildered, and unawed?

   The Poet's soul was with me at that time;
Sweet meditations, the still overflow
Of present happiness, while future years
Lacked not anticipations, tender dreams,   45
No few of which have since been realised;
And some remain, hopes for my future life.[8]
Four years and thirty, told this very week,
Have I been now a sojourner on earth,
By sorrow not unsmitten; yet for me   50
Life's morning radiance hath not left the hills,
Her dew is on the flowers.[9] Those were the days
Which also first emboldened me to trust
With firmness, hitherto but lightly touched
By such a daring thought, that I might leave   55
Some monument behind me which pure hearts
Should reverence. The instinctive humbleness,
Maintained even by the very name and thought
Of printed books and authorship, began
To melt away; and further, the dread awe   60
Of mighty names was softened down and seemed

Approachable, admitting fellowship
Of modest sympathy. Such aspect now,   75
[64] Though not familiarly, my mind put on;
I loved and I enjoyed—that was my chief
And ruling business, happy in the strength
And loveliness of imagery and thought.[1]

All winter long, whenever free to take   80
My choice, did I at nights frequent our groves
And tributary walks—the last, and oft
The only one, who had been lingering there
[70] Through hours of silence till the porter's bell,
A punctual follower on the stroke of nine,   85
Rang with its blunt unceremonious voice,
Inexorable summons. Lofty elms,
Inviting shades of opportune recess,
[75] Did give composure to a neighbourhood
Unpeaceful in itself. A single tree   90
There was, no doubt yet standing there, an ash,
With sinuous trunk, boughs exquisitely wreathed:
[80] Up from the ground and almost to the top
The trunk and master branches everywhere
Were green with ivy, and the lightsome twigs   95
And outer spray profusely tipped with seeds
[84] That hung in yellow tassels and festoons,
Moving or still—a favorite trimmed out
By Winter for himself, as if in pride,
And with outlandish grace. Oft have I stood   100
[86] Foot-bound uplooking at this lovely tree
Beneath a frosty moon. The hemisphere
Of magic fiction, verse of mine perhaps
May never tread,[2] but scarcely Spenser's self
[90] Could have more tranquil visions in his youth,   105
More bright appearances could scarcely see
Of human forms and superhuman powers,
Than I beheld standing on winter nights
Alone beneath this fairy work of earth.

'Twould be a waste of labour to detail   110
[95] The rambling studies of a truant youth—
Which further may be easily divined,
What, and what kind they were. My inner knowledge
(This barely will I note) was oft in depth

---

1. Wordsworth is opposing mental pictures to rational thought-processes. As
both in this instance are set up by literature, his use of "imagery" is closer than
usual to the modern critical term.
2. In the plan for *Lyrical Ballads*, as described in *Biographia Literaria*, chapter
xiv, Wordsworth's half of the poetic universe ("hemisphere") was to be the world
of everyday, Coleridge's the supernatural
(*Biographia*, pp. 168–69).

Approachable, admitting fellowship
Of modest sympathy. Such aspect now,
Though not familiarly, my mind put on,
Content to observe, to admire, and to enjoy.   65

   All winter long, whenever free to choose,
Did I by night frequent the College groves
And tributary walks; the last, and oft
The only one, who had been lingering there
Through hours of silence, till the porter's bell,   70
A punctual follower on the stroke of nine,
Rang with its blunt unceremonious voice,
Inexorable summons! Lofty elms,
Inviting shades of opportune recess,
Bestowed composure on a neighbourhood   75
Unpeaceful in itself. A single tree
With sinuous trunk, boughs exquisitely wreathed,
Grew there; an ash which Winter for himself
Decked as in pride, and with outlandish grace:
Up from the ground, and almost to the top,   80
The trunk and every master branch were green
With clustering ivy, and the lightsome twigs
And outer spray profusely tipped with seeds
That hung in yellow tassels, while the air
Stirred them, not voiceless. Often have I stood   85
Foot-bound uplooking at this lovely tree
Beneath a frosty moon. The hemisphere
Of magic fiction, verse of mine perchance
May never tread;[2] but scarcely Spenser's self
Could have more tranquil visions in his youth,   90
Nor could more bright appearances create
Of human forms with superhuman powers,
Than I beheld loitering on calm clear nights
Alone, beneath this fairy work of earth.

   On the vague reading of a truant youth   95
'Twere idle to descant. My inner judgment
Not seldom differed from my taste in books,

And delicacy like another mind,   115
Sequestered from my outward taste in books—
And yet the books which then I loved the most
[100] Are dearest to me now; for, being versed
In living Nature, I had there a guide
Which opened frequently my eyes, else shut,   120
A standard which was usefully applied,
Even when unconsciously, to other things
Which less I understood. In general terms,
[106] I was a better judge of thoughts than words,
Misled as to these latter not alone   125
By common inexperience of youth,
But by the trade in classic niceties,
Delusion to young scholars incident—
And old ones also—by that overprized
[110] And dangerous craft of picking phrases out   130
From languages that want the living voice
To make of them a nature to the heart,
To tell us what is passion, what is truth,
What reason, what simplicity and sense.[3]

[115]   Yet must I not entirely overlook   135
The pleasure gathered from the elements
Of geometric science. I had stepped
In these inquiries but a little way,
[119] No farther than the threshold—with regret
Sincere I mention this—but there I found   140
Enough to exalt, to chear me and compose.
With Indian[4] awe and wonder, ignorance
Which even was cherished, did I meditate
Upon the alliance of those simple, pure
Proportions and relations, with the frame   145
And laws of Nature—how they could become
Herein a leader to the human mind—
And made endeavours frequent to detect
The process by dark[5] guesses of my own.
Yet from this source more frequently I drew   150
[130] A pleasure calm and deeper, a still sense
Of permanent and universal sway
And paramount endowment in the mind,
An image not unworthy of the one
[135] Surpassing life, which—out of space and time,   155

3. See *Biographia Literaria*, chapter i, where Coleridge refers to a particular conversation with Wordsworth about the style of poetry that consists in "translation of prose thoughts into poetic language." In *1805*, 128, "incident" means "likely to befall"; it is a facetious reference to Shakespeare's *Winter's Tale*, IV, iv, 124–25, "a malady / Most incident to maids."
4. American Indian, as at *1805*, I, 302, above.
5. Uninformed.

As if it appertained to another mind,
And yet the books which then I valued most
Are dearest to me *now*; for, having scanned,   100
Not heedlessly, the laws, and watched the forms
Of Nature, in that knowledge I possessed
A standard, often usefully applied,
Even when unconsciously, to things removed
From a familiar sympathy.—In fine,   105
I was a better judge of thoughts than words,
Misled in estimating words, not only
By common inexperience of youth,
But by the trade in classic niceties,
The dangerous craft of culling term and phrase   110
From languages that want the living voice
To carry meaning to the natural heart;
To tell us what is passion, what is truth,
What reason, what simplicity and sense.[3]

    Yet may we not entirely overlook   115
The pleasure gathered from the rudiments
Of geometric science. Though advanced
In these inquiries, with regret I speak,
No farther than the threshold, there I found
Both elevation and composed delight: 120
With Indian[4] awe and wonder, ignorance pleased
With its own struggles, did I meditate
On the relation those abstractions bear
To Nature's laws, and by what process led,
Those immaterial agents bowed their heads   125
Duly to serve the mind of earth-born man;
From star to star, from kindred sphere to sphere,
From system on to system without end.

    More frequently from the same source I drew
A pleasure quiet and profound, a sense   130
Of permanent and universal sway,
And paramount belief; there, recognised
A type, for finite natures, of the one
Supreme Existence, the surpassing life
Which—to the boundaries of space and time,   135
Of melancholy space and doleful time,
Superior, and incapable of change,[6]

6. A passage that caused Wordsworth considerable trouble. Lines 134–37 belong to his earliest revisions, ca. January 1807; lines 120–33 were reworked chiefly in *MS. D*, but reach their final shape in corrections to *E*, in or after 1839.

Nor touched by welterings of passion—is,
And hath the name of, God. Transcendent peace
[140] And silence did await upon these thoughts
That were a frequent comfort to my youth.

    And as I have read of one by shipwreck thrown   160
With fellow sufferers whom the waves had spared
Upon a region uninhabited,
An island of the deep, who having brought
[145] To land a single volume and no more—
A treatise of geometry—was used,   165
Although of food and clothing destitute,
And beyond common wretchedness depressed,
To part from company and take this book,
[150] Then first a self-taught pupil in those truths,
To spots remote and corners of the isle   170
By the seaside, and draw his diagrams
With a long stick upon the sand, and thus
Did oft beguile his sorrow, and almost
Forget his feeling:[7] even so—if things
[155] Producing like effect from outward cause   175
So different may rightly be compared—
So was it with me then, and so will be
With poets ever. Mighty is the charm
Of those abstractions to a mind beset
[160] With images, and haunted by itself,   180
And specially delightful unto me
Was that clear synthesis built up aloft
So gracefully, even then when it appeared
No more than as a plaything, or a toy
[165] Embodied to the sense—not what it is   185
In verity, an independent world
Created out of pure intelligence.

    Such dispositions then were mine, almost
[170] Through grace of heaven and inborn tenderness.[8]
And not to leave the picture of that time   190
Imperfect, with these habits I must rank
A melancholy, from humours of the blood
In part, and partly taken up, that loved
A pensive sky, sad days, and piping winds,
[175] The twilight more than dawn, autumn than spring—   195
A treasured and luxurious gloom of choice

---

7. The mathematical castaway was John Newton, one-time captain of a slaving ship, who turned evangelical, became curate of Olney, and a close friend of Cowper. Wordsworth in *1805*, 160–74 (*1850*, 143–54) is recalling, at times verbatim, a paragraph from Newton's *Authentic Narrative* which Dorothy had copied into a notebook in 1798–99.
8. Susceptibility to impressions (Johnson's *Dictionary*).

Nor touched by welterings of passion—is,
And hath the name of God. Transcendent peace
And silence did await upon these thoughts   140
That were a frequent comfort to my youth.

'Tis told by one whom stormy waters threw,
With fellow-sufferers by the shipwreck spared,
Upon a desert coast, that having brought
To land a single volume, saved by chance,   145
A treatise of Geometry, he wont,
Although of food and clothing destitute,
And beyond common wretchedness depressed,
To part from company and take this book
(Then first a self-taught pupil in its truths)   150
To spots remote, and draw his diagrams
With a long staff upon the sand, and thus
Did oft beguile his sorrow, and almost
Forget his feeling:[7] so (if like effect
From the same cause produced, 'mid outward things   155
So different, may rightly be compared),
So was it then with me, and so will be
With Poets ever. Mighty is the charm
Of those abstractions to a mind beset
With images, and haunted by herself,   160
And specially delightful unto me
Was that clear synthesis built up aloft
So gracefully; even then when it appeared
Not more than a mere plaything, or a toy
To sense embodied: not the thing it is   165
In verity, an independent world,
Created out of pure intelligence.

Such dispositions then were mine unearned
By aught, I fear, of genuine desert—
Mine, through heaven's grace and inborn aptitudes.   170
And not to leave the story of that time
Imperfect, with these habits must be joined,
Moods melancholy, fits of spleen,[9] that loved
A pensive sky, sad days, and piping winds,
The twilight more than dawn, autumn than spring;   175
A treasured and luxurious gloom of choice

---

9. Gloominess, dejection; by the mid-nineteenth century an archaic and literary word.

And inclination mainly, and the mere
Redundancy of youth's contentedness.
Add unto this a multitude of hours   200
[180] Pilfered away by what the bard who sang
Of the enchanter Indolence hath called
'Good-natured lounging',[1] and behold a map
Of my collegiate life: far less intense
Than duty called for, or, without regard   205
[185] To duty, might have sprung up of itself
By change of accidents; or even—to speak
Without unkindness—in another place.

      In summer among distant nooks I roved—
Dovedale, or Yorkshire dales, or through bye-tracts
[195] Of my own native region—and was blest   210
Between those sundry wanderings with a joy
Above all joys, that seemed another morn
Risen on mid-noon:[3] the presence, friend, I mean
Of that sole sister, she who hath been long
[200] Thy treasure also, thy true friend and mine,   215
Now after separation desolate
Restored to me—such absence that she seemed
A gift then first bestowed.[4] The gentle banks
Of Emont, hitherto unnamed in song,
[205] And that monastic castle, on a flat,   220
Low-standing by the margin of the stream,[5]
A mansion not unvisited of old
By Sidney, where, in sight of our Helvellyn,
Some snatches he might pen for aught we know
[210] Of his *Arcadia*, by fraternal love   225
Inspired[6]—that river and that mouldering dome[7]
Have seen us sit in many a summer hour,
My sister and myself, when, having climbed
In danger through some window's open space,
We looked abroad, or on the turret's head   230

1. Thomson, *The Castle of Indolence* (1748), I, xv. Wordsworth had written an imitation of Thomson's poem in May 1802, and drawn upon it at *1805*, III, 546–49, above.
3. Wordsworth's lines echo beautifully Adam's sense of the presence of Raphael, who in *Paradise Lost*, V, 310–11 "seems another morn / Ris'n on mid-noon."
4. "Now" in *1805*, 216 (*1850*, 201), is summer 1787; for the previous nine years, since the death of their mother, Dorothy had been separated from her brothers, living with cousins in Halifax. Wordsworth puns on the name Dorothy, "gift of God," as Coleridge had done in a letter of July 1803 (Griggs, II, p. 958).
5. Brougham Castle is situated on low ground ("a flat") where the rivers Emont and Lowther meet, just east of Penrith. It is not "monastic" in any normal sense —Wordsworth perhaps means secluded, or austere.
6. Sir Philip Sidney had written his prose romance, *Arcadia* (ca. 1581), for the pleasure of his sister. He was wrongly supposed to have visited Brougham Castle.
7. A building (Johnson's *Dictionary*).

And inclination mainly, and the mere
Redundancy of youth's contentedness.
—To time thus spent, add multitudes of hours   180
Pilfered away, by what the Bard who sang
Of the Enchanter Indolence hath called
'Good-natured lounging',[1] and behold a map
Of my collegiate life—far less intense
Than duty called for, or, without regard   185
To duty, might have sprung up of itself
By change of accidents, or even, to speak
Without unkindness, in another place.
Yet why take refuge in that plea?—the fault,
This I repeat, was mine; mine be the blame.

    In summer, making quest for works of art,   190
Or scenes renowned for beauty, I explored
That streamlet whose blue current works its way
Between romantic Dovedale's spiry rocks;[2]
Pried into Yorkshire dales, or hidden tracts
Of my own native region, and was blest   195
Between these sundry wanderings with a joy
Above all joys, that seemed another morn
Risen on mid noon;[3] blest with the presence, Friend!
Of that sole Sister, she who hath been long
Dear to thee also, thy true friend and mine,   200
Now, after separation desolate,
Restored to me—such absence that she seemed
A gift then first bestowed.[4] The varied banks
Of Emont, hitherto unnamed in song,
And that monastic castle, 'mid tall trees,   205
Low-standing by the margin of the stream,[5]
A mansion visited (as fame reports)
By Sidney, where, in sight of our Helvellyn,
Or stormy Cross-fell, snatches he might pen
Of his Arcadia, by fraternal love   210
Inspired;[6]—that river and those mouldering towers
Have seen us side by side, when, having clomb
The darksome windings of a broken stair,
And crept along a ridge of fractured wall,
Not without trembling, we in safety looked   215
Forth, through some Gothic window's open space,
And gathered with one mind a rich reward
From the far-stretching landscape, by the light
Of morning beautified, or purple eve;
Or, not less pleased, lay on some turret's head,   220

---

2. The rather exaggerated self-reproach of lines 188–89 belongs to 1838/39; for contrast, see *1805*, III, 81–120. The "works of art" of line 190 would be buildings, as opposed to natural scenery. Dovedale is a beauty spot in Derbyshire.

Lay listening to the wild-flowers and the grass
As they gave out their whispers to the wind.
Another maid there was, who also breathed
[225] A gladness o'er that season, then to me   235
By her exulting outside look of youth
And placid under-countenance first endeared[8]—
That other spirit, Coleridge, who is now
So near to us, that meek confiding heart,
[230] So reverenced by us both. O'er paths and fields
In all that neighbourhood, through narrow lanes   240
Of eglantine, and through the shady woods,
And o'er the Border Beacon and the waste
Of naked pools and common crags that lay
[235] Exposed on the bare fell, was scattered love—
A spirit of pleasure, and youth's golden gleam.[9]   245
O friend, we had not seen thee at that time,
And yet a power is on me and a strong
Confusion, and I seem to plant thee there.[1]
[240] Far art thou wandered now in search of health,
And milder breezes[2]—melancholy lot—   250
But thou art with us, with us in the past,
The present, with us in the times to come.
There is no grief, no sorrow, no despair,
[245] No languor, no dejection, no dismay,
No absence scarcely can there be, for those   255
Who love as we do. Speed thee well! divide
Thy pleasure with us; thy returning strength,
Receive it daily as a joy of ours;
[250] Share with us thy fresh spirits, whether gift
Of gales Etesian[3] or of loving thoughts.   260

    I too have been a wanderer, but, alas,
How different is the fate of different men,
Though twins almost in genius and in mind.
Unknown unto each other, yea, and breathing
[255] As if in different elements, we were framed   265
To bend at last to the same discipline,

---

8. Mary Hutchinson, whom Wordsworth married fifteen years later on October 4, 1802.
9. Lines 242–45, written in late March 1804, draw on XI, 315–25, composed for the abandoned five-Book *Prelude* at the beginning of the month; see Composition and Texts: *1805/1850*, Introduction, below. The Border Beacon is the hill above Penrith, scene of *1799*, I, 296–327 (*1805*, XI, 278–315).
1. Wordsworth and Coleridge seem to have met in August–September 1795, but they did not come to know each other well—and Coleridge did not meet Dorothy—until June 1797.
2. Coleridge had set out for the Mediterranean in search of better health—and in the hope of breaking his addiction to opium. He was in fact still in London when these lines were written in late March 1804, but Wordsworth believed him to have sailed. He did not return to England until August 1806.
3. Northwesterly Mediterranean winds.

Catching from tufts of grass and hare-bell flowers
Their faintest whisper to the passing breeze,
Given out while mid-day heat oppressed the plains.

    Another maid there was, who also shed
A gladness o'er that season, then to me,   225
By her exulting outside look of youth
And placid under-countenance, first endeared;[8]
That other spirit, Coleridge! who is now
So near to us, that meek confiding heart,
So reverenced by us both. O'er paths and fields   230
In all that neighbourhood, through narrow lanes
Of eglantine, and through the shady woods
And o'er the Border Beacon, and the waste
Of naked pools, and common crags that lay
Exposed on the bare fell, were scattered love,   235
The spirit of pleasure, and youth's golden gleam.[9]
O Friend! we had not seen thee at that time,
And yet a power is on me, and a strong
Confusion, and I seem to plant thee there.[1]
Far art thou wandered now in search of health   240
And milder breezes,[2]—melancholy lot!
But thou art with us, with us in the past,
The present, with us in the times to come.
There is no grief, no sorrow, no despair,
No languor, no dejection, no dismay,   245
No absence scarcely can there be, for those
Who love as we do. Speed thee well! divide
With us thy pleasure; thy returning strength,
Receive it daily as a joy of ours;
Share with us thy fresh spirits, whether gift   250
Of gales Etesian[3] or of tender thoughts.

    I, too, have been a wanderer; but, alas!
How different the fate of different men.
Though mutually unknown, yea nursed and reared
As if in several[4] elements, we were framed   255
To bend at last to the same discipline,

4. Separate, distinct.

Predestined, if two beings ever were,
To seek the same delights, and have one health,
One happiness. Throughout this narrative,
[260] Else sooner ended, I have known full well   270
For whom I thus record the birth and growth
Of gentleness, simplicity, and truth,
And joyous loves that hallow innocent days
Of peace and self-command. Of rivers, fields,
[265] And groves, I speak to thee, my friend—to thee   275
Who, yet a liveried schoolboy in the depths
Of the huge city, on the leaded roof
Of that wide edifice, thy home and school,
Wast used to lie and gaze upon the clouds
[270] Moving in heaven, or haply, tired of this,   280
To shut thine eyes and by internal light
See trees, and meadows, and thy native stream[5]
Far distant—thus beheld from year to year
Of thy long exile.[6] Nor could I forget
[275] In this late portion of my argument   285
That scarcely had I finally resigned
My rights among those academic bowers
When thou wert thither guided. From the heart
Of London, and from cloisters there, thou cam'st
[280] And didst sit down in temperance and peace,   290
A rigorous student. What a stormy course
Then followed[7]—oh, it is a pang that calls
For utterance, to think how small a change
Of circumstances might to thee have spared
[285] A world of pain, ripened ten thousand hopes   295
For ever withered. Through this retrospect
Of my own college life I still[8] have had
Thy after-sojourn in the self-same place
Present before my eyes, have played with times
(I speak of private business of the thought)   300
[290] And accidents as children do with cards,
Or as a man, who, when his house is built,
A frame locked up in wood and stone, doth still
In impotence of mind by his fireside

5. The river Otter.
6. Coleridge was at "the blue-coat school," Christ's Hospital, in the center of London, 1782–91, and can very seldom have returned home to Devonshire during the holidays. Wordsworth's lines contain literary allusions to Coleridge's *Sonnet: to the River Otter* (1793), *Frost at Midnight* (1798), and *Dejection* (1802).
7. Coleridge entered Jesus College, Cambridge, in September 1791, Wordsworth having left St. John's the previous January. Despite Coleridge's prodigious reading, his university career was not a success. He offended the authorities and his family by becoming a Unitarian and a radical, contracted large debts, contemplated suicide, ran away to join the army, planned (with Robert Southey) to found a communist utopia on the banks of the Susquehanna River, and left in December 1794 without a degree.
8. Always.

Predestined, if two beings ever were,
To seek the same delights, and have one health,
One happiness. Throughout this narrative,
Else sooner ended, I have borne in mind   260
For whom it registers the birth, and marks the growth,
Of gentleness, simplicity, and truth,
And joyous loves, that hallow innocent days
Of peace and self-command. Of rivers, fields,
And groves I speak to thee, my Friend! to thee,   265
Who, yet a liveried schoolboy, in the depths
Of the huge city, on the leaded roof
Of that wide edifice, thy school and home,
Wert used to lie and gaze upon the clouds
Moving in heaven; or, of that pleasure tired,   270
To shut thine eyes, and by internal light
See trees, and meadows, and thy native stream,[5]
Far distant, thus beheld from year to year
Of a long exile.[6] Nor could I forget,
In this late portion of my argument,   275
That scarcely, as my term of pupilage
Ceased, had I left those academic bowers
When thou wert thither guided. From the heart
Of London, and from cloisters there, thou camest,
And didst sit down in temperance and peace,   280
A rigorous student. What a stormy course
Then followed.[7] Oh! it is a pang that calls
For utterance, to think what easy change
Of circumstances might to thee have spared
A world of pain, ripened a thousand hopes,   285
For ever withered. Through this retrospect
Of my collegiate life I still[8] have had
Thy after-sojourn in the self-same place
Present before my eyes, have played with times
And accidents as children do with cards,   290
Or as a man, who, when his house is built,
A frame locked up in wood and stone, doth still,
As impotent fancy prompts, by his fireside,

Rebuild it to his liking. I have thought   305
[295] Of thee, thy learning, gorgeous eloquence,
And all the strength and plumage of thy youth,
Thy subtle speculations, toils abstruse
Among the schoolmen, and Platonic forms[9]
Of wild ideal pageantry, shaped out   310
[300] From things well-matched, or ill, and words for things—
The self-created sustenance of a mind
Debarred from Nature's living images,
Compelled to be a life unto itself,
And unrelentingly possessed by thirst   315
[305] Of greatness, love, and beauty.[1] Not alone,
Ah, surely not in singleness of heart
Should I have seen the light of evening fade
Upon the silent Cam, if we had met,
Even at that early time: I needs must hope,   320
[310] Must feel, must trust, that my maturer age
And temperature less willing to be moved,
My calmer habits, and more steady voice,
Would with an influence benign have soothed
Or chased away the airy wretchedness   325
That battened on[2] thy youth. But thou hast trod,
In watchful meditation thou hast trod,
[315] A march of glory, which doth put to shame
These vain regrets; health suffers in thee, else
Such grief for thee would be the weakest thought   330
That ever harboured in the breast of man.

      A passing word erewhile did lightly touch
[320] On wanderings of my own, and now to these
My poem leads me with an easier mind.
The employments of three winters when I wore   335
A student's gown have been already told,
Or shadowed forth as far as there is need—
When the third summer brought its liberty
A fellow student and myself, he too
A mountaineer, together sallied forth,   340
And, staff in hand on foot pursued our way
[326] Towards the distant Alps.[3] An open slight
Of college cares and study was the scheme,

9. Wordsworth's allusion to Platonic forms, or Ideas, is made without reference to the complex details of Plato's philosophy. "Schoolmen": medieval scholastic philosophers.
1. Because it was starved of natural education and reassurance, Coleridge's mind turned inwards. Creating merely from within himself, he was given to fantasy and idealism, mixing elements that cannot mix, and mistaking words for things.
2. Grew fat upon.
3. "We went staff in hand," Wordsworth recalled in 1847, "and carrying each his needments tied up in a pocket handkerchief, with about twenty pounds apiece in our pockets" (*Memoirs*, I, p. 14). The friend was Robert Jones, who came from a mountainous district of Wales.

Rebuild it to his liking. I have thought
Of thee, thy learning, gorgeous eloquence,   295
And all the strength and plumage of thy youth,
Thy subtle speculations, toils abstruse
Among the schoolmen, and Platonic forms[9]
Of wild ideal pageantry, shaped out
From things well-matched or ill, and words for things,   300
The self-created sustenance of a mind
Debarred from Nature's living images,
Compelled to be a life unto herself,
And unrelentingly possessed by thirst
Of greatness, love, and beauty.[1] Not alone,   305
Ah! surely not in singleness of heart
Should I have seen the light of evening fade
From smooth Cam's silent waters: had we met,
Even at that early time, needs must I trust
In the belief, that my maturer age,   310
My calmer habits, and more steady voice,
Would with an influence benign have soothed,
Or chased away, the airy wretchedness
That battened[2] on thy youth. But thou hast trod
A march of glory, which doth put to shame   315
These vain regrets; health suffers in thee, else
Such grief for thee would be the weakest thought
That ever harboured in the breast of man.

    A passing word erewhile did lightly touch
On wanderings of my own, that now embraced   320
With livelier hope a region wider far.

    When the third summer freed us from restraint,
A youthful friend, he too a mountaineer,
Not slow to share my wishes, took his staff,
And sallying forth, we journeyed side by side,   325
Bound to the distant Alps.[3] A hardy slight
Did this unprecedented course imply
Of college studies and their set rewards;

Nor entertained[4] without concern for those
[332] To whom my worldly interests were dear,[5]   345
But Nature then was sovereign in my heart,
And mighty forms seizing a youthful fancy
[335] Had given a charter to irregular hopes.[6]
In any age, without an impulse sent
From work of nations and their goings-on,   350
I should have been possessed by like desire;
But 'twas a time when Europe was rejoiced,
[340] France standing on the top of golden hours,
And human nature seeming born again.[7]
Bound, as I said, to the Alps, it was our lot   355
[345] To land at Calais on the very eve
Of that great federal day;[8] and there we saw,
In a mean city and among a few,
How bright a face is worn when joy of one
Is joy of tens of millions. Southward thence   360
[350] We took our way, direct through hamlets, towns,
Gaudy with reliques of that festival,
Flowers left to wither on triumphal arcs
And window-garlands.[9] On the public roads—
And once three days successively through paths   365
[355] By which our toilsome journey was abridged—
Among sequestered villages we walked
And found benevolence and blessedness
Spread like a fragrance everywhere, like spring
That leaves no corner of the land untouched.   370
[360] Where elms for many and many a league in files,
With their thin umbrage,[1] on the stately roads
Of that great kingdom rustled o'er our heads,

4. Nor was it entertained.
5. For the concern Wordsworth's trip in
fact caused his family, see *EY*, p. 37.
Coleridge, whose notes on Book VI (only)
of *The Prelude* are preserved in MS. *B*,
found *1805*, 342–45 at first "obscure"
and later "awkwardly expressed." "Thinking dilatation better than awkwardness,"
he "venture[d] to propose" a verbose alternative, much of which was accepted
(see *1850*, 326–32).
6. With *1805*, 346 (*1850*, 333) compare
Tintern Abbey, 73–76, "For Nature
then / * * * To me was all in all." The
"mighty forms" that had seized Wordsworth's fancy (or imagination; no distinction is made here) are mental pictures of the Alps. "Charter": authority,
sanction.
7. *1805*, 353 (*1850*, 340) echoes Shakespeare, sonnet 16, "Now stand you on
the top of happy hours." In its early
phase the French Revolution was peaceful and constitutional (the king was not
deposed for three years, until August

1792). In Britain even Tories assumed
until the publication of Edmund Burke's
Reflections on the Revolution in France
in November 1790 that France was re-
enacting the English "Glorious Revolution" of 1688, at which power had effectively been transferred from the monarchy to Parliament.
8. Wordsworth and Jones landed in
France on July 13, 1790. The fall of the
Bastille (July 14, 1789), and the king's
acceptance of a new, more democratic,
constitution, were celebrated next day at
a massive Fête de la Fédération in Paris,
and throughout the country; see *1805*,
397n, below.
9. The journey was of more than 1,500
miles, through France, Switzerland, Italy,
and Germany, largely on foot, though at
times by water. For Wordsworth's earliest account of the tour, see *Descriptive
Sketches* (1792), on which the *Prelude*
narrative draws heavily at various points.
1. Foliage.

Nor had, in truth, the scheme been formed by me
Without uneasy forethought of the pain, 330
The censures, and ill-omening of those
To whom my worldly interests were dear.[5]
But Nature then was sovereign in my mind,
And mighty forms, seizing a youthful fancy,
Had given a charter to irregular hopes.[6] 335
In any age of uneventful calm
Among the nations, surely would my heart
Have been possessed by similar desire;
But Europe at that time was thrilled with joy,
France standing on the top of golden hours, 340
And human nature seeming born again.[7]

Lightly equipped, and but a few brief looks
Cast on the white cliffs of our native shore
From the receding vessel's deck, we chanced
To land at Calais on the very eve 345
Of that great federal day;[8] and there we saw,
In a mean city, and among a few,
How bright a face is worn when joy of one
Is joy for tens of millions. Southward thence
We held our way, direct through hamlets, towns, 350
Gaudy with reliques of that festival,
Flowers left to wither on triumphal arcs,
And window-garlands.[9] On the public roads,
And, once, three days successively, through paths
By which our toilsome journey was abridged, 355
Among sequestered villages we walked
And found benevolence and blessedness
Spread like a fragrance everywhere, when spring
Hath left no corner of the land untouched:
Where elms for many and many a league in files 360
With their thin umbrage,[1] on the stately roads
Of that great kingdom, rustled o'er our heads,

For ever near us as we paced along,
  'Twas sweet at such a time—with such delights   375
[365] On every side, in prime of youthful strength—
  To feed a poet's tender melancholy
  And fond conceit of sadness, to the noise
  And gentle undulation which they made.
[370] Unhoused beneath the evening star we saw   380
  Dances of liberty, and, in late hours
  Of darkness, dances in the open air.
[375] Among the vine-clad hills of Burgundy,
  Upon the bosom of the gentle Soane   385
  We glided forward with the flowing stream:
  Swift Rhone, thou wert the wings on which we cut
[380] Between thy lofty rocks.[2] Enchanting show
  Those woods and farms and orchards did present,
  And single cottages and lurking towns—
  Reach after reach, procession without end,   390
  Of deep and stately vales. A lonely pair
[385] Of Englishmen we were, and sailed along
  Clustered together with a merry crowd
  Of those emancipated, with a host
  Of travellers, chiefly delegates returning   395
  From the great spousals newly solemnized
[390] At their chief city, in the sight of Heaven.[3]
  Like bees they swarmed, gaudy and gay as bees;
  Some vapoured[4] in the unruliness of joy,
  And flourished with their swords as if to fight   400
  The saucy[5] air. In this blithe company
[395] We landed, took with them our evening meal,
  Guests welcome almost as the angels were
  To Abraham of old.[6] The supper done,
  With flowing cups elate and happy thoughts   405
  We rose at signal given, and formed a ring,
[400] And hand in hand danced round and round the board;
  All hearts were open, every tongue was loud
  With amity and glee. We bore a name
  Honoured in France, the name of Englishmen,   410
  And hospitably did they give us hail
[405] As their forerunners in a glorious course;[7]
  And round and round the board they danced again.

---

2. Coleridge's doubts about the intransitive use of "cut" led to the inclusion of *1850*, 379. Reed, I, p. 101, points out that Wordsworth and Jones cannot in fact have traveled with the *fédérés* down both the Rhône and the Saône.

3. The marriage ("spousals") in Wordsworth's metaphor is between the king, Louis XVI, and the people of France. Louis had sworn fidelity to the new con-

stitution on an altar erected in the Champs de Mars on July 14, 1790.

4. Boasted, bragged, talked fantastically.

5. Impudent.

6. Abraham entertains three angels in Genesis 18:1–15, who tell him that Sarah, though ninety years old and duly incredulous, will bear a son, Isaac.

7. A reference to the "Glorious Revolution" of 1688.

For ever near us as we paced along:
How sweet at such a time, with such delight
On every side, in prime of youthful strength,   365
To feed a Poet's tender melancholy
And fond conceit of sadness, with the sound
Of undulations varying as might please
The wind that swayed them; once, and more than once,
Unhoused beneath the evening star we saw   370
Dances of liberty, and, in late hours
Of darkness, dances in the open air
Deftly prolonged, though grey-haired lookers on
Might waste their breath in chiding.

                       Under hills—
The vine-clad hills and slopes of Burgundy,   375
Upon the bosom of the gentle Soane
We glided forward with the flowing stream.
Swift Rhone! thou wert the *wings* on which we cut
A winding passage with majestic ease
Between thy lofty rocks. Enchanting show   380
Those woods and farms and orchards did present,
And single cottages and lurking towns,
Reach after reach, succession without end
Of deep and stately vales! A lonely pair
Of strangers, till day closed, we sailed along,   385
Clustered together with a merry crowd
Of those emancipated, a blithe host
Of travellers, chiefly delegates returning
From the great spousals newly solemnised
At their chief city, in the sight of Heaven.[3]   390
Like bees they swarmed, gaudy and gay as bees;
Some vapoured[4] in the unruliness of joy,
And with their swords flourished as if to fight
The saucy[5] air. In this proud company
We landed—took with them our evening meal,   395
Guests welcome almost as the angels were
To Abraham of old.[6] The supper done,
With flowing cups elate and happy thoughts
We rose at signal given, and formed a ring
And, hand in hand, danced round and round the board;   400
All hearts were open, every tongue was loud
With amity and glee; we bore a name
Honoured in France, the name of Englishmen,
And hospitably did they give us hail,
As their forerunners in a glorious course;[7]   405
And round and round the board we danced again.

With this same throng our voyage we pursued
At early dawn; the monastery bells   415
Made a sweet jingling in our youthful ears—
[410] The rapid river flowing without noise—
And every spire we saw among the rocks
Spake with a sense of peace, at intervals
[413] Touching the heart amid the boisterous crew   420
With which we were environed. Having parted
From this glad rout, the convent of Chartreuse[8]
Received us two days afterwards, and there
[419] We rested in an awful[9] solitude—
Thence onward to the country of the Swiss.   425

8. Wordsworth did not compose for *The Prelude* an account of the "convent" of Chartreuse, the Carthusian monastery near Grenoble, until 1816/1819. His earliest descriptions of the monastery, however, go back to *Descriptive Sketches* of 1792, from which the *Prelude* account finally draws many of its details.
9. Awesome, awe-inspiring.

With these blithe friends our voyage we renewed
At early dawn. The monastery bells
Made a sweet jingling in our youthful ears;
The rapid river flowing without noise,   410
And each uprising or receding spire
Spake with a sense of peace, at intervals
Touching the heart amid the boisterous crew
By whom we were encompassed. Taking leave
Of this glad throng, foot-travellers side by side,   415
Measuring our steps in quiet, we pursued
Our journey, and ere twice the sun had set
Beheld the Convent of Chartreuse,⁸ and there
Rested within an awful⁹ *solitude*:
Yes, for even then no other than a place   420
Of soul-affecting *solitude* appeared
That far-famed region, though our eyes had seen,
As toward the sacred mansion we advanced,
Arms flashing, and a military glare
Of riotous men commissioned to expel   425
The blameless inmates, and belike subvert
That frame of social being, which so long
Had bodied forth the ghostliness of things
In silence visible and perpetual calm.¹
—'Stay, stay your sacrilegious hands!'—The voice   430
Was Nature's, uttered from her Alpine throne;
I heard it then and seem to hear it now—
'Your impious work forbear, perish what may,
Let this one temple last, be this one spot
Of earth devoted to eternity!'   435
She ceased to speak, but while St. Bruno's pines
Waved their dark tops, not silent as they waved,
And while below, along their several beds,
Murmured the sister streams of Life and Death,²
Thus by conflicting passions pressed, my heart   440
Responded; 'Honour to the patriot's zeal!
Glory and hope to new-born Liberty!
Hail to the mighty projects of the time!
Discerning sword that Justice wields, do thou
Go forth and prosper; and, ye purging fires,   445
Up to the loftiest towers of Pride ascend,
Fanned by the breath of angry Providence.
But oh! if Past and Future be the wings

1. Wordsworth and Jones were at the Grande Chartreuse on August 4 and 5, 1790, and the monks were not in fact expelled until May–October 1792. *Descriptive Sketches*, 60, refers to the expulsion, but does not claim that the poet was present. "Frame of social being" (line 427): in effect, "community." "Bodied forth": embodied. "Ghostliness": spirituality.

2. A reference to actual rivers, the Guiers Vif and the Guiers Mort, that join below the monastery; but to be read as primarily symbolic.

On whose support harmoniously conjoined
Moves the great spirit of human knowledge, spare 450
These courts of mystery, where a step advanced
Between the portals of the shadowy rocks
Leaves far behind life's treacherous vanities,
For penitential tears and trembling hopes
Exchanged—to equalise in God's pure sight 455
Monarch and peasant: be the house redeemed
With its unworldly votaries, for the sake
Of conquest over sense, hourly achieved[3]
Through faith and meditative reason, resting
Upon the word of heaven-imparted truth, 460
Calmly triumphant; and for humbler claim
Of that imaginative impulse sent
From these majestic floods, yon shining cliffs,
The untransmuted shapes of many worlds,
Cerulean ether's pure inhabitants,[4] 465
These forests unapproachable by death,
That shall endure as long as man endures,
To think, to hope, to worship, and to feel,
To struggle, to be lost within himself
In trepidation, from the blank abyss 470
To look with bodily eyes, and be consoled.'
Not seldom since that moment have I wished
That thou, O Friend! the trouble or the calm
Hadst shared, when, from profane regards apart,
In sympathetic reverence we trod 475
The floors of those dim cloisters, till that hour,
From their foundation, strangers to the presence
Of unrestricted and unthinking man.
Abroad, how cheeringly the sunshine lay
Upon the open lawns![5] Vallombre's groves 480
Entering, we fed the soul with darkness; thence
Issued, and with uplifted eyes beheld,
In different quarters of the bending sky,
The cross of Jesus stand erect, as if
Hands of angelic powers had fixed it there,[6] 485
Memorial reverenced by a thousand storms;
Yet then, from the undiscriminating sweep
And rage of one State-whirlwind, insecure.

---

3. Lines 454–58 are an elaboration belonging to 1832; "Life's treacherous vanities" (line 453) replaces "the vanities of life" in Wordsworth's final revisions.
4. Probably a reference to mountaintops that have survived unchanged through many ages, and which inhabit the deep blue ("cerulean") upper air. See *1805,* 572n, below.
5. Lawn: an open space between woods

(Johnson's *Dictionary*).
6. "Alluding to crosses seen on the tops of the spiry rocks of the Chartreuse, which have every appearance of being inaccessible" (Wordsworth's note to *Descriptive Sketches,* 71). Vallombre (line 480) is a valley near the monastery —not to be confused with the more famous Vallombrosa, in Italy.

   'Tis not my present purpose to retrace
[490] That variegated journey step by step;
  A march it was of military speed,
  And earth did change her images and forms
  Before us fast as clouds are changed in heaven.   430
  Day after day, up early and down late,
[495] From vale to vale, from hill to hill we went,
  From province on to province did we pass,
  Keen hunters in a chace of fourteen weeks—
  Eager as birds of prey, or as a ship   435
  Upon the stretch when winds are blowing fair.
[500] Sweet coverts did we cross of pastoral life,
  Enticing vallies—greeted them, and left
  Too soon, while yet the very flash and gleam
  Of salutation were not passed away.   440
  Oh, sorrow for the youth who could have seen
[505] Unchastened, unsubdued, unawed, unraised
  To patriarchal dignity of mind
  And pure simplicity of wish and will,
[508] Those sanctified abodes of peaceful man.   445
  My heart leaped up when first I did look down
  On that which was first seen of those deep haunts,
  A green recess, an aboriginal vale,
[520] Quiet, and lorded over and possessed
  By naked huts, wood-built, and sown like tents   450
  Or Indian cabins over the fresh lawns
  And by the river-side.[7]

        That day we first
[525] Beheld the summit of Mount Blanc, and grieved
  To have a soulless image on the eye
  Which had usurped upon a living thought   455
  That never more could be. The wondrous Vale
  Of Chamouny did, on the following dawn,
[530] With its dumb cataracts and streams of ice—
  A motionless array of mighty waves,
  Five rivers broad and vast—make rich amends,   460
  And reconciled us to realities.

---

7. Compare Dorothy's account in her *Tour of the Continent* (1820) of coming upon this same vale, "this shady deep recess, the very image of pastoral life, stillness and seclusion" (*Journals*, II, p. 280).

    'Tis not my present purpose to retrace
That variegated journey step by step.   490
A march it was of military speed,
And Earth did change her images and forms
Before us, fast as clouds are changed in heaven.
Day after day, up early and down late,
From hill to vale we dropped, from vale to hill   495
Mounted—from province on to province swept,
Keen hunters in a chase of fourteen weeks,
Eager as birds of prey, or as a ship
Upon the stretch, when winds are blowing fair:
Sweet coverts did we cross of pastoral life,   500
Enticing valleys, greeted them and left
Too soon, while yet the very flash and gleam
Of salutation were not passed away.
Oh! sorrow for the youth who could have seen
Unchastened, unsubdued, unawed, unraised   505
To patriarchal dignity of mind,
And pure simplicity of wish and will,
Those sanctified abodes of peaceful man,
Pleased (though to hardship born, and compassed round
With danger, varying as the seasons change),   510
Pleased with his daily task, or, if not pleased,
Contented, from the moment that the dawn
(Ah! surely not without attendant gleams
Of soul-illumination) calls him forth
To industry, by glistenings flung on rocks,   515
Whose evening shadows lead him to repose.

    Well might a stranger look with bounding heart
Down on a green recess, the first I saw
Of those deep haunts, an aboriginal vale,
Quiet and lorded over and possessed   520
By naked huts, wood-built, and sown like tents
Or Indian cabins over the fresh lawns
And by the river side.[7]

                That very day,
From a bare ridge we also first beheld
Unveiled the summit of Mont Blanc, and grieved   525
To have a soulless image on the eye
That had usurped upon a living thought
That never more could be. The wondrous Vale
Of Chamouny stretched far below, and soon
With its dumb cataracts and streams of ice,   530
A motionless array of mighty waves,
Five rivers broad and vast, made rich amends,
And reconciled us to realities;

There small birds warble from the leafy trees,
[535] The eagle soareth in the element,
There doth the reaper bind the yellow sheaf,
The maiden spread the haycock in the sun,   465
While Winter like a tamèd lion walks,
Descending from the mountain to make sport
[540] Among the cottages by beds of flowers.

        Whate'er in this wide circuit we beheld
Or heard was fitted to our unripe state   470
Of intellect and heart. By simple strains
Of feeling, the pure breath of real life,
We were not left untouched. With such a book
Before our eyes we could not chuse but read
[545] A frequent lesson of sound tenderness,   475
The universal reason of mankind,
The truth of young and old. Nor, side by side
Pacing, two brother pilgrims, or alone
Each with his humour,[8] could we fail to abound—
Craft this which hath been hinted at before—   480
[550] In dreams and fictions pensively composed:
Dejection taken up for pleasure's sake,
And gilded sympathies, the willow wreath,[9]
Even among those solitudes sublime,
And sober posies of funereal flowers,   485
[555] Culled from the gardens of the Lady Sorrow,
Did sweeten many a meditative hour.

        Yet still in me, mingling with these delights,
Was something of stern mood, an under-thirst
[559] Of vigour, never utterly asleep.   490
Far different dejection once was mine—
A deep and genuine sadness then I felt—
The circumstances I will here relate
Even as they were. Upturning with a band
Of travellers, from the Valais we had clomb[1]   495
Along the road that leads to Italy;
A length of hours, making of these our guides,
Did we advance, and, having reached an inn
[565] Among the mountains, we together ate
Our noon's repast, from which the travellers rose   500
Leaving us at the board. Erelong we followed,
Descending by the beaten road that led
Right to a rivulet's edge, and there broke off;
[570] The only track now visible was one

8. In the old sense: disposition, state of mind.
9. Willow: a tree [i.e., foliage] worn by forsaken lovers (Johnson's *Dictionary*); here an emblem of luxuriant melancholy.
1. Climbed.

There small birds warble from the leafy trees,
The eagle soars high in the element,   535
There doth the reaper bind the yellow sheaf,
The maiden spread the haycock in the sun,
While Winter like a well-tamed lion walks,
Descending from the mountain to make sport
Among the cottages by beds of flowers.   540

    Whate'er in this wide circuit we beheld,
Or heard, was fitted to our unripe state
Of intellect and heart. With such a book
Before our eyes, we could not choose but read
Lessons of genuine brotherhood, the plain   545
And universal reason of mankind,
The truths of young and old. Nor, side by side
Pacing, two social pilgrims, or alone
Each with his humour,[8] could we fail to abound
In dreams and fictions, pensively composed: 550
Dejection taken up for pleasure's sake,
And gilded sympathies, the willow wreath,[9]
And sober posies of funereal flowers,
Gathered among those solitudes sublime
From formal gardens of the lady Sorrow,   555
Did sweeten many a meditative hour.

    Yet still in me with those soft luxuries
Mixed something of stern mood, an under-thirst
Of vigour seldom utterly allayed.
And from that source how different a sadness   560
Would issue, let one incident make known.
When from the Vallais we had turned, and clomb[1]
Along the Simplon's steep and rugged road,
Following a band of muleteers, we reached
A halting-palce, where all together took   565
Their noon-tide meal. Hastily rose our guide,
Leaving *us* at the board; awhile we lingered,
Then paced the beaten downward way that led
Right to a rough stream's edge, and there broke off;
The only track now visible was one   570

Upon the further side, right opposite,   505
And up a lofty mountain. This we took,
After a little scruple[2] and short pause,
[575] And climbed with eagerness—though not, at length,
Without surprize and some anxiety
On finding that we did not overtake   510
Our comrades gone before. By fortunate chance,
While every moment now encreased our doubts,
A peasant met us, and from him we learned
[580] That to the place which had perplexed us first
We must descend, and there should find the road   515
Which in the stony channel of the stream
Lay a few steps, and then along its banks—
And further, that thenceforward all our course
[585] Was downwards with the current of that stream.
Hard of belief, we questioned him again,   520
And all the answers which the man returned
To our inquiries, in their sense and substance
[590] Translated by the feelings which we had,
Ended in this—that we had crossed the Alps.

      Imagination!—lifting up itself   525
Before the eye and progress of my song
[595] Like an unfathered vapour, here that power,
In all the might of its endowments, came
Athwart me. I was lost as in a cloud,
Halted without a struggle to break through,[3]   530
And now, recovering, to my soul I say
'I recognise thy glory'. In such strength
Of usurpation, in such visitings
[600] Of awful promise, when the light of sense
Goes out in flashes that have shewn to us   535
The invisible world, doth greatness make abode,
There harbours whether we be young or old.
Our destiny, our nature, and our home,
[605] Is with infinitude—and only there;
With hope it is, hope that can never die,   540
Effort, and expectation, and desire,
And something evermore about to be.
The mind beneath such banners militant
[610] Thinks not of spoils or trophies, nor of aught
That may attest its prowess, blest in thoughts   545
That are their own perfection and reward—

---

2. Doubt, difficulty of determination (Johnson's *Dictionary*).
3. Wordsworth switches abruptly from past disappointment (August 1790) to a celebration of present creative power (March 1804). *MS WW* shows, however, that the impressive juxtaposition of *1805*,

524 and 525 (*1850*, 591 and 592) is a second thought. In the original draft the lines are separated by the simile of the cave (finally *1805*, VIII, 711–27; *1850*, VIII, 560–76) in which Wordsworth sought to define his sense of anticlimax at having unknowingly crossed the Alps.

That from the torrent's further brink held forth
Conspicuous invitation to ascend
A lofty mountain. After brief delay
Crossing the unbridged stream, that road we took,
And clomb with eagerness, till anxious fears   575
Intruded, for we failed to overtake
Our comrades gone before. By fortunate chance,
While every moment added doubt to doubt,
A peasant met us, from whose mouth we learned
That to the spot which had perplexed us first   580
We must descend, and there should find the road,
Which in the stony channel of the stream
Lay a few steps, and then along its banks;
And, that our future course, all plain to sight,
Was downwards, with the current of that stream.   585
Loth to believe what we so grieved to hear,
For still we had hopes that pointed to the clouds,
We questioned him again, and yet again;
But every word that from the peasant's lips
Came in reply, translated by our feelings,   590
Ended in this,—*that we had crossed the Alps*.

    Imagination—here the Power so called
Through sad incompetence of human speech,
That awful Power rose from the mind's abyss
Like an unfathered vapour that enwraps,   595
At once, some lonely traveller. I was lost;
Halted without an effort to break through;[3]
But to my conscious soul I now can say—
'I recognise thy glory': in such strength
Of usurpation, when the light of sense   600
Goes out, but with a flash that has revealed
The invisible world, doth greatness make abode,
There harbours, whether we be young or old.[4]
Our destiny, our being's heart and home,
Is with infinitude, and only there;   605
With hope it is, hope that can never die,
Effort, and expectation, and desire,
And something evermore about to be.
Under such banners militant, the soul
Seeks for no trophies, struggles for no spoils   610
That may attest her prowess, blest in thoughts
That are their own perfection and reward,

4. Wordsworth's revisions of *1805*, 532–37 —especially his elimination of "such visitings," the plural "flashes," and "shewn *to us*" (*1805*, 533–35)—make an important difference. In *1805* the experience described is recurrent, and available to others; in *1850*, the lines can be read as referring to a single apocalyptic event.

Strong in itself, and in the access of joy
Which hides it like the overflowing Nile.

[617]   The dull and heavy slackening which ensued
Upon those tidings by the peasant given   550
Was soon dislodged; downwards we hurried fast,
[620] And entered with the road which we had missed
Into a narrow chasm. The brook and road
Were fellow-travellers in this gloomy pass,
And with them did we journey several hours   555
At a slow step. The immeasurable height
[625] Of woods decaying, never to be decayed,
The stationary blasts of waterfalls,
And everywhere along the hollow rent
Winds thwarting winds, bewildered and forlorn,   560
The torrents shooting from the clear blue sky,
[630] The rocks that muttered close upon our ears—
Black drizzling crags that spake by the wayside
As if a voice were in them—the sick sight
And giddy prospect of the raving stream,[5]   565
The unfettered clouds and region of the heavens,
[635] Tumult and peace, the darkness and the light,
Were all like workings of one mind, the features
Of the same face, blossoms upon one tree,
Characters of the great apocalypse,   570
The types and symbols of eternity,
[640] Of first, and last, and midst, and without end.[6]

     That night our lodging was an alpine house,
An inn, or hospital (as they are named),
Standing in that same valley by itself,   575
And close upon the confluence of two streams—
[645] A dreary mansion, large beyond all need,
With high and spacious rooms, deafened and stunned
By noise of waters, making innocent sleep
Lie melancholy among weary bones.[7]   580

5. Compare *Descriptive Sketches*, 243–62, and the magnificent lines that Wordsworth inserted at this point ca. January 1807, but cut in 1832 or 1839: "And ever as we halted, or crept on, / Huge fragments of primaeval mountain spread / In powerless ruin, blocks as huge aloft / Impending, nor permitted yet to fall, / The sacred-death-cross, monument forlorn / Though frequent of the perished traveller * * *"
6. Wordsworth's claims in *1805*, 570–72 (*1850*, 638–40) are less extravagant than perhaps they may seem. Contemporary geological theory held that all but the highest alpine peaks had been created by the retreating waters of the Flood. The features of the landscape would have been engraved, "charactered," by the *first* great apocalyptic event: they would also be in a different sense "characters," or symbols, of the *last*—the millennium yet to come. *1805*, 572 (*1850*, 640) is drawn almost verbatim from Milton's description of God in *Paradise Lost*, V, 165.
7. The Wordsworths visited this "dreary mansion" on their continental tour of 1820, but Dorothy could not persuade her brother to go inside (*Journals*, II, pp. 258–59). "Innocent sleep": from *Macbeth*, II, ii, 36.

Strong in herself and in beatitude
That hides her, like the mighty flood of Nile
Poured from his fount of Abyssinian clouds   615
To fertilise the whole Egyptian plain.

    The melancholy slackening that ensued
Upon those tidings by the peasant given
Was soon dislodged. Downwards we hurried fast,
And, with the half-shaped road which we had missed,   620
Entered a narrow chasm. The brook and road
Were fellow-travellers in this gloomy strait,
And with them did we journey several hours
At a slow pace. The immeasurable height   625
Of woods decaying, never to be decayed,
The stationary blasts of waterfalls,
And in the narrow rent at every turn
Winds thwarting winds, bewildered and forlorn,
The torrents shooting from the clear blue sky,
The rocks that muttered close upon our ears,   630
Black drizzling crags that spake by the way-side
As if a voice were in them, the sick sight
And giddy prospect of the raving stream,[5]
The unfettered clouds and region of the Heavens,
Tumult and peace, the darkness and the light—   635
Were all like workings of one mind, the features
Of the same face, blossoms upon one tree;
Characters of the great Apocalypse,
The types and symbols of Eternity,
Of first, and last, and midst, and without end.[6]   640

    That night our lodging was a house that stood
Alone within the valley, at a point
Where, tumbling from aloft, a torrent swelled
The rapid stream whose margin we had trod;
A dreary mansion, large beyond all need,   645
With high and spacious rooms, deafened and stunned
By noise of waters, making innocent sleep
Lie melancholy among weary bones.[7]

Uprisen betimes, our journey we renewed,
[650] Led by the stream, ere noon-day magnified
Into a lordly river, broad and deep,
Dimpling along in silent majesty
With mountains for its neighbours, and in view   585
Of distant mountains and their snowy tops,
[655] And thus proceeding to Locarno's lake,
Fit resting-place for such a visitant.[8]
Locarno, spreading out in width like heaven,
[660] And Como thou—a treasure by the earth   590
Kept to itself, a darling bosomed up
In Abyssinian privacy[9]—I spake
Of thee, thy chestnut woods and garden plots
Of Indian corn tended by dark-eyed maids,
[665] Thy lofty steeps, and pathways roofed with vines   595
Winding from house to house, from town to town
(Sole link that binds them to each other), walks
League after league, and cloistral avenues
Where silence is if music be not there:
[670] While yet a youth undisciplined in verse,   600
Through fond ambition of my heart I told
Your praises,[1] nor can I approach you now
Ungreeted by a more melodious song,
Where tones of learned art and Nature mixed
[675] May frame enduring language. Like a breeze   605
Or sunbeam over your domain I passed
In motion without pause; but ye have left
Your beauty with me, an impassioned sight
[680] Of colours and of forms, whose power is sweet
And gracious, almost, might I dare to say,   610
As virtue is, or goodness—sweet as love,
Or the remembrance of a noble deed,
Or gentlest visitations of pure thought
[685] When God, the giver of all joy, is thanked
Religiously in silent blessedness—   615
Sweet as this last itself, for such it is.[2]

      Through those delightful pathways we advanced
Two days, and still in presence of the lake,
[690] Which winding up among the Alps now changed

---

8. The river Tusa finds its resting place in Lake Maggiore.
9. An allusion to Milton's description of Abyssinia as the place where Paradise was mistakenly supposed to have been located, in *Paradise Lost*, IV, 280–82: "Nor where Abassin kings their issue guard, / Mount Amara, though this by some supposed / True Paradise * * *"

1. A reference to *Descriptive Sketches*, 80–161, written when the poet was twenty-one or twenty-two.
2. "It" refers to beauty's "power" in *1805*, 609 (*1850*, 680) which is as sweet as the silent prayer of thankfulness to God, because the power of such beauty in fact consists in drawing from the observer this prayerful response.

    Uprisen betimes, our journey we renewed,
Led by the stream, ere noon-day magnified   650
Into a lordly river, broad and deep,
Dimpling along in silent majesty,
With mountains for its neighbours, and in view
Of distant mountains and their snowy tops,
And thus proceeding to Locarno's Lake,   655
Fit resting-place for such a visitant.[8]
Locarno! spreading out in width like Heaven,
How dost thou cleave to the poetic heart,
Bask in the sunshine of the memory;
And Como! thou, a treasure whom the earth   660
Keeps to herself, confined as in a depth
Of Abyssinian privacy,[9] I spake
Of thee, thy chestnut woods, and garden plots
Of Indian corn tended by dark-eyed maids;
Thy lofty steeps, and pathways roofed with vines,   665
Winding from house to house, from town to town,
Sole link that binds them to each other; walks,
League after league, and cloistral avenues,
Where silence dwells if music be not there:
While yet a youth undisciplined in verse,   670
Through fond ambition of that hour, I strove
To chant your praise;[1] nor can approach you now
Ungreeted by a more melodious Song,
Where tones of Nature smoothed by learned Art
May flow in lasting current. Like a breeze   675
Or sunbeam over your domain I passed
In motion without pause; but ye have left
Your beauty with me, a serene accord
Of forms and colours, passive, yet endowed
In their submissiveness with power as sweet   680
And gracious, almost might I dare to say,
As virtue is, or goodness; sweet as love,
Or the remembrance of a generous deed,
Or mildest visitations of pure thought,
When God, the giver of all joy, is thanked   685
Religiously, in silent blessedness;
Sweet is this last herself, for such it is.[2]

    With those delightful pathways we advanced,
For two days' space, in presence of the Lake,
That, stretching far among the Alps, assumed   690

Slowly its lovely countenance and put on   620
A sterner character. The second night,
In eagerness, and by report[3] misled
Of those Italian clocks that speak the time
In fashion different from ours, we rose
[695] By moonshine, doubting not that day was near,[4]   625
And that, meanwhile, coasting the water's edge
As hitherto, and with as plain a track
To be our guide, we might behold the scene
In its most deep repose. We left the town
[700] Of Gravedona with this hope, but soon   630
Were lost, bewildered among woods immense,
Where, having wandered for a while, we stopped
And on a rock sate down to wait for day.
An open place it was and overlooked
From high the sullen water underneath,   635
[705] On which a dull red image of the moon
Lay bedded, changing oftentimes its form
Like an uneasy snake. Long time we sate,
For scarcely more than one hour of the night—
Such was our error—had been gone when we   640
Renewed our journey. On the rock we lay
[711] And wished to sleep, but could not for the stings
Of insects, which with noise like that of noon
Filled all the woods. The cry of unknown birds,
The mountains—more by darkness visible   645
[715] And their own size, than any outward light[5]—
The breathless wilderness of clouds, the clock
That told with unintelligible voice
The widely parted hours, the noise of streams,
And sometimes rustling motions nigh at hand   650
[720] Which did not leave us free from personal fear,
And lastly, the withdrawing moon that set
Before us while she still was high in heaven—
These were our food, and such a summer night
Did to that pair of golden days succeed,   655
With now and then a doze and snatch of sleep,
[725] On Como's banks, the same delicious lake.

[727]   But here I must break off, and quit at once,
Though loth, the record of these wanderings,
A theme which may seduce me else beyond   660
All reasonable bounds. Let this alone
Be mentioned as a parting word, that not

---

3. Sound, message.
4. A single bell was used to mark the
quarters; 1:45 A.M. (three bells for the
quarters, one for the hour) could thus

have been mistaken for 4:00 A.M.
5. I.e., made visible more by their darkness and their size than by any light that
fell upon them.

A character more stern. The second night,
From sleep awakened, and misled by sound
Of the church clock telling the hours with strokes
Whose import then we had not learned, we rose
By moonlight, doubting not that day was nigh,[4]   695
And that meanwhile, by no uncertain path,
Along the winding margin of the lake,
Led, as before, we should behold the scene
Hushed in profound repose. We left the town
Of Gravedona with this hope; but soon   700
Were lost, bewildered among woods immense,
And on a rock sate down, to wait for day.
An open place it was, and overlooked,
From high, the sullen water far beneath,
On which a dull red image of the moon   705
Lay bedded, changing oftentimes its form
Like an uneasy snake. From hour to hour
We sate and sate, wondering, as if the night
Had been ensnared by witchcraft. On the rock
At last we stretched our weary limbs for sleep,   710
But *could not* sleep, tormented by the stings
Of insects, which, with noise like that of noon,
Filled all the woods. The cry of unknown birds;
The mountains more by blackness visible
And their own size, than any outward light;[5]   715
The breathless wilderness of clouds; the clock
That told, with unintelligible voice,
The widely parted hours; the noise of streams,
And sometimes rustling motions nigh at hand,
That did not leave us free from personal fear;   720
And, lastly, the withdrawing moon, that set
Before us, while she still was high in heaven;—
These were our food; and such a summer's night
Followed that pair of golden days that shed
On Como's Lake, and all that round it lay,   725
Their fairest, softest, happiest influence.

    But here I must break off, and bid farewell
To days, each offering some new sight, or fraught
With some untried adventure, in a course
Prolonged till sprinklings of autumnal snow   730
Checked our unwearied steps. Let this alone
Be mentioned as a parting word, that not

In hollow exultation, dealing forth
Hyperboles of praise comparative;
[735] Not rich one moment to be poor for ever;   665
Not prostrate, overborne—as if the mind
Itself were nothing, a mean pensioner
On outward forms—did we in presence stand
Of that magnificent region.⁶ On the front
[740] Of this whole song is written that my heart   670
Must, in such temple, needs have offered up
A different worship. Finally, whate'er
I saw, or heard, or felt, was but a stream
[744] That flowed into a kindred stream, a gale
That helped me forwards, did administer   675
To grandeur and to tenderness—to the one
Directly, but to tender thoughts by means
[750] Less often instantaneous in effect—
Conducted me to these along a path
Which, in the main, was more circuitous.   680

    Oh most belovèd friend, a glorious time,
[755] A happy time that was. Triumphant looks
Were then the common language of all eyes:
As if awaked from sleep, the nations hailed
Their great expectancy; the fife of war   685
Was then a spirit-stirring sound indeed,
[760] A blackbird's whistle in a vernal grove.
We left the Swiss exulting in the fate
Of their neighbours, and, when shortening fast
Our pilgrimage—nor distant far from home—   690
We crossed the Brabant armies on the fret⁷
[765] For battle in the cause of Liberty.⁸
A stripling, scarcely of the household then
Of social life,⁹ I looked upon these things
As from a distance—heard, and saw, and felt,   695
Was touched but with no intimate concern—
[770] I seemed to move among them as a bird
Moves through the air, or as a fish pursues
Its business in its proper¹ element.
I needed not that joy, I did not need   700
[774] Such help: the ever-living universe
And independent spirit of pure youth
Were with me at that season, and delight
Was in all places spread around my steps
As constant as the grass upon the fields.   705

6. An important restatement at the center of the poem of Wordsworth's continuing theme: the creative interplay
between the mind and the forms of external ("outward") Nature.
7. Eagerly anticipating.

8. Republican troops of the short-lived
États Belgiques Unis, which included
Brabant. Leopold II restored Austrian
rule two months later, in December 1790.
9. Scarcely initiated into adult life.
1. Own; French *propre*.

In hollow exultation, dealing out
Hyperboles of praise comparative;
Not rich one moment to be poor for ever; 735
Not prostrate, overborne, as if the mind
Herself were nothing, a mere pensioner
On outward forms—did we in presence stand
Of that magnificent region.[6] On the front
Of this whole Song is written that my heart 740
Must, in such Temple, needs have offered up
A different worship. Finally, whate'er
I saw, or heard, or felt, was but a stream
That flowed into a kindred stream; a gale,
Confederate with the current of the soul, 745
To speed my voyage; every sound or sight,
In its degree of power, administered
To grandeur or to tenderness,—to the one
Directly, but to tender thoughts by means
Less often instantaneous in effect; 750
Led me to these by paths that, in the main,
Were more circuitous, but not less sure
Duly to reach the point marked out by Heaven.

Oh, most belovèd Friend! a glorious time,
A happy time that was; triumphant looks 755
Were then the common language of all eyes;
As if awaked from sleep, the Nations hailed
Their great expectancy: the fife of war
Was then a spirit-stirring sound indeed,
A black-bird's whistle in a budding grove. 760
We left the Swiss exulting in the fate
Of their near neighbours; and, when shortening fast
Our pilgrimage, nor distant far from home,
We crossed the Brabant armies on the fret[7]
For battle in the cause of liberty.[8] 765
A stripling, scarcely of the household then
Of social life,[9] I looked upon these things
As from a distance; heard, and saw, and felt,
Was touched, but with no intimate concern;
I seemed to move among them, as a bird 770
Moves through the air, or as a fish pursues
Its sport, or feeds in its proper[1] element;
I wanted not that joy, I did not need
Such help; the ever-living universe,
Turn where I might, was opening out its glories, 775
And the independent spirit of pure youth
Called forth, at every season, new delights
Spread round my steps like sunshine o'er green fields.

Book Seventh

Residence in London

Five years are vanished since I first poured out,
Saluted by that animating breeze
Which met me issuing from the city's walls,
A glad preamble to this verse.[2] I sang
[5] Aloud in dithyrambic fervour,[3] deep   5
But short-lived uproar, like a torrent sent
Out of the bowels of a bursting cloud
Down Scawfell or Blencathara's[4] rugged sides,
A waterspout from heaven. But 'twas not long
Ere the interrupted strain broke forth once more,   10
[10] And flowed awhile in strength; then stopped for years—
Not heard again until a little space
Before last primrose-time.[5] Belovèd friend,
The assurances then given unto myself,
Which did beguile me of some heavy thoughts   15
At thy departure to a foreign land,
[15] Have failed; for slowly doth this work advance.
Through the whole summer have I been at rest,
Partly from voluntary holiday
And part through outward hindrance.[6] But I heard   20
After the hour of sunset yester-even,
[20] Sitting within doors betwixt light and dark,
A voice that stirred me. 'Twas a little band,
A quire[7] of redbreasts gathered somewhere near
My threshold, minstrels from the distant woods   25
And dells, sent in by Winter to bespeak

2. Writing in October 1804 (see *1805*, 50n, below), Wordsworth looks back five years to the composition of his "Glad Preamble" (*1805*, I, 1–54; *1850*, I, 1–51) ca. November 18, 1799. For comment on "the city's walls" (line 3), see *1805*, I, 8n, above.
3. Dithyrambic: wild, enthusiastick (Johnson's *Dictionary*).
4. Scafell and Blencathra are peaks in the Lake District.
5. The pattern of composition that Wordsworth describes in *1805*, 1–13 (*1850*, 1–12) is broadly accurate, but distorted by his implication—required, of course, by the structure of the poem— that the Preamble (*1805*, I, 1–54) was the first part of *The Prelude* to be written. The two early bursts of composition referred to in lines 4–11 are Parts I and II of *1799*, separated by six months; and the new beginning after a silence of years (lines 12–13) is the start of the five-Book *Prelude* in January 1804. It is Wordsworth's incorporation of specific

dates that makes it clear that he is re-ordering the past. "*Five* years" (*1805*, line 1) refers the reader back correctly from October 1804 to the writing of the Preamble, November 1799, but obscures the true beginnings of *The Prelude* in October 1798; "*Six* changeful years" (the very late emendation found in *1850*, line 1) misdates the Preamble, but accurately reflects the dating of *1799*, I.
6. Wordsworth in January–early March 1804 had assured himself that his poem could be completed in five Books before Coleridge left England; then in March, partly to distract himself as Coleridge's departure grew near (see Composition and Texts: *1805/1850*, Introduction, below) he had decided to create a new longer poem. Work had proceeded fast until mid-June, but then had been shelved. "Outward hindrance" had included visitors to Dove Cottage, and the birth of the poet's daughter Dora on August 16 (*EY*, p. 511).
7. Choir.

Book Seventh

Residence in London

Six changeful years[1] have vanished since I first
Poured out (saluted by that quickening breeze
Which met me issuing from the City's walls)
A glad preamble to this Verse:[2] I sang
Aloud, with fervour irresistible   5
Of short-lived transport, like a torrent bursting,
From a black thunder-cloud, down Scafell's side
To rush and disappear. But soon broke forth
(So willed the Muse) a less impetuous stream,
That flowed awhile with unabating strength,   10
Then stopped for years; not audible again
Before last primrose-time.[5] Belovèd Friend!
The assurance which then cheered some heavy thoughts
On thy departure to a foreign land
Has failed; too slowly moves the promised work.   15
Through the whole summer have I been at rest,
Partly from voluntary holiday,
And part through outward hindrance.[6] But I heard,
After the hour of sunset yester-even,
Sitting within doors between light and dark,   20
A choir of redbreasts gathered somewhere near
My threshold,—ministrels from the distant woods

---

1. See *1805*, line 13*n*, below.

For the old man a welcome, to announce
With preparation artful and benign—
Yea, the most gentle music of the year—
[25] That their rough lord had left the surly north,   30
And hath begun his journey. A delight
At this unthought-of greeting unawares
Smote me, a sweetness of the coming time,
And, listening, I half whispered, 'We will be,
Ye heartsome choristers, ye and I will be   35
[30] Brethren, and in the hearing of bleak winds
Will chaunt together.' And, thereafter, walking
By later twilight on the hills I saw
A glow-worm, from beneath a dusky shade
Or canopy of the yet unwithered fern   40
[35] Clear shining, like a hermit's taper seen
Through a thick forest. Silence touched me here
No less than sound had done before: the child
Of summer, lingering, shining by itself,
The voiceless worm on the unfrequented hills,   45
[40] Seemed sent on the same errand with the quire
Of winter that had warbled at my door,
And the whole year seemed tenderness and love.
The last night's genial feeling[8] overflowed
Upon this morning,[9] and my favorite grove—   50
[45] Now tossing its dark boughs in sun and wind—
Spreads through me a commotion like its own,
Something that fits me for the poet's task,[1]
Which we will now resume with chearful hope,
Nor checked by aught of tamer argument   55
[50] That lies before us, needful to be told.

      Returned from that excursion, soon I bade
Farewell for ever to the private bowers
[54] Of gownèd students—quitted these, no more
To enter them, and pitched my vagrant tent,   60
A casual dweller and at large, among
The unfenced regions of society.[2]

---

8. Warmth, cheerfulness, perhaps also with the implication of creativity (*NED*).
9. Lines 1–50 were originally written as the opening to Book VIII, the first Book to be composed when Wordsworth resumed work on *The Prelude* in early October 1804. For the original opening of VII, and the date at which the openings were transferred, see Composition and Texts: *1805/1850*, Introduction, below.
1. The grove of firs in Ladywood, half a mile from Dove Cottage, was Words-worth's favorite, for the sake of his brother John, who had worn a path by walking there in 1800; see "When to the attractions of the busy world," *Poems on the Naming of Places*, VI.
2. Wordsworth took his B.A. in January 1791, three months after returning from his French "excursion" (*1805*, 57; *1850*, 52), subject of Book VI. "Unfenced regions": commons, as opposed to the enclosed, and privileged, academic bowers of Cambridge.

Sent in on Winter's service, to announce,
With preparation artful and benign,
That the rough lord had left the surly North   25
On his accustomed journey. The delight,
Due to this timely notice, unawares
Smote me, and, listening, I in whispers said,
'Ye heartsome Choristers, ye and I will be
Associates, and, unscared by blustering winds,   30
Will chant together.' Thereafter, as the shades
Of twilight deepened, going forth, I spied
A glow-worm underneath a dusky plume
Or canopy of yet unwithered fern,
Clear-shining, like a hermit's taper seen   35
Through a thick forest. Silence touched me here
No less than sound had done before; the child
Of Summer, lingering, shining by herself,
The voiceless worm on the unfrequented hills,
Seemed sent on the same errand with the choir   40
Of Winter that had warbled at my door,
And the whole year breathed tenderness and love.

    The last night's genial[8] feeling overflowed
Upon this morning, and my favourite grove,
Tossing in sunshine its dark boughs aloft,   45
As if to make the strong wind visible,
Wakes in me agitations like its own,
A spirit friendly to the Poet's task,[1]
Which we will now resume with lively hope,
Nor checked by aught of tamer argument   50
That lies before us, needful to be told.

    Returned from that excursion, soon I bade
Farewell for ever to the sheltered seats
Of gownèd students, quitted hall and bower,
And every comfort of that privileged ground,   55
Well pleased to pitch a vagrant tent among
The unfenced regions of society.[2]

Yet undetermined to what plan of life
I should adhere, and seeming thence to have
[60] A little space of intermediate time   65
Loose and at full command, to London first
I turned, if not in calmness, nevertheless
In no disturbance of excessive hope—
At ease from all ambition personal,
Frugal as there was need, and though self-willed,   70
Yet temperate and reserved, and wholly free
[65] From dangerous passions. 'Twas at least two years
Before this season when I first beheld
That mighty place, a transient visitant;[3]
And now it pleased me my abode to fix   75
Single in the wide waste. To have a house,
It was enough—what matter for a home?—
That owned me, living chearfully abroad
[75] With fancy on the stir from day to day,
And all my young affections out of doors.   80

    There was a time when whatso'er is feigned
Of airy palaces and gardens built
By genii of romance, or hath in grave
[80] Authentic history been set forth of Rome,
Alcairo, Babylon, or Persepolis,   85
Or given upon report by pilgrim friars
Of golden cities ten months' journey deep
Among Tartarean wilds,[4] fell short, far short,
[85] Of that which I in simpleness believed
And thought of London—held me by a chain   90
Less strong of wonder and obscure delight.
I know not that herein I shot beyond
The common mark of childhood, but I well
[90] Remember that among our flock of boys
Was one, a cripple from the birth, whom chance   95
Summoned from school to London—fortunate
And envied traveller—and when he returned,
After short absence, and I first set eyes
Upon his person, verily, though strange
[95] The thing may seem, I was not wholly free   100
From disappointment to behold the same
Appearance, the same body, not to find
Some change, some beams of glory brought away
From that new region. Much I questioned him,

3. Wordsworth apparently visited London first in 1788.
4. Alcairo: Memphis, near the site of modern Cairo, mentioned with Babylon for its magnificence in *Paradise Lost*, I, 717–18. Persepolis: capital of the Persian Empire, sacked by Alexander the Great in 331 B.C. In his reference to "pilgrim friars," "golden cities," and "Tartarean wilds," Wordsworth has in mind *Purchas His Pilgrimes* (1625), source of the opening lines of *Kubla Khan*.

Yet undetermined to what course of life
I should adhere, and seeming to possess
A little space of intermediate time   60
At full command, to London first I turned,
In no disturbance of excessive hope,
By personal ambition unenslaved,
Frugal as there was need, and, though self-willed,
From dangerous passions free. Three years had flown   65
Since I had felt in heart and soul the shock
Of the huge town's first presence, and had paced
Her endless streets, a transient visitant:[3]
Now, fixed amid that concourse of mankind
Where Pleasure whirls about incessantly,   70
Or life and labour seem but one, I filled
An idler's place; an idler well content
To have a house (what matter for a home?)
That owned him; living cheerfully abroad
With unchecked fancy ever on the stir,   75
And all my young affections out of doors.

      There was a time when whatso'er is feigned
Of airy palaces, and gardens built
By Genii of romance; or hath in grave
Authentic history been set forth of Rome,   80
Alcairo, Babylon, or Persepolis;
Or given upon report by pilgrim friars,
Of golden cities ten months' journey deep
Among Tartarian wilds[4]—fell short, far short,
Of what my fond simplicity believed   85
And thought of London—held me by a chain
Less strong of wonder and obscure delight.
Whether the bolt of childhood's Fancy shot
For me beyond its ordinary mark,
'Twere vain to ask; but in our flock of boys   90
Was One, a cripple from his birth, whom chance
Summoned from school to London; fortunate
And envied traveller! When the Boy returned,
After short absence, curiously I scanned
His mien and person, nor was free, in sooth,   95
From disappointment, not to find some change
In look and air, from that new region brought,
As if from Fairy-land. Much I questioned him;

And every word he uttered, on my ears   105
[100] Fell flatter than a cagèd parrot's note,
That answers unexpectedly awry,
And mocks the prompter's listening. Marvellous things
My fancy had shaped forth of sights and shows,
Processions, equipages,[5] lords and dukes,   110
The King and the King's palace, and not last
[110] Or least, heaven bless him! the renowned Lord Mayor—
Dreams hardly less intense than those which wrought
A change of purpose in young Whittington
When he in friendlessness, a drooping boy,   115
Sate on a stone and heard the bells speak out
[115] Articulate music.[6] Above all, one thought
Baffled my understanding, how men lived
Even next-door neighbours, as we say, yet still
Strangers, and knowing not each other's names.   120

    Oh wondrous power of words, how sweet they are
According to the meaning which they bring—
[121] Vauxhall and Ranelagh, I then had heard
Of your green groves and wilderness of lamps,
[124] Your gorgeous ladies, fairy cataracts,   125
And pageant fireworks.[7] Nor must we forget
Those other wonders, different in kind
Though scarcely less illustrious in degree,
The river proudly bridged, the giddy top
[130] And Whispering Gallery of St Paul's, the tombs   130
Of Westminster, the Giants of Guildhall,
Bedlam and the two figures at its gates,[8]
Streets without end and churches numberless,
[135] Statues with flowery gardens in vast squares,
The Monument, and Armoury of the Tower.[9]
These fond imaginations, of themselves,
Had long before given way in season due,
Leaving a throng of others in their stead;
And now I looked upon the real scene,
[145] Familiarly perused it day by day,   140

5. Carriages with attendant servants.
6. According to the legend of Dick Whittington, the bells' message was "Turn again Whittington, / Lord Mayor of London." The historical Richard Whittington was at no stage friendless; he was three times Lord Mayor, and died in 1423.
7. Vauxhall and Ranelagh were fashionable pleasure gardens on the Thames, which provided entertainments of many kinds. On fireworks nights there was an additional charge.
8. The Whispering Gallery goes around inside the dome of St. Paul's; the unusual accoustics mean that a whisper will travel the entire circumference of the dome, returning to the point at which it was made. The Giants of Guildhall were carved wooden figures of Gog and Magog, who have a biblical source in Revelation 20:7–9 but have become a part of popular tradition. Bedlam, the Bethlehem hospital for the insane in Moorfields, was a popular tourist attraction, and had carved stone figures of maniacs lying at the gates (see *1850*).
9. The London Monument was erected by Sir Christopher Wren in 1671–77, to commemorate the great fire of London in 1666. The "Armoury" (*1805*, 135) is one of the showpieces of the Tower of London.

And every word he uttered, on my ears
Fell flatter than a cagèd parrot's note,   100
That answers unexpectedly awry,
And mocks the prompter's listening. Marvelous things
Had vanity (quick Spirit that appears
Almost as deeply seated and as strong
In a Child's heart as fear itself) conceived   105
For my enjoyment. Would that I could now
Recal what then I pictured to myself
Of mitred Prelates, Lords in ermine clad,
The King, and the King's Palace, and, not last,
Nor least, Heaven bless him! the renowned Lord Mayor: 110
Dreams not unlike to those which once begot
A change of purpose in young Whittington,
When he, a friendless and a drooping boy,
Sate on a stone, and heard the bells speak out
Articulate music.[6] Above all, one thought   115
Baffled my understanding: how men lived
Even next-door neighbours, as we say, yet still
Strangers, nor knowing each the other's name.

O, wond'rous power of words, by simple faith
Licensed to take the meaning that we love!   120
Vauxhall and Ranelagh![7] I then had heard
Of your green groves, and wilderness of lamps
Dimming the stars, and fireworks magical,
And gorgeous ladies, under splendid domes,
Floating in dance, or warbling high in air   125
The songs of spirits! Nor had Fancy fed
With less delight upon that other class
Of marvels, broad-day wonders permanent:
The River proudly bridged; the dizzy top
And Whispering Gallery of St. Paul's; the tombs   130
Of Westminster; the Giants of Guildhall;
Bedlam, and those carved maniacs at the gates,
Perpetually recumbent;[8] Statues—man,
And the horse under him—in gilded pomp
Adorning flowery gardens, 'mid vast squares;   135
The Monument, and that Chamber of the Tower
Where England's sovereigns sit in long array,
Their steeds bestriding,[9]—every mimic shape
Cased in the gleaming mail the monarch wore,
Whether for gorgeous tournament addressed,   140
Or life or death upon the battlefield.
Those bold imaginations in due time
Had vanished, leaving others in their stead:
And now I looked upon the living scene;
Familiarly perused it; oftentimes,   145

With keen and lively pleasure even there
Where disappointment was the strongest, pleased
Through courteous self-submission, as a tax
[148] Paid to the object by prescriptive right,
A thing that ought to be. Shall I give way,   145
Copying the impression of the memory—
Though things remembered idly do half seem
The work of fancy—shall I, as the mood
Inclines me, here describe for pastime's sake,
Some portion of that motley imagery,   150
A vivid pleasure of my youth, and now,
Among the lonely places that I love,
A frequent daydream for my riper mind?
And first, the look and aspect of the place—
The broad highway appearance, as it strikes   155
On strangers of all ages, the quick dance
[155] Of colours, lights and forms, the Babel din,
The endless stream of men and moving things,
From hour to hour the illimitable walk
Still among streets, with clouds and sky above,   160
The wealth, the bustle and the eagerness,
The glittering chariots with their pampered steeds,
Stalls, barrows, porters, midway in the street
The scavenger that begs with hat in hand,
The labouring hackney-coaches,[1] the rash speed   165
Of coaches travelling far, whirled on with horn
Loud blowing, and the sturdy drayman's team
Ascending from some alley of the Thames
And striking right across the crowded Strand
Till the fore-horse veer round with punctual skill: 170
Here, there, and everywhere, a weary throng,
[156] The comers and the goers face to face—
Face after face—the string of dazzling wares,
Shop after shop, with symbols, blazoned names,
And all the tradesman's honours overhead: 175
[160] Here, fronts of houses, like a title-page
With letters huge inscribed from top to toe;
Stationed above the door like guardian saints,
There, allegoric shapes, female or male,
Or physiognomies of real men,   180
[165] Land-warriors, kings, or admirals of the sea,
Boyle, Shakespear, Newton, or the attractive head
Of some quack-doctor, famous in his day.[3]

1. Coaches for hire, as opposed to the "chariots" of line 162, the carriages of the wealthy.
3. Robert Boyle (1627–91) was a chemist, founder-member of the Royal Society, and originator of "Boyle's Law." "Quack" is an early correction by Dorothy of "Scotch." The reference is specifically to John Graham (1745–94), handsome, Scottish, and an impudent pretender to remarkable medical cures, who set up a Temple of Health at the Adelphi in 1779, and is referred to in Wordsworth's *Imitation of Juvenal* (1796).

In spite of strongest disappointment, pleased
Through courteous self-submission, as a tax
Paid to the object by prescriptive right.

   Rise up, thou monstrous ant-hill on the plain
Of a too busy world! Before me flow, 150
Thou endless stream of men and moving things!
Thy every-day appearance, as it strikes—
With wonder heightened, or sublimed by awe—
On strangers, of all ages; the quick dance
Of colours, lights, and forms; the deafening din;[2] 155
The comers and the goers face to face,
Face after face; the string of dazzling wares,
Shop after shop, with symbols, blazoned names,
And all the tradesman's honours overhead:
Here, fronts of houses, like a title-page, 160
With letters huge inscribed from top to toe;
Stationed above the door, like guardian saints,
There, allegoric shapes, female or male,
Or physiognomies of real men,
Land-warriors, kings, or admirals of the sea, 165
Boyle, Shakespeare, Newton, or the attractive head
Of some quack-doctor, famous in his day.[3]

2. Wordsworth's text of lines 149–55 reaches its final shape, after many revisions, in 1839. *1805*, lines 163–71 are cut by 1816/19.

Meanwhile the roar continues, till at length,
Escaped as from an enemy, we turn   185
[170] Abruptly into some sequestered nook,
Still as a sheltered place when winds blow loud.
At leisure thence, through tracts of thin resort,[4]

And sights and sounds that come at intervals,
We take our way—a raree-show[5] is here   190
[175] With children gathered round, another street
Presents a company of dancing dogs,
Or dromedary with an antic[6] pair
Of monkies on his back, a minstrel-band
Of Savoyards,[7] single and alone,   195
[180] An English ballad-singer. Private courts,[8]
Gloomy as coffins, and unsightly lanes
Thrilled by some female vendor's scream—belike
The very shrillest of all London cries[9]—
May then entangle us awhile,   200
[185] Conducted through those labyrinths unawares
To privileged regions and inviolate,
Where from their aery lodges studious lawyers
Look out on waters, walks, and gardens green.[1]

Thence back into the throng, until we reach—   205
[190] Following the tide that slackens by degrees—
Some half-frequented scene where wider streets
Bring straggling breezes of suburban air.[2]
Here files of ballads dangle from dead walls;[3]
Advertisements of giant size, from high   210
[195] Press forward in all colours on the sight—
These, bold in conscious merit—lower down,
That, fronted with a most imposing word,
Is peradventure one in masquerade.[4]
As on the broadening causeway we advance,   215
[200] Behold a face turned up towards us, strong
In lineaments, and red with over-toil:
'Tis one perhaps already met elsewhere,

4. Places where few people went.
5. A peep show, carried about in a box.
6. Buffooning.
7. Traveling minstrel bands from Savoy,
a region in southeast France.
8. Courtyards.
9. Hawkers' proclamation of wares to be
sold in the street (Johnson's *Dictionary*).
"Thrilled" (*1805*, 198; *1850*, 182):
pierced.
1. Wordsworth seems to have lived with
his brother Richard at Staple Inn after
his return from France at the end of
1792, and with Basil Montagu at Lincoln's Inn early in 1795 (Reed, I, pp.

138, 163). The inns of court are still remarkably secluded.
2. Fresh air from outside the city.
3. Walls without doors or windows, used
by the ballad sellers to display their
wares.
4. Wordsworth is pointing out advertisements: *these* on the one hand, *that* on
the other. *MS. X* shows the "most imposing word" of *1805*, 213 (*1850*, 197) to
have been "Inviting." The poster was "in
masquerade" (a "joker") in that it disguised the true nature of the goods on
sale.

Meanwhile the roar continues, till at length,
Escaped as from an enemy, we turn
Abruptly into some sequestered nook,   170
Still as a sheltered place when winds blow loud!
At leisure, thence, through tracts of thin resort,[4]
And sights and sounds that come at intervals,
We take our way. A raree-show[5] is here,
With children gathered round; another street   175
Presents a company of dancing dogs,
Or dromedary, with an antic[6] pair
Of monkeys on his back; a minstrel band
Of Savoyards;[7] or, single and alone,
An English ballad-singer. Private courts,[8]   180
Gloomy as coffins, and unsightly lanes
Thrilled by some female vendor's scream, belike
The very shrillest of all London cries,[9]
May then entangle our impatient steps;
Conducted through those labyrinths, unawares,   185
To privileged regions and inviolate,
Where from their airy lodges studious lawyers
Look out on waters, walks, and gardens green.[1]

Thence back into the throng, until we reach,
Following the tide that slackens by degrees,   190
Some half-frequented scene, where wider streets
Bring straggling breezes of suburban air.[2]
Here files of ballads dangle from dead walls;[3]
Advertisements, of giant-size, from high
Press forward, in all colours, on the sight;   195
These, bold in conscious merit, lower down
That, fronted with a most imposing word,
Is, peradventure, one in masquerade.[4]
As on the broadening causeway we advance,
Behold, turned upwards, a face hard and strong   200
In lineaments, and red with over-toil.
'Tis one encountered here and everywhere;

A travelling cripple, by the trunk cut short,
And stumping with his arms.[5] In sailor's garb   220
[205] Another lies at length beside a range
Of written characters, with chalk inscribed
Upon the smooth flat stones. The nurse is here,
The bachelor that loves to sun himself,
The military idler, and the dame   225
[210] That field-ward takes her walk in decency.[6]

   Now homeward through the thickening hubbub,[7] where
See—among less distinguishable shapes—
[215] The Italian, with his frame of images[8]
Upon his head; with basket at his waist,   230
The Jew; the stately and slow-moving Turk,
With freight of slippers piled beneath his arm.
Briefly, we find (if tired of random sights,
And haply to that search our thoughts should turn)
[221] Among the crowd, conspicuous less or more   235
As we proceed, all specimens of man
Through all the colours which the sun bestows,
And every character of form and face:
The Swede, the Russian; from the genial[9] south,
[225] The Frenchman and the Spaniard; from remote   240
America, the hunter Indian; Moors,
Malays, Lascars,[1] the Tartar and Chinese,
And Negro ladies in white muslin gowns.

   At leisure let us view from day to day,
As they present themselves, the spectacles   245
[230] Within doors: troops of wild beasts, birds and beasts
Of every nature from all climes convened,
And, next to these, those mimic sights that ape
The absolute presence of reality,
Expressing as in mirror sea and land,   250
[235] And what earth is, and what she hath to shew—
I do not here allude to subtlest craft,
By means refined attaining purest ends,
But imitations fondly made in plain
Confession of man's weakness and his loves.   255
[240] Whether the painter—fashioning a work
To Nature's circumambient[2] scenery,

---

5. The cripple, as Maxwell points out, was Samuel Horsey, "King of the Beggars," described by Lamb in his essay, "A Complaint of the Decay of Beggars in the Metropolis," *Elia* (1823).
6. Modesty, propriety.
7. The "hubbub" of London is related in Wordsworth's mind to the "universal hubbub wild" of Chaos (*Paradise Lost*, II, 951).
8. Statuettes.
9. Warm.
1. East Indian sailors (*NED*), but it is doubtful whether Wordsworth had anything so specific in mind.
2. Surrounding.

A travelling cripple, by the trunk cut short,
And stumping on his arms.[5] In sailor's garb
Another lies at length, beside a range   205
Of well-formed characters, with chalk inscribed
Upon the smooth flat stones: the Nurse is here,
The Bachelor, that loves to sun himself,
The military Idler, and the Dame,
That field-ward takes her walk with decent steps.   210

    Now homeward through the thickening hubbub,[7] where
See, among less distinguishable shapes,
The begging scavenger, with hat in hand;
The Italian, as he thrids his way with care,
Steadying, far-seen, a frame of images[8]   215
Upon his head; with basket at his breast
The Jew; the stately and slow-moving Turk,
With freight of slippers piled beneath his arm!

    Enough;—the mighty concourse I surveyed
With no unthinking mind, well pleased to note   220
Among the crowd all specimens of man,
Through all the colours which the sun bestows,
And every character of form and face:
The Swede, the Russian; from the genial[9] south,
The Frenchman and the Spaniard; from remote   225
America, the Hunter-Indian; Moors,
Malays, Lascars,[1] the Tartar, the Chinese,
And Negro Ladies in white muslin gowns.

    At leisure, then, I viewed, from day to day,
The spectacles within doors,—birds and beasts   230
Of every nature, and strange plants convened
From every clime; and, next, those sights that ape
The absolute presence of reality,
Expressing, as in mirror, sea and land,
And what earth is, and what she has to shew.   235
I do not here allude to subtlest craft,
By means refined attaining purest ends,
But imitations, fondly made in plain
Confession of man's weakness and his loves.
Whether the Painter, whose ambitious skill   240

And with his greedy pencil[3] taking in
A whole horizon on all sides—with power
Like that of angels or commissioned[4] spirits,   260
Plant us upon some lofty pinnacle
[245] Or in a ship on waters, with a world
Of life and lifelike mockery to east,
To west, beneath, behind us, and before,[5]
Or more mechanic artist represent   265
By scale exact, in model, wood or clay,
[250] From shading colours also borrowing help,
Some miniature of famous spots and things,
Domestic, or the boast of foreign realms:
The Firth of Forth, and Edinburgh, throned   270
On crags, fit empress of that mountain land;
St Peter's Church; or, more aspiring aim,
In microscopic vision, Rome itself;
Or else, perhaps, some rural haunt, the Falls
[255] Of Tivoli, and dim Frescati's bowers,
And high upon the steep that mouldering fane,   275
The Temple of the Sibyl[6]—every tree
Through all the landscape, tuft, stone, scratch minute,
And every cottage, lurking in the rocks—
All that the traveller sees when he is there.   280

[260]   And to these exhibitions mute and still
Others of wider scope, where living men,
Music, and shifting pantomimic scenes,
Together joined their multifarious aid
To heighten the allurement. Need I fear   285
To mention by its name, as in degree
[265] Lowest of these, and humblest in attempt—
Yet richly graced with honours of its own—
Half-rural Sadler's Wells?[7] Though at that time
Intolerant, as is the way of youth   290
[269] Unless itself be pleased, I more than once
Here took my seat, and, maugre[8] frequent fits
Of irksomeness, with ample recompense
Saw singers, rope-dancers, giants and dwarfs,

3. Paintbrush (the primary meaning, in Johnson's *Dictionary*).
4. With commissions, tasks, to perform.
5. Panoramas were a novelty at the end of the eighteenth century, and frequently, as in Wordsworth's description, encompassed the view on all sides of the spectator. Thomas Girtin's *Eidometropolis*, a view of London, painted from Blackfriars Bridge, was 9 feet high and 216 in circumference. Wordsworth may well have seen it, as it was probably on exhibition when he and Dorothy were being shown the sights of the town by Lamb in September 1802.
6. Tivoli and Frascati are towns respectively in the Sabine and Alban hills near Rome. The temple or "fane" of the Sybil at Tivoli was a very frequent subject for British painters of the eighteenth century.
7. Sadler's Wells was in Islington, a suburb in the 1790s; and it offered more popular entertainment than the central London theatres.
8. Despite; pronounced "maúgĕr."

Submits to nothing less than taking in
A whole horizon's circuit, do with power,
Like that of angels or commissioned[4] spirits,
Fix us upon some lofty pinnacle,
Or in a ship on waters, with a world   245
Of life, and life-like mockery beneath,
Above, behind, far stretching and before;[5]
Or more mechanic artist represent
By scale exact, in model, wood or clay,
From blended colours also borrowing help,   250
Some miniature of famous spots or things,—
St. Peter's Church; or, more aspiring aim,
In microscopic vision, Rome herself;
Or, haply, some choice rural haunt,—the Falls
Of Tivoli; and, high upon that steep,   255
The Sibyl's mouldering Temple![6] every tree,
Villa, or cottage, lurking among rocks
Throughout the landscape; tuft, stone, scratch minute—
All that the traveller sees when he is there.

   Add to these exhibitions, mute and still,   260
Others of wider scope, where living men,
Music, and shifting pantomimic scenes,
Diversified the allurement. Need I fear
To mention by its name, as in degree
Lowest of these and humblest in attempt,   265
Yet richly graced with honours of her own,
Half-rural Sadler's Wells?[7] Though at that time
Intolerant, as is the way of youth
Unless itself be pleased, here more than once
Taking my seat, I saw (nor blush to add,   270
With ample recompense) giants and dwarfs,

Clowns, conjurors, posture-masters, harlequins,[9]   295
Amid the uproar of the rabblement,
Perform their feats. Nor was it mean delight
[275] To watch crude Nature work in untaught minds,
To note the laws and progress of belief—
Though obstinate on this way, yet on that   300
How willingly we travel, and how far!—
To have, for instance, brought upon the scene
[280] The champion, Jack the Giant-killer: lo,
He dons his coat of darkness, on the stage
Walks, and atchieves his wonders, from the eye   305
Of living mortal safe as is the moon
'Hid in her vacant interlunar cave'.[1]
[285] Delusion bold (and faith must needs be coy)[2]
How is it wrought?—his garb is black, the word
INVISIBLE flames forth upon his chest.   310

        Nor was it unamusing here to view
Those samples, as of the ancient comedy
[290] And Thespian times,[4] dramas of living men
And recent things yet warm with life: a sea-fight,
Shipwreck, or some domestic incident   315
The fame of which is scattered through the land,
Such as this daring brotherhood of late
[295] Set forth—too holy theme for such a place,
And doubtless treated with irreverence,
Albeit with their very best of skill—   320
I mean, O distant friend, a story drawn
From our own ground, the Maid of Buttermere,
And how the spoiler came, 'a bold bad man'
To God unfaithful, children, wife, and home,
[300] And wooed the artless daughter of the hills,   325
And wedded her, in cruel mockery
Of love and marriage bonds.[5] O friend, I speak
With tender recollection of that time
When first we saw the maiden, then a name
[305] By us unheard of—in her cottage-inn   330

9. "Posture-masters": contortionists. "Harlequins": clowns, traditionally in parti-colored costume.
1. Quoted from Milton's *Samson Agonistes*, 89.
2. Wordsworth's parenthesis, rightly discarded in *1850*, is very difficult to construe. Either, faith, *as opposed to* the delusion being practiced, has to be modest ("coy"); or, faith *in* the delusion—the audience's credulity—shows its modesty in the quiet acceptance of the trick.
4. Thespis was a Greek dramatist (in fact a tragedian) of the sixth century B.C. "Here" (line 311): at Sadler's Wells.

5. A melodrama in rhyme called *Edward and Susan, or The Beauty of Buttermere* was performed in April–June 1803 by the actors of Sadler's Wells (the "daring brotherhood" of *1805*, 317; *1850*, 299) based on the story of Mary Robinson, daughter of the innkeeper of Buttermere, who the previous October had been tricked into a bigamous marriage by a certain John Hatfield, posing as a Scottish M.P. Wordsworth and Coleridge were both extremely interested in the case, and Mary Lamb wrote describing the play in July 1803.

Clowns, conjurors, posture-masters, harlequins,[9]
Amid the uproar of the rabblement,
Perform their feats. Nor was it mean delight
To watch crude Nature work in untaught minds;   275
To note the laws and progress of belief;
Though obstinate on this way, yet on that
How willingly we travel, and how far!
To have, for instance, brought upon the scene
The champion, Jack the Giant-killer: Lo!   280
He dons his coat of darkness; on the stage
Walks, and achieves his wonders from the eye
Of living Mortal covert, as the moon
Hid in her 'vacant interlunar cave'.[1]
Delusion bold! and how can it be wrought?   285
The garb he wears is black as death, the word
'*Invisible*' flames forth upon his chest.

Here, too, were 'forms and pressures of the time',[3]
Rough, bold, as Grecian comedy displayed
When Art was young; dramas of living men,   290
And recent things yet warm with life; a sea-fight,
Shipwreck, or some domestic incident
Divulged by Truth and magnified by Fame,
Such as the daring brotherhood of late
Set forth, too serious theme for that light place—   295
I mean, O distant Friend! a story drawn
From our own ground,—the Maid of Buttermere,—
And how, unfaithful to a virtuous wife
Deserted and deceived, the spoiler came
And wooed the artless daughter of the hills,   300
And wedded her, in cruel mockery
Of love and marriage bonds.[5] These words to thee
Must needs bring back the moment when we first,
Ere the broad world rang with the maiden's name,
Beheld her serving at the cottage inn,   305

---

3. An inexact quotation from *Hamlet*, III, ii, 24 ff., where the Players are being instructed: the "purpose of playing" is "to hold * * * the mirror up to nature; to show virtue her own feature, scorn her own image, *and the very age and body of the time his form and pressure.*"

Were welcomed, and attended on by her,
Both stricken with one feeling of delight,
An admiration of her modest mien
And carriage, marked by unexampled grace.[6]
Not unfamiliarly we since that time   335
[310] Have seen her, her discretion have observed,
Her just opinions, female modesty,
Her patience, and retiredness of mind
[313] Unsoiled by commendation and excess
Of public notice. This memorial verse   340
Comes from the poet's heart, and is her due;
For we were nursed—as almost might be said—
On the same mountains, children at one time,
Must haply often on the self-same day
Have from our several dwellings gone abroad   345
To gather daffodils on Coker's stream.[7]

These last words uttered, to my argument
[317] I was returning, when—with sundry forms
Mingled, that in the way which I must tread
Before me stand—thy image rose again,   350
[320] Mary of Buttermere! She lives in peace
Upon the spot where she was born and reared;
Without contamination does she live
In quietness, without anxiety.
Beside the mountain chapel sleeps in earth   355
[325] Her new-born infant, fearless as a lamb
That thither comes from some unsheltered place
To rest beneath the little rock-like pile
When storms are blowing. Happy are they both,
Mother and child![8] These feelings, in themselves   360
[330] Trite, do yet scarcely seem so when I think
Of those ingenuous moments of our youth
Ere yet by use we have learnt to slight the crimes
And sorrows of the world. Those days are now
My theme, and, 'mid the numerous scenes which they   365
Have left behind them, foremost I am crossed
Here by remembrance of two figures: one
A rosy babe, who for a twelvemonth's space
Perhaps had been of age to deal about
[339] Articulate prattle,[9] child as beautiful   370

6. Wordsworth and Coleridge were at Buttermere during their walking tour of November 1799. "Mien": air, manner.
7. Mary Robinson was two years younger than Wordsworth. The river Cocker flows from Buttermere to his birthplace, Cockermouth. Lines 342–43 recall Milton's *Lycidas*, 23, "For we were nursed upon the selfsame hill." "Several" (line 345): different.

8. There are no records of Mary's having had a child by Hatfield, but Wordsworth presumably had local knowledge. Despite the seeming implication of "memorial" (*1805*, 340; *1850*, 316), Mary lived on, and married a local farmer.
9. I.e., the child for the space of perhaps a year had been able to make himself understood.

Both stricken, as she entered or withdrew,
With admiration of her modest mien
And carriage, marked by unexampled grace.[6]
Not unfamiliarly we since that time
Have seen her,—her discretion have observed,   310
Her just opinions, delicate reserve,
Her patience, and humility of mind
Unspoiled by commendation and the excess
Of public notice—an offensive light
To a meek spirit suffering inwardly.   315

    From this memorial tribute to my theme
I was returning, when, with sundry forms
Commingled—shapes which met me in the way
That we must tread—thy image rose again,
Maiden of Buttermere! She lives in peace   320
Upon the spot where she was born and reared;
Without contamination doth she live
In quietness, without anxiety:
Beside the mountain chapel, sleeps in earth
Her new-born infant, fearless as a lamb   325
That, thither driven from some unsheltered place,
Rests underneath the little rock-like pile
When storms are raging. Happy are they both—
Mother and child![8]—These feelings, in themselves
Trite, do yet scarcely seem so when I think   330
On those ingenuous moments of our youth
Ere we have learnt by use to slight the crimes
And sorrows of the world. Those simple days
Are now my theme; and, foremost of the scenes,
Which yet survive in memory, appears   335
One, at whose centre sate a lovely Boy,
A sportive infant, who, for six months' space,
Not more, had been of age to deal about
Articulate prattle[9]—Child as beautiful

As ever sate upon a mother's knee;
The other was the parent of that babe—
But on the mother's cheek the tints were false,
A painted bloom. 'Twas at a theatre
That I beheld this pair; the boy had been[1]   375
The pride and pleasure of all lookers-on
In whatsoever place, but seemed in this
[350] A sort of alien scattered from the clouds.
Of lusty vigour, more than infantine,
He was in limbs, in face a cottage rose   380
Just three parts blown—a cottage-child, but ne'er
[355] Saw I by cottage or elsewhere a babe
By Nature's gifts so honored. Upon a board,
Whence an attendant of the theatre
Served out refreshments, had this child been placed,   385
And there he sate environed with a ring
[360] Of chance spectators, chiefly dissolute men
And shameless women—treated[2] and caressed—
Ate, drank, and with the fruit and glasses played,
While oaths, indecent speech, and ribaldry   390
Were rife about him as are songs of birds
[365] In springtime after showers. The mother, too,
Was present, but of her I know no more
Than hath been said, and scarcely at this time
Do I remember her; but I behold   395
The lovely boy as I beheld him then,
Among the wretched and the falsely gay,
Like one of those who walked with hair unsinged
[370] Amid the fiery furnace.[3] He hath since
Appeared to me ofttimes as if embalmed   400
[375] By Nature—through some special privilege
Stopped at the growth he had—destined to live,
To be, to have been, come, and go, a child
And nothing more, no partner in the years
That bear us forward to distress and guilt,   405
Pain and abasement; beauty in such excess
Adorned him in that miserable place.
So have I thought of him a thousand times—
And seldom otherwise—but he perhaps,
Mary, may now have lived till he could look   410
[380] With envy on thy nameless babe that sleeps
Beside the mountain chapel undisturbed.

1. I.e., would have been.
2. Presumably, given treats of food.
3. Shadrach, Meshach, and Abednego, who had been cast by King Nebuchadnezzar into the fiery furnace but emerged unharmed: Daniel 3:23–26.

As ever clung around a mother's neck, 340
Or father fondly gazed upon with pride.
There, too, conspicuous for stature tall
And large dark eyes, beside her infant stood
The mother; but, upon her cheeks diffused,
False tints too well accorded with the glare 345
From play-house lustres thrown without reserve
On every object near. The Boy had been[1]
The pride and pleasure of all lookers-on
In whatsoever place, but seemed in this
A sort of alien scattered from the clouds. 350
Of lusty vigour, more than infantine,
He was in limb, in cheek a summer rose
Just three parts blown—a cottage-child—if e'er,
By cottage-door on breezy mountain side,
Or in some sheltering vale, was seen a babe 355
By Nature's gifts so favoured. Upon a board
Decked with refreshments had this child been placed,
His little stage in the vast theatre,
And there he sate surrounded with a throng
Of chance spectators, chiefly dissolute men 360
And shameless women; treated[2] and caressed,
Ate, drank, and with the fruit and glasses played,
While oaths and laughter and indecent speech
Were rife about him as the songs of birds
Contending after showers. The mother now 365
Is fading out of memory, but I see
The lovely Boy as I beheld him then
Among the wretched and the falsely gay,
Like one of those who walked with hair unsinged
Amid the fiery furnace.[3] Charms and spells 370
Muttered on black and spiteful instigation
Have stopped, as some believe, the kindliest growths;
Ah, with how different spirit might a prayer
Have been preferred, that this fair creature, checked
By special privilege of Nature's love, 375
Should in his childhood be detained for ever!
But with its universal freight the tide
Hath rolled along, and this bright innocent,[4]
Mary! may now have lived till he could look
With envy on thy nameless babe that sleeps, 380
Beside the mountain chapel, undisturbed.

---

4. Wordsworth's *1805* vision of the child embalmed by imagination was replaced as early as 1816/19 by a version of 1850. "Preferred" (line 374): submitted, presented.

It was but little more than three short years
Before the season which I speak of now
When first, a traveller from our pastoral hills,   415
Southward two hundred miles I had advanced,[5]
And for the first time in my life did hear
[385] The voice of woman utter blasphemy—
Saw woman as she is to open shame
Abandoned, and the pride of public vice.   420
Full surely from the bottom of my heart
I shuddered; but the pain was almost lost,
Absorbed and buried in the immensity
Of the effect: a barrier seemed at once
Thrown in, that from humanity divorced   425
[390] The human form, splitting the race of man
In twain, yet leaving the same outward shape.
Distress of mind ensued upon this sight,
And ardent meditation—afterwards
A milder sadness on such spectacles   430
[395] Attended: thought, commiseration, grief,
For the individual and the overthrow
Of her soul's beauty—farther at that time
Than this I was but seldom led; in truth
The sorrow of the passion stopped me here.   435

[400]   I quit this painful theme, enough is said
To shew what thoughts must often have been mine
At theatres, which then were my delight—
A yearning made more strong by obstacles
Which slender funds imposed. Life then was new,   440
The senses easily pleased; the lustres,[6] lights,
The carving and the gilding, paint and glare,
And all the mean upholstery of the place,
[410] Wanted not animation in my sight,
Far less the living figures on the stage,   445
Solemn or gay—whether some beauteous dame
Advanced in radiance through a deep recess
[415] Of thick-entangled forest, like the moon
Opening the clouds; or sovereign king, announced
With flourishing trumpets, came in full-blown state   450
Of the world's greatness, winding round with train
Of courtiers, banners, and a length of guards;
[420] Or captive led in abject weeds, and jingling
His slender manacles; or romping girl
Bounced, leapt, and pawed the air; or mumbling sire,   455
A scarecrow pattern of old age, patched up
Of all the tatters of infirmity,

5. Wordsworth journeyed south to Cam-   6. Chandeliers.
bridge in October 1787.

Four rapid years had scarcely then been told
Since, travelling southward from our pastoral hills,[5]
I heard, and for the first time in my life,
The voice of woman utter blasphemy—   385
Saw woman as she is to open shame
Abandoned, and the pride of public vice;
I shuddered, for a barrier seemed at once
Thrown in, that from humanity divorced
Humanity, splitting the race of man   390
In twain, yet leaving the same outward form.
Distress of mind ensued upon the sight
And ardent meditation. Later years
Brought to such spectacle a milder sadness,
Feelings of pure commiseration, grief   395
For the individual and the overthrow
Of her soul's beauty; farther I was then
But seldom led, or wished to go; in truth
The sorrow of the passion stopped me there.

But let me now, less moved, in order take   400
Our argument. Enough is said to show
How casual incidents of real life,
Observed where pastime only had been sought,
Outweighed, or put to flight, the set events
And measured passions of the stage, albeit   405
By Siddons trod in the fulness of her power.[7]
Yet was the theatre my dear delight;
The very gilding, lamps and painted scrolls,
And all the mean upholstery of the place,
Wanted not animation, when the tide   410
Of pleasure ebbed but to return as fast
With the ever-shifting figures of the scene,
Solemn or gay: whether some beauteous dame
Advanced in radiance through a deep recess
Of thick entangled forest, like the moon   415
Opening the clouds; or sovereign king, announced
With flourishing trumpet, came in full-blown state
Of the world's greatness, winding round with train
Of courtiers, banners, and a length of guards;
Or captive led in abject weeds, and jingling   420
His slender manacles; or romping girl
Bounced, leapt, and pawed the air; or mumbling sire,
A scare-crow pattern of old age dressed up
In all the tatters of infirmity

7. Mrs. Siddons (1755–1831) was the most famous actress of her day; it is not certain that Wordsworth ever saw her, but Dorothy did so twice when they were in London together in November 1797 (*EY*, p. 196).

[425] All loosely put together, hobbled in
Stumping upon a cane, with which he smites
From time to time the solid boards and makes them   460
Prate somewhat loudly of the whereabout[8]
Of one so overloaded with his years.
[430] But what of this?—the laugh, the grin, grimace,
And all the antics and buffoonery,
The least of them not lost, were all received   465
With charitable pleasure. Through the night,
Between the show, and many-headed mass
[435] Of the spectators, and each little nook
That had its fray or brawl, how eagerly
And with what flashes, as it were, the mind   470
Turned this way, that way—sportive and alert
And watchful, as a kitten when at play,
[440] While winds are blowing round her, among grass
And rustling leaves.[9] Enchanting age and sweet—
Romantic almost, looked at through a space,
How small, of intervening years! For then,
Though surely no mean progress had been made
[445] In meditations holy and sublime,
Yet something of a girlish childlike gloss
Of novelty survived for scenes like these—   480
Pleasure that had been handed down from times
[449] When at a country playhouse, having caught
In summer through the fractured wall a glimpse
Of daylight, at the thought of where I was
I gladdened more than if I had beheld   485
[455] Before me some bright cavern of romance,
Or than we do when on our beds we lie
At night, in warmth, when rains are beating hard.

    The matter which detains me now will seem
To many neither dignified enough   490
[460] Nor arduous, and is doubtless in itself
Humble and low—yet not to be despised
By those who have observed the curious props
By which the perishable hours of life
Rest on each other, and the world of thought   495
[465] Exists and is sustained.[1] More lofty themes,
Such as at least do wear a prouder face,
Might here be spoken of; but when I think
Of these I feel the imaginative power
Languish within me. Even then it slept,   500

---

8. Compare *Macbeth*, II, i, 58: "Thy
very stones prate of my whereabout."
"Prate": chatter.
9. Wordsworth's imagery shows a connection between Book VII and *Kitten*

and the Falling Leaves, probably also
written in autumn 1804.
1. Lines 492–96 were written for *The
Ruined Cottage* in February–March 1798.

All loosely put together, hobbled in,   425
Stumping upon a cane with which he smites,
From time to time, the solid boards, and makes them
Prate somewhat loudly of the whereabout[8]
Of one so overloaded with his years.
But what of this! the laugh, the grin, grimace,   430
The antics striving to outstrip each other,
Were all received, the least of them not lost,
With an unmeasured welcome. Through the night,
Between the show, and many-headed mass
Of the spectators, and each several nook   435
Filled with its fray or brawl, how eagerly
And with what flashes, as it were, the mind
Turned this way—that way! sportive and alert
And watchful, as a kitten when at play,
While winds are eddying round her, among straws   440
And rustling leaves. Enchanting age and sweet!
Romantic almost,[9] looked at through a space,
How small, of intervening years! For then,
Though surely no mean progress had been made
In meditations holy and sublime,   445
Yet something of a girlish child-like gloss
Of novelty survived for scenes like these;
Enjoyment haply handed down from times
When at a country-playhouse, some rude barn
Tricked out for that proud use, if I perchance   450
Caught, on a summer evening through a chink
In the old wall, an unexpected glimpse
Of daylight, the bare thought of where I was
Gladdened me more than if I had been led
Into a dazzling cavern of romance,   455
Crowded with Genii busy among works
Not to be looked at by the common sun.

    The matter that detains us now may seem,
To many, neither dignified enough
Nor arduous, yet will not be scorned by them,   460
Who, looking inward, have observed the ties
That bind the perishable hours of life
Each to the other, and the curious props
By which the world of memory and thought
Exists and is sustained. More lofty themes,   465
Such as at least do wear a prouder face,
Solicit our regard; but when I think
Of these, I feel the imaginative power
Languish within me; even then it slept,

[470] When, wrought upon by tragic sufferings,
The heart was full—amid my sobs and tears
It slept, even in the season of my youth.
For though I was most passionately moved,
And yielded to the changes of the scene   505
[475] With most obsequious feeling, yet all this
Passed not beyond the suburbs of the mind.[2]
If aught there were of real grandeur here
'Twas only then when gross realities,
The incarnation of the spirits that moved   510
[480] Amid the poet's beauteous world—called forth
With that distinctness which a contrast gives,
Or opposition—made me recognise
As by a glimpse, the things which I had shaped
And yet not shaped, had seen and scarcely seen,   515
[485] Had felt, and thought of in my solitude.[3]

          Pass we from entertainments that are such
Professedly, to others titled higher,
Yet, in the estimate of youth at least,
More near akin to these than names imply—   520
[490] I mean the brawls of lawyers in their courts
Before the ermined judge, or that great stage
Where senators, tongue-favored men, perform,
Admired and envied. Oh, the beating heart,
When one among the prime of these rose up,   525
[495] One of whose name from childhood we had heard
Familiarly, a household term, like those—
The Bedfords, Glocesters, Salisburys of old—
Which the fifth Harry talks of.[4] Silence, hush,
This is no trifler, no short-flighted wit,   530
[500] No stammerer of a minute, painfully
Delivered. No, the orator hath yoked
The hours, like young Aurora, to his car—
O presence of delight, can patience e'er
Grow weary of attending on a track   535
[505] That kindles with such glory?[5] Marvellous,

2. Compare "Dwell I but in the suburbs / Of your good pleasure?" (*Julius Caesar*, II, i, 285–86).
3. I.e., he was deeply moved only when the imaginative world of the poet (Shakespeare, no doubt, as at *1850*, 484) enabled him to identify things half-pictured or half-articulated within his own mind. The "gross realities" of stage presentation draw attention to the spiritual quality of Shakespeare's imagination through the very clumsiness with which they embody, "incarnate," his ideal world.
4. The king in Shakespeare's *Henry V*, IV, iii, 51–55, predicts that Bedford, Salisbury, Gloucester, and others will become "household words" for their part in the Battle of Agincourt. For Wordsworth's response to the play, see Dorothy Wordsworth's *Journal*, May 8, 1802. The orator with a household name (*1805*, 525–27; *1850*, 495–96) is William Pitt the younger, prime minister (with one short break) from 1783 till his death in 1806.
5. Aurora, goddess of the dawn, was traditionally shown as rising from the sea in her chariot ("car"); her track would kindle with the morning light. The overall sense is that Pitt, unlike the "stammerer of a minute" (*1805*, 531; *1850*, 500), is borne along by time, i.e., is capable of talking at length.

When, pressed by tragic sufferings, the heart   470
Was more than full; amid my sobs and tears
It slept, even in the pregnant season of youth.
For though I was most passionately moved
And yielded to all changes of the scene
With an obsequious promptness, yet the storm   475
Passed not beyond the suburbs of the mind;[2]
Save when realities of act and mien,
The incarnation of the spirits that move
In harmony amid the Poet's world,
Rose to ideal grandeur, or, called forth   480
By power of contrast, made me recognise,
As at a glance, the things which I had shaped,
And yet not shaped, had seen and scarcely seen,
When, having closed the mighty Shakespear's page,
I mused, and thought, and felt, in solitude.[3]   485

    Pass we from entertainments, that are such
Professedly, to others titled higher,
Yet, in the estimate of youth at least,
More near akin to those than names imply,—
I mean the brawls of lawyers in their courts   490
Before the ermined judge, or that great stage
Where senators, tongue-favoured men, perform,
Admired and envied. Oh! the beating heart,
When one among the prime of these rose up,—
One, of whose name from childhood we had heard   495
Familiarly, a household term, like those,
The Bedfords, Glosters, Salisburys, of old
Whom the fifth Harry talks of.[4] Silence! hush!
This is no trifler, no short-flighted wit,
No stammerer of a minute, painfully   500
Delivered. No! the Orator hath yoked
The Hours, like young Aurora, to his car:
Thrice welcome Presence! how can patience e'er
Grow weary of attending on a track
That kindles with such glory![5] All are charmed,   505

The enchantment spreads and rises—all are rapt
Astonished—like a hero in romance
He winds away his never-ending horn:
Words follow words, sense seems to follow sense—   540
What memory and what logic!—till the strain
[510] Transcendent, superhuman as it is,
Grows tedious even in a young man's ear.

Astonished; like a hero in romance,
He winds away his never-ending horn;
Words follow words, sense seems to follow sense:
What memory and what logic! till the strain
Transcendent, superhuman, as it seemed,   510
Grows tedious even in a young man's ear.

    Genius of Burke![6] forgive the pen seduced
By specious wonders, and too slow to tell
Of what the ingenuous, what bewildered men,
Beginning to mistrust their boastful guides,   515
And wise men, willing to grow wiser, caught,
Rapt auditors! from thy most eloquent tongue—
Now mute, for ever mute in the cold grave.
I see him,—old, but vigorous in age,—
Stand like an oak whose stag-horn branches start   520
Out of its leafy brow, the more to awe
The younger brethren of the grove. But some—
While he forewarns, denounces, launches forth,
Against all systems built on abstract rights,
Keen ridicule; the majesty proclaims   525
Of Institutes and Laws, hallowed by time;
Declares the vital power of social ties
Endeared by Custom; and with high disdain,
Exploding upstart Theory, insists
Upon the allegiance to which men are born—   530
Some—say at once a froward multitude—
Murmur (for truth is hated, where not loved)
As the winds fret within the Æolian cave,
Galled by their monarch's chain.[7] The times were big
With ominous change, which, night by night, provoked   535
Keen struggles, and black clouds of passion raised;
But memorable moments intervened,
When Wisdom, like the Goddess from Jove's brain,
Broke forth in armour of resplendent words,
Startling the Synod.[8] Could a youth, and one   540
In ancient story versed, whose breast had heaved
Under the weight of classic eloquence,
Sit, see, and hear, unthankful, uninspired?

    Nor did the Pulpit's oratory fail
To achieve its higher triumph. Not unfelt   545

6. Lines 512–43 appear in their earliest form in 1832. They record an admiration certainly not felt by the younger, republican Wordsworth for Edmund Burke (1729–97), whose *Reflections on the Revolution in France* (1790) had been largely responsible for turning English political opinion against the Revolution.
7. Aeolus, classical god of winds, kept them chained in a cave.
8. Athena was said to have sprung fully armed from the head of Zeus, and was on occasion allegorized as Wisdom. "Synod": assembly; here, Parliament.

These are grave follies; other public shows
The capital city teems with of a kind   545
More light—and where but in the holy church?
[551] There have I seen a comely bachelor,
Fresh from a toilette of two hours, ascend
The pulpit, with seraphic glance look up,
And in a tone elaborately low   550
[555] Beginning, lead his voice through many a maze
A minuet course, and, winding up his mouth
From time to time into an orifice
Most delicate, a lurking eyelet, small
And only not invisible, again   555
[560] Open it out, diffusing thence a smile
Of rapt irradiation exquisite.[1]
Meanwhile the Evangelists, Isaiah, Job,
Moses, and he who penned the other day
The Death of Abel, Shakespear, Doctor Young,   560
And Ossian—doubt not, 'tis the naked truth—
Summoned from streamy Morven, each and all
Must in their turn lend ornament and flowers
[570] To entwine the crook of eloquence with which
This pretty shepherd, pride of all the plains,   565
Leads up and down his captivated flock.[2]

    I glance but at a few conspicuous marks,
Leaving ten thousand others that do each—
[575] In hall or court, conventicle,[3] or shop,
In public room or private, park or street—   570
With fondness reared on his own pedestal,[4]
Look out for admiration. Folly, vice,
Extravagance in gesture, mien and dress,
[580] And all the strife of singularity—
Lies to the ear, and lies to every sense—   575
Of these and of the living shapes they wear
There is no end. Such candidates for regard,
Although well pleased to be where they were found,
[585] I did not hunt after or greatly prize,
Nor made unto myself a secret boast   580

1. Wordsworth has in mind Cowper's satirical portrait of a self-consciously theatrical preacher, *The Task*, II, 430–54.
2. The parson's eloquence is seen in Wordsworth's metaphor as a shepherd's crook entwined with "flowers" culled from other men's writings. *The Death of Abel* (1805, 560; 1850, 564), source of Coleridge's *Wanderings of Cain* (1797), was written in 1758 by the German Solomon Gessner, and went through many English editions. Edward Young ("The Bard" of 1850, 564), wrote *Night Thoughts* (1742–45); the poem was immensely popular, and is footnoted in *Lyrical Ballads* as the source of *Tintern Abbey*, 107. "Morven" (1805, 562; 1850, 568) is Macpherson's name for the northwest coast of Scotland, over which Fingal rules in the spurious epics of "Ossian" (1762–63).
3. A place of worship for Protestant nonconformists.
4. I.e., raised on a pedestal by his self-love.

Were its admonishments, nor lightly heard
The awful truths delivered thence by tongues
Endowed with various power to search the soul;
Yet ostentation, domineering, oft
Poured forth harangues, how sadly out of place!—⁹ 550
There have I seen a comely bachelor,
Fresh from a toilette of two hours, ascend
His rostrum, with seraphic glance look up,
And, in a tone elaborately low
Beginning, lead his voice through many a maze 555
A minuet course; and, winding up his mouth,
From time to time, into an orifice
Most delicate, a lurking eyelet, small,
And only not invisible, again
Open it out, diffusing thence a smile 560
Of rapt irradiation, exquisite.¹
Meanwhile the Evangelists, Isaiah, Job,
Moses, and he who penned, the other day,
The Death of Abel, Shakespear, and the Bard
Whose genius spangled o'er a gloomy theme 565
With fancies thick as his inspiring stars,
And Ossian (doubt not, 'tis the naked truth)
Summoned from streamy Morven—each and all
Would, in their turns, lend ornaments and flowers
To entwine the crook of eloquence that helped 570
His pretty Shepherd, pride of all the plains,
To rule and guide his captivated flock.²

   I glance but at a few conspicuous marks,
Leaving a thousand others, that, in hall,
Court, theatre, conventicle,³ or shop, 575
In public room or private, park or street,
Each fondly reared on his own pedestal,⁴
Looked out for admiration. Folly, vice,
Extravagance in gesture, mien, and dress,
And all the strife of singularity, 580
Lies to the ear, and lies to every sense—
Of these, and of the living shapes they wear,
There is no end. Such candidates for regard,
Although well pleased to be where they were found,
I did not hunt after, nor greatly prize, 585
Nor made unto myself a secret boast

9. Lines 544–50 were inserted in *MS. D*, in 1838/39, to replace *1805*, lines 544–46, and to counterbalance the satirical por-trait of the church that follows in both texts.

Of reading them with quick and curious eye,
But as a common produce—things that are
Today, tomorrow will be—took of them
[590] Such willing note as, on some errand bound
Of pleasure or of love, some traveller might,   585
Among a thousand other images,
Of sea-shells that bestud the sandy beach,
Or daisies swarming through the fields in June.

But foolishness, and madness in parade,
[595] Though most at home in this their dear domain,   590
Are scattered everywhere, no rarities,
[597] Even to the rudest novice of the schools.
O friend, one feeling was there which belonged
To this great city by exclusive right:
[626] How often in the overflowing streets   595
Have I gone forwards with the crowd, and said
Unto myself, 'The face of every one
That passes by me is a mystery.'
[630] Thus have I looked, nor ceased to look, oppressed
By thoughts of what, and whither, when and how,   600
Until the shapes before my eyes became
A second-sight procession, such as glides
Over still mountains,[6] or appears in dreams,

6. See the Lake District tradition of spectral horsemen recorded by Wordsworth in
Evening Walk, 179–87.

Of reading them with quick and curious eye;
But, as a common produce, things that are
To-day, to-morrow will be, took of them
Such willing note, as, on some errand bound   590
That asks not speed, a traveller might bestow
On sea-shells that bestrew the sandy beach,
Or daisies swarming through the fields of June.

    But foolishness and madness in parade,
Though most at home in this their dear domain,   595
Are scattered everywhere, no rarities,
Even to the rudest novice of the Schools.
Me, rather it employed, to note, and keep
In memory, those individual sights
Of courage, or integrity, or truth,   600
Or tenderness, which there, set off by foil,
Appeared more touching. One will I select;
A Father—for he bore that sacred name—
Him saw I, sitting in an open square,
Upon a corner-stone of that low wall,   605
Wherein were fixed the iron pales that fenced
A spacious grass-plot; there, in silence, sate
This One Man, with a sickly babe outstretched
Upon his knee, whom he had thither brought
For sunshine, and to breathe the fresher air.   610
Of those who passed, and me who looked at him,
He took no heed; but in his brawny arms
(The Artificer was to the elbow bare,
And from his work this moment had been stolen)
He held the child, and, bending over it,   615
As if he were afraid both of the sun
And of the air, which he had come to seek,
Eyed the poor babe with love unutterable.

    As the black storm upon the mountain top
Sets off the sunbeam in the valley, so   620
That huge fermenting mass of human-kind
Serves as a solemn back-ground, or relief,
To single forms and objects, whence they draw,
For feeling and contemplative regard,
More than inherent liveliness and power.[5]   625
How oft, amid those overflowing streets,
Have I gone forward with the crowd, and said
Unto myself, 'The face of every one
That passes by me is a mystery!'

---

5. In their original form lines 598–618 are found at *1805*, VIII, 837–59; they were transferred, and 619–25 added, in Wordsworth's final revisions (1839 or later).

And all the ballast of familiar life—
The present, and the past, hope, fear, all stays,   605
All laws of acting, thinking, speaking man—
Went from me, neither knowing me, nor known.
[635] And once, far travelled in such mood, beyond
The reach of common indications, lost
Amid the moving pageant, 'twas my chance   610
Abruptly to be smitten with the view
Of a blind beggar, who, with upright face,
[640] Stood propped against a wall, upon his chest
Wearing a written paper, to explain
The story of the man, and who he was.   615
My mind did at this spectacle turn round
As with the might of waters, and it seemed
To me that in this label was a type
[645] Or emblem of the utmost that we know
Both of ourselves and of the universe,[7]   620
And on the shape of this unmoving man,
His fixèd face and sightless eyes, I looked,
As if admonished from another world.[8]

[650]   Though reared upon the base of outward things,
These chiefly are such structures as the mind   625
Builds for itself. Scenes different there are—
Full-formed—which take, with small internal help,
Possession of the faculties: the peace
[655] Of night, for instance, the solemnity
Of Nature's intermediate hours of rest   630
When the great tide of human life stands still,
The business of the day to come unborn,
Of that gone by locked up as in the grave;[9]
[660] The calmness, beauty, of the spectacle,
Sky, stillness, moonshine, empty streets, and sounds   635
Unfrequent as in desarts; at late hours
Of winter evenings when unwholesome rains
Are falling hard, with people yet astir,
[665] The feeble salutation from the voice
Of some unhappy woman now and then   640
Heard as we pass, when no one looks about,
Nothing is listened to. But these I fear
Are falsely catalogued: things that are, are not,

---

7. Wordsworth's original version of lines
617–20 is preserved in *MS. X*: "and I
thought / That even the very most of
what we know / Both of ourselves and of
the universe, / The whole of what is
written to our view, / Is but a label on
a blind man's chest."
8. Compare the Leech Gatherer of spring

1802, who was "like a man from some
far region sent / To give me human
strength by apt admonishment" (*Resolution and Independence*, 118–19).
9. For a comparable response to the
beauty of London in its moments of
calm, see *Sonnet Composed Upon Westminster Bridge*.

Thus have I looked, nor ceased to look, oppressed   630
By thoughts of what and whither, when and how,
Until the shapes before my eyes became
A second-sight procession, such as glides
Over still mountains, or appears in dreams;
And once, far-travelled in such mood, beyond   635
The reach of common indication, lost
Amid the moving pageant, I was smitten
Abruptly, with the view (a sight not rare)
Of a blind Beggar, who, with upright face,
Stood, propped against a wall, upon his chest   640
Wearing a written paper, to explain
His story, whence he came, and who he was.
Caught by the spectacle my mind turned round
As with the might of waters; an apt type
This label seemed of the utmost we can know,   645
Both of ourselves and of the universe;[7]
And, on the shape of that unmoving man,
His steadfast face and sightless eyes, I gazed,
As if admonished from another world.[8]

Though reared upon the base of outward things,   650
Structures like these the excited spirit mainly
Builds for herself; scenes different there are,
Full-formed, that take, with small internal help,
Possession of the faculties,—the peace
That comes with night; the deep solemnity   655
Of nature's intermediate hours of rest,
When the great tide of human life stands still;
The business of the day to come, unborn,
Of that gone by, locked up, as in the grave;[9]
The blended calmness of the heavens and earth,   660
Moonlight and stars, and empty streets, and sounds
Unfrequent as in deserts; at late hours
Of winter evenings, when unwholesome rains
Are falling hard, with people yet astir,
The feeble salutation from the voice   665
Of some unhappy woman, now and then
Heard as we pass, when no one looks about,
Nothing is listened to. But these, I fear,
Are falsely catalogued; things that are, are not,

[670] Even as we give them welcome, or assist— 645
Are prompt, or are remiss. What say you then
To times when half the city shall break out
Full of one passion—vengeance, rage, or fear—
To executions,[1] to a street on fire,
[675] Mobs, riots, or rejoicings? From those sights
Take one, an annual festival, the fair 650
Holden where martyrs suffered in past time,
And named of St Bartholomew,[2] there see
A work that's finished to our hands, that lays,
[680] If any spectacle on earth can do,
The whole creative powers of man asleep. 655
For once the Muse's help will we implore,
And she shall lodge us—wafted on her wings
Above the press and danger of the crowd—
[685] Upon some showman's platform. What a hell
For eyes and ears, what anarchy and din 660
Barbarian and infernal—'tis a dream
Monstrous in colour, motion, shape, sight, sound.
Below, the open space, through every nook
[690] Of the wide area, twinkles, is alive
With heads; the midway region and above 665
Is thronged with staring pictures and huge scrolls,
Dumb proclamations of the prodigies;
And chattering monkeys dangling from their poles,
[695] And children whirling in their roundabouts;[3]
With those that stretch the neck, and strain the eyes, 670
And crack the voice in rivalship, the crowd
Inviting; with buffoons against buffoons
Grimacing, writhing, screaming; him who grinds
[700] The hurdy-gurdy, at the fiddle weaves,
Rattles the salt-box,[4] thumps the kettle-drum, 675
And him who at the trumpet puffs his cheeks,
The silver-collared negro with his timbrel,[5]
Equestrians, tumblers, women, girls, and boys,
[705] Blue-breeched, pink-vested, and with towering plumes.
All moveables of wonder from all parts 680
Are here, albinos, painted Indians, dwarfs,
The horse of knowledge, and the learned pig,[6]

---

1. Public executions continued in England until 1868.
2. St. Bartholomew's Fair, largest of the London fairs, was held at Smithfield, where Protestant martyrs were burned in the reign of Queen Mary (1553–58). Wordsworth and Dorothy were taken to the fair by Charles Lamb in September 1802.
3. Merry-go-rounds.
4. "Hurdy-gurdy": originally a stringed instrument, resembling the lute or guitar, but "ground" by a rosined wheel turned by the left hand. "Salt-box": A wooden box containing salt, that was rattled or beaten; apparently in common use among street musicians.
5. Tambourine.
6. Horses were trained to answer numerical questions by stamping out the answers. "Toby the Sapient Pig," who was exhibited in London in 1817, could allegedly spell, read, cast accounts, and play cards, not to mention reading people's thoughts.

As the mind answers to them, or the heart   670
Is prompt, or slow, to feel. What say you, then,
To times, when half the city shall break out
Full of one passion, vengeance, rage, or fear?
To executions,[1] to a street on fire,
Mobs, riots, or rejoicings? From these sights   675
Take one,—that ancient festival, the Fair,
Holden where martyrs suffered in past time,
And named of St. Bartholomew;[2] there, see
A work completed to our hands, that lays,
If any spectacle on earth can do,   680
The whole creative powers of man asleep!—
For once, the Muse's help will we implore,
And she shall lodge us, wafted on her wings,
Above the press and danger of the crowd,
Upon some showman's platform. What a shock   685
For eyes and ears! what anarchy and din,
Barbarian and infernal,—a phantasma,
Monstrous in colour, motion, shape, sight, sound!
Below, the open space, through every nook
Of the wide area, twinkles, is alive   690
With heads; the midway region, and above,
Is thronged with staring pictures and huge scrolls,
Dumb proclamations of the Prodigies;
With chattering monkeys dangling from their poles,
And children whirling in their roundabouts;[3]   695
With those that stretch the neck and strain the eyes,
And crack the voice in rivalship, the crowd
Inviting; with buffoons against buffoons
Grimacing, writhing, screaming,—him who grinds
The hurdy-gurdy, at the fiddle weaves,   700
Rattles the salt-box,[4] thumps the kettle-drum,
And him who at the trumpet puffs his cheeks,
The silver-collared Negro with his timbrel,[5]
Equestrians, tumblers, women, girls, and boys,
Blue-breeched, pink-vested, with high-towering plumes.   705
All moveables of wonder, from all parts,
Are here—Albinos, painted Indians, Dwarfs,
The Horse of knowledge, and the learned Pig,[6]

The stone-eater, the man that swallows fire,
[710] Giants, ventriloquists, the invisible girl,
The bust that speaks and moves its goggling eyes,   685
The waxwork,[7] clockwork, all the marvellous craft
Of modern Merlins, wild beasts, puppet-shows,
All out-o'-th'-way, far-fetched, perverted things,
[715] All freaks of Nature, all Promethean thoughts
Of man[8]—his dulness, madness, and their feats,   690
All jumbled up together to make up
This parliament of monsters. Tents and booths
Meanwhile—as if the whole were one vast mill[9]—
[720] Are vomiting, receiving, on all sides,
Men, women, three-years' children, babes in arms.   695

    O, blank confusion, and a type not false
Of what the mighty city is itself
To all, except a straggler here and there—
To the whole swarm of its inhabitants—
An undistinguishable world to men,   700
The slaves unrespited[1] of low pursuits,
[725] Living amid the same perpetual flow
Of trivial objects, melted and reduced
To one identity by differences
That have no law, no meaning, and no end—   705
Oppression under which even highest minds
[730] Must labour, whence the strongest are not free.
But though the picture weary out the eye,
By nature an unmanageable sight,
It is not wholly so to him who looks   710
In steadiness, who hath among least things
[735] An under-sense of greatest, sees the parts
As parts, but with a feeling of the whole.
This, of all acquisitions first, awaits
On sundry and most widely different modes   715
Of education—nor with least delight
[740] On that through which I passed. Attention comes,
And comprehensiveness and memory,
From early converse with the works of God
Among all regions, chiefly where appear   720
[744] Most obviously simplicity and power.
By influence habitual to the mind

7. Madame Tussaud brought her collection of wax figures of the leaders and
victims of the French Revolution to London in 1802.
8. Wordsworth has in mind Milton's
Hell, where "nature breeds, / Perverse,
all monstrous, all prodigious things"
(*Paradise Lost*, II, 624–25). "Promethean": inventive; the Titan Prometheus,
in Greek myth, fashioned man out of clay.
9. Factory, as in Blake's "dark satanic
mills."
1. Pronounced "ŭnréspĭttéd": carrying
on with no respite—i.e., ceaselessly. Lines
701–5, with their disdain of city life,
were originally written for *Michael* in
1800; they persist until Wordsworth's
final revisions, in or after 1839.

The Stone-eater, the man that swallows fire,
Giants, Ventriloquists, the Invisible Girl,   710
The Bust that speaks and moves its goggling eyes,
The Wax-work,[7] Clock-work, all the marvellous craft
Of modern Merlins, Wild Beasts, Puppet-shows,
All out-o'-the-way, far-fetched, perverted things,
All freaks of nature, all Promethean thoughts   715
Of man,[8] his dullness, madness, and their feats
All jumbled up together, to compose
A Parliament of Monsters, Tents and Booths
Meanwhile, as if the whole were one vast mill,[9]
Are vomiting, receiving, on all sides,   720
Men, Women, three-years Children, Babes in arms.

    Oh, blank confusion! true epitome
Of what the mighty City is herself
To thousands upon thousands of her sons,
Living amid the same perpetual whirl   725
Of trivial objects, melted and reduced
To one identity, by differences
That have no law, no meaning, and no end—
Oppression, under which even highest minds
Must labour, whence the strongest are not free.   730
But though the picture weary out the eye,
By nature an unmanageable sight,
It is not wholly so to him who looks
In steadiness, who hath among least things
An under-sense of greatest; sees the parts   735
As parts, but with a feeling of the whole.
This, of all acquisitions first, awaits
On sundry and most widely different modes
Of education, nor with least delight
On that through which I passed. Attention springs,   740
And comprehensiveness and memory flow,
From early converse with the works of God
Among all regions;[2] chiefly where appear
Most obviously simplicity and power.
Reflect how everlasting streams and woods,   745

2. It is difficult to know whether the words "Amid the mountains" penciled by Wordsworth at the foot of the page in *E* (in or after 1839) should be regarded as a firm correction. However, it is interesting to know that in his old age Wordsworth really felt God to be most accessible to those who had shared his country upbringing.

The mountain's outline and its steady form
Gives a pure grandeur, and its presence shapes
[755] The measure and the prospect³ of the soul   725
To majesty: such virtue have the forms
Perennial of the ancient hills—nor less
The changeful language of their countenances
Gives movement to the thoughts, and multitude,
[761] With order and relation.⁴. This (if still,   730
As hitherto, with freedom I may speak,
And the same perfect openness of mind,
Not violating any just restraint,
As I would hope, of real modesty),
[765] This did I feel in that vast receptacle.   735
The spirit of Nature was upon me here,
The soul of beauty and enduring life
Was present as a habit, and diffused—
Through meagre lines and colours, and the press
[770] Of self-destroying, transitory things—   740
Composure and ennobling harmony.

---

3. I.e., the external forms of Nature have the power to shape the internal "measure" (dimension) and "prospect" (landscape) of the human soul.
4. Lines 722–30 are drawn from the conclusion of "In storm and tempest," the fragment of third-person narrative belonging to January/February 1798, of which the first twenty lines had already been incorporated in *The Prelude* as *1799*, II, 352–71 (*1805*, II, 322–41).

Stretched and still stretching far and wide, exalt
The roving Indian. On his desert sands
What grandeur not unfelt, what pregnant show
Of beauty, meets the sun-burnt Arab's eye:
And, as the sea propels, from zone to zone,   750
Its currents, magnifies its shoals of life
Beyond all compass spread, and sends aloft
Armies of clouds,—even so, its powers and aspects
Shape for mankind, by principles as fixed,
The views and aspirations of the soul   755
To majesty. Like virtue have the forms
Perennial of the ancient hills; nor less
The changeful language of their countenances
Quickens the slumbering mind, and aids the thoughts,
However multitudinous, to move   760
With order and relation. This, if still,
As hitherto, in freedom I may speak,
Not violating any just restraint,
As may be hoped, of real modesty,—
This did I feel, in London's vast domain.   765
The Spirit of Nature was upon me there;
The soul of Beauty and enduring Life
Vouchsafed her inspiration, and diffused,
Through meagre lines and colours, and the press
Of self-destroying, transitory things,   770
Composure, and ennobling Harmony.

Book Eighth

Retrospect: Love of Nature Leading to Love of Mankind

What sounds are those, Helvellyn, which are heard
Up to thy summit, through the depth of air
Ascending as if distance had the power
To make the sounds more audible? What crowd
[5] Is yon, assembled in the gay green field?   5
Crowd seems it, solitary hill, to thee,
Though but a little family of men—
Twice twenty—with their children and their wives,
[10] And here and there a stranger interspersed.
It is a summer festival, a fair,   10
Such as—on this side now, and now on that,
Repeated through his tributary vales—
Helvellyn, in the silence of his rest
[15] Sees annually, if storms be not abroad
And mists have left him an unshrouded head.[1]   15
Delightful day it is for all who dwell
In this secluded glen, and eagerly
[20] They give it welcome. Long ere heat of noon,
Behold the cattle are driven down; the sheep
That have for traffic been culled out are penned   20
In cotes that stand together on the plain
Ranged side by side; the chaffering[3] is begun;
The heifer lows uneasy at the voice
Of a new master; bleat the flocks aloud.
[25] Booths are there none: a stall or two is here,   25
A lame man, or a blind (the one to beg,
The other to make music); hither too
From far, with basket slung upon her arm
Of hawker's wares—books, pictures, combs, and pins—
[30] Some aged woman finds her way again,   30
Year after year a punctual visitant;
The showman with his freight upon his back,
And once perchance in lapse of many years,
[35] Prouder itinerant—mountebank,[5] or he
Whose wonders in a covered wain[6] lie hid.   35
But one is here, the loveliest of them all,
Some sweet lass of the valley, looking out
For gains—and who that sees her would not buy?

---

1. Helvellyn (3118 feet) is looking down
on Grasmere Fair, then held annually in
early September.
3. Bargaining. "Traffic" (*1805*, 20): sale.
5. Mountebank: a doctor that mounts a
bench in the market and boasts his infallible remedies and cures (Johnson's
Dictionary).
6. Wagon.

Book Eighth

Retrospect.—Love of Nature Leading
to Love of Man

WHAT sounds are those, Helvellyn, that are heard
Up to thy summit, through the depth of air
Ascending, as if distance had the power
To make the sounds more audible? What crowd
Covers, or sprinkles o'er, yon village green?   5
Crowd seems it, solitary hill! to thee,
Though but a little family of men,
Shepherds and tillers of the ground—betimes
Assembled with their children and their wives,
And here and there a stranger interspersed.   10
They hold a rustic fair—a festival,
Such as, on this side now, and now on that,
Repeated through his tributary vales,
Helvellyn, in the silence of his rest,
Sees annually, if clouds towards either ocean   15
Blown from their favourite resting-place, or mists
Dissolved, have left him an unshrouded head.[1]
Delightful day it is for all who dwell
In this secluded glen, and eagerly
They give it welcome. Long ere heat of noon,   20
From byre or field the kine[2] were brought; the sheep
Are penned in cotes; the chaffering[3] is begun.
The heifer lows, uneasy at the voice
Of a new master; bleat the flocks aloud.
Booths are there none; a stall or two is here;   25
A lame man or a blind, the one to beg,
The other to make music; hither, too,
From far, with basket, slung upon her arm,
Of hawker's wares—books, pictures, combs, and pins—
Some aged woman finds her way again,   30
Year after year a punctual visitant!
There also stands a speech-maker by rote,
Pulling the strings of his boxed raree-show;[4]
And in the lapse of many years may come
Prouder itinerant, mountebank,[5] or he   35
Whose wonders in a covered wain[6] lie hid.
But one there is, the loveliest of them all,
Some sweet lass of the valley, looking out
For gains, and who that sees her would not buy?

---

2. Cowshed; "kine": cattle.   4. Peep show.

[40] Fruits of her father's orchard, apples, pears
    (On that day only to such office[7] stooping),   40
    She carries in her basket, and walks round
    Among the crowd, half pleased with, half ashamed
    Of her new calling, blushing restlessly.
    The children now are rich, the old man now
[45] Is generous, so gaiety prevails   45
    Which all partake of, young and old.

                              Immense
[56] Is the recess, the circumambient world
    Magnificent, by which they are embraced.
    They move about upon the soft green field;
    How little they, they and their doings, seem,   50
    Their herds and flocks about them, they themselves,
[60] And all which they can further or obstruct—
    Through utter weakness pitiably dear,
    As tender infants are—and yet how great,
    For all things serve them: them the morning light   55
    Loves as it glistens on the silent rocks,
[65] And them the silent rocks, which now from high
    Look down upon them, the reposing clouds,
    The lurking brooks from their invisible haunts,
    And old Helvellyn, conscious of the stir,   60
    And the blue sky that roofs their calm abode.

[70]   With deep devotion, Nature, did I feel
    In that great city what I owed to thee:
    High thoughts of God and man, and love of man,
    Triumphant over all those loathsome sights   65
    Of wretchedness and vice, a watchful eye,
    Which, with the outside of our human life
    Not satisfied, must read the inner mind.
    For I already had been taught to love
    My fellow-beings, to such habits trained   70
    Among the woods and mountains, where I found
    In thee a gracious guide to lead me forth
    Beyond the bosom of my family,
    My friends and youthful playmates. 'Twas thy power[1]
    That raised the first complacency[2] in me,   75
[124] And noticeable kindliness of heart,

---

7. Task.
1. Though the bulk of Book VIII was composed in October 1804, before the writing of Book VII, lines 1–74 belong to the period of reorganization after VII had been completed. Wordsworth's account of Grasmere Fair thus forms a deliberate link between London's Bar-tholomew Fair (VII, 649–95) and the already existing studies of pastoral life in VIII. For details of the original opening of VIII, see Composition and Texts: *1805/1850*, Introduction, below.
2. Contentedness, satisfaction—without the modern pejorative overtones.

Fruits of her father's orchard, are *her* wares, 40
And with the ruddy produce, she walks round
Among the crowd, half pleased with, half ashamed
Of her new office,⁷ blushing restlessly.
The children now are rich, for the old to-day
Are generous as the young; and if content 45
With looking on, some ancient wedded pair
Sit in the shade together, while they gaze,
'A cheerful smile unbends the wrinkled brow,
The days departed start again to life,
And all the scenes of childhood reappear, 50
Faint, but more tranquil, like the changing sun
To him who slept at noon and wakes at eve.'
Thus gaiety and cheerfulness prevail,
Spreading from young to old, from old to young,
And no one seems to want his share.⁸—Immense 55
Is the recess, the circumambient world
Magnificent, by which they are embraced:
They move about upon the soft green turf:
How little they, they and their doings, seem,
And all that they can further or obstruct! 60
Through utter weakness pitiably dear,
As tender infants are: and yet how great!
For all things serve them: them the morning light
Loves, as it glistens on the silent rocks;
And them the silent rocks, which now from high 65
Look down upon them; the reposing clouds;
The wild brooks prattling from invisible haunts;
And old Helvellyn, conscious of the stir
Which animates this day their calm abode.

With deep devotion, Nature, did I feel 70
In that enormous City's turbulent world
Of men and things, what benefit I owed
To thee, and those domains of rural peace,⁹

---

8. Lines 45–55 were added in Words-worth's final revisions, in 1839 or later; he and his wife—the "ancient wedded pair" of line 46—were both born in 1770. Lines 48–52 are quoted from *Malvern Hills*, 952–56 (1798) by Joseph Cottle, publisher of *Lyrical Ballads*. Writing to Cottle in 1829, Wordsworth said that the poem had always been a favorite of his, and singled out the last of the quoted lines as "super-excellent" (*LY*, I, p. 349). "Want" (line 55): lack.
9. After many attempts at revision, Wordsworth cut *1805*, 64–119 in 1838/39.

Love human to the creature in himself
As he appeared, a stranger in my path,
Before my eyes a brother of this world—
Thou first didst with those motions of delight   80
Inspire me. I remember, far from home
Once having strayed while yet a very child,
I saw a sight—and with what joy and love!
It was a day of exhalations spread
Upon the mountains, mists and steam-like fogs   85
Redounding everywhere, not vehement,[3]
But calm and mild, gentle and beautiful,
With gleams of sunshine on the eyelet spots
And loopholes of the hills, wherever seen,
Hidden by quiet process,[4] and as soon   90
Unfolded, to be huddled up again—
Along a narrow valley and profound
I journeyed, when aloft above my head,
Emerging from the silvery vapours, lo,
A shepherd and his dog, in open day.   95
Girt round with mists they stood, and looked about
From that enclosure small, inhabitants
Of an aërial island floating on,
As seemed, with that abode in which they were,
A little pendant area of grey rocks,   100
By the soft wind breathed forward. With delight
As bland almost, one evening I beheld—
And at as early age (the spectacle
Is common, but by me was then first seen)—
A shepherd in the bottom of a vale,   105
Towards the centre standing, who with voice,
And hand waved to and fro as need required,
Gave signal to his dog, thus teaching him
To chace along the mazes of steep crags
The flock he could not see. And so the brute—   110
Dear creature—with a man's intelligence,
Advancing, or retreating on his steps,
Through every pervious strait,[5] to right or left,
Thridded a way unbaffled, while the flock
Fled upwards from the terror of his bark
Through rocks and seams of turf with liquid gold   115
Irradiate—that deep farewell light by which
The setting sun proclaims the love he bears
To mountain regions.[6]

---

3. Violent, perhaps "swirling." "Redounding": overflowing, eddying in abundance.
4. Change, flux.

5. A narrow place that allows a way through.
6. Lines 117–19 recollect the end of the Coniston episode, *1799*, II, 140–78.

Beauteous the domain
Where to the sense of beauty first my heart   120
[75] Was opened—tract more exquisitely fair
Than is that paradise of ten thousand trees,
Or Gehol's famous gardens,[7] in a clime
Chosen from widest empire, for delight
Of the Tartarian dynasty composed   125
Beyond that mighty wall, not fabulous
[80] (China's stupendous mound!)[8] by patient skill
Of myriads, and boon Nature's lavish help:
Scene linked to scene, and ever-growing change,
Soft, grand, or gay, with palaces and domes   130
[85] Of pleasure spangled over, shady dells
For eastern monasteries, sunny mounds
With temples crested, bridges, gondolas,
Rocks, dens, and groves of foliage, taught to melt
Into each other their obsequious[9] hues—   135
[90] Going and gone again, in subtile[1] chace,
Too fine to be pursued—or standing forth
In no discordant opposition, strong
And gorgeous as the colours side by side
Bedded among the plumes of tropic birds;   140
[95] And mountains over all, embracing all,
And all the landscape endlessly enriched
With waters running, falling, or asleep.
But lovelier far than this the paradise
Where I was reared, in Nature's primitive gifts   145
[100] Favored no less, and more to every sense
Delicious, seeing that the sun and sky,
The elements, and seasons in their change,
Do find their dearest fellow-labourer there
The heart of man—a district on all sides   150
The fragrance breathing of humanity,
Man free, man working for himself, with choice
[105] Of time, and place, and object; by his wants,
His comforts, native occupations, cares,
Conducted on to individual ends   155
Or social, and still followed by a train,[2]
Unwooed, unthought-of even: simplicity,
[110] And beauty, and inevitable grace.[3]

---

7. Pleasure gardens of the emperor at
Gehol, called in Chinese the "paradise
of innumerable trees"; described and illustrated in John Barrow's *Travels in
China* (May 1804).
8. I.e., the Great Wall of China.
"Mound": Anything raised to fortify or
defend; usually a bank of earth or stone
(Johnson's *Dictionary*).

9. Obedient, compliant.
1. Fine, delicate (an earlier—and still,
in 1800, quite common—spelling of
"subtle").
2. Succession.
3. For an important discussion of human
development, "We live by admiration,"
preserved at this point in *MS. Y*, see MS.
Drafts and Fragments, 4(a) below.

Where to the sense of beauty first my heart
Was opened; tract more exquisitely fair   75
Than that famed paradise of ten thousand trees,
Or Gehol's matchless gardens,[7] for delight
Of the Tartarian dynasty composed
(Beyond that mighty wall, not fabulous,
China's stupendous mound)[8] by patient toil   80
Of myriads and boon nature's lavish help;
There, in a clime from widest empire chosen,
Fulfilling (could enchantment have done more?)
A sumptuous dream of flowery lawns, with domes
Of pleasure sprinkled over, shady dells   85
For eastern monasteries, sunny mounts
With temples crested, bridges, gondolas,
Rocks, dens, and groves of foliage taught to melt
Into each other their obsequious[9] hues,
Vanished and vanishing in subtle chase,   90
Too fine to be pursued; or standing forth
In no discordant opposition, strong
And gorgeous as the colours side by side
Bedded among rich plumes of tropic birds;
And mountains over all, embracing all;   95
And all the landscape endlessly enriched
With waters running, falling, or asleep.

   But lovelier far than this, the paradise
Where I was reared; in Nature's primitive gifts
Favoured no less, and more to every sense   100
Delicious, seeing that the sun and sky,
The elements, and seasons as they change,
Do find a worthy fellow-labourer there—
Man free, man working for himself, with choice
Of time, and place, and object; by his wants,   105
His comforts, native occupations, cares,
Cheerfully led to individual ends
Or social, and still followed by a train[2]
Unwooed, unthought-of even—simplicity,
And beauty, and inevitable grace.[3]   110

Yea, doubtless, at an age when but a glimpse
Of those resplendent gardens, with their frame   160
Imperial, and elaborate ornaments,
Would to a child be transport over-great,
When but a half-hour's roam through such a place
Would leave behind a dance of images
[115] That shall break in upon his sleep for weeks,   165
Even then the common haunts of the green earth
With the ordinary human interests
Which they embosom—all without regard
As both may seem—are fastening on the heart
[120] Insensibly, each with the other's help,   170
So that we love, not knowing that we love,
And feel, not knowing whence our feeling comes.
Such league have these two principles of joy[4]
In our affections.[5] I have singled out
Some moments, the earliest that I could, in which   175
Their several currents, blended into one—
Weak yet, and gathering imperceptibly—
Flowed in by gushes. My first human love,
As hath been mentioned, did incline to those
Whose occupations and concerns were most   180
Illustrated by Nature, and adorned,
[128] And shepherds were the men who pleased me first:
Not such as, in Arcadian fastnesses
Sequestered, handed down among themselves,
So ancient poets sing, the golden age;[7]   185
Nor such—a second race, allied to these—
As Shakespeare in the wood of Arden placed,
[141] Where Phoebe sighed for the false Ganymede,
Or there where Florizel and Perdita
Together danced, Queen of the feast and King;   190
Nor such as Spenser fabled.[8] True it is
[145] That I had heard, what he perhaps had seen,
Of maids at sunrise bringing in from far
Their May-bush,[9] and along the streets in flocks
Parading, with a song of taunting rhymes   195
Aimed at the laggards slumbering within doors—
[150] Had also heard, from those who yet remembered,

4. The two "principles," or causes, of joy are "the common haunts of the green earth" (line 166) and "ordinary human interests" (line 167).
5. Emotions, feelings.
7. "Arcadian" (*1805*, 243; *1850*, 133); Arcadia is the traditional setting of Greek and Latin pastoral that looks back to a golden age of innocence and happiness.
8. Wordsworth stresses the unreality of Shakespeare's pastoral world: "the false Ganymede" of *As You Like It* is Rosa-

lind, daughter of the Duke, in male disguise, with whom the shepherdess Phoebe fell in love; Florizel and Perdita in *The Winter's Tale* are heirs to the thrones of Bohemia and Sicilia, as well as king and queen of the sheep-shearing feast. For Spenser's idealization of pastoral life, see especially "May" in *The Shepheard's Calendar*.
9. A branch of hawthorn, or may, used in the May Day festivities.

Yea, when a glimpse of those imperial bowers
Would to a child be transport over-great,
When but a half-hour's roam through such a place
Would leave behind a dance of images,
That shall break in upon his sleep for weeks;   115
Even then the common haunts of the green earth,
And ordinary interests of man,
Which they embosom, all without regard
As both may seem, are fastening on the heart
Insensibly, each with the other's help.   120
For me, when my affections[5] first were led
From kindred, friends, and playmates, to partake
Love for the human creature's absolute self,
That noticeable kindliness of heart
Sprang out of fountains, there abounding most   125
Where sovereign Nature dictated the tasks
And occupations which her beauty adorned,
And Shepherds were the men that pleased me first;
Not such as Saturn ruled 'mid Latian wilds,[6]
With arts and laws so tempered, that their lives   130
Left, even to us toiling in this late day,
A bright tradition of the golden age;
Not such as, 'mid Arcadian fastnesses
Sequestered, handed down among themselves
Felicity, in Grecian song renowned;[7]   135
Nor such as, when an adverse fate had driven,
From house and home, the courtly band whose fortunes
Entered, with Shakespeare's genius, the wild woods
Of Arden, amid sunshine or in shade,
Culled the best fruits of Time's uncounted hours,   140
Ere Phoebe sighed for the false Ganymede;
Or there where Perdita and Florizel
Together danced, Queen of the feast, and King;
Nor such as Spenser fabled.[8] True it is,
That I had heard (what he perhaps had seen)   145
Of maids at sunrise bringing in from far
Their May-bush,[9] and along the street in flocks
Parading with a song of taunting rhymes,
Aimed at the laggards slumbering within doors;
Had also heard, from those who yet remembered,   150

6. Traditionally, Saturn created the Golden Age in Latium (Italy) after being deposed by his son Jupiter; Latium was held to derive from *latio*, "to lie hid."

Tales of the maypole dance, and flowers that decked
The posts and the kirk-pillars,[1] and of youths,
That each one with his maid at break of day,   200
By annual custom, issued forth in troops
[155] To drink the waters of some favorite well,
And hang it round with garlands. This, alas,
Was but a dream: the times had scattered all
These lighter graces, and the rural ways   205
[160] And manners which it was my chance to see
In childhood were severe and unadorned,
The unluxuriant produce of a life
Intent on little but substantial[2] needs,
Yet beautiful—and beauty that was felt.   210
But images of danger and distress
And suffering, these took deepest hold of me,
[165] Man suffering among awful powers and forms:
Of this I heard and saw enough to make
The imagination restless—nor was free   215
Myself from frequent perils. Nor were tales
Wanting, the tragedies of former times,
[170] Or hazards and escapes, which in my walks
I carried with me among crags and woods
And mountains; and of these may here be told   220
One as recorded by my household dame.[3]

   'At the first falling of autumnal snow
A shepherd and his son one day went forth',
Thus did the matron's tale begin, 'to seek
A straggler of their flock. They both had ranged   225
Upon this service the preceding day
All over their own pastures and beyond,
And now, at sunrise sallying out again,
Renewed their search, begun where from Dove Crag—
Ill home for bird so gentle—they looked down   230
On Deepdale Head, and Brothers Water (named
From those two brothers that were drowned therein)
Thence, northward, having passed by Arthur's Seat,
To Fairfield's highest summit. On the right
Leaving St Sunday's Pike, to Grisedale Tarn   235
They shot, and over that cloud-loving hill,
Seat Sandal—a fond lover of the clouds—
Thence up Helvellyn, a superior mount

---

1. Kirk: church.
2. Essential.
3. Ann Tyson; see *1805*, IV, 20*n*, above.
The "Matron's Tale," told in lines 222–
311, was written originally for *Michael*
in October–December 1800. Wordsworth

made small cuts when incorporating the
material in *The Prelude* (October 1804),
and again when preparing the *1805* faircopy, but changed it in no essential.
The tale was cut in 1816/19.

Tales of the May-pole dance, and wreaths that decked
Porch, door-way, or kirk-pillar;[1] and of youths,
Each with his maid, before the sun was up,
By annual custom, issuing forth in troops,
To drink the waters of some sainted well,   155
And hang it round with garlands. Love survives;
But, for such purpose, flowers no longer grow:
The times, too sage, perhaps too proud, have dropped
These lighter graces; and the rural ways
And manners which my childhood looked upon   160
Were the unluxuriant produce of a life
Intent on little but substantial[2] needs,
Yet rich in beauty, beauty that was felt.
But images of danger and distress,
Man suffering among awful Powers and Forms;   165
Of this I heard and saw enough to make
Imagination restless; nor was free
Myself from frequent perils; nor were tales
Wanting,—the tragedies of former times,
Hazards and strange escapes, of which the rocks   170
Immutable and everflowing streams,
Where'er I roamed, were speaking monuments.

With prospect underneath of Striding Edge
And Grisedale's houseless vale, along the brink   240
Of Russet Cove, and those two other coves,
Huge skeletons of crags, which from the trunk
Of old Helvellyn spread their arms abroad
And make a stormy harbour for the winds.[4]
Far went those shepherds in their devious[5] quest,   245
From mountain ridges peeping as they passed
Down into every glen; at length the boy
Said, "Father, with your leave I will go back,
And range the ground which we have searched before."
So speaking, southward down the hill the lad   250
Sprang like a gust of wind, crying aloud,
"I know where I shall find him." 'For take note',
Said here my grey-haired dame, 'that though the storm
Drive one of these poor creatures miles and miles,
If he can crawl he will return again   255
To his own hills, the spots where when a lamb
He learnt to pasture at his mother's side.
After so long a labour suddenly
Bethinking him of this, the boy
Pursued his way towards a brook whose course   260
Was through that unfenced tract of mountain ground
Which to his father's little farm belonged,
The home and ancient birthright of their flock.
Down the deep channel of the stream he went,
Prying through every nook. Meanwhile the rain   265
Began to fall upon the mountain tops,
Thick storm and heavy which for three hours' space
Abated not, and all that time the boy
Was busy in his search, until at length
He spied the sheep upon a plot of grass,   270
An island in the brook. It was a place
Remote and deep, piled round with rocks, where foot
Of man or beast was seldom used to tread;
But now, when everywhere the summer grass
Had failed, this one adventurer, hunger-pressed,   275
Had left his fellows, and made his way alone
To the green plot of pasture in the brook.
Before the boy knew well what he had seen,
He leapt upon the island with proud heart
And with a prophet's joy. Immediately   280
The sheep sprang forward to the further shore
And was borne headlong by the roaring flood—
At this the boy looked round him, and his heart

---

4. The mountains and lakes referred to in lines 229–44 are a little to the north and east of Grasmere. "Cove" (line 241): a sheltered recess formed by the hills.
5. Roving; as at line 347 below.

Fainted with fear. Thrice did he turn his face
To either brink, nor could he summon up   285
The courage that was needful to leap back
Cross the tempestuous torrent: so he stood,
A prisoner on the island, not without
More than one thought of death and his last hour.
Meanwhile the father had returned alone   290
To his own house; and now at the approach
Of evening he went forth to meet his son,
Conjecturing vainly for what cause the boy
Had stayed so long. The shepherd took his way
Up his own mountain grounds, where, as he walked   295
Along the steep that overhung the brook
He seemed to hear a voice, which was again
Repeated, like the whistling of a kite.[6]
At this, not knowing why, as oftentimes
Long afterwards he has been heard to say,   300
Down to the brook he went, and tracked its course
Upwards among the o'erhanging rocks—nor thus
Had he gone far, ere he espied the boy,
Where on that little plot of ground he stood
Right in the middle of the roaring stream,   305
Now stronger every moment and more fierce.
The sight was such as no one could have seen
Without distress and fear. The shepherd heard
The outcry of his son, he stretched his staff
Towards him, bade him leap—which word scarce said,   310
The boy was safe within his father's arms.'

    Smooth life had flock and shepherd in old time,
Long springs and tepid winters on the banks
[175] Of delicate Galesus—and no less
Those scattered along Adria's myrtle shores—   315
Smooth life the herdsman and his snow-white herd,
To triumphs and to sacrificial rites
Devoted, on the inviolable stream
[180] Of rich Clitumnus; and the goatherd lived
As sweetly underneath the pleasant brows   320
Of cool Lucretilis, where the pipe was heard
Of Pan, the invisible God, thrilling the rocks
With tutelary music, from all harm
[185] The fold protecting.[7] I myself, mature

6. Bird of prey, related to the falcon.
7. In *1805*, 312–24 (*1850*, 173–85) Wordsworth shows his love and knowledge of Latin poetry, especially that of Virgil and Horace. Galesus and Clitumnus are rivers in Calabria; the second, according to Virgil (*Georgics*, II, 146–8), was so pure that it whitened the herds feeding on its banks, thus making them fit for sacrifice. Adria is the Adriatic coast of Italy, and Lucretilis the Latin name for Monte Gennaro, the hill above Horace's Sabine farm, mentioned in connection with Pan (Faunus) in Horace's *Odes*, I, xvii, 1–2. "Thrilling": piercing. "Tutelary music": music produced by Pan as guardian deity. "Fold": sheepfold, enclosure for sheep.

Smooth life had flock and shepherd in old time,
Long springs and tepid waters, on the banks
Of delicate Galesus; and no less   175
Those scattered along Adria's myrtle shores:
Smooth life had herdsman, and his snow-white herd
To triumphs and to sacrificial rites
Devoted, on the inviolable stream
Of rich Clitumnus; and the goat-herd lived   180
As calmly, underneath the pleasant brows
Of cool Lucretilis, where the pipe was heard
Of Pan, invisible God, thrilling the rocks
With tutelary music, from all harm
The fold protecting.[7] I myself, mature   185

In manhood then, have seen a pastoral tract   325
Like one of these, where fancy might run wild,
Though under skies less generous and serene;
Yet there, as for herself, had Nature framed
[190] A pleasure-ground, diffused a fair expanse
Of level pasture, islanded with groves   330
And banked with woody risings—but the plain
Endless, here opening widely out, and there
Shut up in lesser lakes or beds of lawn
[195] And intricate recesses, creek or bay
Sheltered within a shelter, where at large   335
The shepherd strays, a rolling hut[8] his home:
Thither he comes with springtime, there abides
All summer, and at sunrise ye may hear
[200] His flute or flagelet[9] resounding far.
There's not a nook or hold of that vast space,   340
Nor strait where passage is, but it shall have
In turn its visitant, telling there his hours
[205] In unlaborious pleasure, with no task
More toilsome than to carve a beechen bowl
For spring or fountain, which the traveller finds,   345
When through the region he pursues at will
His devious course.[1]

                    A glimpse of such sweet life
[210] I saw when, from the melancholy walls
Of Goslar, once imperial, I renewed
My daily walk along that chearful plain,   350
Which, reaching to her gates, spreads east and west
And northwards, from beneath the mountainous verge
[215] Of the Hercynian forest.[2] Yet hail to you,
Your rocks and precipices, ye that seize
The heart with firmer grasp, your snows and streams   355
[220] Ungovernable, and your terrifying winds,
That howled so dismally when I have been
Companionless among your solitudes!
There, 'tis the shepherd's task the winter long
To wait upon the storms: of their approach   360
[225] Sagacious, from the height he drives his flock

---

8. A small hut on wheels, used to enable the shepherd to stay near his flock, especially during lambing time.
9. A kind of recorder, or pipe.
1. *1805*, 324–47 (*1850*, 185–209) apparently recall the scenery encountered by Wordsworth and Dorothy in Germany after leaving the city of Goslar on February 23, 1799 (see 353*n*, below). For seven weeks, between January 27 and ca. April 20, their movements are unknown.
2. *1805*, 347–53 (*1850*, 209–15) have been thought to identify the city walls referred to in the Preamble (*1805*, I, 7, above). It is not clear whether Wordsworth intended his readers to make such a connection, but the experience of being cooped up in Goslar during the winter of 1798–99 certainly contributed to his composite image of the city as a place of bondage. "Once imperial": Goslar had been the seat of Otto I (912–73), crowned emperor of the Franks in 962. "Hercynian": Hartz.

In manhood then, have seen a pastoral tract
Like one of these, where Fancy might run wild,
Though under skies less generous, less serene:
There, for her own delight had Nature framed
A pleasure-ground, diffused a fair expanse   190
Of level pasture, islanded with groves
And banked with woody risings; but the Plain
Endless, here opening widely out, and there
Shut up in lesser lakes or beds of lawn
And intricate recesses, creek or bay   195
Sheltered within a shelter, where at large
The shepherd strays, a rolling hut[8] his home.
Thither he comes with spring-time, there abides
All summer, and at sunrise ye may hear
His flageolet[9] to liquid notes of love   200
Attuned, or sprightly fife resounding far.
Nook is there none, nor tract of that vast space
Where passage opens, but the same shall have
In turn its visitant, telling there his hours
In unlaborious pleasure, with no task   205
More toilsome than to carve a beechen bowl
For spring or fountain, which the traveller finds,
When through the region he pursues at will
His devious course.[1] A glimpse of such sweet life
I saw when, from the melancholy walls   210
Of Goslar, once imperial, I renewed
My daily walk along that wide champaign,
That, reaching to her gates, spreads east and west,
And northwards, from beneath the mountainous verge
Of the Hercynian forest.[2] Yet, hail to you   215
Moors, mountains, headlands, and ye hollow vales,
Ye long deep channels for the Atlantic's voice,
Powers of my native region! Ye that seize
The heart with firmer grasp! Your snows and streams
Ungovernable, and your terrifying winds,   220
That howl so dismally for him who treads
Companionless your awful solitudes!
There, 'tis the shepherd's task the winter long
To wait upon the storms: of their approach
Sagacious, into sheltering coves he drives   225

Down into sheltering coves, and feeds them there
Through the hard time, long as the storm is 'locked'
(So do they phrase it), bearing from the stalls
A toilsome burthen up the craggy ways   365
To strew it on the snow. And when the spring
[230] Looks out, and all the mountains dance with lambs,
He through the enclosures won from the steep waste,
And through the lower heights hath gone his rounds;
And when the flock with warmer weather climbs   370
Higher and higher, him his office leads
To range among them through the hills dispersed,
And watch their goings, whatsoever track
Each wanderer chuses for itself—a work
That lasts the summer through. He quits his home   375
[235] At dayspring, and no sooner doth the sun
Begin to strike him with a fire-like heat,
Than he lies down upon some shining place,
And breakfasts with his dog. When he hath stayed—
As for the most he doth—beyond this time,   380
He springs up with a bound, and then away!
Ascending fast with his long pole in hand,
Or winding in and out among the crags.
[250] What need to follow him through what he does
Or sees in his day's march? He feels himself   385
In those vast regions where his service is
A freeman, wedded to his life of hope
And hazard, and hard labour interchanged
[255] With that majestic indolence so dear
To native man.[5]   390

              A rambling schoolboy, thus
Have I beheld him; without knowing why,
Have felt his presence in his own domain
As of a lord and master, or a power,
Or genius, under Nature, under God,
[260] Presiding—and severest solitude   395
Seemed more commanding oft when he was there.
Seeking the raven's nest and suddenly
Surprized with vapours, or on rainy days
When I have angled up the lonely brooks,
[265] Mine eyes have glanced upon him, few steps off,   400
In size a giant, stalking through the fog,[6]
His sheep like Greenland bears. At other times,

5. To human nature.
6. Wordsworth has in mind Thomson's *Seasons*, III, 725–27, where, because of the mist, "Seen through the turbid air, beyond the life / Objects appear, and, wildered, o'er the waste / The shepherd stalks gigantic * * *" The echo is strengthened in *1850*, 264, "By mists bewildered" (added 1816/19).

His flock, and thither from the homestead bears
A toilsome burden up the craggy ways,
And deals it out, their regular nourishment
Strewn on the frozen snow. And when the spring   230
Looks out, and all the pastures dance with lambs,
And when the flock, with warmer weather, climbs
Higher and higher, him his office leads
To watch their goings, whatsoever track
The wanderers choose. For this he quits his home   235
At day-spring, and no sooner doth the sun
Begin to strike him with a fire-like heat,
Than he lies down upon some shining rock,
And breakfasts with his dog. When they have stolen,
As is their wont, a pittance from strict time,   240
For rest not needed or exchange of love,
Then from his couch he starts; and now his feet
Crush out a livelier fragrance from the flowers
Of lowly thyme, by Nature's skill enwrought
In the wild turf: the lingering dews of morn
Smoke round him, as from hill to hill he hies,   245
His staff portending[3] like a hunter's spear,
Or by its aid leaping from crag to crag,
And o'er the brawling beds of unbridged streams.
Philosophy, methinks, at Fancy's call,
Might deign to follow him through what he does   250
Or sees in his day's march,[4] himself he feels,
In those vast regions where his service lies,
A freeman, wedded to his life of hope
And hazard, and hard labour interchanged
With that majestic indolence so dear   255
To native man.[5] A rambling school-boy, thus
I felt his presence in his own domain,
As of a lord and master, or a power,
Or genius, under Nature, under God,
Presiding; and severest solitude   260
Had more commanding looks when he was there.
When up the lonely brooks on rainy days
Angling I went, or trod the trackless hills
By mists bewildered, suddenly mine eyes
Have glanced upon him distant a few steps,   265
In size a giant, stalking through thick fog,[6]
His sheep like Greenland bears; or, as he stepped

3. Stretching out.
4. Lines 238–51 are gratuitous poetic elaboration that goes back to ca. January 1807, though Wordsworth's final text is reached by successive revisions.

When round some shady promontory turning,[7]
His form hath flashed upon me glorified
[270] By the deep radiance of the setting sun;   405
Or him have I descried in distant sky,
A solitary object and sublime,
Above all height, like an aërial cross,
As it is stationed on some spiry rock
[275] Of the Chartreuse, for worship.[8] Thus was man   410
Ennobled outwardly before mine eyes,
And thus my heart at first was introduced
To an unconscious love and reverence
Of human nature; hence the human form
[280] To me was like an index of delight,   415
Of grace and honour, power and worthiness.
Meanwhile, this creature—spiritual almost
As those of books, but more exalted far,
Far more of an imaginative form—
[285] Was not a Corin of the groves, who lives   420
For his own fancies, or to dance by the hour
In coronal, with Phyllis in the midst,[9]
But, for the purposes of kind,[1] a man
With the most common—husband, father—learned,
[290] Could teach, admonish, suffered with the rest   425
From vice and folly, wretchedness and fear.
Of this I little saw, cared less for it,
But something must have felt.

                       Call ye these appearances
Which I beheld of shepherds in my youth,
[295] This sanctity of Nature given to man,   430
A shadow, a delusion?—ye who are fed
By the dead letter, not the spirit of things,
Whose truth is not a motion or a shape
Instinct with vital functions, but a block
[300] Or waxen image which yourselves have made,   435
And ye adore. But blessèd be the God
Of Nature and of man that this was so,
That men did at the first present themselves
Before my untaught eyes thus purified,
[305] Removed, and at a distance that was fit.   440
And so we all of us in some degree
Are led to knowledge, whencesoever led,
And howsoever—were it otherwise,
And we found evil fast as we find good

---

7. The schoolboy, not the shepherd, is
turning.
8. See *1850*, VI, 480–85 and note, above.
9. Corin and Phyllis are chosen as typical names from pastoral poetry. "Coronal": here a ring formed by the danc-
ers.
1. I.e., "by nature."

Beyond the boundary line of some hill-shadow,
His form hath flashed upon me, glorified
By the deep radiance of the setting sun: 270
Or him have I descried in distant sky,
A solitary object and sublime,
Above all height! like an aerial cross
Stationed alone upon a spiry rock
Of the Chartreuse, for worship.[8] Thus was man   275
Ennobled outwardly before my sight,
And thus my heart was early introduced
To an unconscious love and reverence
Of human nature; hence the human form
To me became an index of delight,   280
Of grace and honour, power and worthiness.
Meanwhile this creature—spiritual almost
As those of books, but more exalted far;
Far more of an imaginative form
Than the gay Corin of the groves, who lives   285
For his own fancies, or to dance by the hour,
In coronal, with Phyllis in the midst[9]—
Was, for the purposes of kind,[1] a man
With the most common; husband, father; learned,
Could teach, admonish; suffered with the rest   290
From vice and folly, wretchedness and fear;
Of this I little saw, cared less for it,
But something must have felt.

                                Call ye these appearances—
Which I beheld of shepherds in my youth,
This sanctity of Nature given to man—   295
A shadow, a delusion, ye who pore
On the dead letter, miss the spirit of things;
Whose truth is not a motion or a shape
Instinct with vital functions, but a block
Or waxen image which yourselves have made,   300
And ye adore! But blessed be the God
Of Nature and of Man that this was so;
That men before my inexperienced eyes
Did first present themselves thus purified,
Removed, and to a distance that was fit: 305
And so we all of us in some degree
Are led to knowledge, whencesoever led,
And howsoever; were it otherwise,
And we found evil fast as we find good

[310] In our first years, or think that it is found,   445
How could the innocent heart bear up and live?
But doubly fortunate my lot: not here
Alone, that something of a better life
Perhaps was round me than it is the privilege
[315] Of most to move in, but that first I looked   450
At man through objects that were great and fair,
First communed with him by their help. And thus
Was founded a sure safeguard and defence
Against the weight of meanness, selfish cares,
[320] Coarse manners, vulgar passions, that beat in   455
On all sides from the ordinary world
In which we traffic. Starting from this point,
I had my face towards the truth, began
With an advantage, furnished with that kind
[325] Of prepossession without which the soul   460
Receives no knowledge that can bring forth good—
No genuine insight ever comes to her—
[330] Happy in this, that I with Nature walked,
Not having a too early intercourse
With the deformities of crowded life,   465
And those ensuing laughters and contempts
Self-pleasing, which if we would wish to think
[335] With admiration and respect of man
Will not permit us, but pursue the mind
That to devotion willingly would be raised,   470
Into the temple and the temple's heart.[2]

[340]   Yet do not deem, my friend, though thus I speak
Of man as having taken in my mind
A place thus early which might almost seem
Preeminent, that this was really so.   475
Nature herself was at this unripe time
But secondary to my own pursuits
And animal activities, and all
[345] Their trivial pleasures. And long afterwards
When those had died away, and Nature did   480
For her own sake become my joy, even then,
And upwards through late youth until not less
Than three-and-twenty summers had been told,
[350] Was man in my affections and regards
Subordinate to her,[3] her awful forms   485

2. Probably a metaphor for the inner-most, sacred, recesses of the mind itself—though it might be those of Nature.
3. In tracing his own development Wordsworth's purpose is seldom to establish biographical fact; see his inept apology in 1805, 472–75. Here, however, he is in broad agreement with the most reliable of his time schemes, that pre-sented in *Tintern Abbey*, where the "music of humanity" becomes audible at some point after his first visit, aged twenty-three, to the river Wye. The reading of 1850, "two-and-twenty summers," shifts the time back to take account of Beaupuy's humanizing influence in 1792; see especially 1805, IX, 511–34 below.

In our first years, or think that it is found, 310
How could the innocent heart bear up and live!
But doubly fortunate my lot; not here
Alone, that something of a better life
Perhaps was round me than it is the privilege
Of most to move in, but that first I looked 315
At Man through objects that were great or fair;
First communed with him by their help. And thus
Was founded a sure safeguard and defence
Against the weight of meanness, selfish cares,
Coarse manners, vulgar passions, that beat in 320
On all sides from the ordinary world
In which we traffic. Starting from this point
I had my face turned toward the truth, began
With an advantage furnished by that kind
Of prepossession, without which the soul 325
Receives no knowledge that can bring forth good,
No genuine insight ever comes to her.
From the restraint of over-watchful eyes
Preserved, I moved about, year after year,
Happy, and now most thankful that my walk 330
Was guarded from too early intercourse
With the deformities of crowded life,
And those ensuing laughters and contempts,
Self-pleasing, which, if we would wish to think
With a due reverence on earth's rightful lord, 335
Here placed to be the inheritor of heaven,
Will not permit us; but pursue the mind,
That to devotion willingly would rise,
Into the temple and the temple's heart.[2]

Yet deem not, Friend! that human kind with me 340
Thus early took a place pre-eminent;
Nature herself was, at this unripe time,
But secondary to my own pursuits
And animal activities, and all
Their trivial pleasures; and when these had drooped 345
And gradually expired, and Nature, prized
For her own sake, became my joy, even then—
And upwards through late youth, until not less
Than two-and-twenty summers had been told—
Was Man in my affections and regards 350
Subordinate to her,[3] her visible forms

And viewless[4] agencies—a passion, she,
A rapture often, and immediate joy
Ever at hand: he distant, but a grace
[355] Occasional, and accidental thought,
His hour being not yet come. Far less had then   490
The inferior creatures, beast or bird, attuned
My spirit to that gentleness of love,
[360] Won from me those minute obeisances
Of tenderness which I may number now
With my first blessings. Nevertheless, on these   495
The light of beauty did not fall in vain,
[364] Or grandeur circumfuse them to no end.[5]

Why should I speak of tillers of the soil?—
The ploughman and his team; or men and boys
In festive summer busy with the rake,   500
Old men and ruddy maids, and little ones
All out together, and in sun and shade
Dispersed among the hay-grounds alder-fringed;
The quarryman, far heard, that blasts the rock;
The fishermen in pairs, the one to row,   505
And one to drop the net, plying their trade
' 'Mid tossing lakes and tumbling boats' and winds
Whistling; the miner, melancholy man,
That works by taper-light, while all the hills
Are shining with the glory of the day.[6]   510

[365] But when that first poetic faculty
Of plain imagination and severe—
No longer a mute influence of the soul,
An element of the nature's inner self—
Began to have some promptings to put on   515
A visible shape, and to the works of art,
[370] The notions and the images of books,
Did knowingly conform itself (by these
Enflamed, and proud of that her new delight),
There came among these shapes of human life   520
A wilfulness of fancy and conceit
Which gave them new importance to the mind[7]—
And Nature and her objects beautified
[375] These fictions, as, in some sort, in their turn

4. Invisible. "Awful": awe-inspiring.
5. For a passage, "Whether the whistling kite," deleted in *MS. Y* at this point, see MS. Drafts and Fragments, 4(b), below.
6. Lines 498–510 were cut in 1832. The quotation in line 507 is from "I'll never love thee more," by James Graham, first Marquis of Montrose (1612–50), which Wordsworth probably read in James Watson's *A Choice Collection of Comic and Serious Scots Poems*, 3 Parts (1706–11), Part III, p. 111. "Whistling wind" (cf. lines 507–8) occurs two lines earlier in Montrose's poem.
7. For the role of the willful fancy, as opposed to the unifying imagination, see *1805*, 586n, below.

And viewless[4] agencies: a passion, she,
A rapture often, and immediate love
Ever at hand; *he*, only a delight
Occasional, an accidental grace,   355
His hour being not yet come. Far less had then
The inferior creatures, beast or bird, attuned
My spirit to that gentleness of love
(Though they had long been carefully observed),   360
Won from me those minute obeisances
Of tenderness, which I may number now
With my first blessings. Nevertheless, on these
The light of beauty did not fall in vain,
Or grandeur circumfuse them to no end.

                                                                    365
  But when that first poetic faculty
Of plain Imagination and severe,
No longer a mute influence of the soul,
Ventured, at some rash Muse's earnest call,
To try her strength among harmonious words;   370
And to book-notions and the rules of art
Did knowingly conform itself; there came
Among the simple shapes of human life
A wilfulness of fancy and conceit;[7]
And Nature and her objects beautified   375
These fictions, as in some sort, in their turn,

They burnished her. From touch of this new power   525
Nothing was safe: the elder-tree that grew
Beside the well-known charnel-house[8] had then
A dismal look, the yew-tree had its ghost
[380] That took its station there for ornament.
    Then common death was none, common mishap,   530
But matter for this humour everywhere,
The tragic super-tragic, else left short.[9]
Then, if a widow staggering with the blow
[385] Of her distress was known to have made her way
To the cold grave in which her husband slept,   535
One night, or haply more than one—through pain
Or half-insensate impotence of mind—
The fact was caught at greedily, and there
[390] She was a visitant the whole year through,
Wetting the turf with never-ending tears,   540
And all the storms of heaven must beat on her.

    Through wild obliquities could I pursue
Among all objects of the fields and groves
These cravings: when the foxglove, one by one,
Upwards through every stage of its tall stem   545
[395] Had shed its bells, and stood by the wayside
Dismantled, with a single one perhaps
Left at the ladder's top, with which the plant
Appeared to stoop, as slender blades of grass
Tipped with a bead of rain or dew, behold,   550
If such a sight were seen, would fancy bring
Some vagrant thither with her babes and seat her
Upon the turf beneath the stately flower,
Drooping in sympathy and making so
A melancholy crest above the head   555
Of the lorn creature, while her little ones,
All unconcerned with her unhappy plight,
[405] Were sporting with the purple cups that lay
Scattered upon the ground.[1] There was a copse,
An upright bank of wood and woody rock   560
That opposite our rural dwelling stood,
In which a sparkling patch of diamond light
Was in bright weather duly to be seen
On summer afternoons, within the wood
At the same place. 'Twas doubtless nothing more   565
Than a black rock, which, wet with constant springs,

---

8. The place where bones were piled when graves were reused.
9. I.e., "the tragic *was* super tragic"—it had to be, or it didn't satisfy.
1. Compare the super-tragic episode of the woman and her babes of *Evening Walk*, 239–300. The juxtaposition in line 556 of the poeticism "lorn" (forlorn) and "creature" (as indulgently applied to a woman) has deliberate sentimental associations.

They burnished her. From touch of this new power
Nothing was safe: the elder-tree that grew
Beside the well-known charnel-house[8] had then
A dismal look: the yew-tree had its ghost,
That took his station there for ornament: 380
The dignities of plain occurrence then
Were tasteless, and truth's golden mean, a point
Where no sufficient pleasure could be found.
Then, if a widow, staggering with the blow
Of her distress, was known to have turned her steps   385
To the cold grave in which her husband slept,
One night, or haply more than one, through pain
Or half-insensate impotence of mind,
The fact was caught at greedily, and there
She must be visitant the whole year through,   390
Wetting the turf with never-ending tears.

    Through quaint obliquities I might pursue
These cravings; when the fox-glove, one by one,
Upwards through every stage of the tall stem,
Had shed beside the public way its bells,   395
And stood of all dismantled, save the last
Left at the tapering ladder's top, that seemed
To bend as doth a slender blade of grass
Tipped with a rain-drop, Fancy loved to seat,
Beneath the plant despoiled, but crested still   400
With this last relic, soon itself to fall,
Some vagrant mother, whose arch little ones,
All unconcerned by her dejected plight,
Laughed as with rival eagerness their hands
Gathered the purple cups that round them lay,   405
Strewing the turf's green slope.

               A diamond light
(Whene'er the summer sun, declining, smote
A smooth rock wet with constant springs) was seen
Sparkling from out a copse-clad bank that rose

Glistered far seen from out its lurking-place
As soon as ever the declining sun
[410] Had smitten it. Beside our cottage hearth
Sitting with open door, a hundred times 570
Upon this lustre have I gazed, that seemed
To have some meaning which I could not find—
And now it was a burnished shield, I fancied,
[415] Suspended over a knight's tomb, who lay
Inglorious, buried in the dusky wood; 575
An entrance now into some magic cave,
Or palace for a fairy of the rock.
Nor would I, though not certain whence the cause
Of the effulgence, thither have repaired
Without a precious bribe, and day by day 580
And month by month I saw the spectacle,
[420] Nor ever once have visited the spot
Unto this hour. Thus sometimes were the shapes
Of wilful fancy grafted upon feelings
Of the imagination, and they rose 585
In worth accordingly.²

          My present theme
Is to retrace the way that led me on
Through Nature to the love of human-kind;
Nor could I with such object overlook
The influence of this power which turned itself 590
[425] Instinctively to human passions, things
Least understood—of this adulterate power,
For so it may be called, and without wrong,
When with that first compared.³ Yet in the midst
Of these vagaries, with an eye so rich 595
As mine was—through the chance, on me not wasted,
Of having been brought up in such a grand
And lovely region—I had forms distinct
[430] To steady me. These thoughts did oft revolve
About some centre palpable, which at once 600
Incited them to motion, and controlled,⁴
And whatsoever shape the fit might take,
And whencesoever it might come, I still

---

2. The imagination, in Wordsworth's horticultural image, is the root stock on which fancies have been grafted. The two faculties had been defined and opposed in his note to *The Thorn* in *Lyrical Ballads* (1800), and again in a Coleridge letter of September 1802 (Griggs, II, pp. 865–66), imagination being presented in each case as constructive in its perception of unity, whereas the fancy is capricious, yoking together ideas and objects essentially dissimilar.

3. Fancy, though "adulterate" by comparison with the purity of imagination (because of its improper yoking of dissimilar elements) is important as an influence (lines 590–91) because of its connection with human emotion.

4. Thus in *1805*, 559–86 (*1850*, 406–23) fancies are incited by the glistening black rock, and also controlled, because it remains a rock.

Fronting our cottage. Oft beside the hearth   410
Seated, with open door, often and long
Upon this restless lustre have I gazed,
That made my fancy restless as itself.
'Twas now for me a burnished silver shield
Suspended over a knight's tomb, who lay   415
Inglorious, buried in the dusky wood:
An entrance now into some magic cave
Or palace built by fairies of the rock;
Nor could I have been bribed to disenchant
The spectacle, by visiting the spot.   420
Thus wilful Fancy, in no hurtful mood,
Engrafted far-fetched shapes on feelings bred
By pure Imagination:² busy Power
She was, and with her ready pupil turned
Instinctively to human passions, then   425
Least understood. Yet, 'mid the fervent swarm
Of these vagaries, with an eye so rich
As mine was through the bounty of a grand
And lovely region, I had forms distinct
To steady me: each airy thought revolved   430
Round a substantial centre, which at once
Incited it to motion, and controlled.⁴

At all times had a real solid world
Of images about me,[5] did not pine   605
As one in cities bred might do—as thou,
Beloved friend, hast told me that thou didst,
[435] Great spirit as thou art—in endless dreams
Of sickness, disjoining, joining things,
Without the light of knowledge. Where the harm   610
If when the woodman languished with disease
From sleeping night by night among the woods
[440] Within his sod-built cabin, Indian-wise,
I called the pangs of disappointed love
And all the long etcetera of such thought   615
To help him to his grave?—meanwhile the man,
If not already from the woods retired
[445] To die at home, was haply, as I knew,
Pining alone among the gentle airs,
Birds, running streams, and hills so beautiful   620
On golden evenings, while the charcoal-pile
Breathed up its smoke, an image of his ghost
[450] Or spirit that was soon to take its flight.

5. Wordsworth is steadied by a world that is solid, objective, but of course subjectively perceived ("images" being landscape as it appears to the beholder, or as —at a secondary stage—it is stored up within the memory).

I did not pine like one in cities bred,
As was thy melancholy lot, dear Friend!
Great Spirit as thou art, in endless dreams   435
Of sickliness, disjoining, joining, things
Without the light of knowledge. Where the harm,
If, when the woodman languished with disease
Induced by sleeping nightly on the ground
Within his sod-built cabin, Indian-wise,   440
I called the pangs of disappointed love,
And all the sad etcetera of the wrong,
To help him to his grave. Meanwhile the man,
If not already from the woods retired
To die at home, was haply, as I knew,   445
Withering by slow degrees, 'mid gentle airs,
Birds, running streams, and hills so beautiful
On golden evenings, while the charcoal pile
Breathed up its smoke, an image of his ghost
Or spirit that full soon must take her flight.   450
Nor shall we not be tending towards that point
Of sound humanity to which our Tale
Leads, though by sinuous ways, if here I shew
How Fancy, in a season when she wove
Those slender cords, to guide the unconscious Boy   455
For the Man's sake, could feed at Nature's call
Some pensive musings which might well beseem
Maturer years.

       A grove there is whose boughs
Stretch from the western marge of Thurston-mere,[6]
With length of shade so thick, that whoso glides   460
Along the line of low-roofed water, moves
As in a cloister. Once—while, in that shade
Loitering, I watched the golden beams of light
Flung from the setting sun, as they reposed
In silent beauty on the naked ridge   465
Of a high eastern hill—thus flowed my thoughts
In a pure stream of words fresh from the heart;
'Dear native Region, wheresoe'er shall close
My mortal course, there will I think on you;
Dying, will cast on you a backward look;   470
Even as this setting sun (albeit the Vale
Is no where touched by one memorial gleam)
Doth with the fond remains of his last power
Still linger, and a farewell lustre sheds
On the dear mountain-tops where first he rose.'[7]   475

6. Coniston Water.
7. Lines 458–75 are a shortened version of *1799*, II, 140–74, without the central section (145–56). The episode had been omitted in *1805*.

There came a time of greater dignity,
Which had been gradually prepared, and now   625
Rushed in as if on wings—the time in which
[480] The pulse of being everywhere was felt,
When all the several frames of things, like stars
Through every magnitude distinguishable,
Were half confounded in each other's blaze,   630
[485] One galaxy of life and joy. Then rose
Man, inwardly contemplated, and present
In my own being, to a loftier height—
As of all visible natures crown, and first
In capability of feeling what   635
Was to be felt, in being rapt away
[491] By the divine effect of power and love—
As, more than any thing we know, instinct
With godhead, and by reason and by will
Acknowledging dependency sublime.⁹   640

[495]   Erelong, transported hence as in a dream,
I found myself begirt with temporal shapes
Of vice and folly thrust upon my view,
Objects of sport and ridicule and scorn,
Manners and characters discriminate,   645
[500] And little busy passions that eclipsed,
As well they might, the impersonated thought,
The idea or abstraction of the kind.¹
An idler among academic bowers,
Such was my new condition—as at large   650
[505] Hath been set forth²—yet here the vulgar light
Of present, actual, superficial life,
Gleaming through colouring of other times,
Old usages and local privilege,
Thereby was softened, almost solemnized,   655
And rendered apt and pleasing to the view.
[510] This notwithstanding, being brought more near
As I was now to guilt and wretchedness,
I trembled, thought of human life at times
With an indefinite terror and dismay,   660
Such as the storms and angry elements
[515] Had bred in me; but gloomier far, a dim
Analogy to uproar and misrule,
Disquiet, danger, and obscurity.

---

9. Man, though "instinct" (imbued) with
the presence of God, acknowledges dependence upon Him—as, for instance, in
Tintern Abbey. In so doing, he demonstrates both "reason in her most exalted
mood" (equated in *1805*, XIII, 166–70
with imagination), and the conscious

will.
1. The idealized vision of mankind ("impersonated thought"), that Wordsworth
had formed unchallenged by experience,
is now eclipsed by living examples
("temporal shapes") of vice and folly.
2. In Book III.

   Enough of humble arguments; recal,
My Song! those high emotions which thy voice
Has heretofore made known; that bursting forth
Of sympathy, inspiring and inspired,
When everywhere a vital pulse was felt,   480
And all the several frames of things, like stars,
Through every magnitude distinguishable,
Shone mutually indebted, or half lost
Each in the other's blaze, a galaxy
Of life and glory. In the midst stood Man,   485
Outwardly, inwardly contemplated,
As, of all visible natures, crown, though born
Of dust, and kindred to the worm,[8] a Being,
Both in perception and discernment, first
In every capability of rapture,   490
Through the divine effect of power and love;
As, more than anything we know, instinct
With godhead, and, by reason and by will,
Acknowledging dependency sublime.[9]

   Ere long, the lonely mountains left, I moved,   495
Begirt, from day to day, with temporal shapes
Of vice and folly thrust upon my view,
Objects of sport, and ridicule, and scorn,
Manners and characters discriminate,
And little bustling passions that eclipsed,   500
As well they might, the impersonated thought,
The idea, or abstraction of the kind.[1]

   An idler among academic bowers,
Such was my new condition, as at large
Has been set forth;[2] yet here the vulgar light   505
Of present, actual, superficial life,
Gleaming through colouring of other times,
Old usages and local privilege,
Was welcome, softened, if not solemnised.
This notwithstanding, being brought more near   510
To vice and guilt, forerunning wretchedness,
I trembled,—thought, at times, of human life
With an indefinite terror and dismay,
Such as the storms and angry elements
Had bred in me; but gloomier far, a dim   515
Analogy to uproar and misrule,
Disquiet, danger, and obscurity.

---

8. One of the most extreme of the Christian revisions of *The Prelude*, introduced in 1838/39.

It might be told (but wherefore speak of things   665
Common to all?) that, seeing, I essayed
To give relief, began to deem myself
[520] A moral agent, judging between good
And evil not as for the mind's delight
But for her safety, one who was to *act*—   670
As sometimes to the best of my weak means
I did, by human sympathy impelled,
[525] And through dislike and most offensive pain
Was to the truth conducted—of this faith
Never forsaken, that by acting well,   675
And understanding, I should learn to love
The end³ of life and every thing we know.

[530]   Preceptress stern, that didst instruct me next,
London, to thee I willingly return.
Erewhile my verse played only with the flowers   680
Enwrought upon thy mantle,⁴ satisfied
[535] With this amusement, and a simple look
Of childlike inquisition now and then
Cast upwards on thine eye to puzzle out
[538] Some inner meanings which might harbour there.   685
Yet did I not give way to this light mood
Wholly beguiled, as one incapable
Of higher things, and ignorant that high things
Were round me. Never shall I forget the hour,
The moment rather say, when, having thridded   690
The labyrinth of suburban villages,
At length I did unto myself first seem
To enter the great city. On the roof
Of an itinerant vehicle I sate,
[545] With vulgar men about me, vulgar forms   695
Of houses, pavement, streets, of men and things,
Mean shapes on every side; but, at the time,
When to myself it fairly might be said
(The very moment that I seemed to know)
'The threshold now is overpast', great God!   700
[550] That aught *external* to the living mind
Should have such mighty sway, yet so it was:
A weight of ages did at once descend
Upon my heart—no thought embodied, no
Distinct remembrans, but weight and power,   705
[555] Power growing with the weight. Alas, I feel
That I am trifling. 'Twas a moment's pause:
All that took place within me came and went

---

3. Purpose, intention.   "mantle hairy * * * Inwrought with fig-
4. A reminiscence of *Lycidas*, 104–5,   ures dim." "Mantle": cloak or covering.
where Camus—the river Cam—has a

It might be told (but whereof speak of things
Common to all?) that, seeing, I was led
Gravely to ponder—judging between good   520
And evil, not as for the mind's delight
But for her guidance—one who was to *act*,
As sometimes to the best of feeble means
I did, by human sympathy impelled:
And, through dislike and most offensive pain,   525
Was to the truth conducted; of this faith
Never forsaken, that, by acting well,
And understanding, I should learn to love
The end³ of life, and every thing we know.

Grave Teacher, stern Preceptress! for at times   530
Thou canst put on an aspect most severe;
London, to thee I willingly return.
Erewhile my verse played idly with the flowers
Enwrought upon thy mantle;⁴ satisfied
With that amusement, and a simple look   535
Of child-like inquisition now and then
Cast upwards on thy countenance, to detect
Some inner meanings which might harbour there.
But how could I in mood so light indulge,
Keeping such fresh remembrance of the day,   540
When, having thridded the long labyrinth
Of the suburban villages, I first
Entered thy vast dominion? On the roof
Of an itinerant vehicle I sate,
With vulgar men about me, trivial forms   545
Of houses, pavement, streets, of men and things,—
Mean shapes on every side: but, at the instant,
When to myself it fairly might be said,
The threshold now is overpast (how strange
That aught external to the living mind   550
Should have such mighty sway! yet so it was),
A weight of ages did at once descend
Upon my heart; no thought embodied, no
Distinct remembrances, but weight and power,—
Power growing under weight: alas! I feel   555
That I am trifling; 'twas a moment's pause,—
All that took place within me came and went

As in a moment, and I only now
Remember that it was a thing divine.   710

[560]   As when a traveller hath from open day
With torches passed into some vault of earth,
The grotto of Antiparos, or the den
Of Yordas among Craven's mountain tracts,[5]
He looks and sees the cavern spread and grow,   715
[565] Widening itself on all sides, sees, or thinks
He sees,[6] erelong, the roof above his head,
Which instantly unsettles and recedes—
Substance and shadow, light and darkness, all
Commingled, making up a canopy   720
[570] Of shapes, and forms, and tendencies to shape,
That shift and vanish, change and interchange
Like spectres—ferment quiet and sublime,
Which, after a short space, works less and less
Till, every effort, every motion gone,   725
[575] The scene before him lies in perfect view
Exposed, and lifeless as a written book.[7]
But let him pause awhile and look again,
And a new quickening shall succeed, at first
Beginning timidly, then creeping fast   730
[580] Through all which he beholds: the senseless mass,
In its projections, wrinkles, cavities,
Through all its surface, with all colours streaming,
Like a magician's airy pageant, parts,
Unites, embodying everywhere some pressure[8]   735
Or image, recognised or new, some type
Or picture of the world—forests and lakes,
[585] Ships, rivers, towers, the warrior clad in mail,
The prancing steed, the pilgrim with his staff,
The mitred bishop and the thronèd king—   740
A spectacle to which there is no end.

[590]   No otherwise had I at first been moved—
With such a swell of feeling, followed soon
By a blank sense of greatness passed away—
And afterwards continued to be moved,   745

5. The grotto on the Aegean island of
Antiparos was, according to the *Encyclopaedia Britannica* (3rd ed., 1797), 120
yards wide and 60 high, and "accounted
one of the greatest natural curiosities in
the world." Yordas is an impressive,
though very much smaller, limestone cave
near Ingleton in northwest Yorkshire,
visited by Wordsworth and his brother
John in May 1800 (*EY*, p. 298).
6. "Sees, or thinks / He sees": from Virgil's *Aeneid*, VI, 454, "*Aut videt, aut*

vidisse putat," copied by Milton, *Paradise Lost*, I, 783–84.
7. Lines 711–27 were drafted late in
March 1804, in an attempt to define
Wordsworth's sense of anticlimax at having unknowingly crossed the Alps in
August 1790 (VI, 511–24). In this original position they precede drafts of the
lines upon imagination (VI, 525–48).
8. Impression, an image that has been
stamped onto a surface.

As in a moment; yet with Time it dwells,
And grateful memory, as a thing divine.

   The curious traveller, who, from open day,   560
Hath passed with torches into some huge cave,
The Grotto of Antiparos, or the Den
In old time haunted by that Danish Witch,
Yordas;[5] he looks around and sees the vault
Widening on all sides; sees, or thinks he sees,[6]   565
Erelong, the massy roof above his head,
That instantly unsettles and recedes,—
Substance and shadow, light and darkness, all
Commingled, making up a canopy
Of shapes and forms and tendencies to shape   570
That shift and vanish, change and interchange
Like spectres,—ferment silent and sublime!
That after a short space works less and less,
Till, every effort, every motion gone,
The scene before him stands in perfect view   575
Exposed, and lifeless as a written book!—
But let him pause awhile, and look again,
And a new quickening shall succeed, at first
Beginning timidly, then creeping fast,
Till the whole cave, so late a senseless mass,   580
Busies the eye with images and forms
Boldly assembled,—here is shadowed forth
From the projections, wrinkles, cavities,
A variegated landscape,—there the shape
Of some gigantic warrior clad in mail,   585
The ghostly semblance of a hooded monk,
Veiled nun, or pilgrim resting on his staff:
Strange congregation! yet not slow to meet
Eyes that perceive through minds that can inspire.

   Even in such sort had I at first been moved,   590
Nor otherwise continued to be moved,

In presence of that vast metropolis,
The fountain of my country's destiny
And of the destiny of earth itself,
That great emporium,⁹ chronicle at once
[595] And burial-place of passions, and their home   750
Imperial, and chief living residence.
With strong sensations teeming as it did
Of past and present, such a place must needs
Have pleased me in those times. I sought not then
[600] Knowledge, but craved for power—and power I found   755
In all things. Nothing had a circumscribed
And narrow influence; but all objects, being
[605] Themselves capacious, also found in me
Capaciousness and amplitude of mind—
Such is the strength and glory of our youth.   760
The human nature unto which I felt
That I belonged, and which I loved and reverenced,
[610] Was not a punctual presence,¹ but a spirit
Living in time and space, and far diffused.
In this my joy, in this my dignity   765
Consisted: the external universe,
By striking upon what is found within,
Had given me this conception, with the help
[616] Of books and what they picture and record.

        'Tis true the history of my native land,   770
With those of Greece compared and popular Rome—
Events not lovely nor magnanimous,
But harsh and unaffecting in themselves;
And in our high-wrought modern narratives
[620] Stript of their humanizing soul, the life   775
Of manners and familiar incidents—
Had never much delighted me.³ And less
Than other minds I had been used to owe
The pleasure which I found in place or thing
To extrinsic transitory accidents,   780
[625] To records or traditions; but a sense
Of what had been here done, and suffered here
Through ages, and was doing, suffering, still,
Weighed with me, could support the test of thought—
[631] Was like the enduring majesty and power   785

---

9. A major center of commerce, a market.
1. I.e., one restricted to a precise moment and place; compare *Paradise Lost*, VIII, 23.
3. I.e., English history (lines 770–77) had never much delighted Wordsworth (a) because it consisted of events which by comparison with those of Greece and republican ("popular") Rome were not high-principled ("magnanimous"—literally, great of mind); and (b) because events had been stripped by historians of their "humanizing soul"—i.e., reference to ordinary human life.

As I explored the vast metropolis,
Fount of my country's destiny and the world's;
That great emporium,[9] chronicle at once
And burial-place of passions, and their home   595
Imperial, their chief living residence.

With strong sensations teeming as it did
Of past and present, such a place must needs
Have pleased me, seeking knowledge at that time
Far less than craving power; yet knowledge came,   600
Sought or unsought, and influxes of power
Came, of themselves, or at her call derived
In fits of kindliest apprehensiveness,
From all sides, when whate'er was in itself
Capacious found, or seemed to find, in me   605
A correspondent amplitude of mind;
Such is the strength and glory of our youth!
The human nature unto which I felt
That I belonged, and reverenced with love,
Was not a punctual presence,[1] but a spirit   610
Diffused through time and space, with aid derived
Of evidence from monuments, erect,
Prostrate, or leaning towards their common rest
In earth, the widely scattered wreck sublime
Of vanished nations, or more clearly drawn   615
From books and what they picture and record.[2]

'Tis true, the history of our native land,
With those of Greece compared and popular Rome,
And in our high-wrought modern narratives
Stript of their harmonising soul,[4] the life   620
Of manners and familiar incidents,
Had never much delighted me. And less
Than other intellects had mine been used
To lean upon extrinsic circumstance
Of record or tradition; but a sense   625
Of what in the Great City had been done
And suffered, and was doing, suffering, still,
Weighed with me, could support the test of thought;
And, in despite of all that had gone by,
Or was departing never to return,   630
There I conversed with majesty and power

2. Lines 611–16 are introduced in a revision of 1838/39. The reference in 612–
13 is to megalithic circles of standing
stones; compare the reference inserted
at *1850*, II, 101–2, above, to the stone
circle at Swinside, west of Duddon
Bridge.

4. The cutting of *1805*, lines 772–73
makes the plural pronoun "their" in line
620 ungrammatical. "Harmonising" in the
same line is a return in *MS. C* (1816/19)
to the original reading of *A* and *B*, "humanizing" (*1805*, 775) being an early
and short-lived correction.

Of independent nature. And not seldom
Even individual remembrances,
By working on the shapes before my eyes,
Became like vital functions of the soul;
And out of what had been, what was, the place   790
Was thronged with impregnations, like those wilds
In which my early feelings had been nursed,
[635] And naked valleys full of caverns, rocks,
And audible seclusions, dashing lakes,
Echoes and waterfalls, and pointed crags   795
[638] That into music touch the passing wind.

    Thus here imagination also found
An element that pleased her, tried her strength
Among new objects, simplified, arranged,
Impregnated my knowledge, made it live—   800
And the result was elevating thoughts
[645] Of human nature. Neither guilt nor vice,
Debasement of the body or the mind,
Nor all the misery forced upon my sight,
Which was not lightly passed, but often scanned   805
Most feelingly, could overthrow my trust
[650] In what we may become, induce belief
That I was ignorant, had been falsely taught,
A solitary, who with vain conceits
Had been inspired, and walked about in dreams.[5]   810
When from that rueful prospect, overcast
And in eclipse, my meditations turned,
[655] Lo, every thing that was indeed divine
Retained its purity inviolate
And unencroached upon, nay, seemed brighter far   815
For this deep shade in counterview, the gloom
Of opposition, such as shewed itself
To the eyes of Adam, yet in Paradise
[660] Though fallen from bliss, when in the East he saw
Darkness ere day's mid course, and morning light   820
More orient in the western cloud, that drew
'O'er the blue firmament a radiant white,
Descending slow with something heavenly fraught.'[6]

[665]   Add also, that among the multitudes
Of that great city oftentimes was seen   825
Affectingly set forth, more than elsewhere
Is possible, the unity of man,
One spirit over ignorance and vice

---

5. A restatement of *Tintern Abbey*, 125–
36, with reference to human, rather than
external, nature.
6. Not just the last two lines (as implied by Wordsworth's quotation marks

in *1805*) but the three previous lines as
well, draw almost verbatim on *Paradise
Lost*, XI, 203–7. "Orient": bright, as
from the rising sun. "Fraught": burdened,
loaded.

Like independent natures. Hence the place
Was thronged with impregnations like the *Wilds*
In which my early feelings had been nursed—
Bare hills and valleys, full of caverns, rocks,   635
And audible seclusions, dashing lakes,
Echoes and waterfalls, and pointed crags
That into music touch the passing wind.
Here then my young imagination found
No uncongenial element; could here   640
Among new objects serve or give command,
Even as the heart's occasions might require,
To forward reason's else too scrupulous march.
The effect was, still more elevated views   645
Of human nature. Neither vice nor guilt,
Debasement undergone by body or mind,
Nor all the misery forced upon my sight,
Misery not lightly passed, but sometimes scanned
Most feelingly, could overthrow my trust   650
In what we *may* become; induce belief
That I was ignorant, had been falsely taught,
A solitary, who with vain conceits
Had been inspired, and walked about in dreams.[5]
From those sad scenes when meditation turned,
Lo! every thing that was indeed divine   655
Retained its purity inviolate,
Nay brighter shone, by this portentous gloom
Set off; such opposition as aroused
The mind of Adam, yet in Paradise
Though fallen from bliss, when in the East he saw   660
Darkness ere day's mid course, and morning light
More orient in the western cloud, that drew
O'er the blue firmament a radiant white,
Descending slow with something heavenly fraught.[6]

   Add also, that among the multitudes   665
Of that huge city, oftentimes was seen
Affectingly set forth, more than elsewhere
Is possible, the unity of man,
One spirit over ignorance and vice

[670] Predominant, in good and evil hearts
    One sense for moral judgments, as one eye   830
    For the sun's light. When strongly breathed upon
    By this sensation—whencesoe'er it comes,
    Of union or communion—doth the soul
    Rejoice as in her highest joy; for there,
    There chiefly, hath she feeling whence she is,   835
[675] And passing through all Nature rests with God.

     And is not, too, that vast abiding-place
    Of human creatures, turn where'er we may,
    Profusely sown with individual sights
[VII, 600] Of courage, and integrity, and truth,   840
    And tenderness, which, here set off by foil,
[VII, 602] Appears more touching?[7] In the tender scenes
    Chiefly was my delight, and one of these
    Never will be forgotten. 'Twas a man,
    Whom I saw sitting in an open square   845
    Close to the iron paling that fenced in
    The spacious grass-plot: on the corner-stone
    Of the low wall in which the pales were fixed
    Sate this one man, and with a sickly babe
    Upon his knee, whom he had thither brought   850
[VII, 610] For sunshine, and to breathe the fresher air.
    Of those who passed, and me who looked at him,
    He took no note; but in his brawny arms
    (The artificer was to the elbow bare,
    And from his work this moment had been stolen)   855
[VII, 615] He held the child, and, bending over it
    As if he were afraid both of the sun
    And of the air which he had come to seek,
    He eyed it with unutterable love.

[676]   Thus from a very early age, O friend,   860
    My thoughts had been attracted more and more
    By slow gradations towards human-kind,
    And to the good and ill of human life.
    Nature had led me on, and now I seemed
[681] To travel independent of her help,   865
    As if I had forgotten her—but no,
    My fellow-beings still were unto me
    Far less than she was: though the scale of love
[685] Were filling fast, 'twas light as yet compared
    With that in which her mighty objects lay.[9]   870

7. The rarity of tenderness in London makes it conspicuous (sets it off by foil), but these lines nevertheless offer a view of the city that comes as a surprise after the satire of disunity in Book VII. It should be remembered that VIII was the first of the two Books to be written.
9. A draft of lines 860–70 preserved in MS. W may well date from ca. January 1804—earlier than the material in the notebook written for the five-Book *Prelude.*

Predominant, in good and evil hearts;   670
One sense for moral judgments, as one eye
For the sun's light. The soul when smitten thus
By a sublime *idea*, whencesoe'er
Vouchsafed for union or communion, feeds
On the pure bliss, and takes her rest with God.   675

    Thus from a very early age, O Friend!
My thoughts by slow gradations had been drawn
To human-kind, and to the good and ill
Of human life: Nature had led me on;
And oft amid the 'busy hum'[8] I seemed   680
To travel independent of her help,
As if I had forgotten her; but no,
The world of human-kind outweighed not hers
In my habitual thoughts; the scale of love,
Though filling daily, still was light, compared   685
With that in which *her* mighty objects lay.

---

8. An allusion to Milton's *L'Allegro*, 117–18: "Towered cities please us then / And
the busy hum of men."

Book Ninth

Residence in France

As oftentimes a river, it might seem,
Yielding in part to old remembrances,
Part swayed by fear to tread an onward road
That leads direct to the devouring sea,
[5] Turns and will measure back his course—far back,   5
Towards the very regions which he crossed
In his first outset—so have we long time
Made motions retrograde, in like pursuit
Detained.[1] But now we start afresh: I feel
An impulse to precipitate[2] my verse.   10
Fair greetings to this shapeless eagerness,
[20] Whene'er it comes, needful in work so long,
Thrice needful to the argument[4] which now
Awaits us—oh, how much unlike the past—
One which though bright the promise, will be found   15
Ere far we shall advance, ungenial, hard
To treat of, and forbidding in itself.

    Free as a colt at pasture on the hills
I ranged at large through the metropolis
[25] Month after month. Obscurely did I live,   20
Not courting the society of men,
By literature, or elegance, or rank,
Distinguished—in the midst of things, it seemed,
Looking as from a distance on the world
That moved about me. Yet insensibly   25
False preconceptions were corrected thus,
And errors of the fancy rectified
(Alike with reference to men and things),
And sometimes from each quarter were poured in
Novel imaginations and profound.   30
A year thus spent,[5] this field, with small regret—
[32] Save only for the bookstalls in the streets
(Wild produce, hedgerow fruit, on all sides hung
To lure the sauntering traveller from his track)—
I quitted, and betook myself to France,   35
Led thither chiefly by a personal wish
To speak the language more familiarly,

---

1. The river is recurrent in *The Prelude* as a symbol both of the poet's mind, and of the form assumed by the poem itself in tracing the progress of that mind— see especially, *1799*, II, 247–49, and the final retrospect, XIII, 171–84.

2. Hasten.
4. Theme.
5. Wordsworth in fact spent only four months in London at this early period, January–May 1791.

Book Ninth

Residence in France

EVEN as a river,—partly (it might seem)
Yielding to old remembrances, and swayed
In part by fear to shape a way direct,
That would engulph him soon in the ravenous sea—
Turns, and will measure back his course, far back,   5
Seeking the very regions which he crossed
In his first outset; so have we, my Friend!
Turned and returned with intricate delay.[1]
Or as a traveller, who has gained the brow
Of some aerial Down, while there he halts   10
For breathing-time, is tempted to review
The region left behind him; and, if aught
Deserving notice have escaped regard,
Or been regarded with too careless eye,
Strives, from that height, with one and yet one more   15
Last look, to make the best amends he may:
So have we lingered.[3] Now we start afresh
With courage, and new hope risen on our toil.
Fair greetings to this shapeless eagerness,
Whene'er it comes! needful in work so long,   20
Thrice needful to the argument[4] which now
Awaits us! Oh, how much unlike the past!

Free as a colt at pasture on the hill,
I ranged at large, through London's wide domain,
Month after month. Obscurely did I live,   25
Not seeking frequent intercourse with men,
By literature, or elegance, or rank,
Distinguished. Scarcely was a year thus spent[5]
Ere I forsook the crowded solitude,
With less regret for its luxurious pomp,   30
And all the nicely-guarded shows of art,
Than for the humble book-stalls in the streets,
Exposed to eye and hand where'er I turned.

France lured me forth; the realm that I had crossed
So lately, journeying toward the snow-clad Alps.   35
But now, relinquishing the scrip and staff,
And all enjoyment which the summer sun
Sheds round the steps of those who meet the day

3. The image of the backward-looking traveler in lines 9–17 is introduced in 1832.

With which intent I chose for my abode
[41] A city on the borders of the Loire.[6]

Through Paris lay my readiest path, and there   40
I sojourned a few days, and visited
In haste each spot of old and recent fame—
[45] The latter chiefly—from the field of Mars
Down to the suburbs of St Anthony,
And from Mont Martyr southward to the Dome   45
Of Geneviève.[7] In both her clamorous halls,
The National Synod and the Jacobins,
[50] I saw the revolutionary power
Toss like a ship at anchor, rocked by storms;[8]
The Arcades I traversed in the Palace huge   50
Of Orleans,[9] coasted round and round the line
Of tavern, brothel, gaming-house, and shop,
[55] Great rendezvous of worst and best, the walk
Of all who had a purpose, or had not;
I stared and listened with a stranger's ears,   55
To hawkers and haranguers, hubbub wild,[1]
And hissing factionists with ardent eyes,
[60] In knots, or pairs, or single, ant-like swarms
Of builders and subverters, every face
That hope or apprehension could put on—   60
Joy, anger, and vexation, in the midst
[66] Of gaiety and dissolute idleness.

Where silent zephyrs sported with the dust
Of the Bastile[2] I sate in the open sun

6. Orleans, which he reached December 6, 1791, and where almost certainly he met Annette Vallon (see *1805*, 555n, below), to whose home town of Blois he moved early in the new year. He had probably come to France chiefly to avoid family discussion of his career, centering at the time on "a paltry curacy" in Harwich (*EY*, p. 59). The scheme to perfect his French, and so qualify as a gentleman's traveling companion or tutor, is mentioned by Dorothy, *EY*, p. 66.
7. The places mentioned are all spots of "recent fame," associated with the still largely peaceful Revolution. The Field of Mars was the place where the Fête de la Fédération had been held, July 14, 1790, to commemorate the fall of the Bastille the previous year; the Faubourg St. Antoine was the militant working-class district next to the Bastille, and the northern suburb of Montmartre was a revolutionary meeting place. The Dome of Geneviève is the Panthéon, a church south of the Seine, chosen for the burial in April 1791 of the Comte de Mirabeau, the great

Revolutionary statesman and orator, and turned into a hall of fame by the re-burials there of Voltaire and Rousseau, both of whom had died in 1778, and were regarded as precursors of the Revolution.
8. First of the two "clamorous halls" was the constitutionally elected National Assembly of 750 deputies (to which Wordsworth was "introduced by a member," *EY*, p. 71); the second was the Jacobin Club (formally, the Society of Friends of the Revolution), which though it did not lay down specific policies, was immensely influential as a meeting place for radical opinion.
9. The arcades of the Palais d'Orleans were the fashionable shopping center and rendezvous of Paris.
1. The phrase "hubbub wild" is from Milton's description of Chaos, *Paradise Lost*, II, 951.
2. The Bastille, fortress-prison and symbol of royal oppression, had been sacked on July 14, 1789, and later demolished.

With motion constant as his own, I went
Prepared to sojourn in a pleasant town,   40
Washed by the current of the stately Loire.[6]

   Through Paris lay my readiest course, and there
Sojourning a few days, I visited,
In haste, each spot of old or recent fame,
The latter chiefly; from the field of Mars   45
Down to the suburbs of St. Anthony,
And from Mont Martyr southward to the Dome
Of Genevieve.[7] In both her clamorous Halls,
The National Synod and the Jacobins,
I saw the Revolutionary Power   50
Toss like a ship at anchor, rocked by storms;[8]
The Arcades I traversed, in the Palace huge
Of Orleans;[9] coasted round and round the line
Of Tavern, Brothel, Gaming-house, and Shop,
Great rendezvous of worst and best, the walk   55
Of all who had a purpose, or had not;
I stared and listened, with a stranger's ears,
To Hawkers and Haranguers, hubbub wild![1]
And hissing Factionists with ardent eyes,
In knots and pairs, or single. Not a look   60
Hope takes, or Doubt or Fear are forced to wear,
But seemed there present; and I scanned them all,
Watched every gesture uncontrollable,
Of anger, and vexation, and despite,
All side by side, and struggling face to face,   65
With gaiety and dissolute idleness.

   Where silent zephyrs sported with the dust
Of the Bastile,[2] I sate in the open sun,

And from the rubbish gathered up a stone,   65
[70] And pocketed the relick in the guise
Of an enthusiast; yet, in honest truth,
Though not without some strong incumbencies,[3]
And glad—could living man be otherwise?—
I looked for something which I could not find,   70
Affecting more emotion than I felt.
[74] For 'tis most certain that the utmost force
Of all these various objects which may shew
The temper of my mind as then it was
Seemed less to recompense the traveller's pains,   75
Less moved me, gave me less delight, than did
A single picture merely, hunted out
Among other sights, the Magdalene of le Brun,
A beauty exquisitely wrought—fair face
[80] And rueful, with its ever-flowing tears.[4]   80

     But hence to my more permanent residence
I hasten: there, by novelties in speech,
Domestic manners, customs, gestures, looks,
And all the attire of ordinary life,
[85] Attention was at first engrossed; and thus   85
Amused and satisfied, I scarcely felt
The shock of these concussions, unconcerned,
Tranquil almost, and careless as a flower
Glassed in a greenhouse, or a parlour-shrub,
[90] When every bush and tree the country through,   90
Is shaking to the roots—indifference this
Which may seem strange, but I was unprepared
With needful knowledge, had abruptly passed
Into a theatre of which the stage
[95] Was busy with an action far advanced.   95
Like others I had read, and eagerly
Sometimes, the master pamphlets of the day,[5]
Nor wanted such half-insight as grew wild
Upon that meagre soil, helped out by talk
[100] And public news; but having never chanced   100
To see a regular chronicle which might shew—
If any such indeed existed then—
Whence the main organs[6] of the public power
Had sprung, their transmigrations, when and how

3. Spiritual broodings; as at *1805*, III,
115, above.
4. A baroque picture of the weeping St.
Mary Magdalene (repentant prostitute
who washed Christ's feet with her tears,
Luke 7:38). It was painted by Charles le
Brun (1616–90). The picture, which is
now in the Louvre, was displayed as a
tourist attraction, apparently to the sound
of religious music (Legouis, p. 194*n*).
5. Wordsworth is presumably referring
to English pamphlets such as Thomas
Paine's *Rights of Man*, Part I, and James
Mackintosh's *Vindiciae Gallicae*, both
1791, written in answer to Burke's attack
on the Revolution.
6. Instruments.

And from the rubbish gathered up a stone,
And pocketed the relic, in the guise   70
Of an enthusiast; yet, in honest truth,
I looked for something that I could not find,
Affecting more emotion than I felt;
For 'tis most certain, that these various sights,
However potent their first shock, with me   75
Appeared to recompense the traveller's pains
Less than the painted Magdalene of Le Brun,
A beauty exquisitely wrought, with hair
Dishevelled, gleaming eyes, and rueful cheek
Pale and bedropped with everflowing tears.[4]   80

But hence to my more permanent abode
I hasten; there, by novelties in speech,
Domestic manners, customs, gestures, looks,
And all the attire of ordinary life,
Attention was engrossed; and, thus amused,   85
I stood, 'mid those concussions, unconcerned,
Tranquil almost, and careless as a flower
Glassed in a green-house, or a parlour shrub
That spreads its leaves in unmolested peace,
While every bush and tree, the country through,   90
Is shaking to the roots: indifference this
Which may seem strange: but I was unprepared
With needful knowledge, had abruptly passed
Into a theatre, whose stage was filled
And busy with an action far advanced.   95
Like others, I had skimmed, and sometimes read
With care, the master pamphlets of the day;[5]
Nor wanted such half-insight as grew wild
Upon that meagre soil, helped out by talk
And public news; but having never seen   100
A chronicle that might suffice to show
Whence the main organs[6] of the public power
Had sprung, their transmigrations, when and how

Accomplished (giving thus unto events   105
[105] A form and body), all things were to me
Loose and disjointed, and the affections left
Without a vital interest. At that time,
Moreover, the first storm was overblown,
And the strong hand of outward violence   110
[110] Locked up in quiet.[7] For myself—I fear
Now in connection with so great a theme
To speak, as I must be compelled to do,
Of one so unimportant—a short time
I loitered, and frequented night by night   115
Routs,[8] card-tables, the formal haunts of men
[115] Whom in the city privilege of birth
Sequestered from the rest, societies
Where, through punctilios of elegance
And deeper causes, all discourse, alike   120
Of good and evil, in the time, was shunned
[120] With studious care. But 'twas not long ere this
Proved tedious, and I gradually withdrew
Into a noisier world, and thus did soon
Become a patriot[9]—and my heart was all
Given to the people, and my love was theirs.   125

[125]   A knot of military officers
That to a regiment appertained which then
Was stationed in the city were the chief
Of my associates; some of these wore swords   130
Which had been seasoned in the wars, and all
Were men well-born, at least laid claim to such
Distinction, as the chivalry[1] of France.
[130] In age and temper differing, they had yet
One spirit ruling in them all—alike   135
(Save only one, hereafter to be named)[2]
Were bent upon undoing what was done.
This was their rest, and only hope; therewith
[135] No fear had they of bad becoming worse,
For worst to them was come—nor would have stirred,   140
Or deemed it worth a moment's while to stir,
In any thing, save only as the act
Looked thitherward. One, reckoning by years,
[140] Was in the prime of manhood, and erewhile
He had sate lord in many tender hearts,   145

---

7. After a brief initial period of violence
in summer 1789, the Revolution continued
peaceful and constitutional until the
massacre of royalist prisoners that followed the final suspension of the king in
August 1792 (see *1805*, X, 48*n*, below).
The Reign of Terror did not begin until

July 1793.
8. Receptions, parties.
9. One who is committed to the Revolution.
1. Nobles.
2. A reference to Michel Beaupuy (see
1805, 296*n*, below, and lines 294–543).

Accomplished, giving thus unto events
A form and body; all things were to me   105
Loose and disjointed, and the affections left
Without a vital interest. At that time,
Moreover, the first storm was overblown,
And the strong hand of outward violence
Locked up in quiet.[7] For myself, I fear   110
Now in connection with so great a theme
To speak (as I must be compelled to do)
Of one so unimportant; night by night
Did I frequent the formal haunts of men,
Whom, in the city, privilege of birth   115
Sequestered from the rest; societies
Polished in arts, and in punctilio versed;
Whence, and from deeper causes, all discourse
Of good and evil of the time was shunned
With scrupulous care; but these restrictions soon   120
Proved tedious, and I gradually withdrew
Into a noisier world, and thus ere long
Became a patriot;[9] and my heart was all
Given to the people, and my love was theirs.

    A band of military Officers,   125
Then stationed in the city, were the chief
Of my associates: some of these wore swords
That had been seasoned in the wars, and all
Were men well-born; the chivalry[1] of France.
In age and temper differing, they had yet   130
One spirit ruling in each heart; alike
(Save only one, hereafter to be named)[2]
Were bent upon undoing what was done:
This was their rest and only hope; therewith
No fear had they of bad becoming worse,   135
For worst to them was come; nor would have stirred,
Or deemed it worth a moment's thought to stir,
In any thing, save only as the act
Looked thitherward. One, reckoning by years,
Was in the prime of manhood, and erewhile   140
He had sate lord in many tender hearts;

Though heedless of such honours now, and changed:
His temper was quite mastered by the times,
And they had blighted him, had eat away
[145] The beauty of his person, doing wrong
Alike to body and to mind. His port,[3]   150
Which once had been erect and open, now
Was stooping and contracted, and a face
By nature lovely in itself, expressed,
[151] As much as any that was ever seen,
A ravage out of season, made by thoughts   155
Unhealthy and vexatious. At the hour,
The most important of each day, in which
[155] The public news was read, the fever came,
A punctual visitant, to shake this man,
Disarmed his voice and fanned his yellow cheek   160
Into a thousand colours. While he read,
Or mused, his sword was haunted by his touch
[160] Continually, like an uneasy place
In his own body. 'Twas in truth an hour
Of universal ferment—mildest men   165
Were agitated, and commotions, strife
Of passion and opinion, filled the walls
[165] Of peaceful houses with unquiet sounds.
The soil of common life was at that time
Too hot to tread upon. Oft said I then,   170
And not then only, 'What a mockery this
Of history, the past and that to come!
[170] Now do I feel how I have been deceived,
Reading of nations and their works in faith—
Faith given to vanity and emptiness—   175
Oh, laughter for the page that would reflect
To future times the face of what now is!'
[175] The land all swarmed with passion, like a plain
Devoured by locusts—Carra, Gorsas[4]—add
A hundred other names, forgotten now,   180
Nor to be heard of more; yet were they powers,
Like earthquakes, shocks repeated day by day,
[180] And felt through every nook of town and field.

---

3. Bearing.
4. Gorsas and Carra were deputies of the
National Assembly, and members of the
idealistic and loosely connected Girondin
group with which Wordsworth and Coleridge were in sympathy. They exercised
considerable power as journalists, and
were executed by Robespierre on October
7 and 31, 1793, respectively. According
to Carlyle (*Reminiscences*, p. 532),
Wordsworth told him ca. 1840 that he
had been present at the death of Gorsas,
and it has been assumed (see especially
Reed, I, p. 147) that Wordsworth made
a brief trip to Paris at this time to see
Annette and Caroline (see *1805, 555n*,
below). Carlyle's account is backed by
circumstantial detail, but only very tenu-
ous evidence has been produced to support the claim that Wordsworth seems to
have made.

Though heedless of such honours now, and changed:
His temper was quite mastered by the times,
And they had blighted him, had eat away
The beauty of his person, doing wrong   145
Alike to body and to mind: his port,[3]
Which once had been erect and open, now
Was stooping and contracted, and a face,
Endowed by Nature with her fairest gifts
Of symmetry and light and bloom, expressed,   150
As much as any that was ever seen,
A ravage out of season, made by thoughts
Unhealthy and vexatious. With the hour,
That from the press of Paris duly brought
Its freight of public news, the fever came,   155
A punctual visitant, to shake this man,
Disarmed his voice and fanned his yellow cheek
Into a thousand colours; while he read,
Or mused, his sword was haunted by his touch
Continually, like an uneasy place   160
In his own body. 'Twas in truth an hour
Of universal ferment; mildest men
Were agitated; and commotions, strife
Of passion and opinion, filled the walls
Of peaceful houses with unquiet sounds.   165
The soil of common life, was, at that time,
Too hot to tread upon. Oft said I then,
And not then only, 'What a mockery this
Of history, the past and that to come!
Now do I feel how all men are deceived,   170
Reading of nations and their works, in faith,
Faith given to vanity and emptiness;
Oh! laughter for the page that would reflect
To future times the face of what now is!'
The land all swarmed with passion, like a plain   175
Devoured by locusts,—Carra, Gorças,[4]—add
A hundred other names, forgotten now,
Nor to be heard of more; yet, they were powers,
Like earthquakes, shocks repeated day by day,
And felt through every nook of town and field.   180

   The men already spoken of as chief
Of my associates were prepared for flight   185
To augment the band of emigrants in arms
Upon the borders of the Rhine, and leagued
[185] With foreign foes mustered for instant war.
   This was their undisguised intent, and they
   Were waiting with the whole of their desires   190
   The moment to depart.[5] An Englishman,
   Born in a land the name of which appeared
[190] To licence some unruliness of mind,
   A stranger, with youth's further privilege,
   And that indulgence which a half-learned speech   195
   Wins from the courteous, I—who had been else
   Shunned and not tolerated—freely lived
[195] With these defenders of the crown, and talked,
   And heard their notions; nor did they disdain
   The wish to bring me over to their cause.   200
   But though untaught by thinking or by books
   To reason well of polity[6] or law,
[200] And nice distinctions—then on every tongue—
   Of natural rights and civil, and to acts
   Of nations, and their passing interests   205
   (I speak comparing these with other things)
   Almost indifferent, even the historian's tale
[205] Prizing but little otherwise than I prized
   Tales of the poets—as it made my heart
   Beat high and filled my fancy with fair forms,   210
   Old heroes and their sufferings and their deeds—
   Yet in the regal sceptre, and the pomp
[210] Of orders and degrees, I nothing found
   Then, or had ever even in crudest youth,
   That dazzled me, but rather what my soul   215
   Mourned for, or loathed, beholding that the best
   Ruled not, and feeling that they ought to rule.

[215]   For, born in a poor district, and which yet
   Retaineth more of ancient homeliness,
   Manners erect, and frank simplicity,   220
   Than any other nook of English land,
   It was my fortune scarcely to have seen
   Through the whole tenor of my schoolday time
[220] The face of one, who, whether boy or man,
   Was vested with attention or respect   225
   Through claims of wealth or blood. Nor was it least

---

5. By April 1792 more than half the 9,000 French army officers had deserted to join the émigrés who were mustering with Austrian and Prussian support at Coblenz for an invasion intended to restore the *ancien régime*.
6. Government.

Such was the state of things. Meanwhile the chief
Of my associates stood prepared for flight
To augment the band of emigrants in arms
Upon the borders of the Rhine, and leagued
With foreign foes mustered for instant war.   185
This was their undisguised intent, and they
Were waiting with the whole of their desires
The moment to depart.[5]

             An Englishman,
Born in a land whose very name appeared
To license some unruliness of mind;   190
A stranger, with youth's further privilege,
And the indulgence that a half-learnt speech
Wins from the courteous; I, who had been else
Shunned and not tolerated, freely lived
With these defenders of the Crown, and talked,   195
And heard their notions; nor did they disdain
The wish to bring me over to their cause.

    But though untaught by thinking or by books
To reason well of polity[6] or law,
And nice distinctions, then on every tongue,   200
Of natural rights and civil; and to acts
Of nations and their passing interests,
(If with unworldly ends and aims compared)
Almost indifferent, even the historian's tale
Prizing but little otherwise than I prized   205
Tales of the poets, as it made the heart
Beat high, and filled the fancy with fair forms,
Old heroes and their sufferings and their deeds;
Yet in the regal sceptre, and the pomp
Of orders and degrees, I nothing found   210
Then, or had ever, even in crudest youth,
That dazzled me, but rather what I mourned
And ill could brook, beholding that the best
Ruled not, and feeling that they ought to rule.

    For, born in a poor district, and which yet   215
Retaineth more of ancient homeliness,
Than any other nook of English ground,
It was my fortune scarcely to have seen,
Through the whole tenor of my school-day time,
The face of one, who, whether boy or man,   220
Was vested with attention or respect
Through claims of wealth or blood; nor was it least

Of many debts which afterwards I owed
To Cambridge and an academic life,
[225] That something there was holden up to view
Of a republic, where all stood thus far   230
Upon equal ground, that they were brothers all
In honour, as of one community—
Scholars and gentlemen—where, furthermore,
[230] Distinction lay open to all that came,
And wealth and titles were in less esteem   235
Than talents and successful industry.
Add unto this, subservience from the first
[235] To God and Nature's single sovereignty
(Familiar presences of awful power),
And fellowship with venerable books   240
To sanction the proud workings of the soul,
And mountain liberty.[8] It could not be
But that one tutored thus, who had been formed
To thought and moral feeling in the way
This story hath described, should look with awe   245
[240] Upon the faculties of man, receive
Gladly the highest promises, and hail
As best the government of equal rights
And individual worth. And hence, O friend,
If at the first great outbreak I rejoiced   250
[245] Less than might well befit my youth, the cause
In part lay here, that unto me the events
Seemed nothing out of nature's certain course—
A gift that rather was come late than soon.
[249] No wonder then if advocates like these   255
Whom I have mentioned, at this riper day
Were impotent to make my hopes put on
The shape of theirs, my understanding bend
In honour to their honour. Zeal which yet
[255] Had slumbered, now in opposition burst   260
Forth like a Polar summer. Every word
They uttered was a dart by counter-winds
Blown back upon themselves; their reason seemed
Confusion-stricken by a higher power
[260] Than human understanding, their discourse   265
Maimed, spiritless—and, in their weakness strong,
I triumphed.

          Meantime day by day the roads,
While I consorted with these royalists,

8. To the alleged egalitarianism of the
Lake District and Cambridge, Wordsworth adds three influences that disposed
him to welcome the Revolution: subservience to God and Nature, fellowship with
books that confirm ("sanction") the
workings of the soul, and finally, the
freedom of spirit associated with mountains.

Of many benefits, in later years
Derived from academic institutes
And rules, that they held something up to view   225
Of a Republic, where all stood thus far
Upon equal ground; that we were brothers all
In honour, as in one community,
Scholars and gentlemen; where, furthermore,
Distinction lay open to all that came,   230
And wealth and titles were in less esteem
Than talents, worth, and prosperous industry.
Add unto this, subservience from the first
To presences of God's mysterious power
Made manifest in Nature's sovereignty,[7]   235
And fellowship with venerable books,
To sanction the proud workings of the soul,
And mountain liberty. It could not be
But that one tutored thus should look with awe
Upon the faculties of man, receive   240
Gladly the highest promises, and hail,
As best, the government of equal rights
And individual worth. And hence, O Friend!
If at the first great outbreak I rejoiced
Less than might well befit my youth, the cause   245
In part lay here, that unto me the events
Seemed nothing out of nature's certain course,
A gift that was rather come late than soon.
No wonder, then, if advocates like these,
Inflamed by passion, blind with prejudice,   250
And stung with injury,[9] at this riper day,
Were impotent to make my hopes put on
The shape of theirs, my understanding bend
In honour to their honour; zeal, which yet
Had slumbered, now in opposition burst   255
Forth like a Polar summer: every word
They uttered was a dart, by counter-winds
Blown back upon themselves; their reason seemed
Confusion-stricken by a higher power
Than human understanding, their discourse   260
Maimed, spiritless; and, in their weakness strong,
I triumphed.

          Meantime, day by day, the roads
Were crowded with the bravest youth of France,

---

7. Lines 233–35 show a careful removal, in 1832, of the pantheist implications of *1805*.
9. As Havens points out, the addition of lines 250–51 (in 1816/19) shows that Wordsworth's growing conservatism did not soften his contempt for the forces of reaction.

Were crowded with the bravest youth of France
And all the promptest of her spirits, linked   270
[265] In gallant soldiership, and posting on
To meet the war upon her frontier-bounds.[1]
Yet at this very moment do tears start
Into mine eyes—I do not say I weep,
I wept not then, but tears have dimmed my sight—   275
[270] In memory of the farewells of that time,
Domestic severings, female fortitude
At dearest separation, patriot love
And self-devotion, and terrestrial hope
Encouraged with a martyr's confidence.[2]   280
[275] Even files of strangers merely, seen but once
And for a moment, men from far, with sound
Of music, martial tunes, and banners spread,
Entering the city, here and there a face
Or person singled out among the rest   285
[280] Yet still a stranger, and beloved as such—
Even by these passing spectacles my heart
Was oftentimes uplifted, and they seemed
Like arguments from Heaven that 'twas a cause
Good, and which no one could stand up against   290
[285] Who was not lost, abandoned, selfish, proud,
Mean, miserable, wilfully depraved,
Hater perverse of equity and truth.

    Among that band of officers was one,
Already hinted at, of other mold—   295
[290] A patriot,[3] thence rejected by the rest,
And with an oriental loathing spurned
As of a different cast.[4] A meeker man
Than this lived never, or a more benign—
Meek, though enthusiastic to the height   300
Of highest expectation. Injuries
[295] Made *him* more gracious, and his nature then
Did breathe its sweetness out most sensibly,[5]
As aromatic flowers on Alpine turf
When foot hath crushed them. He through the events   305
Of that great change wandered in perfect faith,
[300] As through a book, an old romance, or tale

---

1. France declared war against Austria
on April 20, 1792.
2. I.e., Hope for success on earth, supported by confidence such as the Christian martyrs showed. "Self-devotion":
devotion of oneself to a cause.
3. Michel Beaupuy (1755–96) was nobly
born, but came of a family distinguished
for its interest in philosophy and sympathy with the Revolution (Legouis, pp.

201–4); with Coleridge, he is one of
the two great influences on Wordsworth's
intellectual life. "Mold": the earth from
which the human body was regarded as
having been formed.
4. I.e., he was spurned with the kind of
loathing an Oriental might show for a
member of a lower caste.
5. In a way that was particularly apparent to the senses.

And all the promptest of her spirits, linked
In gallant soldiership, and posting on   265
To meet the war upon her frontier bounds.[1]
Yet at this very moment do tears start
Into mine eyes: I do not say I weep—
I wept not then,—but tears have dimmed my sight,
In memory of the farewells of that time,   270
Domestic severings, female fortitude
At dearest separation, patriot love
And self-devotion, and terrestrial hope,
Encouraged with a martyr's confidence;[2]
Even files of strangers merely, seen but once,   275
And for a moment, men from far with sound
Of music, martial tunes, and banners spread,
Entering the city, here and there a face,
Or person singled out among the rest,
Yet still a stranger and beloved as such;   280
Even by these passing spectacles my heart
Was oftentimes uplifted, and they seemed
Arguments sent from Heaven to prove the cause
Good, pure, which no one could stand up against,
Who was not lost, abandoned, selfish, proud,   285
Mean, miserable, wilfully depraved,
Hater perverse of equity and truth.

  Among that band of Officers was one,
Already hinted at, of other mould—
A patriot,[3] thence rejected by the rest,   290
And with an oriental loathing spurned,
As of a different caste.[4] A meeker man
Than this lived never, nor a more benign,
Meek though enthusiastic. Injuries
Made *him* more gracious, and his nature then   295
Did breathe its sweetness out most sensibly,[5]
As aromatic flowers on Alpine turf,
When foot hath crushed them. He through the events
Of that great change wandered in perfect faith,
As through a book, an old romance, or tale   300

Of Fairy,[6] or some dream of actions wrought
Behind the summer clouds. By birth he ranked
With the most noble, but unto the poor   310
Among mankind he was in service bound
[305] As by some tie invisible, oaths professed
To a religious order. Man he loved
As man, and to the mean and the obscure,
And all the homely in their homely works,   315
Transferred a courtesy which had no air
[310] Of condescension, but did rather seem
A passion and a gallantry, like that
Which he, a soldier, in his idler day
Had payed to woman. Somewhat vain he was,   320
Or seemed so—yet it was not vanity,
[315] But fondness, and a kind of radiant joy
That covered him about when he was bent
On works of love or freedom, or revolved
Complacently[7] the progress of a cause   325
Whereof he was a part—yet this was meek
[320] And placid, and took nothing from the man
That was delightful. Oft in solitude
With him did I discourse about the end
Of civil government, and its wisest forms,   330
Of ancient prejudice and chartered rights,
Allegiance, faith, and laws by time matured,
[325] Custom and habit, novelty and change,
Of self-respect, and virtue in the few
For patrimonial honour set apart,   335
And ignorance in the labouring multitude.
For he, an upright man and tolerant,
[330] Balanced these contemplations in his mind,
And I, who at that time was scarcely dipped
Into the turmoil, had a sounder judgement   340
Than afterwards,[8] carried about me yet
With less alloy to its integrity
[335] The experience of past ages, as through help
Of books and common life it finds its way
To youthful minds, by objects over near   345
Not pressed upon, nor dazzled or misled
By struggling with the crowd for present ends.

[340]   But though not deaf and obstinate to find
Error without apology on the side
Of those who were against us, more delight   350
We took, and let this freely be confessed,

---

6. Fairyland; Spenser is in Wordsworth's
mind, as at lines 445–64, below.
7. With enjoyment.

8. I.e., than during 1793–95, the period
treated in Book X.

Of Fairy,[6] or some dream of actions wrought
Behind the summer clouds. By birth he ranked
With the most noble, but unto the poor
Among mankind he was in service bound,
As by some tie invisible, oaths professed   305
To a religious order. Man he loved
As man; and, to the mean and the obscure,
And all the homely in their homely works,
Transferred a courtesy which had no air
Of condescension; but did rather seem   310
A passion and a gallantry, like that
Which he, a soldier, in his idler day
Had paid to woman: somewhat vain he was,
Or seemed so, yet it was not vanity,
But fondness, and a kind of radiant joy   315
Diffused around him, while he was intent
On works of love or freedom, or revolved
Complacently[7] the progress of a cause,
Whereof he was a part: yet this was meek
And placid, and took nothing from the man   320
That was delightful. Oft in solitude
With him did I discourse about the end
Of civil government, and its wisest forms;
Of ancient loyalty, and chartered rights,
Custom and habit, novelty and change;   325
Of self-respect, and virtue in the few
For patrimonial honour set apart,
And ignorance in the labouring multitude.
For he, to all intolerance indisposed,
Balanced these contemplations in his mind;   330
And I, who at that time was scarcely dipped
Into the turmoil, bore a sounder judgment
Than later days allowed;[8] carried about me,
With less alloy to its integrity,
The experience of past ages, as, through help   335
Of books and common life, it makes sure way
To youthful minds, by objects over near
Not pressed upon, nor dazzled or misled
By struggling with the crowd for present ends.

But though not deaf, nor obstinate to find   340
Error without excuse upon the side
Of them who strove against us, more delight
We took, and let this freely be confessed,

In painting to ourselves the miseries
[345] Of royal courts, and that voluptuous life
Unfeeling where the man who is of soul
The meanest thrives the most, where dignity,   355
True personal dignity, abideth not—
A light and cruel world, cut off from all
[350] The natural inlets of just sentiment,
From lowly sympathy, and chastening truth,
When good and evil never have the name,   360
That which they ought to have, but wrong prevails,
And vice at home. We added dearest themes,
[355] Man and his noble nature, as it is[9]
The gift of God and lies in his own power,
His blind desires and steady faculties   365
Capable of clear truth, the one to break
Bondage, the other to build liberty
[360] On firm foundations, making social life,
Through knowledge spreading and imperishable,
As just in regulation, and as pure,   370
As individual in the wise and good.[1]

       We summoned up the honorable deeds
[365] Of ancient story, thought of each bright spot
That could be found in all recorded time,
Of truth preserved and error passed away,   375
Of single spirits that catch the flame from heaven,
And how the multitude of men will feed
[370] And fan each other—thought of sects, how keen
They are to put the appropriate nature on,
Triumphant over every obstacle   380
Of custom, language, country, love and hate,
And what they do and suffer for their creed,
[375] How far they travel, and how long endure—
How quickly mighty nations have been formed
From least beginnings, how, together locked   385
By new opinions, scattered tribes have made
One body, spreading wide as clouds in heaven.
[380] To aspirations then of our own minds
Did we appeal; and, finally, beheld
A living confirmation of the whole   390
Before us in a people risen up
[385] Fresh as the morning star. Elate we looked
Upon their virtues, saw in rudest men
Self-sacrifice the firmest, generous love

9. I.e., insofar as it is.   * * * and pure as individual life is in
1. I.e., "making social life * * * as just   the wise and good."

In painting to ourselves the miseries
Of royal courts, and that voluptuous life   345
Unfeeling, where the man who is of soul
The meanest thrives the most; where dignity,
True personal dignity, abideth not;
A light, a cruel, and vain world cut off
From the natural inlets of just sentiment,   350
From lowly sympathy and chastening truth;
Where good and evil interchange their names,
And thirst for bloody spoils abroad is paired
With vice at home. We added dearest themes—
Man and his noble nature, as it is[9]   355
The gift which God has placed within his power,
His blind desires and steady faculties
Capable of clear truth, the one to break
Bondage, the other to build liberty
On firm foundations, making social life,   360
Through knowledge spreading and imperishable,
As just in regulation, and as pure,
As individual in the wise and good.[1]

    We summoned up the honourable deeds
Of ancient Story, thought of each bright spot,   365
That could be found in all recorded time,
Of truth preserved and error passed away;
Of single spirits that catch the flame from Heaven,
And how the multitudes of men will feed
And fan each other; thought of sects, how keen   370
They are to put the appropriate nature on,
Triumphant over every obstacle
Of custom, language, country, love, or hate,
And what they do and suffer for their creed;
How far they travel, and how long endure;   375
How quickly mighty Nations have been formed,
From least beginnings; how, together locked
By new opinions, scattered tribes have made
One body, spreading wide as clouds in heaven.
To aspirations then of our own minds   380
Did we appeal; and, finally, beheld
A living confirmation of the whole
Before us, in a people from the depth
Of shameful imbecility uprisen,[2]
Fresh as the morning star. Elate we looked   385
Upon their virtues; saw, in rudest men,
Self-sacrifice the firmest; generous love,

---

2. A revision of 1816/19, showing Wordsworth's continued emotional commitment to the Revolution.

And continence of mind,[3] and sense of right   395
Uppermost in the midst of fiercest strife.

[390]   Oh, sweet it is in academic groves—
Or such retirement, friend, as we have known
Among the mountains by our Rotha's stream,
Greta, or Derwent,[4] or some nameless rill—   400
To ruminate, with interchange of talk,
[395] On rational liberty and hope in man,
Justice and peace. But far more sweet such toil
(Toil, say I, for it leads to thoughts abstruse)
If Nature then be standing on the brink   405
Of some great trial, and we hear the voice
[400] Of one devoted, one whom circumstance
Hath called upon to embody his deep sense
In action, give it outwardly a shape,
And that of benediction to the world.   410
Then doubt is not, and truth is more than truth—
[405] A hope it is and a desire, a creed
Of zeal by an authority divine
Sanctioned, of danger, difficulty, or death.
Such conversation under Attic[5] shades   415
Did Dion hold with Plato, ripened thus
[410] For a deliverer's glorious task, and such
He, on that ministry already bound,
Held with Eudemus and Timonides,
Surrounded by adventurers in arms,   420
When those two vessels with their daring freight
[415] For the Sicilian tyrant's overthrow
Sailed from Zacynthus—philosophic war
Led by philosophers.[6] With harder fate,
Though like ambition, such was he, O friend,   425
Of whom I speak. So Beaupuis—let the name
[420] Stand near the worthiest of antiquity—
Fashioned his life, and many a long discourse
With like persuasion honored we maintained,
He on his part accoutred for the worst.   430
He perished fighting, in supreme command,

3. Restraint, self-possession. "Rudest" (*1805*, 393; *1850*, 388): least refined, most ignorant.
4. Lake District rivers that were especially dear to Wordsworth and Coleridge, the Rothay at Grasmere, the Greta near Coleridge's house at Keswick, and the Derwent ("fairest of all rivers," *1799*, I, 2; *1805*, I, 270) at Wordsworth's birthplace, Cockermouth.
5. Greek.
6. *1805*, 415–26 (*1850*, 407–17) are drawn from the *Life of Dion* in North's trans-lation (1579) of Plutarch's *Lives* of eminent Greeks and Romans. Dion liberated Sicily in 357 B.C. from the tyrannical rule of his nephew Dionysius the Younger, after the failure of negotiations in which Plato had taken part. He was supported by "divers of them also that only gave their minds to the studie of Philosophie," among them Eudemus Cyprian and Timonides Leucadian. They sailed in "two great ships of burden" from the Ionian island of Zante—ancient Zacynthus (North, pp. 1038–39).

And continence of mind,[3] and sense of right,
Uppermost in the midst of fiercest strife.

  Oh, sweet it is, in academic groves,   390
Or such retirement, Friend! as we have known
In the green dales beside our Rotha's stream,
Greta, or Derwent,[4] or some nameless rill,
To ruminate, with interchange of talk,
On rational liberty, and hope in man,   395
Justice and peace. But far more sweet such toil—
Toil, say I, for it leads to thoughts abstruse—
If nature then be standing on the brink
Of some great trial, and we hear the voice
Of one devoted,—one whom circumstance   400
Hath called upon to embody his deep sense
In action, give it outwardly a shape,
And that of benediction, to the world.
Then doubt is not, and truth is more than truth,—
A hope it is, and a desire; a creed   405
Of zeal, by an authority Divine
Sanctioned, of danger, difficulty, or death.
Such conversation, under Attic[5] shades,
Did Dion hold with Plato; ripened thus
For a Deliverer's glorious task,—and such   410
He, on that ministry already bound,
Held with Eudemus and Timonides,
Surrounded by adventurers in arms,
When these two vessels with their daring freight,
For the Sicilian Tyrant's overthrow,   415
Sailed from Zacynthus,—philosophic war,
Led by Philosophers.[6] With harder fate,
Though like ambition, such was he, O Friend!
Of whom I speak. So Beaupuis (let the name
Stand near the worthiest of Antiquity)   420
Fashioned his life; and many a long discourse,
With like persuasion honoured, we maintained;
He on his part, accoutred for the worst.
He perished fighting, in supreme command,

[425] Upon the borders of the unhappy Loire,
　For liberty, against deluded men,
　His fellow countrymen; and yet most blessed
　In this, that he the fate of later times　　　　　　435
　Lived not to see, nor what we now behold
[430] Who have as ardent hearts as he had then.[7]

　　Along that very Loire, with festivals
　Resounding at all hours, and innocent yet
　Of civil slaughter, was our frequent walk,　　　　440
　Or in wide forests of the neighbourhood,
[435] High woods and over-arched,[8] with open space
　On every side, and footing many a mile,
　Inwoven roots, and moss smooth as the sea—
　A solemn region. Often in such place　　　　　　445
　From earnest dialogues I slipped in thought,
[439] And let remembrance steal to other times
　When hermits, from their sheds and caves forth strayed,
　Walked by themselves, so met in shades like these,[9]
　And if a devious traveller was heard　　　　　　450
　Approaching from a distance, as might chance,
　With speed and echoes loud of trampling hoofs
[450] From the hard floor reverberated, then
　It was Angelica thundering through the woods
　Upon her palfrey, or that gentler maid　　　　　455
　Erminia, fugitive as fair as she.[1]
　Sometimes I saw methought a pair of knights
[455] Joust underneath the trees, that as in storm
　Did rock above their heads, anon the din
　Of boisterous merriment and music's roar,　　　　460
　With sudden proclamation, burst from haunt
　Of satyrs in some viewless glade, with dance
[460] Rejoicing o'er a female in the midst,
　A mortal beauty, their unhappy thrall.[2]
　The width of those huge forests, unto me　　　　465
　A novel scene, did often in this way
　Master my fancy while I wandered on
[465] With that revered companion. And sometimes
　When to a convent in a meadow green

---

7. Beaupuy became chief of staff in the Republican army during the civil war in the Vendée, but he was in fact killed at Emmendingen on the eastern front, in October 1796. He thus lived to play a part in the wars of conquest which turned the Republic into an imperialist power, and which Wordsworth has in mind in *1805*, 434–37.
8. A reminiscence of *Paradise Lost*, IX, 1106–7: "a pillared shade / High over-arched, and echoing walks between."
9. I.e., met as we ourselves have done, in shades like these.
1. Angelica and Erminia were heroines respectively of Ariosto's *Orlando Furioso* (1532) and Tasso's *Gerusalemme Liberata* (1580–81).
2. Wordsworth probably has in mind the stories of Una and Hellenore, *Faerie Queene*, I, vi, 13, and III, x, 43–44.

Upon the borders of the unhappy Loire,   425
For liberty, against deluded men,
His fellow country-men; and yet most blessed
In this, that he the fate of later times
Lived not to see, nor what we now behold,
Who have as ardent hearts as he had then.[7]   430

    Along that very Loire, with festal mirth
Resounding at all hours, and innocent yet
Of civil slaughter, was our frequent walk;
Or in wide forests of continuous shade,
Lofty and over-arched,[8] with open space   435
Beneath the trees, clear footing many a mile—
A solemn region. Oft amid those haunts,
From earnest dialogues I slipped in thought,
And let remembrances steal to other times,
When, o'er those interwoven roots, moss-clad,   440
And smooth as marble or a waveless sea,
Some Hermit, from his cell forth-strayed, might pace
In sylvan meditation undisturbed;
As on the pavement of a Gothic church
Walks a lone Monk, when service hath expired,   445
In peace and silence. But if e'er was heard,—
Heard, though unseen,—a devious traveller,
Retiring or approaching from afar
With speed and echoes loud of trampling hoofs
From the hard floor reverberated, then   450
It was Angelica thundering through the woods
Upon her palfrey, or that gentle maid
Erminia, fugitive as fair as she.[1]
Sometimes methought I saw a pair of knights
Joust underneath the trees, that as in storm   455
Rocked high above their heads; anon, the din
Of boisterous merriment, and music's roar,
In sudden proclamation, burst from haunt
Of Satyrs in some viewless glade, with dance
Rejoicing o'er a female in the midst,   460
A mortal beauty, their unhappy thrall.[2]
The width of those huge forests, unto me
A novel scene, did often in this way
Master my fancy while I wandered on
With that revered companion. And sometimes—   465
When to a covent in a meadow green,

By a brook-side we came—a roofless pile,   470
And not by reverential touch of time
Dismantled, but by violence abrupt—
[470] In spite of those heart-bracing colloquies,
In spite of real fervour, and of that
Less genuine and wrought up within myself,   475
I could not but bewail a wrong so harsh,
And for the matin-bell—to sound no more—
[475] Grieved, and the evening taper,[3] and the cross
High on the topmost pinnacle, a sign
Admonitory to the traveller,   480
First seen above the woods.[4]

                                And when my friend
[480] Pointed upon occasion to the site
Of Romarentin,[5] home of ancient kings,
To the imperial edifice of Blois,
Or to that rural castle, name now slipped   485
From my remembrance, where a lady lodged
[485] By the first Francis wooed, and bound to him
In chains of mutual passion—from the tower,
As a tradition of the country tells,
Practised to commune with her royal knight   490
By cressets and love-beacons, intercourse
[490] 'Twixt her high-seated residence and his
Far off at Chambord on the plain beneath[6]—
Even here, though less than with the peaceful house
Religious, 'mid these frequent monuments   495
Of kings, their vices and their better deeds,
[495] Imagination, potent to enflame
At times with virtuous wrath and noble scorn,
Did also often mitigate the force
Of civic prejudice, the bigotry,   500
So call it, of a youthful patriot's mind,
[500] And on these spots with many gleams I looked
Of chivalrous delight. Yet not the less,
Hatred of absolute rule, where will of one
Is law for all, and of that barren pride   505
In those who by immunities unjust
[505] Betwixt the sovereign and the people stand,
His helpers and not theirs, laid stronger hold

---

3. Candle.
4. For Wordsworth's regret at the expulsion of the monks from the Grande Chartreuse, see *Descriptive Sketches*, 53–79.
5. Romorantin, small town in the region of the Loire, once a provincial capital.
6. The attempt to identify a particular mistress of Francis I (1514–57), and particular chateau (*1805*, 485; *1850*, 483), is probably futile; the story that Wordsworth heard at Blois in 1792 need have had no basis in fact. "Cressets": torches, beacons. "Chambord": chateau in the Loire valley, built by Francis I.

By a brook-side, we came, a roofless pile,
And not by reverential touch of Time
Dismantled, but by violence abrupt—
In spite of those heart-bracing colloquies,   470
In spite of real fervour, and of that
Less genuine and wrought up within myself—
I could not but bewail a wrong so harsh,
And for the Matin-bell to sound no more
Grieved, and the twilight taper,[3] and the cross   475
High on the topmost pinnacle, a sign
(How welcome to the weary traveller's eyes!)
Of hospitality and peaceful rest.[4]
And when the partner of those varied walks
Pointed upon occasion to the site   480
Of Romorentin,[5] home of ancient kings,
To the imperial edifice of Blois,
Or to that rural castle, name now slipped
From my remembrance, where a lady lodged,
By the first Francis wooed, and bound to him   485
In chains of mutual passion, from the tower,
As a tradition of the country tells,
Practised to commune with her royal knight
By cressets and love-beacons, intercourse
'Twixt her high-seated residence and his   490
Far off at Chambord on the plain beneath;[6]
Even here, though less than with the peaceful house
Religious, 'mid those frequent monuments
Of Kings, their vices and their better deeds,
Imagination, potent to inflame   495
At times with virtuous wrath and noble scorn,
Did also often mitigate the force
Of civic prejudice, the bigotry,
So call it, of a youthful patriot's mind;
And on these spots with many gleams I looked   500
Of chivalrous delight. Yet not the less,
Hatred of absolute rule, where will of one
Is law for all, and of that barren pride
In them who, by immunities unjust,
Between the sovereign and the people stand,   505
His helper and not theirs, laid stronger hold

Daily upon me—mixed with pity too,
And love, for where hope is, there love will be   510
For the abject multitude. And when we chanced
[510] One day to meet a hunger-bitten girl
Who crept along fitting her languid self
Unto a heifer's motion—by a cord
Tied to her arm, and picking thus from the lane   515
Its sustenance, while the girl with her two hands
[515] Was busy knitting in a heartless mood
Of solitude[7]—and at the sight my friend
In agitation said, ' 'Tis against that
Which we are fighting', I with him believed   520
Devoutly that a spirit was abroad
[520] Which could not be withstood, that poverty,
At least like this, would in a little time
Be found no more, that we should see the earth
Unthwarted in her wish to recompense   525
The industrious, and the lowly child of toil,
[525] All institutes for ever blotted out
That legalized exclusion, empty pomp
Abolished, sensual state and cruel power,[8]
Whether by edict of the one or few—   530
And finally, as sum and crown of all,
[530] Should see the people having a strong hand
In making their own laws, whence better days
To all mankind. But, these things set apart,
Was not the single confidence enough   535
To animate the mind that ever turned
[535] A thought to human welfare?—that henceforth
Captivity by mandate without law[9]
Should cease, and open accusation lead
To sentence in the hearing of the world,   540
And open punishment, if not the air
[540] Be free to breathe in, and the heart of man
Dread nothing.[1] Having touched this argument
I shall not, as my purpose was, take note
Of other matters which detained us oft   545
In thought or conversation—public acts,
And public persons, and the emotions wrought
[545] Within our minds by the ever-varying wind
Of record and report which day by day
Swept over us—but I will here instead   550
Draw from obscurity a tragic tale,

7. By an uneasy grammatical transition,
the heifer has become the subject in
Wordsworth's parenthesis. "Heartless":
despondent.
8. I.e., empty pomp abolished, *and with
it*, sensual state.
9. "*Lettres de cachets*"—orders for arrest and imprisonment without trial—
were a frequent weapon of the *ancien
régime*.
1. Wordsworth's implication seems to be
that total freedom and absence from fear
are too much to hope for.

Daily upon me, mixed with pity too
And love; for where hope is, there love will be
For the abject multitude. And when we chanced
One day to meet a hunger-bitten girl,   510
Who crept along fitting her languid gait
Unto a heifer's motion, by a cord
Tied to her arm, and picking thus from the lane
Its sustenance, while the girl with pallid hands
Was busy knitting in a heartless⁷ mood   515
Of solitude, and at the sight my friend
In agitation said, ' 'Tis against *that*
That we are fighting', I with him believed
That a benignant spirit was abroad
Which might not be withstood, that poverty   520
Abject as this would in a little time
Be found no more, that we should see the earth
Unthwarted in her wish to recompense
The meek, the lowly, patient child of toil.
All institutes for ever blotted out   525
That legalised exclusion, empty pomp
Abolished, sensual state and cruel power,⁹
Whether by edict of the one or few;
And finally, as sum and crown of all,
Should see the people having a strong hand   530
In framing their own laws; whence better days
To all mankind. But, these things set apart,
Was not this single confidence enough
To animate the mind that ever turned
A thought to human welfare? That henceforth   535
Captivity by mandate without law
Should cease; and open accusation lead
To sentence in the hearing of the world,
And open punishment, if not the air
Be free to breathe in, and the heart of man   540
Dread nothing.¹ From this height I shall not stoop
To humbler matter that detained us oft
In thought or conversation, public acts,
And public persons, and emotions wrought
Within the breast, as ever-varying winds   545
Of record or report swept over us;
But I will here, instead, repeat a tale,

Not in its spirit singular, indeed,
But haply worth memorial, as I heard
The events related by my patriot friend
And others who had borne a part therein.[2]   555

    Oh, happy time of youthful lovers—thus
My story may begin—oh, balmy time
[555] In which a love-knot[3] on a lady's brow
Is fairer than the fairest star in heaven!
To such inheritance of blessedness   560
Young Vaudracour was brought by years that had
A little overstepped his stripling prime.
A town of small repute in the heart of France
Was the youth's birthplace; there he vowed his love
To Julia, a bright maid from parents sprung   565
Not mean in their condition, but with rights
Unhonoured of nobility—and hence
The father of the young man, who had place
Among that order, spurned the very thought
Of such alliance. From their cradles up,   570
With but a step between their several homes,
The pair had thriven together year by year,
Friends, playmates, twins in pleasure, after strife
And petty quarrels had grown fond again,
Each other's advocate, each other's help,   575
Nor ever happy if they were apart.
A basis this for deep and solid love,
And endless constancy, and placid truth—
But whatsoever of such treasures might,
Beneath the outside[5] of their youth, have lain   580
Reserved for mellower years, his present mind
Was under fascination—he beheld
A vision, and he loved the thing he saw.
Arabian fiction never filled the world
With half the wonders that were wrought for him: 585
Earth lived in one great presence of the spring,

---

2. There is good reason to believe that the events of *Vaudracour and Julia* took place at Blois, and that Wordsworth did hear the story on the spot. Within the context of his autobiography, *Vaudracour and Julia* stands in lieu of an account of his relationship with Annette Vallon, whom he met ca. January 1792, and by whom he had a child, christened in Orleans Cathedral on December 15 as Anne-Caroline Wordsworth. The stories cannot be expected to coincide in any detail, but Annette's two surviving letters, of March 1793 (Émile Legouis, *William Wordsworth and Annette Vallon*, pp. 124–33), are full of tenderness, and it is not difficult to believe that Wordsworth's initial feelings at being separated from her and Caroline by the war of England against France (declared February 1793) were akin to those of Vaudracour. They almost certainly did not meet again till the Peace of Amiens in 1802, the year of Wordsworth's marriage to Mary Hutchinson.
3. A ribbon tied in a particular way and worn as a sign of love.
5. Surface.

Told by my Patriot friend, of sad events,
That prove to what·low depth had struck the roots,
How widely spread the boughs, of that old tree   550
Which, as a deadly mischief, and a foul
And black dishonour, France was weary of.

    Oh, happy time of youthful lovers, (thus
My story may begin) O balmy time,
In which a love-knot,[3] on a lady's brow,   555
Is fairer than the fairest star in Heaven!
So might—and with that prelude *did* begin
The record; and, in faithful verse, was given
The doleful sequel.[4]

---

4. *Vaudracour and Julia* was published
as a separate poem in 1820, and excluded
from *The Prelude* in 1832, when lines
559–85 were composed and the awkward
transition of lines 557–58 was inserted.

Life turned the meanest of her implements
Before his eyes to price above all gold,
The house she dwelt in was a sainted shrine,
Her chamber-window did surpass in glory   590
The portals of the east, all paradise
Could by the simple opening of a door
Let itself in upon him—pathways, walks,
Swarmed with enchantment, till his spirits sunk
Beneath the burthen, overblessed for life.[6]   595
This state was theirs, till—whether through effect
Of some delirious hour, or that the youth,
Seeing so many bars betwixt himself
And the dear haven where he wished to be
In honorable wedlock with his love,   600
Without a certain knowledge of his own
Was inwardly prepared to turn aside
From law and custom and entrust himself
To Nature for a happy end of all,
And thus abated of that pure reserve   605
Congenial to his loyal heart, with which
It would have pleased him to attend the steps
Of maiden so divinely beautiful,
I know not—but reluctantly must add
That Julia, yet without the name of wife,   610
Carried about her for a secret grief
The promise of a mother.

               To conceal
The threatened shame the parents of the maid
Found means to hurry her away, by night
And unforewarned, that in a distant town   615
She might remain shrouded in privacy
Until the babe was born.[7] When morning came
The lover, thus bereft, stung with his loss
And all uncertain whither he should turn,
Chafed like a wild beast in the toils. At length,   620
Following as his suspicions led, he found—
O joy!—sure traces of the fugitives,
Pursued them to the town where they had stopped,
And lastly to the very house itself
Which had been chosen for the maid's retreat.   625
The sequel may be easily divined:
Walks backwards, forwards, morning, noon, and night
(When decency and caution would allow),

6. I.e., his life was blessed to a degree
beyond endurance.
7. Annette, though not subject to the
parental pressures described in this narrative (her father was dead, her mother
had remarried, and she herself was
twenty-six), chose to have her child in
Orleans, not in her home town, Blois.

And Julia, who, whenever to herself
She happened to be left a moment's space,   630
Was busy at her casement as a swallow
About its nest, erelong did thus espy
Her lover; thence a stolen interview
By night accomplished, with a ladder's help.

    I pass the raptures of the pair, such theme   635
Hath by a hundred poets been set forth
In more delightful verse than skill of mine
Could fashion—chiefly by that darling bard
Who told of Juliet and her Romeo,
And of the lark's note heard before its time,   640
And of the streaks that laced the severing clouds
In the unrelenting east.[8] 'Tis mine to tread
The humbler province of plain history,
And, without choice of circumstance, submissively
Relate what I have heard. The lovers came   645
To this resolve—with which they parted, pleased
And confident—that Vaudracour should hie
Back to his father's house, and there employ
Means aptest to obtain a sum of gold,
A final portion even, if that might be;   650
Which done, together they could then take flight
To some remote and solitary place
Where they might live with no one to behold
Their happiness, or to disturb their love.
Immediately, and with this mission charged,   655
Home to his father's house did he return,
And there remained a time without hint given
Of his design. But if a word were dropped
Touching the matter of his passion, still,
In hearing of his father, Vaudracour   660
Persisted openly that nothing less
Than death should make him yield up hope to be
A blessèd husband of the maid he loved.

    Incensed at such obduracy,[9] and slight
Of exhortations and remonstrances,   665
The father threw out threats that by a mandate
Bearing the private signet of the state[1]
He should be baffled of his mad intent—
And that should cure him. From this time the youth
Conceived a terror, and by night or day   670

---

8. See *Romeo and Juliet*, III, v, 1–8.
"Unrelenting": relentless—not willing to
delay the dawn for the sake of the lovers.
9. Scansion: ŏbdúrăcy.

1. A *"lettre de cachet,"* as at 541n above
and 727–28 below; at 676–82 Vaudracour
is therefore resisting arrest. "Signet":
official seal.

Stirred nowhere without arms. Soon afterwards
His parents to their country seat withdrew
Upon some feigned occasion, and the son
Was left with one attendant in the house.
Retiring to his chamber for the night,   675
While he was entering at the door, attempts
Were made to seize him by three armèd men,
The instruments of ruffian power. The youth
In the first impulse of his rage laid one
Dead at his feet, and to the second gave   680
A perilous wound—which done, at sight
Of the dead man, he peacefully resigned
His person to the law, was lodged in prison,
And wore the fetters of a criminal.

    Through three weeks' space, by means which love devised,   685
The maid in her seclusion had received
Tidings of Vaudracour, and how he sped
Upon his enterprize. Thereafter came
A silence; half a circle did the moon
Complete, and then a whole, and still the same   690
Silence; a thousand thousand fears and hopes
Stirred in her mind—thoughts waking, thoughts of sleep,
Entangled in each other—and at last
Self-slaughter seemed her only resting-place:
So did she fare in her uncertainty.   695

    At length, by interference of a friend,
One who had sway at court, the youth regained
His liberty, on promise to sit down
Quietly in his father's house, nor take
One step to reunite himself with her   700
Of whom his parents disapproved—hard law,
To which he gave consent only because
His freedom else could nowise be procured.
Back to his father's house he went, remained
Eight days, and then his resolution failed—   705
He fled to Julia, and the words with which
He greeted her were these: 'All right is gone,
Gone from me. Thou no longer now art mine,
I thine. A murderer, Julia, cannot love
An innocent woman. I behold thy face,   710
I see thee, and my misery is complete.'
She could not give him answer; afterwards
She coupled with his father's name some words
Of vehement indignation, but the youth
Checked her, nor would he hear of this, for thought   715
Unfilial, or unkind, had never once

Found harbour in his breast. The lovers, thus
United once again, together lived
For a few days, which were to Vaudracour
Days of dejection, sorrow and remorse   720
For that ill deed of violence which his hand
Had hastily committed—for the youth
Was of a loyal spirit, a conscience nice,[2]
And over tender for the trial which
His fate had called him to. The father's mind   725
Meanwhile remained unchanged, and Vaudracour
Learned that a mandate had been newly issued
To arrest him on the spot. Oh pain it was
To part!—he could not, and he lingered still
To the last moment of his time, and then,   730
At dead of night, with snow upon the ground,
He left the city, and in villages,
The most sequestered of the neighbourhood,
Lay hidden for the space of several days,
Until, the horseman bringing back report   735
That he was nowhere to be found, the search
Was ended. Back returned the ill-fated youth,
And from the house where Julia lodged—to which
He now found open ingress, having gained
The affection of the family, who loved him   740
Both for his own, and for the maiden's sake—
One night retiring, he was seized.

                              But here
A portion of the tale may well be left
In silence, though my memory could add   745
Much how the youth, and in short space of time,
Was traversed from without[3]—much, too, of thoughts
By which he was employed in solitude
Under privation and restraint, and what
Through dark and shapeless fear of things to come,
And what through strong compunction for the past,   750
He suffered, breaking down in heart and mind.
Such grace, if grace it were, had been vouchsafed—
Or such effect had through the father's want
Of power, or through his negligence, ensued—
That Vaudracour was suffered to remain,   755
Though under guard and without liberty,
In the same city with the unhappy maid
From whom he was divided. So they fared,
Objects of general concern, till, moved
With pity for their wrongs, the magistrate   760

---

2. Fastidious.   3. Crossed, thwarted, by external events.

(The same who had placed the youth in custody)
By application to the minister
Obtained his liberty upon condition
That to his father's house he should return.

    He left his prison almost on the eve   765
Of Julia's travail.⁴ She had likewise been,
As from the time, indeed, when she had first
Been brought for secresy to this abode,
Though treated with consoling tenderness,
Herself a prisoner—a dejected one,   770
Filled with a lover's and a woman's fears—
And whensoe'er the mistress of the house
Entered the room for the last time at night,
And Julia with a low and plaintive voice
Said, 'You are coming then to lock me up',   775
The housewife when these words—always the same—
Were by her captive languidly pronounced,
Could never hear them uttered without tears.
A day or two before her childbed time
Was Vaudracour restored to her, and, soon   780
As he might be permitted to return
Into her chamber after the child's birth,
The master of the family begged that all
The household might be summoned, doubting not
But that they might receive impressions then   785
Friendly to human kindness.⁵ Vaudracour
(This heard I from one present at the time)
Held up the new-born infant in his arms
And kissed, and blessed, and covered it with tears,
Uttering a prayer that he might never be   790
As wretched as his father. Then he gave
The child to her who bare it, and she too
Repeated the same prayer—took it again,
And, muttering something faintly afterwards,
He gave the infant to the standers-by,   795
And wept in silence upon Julia's neck.

    Two months did he continue in the house,
And often yielded up himself to plans
Of future happiness. 'You shall return,
Julia', said he, 'and to your father's house   800
Go with your child; you have been wretched, yet
It is a town where both of us were born—
None will reproach you, for our loves are known.
With ornaments the prettiest you shall dress

---

4. Labor.

5. I.e., that would stimulate kindness
within the beholders.

Your boy, as soon as he can run about,   805
And when he thus is at his play my father
Will see him from the window, and the child
Will by his beauty move his grandsire's heart,
So that it shall be softened, and our loves
End happily, as they began.' These gleams   810
Appeared but seldom; oftener he was seen
Propping a pale and melancholy face
Upon the mother's bosom, resting thus
His head upon one breast, while from the other
The babe was drawing in its quiet food.   815
At other times, when he in silence long
And fixedly had looked upon her face,
He would exclaim, 'Julia, how much thine eyes
Have cost me!' During daytime, when the child
Lay in its cradle, by its side he sate,   820
Not quitting it an instant. The whole town
In his unmerited misfortunes now
Took part, and if he either at the door
Or window for a moment with his child
Appeared, immediately the street was thronged;   825
While others, frequently, without reserve,
Passed and repassed before the house to steal
A look at him. Oft at this time he wrote
Requesting, since he knew that the consent
Of Julia's parents never could be gained   830
To a clandestine marriage, that his father
Would from the birthright of an eldest son
Exclude him, giving but, when this was done,
A sanction to his nuptials. Vain request,
To which no answer was returned.   835

                      And now
From her own home the mother of his love
Arrived to apprise the daughter of her fixed
And last resolve, that, since all hope to move
The old man's heart proved vain, she must retire
Into a convent and be there immured.   840
Julia was thunderstricken by these words,
And she insisted on a mother's rights
To take her child along with her—a grant
Impossible, as she at last perceived.
The persons of the house no sooner heard   845
Of this decision upon Julia's fate
Than everyone was overwhelmed with grief,
Nor could they frame a manner soft enough
To impart the tidings to the youth. But great
Was their astonishment when they beheld him   850

Receive the news in calm despondency,
Composed and silent, without outward sign
Of even the least emotion. Seeing this,
When Julia scattered[6] some upbraiding words
Upon his slackness, he thereto returned   855
No answer, only took the mother's hand
(Who loved him scarcely less than her own child)
And kissed it, without seeming to be pressed
By any pain that 'twas the hand of one
Whose errand was to part him from his love   860
For ever. In the city he remained
A season after Julia had retired
And in the convent taken up her home,
To the end that he might place his infant babe
With a fit nurse; which done, beneath the roof   865
Where now his little one was lodged he passed
The day entire, and scarcely could at length
Tear himself from the cradle to return
Home to his father's house—in which he dwelt
Awhile, and then came back that he might see   870
Whether the babe had gained sufficient strength
To bear removal. He quitted this same town
For the last time, attendant by the side
Of a close chair, a litter or sedan,[7]
In which the child was carried. To a hill   875
Which rose at a league's distance from the town
The family of the house where he had lodged
Attended him, and parted from him there,
Watching below until he disappeared
On the hill-top. His eyes he scarcely took   880
Through all that journey from the chair in which
The babe was carried, and at every inn
Or place at which they halted or reposed
Laid him upon his knees, nor would permit
The hands of any but himself to dress   885
The infant, or undress. By one of those
Who bore the chair these facts, at his return,
Were told, and in relating them he wept.

    This was the manner in which Vaudracour
Departed with his infant, and thus reached   890
His father's house, where to the innocent child
Admittance was denied. The young man spake
No words of indignation or reproof,
But of his father begged, a last request,

---

6. I.e., when Julia, seeing this, scattered.
7. An enclosed ("close") chair carried
on poles by two bearers, one in front, one
behind. "Attendant": watchful, attentive
(the French present participle).

That a retreat might be assigned to him— 895
A house where in the country he might dwell
With such allowance as his wants required—
And the more lonely that the mansion was
'Twould be more welcome. To a lodge that stood
Deep in a forest, with leave given, at the age 900
Of four and twenty summers he retired,
And thither took with him his infant babe
And one domestic for their common needs,
An aged woman. It consoled him here
To attend upon the orphan and perform 905
The office of a nurse to his young child,
Which, after a short time, by some mistake
Or indiscretion of the father, died.
The tale I follow to its last recess
Of suffering or of peace, I know not which— 910
Theirs be the blame who caused the woe, not mine.

From that time forth he never uttered word
To any living. An inhabitant
Of that same town in which the pair had left
So lively a remembrance of their griefs, 915
By chance of business coming within reach
Of his retirement, to the spot repaired
With the intent to visit him; he reached
The house and only found the matron there,
Who told him that his pains were thrown away, 920
For that her master never uttered word
To living soul—not even to her. Behold,
While they were speaking Vaudracour approached,
But, seeing some one there, just as his hand
Was stretched towards the garden-gate, he shrunk 925
And like a shadow glided out of view.
Shocked at his savage outside,[8] from the place
The visitor retired.

Thus lived the youth,
Cut off from all intelligence with man,
And shunning even the light of common day. 930
Nor could the voice of freedom, which through France
Soon afterwards resounded, public hope,
Or personal memory of his own deep wrongs,
Rouze him, but in those solitary shades
His days he wasted, an imbecile[9] mind. 935

---

8. Wild (French *sauvage*) appearance.   9. Pronounced "ĭmbécĭl."

But our little bark
On a strong river boldly hath been launched;   560
And from the driving current should we turn
To loiter wilfully within a creek,
Howe'er attractive, Fellow voyager!
Would'st thou not chide? Yet deem not my pains lost:
For Vaudracour and Julia (so were named   565
The ill-fated pair) in that plain tale will draw
Tears from the hearts of others, when their own
Shall beat no more. Thou, also, there mayst read,
At leisure, how the enamoured youth was driven,
By public power abused, to fatal crime,   570
Nature's rebellion against monstrous law;
How, between heart and heart, oppression thrust
Her mandates, severing whom true love had joined,
Harassing both; until he sank and pressed
The couch his fate had made for him; supine,   575
Save when the stings of viperous remorse,
Trying their strength, enforced him to start up,
Aghast and prayerless. Into a deep wood
He fled, to shun the haunts of human kind;
There dwelt, weakened in spirit more and more;   580
Nor could the voice of Freedom, which through France
Full speedily resounded, public hope,
Or personal memory of his own worst wrongs,
Rouse him; but, hidden in those gloomy shades,
His days he wasted,—an imbecile[9] mind.   585

Book Tenth

Residence in France and French Revolution

It was a beautiful and silent day
That overspread the countenance of earth,
[3] Then fading, with unusual quietness,
When from the Loire I parted, and through scenes
Of vineyard, orchard, meadow-ground and tilth,[1]   5
Calm waters, gleams of sun, and breathless trees,
Towards the fierce metropolis turned my steps
Their homeward way to England.[2] From his throne
[12] The King had fallen; the congregated host—
Dire cloud, upon the front of which was written   10
The tender mercies of the dismal wind
[15] That bore it—on the plains of Liberty
Had burst innocuously.[3] Say more, the swarm
That came elate and jocund, like a band
Of eastern hunters, to enfold in ring   15
Narrowing itself by moments, and reduce
To the last punctual[4] spot of their despair,
A race of victims—so they seemed—themselves
Had shrunk from sight of their own task, and fled
In terror. Desolation and dismay   20
Remained for them whose fancies had grown rank
With evil expectations: confidence
[30] And perfect triumph to the better cause.
The state, as if to stamp the final seal
On her security, and to the world   25
[33] Shew what she was, a high and fearless soul—
Or rather in a spirit of thanks to those
Who had stirred up her slackening faculties
To a new transition—had assumed with joy

1. Ploughed (tilled) land.
2. Wordsworth left Orleans (where Annette had gone in early September, presumably to conceal her pregnancy) at the
end of October 1792, but seems to have
lingered in Paris until late November–
early December, before returning to England.
3. Louis XVI was imprisoned, and ef-

fectively deposed, on August 10, 1792.
The Coalition armies (*1805:* "congregated
host") of Austrian and Prussian troops
invaded France nine days later, but without doing harm ("innocuously") because
on September 20 the French achieved a
highly important victory at Valmy, and
the invaders retreated to the Rhine.
4. Precise; as at VIII, 763, above.

Book Tenth

Residence in France–Continued

It was a beautiful and silent day
That overspread the countenance of earth,
Then fading with unusual quietness,—
A day as beautiful as e'er was given
To soothe regret, though deepening what it soothed,   5
When by the gliding Loire I paused, and cast
Upon his rich domains, vineyard and tilth,[1]
Green meadow-ground, and many-coloured woods,
Again, and yet again, a farewell look;
Then from the quiet of that scene passed on,   10
Bound to the fierce Metropolis.[2] From his throne
The King had fallen, and that invading host—
Presumptuous cloud, on whose black front was written
The tender mercies of the dismal wind
That bore it—on the plains of Liberty   15
Had burst innocuous.[3] Say in bolder words,
They—who had come elate as eastern hunters
Banded beneath the Great Mogul, when he
Erewhile went forth from Agra or Lahore,
Rajahs and Omrahs in his train,[5] intent   20
To drive their prey enclosed within a ring
Wide as a province, but, the signal given,
Before the point of the life-threatening spear
Narrowing itself by moments—they, rash men,
Had seen the anticipated quarry turned   25
Into avengers, from whose wrath they fled
In terror. Disappointment and dismay
Remained for all whose fancies had run wild
With evil expectations; confidence
And perfect triumph for the better cause.   30

    The State, as if to stamp the final seal
On her security, and to the world
Show what she was, a high and fearless soul,
Exulting in defiance, or heart-stung
By sharp resentment, or belike to taunt   35
With spiteful gratitude the baffled League,
That had stirred up 'her slackening faculties
To a new transition, when the King was crushed,
Spared not the empty throne, and in proud haste

5. A direct reference to *Paradise Lost*, XI, 391, "To Agra and Lahor of great mogul," inserted in 1832. "Omrahs": Mohammedan grandees (associated frequently with the Mogul's court).

[40] The body and the venerable name   30
Of a republic.[6] Lamentable crimes,
'Tis true, had gone before this hour—the work
Of massacre, in which the senseless sword
Was prayed to as a judge—but these were past,
[45] Earth free from them for ever (as was thought),   35
Ephemeral monsters, to be seen but once,
Things that could only shew themselves and die.

   This was the time in which, enflamed with hope,
To Paris I returned. Again I ranged,
More eagerly than I had done before,   40
[50] Through the wide city, and in progress passed
The prison where the unhappy monarch lay,
Associate with his children and his wife
In bondage, and the palace, lately stormed
With roar of cannon and a numerous host.   45
[55] I crossed—a black and empty area then—
The square of the Carousel, few weeks back
Heaped up with dead and dying,[7] upon these
And other sights looking as doth a man
Upon a volume whose contents he knows   50
[60] Are memorable but from him locked up,
Being written in a tongue he cannot read,
So that he questions the mute leaves with pain,
And half upbraids their silence. But that night
When on my bed I lay, I was most moved   55
And felt most deeply in what world I was;
[66] My room was high and lonely, near the roof
Of a large mansion or hotel,[8] a spot
That would have pleased me in more quiet times—
Nor was it wholly without pleasure then.   60
[70] With unextinguished taper I kept watch,
Reading at intervals. The fear gone by
Pressed on me almost like a fear to come.
I thought of those September massacres,

6. The Republic was proclaimed on September 22, two days after Valmy, but France was by now a muddled and divided country, and there was no widespread joy to compare with the optimism of 1789 and 1790.

7. The deposition of the king on August 10, 1792, was in effect a second revolution. Constitutional monarchy had failed, the Prussian and Austrian armies were ready to march on Paris, the National Assembly was unable to control the situation, and power passed into the hands of the republican *sections* of Paris. The king and his family sought protection in the newly elected Assembly, leaving the Swiss guard to defend the Palace of the Tuileries, who killed some 400 of the attackers before being slaughtered themselves when they obeyed an order from the king to lay down their arms. In all an estimated 800 defenders and palace employees died in reprisals. To burn the corpses, fires were lit in the Place de Carrousel, a huge square in front of the Tuileries. Louis was imprisoned in the Temple until his execution on January 21, 1793.

8. Town house.

Assumed the body and venerable name   40
Of a Republic.[6] Lamentable crimes,
'Tis true, had gone before this hour, dire work
Of massacre, in which the senseless sword
Was prayed to as a judge; but these were past,
Earth free from them for ever, as was thought,—   45
Ephemeral monsters, to be seen but once;
Things that could only show themselves and die.

    Cheered with this hope, to Paris I returned,
And ranged, with ardour heretofore unfelt,
The spacious city, and in progress passed   50
The prison where the unhappy Monarch lay,
Associate with his children and his wife
In bondage; and the palace, lately stormed
With roar of cannon by a furious host.
I crossed the square (an empty area then!)   55
Of the Carrousel, where so late had lain
The dead, upon the dying heaped,[7] and gazed
On this and other spots, as doth a man
Upon a volume whose contents he knows
Are memorable, but from him locked up,   60
Being written in a tongue he cannot read,
So that he questions the mute leaves with pain,
And half upbraids their silence. But that night
I felt most deeply in what world I was,
What ground I trod on, and what air I breathed.   65
High was my room and lonely, near the roof
Of a large mansion or hotel,[8] a lodge
That would have pleased me in more quiet times;
Nor was it wholly without pleasure then.
With unextinguished taper I kept watch,   70
Reading at intervals; the fear gone by
Pressed on me almost like a fear to come.
I thought of those September massacres,

Divided from me by a little month,[9]   65
[75] And felt and touched them, a substantial dread
(The rest was conjured up from tragic fictions,
And mournful calendars[1] of true history,
Remembrances and dim admonishments):
'The horse is taught his manage, and the wind   70
Of heaven wheels round and treads in his own steps;
Year follows year, the tide returns again,
Day follows day, all things have second birth;
The earthquake is not satisfied at once'[2]—
[85] And in such way I wrought upon myself,   75
Until I seemed to hear a voice that cried
To the whole city, 'Sleep no more!'[3] To this
Add comments of a calmer mind—from which
I could not gather full security—
But at the best it seemed a place of fear,   80
[92] Unfit for the repose of night,
Defenceless as a wood where tigers roam.

      Betimes next morning to the Palace-walk
Of Orleans I repaired, and entering there
Was greeted, among divers other notes,   85
By voices of the hawkers in the crowd
[100] Bawling, *Denunciation of the crimes*
Of Maximilian Robespierre. The speech
Which in their hands they carried was the same
Which had been recently pronounced—the day   90
When Robespierre, well known for what mark
[105] Some words of indirect reproof had been
Intended, rose in hardihood, and dared
The man who had ill surmise of him
To bring his charge in openness. Whereat,   95
When a dead pause ensued and no one stirred,
[110] In silence of all present, from his seat
Louvet walked singly through the avenue
And took his station in the Tribune, saying,
'I, Robespierre, accuse thee!' 'Tis well known   100
What was the issue of that charge, and how
Louvet was left alone without support

---

9. The massacres of September 2–6,
1792 followed the news of the fall of
Verdun. About half the prisoners in
Paris—most of them in fact ordinary
criminals, not royalists—were executed
by the mob, after summary trials. "A
little month": see *Hamlet*, I, ii, 147.
1. Registers.
2. In these magnificent apocalyptic lines

—spoiled in *1850*—Wordsworth is talking to himself. "Manage": the action
and paces to which a horse is trained in
a riding school (*NED*).
3. "Methought I heard a voice cry 'Sleep
no more; / Macbeth doth murder sleep'
* * * Still it cried 'Sleep no more' to
all the house" (*Macbeth*, II, ii, 35–36,
41).

Divided from me by one little month.[9]
Saw them and touched: the rest was conjured up   75
From tragic fictions or true history,
Remembrances and dim admonishments.
The horse is taught his manage, and no star
Of wildest course but treads back his own steps;
For the spent hurricane the air provides   80
As fierce a successor; the tide retreats
But to return out of its hiding-place
In the great deep; all things have second birth;
The earthquake is not satisfied at once;[2]
And in this way I wrought upon myself,   85
Until I seemed to hear a voice that cried,
To the whole city, 'Sleep no more'.[3] The trance
Fled with the voice to which it had given birth;
But vainly comments of a calmer mind
Promised soft peace and sweet forgetfulness.   90
The place, all hushed and silent as it was,
Appeared unfit for the repose of night,
Defenceless as a wood where tigers roam.

   With early morning towards the Palace-walk
Of Orleans eagerly I turned; as yet   95
The streets were still; not so those long Arcades;
There, 'mid a peal of ill-matched sounds and cries,
That greeted me on entering, I could hear
Shrill voices from the hawkers in the throng,
Bawling, 'Denunciation of the Crimes   100
Of Maximilian Robespierre'; the hand,
Prompt as the voice, held forth a printed speech,
The same that had been recently pronounced,
When Robespierre, not ignorant for what mark
Some words of indirect reproof had been   105
Intended, rose in hardihood, and dared
The man who had an ill surmise of him
To bring his charge in openness; whereat,
When a dead pause ensued, and no one stirred,
In silence of all present, from his seat   110
Louvet walked single through the avenue,
And took his station in the Tribune, saying,
'I, Robespierre, accuse thee!' Well is known
The inglorious issue of that charge, and how
He, who had launched the startling thunderbolt,   115
The one bold man, whose voice the attack had sounded,
Was left without a follower to discharge

[120] Of his irresolute friends;[4] but these are things
      Of which I speak only as they were storm   105
      Or sunshine to my individual mind,
      No further. Let me then relate that now—
      In some sort seeing with my proper[5] eyes
[125] That liberty, and life, and death, would soon
      To the remotest corners of the land
      Lie in the arbitrement of those who ruled   110
      The capital city; what was struggled for,
      And by what combatants victory must be won;
[130] The indecision on their part whose aim
      Seemed best, and the straightforward path of those
      Who in attack or in defence alike   115
      Were strong through their impiety—greatly I
      Was agitated. Yea, I could almost
[135] Have prayed that throughout earth upon all souls
      Worthy of liberty, upon every soul
      Matured to live in plainness and in truth,   120
      The gift of tongues might fall,[6] and men arrive
[140] From the four quarters of the winds to do
      For France what without help she could not do,
      A work of honour—think not that to this
      I added, work of safety: from such thought,   125
      And the least fear about the end of things,
[145] I was as far as angels are from guilt.

      Yet did I grieve, nor only grieved, but thought
      Of opposition and of remedies:
      An insignificant stranger and obscure,   130
      Mean as I was, and little graced with powers
[150] Of eloquence even in my native speech,
      And all unfit for tumult and intrigue,
      Yet would I willingly have taken up
      A service at this time for cause so great,   135
      However dangerous. Inly I revolved
[155] How much the destiny of man had still
      Hung upon single persons; that there was,

4. The moderate Louvet denounced Robespierre as a would-be dictator on October 29, 1792, in the National Convention. Robespierre had challenged his enemies to clarify accusations against him made during the previous debate (in which Danton had been indicted as responsible for the September Massacres); Louvet responded, and his speech appeared as the pamphlet that Wordsworth apparently saw (*1805*, 87–90; *1850*, 100–103). Each of the last six paragraphs opens "*Je t'accuse*," and Louvet's final words are, "*Je t'accuse d'avoir evidem-* *ment marché au suprême pouvoir*" ("I accuse you of having clearly aimed at supreme power"). Robespierre asked time to prepare his reply, and produced an extremely skillful defense the following week. He achieved supreme power nine months later, in July 1793; see *1805*, 312*n*, below.
5. Own.
6. God's conferring of the power of the Holy Spirit upon the Apostles at Pentecost showed itself in their sudden ability to prophesy in foreign tongues. See Acts 2:3–4.

His perilous duty,[4] and retire lamenting
That Heaven's best aid is wasted upon men
Who to themselves are false.   120

                        But these are things
Of which I speak, only as they were storm
Or sunshine to my individual mind,
No further. Let me then relate that now—
In some sort seeing with my proper[5] eyes
That Liberty, and Life, and Death would soon   125
To the remotest corners of the land
Lie in the arbitrement of those who ruled
The capital City; what was struggled for,
And by what combatants victory must be won;
The indecision on their part whose aim   130
Seemed best, and the straightforward path of those
Who in attack or in defence were strong
Through their impiety—my inmost soul
Was agitated; yea, I could almost
Have prayed that throughout earth upon all men,   135
By patient exercise of reason made
Worthy of liberty, all spirits filled
With zeal expanding in Truth's holy light,
The gift of tongues might fall,[6] and power arrive
From the four quarters of the winds to do   140
For France, what without help she could not do,
A work of honour; think not that to this
I added, work of safety: from all doubts
Or trepidation for the end of things
Far was I, far as angels are from guilt.   145

    Yet did I grieve, nor only grieved, but thought
Of opposition and of remedies:
An insignificant stranger and obscure,
And one, moreover, little graced with power
Of eloquence even in my native speech,   150
And all unfit for tumult or intrigue,
Yet would I at this time with willing heart
Have undertaken for a cause so great
Service however dangerous. I revolved,
How much the destiny of Man had still   155
Hung upon single persons; that there was,

Transcendent to all local patrimony,
One nature as there is one sun in heaven;   140
That objects, even as they are great, thereby
[160] Do come within the reach of humblest eyes;
That man was only weak through his mistrust
And want of hope, where evidence divine
Proclaimed to him that hope should be most sure;   145
That, with desires heroic and firm sense,
[167] A spirit thoroughly faithful to itself,
Unquenchable, unsleeping, undismayed,
Was as an instinct among men, a stream
That gathered up each petty straggling rill   150
And vein of water, glad to be rolled on
In safe obedience; that a mind whose rest
Was where it ought to be, in self-restraint,
[175] In circumspection and simplicity,
Fell rarely in entire discomfiture   155
Below its aim, or met with from without
A treachery that defeated it or foiled.

[191]   On the other side, I called to mind those truths
Which are the commonplaces of the schools,
A theme[7] for boys, too trite even to be felt,   160
Yet with a revelation's liveliness
[195] In all their comprehensive bearings known
And visible to philosophers of old,
Men who, to business of the world untrained,
Lived in the shade; and to Harmodius known,   165
And his compeer Aristogiton; known
[200] To Brutus[8]—that tyrannic power is weak,

Hath neither gratitude, nor faith nor love,
Nor the support of good or evil men,
To trust in; that the godhead which is ours   170

---

7. I.e., essay topic.
8. Harmodius and Aristogiton, known as the Liberators, were Athenians of noble family who attempted in 504 B.C. to kill the tyrant Hippias; one died in the attempt, the other was arrested and executed. Brutus was a more successful tyrannicide, playing a leading part in the assassination of Julius Caesar in 44 B.C.

Transcendent to all local patrimony,
One nature, as there is one sun in heaven;
That objects, even as they are great; thereby
Do come within the reach of humblest eyes;   160
That man is only weak through his mistrust
And want of hope where evidence divine
Proclaims to him that hope should be most sure;
Nor did the inexperience of my youth
Preclude conviction, that a spirit strong   165
In hope, and trained to noble aspirations,
A spirit thoroughly faithful to itself,
Is for Society's unreasoning herd
A domineering instinct, serves at once
For way and guide, a fluent receptacle   170
That gathers up each petty straggling rill
And vein of water, glad to be rolled on
In safe obedience; that a mind, whose rest
Is where it ought to be, in self-restraint,
In circumspection and simplicity,   175
Falls rarely in entire discomfiture
Below its aim, or meets with, from without,
A treachery that foils it or defeats;
And, lastly, if the means on human will,
Frail human will, dependent should betray   180
Him who too boldly trusted them, I felt
That 'mid the loud distractions of the world
A sovereign voice subsists within the soul,
Arbiter undisturbed of right and wrong,
Of life and death, in majesty severe   185
Enjoining, as may best promote the aims
Of truth and justice, either sacrifice,
From whatsoever region of our cares
Or our infirm affections Nature pleads,
Earnest and blind, against the stern decree.   190

    On the other side, I called to mind those truths
That are the common-places of the schools—
(A theme[7] for boys, too hackneyed for their sires),
Yet, with a revelation's liveliness,
In all their comprehensive bearings known   195
And visible to philosophers of old,
Men who, to business of the world untrained,
Lived in the shade; and to Harmodius known
And his compeer Aristogiton, known
To Brutus[8]—that tyrannic power is weak,   200
Hath neither gratitude, nor faith, nor love,
Nor the support of good or evil men
To trust in; that the godhead which is ours

Can never utterly be charmed or stilled;[9]
[205] That nothing hath a natural right to last
But equity and reason; that all else
Meets foes irreconcilable, and at best
Doth live but by variety of disease.   175

Well might my wishes be intense, my thoughts
[210] Strong and perturbed, not doubting at that time—
Creed which ten shameful years have not annulled—
But that the virtue of one paramount mind
Would have abashed those impious crests, have quelled   180
Outrage and bloody power, and in despite
Of what the people were through ignorance
[216] And immaturity, and in the teeth
Of desperate opposition from without,
Have cleared a passage for just government,   185
And left a solid birthright to the state,
[220] Redeemed according to example given
By ancient lawgivers.[1] In this frame of mind
Reluctantly to England I returned,
Compelled by nothing less than absolute want   190
Of funds for my support;[2] else, well assured
That I both was and must be of small worth,
No better than an alien in the land,
I doubtless should have made a common cause
[230] With some who perished, haply perished too[3]—   195
A poor mistaken and bewildered offering,
Should to the breast of Nature have gone back,
With all my resolutions, all my hopes,
A poet only to myself, to men
Useless, and even, belovèd friend, a soul   200
[235] To thee unknown.

When to my native land,
After a whole year's absence, I returned,
[246] I found the air yet busy with the stir
Of a contention which had been raised up   205
Against the traffickers in Negro blood,

<hr/>

9. I.e., that the divine quality in man can never be totally overpowered ("charmed") or subdued.
1. *1805*, 176–88 (*1850*, 209–21) form a preface to the account that follows of Wordsworth's political feelings 1793–95. Looking back across "ten shameful years" (*1805*, 178), he does not doubt the rightness of the Revolution, but regrets that its clear current should have been muddied and diverted by base men. With hindsight he can see what went wrong, but he remains vehemently committed to his original position—as indeed he does in *1850*, despite the cutting in 1816/19 of line 178.
2. A half-truth. Wordsworth returned to England in late November/early December 1792 looking for funds to support not just himself, but a wife and child (see *1805*, IX, 555n, above). "The land" in *1805*, 193, is England.
3. Almost all the Girondins, with whom Wordsworth was in sympathy, were guillotined or driven to suicide. "Haply": perhaps.

Can never utterly be charmed or stilled;
That nothing hath a natural right to last   205
But equity and reason; that all else
Meets foes irreconcilable, and at best
Lives only by variety of disease.

    Well might my wishes be intense, my thoughts
Strong and perturbed, not doubting at that time   210
But that the virtue of one paramount mind
Would have abashed those impious crests—have quelled
Outrage and bloody power, and, in despite
Of what the People long had been and were
Through ignorance and false teaching, sadder proof   215
Of immaturity, and in the teeth
Of desperate opposition from without—
Have cleared a passage for just government,
And left a solid birthright to the State,
Redeemed, according to example given   220
By ancient lawgivers.[1]

                In this frame of mind,
Dragged by a chain of harsh necessity,
So seemed it,—now I thankfully acknowledge,
Forced by the gracious providence of Heaven,—
To England I returned,[2] else (though assured   225
That I both was and must be of small weight,
No better than a landsman on the deck
Of a ship struggling with a hideous storm)
Doubtless, I should have then made common cause
With some who perished; haply, perished too,[3]   230
A poor mistaken and bewildered offering,—
Should to the breast of Nature have gone back,
With all my resolutions, all my hopes,
A Poet only to myself, to men
Useless, and even, beloved Friend! a soul
To thee unknown!   235

            Twice had the trees let fall
Their leaves, as often Winter had put on
His hoary crown, since I had seen the surge
Beat against Albion's shore, since ear of mine
Had caught the accents of my native speech   240

[250] An effort which, though baffled, nevertheless
Had called back old forgotten principles
Dismissed from service, had diffused some truths,
And more of virtuous feeling, through the heart
Of the English people.⁵ And no few of those,   210
So numerous—little less in verity
Than a whole nation crying with one voice—
Who had been crossed in this their just intent
And righteous hope, thereby were well prepared
To let that journey sleep awhile, and join   215
Whatever other caravan appeared
To travel forward towards Liberty
With more success. For me that strife had ne'er
[255] Fastened on my affections, nor did now
Its unsuccessful issue much excite   220
My sorrow, having laid this faith to heart,
That if France prospered good men would not long
Pay fruitless worship to humanity,
[260] And this most rotten branch of human shame
(Object, as seemed, of a superfluous pains)   225
Would fall together with its parent tree.

    Such was my then belief—that there was one,
And only one, solicitude for all.
And now the strength of Britain was put forth
[265] In league with the confederated host;⁶   230
Not in my single self alone I found,
But in the minds of all ingenuous youth,
Change and subversion from this hour. No shock
Given to my moral nature had I known
[270] Down to that very moment—neither lapse   235
Nor turn of sentiment—that might be named
A revolution, save at this one time:
All else was progress on the self-same path
On which with a diversity of pace
[275] I had been travelling; this, a stride at once   240
Into another region. True it is,
'Twas not concealed with what ungracious eyes
Our native rulers from the very first

---

5. A Society for the Abolition of the Slave Trade had been founded by William Wilberforce, Thomas Clarkson, and others, in 1787. A bill to prohibit slave trading under the British flag had been passed by the House of Commons while Wordsworth was in France, only to be rejected ("baffled," *1805*, 206) by the House of Lords. Success came finally in 1807.

6. France declared war on England and Holland on February 1, 1793. Over the spring and summer England built up a coalition with the various continental powers, notably Prussia and Austria.

Upon our native country's sacred ground.[4]
A patriot of the world, how could I glide
Into communion with her sylvan shades,
Erewhile my tuneful haunt? It pleased me more
To abide in the great City, where I found   245
The general air still busy with the stir
Of that first memorable onset made
By a strong levy of humanity
Upon the traffickers in Negro blood;
Effort which, though defeated, had recalled   250
To notice old forgotten principles,
And through the nation spread a novel heat
Of virtuous feeling.[5] For myself, I own
That this particular strife had wanted power
To *rivet* my affections; nor did now   255
Its unsuccessful issue much excite
My sorrow; for I brought with me the faith
That, if France prospered, good men would not long
Pay fruitless worship to humanity,
And this most rotten branch of human shame,   260
Object, so seemed it, of superfluous pains,
Would fall together with its parent tree.
What, then, were my emotions, when in arms
Britain put forth her free-born strength in league,
Oh, pity and shame! with those confederate Powers![6]   265
Not in my single self alone I found,
But in the minds of all ingenuous youth,
Change and subversion from that hour. No shock
Given to my moral nature had I known
Down to that very moment; neither lapse   270
Nor turn of sentiment that might be named
A revolution, save at this one time;
All else was progress on the self-same path
On which, with a diversity of pace,
I had been travelling: this a stride at once   275
Into another region. As a light
And pliant harebell, swinging in the breeze
On some grey rock—its birth-place—so had I

4. The plain statement of *1805*, "After a whole year's absence," is sacrificed in favour of poetic elaboration that is not even accurate. Wordsworth was in France late November 1791–November/ December 1792.

Had looked upon regenerated France;[7]
Nor had I doubted that this day would come—   245
But in such contemplation I had thought
Of general interests only, beyond this
Had never once foretasted the event.
Now had I other business, for I felt
The ravage of this most unnatural strife   250
In my own heart; there lay it like a weight,
At enmity with all the tenderest springs
Of my enjoyments. I, who with the breeze
Had played, a green leaf on the blessed tree
[280] Of my beloved country—nor had wished   255
For happier fortune than to wither there—
Now from my pleasant station[8] was cut off,
And tossed about in whirlwinds. I rejoiced,
Yes, afterwards, truth painful to record,
[285] Exulted in the triumph of my soul   260
When Englishmen by thousands were o'erthrown,
Left without glory on the field, or driven,
Brave hearts, to shameful flight. It was a grief—
Grief call it not, 'twas any thing but that—
[290] A conflict of sensations without name,   265
Of which he only who may love the sight
Of a village steeple as I do can judge,
When in the congregation, bending all
To their great Father,[9] prayers were offered up
[295] Or praises for our country's victories,   270
And, 'mid the simple worshippers perchance
I only, like an uninvited guest
Whom no one owned, sate silent—shall I add,
Fed on the day of vengeance yet to come!

[300]   Oh, much have they to account for, who could tear   275
By violence at one decisive rent
From the best youth in England their dear pride,
Their joy, in England. This, too, at a time
In which worst losses easily might wear
[305] The best of names; when patriotic love   280
Did of itself in modesty give way
Like the precursor when the deity

---

7. The initial British response to the Revolution had been mistaken, but not in fact "ungracious"—see *1805*, VI, 352n, above. Publication of Burke's *Reflections* in November 1790 was followed by a stiffening of attitudes in the Establishment, but serious repression of left-wing opinion did not begin until 1793. For Wordsworth's vehement comments,
see *1805*, 645–56 below, and his *Letter to the Bishop of Llandaff* of February–March 1793 (*Prose Works*, I, pp. 17–66).
8. Position.
9. "While each to his great father bends," *Ancient Mariner*, 640; for Wordsworth, as for the Mariner, shared worship is symbolic of harmony.

Wantoned, fast rooted on the ancient tower
Of my beloved country, wishing not   280
A happier fortune than to wither there:
Now was I from that pleasant station[8] torn
And tossed about in whirlwind. I rejoiced,
Yea, afterwards—truth most painful to record!—
Exulted, in the triumph of my soul,   285
When Englishmen by thousands were o'erthrown,
Left without glory on the field, or driven,
Brave hearts! to shameful flight. It was a grief,—
Grief call it not, 'twas anything but that,—
A conflict of sensations without name,   290
Of which *he* only, who may love the sight
Of a village steeple, as I do, can judge,
When, in the congregation bending all
To their great Father,[9] prayers were offered up,
Or praises for our country's victories;   295
And, 'mid the simple worshippers, perchance
I only, like an uninvited guest
Whom no one owned, sate silent, shall I add,
Fed on the day of vengeance yet to come.

  Oh! much have they to account for, who could tear, 300
By violence, at one decisive rent,
From the best youth in England their dear pride,
Their joy, in England; this, too, at a time
In which worst losses easily might wear
The best of names, when patriotic love   305
Did of itself in modesty give way,
Like the Precursor when the Deity

Is come, whose harbinger he is—a time
In which apostacy from ancient faith
[310] Seemed but conversion to a higher creed;   285
Withal a season dangerous and wild—
A time in which Experience would have plucked
Flowers out of any hedge to make thereof
A chaplet, in contempt of his grey locks.[1]

[315] Ere yet the fleet of Britain had gone forth   290
On this unworthy service, whereunto
The unhappy counsel of a few weak men
Had doomed it, I beheld the vessels lie—
A brood of gallant creatures—on the deep
I saw them in their rest, a sojourner   295
[320] Through a whole month of calm and glassy days
In that delightful island which protects
Their place of convocation.[3] There I heard
Each evening, walking by the still sea-shore,
A monitory sound which never failed—   300
[325] The sunset cannon. When the orb went down
In the tranquillity of Nature, came
That voice—ill requiem—seldom heard by me
Without a spirit overcast, a deep
Imagination, thought of woes to come,
[330] And sorrow for mankind, and pain of heart.[4]   305

    In France, the men who for their desperate ends
Had plucked up mercy by the roots were glad
Of this new enemy. Tyrants, strong before
In devilish pleas, were ten times stronger now,   310
[335] And thus beset with foes on every side,
The goaded land waxed mad; the crimes of few
Spread into madness of the many; blasts

---

1. Wordsworth makes four remarkably cryptic points in *1805*, 278–89 (*1850*, 303–14), all depending on the fact that he regarded government policy as a reversal of the true interests of the country: (1) *1805*, 278–80 (*1850*, 303–5) Losses could be called gains: i.e., defeats of the French —and thus of republicanism in England and elsewhere—could be described as English victories. (2) *1805*, 280–83 (*1850*, 305–8) In an incongruous image: the true love of one's country gives way to the falsely patriotic wish for victory, as John the Baptist gives place to Christ. (3) *1805*, 283–85 (*1850*, 308–10) Rejection of earlier true belief could thus seem to be conversion to a higher faith (Wordsworth's religious imagery does not link back to the previous lines). (4) *1805*,

286–89 (*1850*, 311–14) "Experience"— those who had grown gray in the service of an earlier ideal—would at this time have adopted any disguise, however inappropriate, so as to lay claim to political innocence.
3. Wordsworth saw the British fleet arming for war off Portsmouth, ca. late June–early August 1793, while staying in the Isle of Wight with William Calvert, who had been his school-mate at Hawkshead Grammar School.
4. Compare, "How sweet the walk along the woody steep," written in 1793: "But hark from yon proud fleet in peal profound / Thunders the sunset cannon; at the sound / The star of life appears to set in blood" (lines 15–17).

Is come Whose harbinger he was; a time
In which apostasy from ancient faith
Seemed but conversion to a higher creed;   310
Withal a season dangerous and wild,
A time when sage Experience would have snatched
Flowers out of any hedge-row to compose
A chaplet in contempt of his grey locks.[1]

    When the proud fleet that bears the red-cross flag[2]   315
In that unworthy service was prepared
To mingle, I beheld the vessels lie,
A brood of gallant creatures, on the deep;
I saw them in their rest, a sojourner
Through a whole month of calm and glassy days   320
In that delightful island which protects
Their place of convocation[3]—there I heard,
Each evening, pacing by the still sea-shore,
A monitory sound that never failed,—
The sunset cannon. While the orb went down   325
In the tranquillity of nature, came
That voice, ill requiem! seldom heard by me
Without a spirit overcast by dark
Imaginations, sense of woes to come,
Sorrow for human kind, and pain of heart.[4]   330

    In France, the men, who, for their desperate ends,
Had plucked up mercy by the roots, were glad
Of this new enemy. Tyrants, strong before
In wicked pleas, were strong as demons now;
And thus, on every side beset with foes,   335
The goaded land waxed mad; the crimes of few
Spread into madness of the many; blasts

2. The white ensign, bearing the red cross of St. George, with the union jack in the top left-hand quarter, although not adopted as the official flag of the Royal Navy till 1864, was used in battle to avoid confusion with the tricolor (supplied to the French fleet in October 1794).

From hell came sanctified like airs from heaven.[5]
The sternness of the just, the faith of those 315
[340] Who doubted not that Providence had times
Of anger and of vengeance, theirs[6] who throned
The human understanding paramount
And made of that their god,[7] the hopes of those
Who were content to barter short-lived pangs 320
[345] For a paradise of ages,[8] the blind rage
Of insolent tempers, the light vanity
Of intermeddlers, steady purposes
Of the suspicious, slips of the indiscreet,
And all the accidents of life, were pressed 325
[350] Into one service, busy with one work.
The Senate was heart-stricken, not a voice
[355] Uplifted, none to oppose or mitigate.
Domestic carnage now filled all the year
With feast-days: the old man from the chimney-nook, 330
The maiden from the bosom of her love,
The mother from the cradle of her babe,
[360] The warrior from the field—all perished, all—
Friends, enemies, of all parties, ages, ranks,
Head after head, and never heads enough 335
For those who bade them fall.[9] They found their joy,
They made it, ever thirsty, as a child—
[365] If light desires of innocent little ones
May with such heinous appetites be matched—
Having a toy, a windmill, though the air 340
[370] Do of itself blow fresh and makes the vane
Spin in his eyesight, he is not content,

5. July 1793 was the month in which Robespierre came to power. The Reign of Terror that followed was from the first justified as the means of saving France from her enemies. Royalist plots, or complicity with Pitt and Coburg (the Austrian commander), were standard pretexts for execution. In *1805*, 309–10 (*1850*, 333–34) an echo of *Paradise Lost*, IV, 394, associates the tyranny of Robespierre in revolutionary France with that of Satan newly landed in Paradise; and *1805*, 313–14 (*1850*, 337–38) draw on *Hamlet*, I, iv, 41: "Bring with thee airs from heaven or blasts from hell."
6. Read: "*and* theirs."
7. The faith of 315–17 is Christianity, that of 317–19 is Reason. Wordsworth's language is not metaphorical: in the summer and autumn of 1793 there was an attempt by certain members of the National Convention to replace Catholicism with a secular religion. Priests, including the Archbishop of Paris, were forced to abjure their faith, images were destroyed, chalices and furnishings confiscated, and at a bizarre ceremony the Cathedral of Notre Dame was renamed the Temple of Reason. Robespierre, who was a deist and detested atheism, disapproved of the process, and brought the major supporters of the new religion to the guillotine during the following year. On June 8, 1794, seven weeks before he was himself executed, he presided at a Festival of the Supreme Being, scarcely less grotesque than the ceremonies of Reason.
8. A reference to patriots who regarded the Terror as a purging of the Revolution before its paradisal future could be achieved.
9. In the Great Terror that followed the law of June 10, 1794, dispensing with defense lawyers and witnesses, and enabling the accused to be condemned in batches, 1,376 people were guillotined in Paris in forty-nine days—100 more than in the previous fifteen months. In other parts of the country the Terror was mainly used against counter-revolutionists, mass executions taking place at Lyons, at Toulon, and in the Vendée.

From hell came sanctified like airs from heaven.[5]
The sternness of the just, the faith of those
Who doubted not that Providence had times   340
Of vengeful retribution, theirs[6] who throned
The human Understanding paramount
And made of that their God,[7] the hopes of men
Who were content to barter short-lived pangs
For a paradise of ages,[8] the blind rage   345
Of insolent tempers, the light vanity
Of intermeddlars, steady purposes
Of the suspicious, slips of the indiscreet,
And all the accidents of life were pressed
Into one service, busy with one work.   350
The Senate stood aghast, her prudence quenched,
Her wisdom stifled, and her justice scared,
Her frenzy only active to extol
Past outrages, and shape the way for new,
Which no one dared to oppose or mitigate.   355

   Domestic carnage now filled the whole year
With feast-days; old men from the chimney-nook,
The maiden from the bosom of her love,
The mother from the cradle of her babe,
The warrior from the field—all perished, all—   360
Friends, enemies, of all parties, ages, ranks,
Head after head, and never heads enough
For those that bade them fall.[9] They found their joy,
They made it proudly, eager as a child,
(If light desires of innocent little ones   365
May with such heinous appetites be compared),
Pleased in some open field to exercise
A toy that mimics with revolving wings
The motion of a wind-mill; though the air
Do of itself blow fresh, and make the vanes   370
Spin in his eyesight, *that* contents him not,

But with the plaything at arm's length he sets
His front against the blast, and runs amain
To make it whirl the faster.   345

                    In the depth
[375] Of these enormities, even thinking minds
Forgot at seasons whence they had their being—
Forgot that such a sound was ever heard
As Liberty upon earth—yet all beneath
Her innocent authority was wrought,   350
[380] Nor could have been, without her blessèd name.
The illustrious wife of Roland, in the hour
Of her composure, felt that agony
And gave it vent in her last words.[1] O friend,
It was a lamentable time for man,   355
[385] Whether a hope had e'er been his or not;
A woeful time for them whose hopes did still
Outlast the shock; most woeful for those few—
They had the deepest feeling of the grief—
Who still were flattered,[2] and had trust in man.   360
[390] Meanwhile the invaders fared as they deserved:
The herculean Commonwealth had put forth her arms,
And throttled with an infant godhead's might
The snakes about her cradle[3]—that was well,
And as it should be, yet no cure for those   365
[395] Whose souls were sick with pain of what would be
Hereafter brought in charge against mankind.
Most melancholy at that time, O friend,
Were my day-thoughts, my dreams were miserable;
Through months, through years, long after the last beat   370
[400] Of those atrocities (I speak bare truth,
As if to thee alone in private talk)
I scarcely had one night of quiet sleep,
Such ghastly visions had I of despair,
And tyranny, and implements of death,   375
[411] And long orations which in dreams I pleaded
Before unjust tribunals, with a voice
Labouring, a brain confounded, and a sense
Of treachery and desertion in the place
[415] The holiest that I knew of—my own soul.   380

---

1. Madame Roland was a major influence behind the moderate Girondins. She was imprisoned in June 1793, and guillotined on November 9. Her last words are said to have been "Oh Liberty, what crimes are committed in thy name!"
2. "Flatter": to raise false hopes (Johnson's *Dictionary*).
3. Hercules was the son of Zeus by the mortal, Alcmene. Hera, wife of Zeus, sent two serpents to kill him in his cradle, but he throttled them. French soil had been cleared of invaders, and the counter-revolution of the Vendée finally suppressed, in autumn 1793; in May–July 1794, the Republican armies turned to the attack. Belgium was taken in the east (Holland too before the end of the year), the Prussians were driven back to the Rhine, Turin was threatened, and Spain invaded at two separate points.

But, with the plaything at arm's length, he sets
His front against the blast, and runs amain,
That it may whirl the faster.

                    Amid the depth
Of those enormities, even thinking minds 375
Forgot, at seasons, whence they had their being;
Forgot that such a sound was ever heard
As Liberty upon earth: yet all beneath
Her innocent authority was wrought,
Nor could have been, without her blessed name. 380
The illustrious wife of Roland, in the hour
Of her composure, felt that agony,
And gave it vent in her last words.[1] O Friend!
It was a lamentable time for man,
Whether a hope had e'er been his or not; 385
A woful time for them whose hopes survived
The shock; most woful for those few who still
Were flattered,[2] and had trust in human kind:
They had the deepest feeling of the grief.
Meanwhile the Invaders fared as they deserved: 390
The Herculean Commonwealth had put forth her arms,
And throttled with an infant godhead's might
The snakes about her cradle;[3] that was well,
And as it should be; yet no cure for them
Whose souls were sick with pain of what would be 395
Hereafter brought in charge against mankind.
Most melancholy at that time, O Friend!
Were my day-thoughts,—my nights were miserable;
Through months, through years, long after the last beat
Of those atrocities, the hour of sleep 400
To me came rarely charged with natural gifts,
Such ghastly visions had I of despair
And tyranny, and implements of death;
And innocent victims sinking under fear,
And momentary hope, and worn-out prayer, 405
Each in his separate cell, or penned in crowds
For sacrifice, and struggling with forced mirth
And levity in dungeons, where the dust
Was laid with tears. Then suddenly the scene
Changed, and the unbroken dream entangled me 410
In long orations, which I strove to plead
Before unjust tribunals,—with a voice
Labouring, a brain confounded, and a sense,
Death-like, of treacherous desertion, felt
In the last place of refuge—my own soul. 415

When I began at first, in early youth,
To yield myself to Nature—when that strong
And holy passion overcame me first—
Neither day nor night, evening or morn,
[420] Were free from the oppression,[4] but, great God,   385
Who send'st thyself into this breathing world
Through Nature and through every kind of life,
And mak'st man what he is, creature divine,
[425] In single or in social eminence,
Above all these raised infinite ascents   390
When reason, which enables him to be,
Is not sequestered—what a change is here!
How different ritual for this after-worship,
[430] What countenance to promote this second love![5]
That first was service but to things which lie   395
At rest, within the bosom of thy will:
Therefore to serve was high beatitude;
The tumult was a gladness, and the fear
[435] Ennobling, venerable; sleep secure,
And waking thoughts more rich than happiest dreams.   400
But as the ancient prophets were enflamed,
[440] Nor wanted consolations of their own
And majesty of mind, when they denounced
On towns and cities, wallowing in the abyss
Of their offences, punishment to come;   405
Or saw like other men with bodily eyes
[445] Before them in some desolated place
The consummation of the wrath of Heaven;
So did some portion of that spirit fall
On me to uphold me through those evil times,   410
And in their rage and dog-day heat I found
Something to glory in, as just and fit,
And in the order of sublimest laws.
And even if that were not, amid the awe
[455] Of unintelligible chastisement   415
I felt a kind of sympathy with power—
Motions raised up within me, nevertheless,
Which had relationship to highest things.
[461] Wild blasts of music thus did find their way
Into the midst of terrible events,   420

4. Dominance.
5. Wordsworth's opposition is between love of Nature, in *1805*, 381–85 (*1850*, 416–20)—and again in *1805*, 395–400 (*1850*, 431–36)—and the "second love," that is far more difficult to achieve, the love of man. Either as an individual, or in social groups, man is potentially god-like (a "creature divine"); and when reason, which differentiates him from the rest of creation, is not dispossessed, cut off ("sequestered"), he is raised infinitely high ("infinite ascents") above other kinds of life. Despite this Wordsworth is led to exclaim at the change as one moves over from love of Nature—at the different form of worship that is implied, the different mode of conduct ("counte-nance") that is appropriate, to furthering this second love.

When I began in youth's delightful prime
To yield myself to Nature, when that strong
And holy passion overcame me first,
Nor day nor night, evening or morn, were free
From its oppression.[4] But, O Power Supreme!   420
Without Whose care this world would cease to breathe,
Who from the fountain of Thy grace dost fill
The veins that branch through every frame of life,
Making man what he is, creature divine,
In single or in social eminence,   425
Above the rest raised infinite ascents
When reason that enables him to be
Is not sequestered—what a change is here!
How different ritual for this after-worship,
What countenance to promote this second love![5]   430
The first was service paid to things which lie
Guarded within the bosom of Thy will.
Therefore to serve was high beatitude;
Tumult was therefore gladness, and the fear
Ennobling, venerable; sleep secure,   435
And waking thoughts more rich than happiest dreams.

But as the ancient Prophets, borne aloft
In vision, yet constrained by natural laws
With them to take a troubled human heart,
Wanted not consolations, nor a creed   440
Of reconcilement, then when they denounced,
On towns and cities, wallowing in the abyss
Of their offences, punishment to come;
Or saw, like other men, with bodily eyes,
Before them, in some desolated place,   445
The wrath consummate and the threat fulfilled;
So, with devout humility be it said,
So, did a portion of that spirit fall
On me uplifted from the vantage-ground
Of pity and sorrow to a state of being   450
That through the time's exceeding fierceness saw
Glimpses of retribution, terrible,
And in the order of sublime behests:
But, even if that were not, amid the awe
Of unintelligible chastisement,   455
Not only acquiescences of faith
Survived, but daring sympathies with power,
Motions not treacherous or profane, else why
Within the folds of no ungentle breast
Their dread vibration to this hour prolonged?   460
Wild blasts of music thus could find their way
Into the midst of turbulent events;

So that worst tempests might be listened to:
Then was the truth received into my heart
[465] That under heaviest sorrow earth can bring,
Griefs bitterest of ourselves or of our kind,
If from the affliction somewhere do not grow   425
Honour which could not else have been—a faith,
An elevation, and a sanctity—
If new strength be not given, or old restored,
[470] The blame is ours, not Nature's. When a taunt
Was taken up by scoffers in their pride,   430
Saying, 'Behold the harvest which we reap
From popular government and equality',
I saw that it was neither these nor aught
[475] Of wild belief engrafted on their names
By false philosophy, that caused the woe,   435
But that it was a reservoir of guilt
And ignorance, filled up from age to age,
That could no longer hold its loathsome charge,
[480] But burst and spread in deluge through the land.

    And as the desert hath green spots, the sea   440
Small islands in the midst of stormy waves,
So that disastrous period did not want
[484] Such sprinklings of all human excellence
As were a joy to hear of. Yet—nor less
For those bright spots, those fair examples given   445
Of fortitude, and energy, and love,
And human nature faithful to itself
[490] Under worst trials—was I impelled to think
Of the glad time when first I traversed France,
A youthful pilgrim; above all remembered   450
[495] That day when through an arch that spanned the street,
A rainbow made of garish ornaments
(Triumphal pomp for Liberty confirmed)
We walked, a pair of weary travellers,
Along the town of Arras—place from which   455
Issued that Robespierre, who afterwards
[502] Wielded the sceptre of the atheist crew.[6]
When the calamity spread far and wide,
And this same city, which had even appeared
[505] To outrun the rest in exultation, groaned   460
Under the vengeance of her cruel son,
As Lear reproached the winds, I could almost

---

6. Wordsworth and his friend, Robert
Jones, had spent the night at Arras on
July 16, 1790 during their walking tour;
for Wordsworth's impressions of France
at that time see *1805*, VI, 352–425 above.
Maximilien Robespierre had been born
at Arras on May 6, 1758; he became a
lawyer and represented the town in the
National Assembly from April 1789. For
his year of power, July 1793–July 1794,
see *1805*, 312*n*, above, and for his death,
535*n*, below.

So that worst tempests might be listened to.
Then was the truth received into my heart,
That, under heaviest sorrow earth can bring, 465
If from the affliction somewhere do not grow
Honour which could not else have been, a faith,
An elevation and a sanctity,
If new strength be not given nor old restored,
The blame is ours, not Nature's. When a taunt 470
Was taken up by scoffers in their pride,
Saying, 'Behold the harvest that we reap
From popular government and equality',
I clearly saw that neither these nor aught
Of wild belief engrafted on their names 475
By false philosophy had caused the woe,
But a terrific reservoir of guilt
And ignorance filled up from age to age,
That could no longer hold its loathsome charge,
But burst and spread in deluge through the land. 480

    And as the desert hath green spots, the sea
Small islands scattered amid stormy waves,
So *that* disastrous period did not want
Bright sprinklings of all human excellence,
To which the silver wands of saints in Heaven 485
Might point with rapturous joy. Yet not the less,
For those examples in no age surpassed
Of fortitude and energy and love,
And human nature faithful to herself
Under worst trials, was I driven to think 490
Of the glad times when first I traversed France
A youthful pilgrim; above all reviewed
That eventide, when under windows bright
With happy faces and with garlands hung,
And through a rainbow-arch that spanned the street, 495
Triumphal pomp for liberty confirmed,
I paced, a dear companion at my side,
The town of Arras, whence with promise high
Issued, on delegation to sustain
Humanity and right, *that* Robespierre, 500
He who thereafter, and in how short a time!
Wielded the sceptre of the Atheist crew.[6]
When the calamity spread far and wide—
And this same city, that did then appear
To outrun the rest in exultation, groaned 505
Under the vengeance of her cruel son,
As Lear reproached the winds—I could almost

Have quarrelled with that blameless spectacle
For being yet an image in my mind
[510] To mock me under such a strange reverse.[7]   465

    O friend, few happier moments have been mine
Through my whole life than that when first I heard
That this foul tribe of Moloch was o'erthrown,
And their chief regent levelled with the dust.[8]
The day was one which haply[9] may deserve   470
A separate chronicle. Having gone abroad
From a small village where I tarried then,
To the same far-secluded privacy
I was returning.[1] Over the smooth sands
[515] Of Leven's ample aestuary[2] lay   475
My journey, and beneath a genial sun,
With distant prospect among gleams of sky
And clouds, and intermingled mountain-tops,
In one inseparable glory clad[3]—
[520] Creatures of one ethereal substance, met   480
In consistory, like a diadem
Or crown of burning seraphs, as they sit
In the empyrean.[4] Underneath this show
Lay, as I knew, the nest of pastoral vales
[525] Among whose happy fields I had grown up   485
From childhood. On the fulgent[5] spectacle,
Which neither changed, nor stirred, nor passed away,
I gazed, and with a fancy more alive
On this account—that I had chanced to find
That morning, ranging through the churchyard graves   490
Of Cartmell's rural town, the place in which
[534] An honored teacher of my youth was laid.[6]
While we were schoolboys he had died among us,
And was born hither, as I knew, to rest
With his own family. A plain stone, inscribed   495
With name, date, office, pointed out the spot,
To which a slip of verses was subjoined—

7. See *King Lear*, III, ii, 16: "I tax not you, you elements, with unkindness." Arras suffered very greatly in the Terror.
8. De Selincourt points out how apt is Wordsworth's allusion to "Moloch, horrid king besmeared with blood / Of human sacrifice" (*Paradise Lost*, I, 392–93).
9. Perhaps.
1. Wordsworth stayed with cousins, August–September 1794, at Rampside, a small village on the coast near Barrow-in-Furness, and opposite Piel Castle.
2. The broad sands of the estuary of the river Leven lie to the southwest of the Lake District.

3. *1805*, 479–88 (*1850*, 519–23) are deliberately Miltonic in diction, containing references to *Paradise Regained* and *At a Solemn Music* as well as *Paradise Lost*.
4. "Creatures": creations. "Consistory": council. "Seraphs": the highest order of angels. "Empyrean": the highest heaven, which consists of the element of fire.
5. Shining, brilliant.
6. The Reverend William Taylor, headmaster of Hawkshead Grammar School, died aged thirty-two in June 1786. He is buried at Cartmel Priory, two miles east of Ulverston over Levens Sands, which Wordsworth had to cross in returning to Rampside along the coast.

Have quarrelled with that blameless spectacle
For lingering yet an image in my mind
To mock me under such a strange reverse.[7]   510

    O Friend! few happier moments have been mine
Than that which told the downfall of this Tribe
So dreaded, so abhorred. The day deserves
A separate record.[1] Over the smooth sands
Of Leven's ample estuary[2] lay   515
My journey, and beneath a genial sun,
With distant prospect among gleams of sky
And clouds, and intermingling mountain tops,
In one inseparable glory clad,[3]
Creatures of one ethereal substance met   520
In consistory, like a diadem
Or crown of burning seraphs as they sit
In the empyrean.[4] Underneath that pomp
Celestial, lay unseen the pastoral vales
Among whose happy fields I had grown up   525
From childhood. On the fulgent[5] spectacle,
That neither passed away nor changed, I gazed
Enrapt; but brightest things are wont to draw
Sad opposites out of the inner heart,
As now their pensive influence drew from mine.   530
How could it otherwise? for not in vain
That very morning had I turned aside
To seek the ground where, 'mid a throng of graves,
An honoured teacher of my youth was laid,[6]

By his desire, as afterwards I learned—
[536] A fragment from the *Elegy* of Gray.[7]
A week, or little less, before his death   500
He had said to me, 'My head will soon lie low';
[540] And when I saw the turf that covered him,
After the lapse of full eight years, those words,
With sound of voice, and countenance of the man,
Came back upon me, so that some few tears   505
Fell from me in my own despite. And now,
[545] Thus travelling smoothly o'er the level sands,
I thought with pleasure of the verses graven
Upon his tombstone, saying to myself,
'He loved the poets, and if now alive   510
Would have loved me, as one not destitute
[550] Of promise, nor belying the kind hope
Which he had formed when I at his command
Began to spin, at first, my toilsome songs.'[8]

Without me and within as I advanced   515
All that I saw, or felt, or communed with,
Was gentleness and peace. Upon a small
[555] And rocky island near, a fragment stood—
Itself like a sea rock—of what had been
A Romish chapel, where in ancient times   520
[560] Masses were said at the hour which suited those
Who crossed the sands with ebb of morning tide.
Not far from this still ruin all the plain
Was spotted with a variegated crowd
Of coaches, wains, and travellers, horse and foot,   525
[565] Wading, beneath the conduct of their guide,
In loose procession through the shallow stream
Of inland water; the great sea meanwhile
Was at safe distance, far retired.[9] I paused,
Unwilling to proceed, the scene appeared   530
So gay and chearful—when a traveller
Chancing to pass, I carelessly inquired
If any news were stirring, he replied
[572] In the familiar language of the day
That, *Robespierre was dead*.[1] Nor was a doubt,   535

7. Gray's *Elegy Written in a Country Churchyard*, 125–28, with adapted first line.
8. Wordsworth's first extant poem is headed *Lines Written as a School Exercise at Hawkshead, Anno Aetatis 14*. Taylor was a man of learning and taste, who encouraged the study of poetry.
9. Wordsworth is describing the guided two-mile passage at low tide across Levens Sands, on the route from Cartmel to Ulverston. The tide goes out a long way, but returns very fast. The oratory on Chapel Island ("Romish chapel") was built by the monks of Furness Abbey; the shallow stream is the Eau, which crosses the Sands, and which has to be waded. "Wains" (*1805*, 525): wagons.
1. Robespierre and twenty-one associates went to the guillotine on July 28, 1794. Though opposition to his policies had been growing, his fall was very sudden. The first report of his death appeared in the *Times* on August 16.

And on the stone were graven by his desire   535
Lines from the churchyard elegy of Gray.[7]
This faithful guide, speaking from his death-bed,
Added no farewell to his parting counsel,
But said to me, 'My head will soon lie low';
And when I saw the turf that covered him,   540
After the lapse of full eight years, those words,
With sound of voice and countenance of the Man,
Came back upon me, so that some few tears
Fell from me in my own despite. But now
I thought, still traversing that widespread plain,   545
With tender pleasure of the verses graven
Upon his tombstone, whispering to myself:
He loved the Poets, and, if now alive,
Would have loved me, as one not destitute
Of promise, nor belying the kind hope   550
That he had formed, when I, at his command,
Began to spin, with toil, my earliest songs.[8]

    As I advanced, all that I saw or felt
Was gentleness and peace. Upon a small
And rocky island near, a fragment stood   555
(Itself like a sea rock) the low remains
(With shells encrusted, dark with briny weeds)
Of a dilapidated structure, once
A Romish chapel, where the vested priest
Said matins at the hour that suited those   560
Who crossed the sands with ebb of morning tide.
Not far from that still ruin all the plain
Lay spotted with a variegated crowd
Of vehicles and travellers, horse and foot,
Wading beneath the conduct of their guide   565
In loose procession through the shallow stream
Of inland waters; the great sea meanwhile
Heaved at safe distance, far retired.[9] I paused,
Longing for skill to paint a scene so bright
And cheerful, but the foremost of the band   570
As he approached, no salutation given,
In the familiar language of the day,
Cried, 'Robespierre is dead!'[1]—nor was a doubt,

On further question, left within my mind
But that the tidings were substantial truth—
[575] That he and his supporters all were fallen.

Great was my glee of spirit, great my joy
In vengeance, and eternal justice, thus   540
Made manifest. 'Come now, ye golden times',
Said I, forth-breathing on those open sands
[580] A hymn of triumph, 'as the morning comes
Out of the bosom of the night, come ye.
Thus far our trust is verified: behold,   545
They who with clumsy desperation brought
Rivers of blood, and preached that nothing else
[585] Could cleanse the Augean stable, by the might
Of their own helper have been swept away.[2]
Their madness is declared and visible;   550
Elsewhere will safety now be sought, and earth
March firmly towards righteousness and pēace.'
[590] Then schemes I framed more calmly, when and how
The madding factions might be tranquillized,
And—though through hardships manifold and long—   555
The mighty renovation would proceed.
Thus, interrupted by uneasy bursts
[595] Of exultation, I pursued my way
Along that very shore which I had skimmed
In former times, when, spurring from the Vale   560
Of Nightshade, and St Mary's mouldering fane,
And the stone abbot, after circuit made
[600] In wantonness of heart, a joyous crew
Of schoolboys, hastening to their distant home,
Along the margin of the moonlight sea,   565
We beat with thundering hoofs the level sand.[3]

2. Robespierre's desperate purging of the Republic in the name of "virtue" is compared to Hercules' cleansing of the stables of King Augeas, accomplished by diverting the rivers Alpheus and Peneus. The "helper" is the guillotine.

3. *1805*, 558–66 (*1850*, 595–603) refer the reader back to *1805*, II, 99–144 (*1799*, II, 98–139); the final line in the earlier texts is repeated verbatim.

After strict question, left within my mind
That he and his supporters all were fallen.   575

   Great was my transport, deep my gratitude
To everlasting Justice, by this fiat
Made manifest. 'Come now, ye golden times',
Said I forth-pouring on those open sands
A hymn of triumph: 'as the morning comes   580
From out the bosom of the night, come ye:
Thus far our trust is verified; behold!
They who with clumsy desperation brought
A river of Blood, and preached that nothing else
Could cleanse the Augean stable, by the might   585
Of their own helper have been swept away;[2]
Their madness stands declared and visible;
Elsewhere will safety now be sought, and earth
March firmly towards righteousness and peace.'—
Then schemes I framed more calmly, when and how   590
The madding factions might be tranquillised,
And how through hardships manifold and long
The glorious renovation would proceed.
Thus interrupted by uneasy bursts
Of exultation, I pursued my way   595
Along that very shore which I had skimmed
In former days, when—spurring from the Vale
Of Nightshade, and St. Mary's mouldering fane,
And the stone abbot, after circuit made
In wantonness of heart, a joyous band   600
Of schoolboys hastening to their distant home
Along the margin of the moonlight sea—
We beat with thundering hoofs the level sand.[3]

From this time forth in France, as is well known,
Authority put on a milder face;[5]
Yet every thing was wanting that might give
Courage to those who looked for good by light   570
[XI, 5] Of rational experience—good I mean
At hand, and in the spirit of past aims.
The same belief I nevertheless retained:
The language of the Senate, and the acts
And public measures of the Government,   575
[10] Though both of heartless omen,[6] had not power
To daunt me. In the people was my trust,
And in the virtues which mine eyes had seen,
And to the ultimate repose of things
I looked with unabated confidence.   580
I knew that wound external could not take
Life from the young Republic, that new foes
[15] Would only follow in the path of shame
Their brethren, and her triumphs be in the end
Great, universal, irresistible.   585
This faith, which was an object in my mind
Of passionate intuition, had effect
Not small in dazzling me; for thus, through zeal,
Such victory I confounded in my thoughts
With one far higher and more difficult: 590
[20] Triumphs of unambitious peace at home,
And noiseless fortitude.[7] Beholding still
Resistance strong as heretofore, I thought
That what was in degree the same was likewise
The same in quality, that as the worse   595
[25] Of the two spirits then at strife remained
Untired, the better surely would preserve
The heart that first had rouzed him[8]—never dreamt
That transmigration could be undergone,
A fall of being suffered, and of hope,   600
By creature[9] that appeared to have received
Entire conviction what a great ascent
Had been accomplished, what high faculties
It had been called to. Youth maintains, I knew,

5. A further eighty-six Robespierrists were guillotined after the execution of their leader and his closest associates on July 28, 1794, but the Terror ceased at once.
6. I.e., depressing in their implication for the future.
7. Wordsworth's faith, as at *1805*, 221–23 above, is that triumph for the Revolution in France would lead to peaceful transformation in Britain.
8. *1805*, 592–98 (*1850*, 21–27) offer two mistaken reasons for assuming that the early idealistic commitment of the Revolution persisted in 1794: (1) that undiminished resistance in the war against Britain implied continuation of the original patriotism; (2) that if the worse "spirit" (Britain) remained tireless in the war, the better one (France) must surely preserve its initial strength of feeling.
9. I.e., the Republic. "Creature": a created being, animate or inanimate (*NED*).

Book Eleventh

France—Concluded

FROM that time forth, Authority in France[4]
Put on a milder face;[5] Terror had ceased,
Yet every thing was wanting that might give
Courage to them who looked for good by light
Of rational Experience, for the shoots   5
And hopeful blossoms of a second spring:
Yet, in me, confidence was unimpaired;
The Senate's language, and the public acts
And measures of the Government, though both
Weak, and of heartless omen,[6] had not power   10
To daunt me; in the People was my trust,
And, in the virtues which mine eyes had seen.
I knew that wound external could not take
Life from the young Republic; that new foes
Would only follow, in the path of shame,   15
Their brethren, and her triumphs be in the end
Great, universal, irresistible.
This intuition led me to confound
One victory with another, higher far,—
Triumphs of unambitious peace at home,   20
And noiseless fortitude.[7] Beholding still
Resistance strong as heretofore, I thought
That what was in degree the same was likewise
The same in quality,—that, as the worse
Of the two spirits then at strife remained   25
Untired, the better, surely, would preserve
The heart that first had roused him.[8] Youth maintains,

---

4. The division of *1805*, X, into *1850*, X
and XI, occurs in *MS. D* of 1832, but on
the evidence of *MS. Z* (April–May 1805)
seems to be a return to the original pattern of December 1805; see Composition
and Texts: *1805/1850*, Introduction, below.

In all conditions of society   605
Communion more direct and intimate
[30] With Nature, and the inner strength she has—
And hence, ofttimes, no less with reason too—
Than age, or manhood even. To Nature then,
Power had reverted: habit, custom, law,   610
Had left an interregnum's open space
For her to stir about in, uncontrolled.[1]
The warmest judgments, and the most untaught,
Found in events which every day brought forth
Enough to sanction them—and far, far more   615
To shake the authority of canons drawn
From ordinary practice. I could see
[35] How Babel-like the employment was of those
Who, by the recent deluge stupefied,
With their whole souls went culling from the day   620
Its petty promises to build a tower
For their own safety[2]—laughed at gravest heads,
[40] Who, watching in their hate of France for signs
Of her disasters, if the stream of rumour
Brought with it one green branch, conceited thence[3]   625
That not a single tree was left alive
In all her forests. How could I believe
[45] That wisdom could in any shape come near
Men clinging to delusions so insane?
And thus, experience proving that no few   630
Of my opinions had been just, I took
Like credit to myself where less was due,
[50] And thought that other notions were as sound—
Yea, could not but be right—because I saw
That foolish men opposed them.   635

                                     To a strain
More animated I might here give way,
And tell, since juvenile errors are my theme,
[55] What in those days through Britain was performed
To turn *all* judgements out of their right course;
But this is passion over near ourselves,   640
Reality too close and too intense,
And mingled up with something, in my mind,
[60] Of scorn and condemnation personal
That would profane the sanctity of verse.

---

1. Habit, custom, law—the usual guides in political matters—having been dethroned by the Revolution, Nature (with whom youth is most closely in touch—*1805*, 604–9; *1850*, 27–30) was left at this period as the basis of political judgment.

2. The allusion is to the Tower of Babel, which men built in the attempt to "reach unto heaven" (Genesis 9:3–9).
3. I.e., fancied on the strength of it; an obsolete usage that implies the poet's contempt.

In all conditions of society,
Communion more direct and intimate
With Nature,—hence, ofttimes, with reason too— 30
Than age, or manhood even. To Nature, then,
Power had reverted: habit, custom, law,
Had left an interregnum's open space
For *her* to move about in, uncontrolled.[1]
Hence could I see how Babel-like their task, 35
Who, by the recent deluge stupified,
With their whole souls went culling from the day
Its petty promises, to build a tower
For their own safety;[2] laughed with my compeers
At gravest heads, by enmity to France 40
Distempered, till they found, in every blast
Forced from the street-disturbing newsman's horn,
For her great cause record or prophecy
Of utter ruin. How might we believe
That wisdom could, in any shape, come near 45
Men clinging to delusions so insane?
And thus, experience proving that no few
Of our opinions had been just, we took
Like credit to ourselves where less was due,
And thought that other notions were as sound, 50
Yea, could not but be right, because we saw
That foolish men opposed them.

                          To a strain
More animated I might here give way,
And tell, since juvenile errors are my theme,
What in those days, through Britain, was performed 55
To turn *all* judgements out of their right course;
But this is passion over-near ourselves,
Reality too close and too intense,
And intermixed with something, in my mind,
Of scorn and condemnation personal, 60
That would profane the sanctity of verse.

Our shepherds (this say merely) at that time 645
Thirsted to make the guardian crook of law
[65] A tool of murder. They who ruled the state,
Though with such awful proof before their eyes
That he who would sow death, reaps death, or worse,
And can reap nothing better, childlike longed 650
[69] To imitate—not wise enough to avoid.
Giants in their impiety alone,
But in their weapons and their warfare base
As vermin working out of reach, they leagued
Their strength perfidiously to undermine 655
Justice, and make an end of liberty.[4]

But from these bitter truths I must return
[75] To my own history.[5] It hath been told
That I was led to take an eager part
In arguments of civil polity 660
Abruptly, and indeed before my time:
I had approached, like other youth, the shield
[80] Of human nature from the golden side,
And would have fought even to the death to attest
The quality of the metal which I saw.[6] 665
What there is best in individual man,
Of wise in passion and sublime in power,
What there is strong and pure in household love,
[85] Benevolent in small societies,
And great in large ones also, when called forth 670
By great occasions—these were things of which
I something knew; yet even these themselves,
Felt deeply,[7] were not thoroughly understood
By reason. Nay, far from it; they were yet,
As cause was given me afterwards to learn, 675
[90] Not proof against the injuries of the day—
Lodged only at the sanctuary's door,
Not safe within its bosom. Thus prepared,
And with such general insight into evil,
And of the bounds which sever it from good, 680

4. Wordsworth's denunciation of Pitt and his government, though toned down for *1850*, is not at all excessive. Like children they mimic the enormities of Robespierre, but they lack the stature to carry their murderous wishes into effect. The rats under the floor boards ("vermin working out of reach") are Home Office agents and informers. One of these—a Mr. Walsh—was sent to investigate Wordsworth and Coleridge at Alfoxden in 1797, on the suspicion that they were spies for the French.
5. Wordsworth returns in *1805*, 657–756

(*1850*, 74–172) to the period in early summer 1792 (described in *1805*, IX, 294–543 above) when firsthand experience, and the influence of Michel Beaupuy, deepened his interest in the Revolution.
6. In the fable that Wordsworth refers to, a two-sided shield—one side gold, one silver—hung up at a crossroads, leads knights approaching from opposite directions to fight "to attest / The quality of the metal" which they see.
7. I.e., "though felt deeply."

Our Shepherds, this say merely, at that time
Acted, or seemed at least to act, like men
Thirsting to make the guardian crook of law
A tool of murder; they who ruled the State,   65
Though with such awful proof before their eyes
That he, who would sow death, reaps death, or worse,
And can reap nothing better, child-like longed
To imitate, not wise enough to avoid;
Or left (by mere timidity betrayed)   70
The plain straight road, for one no better chosen
Than if their wish had been to undermine
Justice, and make an end of Liberty.[4]

 But from these bitter truths I must return
To my own history.[5] It hath been told   75
That I was led to take an eager part
In arguments of civil polity,
Abruptly, and indeed before my time:
I had approached, like other youths, the shield
Of human nature from the golden side,   80
And would have fought, even to the death, to attest
The quality of the metal which I saw.[6]
What there is best in individual man,
Of wise in passion, and sublime in power,
Benevolent in small societies,   85
And great in large ones, I had oft revolved,
Felt deeply, but not thoroughly understood
By reason: nay, far from it; they were yet,
As cause was given me afterwards to learn,
Not proof against the injuries of the day;   90
Lodged only at the sanctuary's door,
Not safe within its bosom. Thus prepared,
And with such general insight into evil,
And of the bounds which sever it from good,

[95] As books and common intercourse with life
Must needs have given (to the noviciate[8] mind,
When the world travels in a beaten road,
Guide faithful as is needed), I began
To think with fervour upon management   685
[100] Of nations—what it is and ought to be,
And how their worth depended on their laws,
And on the constitution of the state.[9]

[105]   O pleasant exercise of hope and joy,
For great were the auxiliars[1] which then stood   690
Upon our side, we who were strong in love.
Bliss was it in that dawn to be alive,
But to be young was very heaven! O times,
[110] In which the meagre, stale, forbidding ways
Of custom, law, and statute took at once   695
The attraction of a country in romance—
When Reason seemed the most to assert her rights
When most intent on making of herself
[115] A prime enchanter to assist the work
Which then was going forwards in her name.   700
Not favored spots alone, but the whole earth,
The beauty wore of promise, that which sets
(To take an image which was felt, no doubt,
[120] Among the bowers of Paradise itself)
The budding rose above the rose full-blown.   705
What temper[2] at the prospect did not wake
To happiness unthought of? The inert
Were rouzed, and lively natures rapt away.[3]
[125] They who had fed their childhood upon dreams—
The playfellows of fancy, who had made   710
All powers of swiftness, subtlety, and strength
Their ministers, used to stir in lordly wise
Among the grandest objects of the sense,
[130] And deal with whatsoever they found there
As if they had within some lurking right   715
To wield it—they too, who, of gentle mood,
Had watched all gentle motions, and to these
Had fitted their own thoughts (schemers more mild,
[135] And in the region of their peaceful selves),
Did now find helpers to their hearts' desire   720

8. Inexperienced, like a novice in a religious order.
9. Compare the account of conversations with Beaupuy, *1805*, IX, 328–36 above.
1. Helpers, allies.
2. Temperament.
3. For a short while the French Revolution seemed to liberals and idealists of every kind to confirm a process towards freedom predicted by Rousseau, and begun in the establishment of the American republic in 1776. "Rapt away": enraptured.

As books and common intercourse with life   95
Must needs have given—to the inexperienced mind,
When the world travéls in a beaten road,
Guide faithful as is needed—I began
To meditate with ardour on the rule
And management of nations; what it is   100
And ought to be; and strove to learn how far
Their power or weakness, wealth or poverty,
Their happiness or misery, depend
Upon their laws, and fashion of the State.⁹

    O pleasant exercise of hope and joy!   105
For mighty were the auxiliars¹ which then stood
Upon our side, we who were strong in love!
Bliss was it in that dawn to be alive,
But to be young was very Heaven! O times,
In which the meagre, stale, forbidding ways   110
Of custom, law, and statute, took at once
The attraction of a country in romance!
When Reason seemed the most to assert her rights
When most intent on making of herself
A prime enchantress—to assist the work,   115
Which then was going forward in her name!
Not favoured spots alone, but the whole Earth,
The beauty wore of promise—that which sets
(As at some moments might not be unfelt
Among the bowers of Paradise itself)   120
The budding rose above the rose full blown.
What temper² at the prospect did not wake
To happiness unthought of? The inert
Were roused, and lively natures rapt away!³
They who had fed their childhood upon dreams,   125
The play-fellows of fancy, who had made
All powers of swiftness, subtilty, and strength
Their ministers,—who in lordly wise had stirred
Among the grandest objects of the sense,
And dealt with whatsoever they found there   130
As if they had within some lurking right
To wield it;—they, too, who of gentle mood
Had watched all gentle motions, and to these
Had fitted their own thoughts, schemers more mild,
And in the region of their peaceful selves;—   135
Now was it that *both* found, the meek and lofty
Did both find helpers to their hearts' desire,

And stuff at hand plastic as they could wish,[4]
Were called upon to exercise their skill
[140] Not in Utopia—subterraneous fields,
Or some secreted island, heaven knows where—
But in the very world which is the world   725
Of all of us, the place in which, in the end,
We find our happiness, or not at all.[5]

[145]   Why should I not confess that earth was then
To me what an inheritance new-fallen
Seems, when the first time visited, to one   730
Who thither comes to find in it his home?
He walks about and looks upon the place
[150] With cordial transport—moulds it and remoulds—
And is half pleased with things that are amiss,
'Twill be such joy to see them disappear.   735

An active partisan, I thus convoked[6]
From every object pleasant circumstance
[155] To suit my ends. I moved among mankind
With genial feelings still[7] predominant,
When erring, erring on the better side,   740
And in the kinder spirit—placable,
Indulgent ofttimes to the worst desires,
As, on one side, not uninformed that men
[160] See as it hath been taught them, and that time
Gives rights to error; on the other hand   745
That throwing off oppression must be work
As well of licence as of liberty;
And above all (for this was more than all),
[165] Not caring if the wind did now and then
Blow keen upon an eminence that gave   750
Prospect so large into futurity—
In brief, a child of Nature, as at first,
Diffusing only those affections wider
[170] That from the cradle had grown up with me,
And losing, in no other way than light   755
Is lost in light, the weak in the more strong.

---

4. As Wordsworth rather clumsily makes clear in *1850*, 136–37, temperaments of two distinct kinds—the grandly imaginative (lines 709–16; *1850*, 125–32), and the gently introspective (lines 716–21; *1850*, 132–35)—both found malleable or "plastic" material for their schemes in the new political situation.
5. Wordsworth is recollecting his Prospectus to *The Recluse* (1800), 38–43, where he had asked why "the very world which is the world / Of all of us" should not, irrespective of political situation, transcend the creations of myth: "Paradise and groves / Elysian, fortunate islands, fields like those of old / In the deep ocean—wherefore should they be / A History, or but a dream, when minds / Once wedded to this outward frame of things / In love, find these the growth of common day?" (*CW*, III, lines 996–1001, p. 102).
6. Summoned.
7. Ever, always.

And stuff at hand, plastic as they could wish,[4]—
Were called upon to exercise their skill,
Not in Utopia,—subterranean fields,—   140
Or some secreted island, Heaven knows where!
But in the very world, which is the world
Of all of us,—the place where, in the end,
We find our happiness, or not at all![5]

    Why should I not confess that Earth was then   145
To me, what an inheritance, new-fallen,
Seems, when the first time visited, to one
Who thither comes to find in it his home?
He walks about and looks upon the spot
With cordial transport, moulds it and remoulds,   150
And is half pleased with things that are amiss,
'Twill be such joy to see them disappear.

    An active partisan, I thus convoked[6]
From every object pleasant circumstance
To suit my ends; I moved among mankind   155
With genial feelings still[7] predominant;
When erring, erring on the better part,
And in the kinder spirit; placable,
Indulgent, as not uninformed that men
See as they have been taught— and that Antiquity[8]   160
Gives rights to error; and aware, no less,
That throwing off oppression must be work
As well of License as of Liberty;
And above all—for this was more than all—
Not caring if the wind did now and then   165
Blow keen upon an eminence that gave
Prospect so large into futurity;
In brief, a child of Nature, as at first,
Diffusing only those affections wider
That from the cradle had grown up with me,   170
And losing, in no other way than light
Is lost in light, the weak in the more strong.

---

8. An alexandrine (six-foot line) in the
manuscripts, but altered to a pentameter
by removal of "and that" in the first edition.

In the main outline, such it might be said
Was my condition, till with open war
[175] Britain opposed the liberties of France.[9]   760
This threw me first out of the pale of love,
Soured and corrupted upwards to the source,
My sentiments; was not,[1] as hitherto,
A swallowing up of lesser things in great,
[180] But change of them into their opposites,
And thus a way was opened for mistakes   765
And false conclusions of the intellect,
As gross in their degree, and in their kind
Far, far more dangerous. What had been a pride
Was now a shame, my likings and my loves
[185] Ran in new channels, leaving old ones dry;   770
And thus a blow, which in maturer age
Would but have touched the judgement, struck more deep
Into sensations near the heart. Meantime,
[189] As from the first, wild theories were afloat,
Unto the subtleties of which at least,   775
I had but lent a careless ear[2]—assured
Of this, that time would soon set all things right,
Prove that the multitude had been oppressed,
And would be so no more. But when events
[195] Brought less encouragement, and unto these   780
The immediate proof of principles no more
Could be entrusted—while the events themselves,
Worn out in greatness, and in novelty,
Less occupied the mind, and sentiments
[200] Could through my understanding's natural growth   785
No longer justify themselves through faith
Of inward consciousness, and hope that laid
Its hand upon its object—evidence
Safer, of universal application, such
[205] As could not be impeached, was sought elsewhere.   790

        And now, become oppressors in their turn,
Frenchmen had changed a war of self-defence
For one of conquest, losing sight of all
Which they had struggled for;[3] and mounted up,

---

9. On February 11, 1793; France had declared war ten days previously. In his
backward glance (begun at *1805*, 657;
1850, 74 above) Wordsworth has worked
through to the period described in *1805*,
227–306.
1. I.e., *there* was not.
2. A reference that has been taken to
anticipate Wordsworth's discussion of
Godwin's political theories in *1805*, 805–
29 below; the passage implies, however,
that the "wild theories" were afloat before the publication of Godwin's *Politi-*

cal Justice in February 1793.
3. A decision renouncing all conquest of
foreign territory had been written into
the French constitution in May 1790. The
occupation of Belgium in November 1792
could perhaps be regarded as part of a
war of self-defense, but in May–July 1794
the Republican armies turned to the attack on a number of different fronts; see
1805, 364n, above. The death of Robespierre (July 1794) did not, as Wordsworth must have hoped, lead to a change
of policy.

   In the main outline, such it might be said
Was my condition, till with open war
Britain opposed the liberties of France.[9]   175
This threw me first out of the pale of love;
Soured and corrupted, upwards to the source,
My sentiments; was not,[1] as hitherto,
A swallowing up of lesser things in great,
But change of them into their contraries;   180
And thus a way was opened for mistakes
And false conclusions, in degree as gross,
In kind more dangerous. What had been a pride,
Was now a shame; my likings and my loves
Ran in new channels, leaving old ones dry;   185
And hence a blow that, in maturer age,
Would but have touched the judgment, struck more deep
Into sensations near the heart: meantime,
As from the first, wild theories were afloat,
To whose pretensions, sedulously urged,   190
I had but lent a careless ear,[2] assured
That time was ready to set all things right,
And that the multitude, so long oppressed,
Would be oppressed no more.

                      But when events
Brought less encouragement, and unto these   195
The immediate proof of principles no more
Could be entrusted, while the events themselves,
Worn out in greatness, stripped of novelty,
Less occupied the mind, and sentiments
Could through my understanding's natural growth   200
No longer keep their ground, by faith maintained
Of inward consciousness, and hope that laid
Her hand upon her object—evidence
Safer, of universal application, such
As could not be impeached, was sought elsewhere.   205

   But now, become oppressors in their turn,
Frenchmen had changed a war of self-defence
For one of conquest, losing sight of all
Which they had struggled for:[3] and mounted up,

[210] Openly in the view of earth and heaven,   795
The scale of Liberty.[4] I read her doom,
Vexed inly somewhat, it is true, and sore,
But not dismayed, nor taking to the shame
[214] Of a false prophet. But, rouzed up, I stuck
More firmly to old tenets, and, to prove   800
Their temper, strained them more;[5] and thus, in heat
Of contest, did opinions every day
[220] Grow into consequence, till round my mind
They clung as if they were the life of it.

This was the time when, all things tending fast   805
To depravation, the philosophy
[225] That promised to abstract the hopes of man
Out of his feelings, to be fixed thenceforth
For ever in a purer element,
Found ready welcome.[6] Tempting region that   810
For zeal to enter and refresh herself,
[230] Where passions had the privilege to work,
And never hear the sound of their own names—
But, speaking more in charity, the dream
Was flattering to the young ingenuous mind   815
Pleased with extremes, and not the least with that
Which makes the human reason's naked self
[235] The object of its fervour. What delight!—
How glorious!—in self-knowledge and self-rule
To look through all the frailties of the world,   820
And, with a resolute mastery shaking off
The accidents of nature, time, and place,
That make up the weak being of the past,
[240] Build social freedom on its only basis:
The freedom of the individual mind,   825
Which, to the blind restraint of general laws
Superior, magisterially[7] adopts
One guide—the light of circumstances, flashed
[244] Upon an independent intellect.[8]

4. The cause of Liberty is being weighed in the balance ("scale") of its own criteria and found to be lightweight.
5. A metaphor from the "proving" (i.e., testing) of tempered steel.
6. The reference is to Godwin's *Enquiry Concerning Political Justice.* By chance, the book came out just after the execution of Louis XVI and the declaration of war with France, and its appeal to British radicals was that it offered them a basis for optimism at a moment when things were going wrong. Godwin's philosophy undertakes to free ("abstract") man's hope—for a future condition of absolute happiness and benevolence—from reliance on his emotional nature, and to ground that hope instead on his reason (" a purer element").
7. Masterfully (as at *1805,* III, 380, above).
8. Despite his claim in *1805,* 814, to be "speaking more in charity," lines 818–29 (*1850,* 235–44) are a mockery of Godwin's position. Wordsworth concludes, significantly, with a quotation from his own post-Godwinian play, *The Borderers,* of autumn 1796–spring 1797, in which the villain Rivers employs rationalism as a means of seducing "the young ingenuous mind" of the hero: "You have obeyed the only law that wisdom / Can ever recognize—the immediate law / Flashed from the light of circumstances / Upon an independent intellect" (*Oxford Wordsworth,* I, p. 187).

Openly in the eye of earth and heaven, 210
The scale of liberty.[4] I read her doom,
With anger vexed, with disappointment sore,
But not dismayed, nor taking to the shame
Of a false prophet. While resentment rose
Striving to hide, what nought could heal, the wounds 215
Of mortified presumption, I adhered
More firmly to old tenets, and, to prove
Their temper, strained them more;[5] and thus, in heat
Of contest, did opinions every day
Grow into consequence, till round my mind 220
They clung, as if they were its life, nay more,
The very being of the immortal soul.

   This was the time, when, all things tending fast
To depravation, speculative schemes—
That promised to abstract the hopes of Man 225
Out of his feelings, to be fixed thenceforth
For ever in a purer element—
Found ready welcome.[6] Tempting region *that*
For Zeal to enter and refresh herself,
Where passions had the privilege to work, 230
And never hear the sound of their own name.
But, speaking more in charity, the dream
Flattered the young, pleased with extremes, nor least
With that which makes our Reason's naked self
The object of its fervour. What delight! 235
How glorious! in self-knowledge and self-rule,
To look through all the frailties of the world,
And, with a resolute mastery shaking off
Infirmities of nature, time, and place,
Build social upon personal Liberty, 240
Which, to the blind restraints of general laws
Superior, magisterially[7] adopts
One guide, the light of circumstances, flashed
Upon an independent intellect.[8]

For howsoe'er unsettled, never once   830
Had I thought ill of human-kind, or been
Indifferent to its welfare, but, enflamed
With thirst of a secure intelligence,
[250] And sick of other passion, I pursued
A higher nature—wished that man should start   835
Out of the worm-like state in which he is,
And spread abroad the wings of Liberty,
Lord of himself, in undisturbed delight.[9]
[255] A noble aspiration!—yet I feel[1]
The aspiration—but with other thoughts   840
And happier: for I was perplexed and sought
To accomplish the transition by such means
As did not lie in nature, sacrificed
The exactness of a comprehensive mind
To scrupulous and microscopic views   845
That furnished out materials for a work
Of false imagination, placed beyond
The limits of experience and of truth.

[259]   Enough, no doubt, the advocates themselves
Of ancient institutions had performed   850
To bring disgrace upon their very names;[2]
Disgrace of which custom, and written law,
And sundry moral sentiments, as props
[265] And emanations of these institutes,
Too justly bore a part. A veil had been   855
Uplifted. Why deceive ourselves?—'twas so,
'Twas even so—and sorrow for the man
Who either had not eyes wherewith to see,
[270] Or seeing hath forgotten. Let this pass,
Suffice it that a shock had then been given   860
To old opinions, and the minds of all men
Had felt it—that my mind was both let loose,
Let loose and goaded.[3] After what hath been
[274] Already said of patriotic love,
And hinted at in other sentiments,   865
We need not linger long upon this theme,
This only may be said, that from the first
Having two natures in me (joy the one,

9. Wordsworth's image of the caterpillar ("worm") turning into a butterfly is derived from Spenser's *Muiopotmos, or, The Tale of the Butterflie*, 209–11.
1. I.e., to this day, I feel.
2. I.e., the names of the institutions.
3. As the *1850* text makes clear, Wordsworth turns in *1805*, 849–63 (*1805*, 259–73) to justification of his earlier radical views. Traditionalists have brought disgrace on the names of the institutions, legal and social, that they uphold, and as a result anything that supports these institutions (custom, law, certain individual emotions) appears tainted as well. In their refusal to acknowledge that the Revolution has lifted a veil, such men must bear responsibility for goading the minds of those who had been shocked out of old ways of thought.

Thus expectation rose again; thus hope,   245
From her first ground expelled, grew proud once more.
Oft, as my thoughts were turned to human kind,
I scorned indifference; but, inflamed with thirst
Of a secure intelligence, and sick
Of other longing, I pursued what seemed   250
A more exalted nature; wished that Man
Should start out of his earthy, worm-like state,
And spread abroad the wings of Liberty,
Lord of himself, in undisturbed delight[9]—
A noble aspiration! *yet* I feel[1]   255
(Sustained by worthier as by wiser thoughts)
The aspiration, nor shall ever cease
To feel it;—but return we to our course.

    Enough, 'tis true—could such a plea excuse
Those aberrations—had the clamorous friends   260
Of ancient Institutions said and done
To bring disgrace upon their very names,[2]
Disgrace, of which, custom and written law,
And sundry moral sentiments as props
Or emanations of those institutes,   265
Too justly bore a part. A veil had been
Uplifted; why deceive ourselves? in sooth,
'Twas even so; and sorrow for the man
Who either had not eyes wherewith to see,
Or, seeing, had forgotten! A strong shock   270
Was given to old opinions; all men's minds
Had felt its power, and mine was both let loose,
Let loose and goaded.[3] After what hath been
Already said of patriotic love,

The other melancholy), and withal
A happy man, and therefore bold to look   870
On painful things—slow, somewhat, too, and stern
In temperament—I took the knife in hand,
And, stopping not at parts less sensitive,
Endeavoured with my best of skill to probe
[281] The living body of society   875
Even to the heart. I pushed without remorse
My speculations forward, yea, set foot
On Nature's holiest places.[4]

                   Time may come
When some dramatic story may afford
Shapes livelier to convey to thee, my friend,   880
[286] What then I learned—or think I learned—of truth,[5]
And the errors into which I was betrayed
By present objects, and by reasonings false
From the beginning, inasmuch as drawn
[290] Out of a heart which had been turned aside   885
From Nature by external accidents,
And which was thus confounded more and more,
Misguiding and misguided. Thus I fared,
Dragging all passions, notions, shapes of faith,
[295] Like culprits to the bar, suspiciously   890
Calling the mind to establish in plain day
Her titles[6] and her honours, now believing,
Now disbelieving, endlessly perplexed
With impulse, motive, right and wrong, the ground
[300] Of moral obligation—what the rule,   895
And what the sanction—till, demanding proof,
And seeking it in every thing, I lost
All feeling of conviction, and, in fine,[7]
Sick, wearied out with contrarieties,
[305] Yielded up moral questions in despair,   900

4. The heart (or mind, or soul) of the individual human being.
5. Wordsworth looks forward to writing *The Excursion*, the "dramatic"—or narrative—section of *The Recluse*, projected as early as March 1804 (*EY*, p. 454), where the Solitary in Books III and IV embodies the failure of hopes in the French Revolution.
6. Deeds to prove legal entitlement.
7. In the end.

Suffice it here to add, that, somewhat stern   275
In temperament, withal a happy man,
And therefore bold to look on painful things,
Free likewise of the world, and thence more bold,
I summoned my best skill, and toiled, intent
To anatomise the frame of social life,   280
Yea, the whole body of society
Searched to its heart. Share with me, Friend! the wish
That some dramatic tale, endued with shapes
Livelier, and flinging out less guarded words
Than suit the work we fashion, might set forth   285
What then I learned, or think I learned, of truth,[5]
And the errors into which I fell, betrayed
By present objects, and by reasonings false
From their beginnings, inasmuch as drawn
Out of a heart that had been turned aside   290
From Nature's way by outward accidents,
And which was thus confounded more and more,
Misguided and misguiding. So I fared,
Dragging all precepts, judgments, maxims, creeds,
Like culprits to the bar; calling the mind,   295
Suspiciously, to establish in plain day
Her titles[6] and her honours; now believing,
Now disbelieving; endlessly perplexed
With impulse, motive, right and wrong, the ground
Of obligation, what the rule and whence   300
The sanction; till, demanding formal *proof*,
And seeking it in every thing, I lost
All feeling of conviction, and, in fine,[7]
Sick, wearied out with contrarieties,
Yielded up moral question in despair.   305

    This was the crisis of that strong disease,
This the soul's last and lowest ebb; I drooped,
Deeming our blessed reason of least use
Where wanted most: 'The lordly attributes
Of will and choice', I bitterly exclaimed,   310
'What are they but a mockery of a Being
Who hath in no concerns of his a test
Of good and evil; knows not what to fear
Or hope for, what to covet or to shun;
And who, if those could be discerned, would yet   315
Be little profited, would see, and ask
Where is the obligation to enforce?
And, to acknowledged law rebellious, still,
As selfish passion urged, would act amiss;
The dupe of folly, or the slave of crime.'   320

And for my future studies, as the sole
Employment of the inquiring faculty,
Turned towards mathematics, and their clear
And solid evidence.[8]

           Ah, then it was
That thou, most precious friend, about this time   905
First known to me, didst lend a living help
To regulate my soul.[9] And then it was
[335] That the belovèd woman in whose sight
Those days were passed—now speaking in a voice
Of sudden admonition like a brook   910
That does but cross a lonely road; and now
Seen, heard and felt, and caught at every turn,
[340] Companion never lost through many a league—
Maintained for me a saving intercourse
With my true self (for, though impaired, and changed   915
Much, as it seemed, I was no further changed
Than as a clouded, not a waning moon);
[345] She, in the midst of all, preserved me still
A poet, made me seek beneath that name
My office upon earth, and nowhere else.[2]   920
And lastly, Nature's self, by human love
Assisted, through the weary labyrinth
Conducted me again to open day,
Revived the feelings of my earlier life,
Gave me that strength and knowledge full of peace,   925
Enlarged, and never more to be disturbed,
Which through the steps of our degeneracy,
All degradation of this age, hath still
[355] Upheld me, and upholds me at this day
In the catastrophe (for so they dream,   930
And nothing less), when, finally to close
And rivet up the gains of France, a Pope
Is summoned in to crown an Emperor—
[360] This last opprobrium, when we see the dog
Returning to his vomit, when the sun   935

---

8. Godwinism having failed to provide Wordsworth the support he needs after the destruction of his faith in the Revolution, he turns to mathematics as the one thing that does seem to provide objective certainty. Lines 888–904 (*1850*, 293–333) have great power, and a pivotal importance in the structure of *The Prelude*, but should probably be read as the dramatization of a process of discovery, not as the record of a single moment of crisis. Whatever the nature of the intellectual episode Wordsworth describes, its date must be spring 1796, at which time he was reading the second edition of *Political Justice* (*EY*, p. 170).

9. An inaccurate statement that is removed by 1816/19. Wordsworth met Coleridge (the "precious friend," line 905) in September 1795; they seem to have corresponded at times in the next two years, but can have exerted no great influence upon each other until June 1797. 2. Wordsworth and Dorothy (the "belovèd woman" of *1805*, 908) moved into Racedown House in southwest Dorset on September 26, 1795. There is no doubt that through her faith in him, and her personal responsiveness to their shared surroundings, Dorothy helped to confirm her brother as a poet.

    Depressed, bewildered thus, I did not walk
With scoffers, seeking light and gay revenge
From indiscriminate laughter, nor sate down
In reconcilement with an utter waste
Of intellect; such sloth I could not brook,   325
(Too well I loved, in that my spring of life,
Pains-taking thoughts, and truth, their dear reward)
But turned to abstract science, and there sought
Work for the reasoning faculty enthroned
Where the disturbances of space and time—   330
Whether in matter's various properties
Inherent, or from human will and power
Derived—find no admission.[8] Then it was—
Thanks to the bounteous Giver of all good![1]—
That the beloved Sister in whose sight   335
Those days were passed, now speaking in a voice
Of sudden admonition—like a brook
That does but *cross* a lonely road, and now
Seen, heard, and felt, and caught at every turn,
Companion never lost through many a league—   340
Maintained for me a saving intercourse
With my true self; for, though bedimmed and changed
Both as a clouded and a waning moon,
She whispered still that brightness would return,
She, in the midst of all, preserved me still   345
A Poet, made me seek beneath that name,
And that alone, my office upon earth;[2]
And, lastly, as hereafter will be shown,
If willing audience fail not, Nature's self,
By all varieties of human love   350
Assisted, led me back through opening day
To those sweet counsels between head and heart
Whence grew that genuine knowledge, fraught with peace,
Which, through the later sinkings of this cause,
Hath still upheld me, and upholds me now   355
In the catastrophe (for so they dream,
And nothing less), when, finally to close
And rivet down[3] the gains of France, a Pope
Is summoned in, to crown an Emperor—
This last opprobrium, when we see a people,   360
That once looked up in faith, as if to Heaven
For manna, take a lesson from the dog
Returning to his vomit; when the sun

---

1. Lines 306–34 are inserted in an original form in 1816/19, but then much revised. For "matter's various properties /
Inherent" (lines 331–32) the first edition,
with no warrant from the manuscripts,
reads "matters various, properties / Inherent."
3. With no warrant from the manuscripts, the first edition prints "And seal
up all" for "And rivet down."

That rose in splendour, was alive, and moved
[365] In exultation among living clouds,
Hath put his function and his glory off,
And, turned into a gewgaw, a machine,
Sets like an opera phantom.⁴   940
                    Thus, O friend,
[370] Through times of honour, and through times of shame,
Have I descended, tracing faithfully
The workings of a youthful mind, beneath
The breath of great events—its hopes no less
Than universal, and its boundless love—   945
A story destined for thy ear,⁵ who now,
[375] Among the basest and the lowest fallen
Of all the race of men, dost make abode
Where Etna looketh down on Syracuse,
The city of Timoleon.⁶ Living God,   950
How are the mighty prostrated!⁷—they first,
[380] They first of all that breathe, should have awaked
When the great voice was heard out of the tombs
Of ancient heroes. If for France I have grieved,
Who in the judgement of no few hath been   955
A trifler only, in her proudest day—
[385] Have been distressed to think of what she once
Promised, now is—a far more sober cause
Thine eyes must see of sorrow in a land
[388] Strewed with the wreck of loftiest years, a land   960
Glorious indeed, substantially renowned
Of simple virtue once, and manly praise,
Now without one memorial hope, not even
A hope to be deferred—for that would serve
To chear the heart in such entire decay.   965

    But indignation works where hope is not,
And thou, O friend, wilt be refreshed. There is

---

4. Napoleon had been emperor since May 1804, but had summoned Pope Pius VII to crown him (lines 930–33) on December 2. To Wordsworth's indignation the French people had not only returned to monarchy, vomited forth (the image is from 2 Peter: 22) in the execution of Louis XVI, but had called on the Church to ratify their backsliding. The glorious sun of the Revolution had declined into a piece of cheap theatrical machinery.
    "Catastrophe" (*1805*, 930; *1850*, 356): dramatic climax—not at this period necessarily tragic ("they", in Wordsworth's parenthesis, are Napoleon's supporters). "Opprobrium" (*1805*, 934; *1850*, 360): disgrace. "Gewgaw" (*1805*, 939; *1850*, 368): plaything, toy.
5. Wordsworth read aloud to Coleridge

the completed thirteen-Book *Prelude* at Coleorton, Christmas 1806; for Coleridge's response, see his poem *To William Wordsworth*.
6. Coleridge had stopped in Sicily on his way home from Malta. North's translation of Plutarch's *Lives* records how Timoleon in 343 B.C. drove the tyrant Dionysius the Younger out of Sicily, defeated the Carthaginians, and established peace and democracy. Sicily in 1804 was part of the kingdom of Naples; its people were regarded by the *Encyclopaedia Britannica*, 3rd ed. (1797) as incapable of progress because of their ignorance, superstition and poverty.
7. Not an improvement on "How are the mighty fallen," of David's lament for Saul and Jonathan, 2 Samuel 1:19 ff.

That rose in splendour, was alive, and moved
In exultation with a living pomp   365
Of clouds—his glory's natural retinue—
Hath dropped all functions by the gods bestowed,
And, turned into a gewgaw, a machine,
Sets like an Opera phantom.[4]

     Thus, O Friend!
Through times of honour and through times of shame   370
Descending, have I faithfully retraced
The perturbations of a youthful mind
Under a long-lived storm of great events—
A story destined for thy ear,[5] who now,
Among the fallen of nations, dost abide   375
Where Etna, over hill and valley, casts
His shadow stretching towards Syracuse,
The city of Timoleon![6] Righteous Heaven!
How are the mighty prostrated![7] They first,
They first of all that breathe should have awaked   380
When the great voice was heard from out the tombs
Of ancient heroes. If I suffered grief
For ill-requited France, by many deemed
A trifler only in her proudest day;
Have been distressed to think of what she once   385
Promised, now is; a far more sober cause
Thine eyes must see of sorrow in a land,
Though with the wreck of loftier years bestrewn,
To the reanimating influence lost
Of memory, to virtue lost and hope.   390

 But indignation works where hope is not,
And thou, O Friend! wilt be refreshed. There is

One great society alone on earth:
The noble living and the noble dead.[8]
Thy consolation shall be there, and time   970
And Nature shall before thee spread in store
Imperishable thoughts, the place itself
Be conscious of thy presence, and the dull
Sirocco air of its degeneracy
Turn as thou mov'st into a healthful breeze   975
To cherish and invigorate thy frame.[9]

[395]   Thine be those motions strong and sanative,[1]
A ladder for thy spirit to reascend
To health and joy and pure contentedness:
To me the grief confined that thou art gone   980
From this last spot of earth where Freedom now
[400] Stands single in her only sanctuary[2]—
A lonely wanderer art gone, by pain
Compelled and sickness, at this latter day,
This heavy time of change for all mankind.   985
I feel for thee, must utter what I feel;
[405] The sympathies, erewhile in part discharged,
Gather afresh, and will have vent again.
My own delights do scarcely seem to me
My own delights: the lordly Alps themselves,   990
Those rosy peaks from which the morning looks
[410] Abroad on many nations, are not now
Since thy migration and departure, friend,
The gladsome image in my memory
Which they were used to be. To kindred scenes,   995
On errand—at a time how different—
Thou tak'st thy way,[3] carrying a heart more ripe
For all divine enjoyment, with the soul
[415] Which Nature gives to poets, now by thought
Matured, and in the summer of its strength.   1000
Oh, wrap him in your shades, ye giant woods,
On Etna's side, and thou, O flowery vale
Of Enna,[4] is there not some nook of thine
[420] From the first playtime of the infant earth
Kept sacred to restorative delight?   1005

8. Echoed in *The Convention of Cintra* (1809): "There is a spiritual community binding together the living and the dead; the good, the brave, and the wise, of all ages. We would not be rejected from this community; and therefore do we hope" (*Prose Works*, I, p. 339).
9. The degeneracy of Sicily is seen in Wordsworth's metaphor as the sirocco (an oppressive wind blowing from the north coast of Africa), which will turn in Coleridge's presence to a life-giving breeze.

1. Healing.
2. Britain was for the moment carrying on alone the war against Napoleon.
3. Wordsworth contrasts his own visit to the Alps in 1790, when France seemed "standing on the top of golden hours" (*1805*, VI, 353), with the political atmosphere of 1804 evoked in *1805*, 929–40 (*1850*, 365–69) above.
4. Where "Proserpine gathering flowers" was kidnapped by Pluto (*Paradise Lost*, IV, 268–71).

One great society alone on earth:
The noble Living and the noble Dead.[8]

    Thine be such converse strong and sanative,[1]   395
A ladder for thy spirit to reascend
To health and joy and pure contentedness;
To me the grief confined, that thou art gone
From this last spot of earth, where Freedom now
Stands single in her only sanctuary;[2]   400
A lonely wanderer art gone, by pain
Compelled and sickness, at this latter day,
This sorrowful reverse for all mankind.
I feel for thee, must utter what I feel:
The sympathies erewhile in part discharged,   405
Gather afresh, and will have vent again:
My own delights do scarcely seem to me
My own delights; the lordly Alps themselves,
Those rosy peaks, from which the Morning looks
Abroad on many nations, are no more   410
For me that image of pure gladsomeness
Which they were wont to be. Through kindred scenes,
For purpose, at a time, how different!
Thou tak'st thy way,[3] carrying the heart and soul
That Nature gives to Poets, now by thought   415
Matured, and in the summer of their strength.
Oh! wrap him in your shades, ye giant woods,
On Etna's side; and thou, O flowery field
Of Enna![4] is there not some nook of thine,
From the first play-time of the infant world   420
Kept sacred to restorative delight,
When from afar invoked by anxious love?

    Child of the mountains, among shepherds reared,
Even from my earliest schoolday time, I loved
To dream of Sicily; and now a sweet
[428] And gladsome promise wafted from that land
Comes o'er my heart. There's not a single name   1010
Of note belonging to that honored isle,
Philosopher or bard, Empedocles,
Or Archimedes—deep and tranquil soul—
[435] That is not like a comfort to my grief.[5]
And, O Theocritus, so far have some   1015
Prevailed among the powers of heaven and earth
By force of graces which were theirs, that they
Have had, as thou reportest, miracles
[440] Wrought for them in old time: yea, not unmoved,
When thinking on my own belovèd friend,   1020
I hear thee tell how bees with honey fed
Divine Comates, by his tyrant lord
Within a chest imprisoned impiously—
[445] How with their honey from the fields they came
And fed him there, alive, from month to month,
Because the goatherd, blessèd man, had lips   1025
Wet with the Muse's nectar.[6]
                        Thus I soothe
The pensive moments by this calm fireside,
[450] And find a thousand fancied images
That chear the thoughts of those I love, and mine.   1030
Our prayers have been accepted: thou wilt stand
Not as an exile but a visitant
On Etna's top; by pastoral Arethuse[7]—
[465] Or if that fountain be indeed no more,
Then near some other spring which by the name   1035
Thou gratulatest, willingly deceived—
Shalt linger as a gladsome votary,[8]
And not a captive pining for his home.

5. Empedocles (ca. 493–ca. 433 B.C.), variously considered a poet and a philosopher writing in verse, was supposed to have thrown himself into the crater of Mount Etna. Archimedes (ca. 287–212 B.C.), the greatest mathematician of the ancient world, was born at Syracuse in Sicily.

6. Theocritus (*1805*, 1015; *1850*, 436), ca. 310–250 B.C., the great Sicilian pastoral poet, tells the story of Comates in *Idyl*, VII, 78–83.

7. A spring at Syracuse, often alluded to in pastoral poetry.

8. Devotee, worshipper. "Thou gratulatest": i.e., "you rejoice over"; a deliberate, and in context appropriate, poeticism.

Child of the mountains, among shepherds reared,
Ere yet familiar with the classic page,
I learnt to dream of Sicily; and lo,   425
The gloom, that, but a moment past, was deepened
At thy command, at her command gives way;
A pleasant promise, wafted from her shores,
Comes o'er my heart: in fancy I behold
Her seas yet smiling, her once happy vales;   430
Nor can my tongue give utterance to a name
Of note belonging to that honoured isle,
Philosopher or Bard, Empedocles,
Or Archimedes, pure abstracted soul!
That doth not yield a solace to my grief:[5]   435
And, O Theocritus, so far have some
Prevailed among the powers of heaven and earth,
By their endowments, good or great, that they
Have had, as thou reportest, miracles
Wrought for them in old time; yea, not unmoved,   440
When thinking on my own beloved friend,
I hear thee tell how bees with honey fed
Divine Comates, by his impious lord
Within a chest imprisoned; how they came
Laden from blooming grove or flowery field,   445
And fed him there, alive, month after month,
Because the goatherd, blessed man! had lips
Wet with the Muses' nectar.[6]

                   Thus I soothe
The pensive moments by this calm fire-side,
And find a thousand bounteous images   450
To cheer the thoughts of those I love, and mine.
Our prayers have been accepted; thou wilt stand
On Etna's summit, above earth and sea,
Triumphant, winning from the invaded heavens
Thoughts without bound, magnificent designs,   455
Worthy of poets who attuned their harps
In wood or echoing cave, for discipline
Of heroes; or, in reverence to the gods,
'Mid temples, served by sapient priests, and choirs
Of virgins crowned with roses. Not in vain   460
Those temples, where they in their ruins yet
Survive for inspiration, shall attract
Thy solitary steps: and on the brink
Thou wilt recline of pastoral Arethuse;[7]
Or, if that fountain be in truth no more,   465
Then, near some other spring, which, by the name
Thou gratulatest, willingly deceived,
I see thee linger a glad votary,[8]
And not a captive pining for his home.

Book Eleventh

Imagination, How Impaired and Restored

Long time hath man's unhappiness and guilt
Detained us: with what dismal sights beset
For the outward view, and inwardly oppressed
With sorrow, disappointment, vexing thoughts,
[5] Confusion of the judgement, zeal decayed—   5
And lastly, utter loss of hope itself
And things to hope for. Not with these began
Our song, and not with these our song must end.[1]
Ye motions of delight, that through the fields
[10] Stir gently, breezes and soft airs that breathe   10
The breath of paradise, and find your way
To the recesses of the soul; ye brooks
Muttering along the stones, a busy noise
[20] By day, a quiet one in silent night;
And you, ye groves, whose ministry it is   15
[25] To interpose the covert of your shades,
Even as a sleep, betwixt the heart of man
And the uneasy world—'twixt man himself,
Not seldom, and his own unquiet heart—
Oh, that I had a music and a voice   20
[30] Harmonious as your own, that I might tell
What ye have done for me. The morning shines,
Nor heedeth man's perverseness; spring returns—
I saw the spring return, when I was dead
To deeper hope, yet had I joy for her   25
And welcomed her benevolence, rejoiced
In common with the children of her love,
[35] Plants, insects, beasts in field, and birds in bower.
So neither were complacency, nor peace,
Nor tender yearnings, wanting for my good   30
[40] Through those distracted times:[3] in Nature still

---

1. An allusion, which Coleridge would enjoy, to *The Idiot Boy*, 445–56, "And with the owls began my song, / And with the owls must end."

3. Wordsworth is referring to spring 1796, and the period of moral crisis described at the end of Book X; see *1805*, X, 904*n*, above.

Book Twelfth

Imagination and Taste, How Impaired and Restored

LONG time have human ignorance and guilt
Detained us, on what spectacles of woe
Compelled to look, and inwardly oppressed
With sorrow, disappointment, vexing thoughts,
Confusion of the judgment, zeal decayed,   5
And, lastly, utter loss of hope itself
And things to hope for! Not with these began
Our song, and not with these our song must end.[1]—
Ye motions of delight, that haunt the sides
Of the green hills; ye breezes and soft airs,   10
Whose subtle intercourse with breathing flowers,
Feelingly watched, might teach Man's haughty race
How without injury to take, to give
Without offence; ye who, as if to show
The wondrous influence of power gently used,   15
Bend the complying heads of lordly pines,
And, with a touch, shift the stupendous clouds
Through the whole compass of the sky; ye brooks,
Muttering along the stones, a busy noise
By day, a quiet sound in silent night;   20
Ye waves, that out of the great deep steal forth
In a calm hour to kiss the pebbly shore,
Not mute, and then retire, fearing no storm;
And you, ye groves, whose ministry it is
To interpose the covert of your shades,   25
Even as a sleep, between the heart of man
And outward troubles, between man himself,
Not seldom, and his own uneasy heart:
Oh! that I had a music and a voice
Harmonious as your own, that I might tell   30
What ye have done for me. The morning shines,
Nor heedeth Man's perverseness; Spring returns,—
I saw the Spring return, and could rejoice,
In common with the children of her love,
Piping on boughs, or sporting on fresh fields,   35
Or boldly seeking pleasure nearer heaven
On wings that navigate cerulean skies.
So neither were complacency,[2] nor peace,
Nor tender yearnings, wanting for my good
Through these distracted times;[3] in Nature still   40

2. Contentedness, satisfaction—as at *1850*, VIII, 75, above.

Glorying, I found a counterpoise in her,
Which, when the spirit of evil was at height,
Maintained for me a secret happiness.
Her I resorted to, and loved so much   35
I seemed to love as much as heretofore—
And yet this passion, fervent as it was,
Had suffered change; how could there fail to be
Some change, if merely hence, that years of life
Were going on, and with them loss or gain   40
Inevitable, sure alternative?

    This history, my friend, hath chiefly told
[45] Of intellectual[5] power from stage to stage
Advancing hand in hand with love and joy,
And of imagination teaching truth
[50] Until that natural graciousness of mind   45
Gave way to over-pressure of the times
And their disastrous issues. What availed,
When spells forbade the voyager to land,[7]
The fragrance which did ever and anon   50
[55] Give notice of the shore, from arbours breathed
Of blessèd sentiment and fearless love?
What did such sweet remembrances avail—
Perfidious then, as seemed—what served they then?
My business was upon the barren seas,   55
My errand was to sail to other coasts.[8]
Shall I avow that I had hope to see
(I mean that future times would surely see)
The man to come parted as by a gulph
[60] From him who had been?—that I could no more   60
Trust the elevation which had made me one
With the great family that here and there
Is scattered through the abyss of ages past,
Sage, patriot, lover, hero; for it seemed
[65] That their best virtues were not free from taint   65
Of something false and weak, which could not stand
The open eye of reason. Then I said,
'Go to the poets, they will speak to thee
More perfectly of purer creatures—yet

---

5. Spiritual—as at *1805*, 168 below, and elsewhere.
7. See *1805*, 67*n*, below.
8. The image of lines 48–56 is drawn from *Paradise Lost*, IV, 156–65, where the scents of Eden are compared to those blowing "from the spicy shore / Of Arabie the blest" to mariners who pass.
9. The arbors of "blessèd sentiment and fearless love" (lines 51–52) from which the poet cut himself off because they seemed perfidious, must be interpreted by reference to lines 57–67. The barren seas he sailed were those of Godwinian rationalism; he was tempted to think himself connected by emotion and love to the "great family" of man (line 62), but sailed on as if bound by a spell (line 49) because man's future behavior was to be so different that even that which seemed best in the past, and the present, was not to be trusted (seemed "perfidious," line 54).

Glorying, I found a counterpoise in her,
Which, when the spirit of evil reached its height,
Maintained for me a secret happiness.[4]

   This narrative, my Friend! hath chiefly told
Of intellectual[5] power, fostering love,   45
Dispensing truth, and, over men and things,
Where reason yet might hesitate, diffusing
Prophetic sympathies of genial faith:
So was I favoured—such my happy lot[6]—
Until that natural graciousness of mind   50
Gave way to overpressure from the times
And their disastrous issues. What availed,
When spells forbade the voyager to land,[7]
That fragrant notice of a pleasant shore
Wafted, at intervals, from many a bower   55
Of blissful gratitude and fearless love?
Dare I avow that wish was mine to see,
And hope that future times *would* surely see,
The man to come, parted, as by a gulph,
From him who had been; that I could no more   60
Trust the elevation which had made me one
With the great family that still survives
To illuminate the abyss of ages past,
Sage, warrior, patriot, hero; for it seemed
That their best virtues were not free from taint   65
Of something false and weak, that could not stand
The open eye of Reason. Then I said,
'Go to the Poets; they will speak to thee
More perfectly of purer creatures;—yet

---

4. The final text of lines 1–43 is the result of many independent revisions, beginning in 1816/19, when the striking poetry of *1805*, 23–28 is reduced to *1850*, 31–34, and *1805*, 35–36 are cut.
6. Lines 45–49 are incorporated in Wordsworth's final revisions, in or after 1839.

[70] If reason be nobility in man,   70
Can aught be more ignoble than the man
Whom they describe, would fasten if they may
Upon our love by sympathies of truth?'

[76]   Thus strangely did I war against myself;
A bigot to a new idolatry,   75
Did like a monk who hath forsworn the world
Zealously labour to cut off my heart
[80] From all the sources of her former strength;
And, as by simple waving of a wand,
The wizard instantaneously dissolves   80
Palace or grove, even so did I unsoul
As readily by syllogistic words
(Some charm of logic, ever within reach)
[85] Those mysteries of passion which have made,
And shall continue evermore to make—   85
In spite of all that reason hath performed,
And shall perform, to exalt and to refine—
One brotherhood of all the human race,[1]
Through all the habitations of past years,
And those to come: and hence an emptiness   90
Fell on the historian's page, and even on that
Of poets, pregnant with more absolute truth.
The works of both withered in my esteem,
Their sentence was, I thought, pronounced—their rights
Seemed mortal, and their empire passed away.   95

    What then remained in such eclipse, what light
To guide or chear? The laws of things which lie
Beyond the reach of human will or power,
The life of Nature, by the God of love
Inspired—celestial presence ever pure—   100
These left, the soul of youth must needs be rich
Whatever else be lost; and these were mine,
Not a deaf echo merely of the thought
(Bewildered recollections, solitary),
But living sounds. Yet in despite of this—   105
This feeling, which howe'er impaired or damped,
Yet having been once born can never die—
'Tis true that earth with all her appanage[3]
Of elements and organs, storm and sunshine,
With its pure forms and colours, pomp of clouds,   110

---

1. Wordsworth has in mind the wizardry
of Prospero in *The Tempest*, IV, i, 148–
56, as he evokes the power of rationalist
language to "unsoul" the mysteries of
passion.
3. Endowment.

If reason be nobility in man,　　　　　　　　　　　70
Can aught be more ignoble than the man
Whom they delight in, blinded as he is
By prejudice, the miserable slave
Of low ambition or distempered love?'

In such strange passion, if I may once more　　75
Review the past, I warred against myself—
A bigot to a new idolatry—
Like a cowled monk who hath forsworn the world,
Zealously laboured to cut off my heart
From all the sources of her former strength;　　80
And as, by simple waving of a wand,
The wizard instantaneously dissolves
Palace or grove, even so could I unsoul
As readily by syllogistic words
Those mysteries of being which have made,　　85
And shall continue evermore to make,
Of the whole human race one brotherhood.[1]

What wonder, then, if, to a mind so far
Perverted, even the visible Universe
Fell under the dominion of a taste　　　　　　90
Less spiritual, with microscopic view
Was scanned, as I had scanned the moral world?[2]

2. Wordsworth's final text of lines 44–92 is not reached until the corrections of *MS. E* in 1839 or later, but dissatisfaction with *1805*, 42–137 shows itself as early as ca. January 1807. There is ex-tensive revision in 1816/19, and again in 1832, this time with an attempt to substitute a version of *1850*, XI, 333–52 for *1805*, 102–37.

Rivers, and mountains, objects among which
It might be thought that no dislike or blame,
No sense of weakness or infirmity
Or aught amiss, could possibly have come,
Yea, even the visible universe was scanned   115
With something of a kindred spirit,[4] fell
[90] Beneath the domination of a taste
Less elevated, which did in my mind
With its more noble influence interfere,
Its animation and its deeper sway.   120

     There comes (if need be now to speak of this
After such long detail of our mistakes),
There comes a time when reason—not the grand
And simple reason, but that humbler power
Which carries on its no inglorious work   125
By logic and minute analysis—
Is of all idols that which pleases most
The growing mind.[5] A trifler would he be
Who on the obvious benefits should dwell
That rise out of this process; but to speak   130
Of all the narrow estimates of things
Which hence originate were a worthy theme
For philosophic verse. Suffice it here
To hint that danger cannot but attend
Upon a function rather proud to be
The enemy of falsehood, than the friend   135
Of truth—to sit in judgement than to feel.

     Oh soul of Nature, excellent and fair,
That didst rejoice with me, with whom I too
[95] Rejoiced, through early youth, before the winds   140
And powerful waters, and in lights and shades
That marched and countermarched about the hills
In glorious apparition, now all eye
[100] And now all ear, but ever with the heart
Employed, and the majestic intellect!   145
O soul of Nature, that dost overflow
With passion and with life, what feeble men
[105] Walk on this earth, how feeble have I been
When thou wert in thy strength! Nor this through stroke
Of human suffering, such as justifies   150
Remissness and inaptitude of mind,

4. I.e., kindred to the spirit described in lines 74–90.
5. The last two-thirds of Book XI—lines 123–388—must coincide almost exactly with the final part of Book V of the five-Book *Prelude*. For the passage used by Wordsworth to link the opening section of his original Book V—corresponding broadly to XIII, 1–165—into the materials now in XI, see MS. Drafts and Fragments, 3(b), below.

O Soul of Nature! excellent and fair!
That didst rejoice with me, with whom I, too,
Rejoiced through early youth, before the winds   95
And roaring waters, and in lights and shades
That marched and countermarched about the hills
In glorious apparition, Powers on whom
I daily waited, now all eye and now
All ear; but never long without the heart   100
Employed, and man's unfolding intellect:
O Soul of Nature! that, by laws divine
Sustained and governed, still dost overflow
With an impassioned life, what feeble ones
Walk on this earth! how feeble have I been   105
When thou wert in thy strength! Nor this through stroke
Of human suffering, such as justifies
Remissness and inaptitude of mind,

But through presumption,[6] even in pleasure pleased
[110] Unworthily, disliking here, and there
Liking, by rules of mimic art transferred
To things above all art. But more—for this,   155
Although a strong infection of the age,
Was never much my habit—giving way
[115] To a comparison of scene with scene,
Bent overmuch on superficial things,
Pampering myself with meagre novelties   160
Of colour and proportion, to the moods
[120] Of Nature, and the spirit of the place,
Less sensible.[7] Nor only did the love
Of sitting thus in judgment interrupt
My deeper feelings, but another cause,   165
More subtle and less easily explained,
[125] That almost seems inherent in the creature,
Sensuous and intellectual as he is,
A twofold frame of body and of mind:
The state to which I now allude was one   170
In which the eye was master of the heart,
When that which is in every stage of life
The most despotic of our senses gained
[130] Such strength in me as often held my mind
In absolute dominion. Gladly here,   175
Entering upon abstruser argument,
Would I endeavour to unfold the means
Which Nature studiously employs to thwart
[135] This tyranny, summons all the senses each
To counteract the other and themselves,   180
And makes them all, and the objects with which all
Are conversant, subservient in their turn
To the great ends of liberty and power.
But this is matter for another song;[8]
Here only let me add that my delights,   185
[141] Such as they were, were sought insatiably.
Though 'twas a transport of the outward sense,
Not of the mind—vivid but not profound—
Yet was I often greedy in the chace,
And roamed from hill to hill, from rock to rock,   190

6. Arrogance, presumptuousness (Johnson's *Dictionary*).
7. Wordsworth moves on in *1805*, 138–63 (*1850*, 83–121) from his preceding discussion of reason as an idol to consider a different but equally destructive, and equally fashionable, form of sitting in judgment. He had not himself subscribed to the cult of the picturesque as defined by William Gilpin—"liking, by rules of mimic art transferred" to Nature (*1805*, 149–57; *1850*, 106–114) but had nevertheless indulged too much in aesthetic comparisons of landscape, and pleasure in transient effects.
"Sensible" (*1805*, 163): responsive; "insensible" (*1850*, 121): unresponsive.
8. Another reference to the prospective but never written philosophical section of *The Recluse*; not removed until Wordsworth's final revision, in 1839 or later.

But through presumption;[6] even in pleasure pleased
Unworthily, disliking here, and there   110
Liking, by rules of mimic art transferred
To things above all art; but more,—for this,
Although a strong infection of the age,
Was never much my habit—giving way
To a comparison of scene with scene,   115
Bent overmuch on superficial things,
Pampering myself with meagre novelties
Of colour and proportion; to the moods
Of time and season, to the moral power,
The affections and the spirit of the place,   120
Insensible.[7] Nor only did the love
Of sitting thus in judgment interrupt
My deeper feelings, but another cause,
More subtle and less easily explained,
That almost seems inherent in the creature,   125
A twofold frame of body and of mind.
I speak in recollection of a time
When the bodily eye, in every stage of life
The most despotic of our senses, gained
Such strength in *me* as often held my mind   130
In absolute dominion. Gladly here,
Entering upon abstruser argument,
Could I endeavour to unfold the means
Which Nature studiously employs to thwart
This tyranny, summons all the senses each   135
To counteract the other, and themselves,
And makes them all, and the objects with which all
Are conversant, subservient in their turn
To the great ends of Liberty and Power.
But leave we this: enough that my delights   140
(Such as they were) were sought insatiably.
Vivid the transport, vivid though not profound;
I roamed from hill to hill, from rock to rock,

Still craving combinations of new forms,[9]
[145] New pleasure, wider empire for the sight,
Proud of its own endowments, and rejoiced
To lay the inner faculties asleep.

Amid the turns and counter-turns, the strife   195
And various trials of our complex being
[150] As we grow up, such thraldom of that sense
Seems hard to shun; and yet I knew a maid,
Who, young as I was then, conversed with things
In higher style.[1] From appetites like these   200
She, gentle visitant, as well she might,
Was wholly free. Far less did critic rules
[155] Or barren intermeddling subtleties
Perplex her mind,[2] but, wise as women are
When genial circumstance[3] hath favored them,   205
She welcomed what was given, and craved no more.
Whatever scene was present to her eyes,
[160] That was the best, to that she was attuned
Through her humility and lowliness,
And through a perfect happiness of soul,   210
Whose variegated feelings were in this
[164] Sisters, that they were each some new delight.
For she was Nature's inmate:[4] her the birds,
And every flower she met with, could they but
Have known her, would have loved. Methought such charm   215
Of sweetness did her presence breathe around
That all the trees, and all the silent hills,
And every thing she looked on, should have had
[170] An intimation how she bore herself
Towards them and to all creatures. God delights   220
In such a being, for her common thoughts
Are piety, her life is blessedness.[5]

Even like this maid, before I was called forth
[175] From the retirement of my native hills

---

9. For this phase of Wordsworth's development, compare *Tintern Abbey*, 68–71, "when like a roe / I bounded o'er the mountains"; and for a clearly deliberate verbal echo, see *To the Daisy* ("In youth from rock to rock"), 1–2.
1. Mary Hutchinson, whom Wordsworth married on October 4, 1802, but whom he had known since childhood (see *1805*, VI, 236n, above). "Young as I was then" (*1805*, 199) is an adjectival clause referring to Mary: she was as young as he was. The clause is emended in one of Wordsworth's earliest revisions, ca. January 1807.
2. Wordsworth is again alluding to one of his own earlier poems, *Tables Turned*, 26–28, "Our meddling intellect / Misshapes the beauteous forms of things— / We murder to dissect."
3. Good fortune.
4. She lived as a companion with Nature.
5. Mary is presented here—as her sister Sara had been two years before in the first version of Coleridge's *Dejection* (April 1802)—as an emblem of innocence. Like Sara, the "conjugal and mother dove" of Coleridge's poem, she is capable of unquestioning responsiveness, the outgoing joy that both poets chiefly value, and that both at times feel themselves to have lost.

Still craving combinations of new forms,[9]
New pleasure, wider empire for the sight, 145
Proud of her own endowments, and rejoiced
To lay the inner faculties asleep.
Amid the turns and counterturns, the strife
And various trials of our complex being,
As we grow up, such thraldom of that sense 150
Seems hard to shun. And yet I knew a maid,
A young enthusiast, who escaped these bonds;[1]
Her eye was not the mistress of her heart;
Far less did rules prescribed by passive taste,
Or barren intermeddling subtleties, 155
Perplex her mind;[2] but, wise as women are
When genial circumstance[3] hath favoured them,
She welcomed what was given, and craved no more;
Whate'er the scene presented to her view,
That was the best, to that she was attuned 160
By her benign simplicity of life,
And through a perfect happiness of soul,
Whose variegated feelings were in this
Sisters, that they were each some new delight.
Birds in the bower, and lambs in the green field, 165
Could they have known her, would have loved; methought
Her very presence such a sweetness breathed,
That flowers, and trees, and even the silent hills,
And every thing she looked on, should have had
An intimation how she bore herself 170
Towards them and to all creatures. God delights
In such a being; for her common thoughts
Are piety, her life is gratitude.[5]

    Even like this maid, before I was called forth
From the retirement of my native hills, 175

I loved whate'er I saw, nor lightly loved,   225
But fervently—did never dream of aught
More grand, more fair, more exquisitely framed,
Than those few nooks to which my happy feet
[180] Were limited. I had not at that time
Lived long enough, nor in the least survived   230
The first diviner influence of this world
As it appears to unaccustomed eyes.
I worshipped then among the depths of things
[185] As my soul bade me; could I then take part
In aught but admiration, or be pleased   235
With any thing but humbleness and love?
I felt, and nothing else; I did not judge,
I never thought of judging, with the gift
[190] Of all this glory filled and satisfied—
And afterwards, when through the gorgeous Alps   240
Roaming, I carried with me the same heart.[7]
In truth, this degradation[8]—howsoe'er
Induced, effect in whatsoe'er degree
[195] Of custom that prepares such wantonness
As makes the greatest things give way to least,   245
Or any other cause that hath been named,
Or, lastly, aggravated by the times,
Which with their passionate sounds might often make
[200] The milder minstrelsies of rural scenes
Inaudible—was transient. I had felt   250
Too forcibly, too early in my life,
Visitings of imaginative power
For this to last: I shook the habit off
[205] Entirely and for ever, and again
In Nature's presence stood, as I stand now,   255
A sensitive, and a *creative* soul.[9]
    There are in our existence spots of time,[1]
Which with distinct preeminence retain
[210] A renovating[2] virtue, whence, depressed

---

7. At the age of twenty, in summer 1790; see *1805*, VI, 428 ff., above.
8. I.e., the decline in responsiveness recorded in *1805*, 152–98 (*1850*, 109–51).
9. The original text of lines 242–56 (as composed for the five-Book *Prelude* in *MS. W*, March 1804) is briefer, and so muted as almost to suggest that Wordsworth had never been subject to the "malady" he describes: "In truth this malady of which I speak / Though aided by the times, whose deeper sound / Without my knowledge sometimes might perchance / Make rural Nature's milder minstrelsies / Inaudible, did never take in me / Deep root, or larger action. I had received / Impressions far too early, and too strong, / For this to last: I threw the habit off / Entirely and for ever, and again / In Nature's presence stood, as I do now, / A meditative and creative soul."
1. The original "spots of time" sequence (corresponding broadly to *1805*, 257–315, 342–88) was written ca. January 1799, and appears as *1799*, I, 288–374.
2. Wordsworth's third attempt at this highly important adjective, and certainly the neatest, though less striking in its implications than either "fructifying" (*1799*) or "vivifying" (the intermediate stage, printed in de Selincourt's text of *1805*, but in fact corrected very early to "renovating" in both faircopies).

I loved whate'er I saw: nor lightly loved,
But most intensely; never dreamt of aught
More grand, more fair, more exquisitely framed
Than those few nooks to which my happy feet
Were limited. I had not at that time   180
Lived long enough, nor in the least survived
The first diviner influence of this world,
As it appears to unaccustomed eyes.
Worshipping then among the depth of things,
As piety ordained;[6] could I submit   185
To measured admiration, or to aught
That should preclude humility and love?
I felt, observed, and pondered; did not judge,
Yea, never thought of judging; with the gift
Of all this glory filled and satisfied.   190
And afterwards, when through the gorgeous Alps
Roaming, I carried with me the same heart:[7]
In truth, the degradation[8]—howsoe'er
Induced, effect, in whatsoe'er degree,
Of custom that prepares a partial scale   195
In which the little oft outweighs the great;
Or any other cause that hath been named;
Or lastly, aggravated by the times
And their impassioned sounds, which well might make
The milder minstrelsies of rural scenes   200
Inaudible—was transient; I had known
Too forcibly, too early in my life,
Visitings of imaginative power
For this to last: I shook the habit off
Entirely and for ever, and again   205
In Nature's presence stood, as now I stand,
A sensitive being, a *creative* soul.

     There are in our existence spots of time,[1]
That with distinct pre-eminence retain
A renovating virtue, whence, depressed   210

---

6. A small but significant emendation of 1816/19.

By false opinion and contentious thought,   260
Or aught of heavier or more deadly weight
In trivial occupations and the round
Of ordinary intercourse, our minds
[215] Are nourished and invisibly repaired—
A virtue, by which pleasure is enhanced,   265
That penetrates, enables us to mount
When high, more high, and lifts us up when fallen.
This efficacious spirit chiefly lurks
[220] Among those passages of life in which
We have had deepest feeling that the mind   270
Is lord and master, and that outward sense
Is but the obedient servant of her will.
Such moments, worthy of all gratitude,
Are scattered everywhere, taking their date
[225] From our first childhood—in our childhood even   275
Perhaps are most conspicuous. Life with me,
As far as memory can look back, is full
Of this beneficent influence.[3]
                     At a time
When scarcely (I was then not six years old)
My hand could hold a bridle, with proud hopes   280
I mounted, and we rode towards the hills:
We were a pair of horsemen—honest James
[230] Was with me, my encourager and guide.[4]
We had not travelled long ere some mischance
Disjoined me from my comrade, and, through fear   285
Dismounting, down the rough and stony moor
I led my horse, and stumbling on, at length
[235] Came to a bottom[5] where in former times
A murderer had been hung in iron chains.
The gibbet-mast was mouldered down, the bones   290
And iron case were gone, but on the turf
Hard by, soon after that fell deed was wrought,
[240] Some unknown hand had carved the murderer's name.
The monumental writing was engraven
In times long past, and still from year to year   295
By superstition of the neighbourhood
The grass is cleared away; and to this hour
[245] The letters are all fresh and visible.
Faltering, and ignorant where I was, at length
I chanced to espy those characters inscribed   300

---

3. Lines 257–78 should be compared with Wordsworth's much briefer original statement, *1799*, I, 288–96. The important new element in *1805* is the emphasis on mind as "lord and master" (line 271).

4. Wordsworth, probably aged five, was staying with his grandparents at **Penrith**. "Honest James" was presumably their servant.

5. Valley bottom.

By false opinion and contentious thought,
Or aught of heavier or more deadly weight,
In trivial occupations, and the round
Of ordinary intercourse, our minds
Are nourished and invisibly repaired;   215
A virtue, by which pleasure is enhanced,
That penetrates, enables us to mount,
When high, more high, and lifts us up when fallen.
This efficacious spirit chiefly lurks
Among those passages of life that give   220
Profoundest knowledge to what point, and how,
The mind is lord and master—outward sense
The obedient servant of her will. Such moments
Are scattered everywhere, taking their date
From our first childhood. I remember well,   225
That once, while yet my inexperienced hand
Could scarcely hold a bridle, with proud hopes
I mounted, and we journeyed towards the hills:
An ancient servant of my father's house
Was with me, my encourager and guide:[4]   230
We had not travelled long, ere some mischance
Disjoined me from my comrade; and, through fear
Dismounting, down the rough and stony moor
I led my horse, and, stumbling on, at length
Came to a bottom,[5] where in former times   235
A murderer had been hung in iron chains.
The gibbet-mast had mouldered down, the bones
And iron case were gone; but on the turf,
Hard by, soon after that fell deed was wrought,

On the green sod:[6] forthwith I left the spot,
And, reascending the bare common, saw
A naked pool that lay beneath the hills,
[250] The beacon on the summit,[7] and more near,   305
A girl who bore a pitcher on her head
And seemed with difficult steps to force her way
Against the blowing wind. It was, in truth,
An ordinary sight, but I should need
[255] Colours and words that are unknown to man
To paint the visionary dreariness   310
Which, while I looked all round for my lost guide,
Did at that time invest the naked pool,
The beacon on the lonely eminence,
[260] The woman, and her garments vexed and tossed
By the strong wind. When, in blessèd season,   315
With those two dear ones[8]—to my heart so dear—
When, in the blessèd time of early love,
Long afterwards I roamed about
In daily presence of this very scene,
Upon the naked pool and dreary crags,   320
[265] And on the melancholy beacon, fell
The spirit of pleasure and youth's golden gleam—
And think ye not with radiance more divine
From these remembrances, and from the power
They left behind? So feeling comes in aid   325
[270] Of feeling, and diversity of strength
Attends us, if but once we have been strong,

Oh mystery of man, from what a depth
Proceed thy honours! I am lost, but see
In simple childhood something of the base   330
[275] On which thy greatness stands—but this I feel,
That from thyself it is that thou must give,
Else never canst receive. The days gone by
Come back upon me from the dawn almost
Of life; the hiding-places of my power   335
[280] Seem open, I approach, and then they close;
I see by glimpses now, when age comes on
May scarcely see at all; and I would give

6. Wordsworth is conflating two separate
murder stories, one belonging to Hawkshead, the other to Penrith; see 1799, I,
310n, above. According to the anonymous
History of Penrith (1858), the letters cut
in the turf—an 1804 addition to the Prelude account—were "TPM," signifying
"Thomas Parker Murdered." The interpretation is not very convincing, but
Wordsworth's statement that the letters
recorded the name of the murderer
(Thomas Nicholson) is suspect too, as
there is no particular reason to suppose
he ever saw them.
7. The impressive stone signal-beacon,
built in 1719 on the hill (737 feet) above
Penrith. Nicholson was hanged a mile
or so to the east, near the Edenhall road.
8. Wordsworth's companions in summer
1787 had been his future wife, Mary
Hutchinson, and Dorothy; see 1805, VI,
236n, above. Dorothy's presence is no
longer mentioned in the 1850 text.

Some unknown hand had carved the murderer's name.[6]   240
The monumental letters were inscribed
In times long past; but still, from year to year,
By superstition of the neighbourhood,
The grass is cleared away, and to that hour
The characters were fresh and visible: 245
A casual glance had shown them, and I fled,
Faltering and faint, and ignorant of the road:
Then, reascending the bare common, saw
A naked pool that lay beneath the hills,
The beacon on its summit,[7] and, more near,   250
A girl, who bore a pitcher on her head,
And seemed with difficult steps to force her way
Against the blowing wind. It was, in truth,
An ordinary sight; but I should need
Colours and words that are unknown to man,   255
To paint the visionary dreariness
Which, while I looked all round for my lost guide,
Invested moorland waste, and naked pool,
The beacon crowning the lone eminence,
The female and her garments vexed and tossed   260
By the strong wind. When, in the blessed hours
Of early love, the loved one at my side,[8]
I roamed, in daily presence of this scene,
Upon the naked pool and dreary crags,
And on the melancholy beacon fell   265
A spirit of pleasure and youth's golden gleam;
And think ye not with radiance more sublime
For these remembrances, and for the power
They had left behind? So feeling comes in aid
Of feeling, and diversity of strength   270
Attends us, if but once we have been strong.
Oh! mystery of man, from what a depth
Proceed thy honours. I am lost, but see
In simple childhood something of the base
On which thy greatness stands; but this I feel,   275
That from thy self it comes, that thou must give,
Else never canst receive. The days gone by
Return upon me almost from the dawn
Of life: the hiding-places of man's power
Open; I would approach them, but they close.   280
I see by glimpses now; when age comes on,
May scarcely see at all; and I would give,

While yet we may, as far as words can give,
A substance and a life to what I feel: 340
[285] I would enshrine the spirit of the past
For future restoration. Yet another
Of these to me affecting incidents,
With which we will conclude.[9]

                             One Christmas-time,
The day before the holidays began,   345
Feverish, and tired, and restless, I went forth
[290] Into the fields, impatient for the sight
Of those two horses which should bear us home,
My brothers and myself.[1] There was a crag,
An eminence, which from the meeting-point   350
Of two highways ascending overlooked
At least a long half-mile of those two roads,
By each of which the expected steeds might come—
[296] The choice uncertain.[2] Thither I repaired
Up to the highest summit. 'Twas a day   355
Stormy, and rough, and wild, and on the grass
I sate half sheltered by a naked wall.
[300] Upon my right hand was a single sheep,
A whistling hawthorn on my left, and there,
With those companions at my side, I watched,   360
Straining my eyes intensely as the mist
Gave intermitting prospect of the wood
[305] And plain beneath. Ere I to school returned
That dreary time, ere I had been ten days
A dweller in my father's house, he died,   365
And I and my two brothers, orphans then,
Followed his body to the grave.[3] The event,
[310] With all the sorrow which it brought, appeared
A chastisement; and when I called to mind
That day so lately past, when from the crag   370
I looked in such anxiety of hope,
With trite reflections of morality,
[315] Yet in the deepest passion, I bowed low

9. Lines 315–44 were written in early
March 1804, just after the completion of
the *Intimations Ode* and composition of
the *Ode to Duty*; for their original context and different conclusion, see Composition and Texts: *1805/1850*, Introduction, below.
1. The date was almost certainly December 19, 1783; Wordsworth was thirteen.
Two of his three brothers, Richard (born
1768) and John (born 1772), were also
at Hawkshead Grammar School at this
time. The horses of *1805*, 348, turn into
the literary "palfreys" of *1850*, 291 as

early as the 1816/19 revisions of *A*; the
emendation "couched" for "was" in line
358 belongs to the same time, as does the
recasting of line 359.
2. Wordsworth was waiting on the ridge
north of Borwick Lodge, a mile and a
half from the school.
3. John Wordsworth, Sr., died on December 30, 1783; Wordsworth's mother
had died five years before. The *1805*
reading "two brothers" is correct, as
against *1850* "three." Richard and John
Wordsworth were present (*MY*, I, p.
185).

While yet we may, as far as words can give,
Substance and life to what I feel, enshrining,
Such is my hope, the spirit of the Past   285
For future restoration.—Yet another
Of these memorials:—

                    One Christmas-time,
On the glad eve of its dear holidays,
Feverish and tired, and restless, I went forth
Into the fields, impatient for the sight   290
Of those led palfreys that should bear us home;
My brothers and myself.[1] There rose a crag,
That, from the meeting-point of two highways
Ascending, overlooked them both, far stretched;[2]
Thither, uncertain on which road to fix   295
My expectation, thither I repaired,
Scout-like, and gained the summit; 'twas a day
Tempestuous, dark, and wild, and on the grass
I sate half-sheltered by a naked wall;
Upon my right hand couched a single sheep,   300
Upon my left a blasted hawthorn stood;
With those companions at my side, I sate
Straining my eyes intensely, as the mist
Gave intermitting prospect of the copse
And plain beneath. Ere we to school returned,—   305
That dreary time,—ere we had been ten days
Sojourners in my father's house, he died,
And I and my three brothers, orphans then,
Followed his body to the grave.[3] The event,
With all the sorrow that it brought, appeared   310
A chastisement; and when I called to mind
That day so lately past, when from the crag
I looked in such anxiety of hope;
With trite reflections of morality,
Yet in the deepest passion, I bowed low   315

To God who thus corrected my desires.
And afterwards the wind and sleety rain,   375
And all the business⁴ of the elements,
The single sheep, and the one blasted tree,
[320] And the bleak music of that old stone wall,
The noise of wood and water, and the mist
Which on the line of each of those two roads   380
Advanced in such indisputable shapes⁵—
All these were spectacles and sounds to which
[325] I often would repair, and thence would drink
As at a fountain. And I do not doubt
That in this later time, when storm and rain   385
Beat on my roof at midnight, or by day
When I am in the woods, unknown to me
[331–32] The workings of my spirit thence are brought.

Thou wilt not languish here, O friend, for whom
I travel in these dim uncertain ways—   390
Thou wilt assist me, as a pilgrim gone
In quest of highest truth. Behold me then
Once more in Nature's presence, thus restored,
Or otherwise,⁷ and strengthened once again
(With memory left of what had been escaped)   395
To habits of devoutest sympathy.

4. I.e., busy-ness, activity.   7. I.e., "restored in this, or in other
5. Scansion: índíspŭtáblĕ shápes."   ways."

To God, Who thus corrected my desires;
And, afterwards, the wind and sleety rain,
And all the business[4] of the elements,
The single sheep, and the one blasted tree,
And the bleak music of that old stone wall,   320
The noise of wood and water, and the mist
That on the line of each of those two roads
Advanced in such indisputable shapes;[5]
All these were kindred spectacles and sounds
To which I oft repaired, and thence would drink,   325
As at a fountain; and on winter nights,
Down to this very time, when storm and rain
Beat on my roof, or, haply, at noon-day,
While in a grove I walk, whose lofty trees,
Laden with summer's thickest foliage, rock   330
In a strong wind, some working of the spirit,
Some inward agitations thence are brought,
Whate'er their office, whether to beguile
Thoughts over busy in the course they took,
Or animate an hour of vacant ease.[6]   335

6. Wordsworth's first expansion of *1805*, 386–88, belongs to 1832, and this final text to 1839 or later.

Book Twelfth

Same Subject (Continued)

From Nature doth emotion come, and moods
Of calmness equally are Nature's gift:
This is her glory—these two attributes
[4] Are sister horns that constitute her strength;
This twofold influence is the sun and shower   5
Of all her bounties, both in origin
And end alike benignant.[1] Hence it is
[5] That genius, which exists by interchange
Of peace and excitation,[2] finds in her
His best and purest friend—from her receives   10
That energy by which he seeks the truth,
Is rouzed, aspires, grasps, struggles, wishes, craves
From her that happy stillness of the mind
[10] Which fits him to receive it when unsought.

    Such benefit may souls of humblest frame   15
Partake of, each in their degree; 'tis mine
To speak of what myself have known and felt—
Sweet task, for words find easy way, inspired
[15] By gratitude and confidence in truth.
Long time in search of knowledge desperate,   20
I was benighted heart and mind, but now
On all sides day began to reappear,[3]
And it was proved indeed that not in vain
[20] I had been taught to reverence a power
That is the very quality and shape   25
And image of right reason,[4] that matures
Her processes by steady laws, gives birth
To no impatient or fallacious hopes,
[25] No heat of passion or excessive zeal,
No vain conceits, provokes to no quick turns   30
Of self-applauding intellect, but lifts
The being into magnanimity,
Holds up before the mind, intoxicate
[30] With present objects and the busy dance
Of things that pass away, a temperate shew   35
Of objects that endure—and by this course
Disposes her, when over-fondly set

---

1. The horns which in line 4 suggest first
twofoldness, and then strength, become
in lines 5–6 "horns of plenty," cornu-
copias.
2. Stimulus, encouragement.
3. Wordsworth is referring to the period
of rehabilitation that followed his moral

crisis of spring 1796, described in *1805*,
X, 888–904 (*1850*, XI, 293–333) above.
4. The power described is Nature, as in
the opening line, above. The phrase
"right reason" is used by Milton to
signify reason that is attuned to intellectual, moral, and religious truth.

Book Thirteenth

*Imagination and Taste, How Impaired
and Restored—Concluded*

F‌ROM Nature doth emotion come, and moods
Of calmness equally are Nature's gift:
This is her glory; these two attributes
Are sister horns that constitute her strength.
Hence Genius, born to thrive by interchange   5
Of peace and excitation,[2] finds in her
His best and purest friend; from her receives
That energy by which he seeks the truth,
From her that happy stillness of the mind
Which fits him to receive it when unsought.   10

   Such benefit the humblest intellects
Partake of, each in their degree; 'tis mine
To speak, what I myself have known and felt;
Smooth task! for words find easy way, inspired
By gratitude, and confidence in truth.   15
Long time in search of knowledge did I range
The field of human life, in heart and mind
Benighted; but, the dawn beginning now
To re-appear,[3] 'twas proved that not in vain
I had been taught to reverence a Power   20
That is the visible quality and shape
And image of right reason;[4] that matures
Her processes by steadfast laws; gives birth
To no impatient or fallacious hopes,
No heat of passion or excessive zeal,   25
No vain conceits; provokes to no quick turns
Of self-applauding intellect; but trains
To meekness, and exalts by humble faith;[5]
Holds up before the mind intoxicate
With present objects, and the busy dance   30
Of things that pass away, a temperate show
Of objects that endure; and by this course
Disposes her, when over-fondly set

---

5. Lines 27–28 belong to 1832, or 1838/39. The strength of *1805*, 31–32, is sacrificed
to neatness and conventional piety.

On leaving her incumbrances behind,
[35] To seek in man, and in the frame of life
Social and individual, what there is   40
Desirable, affecting, good or fair,
Of kindred permanence, the gifts divine
And universal, the pervading grace
That hath been, is, and shall be. Above all
Did Nature bring again this wiser mood,   45
More deeply reestablished in my soul,
[41] Which, seeing little worthy or sublime
In what we blazon with the pompous names
Of power and action, early tutored me
[45] To look with feelings of fraternal love   50
Upon those unassuming things that hold
A silent station in this beauteous world.
    Thus moderated, thus composed, I found
Once more in man an object of delight,
[50] Of pure imagination, and of love;   55
And, as the horizon of my mind enlarged,
Again I took the intellectual eye
For my instructor, studious more to see
Great truths, than touch and handle little ones.
[55] Knowledge was given accordingly: my trust   60
Was firmer in the feelings which had stood
The test of such a trial, clearer far
My sense of what was excellent and right,
The promise of the present time retired
[60] Into its true proportion; sanguine⁶ schemes,   65
Ambitious virtues, pleased me less; I sought
For good in the familiar face of life,
And built thereon my hopes of good to come.

    With settling judgements now of what would last,
[65] And what would disappear; prepared to find   70
Ambition, folly, madness, in the men
Who thrust themselves upon this passive world
As rulers of the world—to see in these
Even when the public welfare is their aim
[70] Plans without thought, or bottomed⁷ on false thought   75
And false philosophy; having brought to test
Of solid life and true result the books
Of modern statists, and thereby perceived
The utter hollowness of what we name
The wealth of nations,⁸ where alone that wealth   80

6. Hopeful.
7. Based.
8. A reference to the most influential of
eighteenth-century "statists" (political
theorists), Adam Smith, whose *Inquiry*

*into the Nature and Causes of the Wealth
of Nations* (1776) not very surprisingly
ignores the spiritual riches chiefly valued
by the poet.

On throwing off incumbrances, to seek
In man, and in the frame of social life,   35
Whate'er there is desirable and good
Of kindred permanence, unchanged in form
And function, or, through strict vicissitude
Of life and death, revolving. Above all
Were re-established now those watchful thoughts   40
Which, seeing little worthy or sublime
In what the Historian's pen so much delights
To blazon—power and energy detached
From moral purpose—early tutored me
To look with feelings of fraternal love   45
Upon the unassuming things that hold
A silent station in this beauteous world.

   Thus moderated, thus composed, I found
Once more in Man an object of delight,
Of pure imagination, and of love;   50
And, as the horizon of my mind enlarged,
Again I took the intellectual eye
For my instructor, studious more to see
Great truths, than touch and handle little ones.
Knowledge was given accordingly; my trust   55
Became more firm in feelings that had stood
The test of such a trial; clearer far
My sense of excellence—of right and wrong:
The promise of the present time retired
Into its true proportion; sanguine[6] schemes,   60
Ambitious projects, pleased me less; I sought
For present good in life's familiar face,
And built thereon my hopes of good to come.

   With settling judgments now of what would last
And what would disappear; prepared to find   65
Presumption, folly, madness, in the men
Who thrust themselves upon the passive world
As Rulers of the world; to see in these,
Even when the public welfare is their aim,
Plans without thought, or built on theories   70
Vague and unsound; and having brought the books
Of modern statists to their proper test,
Life, human life, with all its sacred claims
Of sex and age, and heaven-descended rights,
Mortal, or those beyond the reach of death;   75
And having thus discerned how dire a thing
Is worshipped in that idol proudly named
'The Wealth of Nations',[8] *where* alone that wealth

Is lodged, and how encreased; and having gained
[80] A more judicious knowledge of what makes
The dignity of individual man—
Of man, no composition of the thought,
Abstraction, shadow, image, but the man   85
Of whom we read, the man whom we behold
With our own eyes—I could not but inquire,
[85] Not with less interest than heretofore,
But greater, though in spirit more subdued,
Why is this glorious creature to be found   90
One only in ten thousand? What one is,
Why may not many be? What bars are thrown
[90] By Nature in the way of such a hope?
Our animal wants and the necessities
Which they impose, are these the obstacles?—   95
If not, then others vanish into air.
Such meditations bred an anxious wish
[95] To ascertain how much of real worth,
And genuine knowledge, and true power of mind,
Did at this day exist in those who lived   100
By bodily labour, labour far exceeding
Their due proportion, under all the weight
Of that injustice which upon ourselves
By composition of society
[100] Ourselves entail. To frame such estimate   105
I chiefly looked (what need to look beyond?)
Among the natural abodes of men,
Fields with their rural works—recalled to mind
My earliest notices,[9] with these compared
[105] The observations of my later youth   110
Continued downwards to that very day.

        For time had never been in which the throes
And mighty hopes of nations, and the stir
And tumult of the world, to me could yield—
How far soe'er transported and possessed—   115
[110] Full measure of content, but still I craved
An intermixture of distinct regards[1]
And truths of individual sympathy
Nearer ourselves.[2] Such often might be gleaned

9. His earliest social observations.
1. Sights, or experiences. Wordsworth is
saying that he can grasp the implications
of major political events only if they are
mixed with (or exemplified by) specific,
local experience.
2. In their earliest form 1805, 112–277
had been the conclusion of a sequence
of 206 lines found at the end of MS. Y
of October 1804, and were probably part
of the original version of Book VIII,

written before the full-scale treatment of
London in VII. Wordsworth's subject in
MS. Y had been the unity of man—
more especially the human potential of
unrefined and unpretentious man. The
sequence had begun with the tenderness
of the London artificer (VIII, 824–59),
then moved, via lines that became XI,
9–14 to a consideration of the country
poor whom he had met in his walks and
travels.

Is lodged, and how increased; and having gained
A more judicious knowledge of the worth   80
And dignity of individual man,
No composition of the brain, but man
Of whom we read, the man whom we behold
With our own eyes—I could not but inquire—
Not with less interest than heretofore,   85
But greater, though in spirit more subdued—
Why is this glorious creature to be found
One only in ten thousand? What one is,
Why may not millions be? What bars are thrown
By Nature in the way of such a hope?   90
Our animal appetites and daily wants,
Are these obstructions insurmountable?
If not, then others vanish into air.
'Inspect the basis of the social pile:
Inquire,' said I, 'how much of mental power   95
And genuine virtue they possess who live
By bodily toil, labour exceeding far
Their due proportion, under all the weight
Of that injustice which upon ourselves
Ourselves entail.' Such estimate to frame   100
I chiefly looked (what need to look beyond?)
Among the natural abodes of men,
Fields with their rural works; recalled to mind
My earliest notices;[9] with these compared
The observations made in later youth,   105
And to that day continued.—For, the time
Had never been when throes of mighty Nations
And the world's tumult unto me could yield,
How far soe'er transported and possessed,
Full measure of content; but still I craved   110
An intermingling of distinct regards[1]
And truths of individual sympathy
Nearer ourselves. Such often might be gleaned

From that great city—else it must have been   120
[115] A heart-depressing wilderness indeed,
Full soon to me a wearisome abode—
But much was wanting; therefore did I turn
To you, ye pathways and ye lonely roads,
Sought you enriched with every thing I prized,   125
With human kindness and with Nature's joy.

[120]   Oh, next to one dear state of bliss, vouchsafed
Alas to few in this untoward[3] world,
The bliss of walking daily in life's prime
Through field or forest with the maid we love   130
While yet our hearts are young, while yet we breathe
[125] Nothing but happiness, living in some place,
Deep vale, or anywhere the home of both,
From which it would be misery to stir—
Oh, next to such enjoyment of our youth,   135
In my esteem next to such dear delight,
[130] Was that of wandering on from day to day
Where I could meditate in peace, and find
The knowledge which I love, and teach the sound
[135] Of poet's music to strange fields and groves,   140
Converse with men, where if we meet a face
We almost meet a friend, on naked moors
[140] With long, long ways before, by cottage bench,
Or well-spring where the weary traveller rests.

    I love a public road: few sights there are   145
That please me more—such object hath had power
O'er my imagination since the dawn
[145] Of childhood, when its disappearing line
Seen daily afar off, on one bare steep
Beyond the limits which my feet had trod,[5]   150
[150] Was like a guide into eternity,
At least to things unknown and without bound.
Even something of the grandeur which invests
The mariner who sails the roaring sea
Through storm and darkness, early in my mind   155
Surrounded too the wanderers of the earth—
[155] Grandeur as much, and loveliness far more.
Awed have I been by strolling bedlamites;[6]

---

3. Unfortunate, vexatious.
5. The road which the child Wordsworth could see from the garden at Cockermouth, leading over Hay Hill to the village of Isel.
6. Madmen; so called from the Bethlehem (pronounced "Bedlam") Hospital for the Insane in London.

From the great City, else it must have proved
To me a heart-depressing wilderness;   115
But much was wanting: therefore did I turn
To you, ye pathways, and ye lonely roads;
Sought you enriched with everything I prized,
With human kindnesses and simple joys.

Oh! next to one dear state of bliss, vouchsafed   120
Alas! to few in this untoward³ world,
The bliss of walking daily in life's prime
Through field or forest with the maid we love,
While yet our hearts are young, while yet we breathe
Nothing but happiness, in some lone nook,   125
Deep vale, or any where, the home of both,
From which it would be misery to stir:
Oh! next to such enjoyment of our youth,
In my esteem, next to such dear delight,
Was that of wandering on from day to day   130
Where I could meditate in peace, and cull
Knowledge that step by step might lead me on
To wisdom; or, as lightsome as a bird
Wafted upon the wind from distant lands,
Sing notes of greeting to strange fields or groves,   135
Which lacked not voice to welcome me in turn:
And, when that pleasant toil had ceased to please,
Converse with men, where if we meet a face
We almost meet a friend, on naked heaths
With long long ways before, by cottage bench,   140
Or well-spring where the weary traveller rests.

Who doth not love to follow with his eye
The windings of a public way? the sight
Hath wrought on my imagination since the morn⁴
Of childhood, when a disappearing line,   145
One daily present to my eyes, that crossed
The naked summit of a far-off hill
Beyond the limits that my feet had trod,⁵
Was like an invitation into space
Boundless, or guide into eternity.   150
Yes, something of the grandeur which invests
The mariner who sails the roaring sea
Through storm and darkness, early in my mind
Surrounded, too, the wanderers of the earth;
Grandeur as much, and loveliness far more.   155
Awed have I been by strolling Bedlamites;⁶

---

4. The first edition conflates two versions present in *MS. D* in order to avoid the alexandrine (six-foot) line 144 created by Wordsworth in revision: "Familiar object as it is, hath wrought / On my imagination since the morn * * *."

From many other uncouth vagrants, passed
In fear, have walked with quicker step—but why   160
Take note of this? When I began to inquire,
[160] To watch and question those I met, and held
Familiar talk with them, the lonely roads
Were schools to me in which I daily read
With most delight the passions of mankind,   165
[165] There saw into the depth of human souls—
Souls that appear to have no depth at all
To vulgar⁷ eyes. And now, convinced at heart
[170] How little that to which alone we give
The name of education hath to do   170
With real feeling and just sense, how vain
A correspondence with the talking world
Proves to the most—and called to make good search
[175] If man's estate, by doom of Nature yoked
With toil, is therefore yoked with ignorance,   175
If virtue be indeed so hard to rear,
And intellectual strength so rare a boon—
I prized such walks still more; for there I found
[180] Hope to my hope, and to my pleasure peace
And steadiness, and healing and repose   180
To every angry passion. There I heard,
From mouths of lowly men and of obscure,
A tale of honour—sounds in unison
[185] With loftiest promises of good and fair.

      There are who think that strong affections, love   185
Known by whatever name, is falsely deemed
A gift (to use a term which they would use)
Of vulgar Nature—that its growth requires
[190] Retirement, leisure, language purified
By manners thoughtful and elaborate—   190
That whoso feels such passion in excess
Must live within the very light and air
Of elegances that are made by man.
[195] True is it, where oppression worse than death
Salutes the being at his birth, where grace   195
Of culture hath been utterly unknown,
And labour in excess and poverty
From day to day pre-occupy the ground
[200] Of the affections, and to Nature's self
Oppose a deeper nature—there indeed   200
Love cannot be; nor does it easily thrive
In cities, where the human heart is sick,

7. Common, ordinary.

From many other uncouth vagrants (passed
In fear) have walked with quicker step; but why
Take note of this? When I began to enquire,
To watch and question those I met, and speak   160
Without reserve to them, the lonely roads
Were open schools in which I daily read
With most delight the passions of mankind,
Whether by words, looks, sighs, or tears, revealed;
There saw into the depth of human souls,   165
Souls that appear to have no depth at all
To careless eyes. And—now convinced at heart
How little those formalities, to which
With overweening trust alone we give   170
The name of Education, hath to do
With real feeling and just sense; how vain
A correspondence with the talking world
Proves to the most; and called to make good search
If man's estate, by doom of Nature yoked   175
With toil, is therefore yoked with ignorance;
If virtue be indeed so hard to rear,
And intellectual strength so rare a boon—
I prized such walks still more, for there I found
Hope to my hope, and to my pleasure peace   180
And steadiness, and healing and repose
To every angry passion. There I heard,
From mouths of men obscure and lowly, truths
Replete with honour; sounds in unison
With loftiest promises of good and fair.   185

There are who think that strong affections, love
Known by whatever name, is falsely deemed
A gift, to use a term which they would use,
Of vulgar nature; that its growth requires
Retirement, leisure, language purified   190
By manners studied and elaborate;
That whoso feels such passion in its strength
Must live within the very light and air
Of courteous usages refined by art.
True is it, where oppression worse than death   195
Salutes the being at his birth, where grace
Of culture hath been utterly unknown,
And poverty and labour in excess
From day to day pre-occupy the ground
Of the affections, and to Nature's self   200
Oppose a deeper nature; there, indeed,
Love cannot be; nor does it thrive with ease
Among the close and overcrowded haunts
Of cities, where the human heart is sick,

[205] And the eye feeds it not, and cannot feed:
Thus far, no further, is that inference good.[8]

    Yes, in those wanderings deeply did I feel   205
How we mislead each other, above all
How books mislead us—looking for their fame
To judgements of the wealthy few, who see
[210] By artificial lights—how they debase   210
The many for the pleasure of those few,
Effeminately level down the truth
To certain general notions for the sake
Of being understood at once, or else
[215] Through want of better knowledge in the men   215
Who frame them, flattering thus our self-conceit
With pictures that ambitiously set forth
The differences, the outside marks by which
Society has parted man from man,
[220] Neglectful of the universal heart.[9]

    Here calling up to mind what then I saw   220
A youthful traveller, and see daily now
Before me in my rural neighbourhood—
Here might I pause, and bend in reverence
[225] To Nature, and the power of human minds,
To men as they are men within themselves.   225
How oft high service is performed within
When all the external man is rude in shew,
Not like a temple rich with pomp and gold,
[230] But a mere mountain-chapel such as shields
Its simple worshippers from sun and shower.   230
'Of these,' said I, 'shall be my song. Of these,
If future years mature me for the task,
Will I record the praises, making verse
[235] Deal boldly with substantial things—in truth
And sanctity of passion speak of these,   235
That justice may be done, obeisance paid
Where it is due. Thus haply shall I teach,
Inspire, through unadulterated[1] ears
[240] Pour rapture, tenderness, and hope, my theme
No other than the very heart of man   240
As found among the best of those who live

8. Lines 185–204 go back to *MS. J* of October–December 1800, and like the Matron's Tale (VIII, 222–311, above) are surplus material written for *Michael*.
9. Wordsworth told the diarist, Crabb Robinson, in 1837 that "he did not expect or desire from posterity any other fame than that which would be given him for the way in which his poems ex-hibit man in his essentially human character and relations—as child, parent, husband, the qualities which are common to all men as opposed to those which distinguish one man from another" (*On Books and Their Writers*, ed. E. J. Morley, II, p. 535).
1. Uncorrupted, innocent.

And the eye feeds it not, and cannot feed.   205
—Yes, in those wanderings deeply did I feel
How we mislead each other; above all,
How books mislead us, seeking their reward
From judgments of the wealthy Few, who see
By artificial lights; how they debase   210
The Many for the pleasure of those Few;
Effeminately level down the truth
To certain general notions, for the sake
Of being understood at once, or else
Through want of better knowledge in the heads   215
That framed them; flattering self-conceit with words,
That, while they most ambitiously set forth
Extrinsic differences, the outward marks
Whereby society has parted man
From man, neglect the universal heart.[9]   220

    Here, calling up to mind what then I saw,
A youthful traveller, and see daily now
In the familiar circuit of my home,
Here might I pause, and bend in reverence
To Nature, and the power of human minds,   225
To men as they are men within themselves.
How oft high service is performed within,
When all the external man is rude in show,—
Not like a temple rich with pomp and gold,
But a mere mountain chapel, that protects   230
Its simple worshippers from sun and shower.
Of these, said I, shall be my song; of these,
If future years mature me for the task,
Will I record the praises, making verse
Deal boldly with substantial things; in truth   235
And sanctity of passion, speak of these,
That justice may be done, obeisance paid
Where it is due: thus haply shall I teach,
Inspire, through unadulterated[1] ears
Pour rapture, tenderness, and hope,—my theme   240
No other than the very heart of man,
As found among the best of those who live,

Not unexalted by religious faith,
Nor uninformed by books (good books, though few),
[245] In Nature's presence—thence may I select
Sorrow that is not sorrow but delight,   245
And miserable love that is not pain
To hear of, for the glory that redounds
Therefrom to human-kind and what we are.
[250] Be mine to follow with no timid step
Where knowledge leads me: it shall be my pride   250
That I have dared to tread this holy ground,
Speaking no dream but things oracular,
Matter not lightly to be heard by those
[255] Who to the letter of the outward promise
Do read the invisible soul,[2] by men adroit   255
In speech and for communion with the world
Accomplished, minds whose faculties are then
Most active when they are most eloquent,
[260] And elevated most when most admired.[3]
Men may be found of other mold[4] than these,   260

Who are their own upholders, to themselves
Encouragement, and energy, and will,
Expressing liveliest thoughts in lively words
[265] As native passion dictates.[5] Others, too,
There are among the walks of homely life   265
Still higher, men for contemplation framed,
Shy, and unpractised in the strife of phrase,
Meek men, whose very souls perhaps would sink
[270] Beneath them, summoned to such intercourse:
Theirs is the language of the heavens, the power,   270
The thought, the image, and the silent joy;
Words are but under-agents in their souls—
When they are grasping with their greatest strength
[275] They do not breathe among them.[6] This I speak
In gratitude to God, who feeds our hearts   275
For his own service, knoweth, loveth us,
When we are unregarded by the world.'

---

2. I.e. those who judge a man's inner worth strictly on the evidence of outward appearances.

3. *1805*, 231–59 (*1850*, 232–60) contain several striking echoes of Wordsworth's poetic manifesto of 1800, the Prospectus to *The Recluse* (CW, III, pp. 100–106).

4. The earth from which the human body was regarded as having been formed, as at *1805*, IX, 295, above.

5. Wordsworth's thoughts have moved from the Prospectus to that other great statement of his belief (also of 1800), the Preface to *Lyrical Ballads*: "Low and rustic life was generally chosen because in that situation the essential passions of

the heart find a better soil in which they can attain their maturity, are less under restraint, and speak a plainer and more emphatic language . . ." (*Prose Works*, I, p. 124).

6. "Them" refers back to "words." Wordsworth almost certainly had in mind the deep but inarticulate response of Michael (described in *MS. J*, from which he had drawn lines 185–204, above; see *Oxford Wordsworth*, II, pp. 482–83), and of his own brother John, "the silent poet," who was drowned on February 5, 1805, three months after these lines were composed in *MS. Y*.

Not unexalted by religious faith,
Nor uninformed by books, good books, though few,
In Nature's presence: thence may I select   245
Sorrow, that is not sorrow, but delight;
And miserable love, that is not pain
To hear of, for the glory that redounds
Therefrom to human kind, and what we are.
Be mine to follow with no timid step   250
Where knowledge leads me: it shall be my pride
That I have dared to tread this holy ground,
Speaking no dream, but things oracular;
Matter not lightly to be heard by those
Who to the letter of the outward promise   255
Do read the invisible soul;[2] by men adroit
In speech, and for communion with the world
Accomplished; minds whose faculties are then
Most active when they are most eloquent,
And elevated most when most admired.[3]   260
Men may be found of other mould[4] than these,
Who are their own upholders, to themselves
Encouragement, and energy, and will,
Expressing liveliest thoughts in lively words
As native passion dictates.[5] Others, too,   265
There are among the walks of homely life
Still higher, men for contemplation framed,
Shy, and unpractised in the strife of phrase;
Meek men, whose very souls perhaps would sink
Beneath them, summoned to such intercourse: 270
Theirs is the language of the heavens, the power,
The thought, the image, and the silent joy:
Words are but under-agents in their souls;
When they are grasping with their greatest strength,
They do not breathe among them:[6] this I speak   275
In gratitude to God, Who feeds our hearts
For His own service; knoweth, loveth us,
When we are unregarded by the world.

Also about this time did I receive
[280] Convictions still more strong than heretofore
Not only that the inner frame is good,   280
And graciously composed, but that, no less,
Nature through all conditions hath a power
To consecrate—if we have eyes to see—
[285] The outside of her creatures, and to breathe
Grandeur upon the very humblest face   285
Of human life. I felt that the array
Of outward circumstance and visible form
Is to the pleasure of the human mind
[290] What passion makes it; that meanwhile the forms
Of Nature have a passion in themselves   290
That intermingles with those works of man
To which she summons him, although the works
Be mean, have nothing lofty of their own;
[295] And that the genius of the poet hence
May boldly take his way among mankind   295
Wherever Nature leads—that he hath stood
By Nature's side among the men of old,
And so shall stand for ever.[7] Dearest friend,
Forgive me if I say that I, who long
Had harboured reverentially a thought   300
[301] That poets, even as prophets, each with each
Connected in a mighty scheme of truth,
Have each for his peculiar dower a sense
By which he is enabled to perceive
[305] Something unseen before—forgive me, friend,   305
If I, the meanest of this band, had hope
That unto me had also been vouchsafed
An influx,[8] that in some sort I possessed
A privilege, and that a work of mine,
[310] Proceeding from the depth of untaught things,   310
Enduring and creative, might become
A power like one of Nature's.

           To such mood,
Once above all—a traveller at that time
Upon the plain of Sarum—was I raised:[9]

7. Wordsworth in this important passage, as in *1805*, 231–64 (*1850*, 232–65) is seen defining his rôle as a poet, and the nature of his subject-matter. As M. H. Abrams remarks, "*The Prelude* is a poem which incorporates the discovery of its own *ars poetica*" (*Natural Supernaturalism*, p. 78).
8. Inspiration.
9. Wordsworth crossed Salisbury Plain ("the plain of Sarum") alone and on foot, in a vividly imaginative frame of mind (see *1805*, 318–36 below) in late July or early August 1793 en route from the Isle of Wight to Wales. He was without money or prospects, was parted from Annette Vallon, and for the previous month had watched the British fleet off Portsmouth preparing for a war that went against all his deepest feelings, personal, patriotic, and political (see *1805*, X, 229–306, above).

　　　Also, about this time did I receive
Convictions still more strong than heretofore,　　　　　　280
Not only that the inner frame is good,
And graciously composed, but that, no less,
Nature for all conditions wants not power
To consecrate, if we have eyes to see,
The outside of her creatures, and to breathe　　　　　　285
Grandeur upon the very humblest face
Of human life. I felt that the array
Of act and circumstance, and visible form,
Is mainly to the pleasure of the mind
What passion makes them; that meanwhile the forms　　290
Of Nature have a passion in themselves,
That intermingles with those works of man
To which she summons him; although the works
Be mean, have nothing lofty of their own;
And that the Genius of the Poet hence　　　　　　295
May boldly take his way among mankind
Wherever Nature leads; that he hath stood
By Nature's side among the men of old,
And so shall stand for ever.[7] Dearest Friend!
If thou partake the animating faith　　　　　　300
That Poets, even as Prophets, each with each
Connected in a mighty scheme of truth,
Have each his own peculiar faculty,
Heaven's gift, a sense that fits him to perceive
Objects unseen before, thou wilt not blame　　　　　　305
The humblest of this band who dares to hope
That unto him hath also been vouchsafed
An insight that in some sort he possesses,
A privilege whereby a work of his,
Proceeding from a source of untaught things　　　　　　310
Creative and enduring, may become
A power like one of Nature's. To a hope
Not less ambitious once among the wilds
Of Sarum's Plain, my youthful spirit was raised;[9]

[315] There on the pastoral downs[1] without a track   315
    To guide me, or along the bare white roads
    Lengthening in solitude their dreary line,
    While through those vestiges of ancient times
    I ranged, and by the solitude o'ercome,
    I had a reverie and saw the past,   320
[321] Saw multitudes of men, and here and there
    A single Briton in his wolf-skin vest,
    With shield and stone-ax, stride across the wold;[2]
    The voice of spears was heard, the rattling spear
[325] Shaken by arms of mighty bone, in strength   325
    Long mouldered, of barbaric majesty.
    I called upon the darkness, and it took—
    A midnight darkness seemed to come and take—
    All objects from my sight; and lo, again
[330] The desart visible by dismal flames!   330
    It is the sacrificial altar, fed
    With living men—how deep the groans![3]—the voice
    Of those in the gigantic wicker thrills
    Throughout the region far and near, pervades
    The monumental hillocks,[4] and the pomp   335
[335] Is for both worlds, the living and the dead.
    At other moments, for through that wide waste
    Three summer days I roamed, when 'twas my chance
    To have before me on the downy plain
    Lines, circles, mounts, a mystery of shapes   340
    Such as in many quarters yet survive,
    With intricate profusion figuring o'er
    The untilled ground (the work, as some divine,[5]
    Of infant science,[6] imitative forms
    By which the Druids covertly expressed   345
[341] Their knowledge of the heavens, and imaged forth
    The constellations), I was gently charmed,
    Albeit with an antiquarian's dream,
[345] And saw the bearded teachers, with white wands
    Uplifted, pointing to the starry sky,   350
    Alternately, and plain below, while breath

1. Open hills used only for grazing sheep.
2. A poetic, unspecific word for countryside, here meaning "plain."
3. Wordsworth is drawing heavily—verbatim in these last two lines—on his early poem *Salisbury Plain*, perhaps begun during his wanderings, and certainly completed by April 1794 (see *CW*, I, pp. 26–27). In both poems Wordsworth accepts the common, but false, beliefs that the Druids (*1805*, 345; *1850*, 340) performed human sacrifice, and that Stonehenge was a Druid temple.
4. "The gigantic wicker" (also referred to in *Salisbury Plain*) had been described by Aylett Sammes, *Britannia Antiqua Illustrata* (1676), p. 104: "They made a Statue or Image of a MAN in a vast proportion, whose limbs consisted of Twigs, weaved together in the nature of Basketware: These they fill'd with live Men, and after that, set it on fire, and so destroyed the poor Creatures in the smoak and flames."

"Monumental hillocks": Bronze Age burial mounds, of which there are many on the Plain.
5. Conjecture (a verb).
6. Science in its early stages.

There, as I ranged at will the pastoral downs[1]   315
Trackless and smooth, or paced the bare white roads
Lengthening in solitude their dreary line,
Time with his retinue of ages fled
Backwards, nor checked his flight until I saw
Our dim ancestral Past in vision clear;   320
Saw multitudes of men, and, here and there,
A single Briton clothed in wolf-skin vest,
With shield and stone-axe, stride across the wold;[2]
The voice of spears was heard, the rattling spear
Shaken by arms of mighty bone, in strength,   325
Long mouldered, of barbaric majesty.
I called on Darkness—but before the word
Was uttered, midnight darkness seemed to take
All objects from my sight; and lo! again
The Desert visible by dismal flames;   330
It is the sacrificial altar, fed
With living men—how deep the groans![3] the voice
Of those that crowd the giant wicker thrills
The monumental hillocks,[4] and the pomp
Is for both worlds, the living and the dead.   335
At other moments (for through that wide waste
Three summer days I roamed) where'er the Plain
Was figured o'er with circles, lines, or mounds,
That yet survive, a work, as some divine,[5]
Shaped by the Druids, so to represent   340
Their knowledge of the heavens, and image forth
The constellations; gently was I charmed
Into a waking dream, a reverie
That, with believing eyes, where'er I turned,
Beheld long-bearded teachers, with white wands   345
Uplifted, pointing to the starry sky,
Alternately, and plain below, while breath

Of music seemed to guide them, and the waste
Was cheared with stillness and a pleasant sound.[7]

[350] This for the past, and things that may be viewed,
Or fancied, in the obscurities of time.   355
Nor is it, friend, unknown to thee; at least—
Thyself delighted—thou for my delight
Hast said,[8] perusing some imperfect verse
Which in that lonesome journey was composed,
[355] That also I must then have exercised   360
Upon the vulgar forms of present things
And actual world of our familiar days,
A higher power—have caught from them a tone,
An image, and a character, by books
[360] Not hitherto reflected.[9] Call we this   365
But a persuasion taken up by thee
In friendship, yet the mind is to herself
Witness and judge, and I remember well
That in life's everyday appearances
I seemed about this period to have sight   370
[370] Of a new world—a world, too, that was fit
To be transmitted and made visible
To other eyes, as having for its base
That whence our dignity originates,
That which both gives it being, and maintains   375
[375] A balance, an ennobling interchange
Of action from within and from without:
The excellence, pure spirit, and best power,
Both of the object seen, and eye that sees.

---

7. The transition from Wordsworth's creative reverie of *1805*, 312–36 (*1850*, 312–35) to the merely "antiquarian's dream" of *1805*, 337–53 (*1850*, 336–49) reproduces exactly the progression in Salisbury Plain (see *CW*, I, p. 27).
8. Lines 356–58 are very difficult to construe. "It" ("Nor is *it* * * * unknown to thee") has no antecedent, but presumably refers to the situation in general—"You know about *all this*." "At least / Thyself delighted" can be interpreted, "YOU, at least, were pleased"; but more probably "Thyself delighted" is in parenthesis: "You, being pleased yourself, gave me pleasure by saying." No version of *Salisbury Plain*, the "imperfect verse" of line 358, was published until 1842. See *1805*, 365*n*, below.
9. It is doubtful whether much of *Salis-*

bury Plain was composed during Wordsworth's journey in August 1793, but the extant faircopy belongs to the following April. In its revised and extended form, *Adventures on Salisbury Plain* of ca. November 1795, the poem was read to Coleridge, and *1805*, 360–65 (*1850*, 355–60) suggest that his early reaction was very similar to the famous assessment in *Biographia Literaria* (1817), chapter iv, where Coleridge recollects having been impressed above all by: "the original gift of spreading the tone, the *atmosphere* and with it the depth and height of the ideal world, around forms, incidents and situations of which, for the common view, custom had bedimmed all the lustre, had dried up the sparkle and the dewdrops" (*Biographia*, pp. 48–49).

Of music swayed their motions, and the waste
Rejoiced with them and me in those sweet sounds.[7]

This for the past, and things that may be viewed   350
Or fancied in the obscurity of years
From monumental hints: and thou, O Friend!
Pleased with some unpremeditated strains
That served those wanderings to beguile, hast said
·That then and there my mind had exercised   355
Upon the vulgar forms of present things,
The actual world of our familiar days,
Yet higher power; had caught from them a tone,
An image, and a character, by books
Not hitherto reflected.[9] Call we this   360
A partial judgment—and yet why? for *then*
We were as strangers;[1] and I may not speak
Thus wrongfully of verse, however rude,
Which on thy young imagination, trained
In the great City, broke like light from far.   365
Moreover, each man's Mind is to herself
Witness and judge; and I remember well
That in life's every-day appearances
I seemed about this time to gain clear sight
Of a new world—a world, too, that was fit   370
To be transmitted, and to other eyes
Made visible; as ruled by those fixed laws
Whence spiritual dignity originates,
Which do both give it being and maintain
A balance, an ennobling interchange   375
Of action from without and from within;
The excellence, pure function, and best power
Both of the object seen, and eye that sees.

---

1. Wordsworth and Coleridge had met in September 1795, but did not come to know each other well until June 1797.

Book Thirteenth

Conclusion

In one of these excursions, travelling then
Through Wales on foot and with a youthful friend,
I left Bethkelet's huts at couching-time,
[5] And westward took my way to see the sun
Rise from the top of Snowdon.[1] Having reached
The cottage at the mountain's foot, we there
Rouzed up the shepherd who by ancient right
Of office is the stranger's usual guide,
[10] And after short refreshment sallied forth.

It was a summer's night, a close warm night,
Wan, dull, and glaring,[2] with a dripping mist
Low-hung and thick that covered all the sky,
Half threatening storm and rain; but on we went
Unchecked, being full of heart and having faith
In our tried pilot. Little could we see,
Hemmed round on every side with fog and damp,
[16] And, after ordinary travellers' chat
With our conductor, silently we sunk
Each into commerce with his private thoughts.
Thus did we breast the ascent, and by myself
[20] Was nothing either seen or heard the while
Which took me from my musings, save that once
The shepherd's cur did to his own great joy
Unearth a hedgehog in the mountain-crags,
Round which he made a barking turbulent.
[25] This small adventure—for even such it seemed
In that wild place and at the dead of night—
Being over and forgotten, on we wound
In silence as before. With forehead bent
Earthward, as if in opposition set
[30] Against an enemy, I panted up
With eager pace, and no less eager thoughts,
Thus might we wear perhaps an hour away,

5

10

15

20

25

30

---

1. The Ascent of Mount Snowdon(*1805*,
1–65; *1850*, 1–62), made when he was
twenty-one, had a climactic importance
for Wordsworth. In its original version
the account was written for the five-Book
Prelude at the end of February 1804, to
form the opening of the last Book; and
despite the rearrangement of other five-
Book materials, it has the equivalent position in *1805*. The "youthful friend" was
Robert Jones, with whom Wordsworth
made a walking-tour of North Wales,
June–August 1791, the year after their

tour through France (see *1805*, VI, 342*n*,
above).
"Cambria" (*1850*, 3): Wales. "Huts":
"old rugged and tufted cottages," according to a letter of 1824, in which Wordsworth laments changes at Beddgelert
(LY, I, p. 154). "Couching-time": bed-
time.
2. Maxwell suggests that Wordsworth in
his use of "glaring" was influenced by
northern dialect "glairy," "glaurie,"
meaning (when applied to the weather)
dull or rainy.

Book Fourteenth

Conclusion

In one of those excursions (may they ne'er
Fade from remembrance!) through the Northern tracts
Of Cambria ranging with a youthful friend,
I left Bethgelert's huts at couching-time,
And westward took my way, to see the sun   5
Rise from the top of Snowdon.[1] To the door
Of a rude cottage at the mountain's base
We came, and roused the shepherd who attends
The adventurous stranger's steps, a trusty guide;
Then, cheered by short refreshment, sallied forth.   10

    It was a close, warm, breezeless summer night,
Wan, dull, and glaring,[2] with a dripping fog
Low-hung and thick that covered all the sky;
But, undiscouraged, we began to climb
The mountain-side. The mist soon girt us round,   15
And, after ordinary travellers' talk
With our conductor, pensively we sank
Each into commerce with his private thoughts:
Thus did we breast the ascent, and by myself
Was nothing either seen or heard that checked   20
Those musings or diverted, save that once
The shepherd's lurcher,[3] who, among the crags,
Had to his joy unearthed a hedgehog, teased
His coiled-up prey with barkings turbulent.
This small adventure, for even such it seemed   25
In that wild place and at the dead of night,
Being over and forgotten, on we wound
In silence as before. With forehead bent
Earthward, as if in opposition set
Against an enemy, I panted up   30
With eager pace, and no less eager thoughts.
Thus might we wear a midnight hour away,

3. Mongrel.

459

Ascending at loose distance each from each,
And I, as chanced, the foremost of the band—   35
[35] When at my feet the ground appeared to brighten,
And with a step or two seemed brighter still;
Nor had I time to ask the cause of this,
For instantly a light upon the turf
Fell like a flash. I looked about, and lo,   40
[40] The moon stood naked in the heavens at height
Immense above my head, and on the shore
I found myself of a huge sea of mist,
Which meek and silent rested at my feet.
A hundred hills their dusky backs upheaved   45
All over this still ocean,[4] and beyond,
[45] Far, far beyond, the vapours shot themselves
In headlands, tongues, and promontory shapes,
Into the sea, the real sea, that seemed
To dwindle and give up its majesty,   50
Usurped upon as far as sight could reach.
Meanwhile, the moon looked down upon this shew
In single glory, and we stood, the mist
Touching our very feet; and from the shore
At distance not the third part of a mile   55
Was a blue chasm, a fracture in the vapour,
A deep and gloomy breathing-place, through which
Mounted the roar of waters, torrents, streams
[60] Innumerable, roaring with one voice.[5]
The universal spectacle throughout   60
Was shaped for admiration and delight,
Grand in itself alone, but in that breach
Through which the homeless voice of waters rose,
That dark deep thoroughfare, had Nature lodged
The soul, the imagination of the whole.   65

    A meditation rose in me that night
Upon the lonely mountain when the scene
Had passed away, and it appeared to me
[70] The perfect image of a mighty mind,
Of one that feeds upon infinity,   70
That is exalted by an under-presence,

---

4. Compare the account of the Creation, *Paradise Lost*, VII, 285–87, "the mountains huge appear / Emergent, and their broad bare backs upheave / Into the clouds * * *"
5. For Wordsworth's first account of this scene (interestingly by sunlight), see *Descriptive Sketches*, 492–505, composed in summer 1792, a year after his walking tour in Wales. Almost all the details of the Snowdon landscape are present in this original picturesque scene. Their relationship to Wordsworth's personal experience, however, is not easy to assess, as *Descriptive Sketches* draws very heavily on a literary source, James Beattie's *Minstrel*, Book I (1771), stanza 23. A probable further source, in James Clarke's *Survey of the Lakes* (1787), p. 73, has been suggested by Z. S. Fink, *Early Wordsworthian Milieu*, pp. 45–48.

Ascending at loose distance each from each,
And I as chanced, the foremost of the band;
When at my feet the ground appeared to brighten,   35
And with a step or two seemed brighter still;
Nor was time given to ask or learn the cause,
For instantly a light upon the turf
Fell like a flash, and lo! as I looked up,
The Moon hung naked in a firmament   40
Of azure without cloud, and at my feet
Rested a silent sea of hoary mist.
A hundred hills their dusky backs upheaved
All over this still ocean;[4] and beyond,
Far, far beyond, the solid vapours stretched,   45
In headlands, tongues, and promontory shapes,
Into the main Atlantic, that appeared
To dwindle, and give up his majesty,
Usurped upon far as the sight could reach.
Not so the ethereal vault; encroachment none   50
Was there, nor loss; only the inferior stars
Had disappeared, or shed a fainter light
In the clear presence of the full-orbed Moon,
Who, from her sovereign elevation, gazed
Upon the billowy ocean, as it lay   55
All meek and silent, save that through a rift—
Not distant from the shore whereon we stood,
A fixed, abysmal, gloomy, breathing-place—
Mounted the roar of waters, torrents, streams
Innumerable, roaring with one voice   60
Heard over earth and sea, and, in that hour,
For so it seems, felt by the starry heavens.[6]

When into air had partially dissolved
That vision, given to spirits of the night
And three chance human wanderers, in calm thought   65
Reflected, it appeared to me the type
Of a majestic intellect, its acts
And its possessions, what it has and craves,
What in itself it is, and would become.
There I beheld the emblem of a mind   70
That feeds upon infinity, that broods
Over the dark abyss,[7] intent to hear

6. None of the other great passages of *The Prelude*—indeed of Wordsworth's poetry as a whole—suffered in revision as did the Ascent of Snowdon. From the earliest reworkings (*1850*, 50–53, e.g., belong to 1816/19) to the final concession to orthodoxy in 61–62 (1839 or later), alterations are consistently for the worse. Note also the elaboration of *1805*, 66–73 that results in *1850*, 63–77.
7. Lines 71–72 are a reminiscence of *Paradise Lost*, I, 20–22, in which the Holy Spirit brooding over Chaos makes it fruitful.

The sense of God, or whatsoe'er is dim
Or vast in its own being[8]—above all,
One function of such mind had Nature there
Exhibited by putting forth, and that   75
[80] With circumstance most awful and sublime:[9]
That domination which she oftentimes
Exerts upon the outward face of things,
So moulds them, and endues, abstracts, combines,
Or by abrupt and unhabitual influence   80
Doth make one object so impress itself
Upon all others, and pervades them so,
[85] That even the grossest minds must see and hear,
And cannot chuse but feel. The power which these
Acknowledge when thus moved, which Nature thus   85
Thrusts forth upon the senses, is the express
Resemblance—in the fullness of its strength
Made visible—a genuine counterpart
And brother of the glorious faculty
[90] Which higher minds bear with them as their own.[1]   90
This is the very spirit in which they deal
With all the objects of the universe:
They from their native selves can send abroad
Like transformation, for themselves create
[95] A like existence, and, when'er it is   95
Created for them, catch it by an instinct.[2]
[100] Them the enduring and the transient both
Serve to exalt. They build up greatest things
From least suggestions,[3] ever on the watch,

8. The spatial quality of Wordsworth's language serves to link his "meditation" back into the central experience: the grandeur of Snowdon now evokes an inner vastness (see 96n, below), the "dark deep thoroughfare" (line 64) becomes an "under-presence" within the individual mind.

9. Lines 66–76 do not appear in *MS. W*, and belong probably to May 1805. For the series of six further analogies between the mind of man and Nature, written late February–early March 1804 to follow line 65, see MS. Drafts and Fragments, 3(a), below. The sequence appears to have been cut before the five-Book scheme was abandoned.

1. Nature, as the sea of mist, has transformed the Snowdon landscape, usurping upon the sovereignty of the "real sea," the Irish Channel (*1805*, 42–51; *1850*, 41–49). In the process she has demonstrated by analogy ("Exhibited by putting forth" (*1805*, 75) the power of the human imagination. Compare Coleridge's definition of the secondary imagination, which "dissolves, diffuses, dissipates, in

order to re-create" (*Biographia*, chapter xiii, p. 167).

2. For Wordsworth and Coleridge imagination was at once creative and receptive of what is apprehended through sense experiences. Among many statements that emphasize this central belief, see especially the Infant Babe of *1805*, II, 267–75 above (*1799*, II, 297–305), who "as an agent of the one great mind" is "creator and receiver both," and Coleridge's definition of the primary imagination as "the living power and prime agent of all human perception" but also "a repetition in the finite mind of the eternal act of creation" (*Biographia*, chapter xiii; p. 167). In his imaginative acts, the individual who is endowed with a "higher" mind is at once godlike, and perceptive of the existence of God, draws on the dim and vast in his own being, and experiences "an under-presence, / The sense of God" (*1805*, 71–72, above).

3. "Imagination, by which word I mean the faculty which produces impressive effects out of simple elements" (note to *The Thorn, Lyrical Ballads*, 1800).

Its voices issuing forth to silent light
In one continuous stream; a mind sustained
By recognitions of transcendent power,   75
In sense conducting to ideal form,
In soul of more than mortal privilege.
One function, above all, of such a mind
Had Nature shadowed there, by putting forth,
'Mid circumstances awful and sublime,   80
That mutual domination which she loves
To exert upon the face of outward things,
So moulded, joined, abstracted, so endowed
With interchangeable supremacy,
That men, least sensitive, see, hear, perceive,   85
And cannot choose but feel. The power, which all
Acknowledge when thus moved, which Nature thus
To bodily sense exhibits, is the express
Resemblance of that glorious faculty
That higher minds bear with them as their own.[1]   90
This is the very spirit in which they deal
With the whole compass of the universe:
They from their native selves can send abroad
Kindred mutations; for themselves create
A like existence; and, whene'er it dawns   95
Created for them, catch it, or are caught
By its inevitable mastery.[2]
Like angels stopped upon the wing by sound
Of harmony from Heaven's remotest spheres.
Them the enduring and the transient both   100
Serve to exalt; they build up greatest things
From least suggestions;[3] ever on the watch,

Willing to work and to be wrought upon.   100
They need not extraordinary calls
[105] To rouze them—in a world of life they live,
By sensible impressions not enthralled,
But quickened, rouzed, and made thereby more fit
To hold communion with the invisible world.   105
Such minds are truly from the Deity,
For they are powers; and hence the highest bliss
That can be known is theirs—the consciousness
[115] Of whom they are, habitually infused
Through every image,⁴ and through every thought,   110
And all impressions; hence religion, faith,
And endless occupation for the soul,
[120] Whether discursive or intuitive;⁵
Hence sovereignty within and peace at will,
Emotion which best foresight need not fear,   115
Most worthy then of trust when most intense;
Hence chearfulness in every act of life;
Hence truth in moral judgements; and delight
That fails not, in the external universe.

[130]   Oh, who is he that hath his whole life long   120
Preserved, enlarged, this freedom in himself?—
For this alone is genuine liberty.
Witness, ye solitudes, where I received
[141] My earliest visitations (careless then
Of what was given me), and where now I roam,   125
[143] A meditative, oft a suffering man,
And yet I trust with undiminished powers;⁷

---

4. I.e., through all they see. The "highest bliss" of *1805*, 107 (*1850*, 113) is
self-awareness, "consciousness / Of whom
they are."
5. Wordsworth is echoing a distinction
made in *Paradise Lost*, V, 487–90, between "discursive" reason (belonging
chiefly to man) and the higher "intui-

tive" reason to which man may aspire,
but which is normally angelic.
7. Written in early March 1804, shortly
after the completion of the *Intimations
Ode*, with its similar concerns, and probably a day or two before XI, 335–36
("the hiding-places of my power / Seem
open, I approach, and then they close").

Willing to work and to be wrought upon,
They need not extraordinary calls
To rouse them; in a world of life they live,   105
By sensible impressions not enthralled,
But by their quickening impulse made more prompt
To hold fit converse with the spiritual world,
And with the generations of mankind
Spread over time, past, present, and to come,   110
Age after age, till Time shall be no more.
Such minds are truly from the Deity,
For they are Powers; and hence the highest bliss
That flesh can know is theirs—the consciousness
Of Whom they are, habitually infused   115
Through every image⁴ and through every thought
And all affections, by communion raised
From earth to heaven, from human to divine;
Hence endless occupation for the Soul,
Whether discursive or intuitive;⁵   120
Hence cheerfulness for acts of daily life,
Emotions which best foresight need not fear,
Most worthy then of trust when most intense.
Hence, amid ills that vex and wrongs that crush
Our hearts—if here the words of Holy Writ   125
May with fit reverence be applied—that peace
Which passeth understanding, that repose
In moral judgments which from this pure source
Must come, or will by man be sought in vain.⁶

Oh! who is he that hath his whole life long   130
Preserved, enlarged, this freedom in himself?
For this alone is genuine liberty:
Where is the favoured being who hath held
That course unchecked, unerring, and untired,
In one perpetual progress smooth and bright?—   135
A humbler destiny have we retraced,
And told of lapse and hesitating choice,
And backward wanderings along thorny ways:
Yet—compassed round by mountain solitudes,
Within whose solemn temple I received   140
My earliest visitations, careless then
Of what was given me; and which now I range,
A meditative, oft a suffering man—
Do I declare—in accents which, from truth
Deriving cheerful confidence, shall blend   145
Their modulation with these vocal streams—

6. Lines 124–29 are produced by a revision of 1838/39, and the similarly pious phrasing of line 114, "That flesh can know," is probably 1832 (Wordsworth tried first "man," then "earth," before arriving at "flesh").

Witness—whatever falls my better mind,
Revolving with the accidents of life,
May have sustained—that, howsoe'er misled,   130
[150] I never in the quest of right and wrong
Did tamper with myself from private aims;[8]
Nor was in any of my hopes the dupe
Of selfish passions; nor did wilfully
Yield ever to mean cares and low pursuits;   135
[155] But rather did with jealousy shrink back
From every combination that might aid
The tendency, too potent in itself,
Of habit to enslave the mind—I mean
Oppress it by the laws of vulgar sense,   140
[160] And substitute a universe of death,
The falsest of all worlds, in place of that
Which is divine and true.[9] To fear and love
(To love as first and chief, for there fear ends)
Be this ascribed, to early intercourse   145
[165] In presence of sublime and lovely forms
With the adverse principles of pain and joy—
Evil as one is rashly named by those
Who know not what they say.[1] From love, for here
Do we begin and end, all grandeur comes,   150
All truth and beauty—from pervading love—
[170] That gone, we are as dust. Behold the fields
In balmy springtime, full of rising flowers
And happy creatures; see that pair, the lamb
And the lamb's mother, and their tender ways   155
Shall touch thee to the heart; in some green bower
Rest, and be not alone, but have thou there
[178] The one who is thy choice of all the world—
There linger, lulled, and lost, and rapt away—
Be happy to thy fill; thou call'st this love,   160
[175] And so it is, but there is higher love
Than this, a love that comes into the heart
With awe and a diffusive sentiment.[2]

8. Wordsworth's meaning—that he never attempted to buy off his conscience—is established by *1850*, 151.
9. Wordsworth's "universe of death" (in *Paradise Lost*, II, 622, the phrase is used to describe Hell) is one in which the individual is enslaved by unimaginative reliance on the senses and on purely habitual perception.
1. A reference back to *1805*, I, 305–6, above: "Fair seed-time had my soul, and I grew up / Fostered alike by beauty and by fear * * *" In *1805*, 143–49 (*1850*, 162–68), "beauty" is assimilated to the principles of joy and love, and "fear" is related to pain. Wordsworth, however, denies that fear and pain are in them-selves "evil," since, subordinated to the ultimate principle of love, these aspects of human experience are necessary to the formation of the mature and imaginative mind. Wordsworth's justification of pain and fear as ultimately serving love is parallel to Milton's justification of God's ways to men, *Paradise Lost*, XII, 469 ff: "goodness infinite, goodness immense! / That all this good of evil shall produce, / And evil turn to good."
2. Probably an emotion that is diffused —"Felt in the blood, and felt along the heart," *Tintern Abbey*, 29. "Diffusive" at times has the implication of bountiful dispensing (*NED*).

That, whatsoever falls my better mind,
Revolving with the accidents of life,
May have sustained, that, howsoe'er misled,
Never did I, in quest of right and wrong,   150
Tamper with conscience from a private aim;
Nor was in any public hope the dupe
Of selfish passions; nor did ever yield
Wilfully to mean cares or low pursuits,
But shrunk with apprehensive jealousy   155
From every combination which might aid
The tendency, too potent in itself,
Of use and custom to bow down the soul
Under a growing weight of vulgar sense,
And substitute a universe of death   160
For that which moves with light and life informed,
Actual, divine, and true.[9] To fear and love,
To love as prime and chief, for there fear ends,
Be this ascribed; to early intercourse,
In presence of sublime or beautiful forms,   165
With the adverse principles of pain and joy—
Evil as one is rashly named by men
Who know not what they speak.[1] By love subsists
All lasting grandeur, by pervading love;
That gone, we are as dust,—Behold the fields   170
In balmy spring-time full of rising flowers
And joyous creatures; see that pair, the lamb
And the lamb's mother, and their tender ways
Shall touch thee to the heart; thou callest this love,
And not inaptly so, for love it is,   175
Far as it carries thee. In some green bower
Rest, and be not alone, but have thou there
The One who is thy choice of all the world:
There linger, listening, gazing, with delight
Impassioned, but delight how pitiable!   180
Unless this love by a still higher love
Be hallowed, love that breathes not without awe;
Love that adores, but on the knees of prayer,
By heaven inspired; that frees from chains the soul,
Bearing, in union with the purest, best,   185

Thy love is human merely: this proceeds
More from the brooding soul, and is divine.[3]   165

    This love more intellectual cannot be
Without imagination, which in truth
[190] Is but another name for absolute strength
And clearest insight, amplitude of mind,
And reason in her most exalted mood.[5]   170
This faculty hath been the moving soul
Of our long labour: we have traced the stream
From darkness, and the very place of birth
[195] In its blind cavern, whence is faintly heard
The sound of waters; followed it to light   175
And open day, accompanied its course
Among the ways of Nature, afterwards
Lost sight of it bewildered and engulphed,
[200] Then given it greeting as it rose once more
With strength, reflecting in its solemn breast   180
The works of man, and face of human life;
And lastly, from its progress have we drawn
The feeling of life endless, the one thought
[205] By which we live, infinity and God.[6]

    Imagination having been our theme,   185
So also hath that intellectual love,
For they are each in each, and cannot stand
Dividually.[7] Here must thou be, O man,
[210] Strength to thyself—no helper hast thou here—
Here keepest thou thy individual state: 190
No other can divide with thee this work,
No secondary hand can intervene
To fashion this ability.[8] 'Tis thine,

---

3. At this point in the five-Book *Prelude* Wordsworth turned to consider the factors which in practice conspire to thwart the "divine" love of lines 161–65. The passage is not fully legible in *MS. W* (see MS. Drafts and Fragments, 3[b], below), but leads into a version of XI, 175–83 and on, through drafts that may never have reached a final shape, into the "spots of time" sequence that formed the climax of the five-Book poem; see Composition and Texts: *1805/1850*, Introduction, below, and XI, 128*n*, above.
5. I.e., the higher reason—as opposed to understanding—later to be associated with the primary imagination in *Biographia Literaria*, and already by 1805 reinforced for Coleridge (and thus presumably for Wordsworth): by the Kantian distinction between *Vernunft* and *Verstand*. "Intellectual" (*1805*, 166): spiritual, as elsewhere in *The Prelude*.
6. Wordsworth's use of the river to image the progress of his mind appears as early as *1799*, II, 247–49, and is recurrent in

1805; see e.g., III, 10–12, IV, 39–55, VI, 672–80, IX, 1–9. "Life endless" (*1805*, 183; *1850*, 204): a reference to the afterlife which emerges very suddenly in the context of the poem as a whole, but which is explained by Wordsworth's urgent need to believe in the survival of his brother John, drowned on February 5, 1805, some three months before these lines were written (*EY*, p. 556).
7. Spiritual love for Wordsworth, as for Coleridge, is the principle which unites an individual man both to other men and to Nature; it is experienced as joy, and empowers the imagination. The point is made most clearly in *Dejection* (April 1802), 231–42, 296–323, but is everywhere implicit in the work of both poets. "Dividually": separately, apart; a reminiscence of *Paradise Lost*, XII, 85.
8. The reference in *1805*, 188–93 (*1850*, 209–14) is consistently to spiritual love, which the individual must develop within himself, and by himself.

Of earth-born passions, on the wings of praise
A mutual tribute to the Almighty's Throne.[4]

This spiritual Love acts not nor can exist
Without Imagination, which, in truth,
Is but another name for absolute power   190
And clearest insight, amplitude of mind,
And Reason in her most exalted mood.[5]
This faculty hath been the feeding source
Of our long labour: we have traced the stream
From the blind cavern whence is faintly heard   195
Its natal murmur; followed it to light
And open day; accompanied its course
Among the ways of Nature, for a time
Lost sight of it bewildered and engulphed:
Then given it greeting as it rose once more   200
In strength, reflecting from its placid breast
The works of man and face of human life;
And lastly, from its progress have we drawn
Faith in life endless, the sustaining thought
Of human Being, Eternity, and God.[6]   205

Imagination having been our theme,
So also hath that intellectual Love,
For they are each in each, and cannot stand
Dividually.[7]—Here must thou be, O Man!
Power to thyself; no Helper hast thou here;   210
Here keepest thou in singleness thy state:
No other can divide with thee this work:
No secondary hand can intervene
To fashion this ability;[8] 'tis thine,

---

4. Wordsworth's redefinition of the "higher love" of *1805*, 161, in specifically Christian terms takes place as early as 1816/19: "Passion from all disturbing influence pure, / Foretaste of beatific sentiment / Bestowed in mercy on a world condemned / To mutability, pain and grief, / Terrestrial nature's sure inheritance" (*A* revisions).

[215] The prime and vital principle is thine
In the recesses of thy nature, far   195
From any reach of outward fellowship,
Else 'tis not thine at all. But joy to him,
O, joy to him who here hath sown—hath laid
[220] Here the foundations of his future years—
For all that friendship, all that love can do,   200
All that a darling countenance can look
Or dear voice utter, to complete the man,
Perfect him, made imperfect in himself,
[225] All shall be his. And he whose soul hath risen
Up to the height of feeling intellect   205
Shall want no humbler tenderness, his heart
Be tender as a nursing mother's heart;
Of female softness shall his life be full,[9]
[230] Of little loves and delicate desires,
Mild interests and gentlest sympathies.   210

Child of my parents, sister of my soul,
Elsewhere have strains of gratitude been breathed
To thee for all the early tenderness
[235] Which I from thee imbibed.[1] And true it is
That later seasons owed to thee no less;   215
For, spite of thy sweet influence and the touch
Of other kindred hands that opened out
The springs of tender thought in infancy,
[240] And spite of all which singly I had watched
Of elegance, and each minuter charm   220
In Nature or in life, still to the last—
Even to the very going-out of youth,
The period which our story now hath reached[2]—
I too exclusively esteemed that love,
[245] And sought that beauty, which as Milton sings   225
Hath terror in it.[3] Thou didst soften down
This over-sternness; but for thee, sweet friend,
My soul, too reckless of mild grace, had been
Far longer what by Nature it was framed—
[250] Longer retained its countenance severe—   230
A rock with torrents roaring, with the clouds

9. Compare *Michael*, 162–68, where the old shepherd is praised for doing "female service" to Luke when he was a baby.
1. Wordsworth had often· expressed "strains of gratitude" to Dorothy—in *1805*, VI, 210–18, X, 908–15, above, for instance, as well as *Tintern Abbey* and *Home at Grasmere*—but the reference to imbibing early tenderness suggests that he has in mind the lyrics of spring 1802; see especially *The Sparrow's Nest* (quoted at *1850*, 230) and *To a Butterfly*.
2. Though the recent experience in the reader's mind will be the Ascent of Snowdon in 1791, and the journey across Salisbury Plain in 1793 (*1805*, XII, 312–53; *1850*, XIII, 312–49), Wordsworth regards his story as having reached the period of 1796–97; see 246*n*, below.
3. Rather surprisingly it is the serpent who, at *Paradise Lost*, IX, 490–91, remarks "though terror be in love / And beauty * * *."

The prime and vital principle is 'thine   215
In the recesses of thy nature, far
From any reach of outward fellowship,
Else is not thine at all. But joy to him,
Oh, joy to him who here hath sown, hath laid
Here, the foundation of his future years!   220
For all that friendship, all that love can do,
All that a darling countenance can look
Or dear voice utter, to complete the man,
Perfect him, made imperfect in himself,
All shall be his: and he whose soul hath risen   225
Up to the height of feeling intellect
Shall want no humbler tenderness; his heart
Be tender as a nursing mother's heart;
Of female softness shall his life be full,[9]
Of humble cares and delicate desires,   230
Mild interests and gentlest sympathies.

   Child of my parents! Sister of my soul!
Thanks in sincerest verse have been elsewhere
Poured out for all the early tenderness
Which I from thee imbibed:[1] and 'tis most true   235
That later seasons owed to thee no less;
For, spite of thy sweet influence and the touch
Of kindred hands that opened out the springs
Of genial thought in childhood, and in spite
Of all that unassisted I had marked   240
In life or nature of those charms minute
That win their way into the heart by stealth
(Still to the very going-out of youth),[2]
I too exclusively esteemed *that* love,
And sought that beauty, which, as Milton sings,   245
Hath terror in it.[3] Thou didst soften down
This over-sternness; but for thee, dear Friend!
My soul, too reckless of mild grace, had stood
In her original self too confident,
Retained too long a countenance severe;   250
A rock with torrents roaring, with the clouds

Familiar, and a favorite of the stars;
But thou didst plant its crevices with flowers,
Hang it with shrubs that twinkle in the breeze,
[255] And teach the little birds to build their nests   235
And warble in its chambers. At a time
When Nature, destined to remain so long
Foremost in my affections, had fallen back
Into a second place, well pleased to be
[260] A handmaid to a nobler than herself—   240
When every day brought with it some new sense
Of exquisite regard for common things,
And all the earth was budding with these gifts
Of more refined humanity—thy breath,
[265] Dear sister, was a kind of gentler spring   245
That went before my steps.[4]
[275]   With such a theme
Coleridge—with this my argument—of thee
Shall I be silent? O most loving soul,
Placed on this earth to love and understand,
And from thy presence shed the light of love,   250
[280] Shall I be mute ere thou be spoken of?
Thy gentle spirit to my heart of hearts
Did also find its way; and thus the life
Of all things and the mighty unity
In all which we behold, and feel, and are,   255
[288] Admitted more habitually a mild
Interposition, closelier gathering thoughts
[290] Of man and his concerns,[6] such as become
A human creature, be he who he may,
Poet, or destined to an humbler name;   260
And so the deep enthusiastic joy,
The rapture of the hallelujah sent
[295] From all that breathes and is, was chastened, stemmed,
And balanced, by a reason which indeed
Is reason, duty, and pathetic truth—[7]   265
And God and man divided, as they ought,
Between them the great system of the world,
Where man is sphered, and which God animates.

---

4. With *1805*, 236–46 (*1850*, 256–66),
compare *Tintern Abbey*, 73–94, in which
Nature, once "all in all," gives place to
other gifts, among them the ability to
hear "the still, sad music of humanity."
Wordsworth's reference is to the period
between his moral crisis (whatever its
actual strength) in spring 1796, and July
1798 when he and Dorothy left Alfoxden.
"Humanity" is more refined than the
"common things," being quiet and serious ("sad"), and nobler than the mere

handmaid Nature.
6. I.e., were gently and more habitually
mediated to me, bringing more close to
me thoughts of man and his concerns.
Wordsworth had already paid tribute to
Coleridge at *1805*, X, 904–7.
7. Reason in its most exalted mood may
be imagination (lines 167–70, above),
but in its chastening personal aspect, it
is "duty, and pathetic truth"—truth, to,
and of, the emotions.

Familiar, and a favourite of the stars:
But thou didst plant its crevices with flowers,
Hang it with shrubs that twinkle in the breeze,
And teach the little birds to build their nests   255
And warble in its chambers. At a time
When Nature, destined to remain so long
Foremost in my affections, had fallen back
Into a second place, pleased to become
A handmaid to a nobler than herself,   260
When every day brought with it some new sense
Of exquisite regard for common things,
And all the earth was budding with these gifts
Of more refined humanity, thy breath,
Dear Sister! was a kind of gentler spring   265
That went before my steps.⁴ Thereafter came
One whom with thee friendship had early paired;
She came, no more a phantom to adorn
A moment, but an inmate of the heart,
And yet a spirit, there for me enshrined   270
To penetrate the lofty and the low;
Even as one essence of pervading light
Shines, in the brightest of ten thousand stars,
And, the meek worm that feeds her lonely lamp
Couched in the dewy grass.⁵

              With such a theme,   275
Coleridge! with this my argument, of thee
Shall I be silent? O capacious Soul!
Placed on this earth to love and understand,
And from thy presence shed the light of love,
Shall I be mute, ere thou be spoken of?   280
Thy kindred influence to my heart of hearts
Did also find its way. Thus fear relaxed
Her overweening grasp; thus thoughts and things
In the self-haunting spirit learned to take
More rational proportions; mystery,   285
The incumbent mystery of sense and soul,
Of life and death, time and eternity,
Admitted more habitually a mild
Interposition—a serene delight
In closelier gathering cares, such as become   290
A human creature, howsoe'er endowed,
Poet, or destined for a humbler name;
And so the deep enthusiastic joy,
The rapture of the hallelujah sent

5. Wordsworth's tribute to his wife, with the allusion in lines 268–9 to "She was a phantom of delight," 1–4, was added in 1816/19, but later considerably revised. "Worm": glowworm.

And now, O friend, this history is brought
To its appointed close: the discipline   270
And consummation of the poet's mind
[305] In every thing that stood most prominent
Have faithfully been pictured. We have reached
The time, which was our object from the first,   275
When we may (not presumptuously, I hope)
Suppose my powers so far confirmed, and such
[310] My knowledge, as to make me capable
Of building up a work that should endure.[9]
Yet much hath been omitted, as need was—
Of books how much![1] and even of the other wealth   280
Which is collected among woods and fields,
[315] Far more. For Nature's secondary grace,
That outward illustration which is hers,
Hath hitherto been barely touched upon:
The charm more superficial, and yet sweet,
Which from her works finds way, contemplated[2]   285
As they hold forth a genuine counterpart
And softening mirror of the moral world.[3]

Yes, having tracked the main essential power—
Imagination—up her way sublime,   290
In turn might fancy also be pursued
Through all her transmigrations, till she too
Was purified, had learned to ply her craft
By judgement steadied. Then might we return,
And in the rivers and the groves behold   295
Another face, might hear them from all sides
Calling upon the more instructed mind
To link their images—with subtle skill
Sometimes, and by elaborate research—
With forms and definite appearances   300
Of human life, presenting them sometimes
To the involuntary sympathy
Of our internal being, satisfied
And soothed with a conception of delight
Where meditation cannot come, which thought   305
Could never heighten.[4] Above all, how much
Still nearer to ourselves is overlooked

9. Among Wordsworth's earlier statements of his poetic intention, see especially *1799*, I, 459–64, and *1805*, I, 123–
271, written ca. December 1798 and January 1804 respectively.
1. A reference to the inadequacies of
Book V, where scanty treatment is given
to the influence of literature; see *1805*, V,
169n, above.
2. Scansion: cŏntĕmplătĕd.
3. Wordsworth did not share Coleridge's
fondness for viewing the objects of Nature as symbolic of moral truths. See,
e.g., Coleridge's *Destiny of Nations*, 18–
20: "For all that meets the bodily sense
I deem / Symbolical, one mighty alpha-
bet / For infant minds * * *."
4. The drift of Wordsworth's thought is
clearer if one remembers that fancy (line
291) is described at VIII, 590–91 as the
power that turns "itself / Instinctively to
human passions."

From all that breathes and is, was chastened, stemmed   295
And balanced by pathetic truth, by trust
In hopeful reason, leaning on the stay
Of Providence; and in reverence for duty,
Here, if need be, struggling with storms, and there
Strewing in peace life's humblest ground with herbs,   300
At every season green, sweet at all hours![8]

   And now, O Friend! this history is brought
To its appointed close: the discipline
And consummation of a Poet's mind,
In everything that stood most prominent,   305
Have faithfully been pictured; we have reached
The time (our guiding object from the first)
When we may, not presumptuously, I hope,
Suppose my powers so far confirmed, and such
My knowledge, as to make me capable   310
Of building up a Work that shall endure.[9]
Yet much hath been omitted, as need was;
Of books how much![1] and even of the other wealth
That is collected among woods and fields,
Far more: for Nature's secondary grace   315
Hath hitherto been barely touched upon,
The charm more superficial that attends
Her works, as they present to Fancy's choice
Apt illustrations of the moral world,
Caught at a glance, or traced with curious pains.[3]   320

---

8. This revised, and (especially in lines 285–87) far less accurate, assessment of Coleridge's influence belongs probably to 1838/39, nearly five years after his death in July 1834.

In human nature and that marvellous world
[325] As studied first in my own heart, and then
In life, among the passions of mankind   310
And qualities commixed and modified
By the infinite varieties and shades
Of individual character. Herein
It was for me (this justice bids me say)
No useless preparation to have been   315
The pupil of a public school,[5] and forced
In hardy independence to stand up
Among conflicting passions and the shock
[335] Of various tempers, to endure and note
What was not understood, though known to be—   320
Among the mysteries of love and hate,
Honour and shame, looking to right and left,
Unchecked by innocence too delicate,
[340] And moral notions too intolerant,
Sympathies too contracted. Hence, when called   325
To take a station among men, the step
Was easier, the transition more secure,
More profitable also; for the mind
[345] Learns from such timely exercise to keep
In wholesome separation the two natures—   330
The one that feels, the other that observes.

    Let one word more of personal circumstance—
Not needless, as it seems—be added here.
[349] Since I withdrew unwillingly from France,
The story hath demanded less regard   335
To time and place; and where I lived, and how,
Hath been no longer scrupulously marked.
Three years, until a permanent abode
Received me with that sister of my heart
Who ought by rights the dearest to have been   340
Conspicuous through this biographic verse—
Star seldom utterly concealed from view—
I led an undomestic wanderer's life.
In London chiefly was my home, and thence
Excursively, as personal friendships, chance   345
Or inclination led, or slender means
Gave leave, I roamed about from place to place,
Tarrying in pleasant nooks, wherever found,
Through England or through Wales.[6] A youth—he bore

5. Hawkshead, where Wordsworth was a pupil May 1779–June 1787, was a Free Grammar School—i.e., an endowed foundation, open (theoretically at least) to able pupils, whether rich or poor. "Public" is thus used in its original (and logical) sense, which survives in American, but not in modern British usage.
6. Wales was the home of Robert Jones (see *1805*, VI, 342n, above). "Cambrian" (*1850*): "Welsh."

Finally, and above all, O Friend! (I speak
With due regret) how much is overlooked
In human nature and her subtle ways,
As studied first in our own hearts, and then
In life among the passions of mankind,   325
Varying their composition and their hue,
Where'er we move, under the diverse shapes
That individual character presents
To an attentive eye. For progress meet,
Along this intricate and difficult path,   330
Whate'er was wanting, something had I gained,
As one of many schoolfellows compelled,
In hardy independence, to stand up
Amid conflicting interests, and the shock
Of various tempers; to endure and note   335
What was not understood, though known to be;
Among the mysteries of love and hate,
Honour and shame, looking to right and left,
Unchecked by innocence too delicate,
And moral notions too intolerant,   340
Sympathies too contracted. Hence, when called
To take a station among men, the step
Was easier, the transition more secure,
More profitable also; for, the mind
Learns from such timely exercise to keep   345
In wholesome separation the two natures,
The one that feels, the other that observes.

Yet one word more of personal concern—
Since I withdrew unwillingly from France,
I led an undomestic wanderer's life,   350
In London chiefly harboured, whence I roamed,
Tarrying at will in many a pleasant spot
Of rural England's cultivated vales
Or Cambrian solitudes.[6] A youth (he bore

[355] The name of Calvert; it shall live, if words   350
Of mine can give it life—without respect
To prejudice or custom, having hope
That I had some endowments by which good
Might be promoted, in his last decay
From his own family withdrawing part   355
[360] Of no redundant patrimony,[7] did
By a bequest sufficient for my needs
Enable me to pause for choice, and walk
At large and unrestrained, nor damped too soon
By mortal cares.[8] Himself no poet, yet   360
[365] Far less a common spirit of the world,
He deemed that my pursuits and labors lay
Apart from all that leads to wealth, or even
Perhaps to necessary maintenance,
Without some hazard to the finer sense,   365
[370] He cleared a passage for me, and the stream
Flowed in the bent of Nature.

                          Having now
Told what best merits mention, further pains
Our present labour seems not to require,
And I have other tasks.[9] Call back to mind   370
[375] The mood in which this poem was begun,
O friend—the termination of my course
Is nearer now, much nearer, yet even then
In that distraction and intense desire
I said unto the life which I had lived,   375
[380] 'Where art thou? Hear I not a voice from thee
Which 'tis reproach to hear?' Anon I rose
As if on wings, and saw beneath me stretched
Vast prospect of the world which I had been,
And was; and hence this song, which like[1] a lark   380
[385] I have protracted, in the unwearied heavens
Singing, and often with more plaintive voice
Attempered to the sorrows of the earth—
Yet centring all in love, and in the end
All gratulant[2] if rightly understood.   385

[390]   Whether to me shall be allotted life,
And with life power to accomplish aught of worth
Sufficient to excuse me in men's sight

---

7. I.e., an inheritance which was not in excess of his needs.
8. Raisley Calvert was the brother of the school friend, William Calvert, with whom Wordsworth spent a month on the Isle of Wight in July 1793 (see *1805*, X, 290–306, above). Raisley died of con-

sumption in January 1795, leaving Wordsworth £900.
9. Primarily the philosophical section of *The Recluse.*
1. Unsupported alternative reading, "for."
2. Expressive of joy.

The name of Calvert—it shall live, if words   355
Of mine can give it life) in firm belief
That by endowments not from me withheld
Good might be furthered—in his last decay
Withdrawing, and from kindred whom he loved,
A part of no redundant patrimony,[7]   360
By a bequest sufficient for my needs
Enabled me to pause for choice, and walk
At large and unrestrained, nor damped too soon
By mortal cares.[8] Himself no Poet, yet
Far less a common follower of the world,   365
He deemed that my pursuits and labours lay
Apart from all that leads to wealth, or even
A necessary maintenance insures,
Without some hazard to the finer sense;
He cleared a passage for me, and the stream   370
Flowed in the bent of Nature.

                      Having now
Told what best merits mention, further pains
Our present purpose seems not to require,
And I have other tasks.[9] Recall to mind
The mood in which this labour was begun,   375
O Friend! The termination of my course
Is nearer now, much nearer; yet even then,
In that distraction and intense desire,
I said unto the life which I had lived,
Where art thou? Hear I not a voice from thee   380
Which 'tis reproach to hear? Anon I rose
As if on wings, and saw beneath me stretched
Vast prospect of the world which I had been
And was; and hence this Song, which like[1] a lark
I have protracted, in the unwearied heavens   385
Singing, and often with more plaintive voice
To earth attempered and her deep-drawn sighs,
Yet centring all in love, and in the end
All gratulant,[2] if rightly understood.

    Whether to me shall be allotted life,   390
And, with life, power to accomplish aught of worth,
That will be deemed no insufficient plea

For having given this record of myself,
Is all uncertain;[3] but, belovèd friend,   390
[395] When looking back thou seest, in clearer view
That any sweetest sight of yesterday,
That summer when on Quantock's grassy hills
Far ranging, and among the sylvan coombs,
[400] Thou in delicious words, with happy heart,   395
Didst speak the vision of that ancient man,
The bright-eyed Mariner, and rueful woes
Didst utter of the Lady Christabel;[4]
And I, associate in such labour, walked
[406] Murmuring of him, who—joyous hap—was found,   400
After the perils of his moonlight ride,
Near the loud waterfall, or her who sate
In misery near the miserable thorn;[5]
[410] When thou dost to that summer turn thy thoughts,
And hast before thee all which then we were,   405
To thee, in memory of that happiness,
It will be known—by thee at least, my friend,
Felt—that the history of a poet's mind
[415] Is labour not unworthy of regard:
To thee the work shall justify itself.   410

     The last and later portions of this gift
Which I for thee design have been prepared
In times which have from those wherein we first
[420] Together wandered in wild poesy
Differed thus far, that they have been, my friend,   415
Times of much sorrow, of a private grief
Keen and enduring, which the frame of mind
That in this meditative history
Hath been described, more deeply makes me feel,
[425] Yet likewise hath enabled me to bear   420
More firmly; and a comfort now, a hope,
One of the dearest which this life can give,
Is mine: that thou art near, and wilt be soon
Restored to us in renovated health—

---

3. "This Poem will not be published these many years, and never during my lifetime, till I have finished a larger and more important work to which it is tributary," Wordsworth to De Quincey, March 1804 (*EY*, p. 454). He never changed the view that the egocentricity of *The Prelude* could be justified only by its position as part of *The Recluse*; hence the postponement of its publication until after his death in 1850.
4. Only Part I of *Christabel* was written among the "sylvan coombs" (wooded valleys) of the Quantocks. Wordsworth is looking back to the period of his and Coleridge's closest relationship, at Alfoxden in Somerset in the spring and early summer of 1798—the period of *Lyrical Ballads*, and of the drawing up of the scheme of *The Recluse* (*EY*, p. 212).
5. Coleridge would enjoy the humour and self-mockery of Wordsworth's allusion to *The Thorn*, and Martha Ray's "doleful cry": "Oh misery! oh misery! / Oh woe is me! oh misery!"
     It was Johnny of *The Idiot Boy* (line 442) who was found "Near the loud waterfall."

For having given this story of myself,
Is all uncertain:[3] but, beloved Friend!
When, looking back, thou seest, in clearer view   395
Than any liveliest sight of yesterday,
That summer, under whose indulgent skies,
Upon smooth Quantock's airy ridge we roved
Unchecked, or loitered 'mid her sylvan coombs,
Thou in bewitching words, with happy heart,   400
Didst chaunt the vision of that Ancient Man,
The bright-eyed Mariner, and rueful woes
Didst utter the Lady Christabel;[4]
And I, associate with such labour, steeped
In soft forgetfulness the livelong hours,   405
Murmuring of him who, joyous hap, was found,
After the perils of his moonlight ride,
Near the loud waterfall; or her who sate
In misery near the miserable Thorn;[5]
When thou dost to that summer turn thy thoughts,   410
And hast before thee all which then we were,
To thee, in memory of that happiness,
It will be known, by thee at least, my Friend!
Felt, that the history of a Poet's mind
Is labour not unworthy of regard: 415
To thee the work shall justify itself.

      The last and later portions of this gift
Have been prepared, not with the buoyant spirits
That were our daily portion when we first
Together wantoned in wild Poesy,   420
But under pressure of a private grief,
Keen and enduring, which the mind and heart,
That in this meditative history
Hath been laid open, needs must make me feel
More deeply, yet enable me to bear   425
More firmly; and a comfort now hath risen
From hope that thou art near, and wilt be soon
Restored to us in renovated health;

When, after the first mingling of our tears,   425
[430] 'Mong other consolations, we may find
Some pleasure from this offering of my love.[6]

Oh, yet a few short years of useful life,
And all will be complete—thy race be run,
Thy monument of glory will be raised.   430
[435] Then, though too weak to tread the ways of truth,
This age fall back to old idolatry,
Though men return to servitude as fast
As the tide ebbs, to ignominy and shame
By nations sink together, we shall still   435
[440] Find solace in the knowledge which we have,
Blessed with true happiness if we may be
United helpers forward of a day
Of firmer trust, joint labourers in the work—
Should Providence such grace to us vouchsafe—   440
[445] Of their redemption, surely yet to come.[7]
Prophets of Nature, we to them will speak
A lasting inspiration, sanctified
By reason and by truth; what we have loved
Others will love, and we may teach them how: 445
[450] Instruct them how the mind of man becomes
A thousand times more beautiful than the earth
On which he dwells, above this frame of things
(Which, 'mid all revolutions in the hopes
And fears of men, doth still remain unchanged)   450
[455] In beauty exalted, as it is itself
Of substance and of fabric more divine.[9]

6. For the pleasure given to Coleridge by *The Prelude*, the "offering" of Wordsworth's love, see *To William Wordsworth*.
7. "Their redemption" (*1850*, "deliverance"): that of mankind. The millennial optimism of this passage is based on the conclusion of *1799*; see *1799*, II, 484n, above, for its original source.
9. Though speaking as "Prophets of Nature" (*1805*, 442; *1850*, 446), Wordsworth and Coleridge will instruct their readers about the mind of man, which is not just more beautiful than the natural world, but inherently more divine, in that it can—through an act of the creative and responsive imagination—perceive the existence of God. Compare Wordsworth's most deliberately challenging statement of this central theme, in the Prospectus to *The Recluse* (*CW*, III, 100 and 102, lines 973–90), where the mind of man is offered not only as "the main haunt and region" of the poet's song, but as a replacement of the subject-matter of Milton's Christian epic.

When, after the first mingling of our tears,
'Mong other consolations, we may draw   430
Some pleasure from this offering of my love.[6]

Oh! yet a few short years of useful life,
And all will be complete, thy race be run,
Thy monument of glory will be raised;
Then, though (too weak to tread the ways of truth)   435
This age fall back to old idolatry,
Though men return to servitude as fast
As the tide ebbs, to ignominy and shame
By nations sink together, we shall still
Find solace—knowing what we have learnt to know,   440
Rich in true happiness if allowed to be
Faithful alike in forwarding a day
Of firmer trust, joint labourers in the work
(Should Providence such grace to us vouchsafe)
Of their deliverance, surely yet to come.[7]   445
Prophets of Nature, we to them will speak
A lasting inspiration, sanctified
By reason, blest by faith:[8] what we have loved,
Others will love, and we will teach them how;
Instruct them how the mind of man becomes   450
A thousand times more beautiful than the earth
On which he dwells, above this frame of things
(Which, 'mid all revolutions in the hopes
And fears of men, doth still remain unchanged)
In beauty exalted, as it is itself   455
Of quality and fabric more divine.[9,1]

8. The last substantial change in the *Prelude* text, belonging probably to 1832.
1. Both *D* and *E* conclude in a statement, "The Composition of this Poem was finished early in the year *1805*—it having been begun about 1798." Below this in *E* is written: "The Life is brought up to the time of the Composition of the first Edition of the Lyrical Ballads."

MS. Drafts and Fragments
1798-1804

Reproduced below are important drafts from the working notebooks of *The Prelude* that are too long to be presented in the notes. Section 1 is of unique significance in that MS. *JJ* enables us to trace the beginnings of *Prelude* composition in October 1798. Sections 2–4 are similarly interesting for what they reveal of Wordsworth's changing intentions, and also because each incorporates memorable poetry that does not appear in any surviving completed version of *The Prelude*. Punctuation as elsewhere in this volume is editorial. Words placed within square brackets (except in the special case of Section 4 below) are supplied by the editor. A question mark preceding the enclosed word indicates a conjectural reading; a question mark on its own, an illegibile word; and a blank space within brackets, a gap in the manuscript.

1. The Beginnings of *The Prelude*: 1799 Drafts and Related Materials in MS. *JJ*, October 1798

Starting at the end of a notebook later used by Dorothy for her *Journal* of spring 1802, working backwards and forwards in an irregular progression, and writing across or along the page as the fancy took him, Wordsworth in October–November 1798 made a series of drafts, grouped below under headings (a) to (h). The relationship of the different entries to each other, and to 1799, I, as it took shape in the mind of the poet, is often very difficult to assess. It is possible that some portions of (h) preceded (a); and it cannot be proven that (c) and (d), (f) and (g), should not be the other way round. The material is presented below in its unrevised form, except on occasions—notably (a), 43–46, 59–75, and (c) 26–46—where second thoughts occurred before the original narrative or sentence structure had been established.

In effect (a) is a short version of 1799, I, as a whole; it served as a framework that Wordsworth later filled up by inserting further episodes and discursive sequences. At first Wordsworth almost certainly did not

know that he was undertaking a poem of considerable scope. His opening question—"was it for this / That one the fairest of all rivers . . ."—
begins in mid-line, in the lower case, and requires an antecedent to "this"
that is never supplied. After 94 lines, however (which include the Birds-
nesting and Woodcock-snaring episodes, but do not coincide with 1799,
I, 1–94), he reckoned his total, and set out afresh with evident sense of
purpose: "Nor while, though doubting yet not lost, I tread / The mazes
of this argument . . . " After 150 lines the main text gives place to revisions ([b], i–iii, below) that result in the drafting of 1799, I, 68–80
([b], iv). This passage forms the introduction to Boat-stealing (I, 81–129)
in the final text, and it may have done so here, as the episode ([c], below)
seems to have come next in order of composition; there can be no certainty, however, since in (e) Wordsworth tries out the same passage as a
preface to Birds-nesting. Draft (d) is "There was a boy" (1805, V, 389–
413); it is not in any obvious way connected with the other drafts, but is
told in the first person and presumably also intended for insertion within
the framework of (a). Draft (f) is a version of the concluding lines of
Part I; (g) is the opening of "I would not strike a flower" (*Oxford "Prelude,"* p. 612), a poem which is normally considered to be surplus material
from *Nutting*; on the evidence of this MS., however, it may well have been
the starting-point of Wordsworth's thoughts about doing violence to Nature, and conceived of originally within the structure of Part I. (The Fenwick Note of 1843 claims that *Nutting* was itself intended for *The Prelude*).

It is the five fragments of (h) that provide the most difficult problems.
They are of special importance because numbers i–iii contribute lines to
the opening of *The Prelude* of 1805, Wordsworth's "Glad Preamble"; and
it is particularly intriguing that they should be found on the last page of
the notebook—that is to say, working backwards (as Wordsworth was
doing at this time), they occur on the page *before* the passage which became the opening of 1799. Because of this juxtaposition it is tempting to
assume that the fragments bore something of the same relation to 1799 as
the Preamble bears to 1805; this, however, seems highly improbable. The
Preamble in its present form was written on, or shortly after, November 18,
1799 (see 1805, I, 54n, above); if it had been associated by Wordsworth
with *The Prelude*, there would have been time to incorporate it in 1799
before the faircopies V and U of the following month, either in the conclusion to Part II, which had yet to be composed, or in an introductory
section.

Nor is it clear, despite their position on the final page, that the JJ fragments which became part of the Glad Preamble did in fact precede the
other materials in the notebook. It could well be that Wordsworth at first
left the page blank, intending later to write a brief account of the sense of
failure and inadequacy that lie behind the hanging "this" at the opening
of 1799. The facing outer cover was certainly used for trial lines during
the composition of draft (a), and the fragments of (h) may similarly comprise jottings made by the poet when already at work on his main sequence.
Their mood, and theme, of exalted creativity can hardly square with the
self-reproach "was it for this," but could very plausibly represent Wordsworth's excitement as the great poetry began to flow. It is noticeable that
the last jotting on the page reappears at (a), 62–63.

(a) A connected sequence of 150 lines, corresponding to 1799, I,
1–26 (with 4 extra lines), 50–66, 130–41, 186–98 (4 extra
lines), 28–49, a twenty-five-line version of 375–90, 391–412 (5
extra lines).

was it for this

That one, the fairest of all rivers, loved
To blend his murmurs with my nurse's song,
And from his alder shades and rocky falls,
And from his fords and shallows, sent a voice   5
To intertwine my dreams? For this didst thou,
O Derwent, travelling over the green plains
Near my sweet birth-place, didst thou, beauteous stream,
Give ceaseless music to the night and day,
Which with its steady cadence tempering   10
Our human waywardness, composed my thoughts
To more than infant softness, giving me
Amid the fretful tenements of man
A knowledge, a dim earnest, of the calm
That Nature breathes among her woodland h[aunts]?   15
Was it for this—and now I speak of things
That have been, and that are, no gentle dreams
Complacent fashioned fondly to adorn
The time of unrememberable being—
Was it for this that I, a four years' child,   20
Beneath thy scars and in thy silent pools
Made one long bathing of a summer's day,
Basked in the sun, or plunged into thy streams,
Alternate, all a summer's day, or coursed
Over thy sandy plains, and dashed the flowers   25
Of yellow grundsel; or, when the hill-tops,
The woods, and all the distant mountains,
Were bronzed with a deep radiance, stood alone
A naked savage in the thunder shower?

For this in springtime, when on southern banks   30
The shining sun had from his knot of leaves
Decoyed the primrose flower, and when the vales
And woods were warm, was I a rover then
In the high places, on the lonely peaks,
Among the mountains and the winds. Though mean   35
And though inglorious were my views, the end
Was not ignoble. Oh, when I have hung
Above the raven's nest, have hung alone
By half-inch fissures in the slippery rock
But ill sustained, and almost, as it seemed,   40
Suspended by the wind which blew amain
Against the naked cragg, ah, then,
While on the perilous edge I hung alone,
With what strange utterance did the loud dry wind

Blow through my ears; the sky seemed not a sky   45
Of earth, and with what motion moved the clouds!

   Ah, not in vain ye beings of the hills,
And ye that walk the woods and open heaths
By moon or starlight, thus, from my first day
Of childhood, did ye love to interweave   50
The passions [   ]
Not with the mean and vulgar works of man,
But with high objects, with eternal things,
With life and Nature, purifying thus
The elements of feeling and of thought,   55
And sanctifying by such discipline
Both pain and fear, untill we recognize
A grandeur in the beatings of the heart.
Ah, not in vain ye spirits of the springs,
And ye that have your voices in the clouds,   60
And ye that are familiars of the lakes
And standing pools, ah, not for trivial ends
Through snow and sunshine and the sparkling plains
Of moonlight frost, and through the stormy day,
Did ye with such assiduous love pursue   65
Your favorite and your joy. I may not think
A vulgar hope was yours when ye employed
Such ministry, when ye through many a year
Thus, by the agency of boyish sports,
Impressed upon the streams, the woods, the hills—   70
Impressed upon all forms—the characters
Of danger and desire, and thus did make
The surface of the universal earth
With meanings of delight, of hope and fear,
Work like a sea.   75

   For this, when on the withered mountain slope
The frost and breath of frosty wind had nipped
The last autumnal crocus, did I love
To range through half the night among the cliffs
And the smooth hollows where the woodcocks ran   80
Along the moonlight turf? In thought and wish
That time, my shoulder all with springes hung,
I was a fell destroyer. Gentle powers,
Who give us happiness and call it peace,
When scudding on from snare to snare I plied   85
My anxious visitation, hurrying on,
Still hurrying, hurrying onward, how my heart
Panted: among the lonely eugh-trees and the crags
That looked upon me, how my bosom beat
With hope and fear! Sometimes strong desire   90

Resistless overcame me and the bird
Th[at] was the captive of another's toils
Became my prey, and when the deed [was done]
I heard among the solitary hills
Low breathings coming after me and sounds   95
Of undistinguishable motion, steps
Almost as silent as the turf they trod.

   Nor while, thou[gh] doubting yet not lost, I tread
The mazes of this argument, and paint
How Nature by collateral interest   100
And by extrinsic passion peopled first
My mind with beauteous objects, may I well
Forget what might demand a loftier song,
How oft the eternal spirit—he that has
His life in unimaginable things,   105
And he who painting what he is in all
The visible imagery of all the worlds
Is yet apparent chiefly as the soul
Of our first sympathies—oh bounteous power,
In childhood, in rememberable days,   110
How often did thy love renew for me
Those naked feelings which when thou wouldst form
A living thing thou sendest like a breeze
Into its infant being. Soul of things,
How often did thy love renew for me   115
Those hallowed and pure motions of the sense
Which seem in their simplicity to own
An intellectual charm—that calm delight
Which if I err not surely must belong
To those first-born affinities which fit   120
Our new existence to existing things,
And in our dawn of being constitute
The bond of union betwixt life and joy.

   Yes, I remember when the changeful earth
And twice five seasons on my mind had stamped   125
The faces of the changeful year, even then,
A child, I held unconscious intercourse
With the eternal beauty, drinking in
A pure organic pleasure from the lines
Of curling mist, or from the smooth expanse   130
Of waters coloured by the cloudless moon.
The sands of Westmoorland, the creeks and bays
Of Cumbria's rocky limits, they can tell
How when the sea threw off his evening shade
And to the shepherd's hut beneath the craggs   135
Did send sweet notice of the rising moon,

How I have stood, to images like this
A stranger, linking with the spectacle
No body of associated forms,
And bearing with [me] no peculiar sense   140
Of quietness or peace—yet I have stood
Even while my eye has moved o'er three long leagues
Of shining water, gathering, as it seemed,
[   ]
New pleasure like a bee among the flowers.   145
Nor unsubservient even to noblest ends
Are these primordial feelings. How serene,
How calm these seem amid the swell
Of human passion—even yet I feel
Their tranquillizing power.   150

(b) *Revisions of (a), 102–15 towards 1799, I, 375–82, resulting en route in a version of I, 68–80.*

i

How while I ran where'er the working heat
Of passion drove me at that thoughtless time
A power unknown would open out the clouds
As with the touch of lightning, seeking me
With gentle visitation then unknown   5

ii

Nor in that thoughtless season [? may I well]
Forget that other pleasures have been mine
And joys of purer origin, for oft
While thus I wandered doubting

iii

for often-times
In that tempestuous season I have felt

iv

Yes, there are genii which when they would form
A favoured spirit open out the clouds
As with the touch of lightning, seeking him
With gentle visitation. Others use,
Though haply aiming at the self-same end,   5
[?Severer] interference, ministry
Of grosser kind, and of their school was [I].

v

And made me love them

(c) *Lines that became* 1799, I, 82–129; *presumably written for insertion in the consecutive text of* (a), *and perhaps—as finally in* 1799—*to be introduced by* (b), iv, *above (however, see* [e], *below). Lines 26–46 below are presented in Wordsworth's second draft, since the first draft in the MS. breaks down before the sequence is established.*

I went alone into a shepherd's boat,
A skiff, which to a willow-tree was tied
With[in] [   ], its usual home.
The moon was up, the lake was shining clear
Among the hoary mountains; from the shore   5
I pushed, and struck the oars, and struck again
In cadence, and my little boat moved on
Just like a man who walks with stately step
Though bent on speed. It was an act of stealth
And troubled pleasure. Not without the voice   10
Of mountain echoes did my boat move on,
Leaving behind [her] still on either side
Small circles glittering idly in the moon,
Untill they melted all into one track
Of sparkling light. A rocky steep uprose   15
Above the cavern of the willow-tree,
And as beseemed a man who proudly rowed
With his best speed, I fixed a steady view
Upon the top of that same shaggy ridge,
The bound of the horizon—for behind   20
Was nothing but the stars and the grey sky.
She was an elfin pinnace; twenty times
I dipped my oars into the silent lake,
And [as] I rose upon the stroke my boat
Went heaving through the water like a swan—   25
When from behind that rocky steep, till then
The bound of the horizon, a huge cliff,
As if with voluntary power instinct,
Upreared its head. I struck, and struck again,
And, growing still in stature, the huge cliff   30
Rose up between me and the stars, and still,
With measured motion, like a living thing
Strode after me. With trembling hands I turned,
And through the silent water stole my way
Back to the willow-tree, the mooring-place   35
Of my small bark.
                    Unusual was the power
Of that strange sight: for many days my brain
Worked with a dim and undetermined sense
Of unknown modes of being. In my thoughts

There was a darkness—call it solitude,   40
Or [?strange] desertion—no familiar shapes
Of hourly objects, images of trees,
Of sea or sky, no colours of green fields,
But huge and mighty forms that do not live
Like living men moved slowly through my mind   45
By day, and were the trouble of my dreams.

(d) *Lines that finally became* 1805, V, 389–413; *probably written for* 1799, *but excluded on grounds no longer obvious.*

There was a boy—ye knew him well, ye rocks
And islands of Winander, and ye green
Peninsulas of Esthwaite—many a time
[   ] when the stars began
To move along the edges of the hills,   5
Rising or setting, would he stand alone
Beneath the trees or by the glimmering lakes,
And through his fingers woven in one close knot
Blow mimic hootings to the silent owls,
And bid them answer him. And they would shout   10
Across the wat'ry vale, and shout again,
Responsive to my call, with tremulous sobs
And long halloos, and screams, and echoes loud,
Redoubled and redoubled—a wild scene
Of mirth and jocund din. And when it chanced   15
That pauses of deep silence mocked my skill,
Then often in that silence, while I hung
Listening, a sudden shock of mild surprize
Would carry far into my heart the voice
Of mountain torrents; or the visible scene   20
Would enter unawares into my mind
With all its solemn imagery, its rocks,
Its woods, and that uncertain heaven, received
Into the bosom of the steady lake.

(e) *Version of* 1799, I, 67–80, *copied by Dorothy from dictation in state intermediate between* (b), iv, *above and the final text, and leading at this stage into* I, 28ff.

The soul of man is fashioned and built up
Just like a strain of music. I believe
That there are spirits which, when they would form
A favored being, open out the clouds
As at the touch of lightning, seeking him   5
With gentle visitation; and with such,
Though rarely, in my wanderings I have held
Communion. Others too there are who use,

Yet haply aiming at the self-same end,
Severer interventions, ministry   10
Of grosser kind—and of their school was I.
And oft when on the withered mountain slope
The frost and breath

(f) Eight-line version of 1799, I, 460–64 (conclusion of Part I).

i

Those beauteous colours of my early years
Which make the starting-place of being fair
And worthy of the goal to which the[y] tend—
Those recollected hours that have the charm
Of visionary things, and lovely forms   5
And sweet sensations, which throw back our life
And make our infancy a visible scene
On which the sun is shining.

ii

        islands in the unnavigable depth
Of our departed time

(g) "I would not strike a flower" (Oxford "Prelude," pp. 612–14),
    lines 1–12, with five additional lines, plus two separate drafts,
    the second contributing to "I would not strike," 14–15. A con-
    nection between these passages and 1799 is not to be ruled out.

i

I would not strike a flower
As many a man would strike his horse; at least
If from the wantonness in which we play
With things we love, or from a freak of power,
Or from involuntary act of hand,   5
Or foot unruly with excess of life,
It e'er should chance that I ungently used
A tuft of [   ], or snapped the stem
Of foxglove bending o'er his native rill,
I should be loth to pass along my road   10
With unreproved indifference—I would stop
Self-questioned, asking wherefore that was done.
For, seeing little worthy or sublime
In what we blazon with the names of power
And action, I was early taught to love   15
Those unassuming things, that occupy
A silent station in this beauteous world.

ii

let each thing have
Its little lot of life, but more than all,
The things that live in peace

iii

Then dearest maiden on whose lap I rest
My head [   ], do not deem that these
Are idle sympathies

(h) *Six separate jottings made probably during the composition of*
    (a), above, numbers i–iii providing finally lines 20 and 43–47 of
    the Glad Preamble (1805, I, 1–54), v contributing, less certainly,
    to 1805, III, 546–49, and vi becoming (a) lines 61–62, above.

i

a mild creative breeze,
A vital breeze that passes gently on
O'er things which it has made, and soon becomes
A tempest, a redundant energy,
Creating not but as it may [   ],   5
Disturbing things created

ii

a storm not terrible but strong,
With lights and shades, and with a rushing power

iii

trances of thought
And mountings of the mind, compared to which
The wind that drives along th'autumnal leaf
Is meekness

iv

what there is
Of subtler feeling, of remembered joy,
Of soul and spirit, in departed sound
That cannot be remembered

v

a plain of leaves
Whose matted surface spreads for many leagues,
A level prospect such as shepherds view
From some high promontory when the sea
Flames, and the sun is setting   5

vi

familiars of the standing pools

2. Fragments from *Peter Bell MS. 2*, ca. February 1799

Four distinct passages copied on two facing pages, and apparently belonging to the late Goslar period after the completion of 1799, Part I. Fragments (a) and (c) probably reflect failure to begin work on Part II, and may, conceivably represent an early attempt to write an introductory section for 1799 in the manner of 1805, I, 238–71. Fragment (d) is of special interest, both for its extreme pantheist viewpoint, and because for a time it was incorporated in Part II (see 1799, 464–5n, above).

(*a*)

               nor had my voice
Been silent—oftentimes had I burst forth
In verse which with a strong and random light
Touching an object in its prominent parts
Created a memorial which to me   5
Was all sufficient, and, to my own mind
Recalling the whole picture, seemed to speak
An universal language. Scattering thus
In passion many a desultory sound,
I deemed that I had adequately cloathed   10
Meanings at which I hardly hinted, thoughts
And forms of which I scarcely had produced
A monument and arbitrary sign.

(*b*)

In that considerate and laborious work,
That patience which, admitting no neglect,
[? By] slow creation doth impart to speach
Outline and substance, even till it has given
A function kindred to organic power—   5
The vital spirit of a perfect form

(*c*)

             I knew not then
What fate was mine, nor that the day would come
When after-loathings, damps of discontent
Returning ever like the obstinate pains
Of an uneasy spirit with a force   5
Inexorable, would from hour to hour
For ever summon my exhausted mind.

(d)

                    I seemed to learn
That what we see of forms and images
Which float along our minds, and what we feel
Of active or recognizable thought,
Prospectiveness, or intellect, or will,   5
Not only is not worthy to be deemed
Our being, to be prized as what we are,
But is the very littleness of life.
Such consciousness I deem but accidents,
Relapses from that one interior life   10
That lives in all things, sacred from the touch
Of that false secondary power by which
In weakness we create distinctions, then
Believe that all our puny boundaries are things
Which we perceive, and not which we have made—   15
In which all beings live with God, themselves
Are God, existing in one mighty whole,
As undistinguishable as the cloudless east
At noon is from the cloudless west, when all
The hemisphere is one cerulean blue.   20

3. Draft Material from the Five-Book *Prelude* in MS. W, February 1804

(a) *"Even yet thou wilt vouchsafe an ear"*

Written in late February / very early March 1804 for Book V of the five-Book *Prelude*. The sequence was intended to follow the Ascent of Snowdon (finally XIII, 1–65) and provide further analogies "betwixt / The mind of man and Nature"; but despite extensive revision, and the recopying of lines 74–106 of the text presented below, it was cut before the five-Book scheme was abandoned, in favor of a version of XIII, 77–165. The text printed is from Wordsworth's original copy; no attempt has been made to reproduce his numerous corrections.

   In his last four "analogies," lines 75–130, Wordsworth drew, at times verbatim, on Ferdinand Columbus, *Life and Actions of Christopher Columbus*, 1571 (*Collection of Voyages and Travels* [1704], II, p. 58), Richard Hakluyt's *Principall Navigations* (1589), p. 580; Mungo Park, *Travels in the Interior of Africa* (1799), p. 177; and William Dampier, *A New Voyage round the World* (1697), pp. 494–98.

Even yet thou wilt vouchsafe an ear, O friend,
And something too of a submissive mind,
As in thy mildness thou I know hast done,
While with a winding but no devious song
Through [   ] processes I make my way   5

By links of tender thought. My present aim
Is to contemplate for a needful while
(Passage which will conduct in season due
Back to the tale which I have left behind)
The diverse manner in which Nature works   10
Oft times upon the outward face of things,
I mean so moulds, exalts, endues, combines,
Impregnates, separates, adds, takes away,
And makes one object sway another so
By unhabitual influence or abrupt,   15
That even the grossest minds must see and hear
And cannot chuse but feel. The power which these
Are touched by, being so moved—which Nature thus
Puts forth upon the senses (not to speak
Of finer operations)—is in kind   20
A brother of the very faculty
Which higher minds bear with them as their own.
These from their native selves can deal about
Like transformation, to one life impart
The functions of another, shift, create,   25
Trafficking with immeasurable thoughts.
Oft tracing this analogy betwixt
The mind of man and Nature, doth the scene
Which from the side of Snowdon I beheld
Rise up before me, followed too in turn   30
By sundry others, whence I will select
A portion, living pictures, to embody
This pleasing argument.
                                  It was a day
Upon the edge of autumn, fierce with storm;
The wind blew down the vale of Coniston   35
Compressed as in a tunnel; from the lake
Bodies of foam took flight, and every thing
Was wrought into commotion high and low,
A roaring wind, mist, and bewildered showers,
Ten thousand thousand waves, mountains and crags,   40
And darkness and the sun's tumultuous light.
Green leaves were rent in handfuls from the trees;
The mountains all seemed silent, din so near
Pealed in the traveller's ear, the clouds [? ?],
The horse and rider staggered in the blast,   45
And he who looked upon the stormy lake
Had fear for boat or vessel where none was.
Meanwhile, by what strange chance I cannot tell,
What combination of the wind and clouds,
A large unmutilated rainbow stood   50
Immoveable in heaven, [?] [? been] [?]
With stride colossal bridging the whole vale.

The substance thin as dreams, lovelier than day,
Amid the deafening uproar stood unmoved,
Sustained itself through many minutes space,   55
As if it were pinned down by adamant.

   One evening, walking in the public way,
A peasant of the valley where I dwelt
Being my chance companion, he stopped short
And pointed to an object full in view   60
At a small distance. 'Twas a horse, that stood
Alone upon a little breast of ground
With a clear silver moonlight sky behind.
With one leg from the ground the creature stood,
Insensible and still; breath, motion gone,   65
Hairs, colour, all but shape and substance gone,
Mane, ears, and tail, as lifeless as the trunk
That had no stir of breath. We paused awhile
In pleasure of the sight, and left him there,
With all his functions silently sealed up,   70
Like an amphibious work of Nature's hand,
A borderer dwelling betwixt life and death,
A living statue or a statued life.

   Add others still more obvious, those I mean
Which Nature forces on the sight when she   75
Takes man into the bosom of her works—
Man suffering or enjoying. Meanest minds
Want not these moments, if they would look
Back on the past, and books are full of them.
Such power to pass at once from daily life,   80
Such power was with Columbus and his crew
When first, far travelled into unknown seas,
They saw the needle faltering in its office,
Turn from the Pole. What chivalry was seen
With English heroes in thy golden times   85
Elizabeth—such perhaps to those behind
That followed closely in a second ship,
Tried comrades in his perils, did present
Sir Humphrey Gilbert, that bold voyager,
When they beheld him in the furious storm   90
Upon the deck of his small pinnace sitting
In calmness, with a book upon his knee—
The ship and he a moment afterwards
Engulphed and seen no more.
               Like spectacle
That traveller yet living doth appear   95
To the mind's eye, when from the Moors escaped,
Alone, and in the heart of Africa,

And overcome with weariness and pain
That he [?] at length the sense of life,
Sunk to the earth, did find when he awaked   100
His horse in quiet standing at his side,
His arm within the bridle, and the sun
Setting upon the desart. Kindred power
Was present for the suffering and distress
In those who read the story at their ease   105
When, flying in his Nicobar canoe
With three Malayan helpers, Dampier saw
Well in those portents of the broken wheel
Girding the sun, and afterwards the sea
Roaring and whitening at the night's approach,   110
And danger coming on, not in a shape
Which in the heat and mettle of the blood
He oft had welcomed, but deliberate,
With dread and leisurely solemnity.
Bitter repentance for his roving life   115
Seized then upon the vent'rous mariner,
Made calm at length by prayer and trust in God.
Meanwhile the bark went forward like an arrow,
For many hours abandoned to the wind,
Her steersman. But a slackening of the storm   120
Encouraged them at length to cast a look
Upon the compass, by a lighted match
Made visible, which they in their distress
Kept burning for the purpose. Thus they fared
Sitting all night upon the lap of death   125
In wet and starveling plight, wishing for dawn,
A dawn that came at length, with gloomy clouds
Blackening the horizon; the first glimpse
Far from the horizon's edge, high up in heaven—
High dawn, prognosticating winds as high.   130

(b) "The unremitting warfare"

Written in early March 1804 for Book V of the five-Book *Prelude*
to follow a version of 1805, XIII, 1–165 and lead (perhaps *via* a
shorter version of 1805, XI, 42–120) into lines that became XI,
123–388.

The unremitting warfare from the first
Waged with this faculty, its various foes
Which for the most continue to increase
With growing life and burthens which it brings
Of petty duties and degrading cares,   5
Labour and penury, disease and grief,
Which to one object chain the impoverished mind

Enfeebled and [?], vexing strife
At home, and want of pleasure and repose,
And all that eats away the genial spirits,   10
May be fit matter for another song;
Nor less the misery brought into the world
By degradation of this power misplaced
And misemployed [?where] [? ?]
Blind [?], ambition obvious,   15
And all the superstitions of this life,
A mournful catalogue.

4. Rejected Drafts for 1805, Book VIII, in *MS. Y*, October 1804

(a) "*We live by admiration*"

Transcribed in October 1804 between 1805, VIII, 158 and a version of
174–221 (on reaching line 221 in his transcription, Wordsworth went
back, cut "We live by admiration," composed 159–74, redrafted the lines
that follow, and proceeded with his poem). Especially remarkable, when
considered in the context of Book VIII—"Love of Nature leading to Love
of Man"—is the statement in lines 191–202 below that Nature's devotee
will, "Like earlier priest or monk," sequester himself from "sordid men."
Wordsworth's original text is presented below. He left a number of gaps
(never filled, though there was substantial later correction), and water
staining on the upper portion of the leaves makes them at times very difficult to decipher. Words that were legible to de Selincourt (*Oxford "Prelude,*" pp. 571–78), but cannot now be read, have been placed in brackets.
Corrections made during composition have been accepted.

We live by admiration and by love,
And even as these are well and wisely fixed,
In dignity of being we ascend.
There doth our life begin: how long it is,
To pass things nearer by, ere the delight   5
Abate, or with less eagerness return,
Which flashes from the eyes of babes in arms
When they have caught, held up for that intent,
A prospect of the moon, or that with which,
When borne about on [   ] days, they greet   10
All uninvited, of their own accord,
Some unregarded sight—a little rill
Of water sparkling down a rocky slope
By the wayside, a beast, a bird, a flower.
When these few works of earliest [?dawn],   15
Gifts and enchanting toys by Nature [? sent]
Thus [   ],

Become familiar, agitate us less,
Then doth an after-transport, to the first
Succeeding lawfully, nor less intense,   20
Attend the child, when he can stir about
Braced, startled into notice, lifted up
As if on plumes by sudden gift of [?flight]
By things of Nature's rarer workmanship,
Her scattered accidents of sight and sound: 25
The peacock's fan with all its [   ] eyes
Unfurled, the rainbow or the cuckoo's shout,
An echo or the glowworm's faery lamp,
Or some amazement and surprize of sense
When it hath passed away returns again   30
In later days—the fluid element
That yields not when we touch it, lake or pool
[?Frozen], transparent as [the liquid deep],
And safe with all its dangers under foot.
Then everyday appearances, which now   35
The spirit of thoughtful wonder first pervades,
Crowd in and give the mind its needful food—
Nature's unfathomable works, or man's,
Mysterious as her own—a ship that sails
The sea, the lifeless arch of stones in air   40
Suspended, the cerulean firmament
And what it is, the river that flows on
Perpetually (whence comes it? whither tends?—
Going and never gone), the fish that moves
And lives as in an element of death,   45
Or aught of more refined astonishment,
Such as the skylark breeds singing aloft
As if the bird were roosted in the heavens,
There planted like a star. With these combine
Objects of fear yet not without their own   50
Enjoyment—lightning and the thunder's roar,
Snow, cloud, and rain, and storm implacable—
These also in their return find less [?],
Becoming somewhat like a [?book] [?new] [   ],
The faith in turn less passionately [?felt],   55
And the world's native produce as it meets
The sense with less habitual stretch of mind
Is pondered as a miracle, and words
By frequent repetition take the place
Of theories, repeated till faith grows   60
Through acquiescence, and the name of God
Stands fixed, a keystone of the mighty arch.

    Meantime, while we have been advancing thus
Through hesitations that do evermore

Revive, and when the impersonating power,   65
The faculty that gives sense, motion, will,
And [? ?] is at length
[? ? ?] betwixt the depth
[?Of our] existence, and admits though loth
Divided sway—things, qualities that are,   70
And not as we are—when the child hath long
Ceased to enquire of his own thoughts whence day,
Whence night, and whither they betake themselves,
Or, told of something pleasant to be done
When summer come, no more within himself   75
Marvels what summer is, and when, in fine,
That great magician the revolving year
Hath in our presence played his changes off
Till they excite less passionate regard,
Then attestations new of growing life,   80
Distinct impressions and unbounded thought,
To appease the absolute necessities
That struggle in us, opportunely come
From the universe of fable and [?romance]:
Trees that bear gems for fruit, rocks spouting milk,   85
And palaces of diamond, birds that sing
With human voices, formidable hills
Of magnets which, leagues off, can witch away
Iron, disjointing in a moment's space
The unhappy ship that comes within their reach,   90
Enchanted armour, talismanic rings,
Dwarfs, giants, genii, creatures that can shape
Themselves and be or not be at their will;
Others, the slaves and instruments of these,
That neither are beast, bird, insect, or worm,   95
But shapes and powers of these intemperately
Upon each other heaped, or parcelled out
In boundless interchange. Nor less esteem
[Bear] at this season the more sober tales
Of travellers through foreign climes, that shew   100
A[face] as if it were another earth,
As if another Nature flourished there:
Bananas, palm trees, citrons, orange groves
And jasmine bowers, or desert wastes of sand
Helpless and hopeless, or in desert woods   105
The enormous snake that is a tree in size,
The burning mountain, the huge cataract,
Or lands that see the sun through half a year
And lie as long in night beneath the stars.

    Meantime the spirits are in dance if aught   110
At home of glaring spectacle, or new,

Be interwoven with the common sights .
Which earth presents; and contrasts strong and harsh,
And fanciful devices, temples, grots,
Statue and terrace, sward and trim cascade,   115
In short whatever object savours least
Of mind's right understanding and [?],
Is least in Nature, seems to please [us] most,
Affects us with most vehement delight.
Untutored minds stop here, and after life   120
Leads them no farther; vivid images
To them and strong sensations must be given
They cannot [?make these], walking without harm
In the eye of Nature. Fast outstripping these
The child, by constitution of his frame   125
And circumstances favored from the first,
Grows in the common [   ], an animal
Like others, only [   ]
Burning within to irradiate all without,
Vulgar impostor seems and unrefined,   130
Careless of Nature's presence, and unawed,
Best pleased when his [?] way [?]
And his own person, senses, faculties,
Centre and soul of all, yet haunted oft
By what has been his life at every turn,   135
Unfolding a proud length of [?].
Why need we track the process? Then will come
Another soul, spring, centre of his being,
And that is Nature. As his powers advance
He is not like a man who sees in the heavens   140
A blue vault merely and a glittering cloud,
One old familiar likeness over all,
A superficial pageant, known too well
To be regarded—he looks nearer, calls
The stars out of their shy retreats and parts   145
The milky stream into its separate forms,
Loses and finds again, when baffled most
Not least delighted. Finally he takes
The optic tube of thought, that patient men
Have furnished with the toil of [?],   150
Without the glass of Galileo sees
What Galileo saw, and, as it were,
Resolving into one great faculty
Of being bodily eye and spiritual need,
The converse which he holds is limitless—   155
Nor only with the firmament of [thought],
But nearer home he looks with the same eye
Through the entire abyss of things.

And now

The first and earliest motions of his life,
I mean of his rememberable time,   160
Redound upon him with a stronger flood.
In speculation he is like a child—
With this advantage, that he now can rest
Upon himself. Authority is none
To cheat him of his boldness, or hoodwink   165
His intuitions, or to lay asleep
The [unquiet] stir of his perplexities;
And in this season of his second birth,
[?] submission and a slavish world,
He feels that be his mind however great   170
In aspiration, the universe in which
He lives is equal to his mind, that each
Is worthy of the other—if the one
Be insatiate, the other is inexhaustible.
Whatever dignity there be [   ]   175
Within himself from which he gathers hope,
There doth he feel its counterpart, the same
In kind before him outwardly expressed,
With difference that makes the likeness clear,
Sublimity, grave beauty, excellence   180
Not taken upon trust, but self-displayed
Before his proper senses; transcripts
And imitations are not here that mock
Their archetypes, no single residue
Of a departed glory, but a world   185
Living and to live, no [? ? ?]
What hidden greater far than what is seen,
No false subordination, fickleness,
Or thwarted virtue, but inveterate power
Directed to best ends, and all things good,   190
Pure, and consistent.

If upon mankind

He looks, and on the human maladies
Before his eyes, what finds he there to this
Framed answerably?—what but sordid men,
And transient occupations, and desires   195
Ignoble and depraved. Therefore he cleaves
Exclusively to Nature, as in her
Finding his image, what he has, what lacks,
His rest and his perfection. From mankind,
Like earlier monk or priest, as if by birth   200
He is sequestered, to her altar's laws
Bound by an irrefutable decree.
No fellow labourer of the brotherhood,

Single he is in state, monarch and king,
Or like an Indian when in solitude   205
And individual glory he looks [out]
From some high eminence upon a tract
Boundless of unappropriated earth—
So doth he measure the vast universe,
His own by right of spiritual sovreignty.   210
Yet who can tell while he this path
Hath been ascending, in apparent slight
Of man and all the mild humanities
That overspread the surface of the [heart],
What subtle virtues from the first have been   215
In midst of this and in despite of [?all],
At every moment finding out their way
Insensibly to nourish in the heart
Its tender sympathies, to keep alive
Those yearnings, and to strengthen them and shape,   220
Which from the mother's breast were first received?
The commonest images of Nature, all
No doubt are with this office charged: a path,
A taper burning through the gloom of night,
Smoke breathing up by day from cottage trees,   225
A beauteous sunbeam in a sunny shed,
A garden with its walks and banks of flowers,
A churchyard and the bell that [?] to church,
The roaring ocean and waste wilderness,
Familiar things and awful, the minute   230
And grand, are destined here to meet, are all
Subservient to this end, near or remote,
Namely to make those gracious charities,
Habits of eye and ear and every sense,
Endearing union without which the earth   235
Is valueless, even in its Maker's eye.

(b) *"Whether the whistling kite"*

Preserved in MS. Y, first as an incomplete draft, then as part of Wordsworth's established text at 1805, VIII, 497/98. Cut probably during the
preparation of MS. A in 1805, and finally used in *Excursion*, IV, 402–12
and IX, 437–48. The bracketed words in lines 8–9 below are supplied
from an *Excursion* notebook (Dove Cottage MS. 70) of ca. 1812.

Whether the whistling kite wheeled in the storm,
Maze intricate above me or below,
As if in mockery or in proud display
Of his own gifts compared with feeble man;
Or facing some huge breast of rock I heard,   5
As I have sometimes done, a solemn bleat

Sent forth as if it were the mountain's voice,
As if the visible [mountain made the cry]
And hark, again [that solemn bleat, there is]
No other, and the region all about   10
Is silent, empty of all shape of life—
It is a lamb left somewhere to itself,
The plaintive spirit of the solitude.
In those same careless rambles of my youth,
Once coming to a bridge that overlooked   15
A mountain torrent where it was becalmed
By a flat meadow, at a glance I saw
A twofold image; on the grassy bank
A snow-white ram and in the peaceful flood
Another and the same. Most beautiful   20
The breathing creature was, as beautiful
Beneath him was his shadowy counterpart;
Each had his glowing mountains, each his sky,
And each seemed centre of his own fair world.
A stray temptation seized me to dissolve   25
The vision, but I could not, and the stone
Snatched up for that intent dropped from my hand.

Manuscripts of *The Prelude,* 1798-1850

(Note: The numbers in parentheses preceded by "D.C." refer to the Wordsworth archive at Dove Cottage, Grasmere, and are offered for convenience in addition to the name or number by which the manuscript has commonly been known.) The later *Prelude* MSS. C, D, and E are not yet part of the new classification.

MS. JJ (D.C. MS. 19) The original drafts of 1799, Part I, belonging to October–November 1798. Described and edited in MS. Drafts and Fragments 1, above.

Christabel Notebook (D.C. MS. 15) A notebook similarly in use at Goslar, originally containing 1799 material on seven consecutive leaves, dating probably from late November–early December 1798. Six leaves were later cut out, but initial letters on the stubs suggest that Wordsworth used the notebook to rationalize his *JJ* drafts, and to construct the first coherent version of Part I, consisting broadly of 1799, I, 1–198, 376–464.

MS. 18A (D.C. MS. 16) The companion volume to the *Christabel Notebook*, containing frequently the same materials at a slightly later stage of composition or revision. 1799 faircopy, again represented by remaining stubs and a single extant leaf, dates from late December 1798–early February 1799. A 400-line version of Part I of 1799 is implied, including for the first time the "spots of time" sequence, 1799, I, 234–374. A rough pencil draft of 1805, III, 6–15, on the inner cover belongs to December 1801.

Peter Bell MS. 2 (D.C. MS. 33) Contains four related fragments of blank verse of ca. February 1799, perhaps all written with 1799, II, in mind, but only one contributing finally to the text. Edited in MS. Drafts and Fragments 2, above.

MS. RV (D.C. MS. 21) The original faircopy of 1799, II belonging to ca. September–early December 1799, completed first in 453 lines, then expanded to 491 lines.

MS. V (D.C. MS. 22) Dorothy's faircopy of 1799, and base text of the poem as printed in this volume, belonging to late November–early December 1799. Revised in March–May 1801; in use during composition of the five-Book *Prelude*, January–early March 1804, and perhaps again in late April of the following year, when Wordsworth was at work on 1805, XI.

MS. U (*D.C. MS.* 23) Mary Hutchinson's duplicate faircopy of 1799, transcribed concurrently with MS. V in late November–early December. Normally, though not invariably, the later of these two manuscripts, and, to judge from the comparative lack of revision, regarded by Wordsworth as the less authoritative.

MS. WW (*D.C. MS.* 43) Fragmentary and often illegible pencil drafts on twenty-three leaves cut from a small pocket notebook used first by Dorothy on the Scottish tour of autumn 1803, then by Wordsworth for composition outdoors in January–March 1804. Surviving materials are mainly drafts of the five-Book *Prelude*, but include work towards 1805, VI, carried out after the poem in five Books was abandoned ca. March 10.

MS. W (*D.C. MS.* 38) Badly mutilated notebook used by Wordsworth to assemble faircopy of Books III (probably), IV, and V of the five-Book *Prelude*, February–early March 1804. Probably filled before the five-Book scheme was abandoned, showing no sign of the reorganization of material to form 1805, I–V, that took place ca. March 10–18.

MS. M (*D.C. MS.* 44) Contains Mary Wordsworth's faircopy of 1805, I–V—Dorothy's companion version is lost—transcribed for Coleridge, March 1804, and sent to him in packets, the last dispatched on the eighteenth.

MS. Y (*D.C. MS.* 48) Mutilated notebook of October 1804, that contained a version of 1805, IX, 294–55 (the account of Michel Beaupuy), followed by an early form of Book VIII, with lines that became VII, 1–50 in place of lines 1–74, and including at lines 158–74 and 197–98 respectively sequences printed as MS. Drafts and Fragments 4, (a) and (b) above. Copy breaks off at lines 661, to be followed by missing leaves, lines 824–59, and materials finally used in Books XI and XII.

MS. X(*D.C. MS.* 47) Notebook of November 1804, containing an early form of 1805, Book VII, opening with lines that became VIII, 711–51 in place of lines 1–50 (yet to be transferred from Book VIII). Stubs show that at the front of the notebook, before these materials, stood a reworking of the introductory lines to Book VI.

D.C. MS. 74B Loose double sheet containing drafts of 1805, X, 444–65, 567–73 belonging probably to ca. December 1804.

Windy Brow Notebook (*D.C. MS.* 10) Notebook of 1794 containing on spare paper a stray draft of 1805, XI, 163–89 belonging probably to January–early February, or late April 1805.

MS. Z (*D.C. MS.* 49) Homemade notebook containing 1805, Books XI and XII—here numbered XII and XIII—as they stood in late April–early May 1805. Incorporated in the notebook are leaves from a slightly earlier manuscript on similar paper that had been used to assemble the latter part of Book X, as well as what was presumably the original faircopy of XI.

MS. A (*D.C. MS.* 52) Dorothy's faircopy of 1805, belonging to late November 1805–February 1806. Used as base text for the 1805 version in this volume. Revised extensively in 1816/19 in preparation for MS. C, and probably revised also from time to time during the previous ten years. The earliest datable corrections show the influence of Coleridge, ca. January 1807.

MS. B (D.C. MS. 53) Mary's duplicate faircopy of 1805, belonging to the same period as MS. A, and containing a small number of independent readings. Less extensively revised than A.

MS. C Transcription in 1816 / 19 by Wordsworth's clerk, John Carter, of the revised MS. A, ending abruptly at 1805, XII, 187, and including for the first time a version of 1850, 420–88, on the Grande Chartreuse. Used in preparation of *Vaudracour and Julia* (1805, 556–935, published separately 1820), and containing on final blank leaves drafts of 1832, but surprisingly little revised.

MS. D Faircopy of *The Prelude* in fourteen Books made by Mary early in 1832. Very extensively revised, both in 1832 and 1838/39, in preparation for MS. E.

MS. E Hasty and inaccurate transcription of the final state of D made by Wordsworth's daughter, Dora, and her cousin Elizabeth Cookson, in the poet's absence, late March–May 1839. Revised on a number of occasions, but never consistently proof-read. Used as the printer's copy for the first edition, and containing, in addition to corrections of Wordsworth and his amanuenses, certain queries made by his clerk, Carter, ca. late April 1850, just before the poem went to press.

The Texts:
History and Presentation

General Editorial Procedures

There can be no prefect edition of any of the three major states of *The Prelude*. The published text of 1850 might be expected to be authoritative, but was seen through the press after the poet's death by executors whose editorial decisions certainly do not always reflect his intentions; and in addition, the printer's copy, *MS. E*, is at times demonstrably inaccurate. With the two early versions, the poem of 1799 in two Parts, and the thirteen-Book poem of 1805, the problems are no simpler. Both texts are preserved in duplicate faircopies, but in neither case are the duplicates identical. To confuse things further, the manuscripts of all three versions of *The Prelude* contain revisions and inserted material that cannot be dated with certainty. In the circumstances the editor's task must be to arrive at the most helpful criteria and state them with clarity, to stick by them firmly but not inflexibly, and to note scrupulously where and why he departs from them on particular occasions.

The text of each of the three *Preludes* is discussed below in some detail, but certain general points may be made. As regards the texts of 1799 and 1805, it is clear that Dorothy Wordsworth's faircopies of each text—MSS. V and A, respectively—were begun slightly earlier, and remain more authoritative, than MSS. U and B, transcribed by Mary Hutchinson Wordsworth. In neither poem, however, can Dorothy's original text be established, as the first corrections in the manuscripts were entered over careful erasure of the original—in 1805, at least, clearly before the faircopy as a whole was complete. 1799 is printed above as it may be presumed to have stood between the initial corrections (ca. mid-December 1799) and the revisions of March–May 1801. 1805 is printed in the version that seems likely to have stood for a rather shorter period—between ca. February 1806 (when transcription of MSS. A and B was completed) and the revisions of ca. January 1807 (which take into account suggestions made by Coleridge on returning from Malta).

The text of 1805 will be found to differ in very numerous minor points, but few striking instances, from that of the revised Oxford *Prelude* (1959). Three lines are added at the conclusion of Book I; Books VII and IX are one line longer, and Books X and XI one line shorter, than in the Oxford text. The most notable textual change concerns de Selincourt's "*vivifying* virtue" in the "spots of time" sequence (XI, 259); this was clearly corrected very early to "*renovating* virtue," as in 1850, and must give way to the latter reading in 1805 as well. In 1799 the spelling of the manuscript has been retained throughout, and in 1805 an exception has been made only in a few cases of major confusion. Ampersands have been eliminated, and it has seemed more useful to mark the occasional "èd" that requires a stress than to preserve apostrophe "d" for the many that don't.

Punctuation in the printed texts of 1799 and 1805 is editorial. The presence of a particular stop in a manuscript may be useful evidence—the colon in 1799, I, 39–40, "how my heart / Panted: among the scattered yew-trees . . ." is found in *MS. JJ*, and precludes the alternative reading, "how my heart / Panted among . . ."—but punctuation in the manuscripts is so spasmodic that its absence tells us nothing. Wordsworth seems not to have believed that his poetry could be misread (for instance, asking Humphrey Davy, whom he had never met, to correct the punctuation of *Lyrical Ballads* 1800); and with *The Prelude*, his amanuenses knew that they were preparing texts that would be read only by members of their circle. Editorial punctuation can, of course, radically change the writer's meaning. At 1805, IV, 105 in the Oxford *Prelude* the absence of a single comma causes the youthful poet to leap forward like Venus from the sea, to pat his dog:

> and at once
> Some fair enchanting image in my mind
> Rose up, full form'd, like Venus from the sea
> Have I sprung forth towards him, and let loose
> My hand upon his back with stormy joy * * *

The results of mismanaged pointing are not usually so dramatic, but it is among the more important features of this edition that punctuation has been systematically reconsidered.

Capitalization can be similarly misleading, and here again the manuscripts are wayward. Initial capitals in 1799 and 1805 have been retained only for the terms "God" and "Nature," and for personifications that are clearly presented by the poetry *as* personifications. Even here there are problems. At times the lower case "nature of things" may shade imperceptibly into "Nature" with a capital N; or, to take a specific case, capitals would change "the eternal beauty" of 1799, I, 395 into a Platonic concept of God, warranted probably by Wordsworth's views when the line was composed in *MS. JJ* (October–November 1798), but far less certainly when 1799 was transcribed the following year.

Previous editors of 1850 have offered the text of the first edition, although it was printed after Wordsworth's death, and manifestly does not in all cases represent his intentions. The survival of *MS. E*, the printer's copy, enables us to isolate changes made by the poet's executors who saw the poem through the press, and there are sixty odd that are quite unwarranted. Clearly the first edition of *The Prelude* (July 1850) has its own integrity—it is an established fact of literary history—but should its readings be preferred to Wordsworth's own wishes? In the opening lines, for example, the "mild creative breeze" that greets the poet issuing from the city's walls is referred to three times by Wordsworth as "he;" in the first edition the pronoun is "it." If this correction is reversed, and Wordsworth's animism restored, others are bound to follow. The poet's executors (chiefly his nephew, Christopher, later Bishop of Lincoln), rewrote, reordered, and omitted lines, reinstated earlier readings as they chose, altered words that did not please them, and tidied up meter and syntax. If the decision is taken—as it surely must be—to return in all such cases to Wordsworth's intentions, it follows that an attempt should be made to establish where not only the first edition, but the printer's copy, is at fault. Except where it has been corrected, either by the poet or by an amanuensis, *MS. E* has no authority against the final state of *D*, from which it was carelessly transcribed.

The 1850 text printed here is therefore that of the first edition, refined by collation with *E*, and further checked against *D*; on very exceptional occasions it has been necessary to go back a stage further to see if *D* itself perpetuated an error. The line count will be found to differ from that of the first edition (and the Oxford *Prelude*) in Books I, IV, V, XI, and XIV. Among the more striking differences of wording is the reference at II, 342, which the poet's executors declined to print, to the thrush's "shrill *reveillé*." The spelling and capitalization of the first edition have been preserved throughout, as has punctuation except in cases—again roughly sixty in number—where manuscript evidence shows the printed text to be certainly wrong.

Composition and Texts: The Two-Part *Prelude* of 1799

Introduction

The Prelude survives in three forms: the much revised official text (1850), published in fourteen Books by Wordsworth's executors after his death; the version in thirteen Books (1805), first printed by Ernest de Selincourt in 1926; and the two-Part poem (1799). 1805 remained in manuscript for 120 years, 1799 has had to wait another fifty. Though a great poem in its own right, it has been known to few, and very little discussed. In 1958 Helen Darbishire commented in passing that the two Parts formed "one vital and self-contained whole," but it was left to J. R. MacGillivray ("The Three Forms of *The Prelude*," 1964) to make the first critical assessment of the poem of 1799. "In this proto-*Prelude*," he writes,

> one observes a much more unified theme and a much stronger sense of formal structure than in the poem completed first in 1805, and published in 1850. The time covered is restricted to childhood and school days only. The single theme is the awakening of the imagination. Each of the two parts has its own limit in time: the first being of childhood and to the age of about ten, the second until the end of school days when the narrator was seventeen. The whole poem, and each separate part, shows an unusual number, for Wordsworth at least, of devices of formal structure, used, I think, with considerable success.

1799 is a separate and internally coherent early form of *The Prelude*. Part I was written at Goslar in Germany, October 1798–ca. January 1799; Part II at Sockburn, County Durham, home of Wordsworth's future wife,

Mary Hutchinson, ca. September–December 1799. Wordsworth's theme is, as MacGillivray points out, the awakening of imagination; 1799 offers a treatment that is at once fuller and more concentrated than that presented in the first two Books of 1805, to which it roughly corresponds. The poem has no formal introduction, opening abruptly (at what in the 1805 text is I, 271) in a mood of self-dissatisfaction. Wordsworth has been unable to start the main section of *The Recluse*, the great philosophical work planned with Coleridge at Alfoxden the previous spring. Present inaction does not square with his strong sense of having been singled out by a favored upbringing—

> was it for this
> That one, the fairest of all rivers, loved
> To blend his murmurs with my nurse's song?

—and he turns to his childhood experience to examine the sources of creativity and adult consciousness. Part I contains not only the incidents associated with Book I of 1805—notably the Woodcock-snaring, Birds-nesting, Boat-stealing, and Skating episodes—but also the doctrinal passage, "There are in our existence spots of time . . .," together with the two illustrative "spots" (XI, 257–315, 342–88, in the later poem), and preceded by the child's discovery of the Drowned Man (1805, V, 450–73). Part II, though including at lines 140–78 a major passage that was later cut, is substantially similar to Book II of 1805. Its discussion of adolescent perception and creativeness is, however, qualified by the presence in Part I of Wordsworth's central definition; and the structural implications, especially of the conclusion, are naturally more apparent in the shorter original poem. The final lines of 1799 are tied back to the opening by quotations from Coleridge's *Frost at Midnight* at I, 8 and II, 496–97, and the poem ends in a moving farewell that reaffirms the shared aims of the two poets, while admitting Coleridge's very different character and needs.

Despite the deliberate formal rounding at the end of 1799, and despite the fact that Wordsworth had duplicate faircopies made of the poem, there is some difficulty in the assumption that it is a completed work. The reiterated "this" of lines 1, 6, and 17 has no antecedent, and the opening, though drawing on a rhetorical pattern that goes back to Milton, Ariosto, and Virgil, is undeniably abrupt. But though Wordsworth clearly thought for a time that an antecedent should be supplied—the first line begins in the lower case in both early manuscripts—his failure to write an introduction while carrying out other needful alterations in December 1799 suggests that he himself came to find the abruptness acceptable. A more significant difficulty is the fact that Dorothy Wordsworth concluded her faircopy of 1799 (MS. V, printed here) not, as might be expected, with "The End," but with "End of the second Part"—implying, it would seem, that she at least thought the poem might be continued at a future date. For this reason 1799 is presented here not as a finished work, but as one that Wordsworth regarded as for the time complete—hence the rounding off, and the faircopies—and which was in the event not continued, but taken apart and redistributed, in the construction of 1805.

Composition

The history of 1799 goes back to October–November 1798, when in MS. JJ (MS. Drafts and Fragments 1, above), Wordsworth composed lines corresponding to I, 1–26, 50–66 ("Birds-nesting"), 130–41, 186–98, 28–49 ("Woodcock-snaring"), and 375–412. Though not in their final order, and clearly still in the process of composition, these drafts in MS. JJ form a coherent sequence of 150 lines, the first 94 being numbered by the poet. They are followed by a version of I, 68–80, 82–129 ("Boat-stealing"), and other material, some of it important, that was not in the event used for 1799. The fragmentary *Christabel Notebook* shows that by mid-December the JJ drafts had become a version of Part I, lacking: the "spots of time" (1799, I, 234–374—written soon after), "Skating" (I, 150–85—already written, but not incorporated until December 1799), the transition passage (I, 142–49) and the card-playing sequence (I, 206–33—both late 1799). A final Goslar faircopy, in MS. 18A, dating from ca. January 1799, shows the "spots of time" and I, 198–205 to have been composed, and implies a fully worked out Part I of 390 to 400 lines; the notebook also preserves an unsuccessful attempt to begin Part II, dating from ca. May 1799, after the Wordsworths' return to England.

The working drafts of Part II are lost, but the evidence of Wordsworth's faircopy, MS. RV, suggests that serious composition did not begin until the end of the summer. At the time of Coleridge's sudden arrival in the north on October 25–26, little more than half the text of Part II had been transcribed, but on Wordsworth's return a month later from a subsequent walking tour in the Lake District the poem seems very quickly to have been completed; no doubt some of the final portion already existed in draft (II, 446–64 had been written in February / March 1798). To late November–early December 1799 must belong, among other less important passages, II, 6–45 (inserted as a result of Wordsworth's recent visit to Hawkshead), the concluding lines (II, 496–514), and insertions at II, 250–55, 333–51, and 425–37.

Almost certainly the completion of RV was followed at once by the transcription in MSS. V and U of the full text of 1799. Wordsworth at this stage made the three additions to Part I mentioned above, cut an important pantheist sequence that had been incorporated in RV (MS. Drafts and Fragments 2[d], above) and inserted II, 140–78. The text of 1799 is established in MS. V, copied by Dorothy, from which Mary Hutchinson's MS. U, though containing certain independent readings, normally—perhaps invariably—derives. As in the case of MS. A (see Note on the Printed Text, 1805, below) the earlier manuscript remains the more authoritative, since it contains fewer gaps in transcription and has been corrected with greater consistency. Both manuscripts of 1799 seem to have been complete when the Wordsworths left Sockburn for Grasmere on December 17, 1799.

The letters of John Wordsworth show 1799 to have been to some extent revised in spring 1801; they provide too the earliest reference to the work as "The Poem to Coleridge," the name by which *The Prelude* in all its forms is henceforth known throughout the poet's lifetime. The first hint of work towards a longer poem comes in December 1801, when 1805, III, 1–167 is almost certainly written, bringing the narrative up to Wordsworth's Cambridge period. For the later merging of 1799 in 1805, see Composition and Texts: 1805/1850, Introduction, below; and for a detailed account of the origin and composition of 1799, see Jonathan Wordsworth and Stephen Gill, "The Two-Part *Prelude* of 1798–99," *JEGP*, LXXII (1973), pp. 503–25, and *CW*, II, which incorporates in addition photographs of the more important manuscript stages.

Note on the Printed Text

The 1799 text printed above corresponds to MS V faircopy, after small immediate corrections (frequently over erasure), but before the revisions of spring 1801. MS. U has been taken as a means of checking the date of corrections in V; "soul" at II, 377 and "waste" at II, 479, for instance, though merely penciled into V, are found in U faircopy. Two U readings that do not appear in V have been accepted: at II, 322 a gap is left in V, but the deleted RV reading "obscure" is reincorporated in U; and at II, 456 "that" has been preferred to "which," again on the grounds that the reading is supported by both earlier and later manuscripts. In Part I, line 375 is defective in both 1799 manuscripts, and is supplied from MS. M of March 1804. The first fifty-three lines of Part II have been cut out of MS. V, and are therefore printed from U. At II, 7 a/b MS. U preserves a deleted reading which has been omitted in the printed text, on the grounds that the mode of crossing-out is associated in V with early corrections, and the lines had probably been deleted there as well; see II, 7n.

Composition and Texts:
The Prelude of 1805 and 1850

Introduction, 1805/1850

The thirteen-Book *Prelude* (1805) is found, like *The Prelude* of 1799, in duplicate faircopies—MSS. A and B, of November 1805–February 1806. The poem had been finished the previous May after three distinct phases of composition: 1801–3, in which 1799 was revised and extended; January–March 1804, when Wordsworth reorganized his material, and at least very nearly completed a *Prelude* in five Books; and March 1804–May 1805, when the thirteen-Book poem was created by new composition and further redistribution of existing materials. It is doubtful if Wordsworth could have guessed at either the shape or the scope of his eventual work much before Christmas 1804, by which time nine-tenths of the poetry had been written. The probable order of composition of his last eight Books is VI, IX, the first half of X, VIII, VII, the second half of X, XI, XII, XIII. Not that the individual Books were normally of a single moment: most contain earlier work, and many the work of several earlier periods. There is nothing careless or piecemeal about the structure of 1805, but it is the result of frequent rethinking, not of a single well-executed plan.

1799 was probably extended in December 1801 by the addition of 1805, III, 1–167, bringing the poet's autobiography up to the Cambridge period. Further work on *The Prelude* seems to have taken place in January 1803, and again in the summer; but if anything of great importance had been achieved at this period, Wordsworth would presumably not in October 1804 have described the flow of composition as having "stopped for years . . . until a little space / Before last primrose-time" (1805, VII, 9–13). A new impetus was given to *The Prelude* by Coleridge's decision at Christmas 1803 to go abroad in search of health, and, more specifically, by Wordsworth's reading to Coleridge Part II of 1799 at Grasmere on January 4, 1804.

i. *The Five-Book* Prelude (*January–early March* 1804)

The five-Book *Prelude* cannot be printed, as can 1799 and 1805, because only parts of it survive in faircopy; but it can be reconstructed in considerable detail. The project was abandoned very suddenly when ca. March 10, 1804, Wordsworth decided that he would work towards a longer poem. At this point his material for the five-Book *Prelude* must have been complete, although we cannot know whether certain drafts in the middle of his last Book had reached their final shape. The poem was the most carefully structured of the different *Prelude* versions; it began and ended with the early memories that were the source of Wordsworth's creative power, and attempted *en route* to define the nature of their restorative effect. Books I–III were identical to 1805 (Book I is the creation of January 1804, more than half the material being new since 1799; Book II lacks 1799, II, 140–78, but is otherwise little changed; the bulk of Book III is recent composition). Book IV, finished by March 1, was a version in 650 lines of what became 1805 IV and V. Of the major 1805 sequences—the moment of dedication (IV, 314–45, recent work), Discharged Soldier (IV, 360–504, early 1798), Quixote dream (V, 49–165, recent work), Infant Prodigy (V, 294–369, recent work), "There was a boy" (V, 370–422, late 1798), and the Drowned Man (V, 450–73, originally 1799, I, 258–79)—only the dream remained to be incorporated; the other sequences were merely grouped a little more tightly. The opening of Wordsworth's fourth Book is not preserved, but the first extant lines (see IV, 270n, above) imply a preceding account in some detail of the poet's return to Hawkshead described in 1805, IV, 1–268. For the transition between the Discharged Soldier and the second half of the original Book IV, see V, 1n.

In terms of the structure of 1805, the last Book of this intermediate five-Book *Prelude* consisted of the first third of XIII *plus* the last two-thirds of XI, opening with the Ascent of Snowdon (XIII, 1–65, recently composed) and concluding in the "spots of time" (1799, I, 288–374). An important section of 130 lines following the Ascent of Snowdon was discarded during composition (MS. Drafts and Fragments, 3[a], above) in favor of a version of XIII, 74–165; and Wordsworth then turned to consider the "unremitting warfare" waged against the imaginative faculty (MS. Drafts and Fragments, 3[b]). Drafts of this central section did not reach a completed form in the extant notebook, MS. W, but could well have done so elsewhere, as at least two manuscripts of spring 1804 have been lost. The remainder of Book V must have coincided almost exactly with 1805, XI, 123–388. Newly composed is the passage, "When in a blessed season" (XI, 315–44), inserted between the two 1799 "spots of time," and ending in this original version:

> the hiding-places of my power
> Seem open, I approach, and then they close;
> Yet have I singled out—not satisfied
> With general feelings, here and there have culled—
> Some incidents that may explain whence come
> My restorations, and with yet one more of these
> Will I conclude. One Christmas time . . .

Looking back over his five-Book poem, Wordsworth sees its various episodes as illustrations of his central theme of developing imagination; the "spots of time" LXXVI (1977), are here a culmination of all that has gone before. For a reconstruction in detail of this version of the poem, see Jonathan Wordsworth, "The Five-Book *Prelude* of Early Spring 1804," *JEGP*, LXXVI (1977), pp. 1–25.

ii. *Reorganization and Expansion, March 1804–May 1805, Leading to the* Prelude *of 1805*

The five-Book *Prelude* was abandoned ca. March 10, 1804, the fifth Book being set aside for future use, the fourth split in two and reworked to form 1805 IV and V. By March 18 Coleridge had been sent 1805 I–V to take with him to Malta, and ten days later Book VI was well under way. The factors that seem chiefly to have influenced Wordsworth in deciding to work towards a longer poem were his unwillingness, in the absence of Coleridge, to make another attempt at the main section of *The Recluse*, the wish nevertheless to do something on his friend's behalf, and his dissatisfaction at having left out of *The Prelude* important biographical material, especially his visit to France and the Alps in 1790.

Though its introduction seems to have been reworked in the late autumn, a version of Book VI was finished by April 29, 1804. At this time Wordsworth claimed to have written during the previous ten weeks, "between two and three thousand lines, accurately near three thousand . . . namely 4 books, and a third of another." The time of composition had in fact been fourteen weeks, not ten, but Wordsworth's estimate is almost exact. His reference is to work within the new scheme, and (if we do not count the XIII–XI materials which he took largely ready-made, from the five-Book *Prelude*) he had since January written 1805 III–VI, plus I, 1–271—four Books, and rather more than one-third of another, totalling (if VI had at this stage the 705 lines of MS. A) 2,791 lines, which is indeed "accurately near three thousand." A similar figure would be reached if one assumed that Wordsworth regarded work on Book I as revision, and the "third" of a Book that he mentions was material already composed towards a seventh Book.

Of Books VII to X, only VIII can be dated with certainty. It belongs to October 1804, and its original form can to a large extent be reconstructed from MS. Y. The central section corresponded broadly to VIII, 75–661; "Whether the whistling kite" (MS. Drafts and Fragments, 4[b]) was included at 497–98, and "We live by admiration" (MS. Drafts and Fragments, 4[a]), was written for 158–74, but discarded during the original period of composition. It is not clear how the Book ended, but the probability is that it included the sequence that follows almost immediately in Y consisting of VIII, 824–59, leading through a version of XI, 9–14 to XII, 112–277. The opening of Book VIII consisted at this stage of the famous lines later transferred to VII, announcing the poet's return to work after the summer's pause: VII, 43–50 (which imply that 1–50 were originally present) lead in Y through a consecutive sequence of 54 lines later reworked as XIII, 334–67 and *Excursion*, II, 1–26, and on into the center of VIII. No passage in *The Prelude* is of greater chronological importance than these early lines. In VII, 1–13 Wordsworth looks back over the period of composition 1798–1804, confirming that there had been a gap between Parts I and II of 1799, and a long period of silence before work began on the five-Book *Prelude* in January 1804. Lines 17–48 provide the information that it is autumn, and that work has been shelved all summer. And the passage that follows contains references that are vital to a dating of Books IX and X:

> The last night's genial feeling overflows
> Upon this morning, *efficacious more*
> *By reason that my song must now return*
> *If she desert not her appointed path*
> *Back into Nature's bosom.*
>
> Since the time
> When with reluctance I withdrew from France
> The story hath demanded less regard
> To time and place; and where I lived, and how,
> Hath been no longer scrupulously traced.
>
> (VII, 49–50, XIII, 334–37,
> italicized lines not in 1805)

"When with reluctance I withdrew" refers to, and echoes, "In this frame of mind / Reluctantly to England I returned" at X, 188–89; and only the succeeding narrative in X can have been intended by the poet's reference to an account of life after his return, that had less regard to time and place. The second half of the Book (corresponding to 1850, XI) belongs in all probability to late November–December 1804, but a version of 1805, X, 1–566 must have existed in the early summer. Inevitably this implies the existence of a narrative corresponding to Book IX, describing Wordsworth's French experiences of 1791–92; and the fact that 294–555 once stood at the beginning of *MS. Y* is strong corroborative evidence that a version of IX had indeed been written early in the summer. In context this central section on Michel Beaupuy (IX, 294–555) has the look of an afterthought (see IX, 136n, below), and it is certainly not likely to have been written before lines 18–293. There is no means of dating *Vaudracour and Julia* (IX, 556–935), the completely separate episode that tells by implication the story of Wordsworth's love for Annette Vallon, but equally there is no reason to suppose that it is a later addition. The likelihood is that completion of Book VI in late April 1804 was followed by composition of IX, 18–293, 556–end, plus a version of X, 1–566, and that at a final stage ca. early June (or conceivably at the beginning of October) IX, 294–555 were inserted. To move on from describing unpolitical response to the Revolution in 1790, to an account of increasing awareness and final identification in 1791–94, might anyway seem natural; but there is also the interesting possibility that the two and a half French Books were composed in a single manuscript, now lost. Books I–V, VII, VIII, XI–XII are preserved in manuscripts that antedate the *Prelude* faircopies, A and B; no manuscript survives for VI, IX and X (or the latter part of XIII).

Book VII belongs almost certainly to November 1804. Wordsworth's treatment of his London experiences in *MS. Y* (October) implies very strongly that he has not yet decided to give them a Book in their own right, or to present them in a satirical context. In the original opening to VIII, partly quoted above, he attempts to gloss over the whole period, November 1792–September 1795, between returning from France and going to live at Racedown; in VIII, 689–706 we come suddenly on the poet's first entry into London; and in VIII, 824–59, XII, 112–22 (from the same long sequence in *MS. Y*) London is represented as part of the brotherhood of man, though VII is almost consistently a satire of disunity. On November 30 Wordsworth claimed to have written 1,600 or 1,700 lines during the recent period of composition, which would be a close approximation of Book VIII and related materials in *MS. Y*, plus the version of Book VII that stands in *MS. X*.

In fact, the probable sequence of *Prelude* work in autumn 1804 is: *October:* composition of VIII and related materials in *MS. Y. Late October–early November:* composition or reworking in *MS. X* of introduction to Book VI. *November:* composition in *MS. X* of Book VII, opening with lines that became finally VIII, 711–51 (VIII, 711–41, had been written in March for VI, 524–25; lines 742–51 are newly composed). Ca. *late November:* a new opening (lines 1–61) is written for Book VIII (Wordsworth's account of a country fair at Grasmere, linking back to Bartholomew Fair, VII, 649–95), the original opening is transferred to Book VII (as lines 1–50), and the original opening of VII is relegated to its final position as VIII, 711–51. *December:* composition of the latter part of X (567–end) as a separate Book. This last section, describing the period of rationalism and moral crisis, 1794–96, contains a reference to the Pope's coronation of Napoleon on December 2, 1802 (X, 930–33), and presumably accounts for the difference between Wordsworth's November 30 estimate of recent work (1,600 or 1,700 lines) and his "upwards of 2,000 verses" on Christmas Day.

Very little is known to have been written between Christmas 1804 and February 11, 1805, when the news of John Wordsworth's death reached Grasmere. A start may have been made on Book XI, but Wordsworth's major task at this period was probably consolidation. By April 11 he is back at work, "though not in the regular way," his thoughts being dominated by John. Then on May 1 he tells Beaumont that 300 lines have been added in the past week, and that two further Books will complete the poem. By ca. May 19, 1805 is finished, three quarters of Book XI and the whole of XII–XIII belonging apparently to the final month of composition.

The last three Books of 1805 are the shortest in the poem, and all contain much old material. Wordsworth had reserved, as his conclusion the great final section of the five-Book *Prelude*. The "spots of time" sequence, formerly the climax, is used earlier now (in Book XI), but the Ascent of Snowdon—more important than ever because of the new domi-ant role of imagination—retains its position as the opening of the last Book (XIII). Books XI and XII are preserved in MS. Z of April–May, headed respectively "Book 12th" and "Book 13th" because of the division of X. Book XI opens in the original copy at line 42, "This history, my friend, hath chiefly told . . ."; a consistent shorter version of lines 42–120 may well have been composed for the five-Book *Prelude*, and lines 123–388 formed the conclusion of the earlier poem (lines 257–315, 344–88 of course going back to 1799). Of Book XII Wordsworth had 200 lines to write in early May 1805—a little over half, lines 112–277 having been drafted at the end of MS. Y the previous October (probably for the original version of VIII). Lines 1–65 of Book XIII are drawn from the last section of the five-Book *Prelude*, and lines 74–165 are probably a revised and extended version of material in the earlier poem; at XIII, 236–40 and 334–67, ma-terial is included from MS. Y. Wordsworth's new work emphasizes in retro-spect the thematic and structural role of imagination, acknowledges the importance of Dorothy and then Coleridge in the years following the crisis of 1796, and concludes in tones of millennial aspiration that triumphantly recreate the final lines of 1799. As "prophets of Nature" Wordsworth and Coleridge will instruct their listeners "how the mind of man becomes / A thousand times more beautiful than the earth / On which he dwells," and becomes so because it is "Of substance and of fabric more divine" (XIII, 442–52).

iii. The Prelude *and* The Recluse, 1805–50

The thirteen-Book *Prelude* was finished ca. May 19, 1805, and copied November–February 1805-6, leaving Wordsworth once more free to write the main philosophical section of *The Recluse*, which alone could justify (during the poet's lifetime) publication of his autobiography. Wordsworth at Christmas 1805 was, according to Dorothy, "very anxious to get forward with The Recluse," and "reading for the nourishment of his mind, preparatory to beginning" (*EY*, p. 664). In the summer of 1806 he did complete *Home at Grasmere*, the first Book of the *Recluse*; but his task was mainly one of rationalization. Almost at once he seems to have turned back to the text of *The Prelude.* In November Joseph Farington reports that Wordsworth is "employed on a poem—*the progress of His own Mind*" (Greig, IV, p. 42); and ca. January 1807 comes what seems to be the earliest consistent revision of *The Prelude,* which takes account of certain suggestions by Coleridge preserved in *MS. B,* and almost certainly belongs to the time of Coleridge's reunion with the Wordsworths at Coleorton. No further revisions can be dated until those of 1816/19 that precede the transcription of *MS. C,* though no doubt Wordsworth did in that interval take the poem up from time to time. In the summer of 1808 he made a further attempt at the philosophical center of *The Recluse,* producing the rather desultory *Tuft of Primroses;* but the major achievement of these middle years was *The Excursion,* the narrative—or, in Wordsworth's terms, "dramatic"—section of *The Recluse,* which had been planned as early as 1804, and was founded on *The Ruined Cottage* of 1797–98.

Publication of *The Excursion* in 1814 left Wordsworth with the main philosophical section of *The Recluse* hardly begun. He could no longer hope that material would be provided by Coleridge, with whom he had quarreled, and was no closer himself to having a system to expound; yet he went out of his way to advertize the poem that for sixteen years he had been unable to write. Not only does he print with *The Excursion* a grandiose "Prospectus" to *The Recluse,* he effectively doubles what had been the intended scope of his yet unwritten work. In 1804 it had been clear that *The Prelude,* though the "least important," was one of the three sections of *The Recluse;* now, ten years later, it seems that it is merely introductory and not part of the major work at all. *The Excursion,* in which "something of a dramatic form [is] adopted," is now to be flanked by two "meditations in the Author's own Person," neither of which has yet been written. The first meditation is to be the main philosophical section; of the second we know nothing, except that it long continued to have an existence in the poet's own mind, and to increase the pressures he felt to be upon him.

Wordsworth's hopes and aspirations to carry on with *The Recluse* continue, and there is evidence in the shape of a new manuscript of his going back in 1812/16 to *Home at Grasmere* in an attempt to get ·under way; but once again we hear of the family's anxieties about the project, and, as in the period following the completion of 1805, there is ominous talk of the poet's reading for the nourishment of his mind. There can have been no significant work at this period on the main sections of *The Recluse;* instead we have the first of the three major revisions of *The Prelude. MS. A* is reworked extensively in 1816/19 (and certain areas of *B* as well) in preparation for a new faircopy, *C.* Drafted at this time are versions of 1850, VI, 420–88, on the desecration of the Grande Chartreuse, and 1850, VII, 512–43, "Genius of Burke!", this second passage strikingly at odds with Wordsworth's earlier political views. The mood of the 1820's is probably well represented by Dorothy's comments of December 1824— "My brother has not yet looked at *The Recluse;* he seems to feel the task so weighty that he shrinks from beginning with it * * * ." Then, at the end of 1831, Wordsworth makes one last attempt, going back yet again to *Home at Grasmere* and *The Tuft of Primroses,* and yet again turning from them to the poem that he had always found easier to write. "Father is particularly well," writes his daughter Dora in February 1832,

> and busier than 1000 bees. Mother and he work like slaves from morning to night—an arduous work—correcting a long Poem written thirty years back and which is not to be published during his life—The Growth of his own Mind—The ante-chapel as he calls it to *The Recluse*.
>
> (MS. University of California, Davis)

At some level Wordsworth had conceded that the main church to which *The Prelude* was ante-chapel would never be built—in 1836 *The Excursion* was reprinted without the words "Being a portion of THE RECLUSE" on the title—and from now on we see him lavishing on the subordinate poem the care that he hopes will make it sufficient in itself as his gift to posterity. *MS. D*, the result of Wordsworth and his wife working like slaves through the winter of 1832, contains only two structural changes—*Vaudracour and Julia* (*1805*, IX, 556–935), had been published separately in 1820, and disappears from the text, and Book X of *1805* is redivided, making a fourteen-Book poem—but is responsible for a large number of the minor revisions that give *1850* its characteristic tone. The manuscript has been very extensively corrected, and it is often not possible to distinguish between immediate revisions and the later ones of 1838/9 that led to the transcription of *E*, the final manuscript of *The Prelude*.

In May 1838 Wordsworth told an American visitor, George Ticknor, that in *The Recluse* "he had undertaken something beyond his powers to accomplish" (*Life, Letters and Journals* [Boston, 1876], II, p. 167); and very soon afterwards he started making *The Prelude* ready for posthumous publication. *MS. E*, the printer's copy, was transcribed by Dora and her friend Elizabeth Cookson in spring 1839. It contains a large number of errors, and though the poet reworked many passages, there seems to have been no consistent attempt to proof-read *E* against the final state of *D*. It is a fair assumption that all substantial revisions in *E* were made during Wordsworth's lifetime. Copy was sent to press very soon after his death on April 23, 1850. Proofs were read by Christopher Wordsworth (the poet's nephew), Edward Quillinan (the poet's son-in-law), and John Carter (Wordsworth's clerk for many years, and copyist in 1816/19 of *MS. C*). Christopher Wordsworth, senior partner in the enterprise, seems to have been responsible at least for most of the unwarranted changes that were introduced in proof and appear in the text of the first edition.

iv. 1850 versus 1805

The relation of 1850 to 1805 has been well summed up by Herbert Lindenberger:

> the later Wordsworth had forgotten much that the younger poet was trying to do in *The Prelude*. For one thing, in the process of tidying up stray phrases here and there, he had forgotten that much of the success of the poem—especially of the mystical passages and those of

inner turmoil—depends upon the conversational tone, the off-handedness, the struggle towards definition.

(On Wordsworth's "Prelude," pp. 297–98)

1850, IV, 323–28 provides an example:

Magnificent
The morning *rose*, in memorable pomp,
Glorious as e'er I had beheld—in front
The sea *lay* laughing at a distance; near,
The solid mountains *shone*, bright as the clouds,
Grain-tinctured, drenched in empyrean light.

Three times in the space of four lines Wordsworth has altered his original text to remove the verb *to be*. To de Selincourt in 1926 these changes seemed clearly an improvement; now surely the matter is open to question. There is an elemental strength, unvivid perhaps, but very sure, about "Magnificent / The morning *was*." When he changed it, Wordsworth had forgotten the former self who wrote of the Leech Gatherer in June 1802: " 'A lonely place, a Pond' 'by which an old man *was*, far from all house or home'—not stood, not sat, but '*was*'—the figure presented in the most naked simplicity possible" (*EY*, p. 366; Wordsworth's italics).

1850 is a more formal poem than 1805, frequently tighter in syntax, but seldom more accurately reflecting the thought processes it had been Wordsworth's original intention to evoke. The diction is weightier, and there is more pomposity, far more poeticism. The alpine shepherd of 1805, VIII, 381, "springs up with a bound, and then away!," in 1850 he can do nothing so simple:

Then from his couch he starts; and now his feet
Crush out a livelier fragrance from the flowers
Of lowly thyme, by Nature's skill enwrought
In the wild turf.

(1850, VIII, 241–44)

A few majestic lines appear for the first time—Newton's statue as

The marble index of a mind for ever
Voyaging through strange seas of Thought alone . . .

(1850, III, 62–63)

and "Clothed in the sunshine of the withering fern" (1850, VI, 11)—but far more often sound has been deadened, neatness achieved at the expense of spontaneity and strength. None of the great characteristically Wordsworthian early passages gains in power, and some lose disastrously; compare 1805, XIII, 41–73 for instance, in the Ascent of Snowdon, with 1850, XIV, 40–77. In terms of content there is of course a movement in 1850 towards orthodoxy and Victorian proprieties, but too much can be made of Wordsworth's later conservatism; he was not an unthinking apostate, not the "Lost Leader" of Browning's poem. His vision never became typical of the age—he was prepared, for instance, despite his brother's position as head of a Cambridge college, to leave the wonderful description of Cambridge dons as "grave Elders, men unscoured, grotesque / In character, tricked out like aged trees" (1850, III, 545–56)—and it is doubtful if he ever rejected his pantheist and near-pantheist beliefs of 1798–1805. He came to see them, however, in a new context; and he became increasingly self-conscious about how such beliefs might seem to the orthodox. The result is countless little fudgings, insertions of reassuring Christian reference. Man now is "born / Of dust, and kindred to the worm" (1850, VIII, 487–88); he is prompted to worship not by instinctive feeling—

> I worshipped then among the depth of things
> As my soul bade me . . .
>
> (1805, XI, 233–34)

—but by duty to institutionalized religion:

> Worshipping then among the depth of things
> As piety ordained.
>
> (1850, XII, 184–85)

The last word may fittingly be given to de Selincourt:

> The revised *Prelude* represents another, less independent creed. The position into which he had now withdrawn was not for him a false position. He was sincere, now as ever. But if he was conscious of a change, as it is abundantly clear that he was, he would surely have done better to leave as it stood what he had first written for Coleridge, and, instead of disguising his former faith, to have expounded in a book of *The Recluse*, or elsewhere, the reasons that led him to move from it, and the manner in which it could be reconciled with the tenets of an historic Church.
>
> (*Oxford "Prelude,"* p. lxxiv)

Note on the Text of 1805

Two copies of 1805 were made between November 1805 and February 1806, MS. A by Dorothy Wordsworth, MS. B by Mary. The relationship of the two manuscripts is by no means simple, but as with V and U of 1799 —and, one may infer, with the two early versions of 1805, I–V, Dorothy's text (now missing) and Mary's MS. M—it appears that Dorothy's copy was more carefully transcribed, received more attention from the poet in terms of subsequent correction, and is in general the more authoritative. MS. B, though incorporating as base text many of the corrections in A, and, more surprisingly, containing a number of wholly independent readings, has also a far higher proportion than A of uncorrected errors; and it was significantly from A, not B, that MS. C was transcribed in 1816/19. B is of great importance, but in some sense outside the mainstream of *Prelude* manuscripts. It has been used in this volume as a means of checking and dating corrections in A, and its independent readings have been noted where they seem of sufficient interest, but with a single exception (mentioned below) they have not been included in the text.

The original faircopy of MS. A cannot be retrieved, as the early corrections were made by Dorothy over erasure; in fact it can never have existed as a totality, because the first revisions were entered long before the manuscript was complete. The text presented above is that of MS. A as it may be presumed to have stood after the immediate corrections of 1805–6. Emendations made by Dorothy over erasure are undoubtedly early, and have been accepted even where—as in "strain" for "stream" at VII, 10—later revisions return to the original reading. Corrections made in the hand of the poet himself have been accepted where an early date is confirmed by their appearance over erasure in the original faircopy, or in MS. B. In certain other cases, reference to a previous manuscript establishes that inserted words or lines had been omitted in error (or because the poet was temporarily seeking an alternative). No doubt further changes in MSS. A and B belong to this earliest period, but no sure means exists of identifying them. Corrections made by the original copyist during transcription are normally easy to identify, and have been silently accepted.

At II, 246 and VII, 275 it has been necessary to fill gaps left in MS. A from, respectively, MS. M and MS. X. On five occasions—at VIII, 758; X, 230, 248, 715; XI, 216—changes involving a single word have been accepted (with no guarantee that they belong to the early period) because they make up defective lines. At IV, 148 "weariness" has been preferred to "weakness," and at IX, 187 "Rhine" to "Loire," because the original readings derive almost certainly from copyist's errors; at XII, 242 the correction "faith" has been accepted because it removes a repetition of "hope" three lines before; and at VI, 170 the B reading "isle" is preferred on the grounds that "island" in A creates a hypermetrical (and ugly) line that is unlikely to have been intended. A case of especial textual interest is noted at XI, 259.

As with the text of 1799, punctuation and capitalization are editorial; the original spelling has been retained except in a very few cases that show, or might create, confusion: "peeling" for "pealing" at III, 322, "wrapped" for "rapt" at IV, 153.

Note on the Printed Text of 1850

The 1850 text presented above is the result of collating the first edition of *The Prelude* with the printer's copy, MS E, to remove misprints, misreadings, and the sixty-odd changes of varying importance made by Wordsworth's executors. It has been assumed, for reasons given above, that revisions in MS. E were made either by the poet or by a copyist working from his dictation, and except in a very few cases—where readings are so faint as to make it probable that they were erased, or where drafts seem never to have been fitted into the base text—the latest corrections have been taken to represent Wordsworth's final intentions, despite the fact that in many cases the original reading was not erased. (The danger of this assumption—which cannot be avoided—is that certain of the corrections accepted as second thoughts will be cases in which Wordsworth was not in fact clear which reading he preferred.) MS. E, where unrevised, has no textual authority in cases where it differs from the final state of MS. D, from which it was transcribed, and D has therefore been used as a further check on the printed version. On three occasions, it has been assumed that *D* too incorporates mistranscription, "whencesoever" and "eclipsed" (VII, 307, 500) being supplied from MS. *C*, and "light" in X, 365 from MS. *A*.

Changes made by Wordsworth's executors that involve significant rewriting are noted at I, 6, 617; II, 342; XI, 343, 358; XIII, 144; and XIV, 185–87; a dozen similar cases involving mainly a single word—"famous" for Wordsworth's "froward," at IV, 51, for example—have been silently corrected. At XI, 388–90 lines were reordered for no apparent reason; at XIV, 359–60 two lines were omitted; and at IV, 352–53 and XIII, 143–44 single lines were included even though they had certainly been cut by the poet himself—these last being among ten instances in which the executors showed an arbitrary preference for an earlier manuscript state. At VII, 752 serious misunderstanding by the executors of Wordsworth's syntax has had to be corrected. Of the remaining intrusions, the majority show an urge to tidy up grammar, spelling, and meter.

One particularly difficult case, in which the executors' decision has been accepted, is the opening of Book V, where lines 1–11a were reinstated in proof, after having been crossed out in MS. *D* and omitted in *E*. It is possible that the lines were left out of *E* by mistake, but immediately above the altered opening is written the word "Reviewed," implying presumably that the poet had seen and authorized the cut-down version. There is evidence, however, that at a still later stage Wordsworth went back and revised the opening lines in *D*; and it may have been the existence of these final reworkings that led his executors to reinstate the passage. On balance, perhaps they were right to do so.

Punctuation of the first edition has been retained except in cases where the poet's intention is clearly misrepresented. Fifty-five of these have been silently corrected on the authority of the manuscripts (normally in fact of MS. *D*, which was punctuated with considerable care); changes at IV, 339 and XI, 331–32 have been noted; and others made (with confidence) at V, 169, 517–18; VII, 196 and XI, 11–12, 31.

Context and
Reception

References to The Prelude
in Process: 1799-1850

Almost to the end of his life Wordsworth regarded *The Prelude* as a merely subordinate part of his great philosophical work, *The Recluse*. There could, he declared in 1805, be no question of publishing such an egocentric poem during his lifetime unless *The Recluse* had been completed. As a result of this decision, *The Prelude* lay in manuscript until after his death in 1850, and was known only to his family and closest friends. References to the circumstances of its composition and to its development over the years are found either within the poem itself, or in letters of the poet and members of his circle. The list presented below is not inclusive, but contains those references that are most significant from a scholarly point of view, or that tell us most about Wordsworth's own changing attitude to his poem.

1. The Two-Part *Prelude* of 1799

Coleridge to Wordsworth, October 12, 1799:

I long to see what you have been doing. O let it be the tail-piece of 'The Recluse!',[1] for of nothing but 'The Recluse' can I hear patiently. That it is to be addressed to me makes me more desirous that it should not be a poem of itself. To be addressed, as a beloved man, by a thinker, at the close of such a poem as 'The Recluse', a poem *non unius populi*,[2] is the only event, I believe, capable of inciting in me an hour's vanity—vanity, nay, it is too good a feeling to be so called; it would indeed be a self-elevation produced *ab extra*.[3]

(Griggs, I, p. 538)

Coleridge Notebooks, January 4, 1804:

in the highest and outermost of Grasmere Wordsworth read to me the second Part of his divine Self-biography * * *[4]

(I, entry 1801)

---

1. On *The Recluse* see Composition and Texts: *1799*, Introduction, above.
2. Literally, "not of one people"; Coleridge means that *The Recluse* will not be limited to a single audience, but be for all time.
3. "From without."
4. At this stage Wordsworth had probably made little progress in adding a third Part to *1799*; see Composition and

Coleridge to Lady Beaumont,[5] *March 26, 1804:*

I have left your Ladyship the two first Parts of the biographical, or philosophico-biographical Poem to be prefixed or annexed to the Recluse: your Ladyship may perhaps wish to *look* them over.[6]

(Griggs, II, p. 1104)

2. Evidence of Work Towards an Extended Version of 1799

Dorothy Wordsworth's Journal, December 26, 1801:

Wm wrote part of the poem to Coleridge.

December 27, 1801:

Mary wrote some lines of the 3ᵈ part of Wm's poem, which he brought to read to us when we came home.

Dorothy Wordsworth to Catherine Clarkson,[7] *March 25, 1804:*

A great addition to the poem on my Brother's life he has made since C. left us [January 14], 1500 Lines; and since we parted from you [mid-July 1803] a still greater—he has also written a few small poems.

(EY, p. 459)

3. Evidence of Work Towards a Five-Book *Prelude*

Wordsworth to Wrangham,[8] *January 24–February 7, 1804:*

I have great things in meditation, but as yet I have only been doing little ones. At present I am engaged in a Poem on my own earlier life which will take five parts or books to complete, three of which are nearly finished.

(EY, p. 436)

Texts: *1799*, Introduction, above. Coleridge was seriously ill, and en route for the Mediterranean in search of a drier climate. In the circumstances, Part II, which recalled an earlier leave-taking between the two poets and concluded in a reaffirmation of their shared ideals (*1799*, II, 496–514), would have been specially appropriate reading.

5. Wife of Sir George Beaumont (1753–1827), friend of Coleridge and Wordsworth, and influential patron of the arts.

6. Coleridge had just been sent a copy of the first five Books of *1805* (MS. M) to take with him to Malta, and apparently decided to leave behind his text of *1799*. The manuscript in question has disappeared.

7. Close friend of Dorothy Wordsworth, and wife of Thomas Clarkson (1760–1846), who with William Wilberforce was chiefly instrumental in bringing about the abolition of the British slave trade in 1807.

8. Francis Wrangham (1769–1842) had collaborated with Wordsworth in 1795–96 in his attempted *Imitations of Juvenal.*

Dorothy Wordsworth to Catherine Clarkson, February 13, 1804:

William * * * is chearfully engaged in composition, and goes on with great rapidity. He is writing the Poem on his own early life which is to be an appendix to the Recluse. He walks out every morning, generally alone, and brings us in a large treat almost every time he goes.

(EY, p. 440)

Wordsworth to Hazlitt, ⁹ March 5, 1804:

I have been tolerably busy this last month, having written about 1,200 Lines of the Poem on my own life.

(EY, p. 447)

Wordsworth to Coleridge, March 6, 1804:

I finished five or six days ago another Book of my Poem, amounting to 650 lines. And now I am positively arrived at the subject I spoke of in my last. When this next book is done, which I shall begin in two or three days time, I shall consider the work as finished. Farewell.

I am very anxious to have your notes for the Recluse. I cannot say how much importance I attach to this * * *

(EY, pp. 448–51, 452)

4. Development Leading to the Thirteen-Book
Prelude of 1805

Wordsworth to De Quincey,¹ March 6, 1804:

I am now writing a Poem on my own earlier life; and have just finished that part in which I speak of my residence at the University. * * * This Poem will not be published these many years, and never during my lifetime, till I have finished a larger and more important work to which it is tributary. Of this larger work [*The Recluse*] I have written one Book and several scattered fragments: it is a moral and Philosophical Poem; the subject whatever I find most interesting in Nature, Man, Society, most adapted to Poetic illustration. To this work I mean to devote the Prime of my life and the chief force of my mind. I have also arranged the plan of a narrative Poem [*The Excursion*]. And if I live to finish these three principal

9. William Hazlitt (1778–1830) met Wordsworth as early as June 1798 when he visited Coleridge at Nether Stowey (see *My First Acquaintance with Poets*, 1823), but never became a close friend.
1. Thomas De Quincey (1785–1859), whose *Confessions of An English Opium-Eater* (1821) is the single literary work to be influenced by *The Prelude* before its publication in 1850, had first written to Wordsworth in May 1803 at the age of seventeen.

works I shall be content. That on my own life, the least important of the three, is better [than] half complete: viz 4 Books amounting to about 2500 lines.

(EY, p. 454)

Dorothy Wordsworth to Catherine Clarkson, March 25, 1804:

We have been engaged, Mary and I, in making a complete copy of William's Poems for poor Coleridge, to be his companions in Italy. * * * The last pacquet we sent off would arrive in London, as we now learn, three days before his departure. * * * A great addition to the poem on my Brother's life he has made since C. left us, 1500 Lines * * *

(EY, pp. 458–59)[2]

Wordsworth to Sharp,[3] April 29, 1804:

I have been very busy these last 10 weeks, [having] written between two and three thousand lines, accurately near three thousand, in that time, namely 4 books, and a third of another, of the Poem, which I believe I mentioned to you, on my own early life. I am at present in the 7th book of this work, which will turn out far longer than I ever dreamt of: it seems a frightful deal to say about one's self, and of course will never be published (during my lifetime, I mean), till another work [*The Recluse*] has been written and published, of sufficient importance to justify me in giving my own history to the world.

(EY, p. 470)

Dorothy Wordsworth to Lady Beaumont, May 25, 1804:

You will rejoice to hear that [William] has gone on regularly, I may say rapidly, with the poem of which Coleridge shewed you a part. * * * In wet weather he takes out an umbrella, chuses the most sheltered spot, and there walks backwards and forwards; and though the length of his walk be sometimes a quarter or half of a mile, he is as fast bound within the chosen limits as if by prison walls. He generally composes his verses out of doors, and while he is so engaged he seldom knows how the time slips away, or hardly whether it is rain or fair.

(EY, p. 477)

2. Dorothy thought Coleridge to have left England on March 21 or 22. He had left Grasmere on January 14. See also Griggs, II, pp. 1065, 1094–95, 1096–97, 1115.

3. Richard Sharp (1759–1835), conversationalist and friend since June 1801 of both Wordsworth and Coleridge.

Prelude *address to Coleridge, early October 1804:*

> Five years[4] are vanished since I first poured out,
> Saluted by that animating breeze
> Which met me issuing from the city's walls,
> A glad preamble to this verse. I sang
> Aloud in dithyrambic fervour, deep
> But short-lived uproar. * * *
>
> But 'twas not long
> Ere the interrupted strain broke forth once more,
> And flowed awhile in strength; then stopped for years—
> Not heard again until a little space
> Before last primrose-time.
> * * * slowly doth this work advance.
> Through the whole summer have I been at rest,
> Partly from voluntary holiday
> And part through outward hindrance.
>
> (1805, VII, 1–6, 9–13, 17–20)

Wordsworth to Sir George Beaumont, December 25, 1804:

You will be pleased to hear that I have been advancing with my Work: I have written upwards of 2,000 verses during the last ten weeks. I do not know if you are exactly acquainted with the plan of my poetical labours; it is twofold, first a Poem to be called, *The Recluse*, in which it will be my object to express in verse my most interesting feelings concerning Man, Nature, and society; and next, a Poem (in which I am at present chiefly engaged) on my earlier life, or the growth of my own mind, taken up upon a large scale; this latter work I expect to have finished before the Month of May; and then I purpose to fall with all my might on the former, which is the chief object upon which my thoughts have been fixed these many years.

(EY, pp. 517–18)

Dorothy Wordsworth to Lady Beaumont, April 11, 1805:

It will give you great pleasure to hear that my Brother has resumed his old employments, having taken up again the Task of his life, though not in the regular way. Till he has unburthened his heart of its feelings on our loss he cannot go on with other things, and it does him good to speak of John as he was, therefore he is now writing a poem upon him. * * * I doubt not, when this labour of love is finished, that he will go on with more firmness and devotion than he has ever yet done * * *

(EY, p. 576)

---

4. See note to *1805/1850*, VII, 1.

Wordsworth to Sir George Beaumont, May 1, 1805:

Unable to proceed with this work [an elegy on his brother John],
I turned my thoughts again to the Poem on my own life, and you
will be glad to hear that I have added 300 lines to it in the course
of last week. Two Books more will conclude it. It will not be much
less than 9,000 lines * * * an alarming length! and a thing unprecedented in Literary history that a man should talk so much
about himself. It is not self-conceit, as you will know well, that has
induced [me] to do this, but real humility: I began the work because I was unprepared to treat any more arduous subject, and
diffident of my own powers. Here at least I hoped that to a certain
degree I should be sure of succeeding, as I had nothing to do but
describe what I had felt and thought, therefore could not easily be
bewildered. This might certainly have been done in narrower compass by a man of more address, but I have done my best. If when
the work shall be finished it appears to the judicious to have re-
dundancies they shall be lopped off, if possible. But this is very
difficult to do when a man has written with thought, and this
defect, whenever I have suspected it or found it to exist in any
writings of mine, I have always found incurable. The fault lies too
deep, and is in the first conception.

(EY, pp. 586–87)

Wordsworth to Sir George Beaumont, June 3, 1805:

I have the pleasure to say that I finished my Poem about a fortnight
ago. I had looked forward to the day as a most happy one; and I
was indeed grateful to God for giving me life to complete the work,
such as it is; but it was not a happy day for me—I was dejected on
many accounts; when I looked back upon the performance it seemed
to have a dead weight about it, the reality so far short of the expectation; it was the first long labour that I had finished, and the
doubt whether I should ever live to write the Recluse, and the sense
which I had of this Poem being so far below what I seemed capable
of executing, depressed me much: above all, many heavy thoughts
of my poor departed Brother hung upon me; the joy which I should
have had in shewing him the Manuscript, and a thousand other
vain fancies and dreams. I have spoken of this because it was a state
of feeling new to me, the occasion being new. This work may be
considered as a sort of portico to the Recluse, part of the same
building, which I hope to be able erelong to begin with, in earnest;
and if I am permitted to bring it to conclusion, and to write, further, a narrative Poem of the Epic kind, I shall consider the *task*
of my life as over.

(EY, pp. 594–95)

5. *The Prelude*, 1805–50

Dorothy Wordsworth to Lady Beaumont, November 29, 1805:

I am now engaged in making a fair and final transcript of the Poem on his own Life. I mean *final*, till it is prepared for the press, which will not be for many years. No doubt before that time he will, either from the suggestions of his Friends or his own or both have some alterations to make, but it appears to us at present to be finished.

(EY, p. 650)

Dorothy Wordsworth to Lady Beaumont, December 26, 1805:

I have transcribed two thirds of the Poem addressed to Coleridge, and am far more than pleased with it as I go along. * * * He is very anxious to get forward with The Recluse, and is reading for the nourishment of his mind, preparatory to beginning; but I do not think he will be able to do much more till we have heard of Coleridge.

(EY, p. 664)

Wordsworth, Preface to The Excursion, *1814:*

It may be proper to state whence the Poem, of which The Excursion is a part, derives its Title of THE RECLUSE—Several years ago, when the Author retired to his native Mountains, with the hope of being enabled to construct a literary Work that might live, it was a reasonable thing that he should take a review of his own Mind, and examine how far Nature and Education had qualified him for such employment. As subsidiary to this preparation, he undertook to record, in Verse, the origin and progress of his own powers, as far as he was acquainted with them. That Work, addressed to a dear Friend, most distinguished for his knowledge and genius, and to whom the Author's Intellect is deeply indebted, has been long finished; and the result of the investigation which gave rise to it was a determination to compose a philosophical Poem, containing views of Man, Nature, and Society; and to be entitled, The Recluse; as having for its principal subject the sensations and opinions of a Poet living in retirement.—The preparatory Poem is biographical, and conducts the history of the Author's mind to the point when he was emboldened to hope that his faculties were sufficiently matured for entering upon the arduous labour which he had proposed to himself; and the two Works have the same kind of relation to each other, if he may so express himself, as the Anti-chapel [*sic*] has to the body of a gothic church.

Dorothy Wordsworth to Mrs. Clarkson, March 27, 1821:

William is quite well, and very busy, though he has not looked at *The Recluse* or the poem on his own life; and this disturbs us. After fifty years of age there is no time to spare, and unfinished works should not, if it be possible, be left behind. This he feels, but the will never governs *his* labours. How different from Southey, who can go as regularly as clockwork, from history to poetry, from poetry to criticism, and so on to biography, or anything else. If their minds could each spare a little to the other, how much better for both!

(LY, I, p. 28)

Dora Wordsworth to Maria Kinnaird, February 17, 1832:

Father is particularly well and busier than 1000 bees. Mother and he work like slaves from morning to night—an arduous work— correcting a long Poem written thirty years back and which is not to be published during his life—'The Growth of his own Mind'— The 'ante-chapel' as he calls it to the 'Recluse'.

(MS. University of California, Davis)

Christopher Wordsworth to Christopher Wordsworth, Jr.,[5]
April 18, 1832:

They were very loath to part with him [John, brother to Christopher Jr.] at Rydal for he has been of great value to all the family—more especially to your uncle—who having John to talk to in his walks, was very industrious through the whole winter at all other times of the day—and worked very hard, especially in the revising and finishing of his long autobiographic poem * * *

(B.M. Add. MSS. 46137)

Isabella Fenwick[6] to Henry Taylor, June 29, 1838:

From time to time I have heard portions of that marvellous work of his which is to appear when he ceases to be, and I am to hear it all * * *

(*Correspondence of Henry Taylor,* pp. 86–87)

---

5. The poet's brother Christopher (1774–1846), Master of Trinity College, Cambridge, writing to his son (1807–85), author of *Memoirs of William Wordsworth* (1851), and later Bishop of Lincoln.

6. First visited Rydal Mount in 1833, aged fifty. Close friend of Wordsworth's later years, and transcriber of the "Fenwick Notes" on his poetry (1843).

Isabella Fenwick to Henry Taylor, August 18, 1838:

I have had so much to interest me the last two months that I have taken little heed of the weather. * * * Some interruption there has been to my enjoyment the last ten days from an attack of illness this dear great man here has had, almost, I believe, the only one he has ever had. * * * Every day that I am with him I am more and more struck with the *truth* of his writings; they are from the abundance of his heart; yet (as he said last night) how small a portion of what he has felt or thought has he been able to reveal to the world; and he will leave it, his tale still untold. His illness has been an interruption to his continuing to read to me his unpublished poetry; indeed, without this illness, he is so beset with visitors at this season that he has very little leisure time. Some days there are in the course of the day between twenty and thirty people at the Mount. * * * Now that he is well again, I may hear 'how his heart was nursed in genuine freedom,' and 'how his immortal spirit was built up.' * * *

The beloved old poet has again begun to read me his MS., so in time I hope to hear it all. You will read it in time, my dear cousin, but I fear you may never *hear* that 'song divine of high and passionate thoughts, to their own music chanted,'[7] as I have heard it. It was almost too much emotion for me to see and hear this fervent old man, the passionate feelings of his youth all come back to him, making audible this 'linked lay of truth.' * * * He has been working hard this last month at this poem, that he may leave it in a state fit for publication so far as it is written—that is, fifteen books. May God grant him life to write many more! He seems still to have a great power of working; he can apply himself five, six, or seven hours a day to composition, and yet be able to converse all the evening.

(*Correspondence of Henry Taylor,* pp. 93–97)

Isabella Fenwick to Henry Taylor, March 28, 1839:

Our journey was postponed for a week, that the beloved old poet might accomplish the work that he had in hand, the revising of his grand autobiographical poem, and leaving it in a state fit for publication. At this he has been labouring for the last month, seldom less than six or seven hours in the day, or rather one ought to say the whole day, for it seemed always in his mind—quite a possession; and much, I believe, he has done to it, expanding it in some parts, retrenching it in others, and perfecting it in all. * * * Nothing

---

7. From Coleridge's "To William Wordsworth," lines 46–47, written after he had heard Wordsworth read *The Prelude* aloud in January, 1807.

appears more remarkable to me in him than the constant and firm persuasion of his own *greatness*, which maintained itself through neglect and ridicule and contempt, and when in devoting himself to that culture which he conceived best adapted to it he encountered a life of poverty and obscurity, and must have incurred the censure of his friends, as leading a life of idleness originating in self-conceit and vanity. And yet who in all other things desires sympathy more earnestly, or is more sensible to praise? The other evening I was peculiarly struck by his sensibility on this point, and I cannot forbear giving you the little trait. On his arrival I saw something had occurred which had delighted him exceedingly. He had appeared quite radiant with joy, and I told him I saw that he had been very successful in his morning's work; he said he had indeed, and that he was sure that he had never done better in his life, and then he continued: 'And I must tell you what Mary said when I was dictating to her this morning' (she always writes for him). ' "Well, William, I declare you are cleverer than ever",' and the tears started into his eyes, and he added: 'It is not often I have had such praise; she has always been sparing of it.'

(*Correspondence of Henry Taylor*, pp. 117–18)

Wordsworth to Thomas Noon Talfourd, April 11, 1839:

in the year 1805, I concluded a long poem upon the formation of my own mind, a small part of which you saw in manuscript, when I had the pleasure of a visit from you at Rydal. That book still exists in manuscript. Its publication has been prevented merely by the personal character of the subject.

(LY, II, p. 969)

Wordsworth to Aubrey de Vere, November 16, 1842:

You enquire after my MS. poem on my own life. It is lying, and in all probability will lie, where my 'Tragedy' [*The Borderers*, publ. 1842] and other 'Poems' lay ambushed for more than a generation of years.

(LY, III, pp. 1386–87)

Edward Moxon to John Carter, June 7, 1850:[8]

With this you will receive proofs of the first 4 sheets of Mr. Wordsworth's unpublished Poem. Proofs, together with the copy, have also been sent to Dr. Wordsworth [Christopher, Jr.]. I shall be glad to hear that you and Mrs. Wordsworth approve of the size, type, etc. The entire Poem will make about 380 pages.

(D.C. Papers)

8. Wordsworth had died on April 23, 1850.

Edward Quillinan's Diary, June 10, 1850:

Revised first six sheets of Wordsworth's posthumous Poem 'Growth of the Poet's Mind', at Mrs. W's request.

(D.C. Papers)

Christopher Wordsworth, Jr., to Joshua Watson, June 14, 1850:

Susan and I are at the Mount: we found my Aunt in her usual placid state of mind, and with her cousin and sister-in-Law Mrs Hutchinson, and Miss Fenwick: and as an occasional guest Mr Carter, who was for many years my Uncle's assistant and right-hand in the Stamp Office, and is now invaluable in all matters of business, and also in literary matters, to the Poet's Widow.

My first duty here is conjointly with Mr. Carter and Mr. Quillinan to prepare the posthumous Poem for publication, I mean so far as revising the Proof Sheets is concerned; for it was left ready for the Press by the Author. It consists of 14 Books, and gives the history of the growth of the Poet's mind from childhood to the time of the Publication of the Lyrical Ballads: it will appear in about a month's time.

(B.M. Add. MS. 46137)

Edward Quillinan's Diary, July 9, 1850:

Finished the Revisal of 'The Prelude or Growth of a Poet's Mind'—the last proof this day, having as well as Dr. C[hristopher] W[ordsworth] & Mr. Carter revised the whole carefully.

(D.C. Papers)

Christopher Wordsworth, Jr., 1851:

Its title, 'The Prelude', had not been fixed on by the author himself: the Poem remained anonymous till his death. The present title has been prefixed to it at the suggestion of the beloved partner of his life, and the best interpreter of his thoughts,[9] from considerations of its tentative and preliminary character. Obviously it would have been desirable to mark its relation to 'The Recluse' by some analogous appellation; but this could not easily be done, at the same time that its other essential characteristics were indicated, Besides, the appearance of this poem, *after* the author's death, might tend to lead some readers into an opinion that it was his *final* production, instead of being, as it really is, one of his *earlier* works. They were to be guarded against this supposition. Hence a name has been adopted, which may serve to keep the true nature and

9. I.e., Wordsworth's wife, Mary.

position of the poem constantly before the eye of the reader; and "THE PRELUDE" will now be perused and estimated with the feelings properly due to its preparatory character, and to the period at which it was composed.

(*Memoirs,* I, p. 313)

The Early Reception

Coleridge's ode "To W. Wordsworth" was written in early January, 1807, just after Coleridge had heard his friend read *The Prelude* aloud during the evenings of almost two weeks. Of the comments reprinted in this section, this and De Quincey's are the only ones written in response to the MS. version of *The Prelude* that Wordsworth completed in 1805. Of the other comments all but the last two are by reviewers and individual readers of the first published version of *The Prelude*, when it was issued in 1850, forty-five years after its original composition and three months after Wordsworth's death. These estimates of the poem express the views of mid-Victorian readers who, although they take for granted Wordsworth's greatness, look upon *The Prelude* as a poetic relic which does not speak directly to the tastes and concerns of their own time; they do not allow it to alter the prior conceptions of Wordsworth as a poet which they had based on his shorter poems and on *The Excursion*.* The selection from Matthew Arnold shows that, so late as 1879, Arnold's influential estimate of Wordsworth as an uncomplicated poet of nature and of "the simple primary affections and duties," is grounded entirely on his lyrics and shorter narrative poems. Not until A. C. Bradley's essay (published in 1909, but delivered in a course of lectures in 1903), do we find *The Prelude* put at the center of Wordsworth's achievement. Bradley develops a brilliant sketch of Wordsworth as most of us read him today—a visionary poet who indeed celebrates nature and the elemental feelings, yet is deeply aware of the paradoxes and anguish of the human lot in this world.

* See Herbert Lindenberger, "The Reception of *The Prelude*," *Bulletin of the* *New York Public Library*, LXIV (1960), 196–208.

SAMUEL TAYLOR COLERIDGE

To William Wordsworth†

LINES COMPOSED, FOR THE GREATER PART ON THE NIGHT,

ON WHICH HE FINISHED THE RECITATION OF HIS POEM

(IN THIRTEEN BOOKS) CONCERNING THE GROWTH

AND HISTORY OF HIS OWN MIND

Jan^{ry}, 1807. Cole-orton, near Ashby de la Zouch.

O FRIEND! O Teacher! God's great Gift to me!
Into my heart have I receiv'd that Lay
More than historic, that prophetic Lay,
Wherein (high theme by Thee first sung aright)
Of the Foundations and the Building-up   5
Of thy own Spirit, thou hast lov'd to tell
What may be told to th' understanding mind
Revealable; and what within the mind
May rise enkindled. Theme as hard as high!
Of Smiles spontaneous, and mysterious Fear;   10
(The First-born they of Reason, and Twin-birth)
Of Tides obedient to external Force,
And Currents self-determin'd, as might seem,
Or by interior Power: of Moments aweful.
Now in thy hidden Life; and now abroad,   15
Mid festive Crowds, *thy* Brows too garlanded,
A Brother of the Feast: of Fancies fair,
Hyblæan[1] Murmurs of poetic Thought,
Industrious in its Joy, by lilied Streams
Native or outland, Lakes and famous Hills!   20
Of more than Fancy, of the Hope of Man
Amid the tremor of a Realm aglow—
Where France in all her Towns lay vibrating,
Ev'n as a Bark becalm'd on sultry seas

---

† The standard text of this poem, as printed by E. H. Coleridge, editor, *The Complete Poetical Works of Samuel Taylor Coleridge* (Oxford, 1912), is based on the version printed in the Pickering edition of Coleridge's *Poetical Works* (1834). The version here reproduced is transcribed (with permission of the trustees) from a MS., now in the Dove Cottage Library, which Coleridge sent to William Wordsworth; it was reprinted, with some errors of transcription, in appendix I of E. H. Coleridge's edition of *The Complete Poetical Works*. This version is the closest we can come to the poem Coleridge wrote down just after hearing *The Prelude* read aloud. It is a remarkably insightful comment on, as well as a personal response to, the crucial events and major themes of the work which in 1807 was still called "the poem to Coleridge."

1. Honeyed; Hybla, in ancient Sicily, was noted for its honey.

Beneath the voice from Heaven, the bursting Crash   25
Of Heaven's immediate thunder! when no Cloud
Is visible, or Shadow on the Main!
Ah! soon night roll'd on night, and every Cloud
Open'd its eye of Fire: and Hope aloft
Now flutter'd, and now toss'd upon the Storm   30
Floating! Of Hope afflicted, and struck down,
Thence summon'd homeward—homeward to thy Heart,
Oft from the Watch-tower of Man's absolute Self,
With Light unwaning on her eyes, to look
Far on—herself a Glory to behold,   35
The Angel of the Vision![2] Then (last strain!)
Of *Duty*, chosen Laws controlling choice,
Virtue and Love! An Orphic[3] Tale indeed,
A Tale divine of high and passionate Thoughts
To their own music chaunted!

                Ah great Bard!   40
Ere yet that last Swell dying aw'd the Air,
With stedfast ken I view'd thee in the Choir
Of ever-enduring Men. The truly Great
Have all one Age, and from one visible space
Shed influence: for they, both power and act,   45
Are permanent, and Time is not with them,
Save as it worketh for them, they in it.
Nor less a sacred Roll, than those of old,
And to be plac'd, as they, with gradual fame
Among the Archives of mankind, thy Work   50
Makes audible a linked Song of Truth.
Of Truth profound a sweet continuous Song
Not learnt, but native, her own natural notes!
Dear shall it be to every human Heart.
To me how more than dearest! Me, on whom   55
Comfort from Thee and utterance of thy Love
Came with such heights and depths of Harmony
Such sense of Wings uplifting, that the Storm
Scatter'd and whirl'd me, till my Thoughts became
A bodily Tumult! and thy faithful Hopes,   60
Thy Hopes of me, dear Friend! by me unfelt
Were troubles to me, almost as a Voice
Familiar once and more than musical
To one cast forth, whose hope had seem'd to die,
A Wanderer with a worn-out heart,   65
Mid Strangers pining with untended Wounds!

O Friend! too well thou know'st, of what sad years
The long suppression had benumm'd my soul,

---

2. Probably an allusion to "the great vision of the guarded mount" in Milton's *Lycidas*, line 161.

3. As oracular as the song of the legendary Orpheus.

That even as Life returns upon the Drown'd,
Th' unusual Joy awoke a throng of Pains—   70
Keen Pangs of Love, awakening, as a Babe,
Turbulent, with an outcry in the Heart:
And Fears self-will'd, that shunn'd the eye of Hope,
And Hope, that would not know itself from Fear:
Sense of pass'd Youth, and Manhood come in vain;   75
And Genius given, and Knowledge won in vain;
And all, which I had cull'd in Wood-walks wild,
And all, which patient Toil had rear'd, and all
Commune with Thee had open'd out, but Flowers
Strew'd on my Corse, and borne upon my Bier,   80
In the same Coffin, for the self-same Grave!

—That way no more! and ill beseems it me,
Who came a Welcomer in Herald's Guise
Singing of Glory and Futurity,
To wander back on such unhealthful Road   85
Plucking the Poisons of Self-harm! and ill
Such Intertwine beseems triumphal wreaths
Strew'd before thy Advancing! Thou too, Friend!
O injure not the memory of that Hour
Of thy communion with my nobler mind[4]   90
By pity or grief, already felt too long!
Nor let my words import more blame than needs.
The Tumult rose and ceas'd: for Peace is nigh
Where Wisdom's Voice has found a list'ning Heart.
Amid the howl of more than wintry Storms,   95
The Halcyon[5] hears the voice of vernal Hours,
Already on the wing!
                    Eve following eve,[6]
Dear tranquil Time, when the sweet sense of Home
Becomes most sweet! hours for their own sake hail'd,
And more desir'd, more precious, for thy song!   100
In silence list'ning, like a devout Child,
My soul lay passive, by thy various strain
Driven as in surges now, beneath the stars,
With momentary Stars of my own Birth,
Fair constellated Foam still darting off   105
Into the darkness! now a tranquil Sea
Outspread and bright, yet swelling to the Moon!

And when O Friend! my Comforter! my Guide!
Strong in thyself and powerful to give strength!
Thy long sustained Lay finally clos'd   110
And thy deep Voice had ceas'd—(yet thou thyself

4. I.e., during the early association between the two poets, 1797–98.
5. A legendary bird, able to calm the
sea where it nested in winter.
6. The evenings during which Wordsworth recited *The Prelude*.

Wert still before mine eyes, and round us both
That happy Vision of beloved Faces!
All, whom I deepliest love, in one room all!),
Scarce conscious and yet conscious of it's Close, 115
I sate, my Being blended in one Thought,
(Thought was it? or aspiration? or Resolve?)
Absorb'd, yet hanging still upon the sound:
And when I rose, I found myself in Prayer!

THOMAS DE QUINCEY

William Wordsworth†

* * * About the year 1810, by way of expressing an interest in
The Friend, which Coleridge was just at that time publishing in
weekly numbers, Wordsworth allowed Coleridge to print an extract
from the poem on his own life, descriptive of the games celebrated
upon the ice of Esthwaite by all who were able to skate:[1] the mimic
chases of hare and hounds, pursued long after the last orange gleam
of light had died away from the western horizon—oftentimes far
into the night—a circumstance which does not speak much for the
discipline of the schools—or rather, perhaps, *does* speak much for
the advantages of a situation so pure, and free from the usual perils
of a town, as this primitive village of Hawkshead. Wordsworth, in
this descriptive passage—which I wish that I had at this moment the
means of citing, in order to amplify my account of his earliest
tyrocinium[2]—speaks of himself as frequently wheeling aside from
his joyous companions to cut across the image of a star; and thus
already, in the midst of sportiveness, and by a movement of sportiveness, half unconsciously to himself expressing the growing
necessity of retirement to his habits of thought. At another period
of the year, when the golden summer allowed the students a long

---

† De Quincey contributed a three-part
essay on Wordsworth to *Tait's Edinburgh Magazine*; this selection is from
the second part, appearing in volume VI
(1839), pp. 90–103. De Quincey had
read *The Prelude* in manuscript during
the period, approximately 1809–15, while
he was a neighbor of Wordsworth in the
Lake Country, and before his friendship
with the poet was broken off because of
De Quincey's affair with the daughter of
a local farmer. The differences in De
Quincey's quotations from the manuscript
Prelude of 1805, as well as from the other
manuscript versions available to him, indicate that De Quincey may have been
accurate in claiming that he is quoting
from memory a poem he had not seen
"for more than twenty years." It is probable, however, that De Quincey made use
of notes that he had taken while reading
Wordsworth's manuscripts; see John
Edwin Wells, "De Quincey and *The Prelude* in 1839," *Philological Quarterly*,
XX (1941), 1–24.
1. See *The Prelude* (1805), I, 452–89.
Coleridge printed a slightly different version of this passage in his periodical *The
Friend*, no. 19 (December 28, 1809), and
again in the revised *Friend* of 1818.
2. A medieval Latin word: apprentice-
ship, training for a vocation.

season of early play before the studies of the day began, he describes himself as roaming, hand-in-hand, with one companion, along the banks of Esthwaite Water, chanting, with one voice, the verses of Goldsmith and of Gray[3]—verses which, at the time of recording the fact, he had come to look upon as either in parts false in the principles of their composition, or, at any rate, as wofully below the tone of high poetic passion; but which, at that time of life, when the profounder feelings were as yet only germinating, filled them with an enthusiasm which he describes as brighter than the dreams of fever or of wine.

* * * Wordsworth was a profound admirer of the sublimer mathematics; at least of the higher geometry. The secret of this admiration for geometry lay in the antagonism between this world of bodiless abstraction and the world of passion. And here I may mention appropriately, and I hope without any breach of confidence, that, in a great philosophic poem of Wordsworth's, which is still in MS., and will remain in MS. until after his death, there is, at the opening of one of the books, a dream, which reaches the very *ne plus ultra* of sublimity in my opinion, expressly framed to illustrate the eternity and the independence of all social modes or fashions of existence, conceded to these two hemispheres, as it were, that compose the total world of human power—mathematics on the one hand, poetry on the other.[4]

> "The one that held acquaintance with the stars
> ————undisturbed by space or time;
> The other that was a god—yea, many gods—
> Had voices more than all the winds, and was
> A joy, a consolation, and a hope."

I scarcely know whether I am entitled to quote—as my memory (though not refreshed by a sight of the poem for more than twenty years) would well enable me to do—any long extract; but thus much I may allowably say, as it cannot in any way affect Mr Wordsworth's interests, that the form of the dream is as follows; and, by the way, even this form is not arbitrary; but, with exquisite skill in the art of composition, is made to arise out of the situation in which the poet had previously found himself, and is faintly prefigured in the elements of that situation. He had been reading "Don Quixote" by the seaside; and, oppressed by the heat of the sun, he had fallen asleep whilst gazing on the barren sands before him. He dreams that, walking in some sandy wilderness of Africa, some endless Zaarrah,[5] he sees, at a distance

3. See *The Prelude* (1805), II, 348–53; V, 582–601.
4. The reference is to Wordsworth's description in *The Prelude* (1805) of his dream of the Arab, V, 55–139.
5. Sahara.

"An Arab of the desert, lance in rest,
Mounted upon a dromedary."

The Arab rides forward to meet him; and the dreamer perceives, in the countenance of the rider, the agitation of fear, and that he often looks behind him in a troubled way, whilst in his hand he holds two books—one of which is Euclid's "Elements;" the other, which is a book and yet not a book, seeming, in fact, a shell as well as a book, sometimes neither, and yet both at once. The Arab directs him to apply his ear; upon which—

"In an unknown tongue, which yet I understood," the dreamer says that he heard

"A wild prophetic blast of harmony,
An ode, as if in passion utter'd, that foretold
Destruction to the people of this earth
By deluge near at hand."

The Arab, with grave countenance, assures him that it is even so; that all was true which had been said; and that he himself was riding upon a divine mission, having it in charge

"To bury those two books;
"The one that held acquaintance with the stars," &c.—

that is, in effect, to secure the two great interests of poetry and mathematics from sharing in the watery ruin. As he talks, suddenly the dreamer perceives that the Arab's

————"countenance grew more disturb'd,"

and that his eye was often reverted; upon which the dreaming poet also looks along the desert in the same direction; and in the far horizon he descries

————"a glittering light."

What is it? he asks of the Arab rider. "It is," said he, "the waters of the earth," that even then were travelling on their awful errand. Upon which, the poet sees this apostle of the desert riding off,

"With the fleet waters of the world in chase of him."

* * *

From the *Eclectic Review*†

For well nigh thirty-four years the public curiosity has been excited by the knowledge that there existed in MS. an unfinished

† *"The Prelude," Eclectic Review,* XXVIII (1850), 550–62.

poem, of very high pretensions, and extraordinary magnitude, from the pen of the late—is he to be the last?—poet-laureate of Britain. At the tidings, Lord Jeffrey[1] made himself very merry, and sought for a powerful calculus to compute the supposed magnitude of the poem. De Quincey, on the other hand, had read it, and, both in his writings and conversation, was in the habit of alluding to, quoting, and panegyrizing it as more than equal to Wordsworth's other achievements.[2] All of it that is publishable, or shall ever be published, now lies before us; and we approach it with curiously-mingled emotions—mingled, because although a fragment, it is so vast, and in parts so finished, and because it may be regarded as at once an early production of his genius, and its latest legacy to the world. It seems a large fossil relic—imperfect and magnificent—newly dug up, and with the fresh earth and the old dim subsoil meeting and mingling around it.

The 'Prelude' is the first *regular*[3] *versified* autobiography we remember in our language. Passages, indeed, and parts of the lives of celebrated men, have been at times represented in verse, but in general a veil of fiction has been dropt over the real facts, as in the case of Don Juan[4]; and in all the revelation made has resembled rather an escapade or a partial confession than a systematic and slowly-consolidated life. The mere circumstances, too, of life, have been more regarded than the inner current of life itself. We class the 'Prelude' at once with Sartor Resartus[5]—although the latter wants the poetic *form*—as the two most interesting and faithful records of the individual experience of men of genius which exist.

And yet, how different the two men, and the two sets of experience. Sartor resembles the unfilled and yawning crescent moon, Wordsworth the rounded harvest orb: Sartor's cry is 'Give, give!' Wordsworth's, 'I have found it, I have found it!' Sartor cannot, amid a universe of work, find a task fit for him to do, and yet can much less be utterly idle; while to Wordsworth, basking in the sun, or loitering near an evening stream, is sufficient and satisfactory work. To Sartor, Nature is a divine tormentor—her works at once inspire and agonize him; Wordsworth loves her with the passion of a perpetual honeymoon. Both are intensely self-conscious; but Sartor's is the consciousness of disease, Wordsworth's of high health standing before a mirror. Both have 'a demon,'[6] but Sartor's is exceedingly fierce, dwelling among the tombs—Wordsworth's a

---

1. Francis Jeffrey (1773–1850), who became Lord Jeffrey, influential editor of the *Edinburgh Review* from its founding in 1802 until 1829. He had attacked Wordsworth's poetry, especially in a notorious review of *The Excursion* which began, "This will never do."
2. See the selection from De Quincey, above.
3. Systematic, fully developed.
4. Byron's *Don Juan* (1818–23).
5. Thomas Carlyle's *Sartor Resartus*, which was published serially in 1833–34 and as a separate volume in 1836.
6. A daemon; an indwelling spirit or power.

mild eremite, loving the rocks and the woods. Sartor's experience has been frightfully peculiar, and Wordsworth's peculiarly felicitous. Both have passed through the valley of the shadow of death; but the one has found it as Christian found it, dark and noisy,—the other has passed it, with Faithful, by daylight.[7] * * *

We grant, then, to Wordsworth's detractors, that his eye was introverted, that he studied himself more profoundly than aught else but nature—that his genius was neither epic, nor lyric, nor dramatic —that he did not 'look abroad into universality'—that he is monotonous—and that to sympathize fully with his strains, requires a certain share both of his powers and of their peculiar training. But all this we look at as only a needful statement of his limitations; and we pity those who produce it for any other purpose. Future ages will be thankful that a formation so peculiar, has been so carefully preserved. The 'moods' of such a mind will be ranked with the dramas, lyrics, and epics of inferior poets. His monotony will be compared to that of the ocean surges, which break now on the shore to the same tune as they did the eve before the deluge. His obscurities will appear jet black ornaments. His fragments will be valued as if they were bits of the ark. * * *

* * *

In reading the 'Prelude,' we should never forget that his object is not to weave an artful and amusing story, but sternly and elaborately to trace the 'growth of a poet's mind.' This is a metaphysical more than a biographical purpose. He leads us accordingly, not so much from incident to incident, as from thought to thought, along the salient points of his mental history. Skiddaw, Cambridge, Paris, London, the Alps, are but milestones marking his progress onwards, from the measured turbulence of his youth, to the calm 'philosophic mind' brought him by the 'years' of his manhood. No object, however august, is here described solely for its intrinsic charms, or made awkwardly to outstand from the main current of the story. Were Ossa[8] an excrescence, he would treat it as if it were a wart—were a wart a point of interest, he would dilate on it as if it were an Ossa. His strong personal feeling bends in all that is needful to his purpose, and rejects all that is extraneous. * * *

The book is thus a record of 'moods of his own mind,'[9] selected from a life composed of little else, upon the principle of showing how, succeeding and supplanting each other, they move 'Hyperion-like[1] on high.' Very lofty mountains are jagged, torn, and precipi-

7. In John Bunyan's *Pilgrim's Progress* (1678).
8. High mountain in Sicily; in the myth, the giants pile Mount Ossa on Mount Pelion in their endeavor to reach heaven.
9. In his *Poems in Two Volumes* of 1807

Wordsworth had printed one group of poems under the heading "Moods of My Own Mind."
1. Hyperion: In Greek myth, one of the Titans, often identified with the sun.

tous; loftier ones still are rounded off on their summits into the smoothest of contours. Thus Wordsworth shows himself rising gradually into the measure and the stature of supernal unity and peace.

The chapters of the poem might have been very properly entitled, 'Moods in Boyhood,' 'Moods in Cambridge,' 'Moods among my Books,' 'Moods among the Alps,' 'Moods in France,' &c. Characters, indeed, rush occasionally across those moods. Now it is his humble 'dame'[2]—now it is his amiable sister—now it is a friend of youth, departed—and now the 'rapt one with the Godlike forehead,'[3] the wondrous Coleridge; but they come like shadows, and like shadows depart, nor does their presence prevail for more than a moment to burst the web of the great soliloquy. Indeed, whether with them or without them, among mountains or men, with his faithful terrier, and talking to himself by the wayside, or pacing the Palais Royale, Wordsworth is equally and always alone. * * *

In contemplating the 'Prelude' as a whole, we feel that all our formerly-expressed notions of his poetry are confirmed. The slow motion, as of a fleet leaving the harbour—the cumbrous manner in which he relates little things—the clumsiness of the connecting links in the history—the deliberate dallyings with his subject, till he has accumulated strength and breath for a great effort—the superb and elaborate architecture of particular passages—the profundity of certain individual thoughts, and the weight and strength of particular lines, which seem to lie on his page *salted in glory*, and cast a lustre all around them—the sympathy with the lowlier passages of human life, and the simpler forms of nature—his profound natural piety and almost superhuman purity, are all found written large in the 'Prelude.' We find, too, in it, what we may call his peculiar differentia as an artist, which seems to be his *uniform subordination of the materials of art to art itself*. Other poets worship the materials which they transmute into song, and cannot work except on a certain set of materials, which they deem poetical. Wordsworth can extract poetry from anything in the heaven above, the earth below, or the waters under the earth. His eye anoints every object it encounters. He bends and broods over things, till they tell him all the mystery and beauty which are in their hearts. * * *

From *Tait's Edinburgh Magazine*†

* * * Of the whole, he says, in the preface to "The Excursion," with his usual fondness for fancied affinities, that "The Prelude"

---

2. See *The Prelude* (1850), IV, 27–39.
3. Wordsworth's *Extempore Effusion upon the Death of James Hogg* (1835),

line 17.
† "*The Prelude*," from *Tait's Edinburgh Magazine*, XVII (1850), 521–27.

and "The Recluse" may be considered to be in the relation to each other of a Gothic ante-chapel and chapel, and that the minor pieces may be likened to little cells and oratories.

We have already observed, in a previous paper (vol. 17, page 395), that we entertain, like many other devotees, a decided preference for these little cells and oratories, as compared with the more extensive and ambitious aisles; and, though we now have an opportunity of carefully perusing the ante-chapel, we see no reason to alter our judgment. As "The Prelude" is not, nor pretends to be, a tale of stirring interest, and as it is also of very considerable length, it necessarily requires all legitimate aids of poetic art to sustain the continued attention of the reader. Unfortunately, Wordsworth never attributed to these their just importance; and, accordingly, in "The Prelude," as in all his longer pieces, we cannot conceal from ourselves that the bard is sometimes prolix, and sometimes careless, in the selection of his phrase, and still more often we find his humbler themes become almost trivial from his want of that nameless tact possessed in so high a degree by Addison and Cowper.[1] * * *

* * * The walk which Wordsworth selected was very limited, though by no means unworthy. He is the poet of the external phases of Nature, but only in her milder moods. He cannot make, as Byron did, "the live thunder leap from crag to crag,"[2] but he serenely gazes with artless joy on the sun sinking behind the dark outline of a Cumbrian fell,[3] and his soul hovers in rapture over the silvery mist that fills the vale at daybreak. In dealing with human passions, the noblest, in fact the only real theme of song (for the external imageries of the visible are but accessories deriving their interest only from their relation to the sentient soul of man), the power of Wordsworth is voluntarily confined to tales of simple pathos and subdued sorrow, or tranquil enjoyment. The texture of his compositions is in general eminently artless. From multiplicity he shrinks as from confusion; and in no instance does he summon thoughts and feelings from various regions to converge like troops in a campaign, and to bear with irresistible effect on a point long since predetermined. His is the ripple of the brook, and not the collective might of waters slowly gathering to break in one huge billow on the shore.

There is, however, a charm about Wordsworth that amply compensates for the absence of those vivid and passionate passages which stir us powerfully in more vigorous poets. Much of our life is work-a-day and weary; we are daily racked by the apprehension of

---

1. Joseph Addison (1672–1719), best known for his essays in *The Spectator*. William Cowper (1731–1800), author of *The Task*.
2. Byron, *Childe Harold's Pilgrimage*, III, 864–65: "From peak to peak, the rattling crags among,/ Leaps the live thunder!"
3. A Cumberland mountain.

real calamities, and in our struggles to avoid them our moral nature has a tendency to become soured and perverted from very suffering. It is in these phases of mind that Wordsworth's gentle pages cast a soothing influence upon the troubled spirit, and supply that invigorating repose which enables us to withstand the recurring fever of life's turmoil. In this respect "The Prelude," as we have seen, a tale of childhood, boyhood, and youth, tranquil, happy, and innocent, will minister to minds diseased[4] as effectively as its predecessors have done.

* * *

From the *Gentleman's Magazine*†

* * *

Such is the general outline of the Prelude. Its component parts—its tone and impasto,[1] to borrow a painter's phrase, are at least equal to the best of Wordsworth's earlier published works, and, in our opinion at least, superior to all of them, except his best lyrical ballads, his best sonnets, and his Ode to Immortality. * * *

In the Prelude, however, as well as in Wordsworth's poetry generally, there are peculiar and characteristic defects. There is an occasional laxity of phrase, there is a want of precision in form, and there is an absence of deep and vital sympathy with men, their works and ways. * * * His lyric emotion is brief; his speculative contemplation is infinite; he evinces awakened curiosity rather than spiritual fellowship. In Shelley's poetry, especially in his "Prometheus" and "Revolt of Islam," we seem, as it were, to be confronted by that yawning and roaring furnace into which the opinions and institutions of the past were being hurled. In Wordsworth's most excited mood we have rather the reflexion of the flame than the authentic or derivative fire itself. Its heat and glare pass to us through some less pervious and colder lens. In Shelley again—we are contrasting not his poetry but his idiosyncrasy with that of Wordsworth—we encounter in its full vigour the erotic element of poetry, the absence of which in Wordsworth is so remarkable, that of all poets of equal rank and power in other respects, he, and he alone, may be said to have dispensed with it altogether. The sensuous element was omitted in his composition. His sympathies are absorbed by the magnificence and the mystery of external nature, or by the vigour and freshness of the human soul when under immediate contact with nature's elemental forms and influences. Neither

---

4. *Macbeth*, V, iii, 40: "Cans't thou not minister to a mind diseased?"
† "Wordsworth's Autobiographical Poem," from the *Gentleman's Magazine*, XXXIV

(1850), 459–68.
1. Thick application of pigment in a painting.

was there ever any poet of his degree less dramatic than Wordsworth. All the life in his ballads, in his narrative poems, in his Excursion, is the reflex of his own being. The actors in his scenes are severe, aloof, stately, and uniform; grand in their isolation, dignified in their sorrows. They are not creatures of the market or the haven, of the senate or the forum. * * * But the French Revolution was an electric shock to his whole spiritual being, perversive in its immediate, and permanent in its remote effects. It led him, both in its transit and catastrophe, to meditate deeply on the destinies and capacities of man; upon the powers and duties of the poet; upon the relations of society and nature; upon all that keeps man little, and upon all that might render him great. The lyrical ballads, the critical prefaces, and the renown of Wordsworth, have wrought one of the greatest literary revolutions the world has ever seen: and the nerve and purpose to work it were braced and formed under the influence of a corresponding convulsion in politics. Men had already asked themselves the question, shall we continue to obey phantasms, or shall we search for realities; and poets also were beginning to say, at least in Germany and England, is our vocation for the apparent only, or for the true? Verse was regarded no longer as an elegant accomplishment, or the poet merely as one who could *amuse* a vacant hour, but not instruct a thoughtful one. Childish things were put away; and poetry resumed the dignity, and almost the stature, of its first manhood. * * * It is seldom that we have the privilege of noticing so masterly a work as this poem, still less seldom do we meet with one so rich in both historical and psychological interest. But we must now conclude, partly rejoicing, and partly regretting, that the late venerable Laureate should not have printed, in his lifetime, this record of his mind's growth. * * * The Prelude therefore, complete as it is with regard to a brief period of the poet's life, is only a fragment, and one more example of the many which the last generation could produce of the uncertainty of human projects and of the contrast between the promise of youth and the accomplishment of manhood. Such as it is, we rejoice to welcome it, while we regret that the greeting and applause with which it has been universally hailed, can no longer soothe and strengthen the soul of the great regenerator of English poetry— William Wordsworth.

From *Graham's Magazine*†

* * * The character of the poem is essentially psychological, the object being to notice only those events and scenes which fed and

† *"The Prelude,"* from *Graham's Magazine* (Philadelphia), XXXVII (1850), 322–23.

directed the poet's mind, and to regard them, not so much in their own nature, as in their influence on the nature of the poet. The topics, therefore, though trite in themselves, are all made original from the peculiarities of the person conceiving them. His childhood and school-time, his residence at the university, his summer vacation, his visit to the Alps, his tour through France, his residence in London and France, are the principal topics; but the enumeration of the topics can convey no impression of the thought, observation, and imagination, the eloquent philosophy, vivid imagery, and unmistakable *Wordsworthianism*, which characterize the volume.

It must be admitted, however, that "The Prelude," with all its merits, does not add to the author's great fame, however much it may add to our knowledge of his inner life. As a poem it cannot be placed by the side of The White Doe, or The Excursion, or the Ode on Childhood, or the Ode on the Power of Sound; and the reason is to be found in its strictly didactic and personal character, necessitating a more constant use of analysis and reflection, and a greater substitution of the metaphysical for the poetic process, than poetry is willing to admit. Though intended as an introduction to "The Excursion," it has not its sustained richness of diction and imagery; and there is little of that easy yielding of the mind to the inspiration of objects, and that ecstatic utterance of the emotions they excite, which characterize passages selected at random from the latter poem— * * *

If "The Prelude" has thus fewer "trances of thought and mountings of the mind"[1] than "The Excursion," it still bears the marks of the lofty and thoughtful genius of the author, and increases our respect for his personal character. The books devoted to his residence in Cambridge, his tour to the Alps, and to the influence of the French Revolution upon his genius and character, are additions to the philosophy of the human mind. We believe that few metaphysicians ever scanned their consciousness with more intensity of vision, than Wordsworth was wont to direct upon his; and in the present poem he has subtly noted, and firmly expressed, many new psychological laws and processes. The whole subject of the development of the mind's creative faculties, and the vital laws of mental growth and production, has been but little touched by professed metaphsicians; and we believe "The Prelude" conveys more real available knowledge of the facts and laws of man's internal constitution, than can be found in Hume or Kant.[2]

---

1. *The Prelude* (1850), I, 19.
2. The philosophers David Hume (1711–76) and Immanuel Kant (1724–1804).

From the *British Quarterly Review*†

* * * Respecting 'The Prelude,' then, as we now have it, it is important to bear this in mind, that, though given to the world as the legacy of an old man, it is in reality the autobiography of a poet only up to his thirtieth year, and written by him between his thirtieth and thirty-sixth. It is neither, on the one hand, a complete autobiography of the poet; nor is it, on the other, like Goethe's *Dichtung und Wahrheit*, an autobiography of his early years, written by him in old age. It is true that, in leaving instructions that it should be published, the author virtually gave it the sanction of his maturer approbation, and also that, while lying by him in manuscript, it may have received the benefit of his revision. Essentially, however, it is the composition of a young man; and it bears marks of being so.

* * *

Regarding the work before us, we have first to say that it is not so much a complete autobiography of the poet up to his thirtieth year, as a theoretic retrospect of what the poet himself considered significant in that portion of his life. That he was born amid scenes of natural beauty; that as soon as the mere sense of animal activity was subdued in him, all his affections were bestowed on inanimate nature, to the exclusion, for the greater part, of any interest in human beings or their affairs; that thence by a long course of training he was led on, and as it were violently compelled to feel the force of the social sentiment; but that still Nature was his goddess, and that ultimately she regained her sway over him, and made him the poet he was—such, in substance, is the autobiographic view which 'the Prelude,' was written to illustrate. And here again, keeping up the instructive contrast between Goethe and Wordsworth, one sees the difference between the two poets. Goethe, the larger and more complex nature, writes an autobiography full of facts, incidents, sketches, episodes; advancing, openly at least, no theory of the course of his genius, but artistically evoking out of his past life the most beautiful and sweet of its multitudinous recollections. Wordsworth, a poet too, but of a mind more meagre and didactic, first stretches as it were a line of bare autobiographic theory along the period he means to traverse, and then hangs upon it a few reminiscences that shall be ornamental and illustrative. And among these reminiscences, it will have been remarked with curiosity, there

† *"The Prelude,"* from the *British Quarterly Review*, XII (1850), 549–79. This anonymous review is reliably attributed to David Masson by A.T.C. Pratt, *People of the Period* (2 vols.; London, 1897), II, 148.

is hardly one of the species usually deemed more important than any other in the retrospect of a man's life, and so amply done justice to by Goethe in *his* autobiographic narrative. Gretchen, Rica, Lilli —what reader of the '*Dichtung und Wahrheit*' can ever forget these dead German maidens, or their influence on the life of Goethe? But not one such love-experience of our English author is there recorded in 'the Prelude.' * * *

'The Prelude,' we will venture to say, ought, like the 'Dichtung und Wahrheit,' to have been written in prose. It is true there are many passages of fine poetry in the volume, which, on account of the necessary restrictions of prose, we should in that case have been obliged to dispense with; but, on the other hand, we should necessarily have had then a more rich and perfect autobiography of the poet than the work as it is can be said to furnish. That Wordsworth should have made such an attempt in verse at all, is to be regarded as a consequence of his peculiar theory of poetic diction, and as a proof how thoroughly he believed in that theory. According to that theory, large portions of the poem which, from another point of view, would appear decidedly cold and prosaic, are strictly and sufficiently poetical. Still even Wordsworth himself, with all his faith in the title of verse to be made a vehicle even for the most ordinary circumstances and statements, might have seen that, by preferring the element of prose, he could have been more anecdotic, interesting, and communicative. * * *

After all, however, 'the Prelude' is a sterling book, worthy of the reputation of its author, and of a place among the most remarkable poems in our language. It will stand, we believe, as a production *sui generis* in our literature, a memorial, executed by his own hands, egotistically perhaps, but still truly (and Wordsworth's very egotism is capable of a reverent interpretation), of the early life of a good and highly-gifted man. Passages might be extracted from it, illustrative of all the merits exhibited in such high measure by the other works of the author—of his large imaginative power; of his accurate eye for the varying aspects of nature; of his general intellectual vigour, and the extent even of his formal acquisitions; of the fine pensive cast of his spirit and the pure and religious air of contemplation which he breathed; of his intimate acquaintance with the joys and sorrows of rural English life; of his manly love for all that is noble and stirring in English history; and of his admirable and exquisite mastery over the resources of the English tongue. In these respects 'the Prelude' is inferior, among the author's writings, only perhaps to 'the Excursion.'

From the *Dublin University Magazine*†

* * *

The poem, now first published in the goodly tome before us, contains about nine thousand lines of blank verse, divided into fourteen books. It was completed some five-and-forty years ago, when the author was thirty-five years old, his genius matured by reflection, and his intellectual character fixed and determined. We may expect, then, to find the full fruitage of the poetic faculty he possessed, and herein no reader capable of appreciating the highest order of poetry will be disappointed. But he will also find more of the eccentricities of this great author than his own later judgment would probably have approved. There are many heavy and prosaic passages, and some matters of familiar, and not very important, narrative are given with a solemnity which cannot but provoke a smile. But these are but casual clouds floating in the pure Wordsworthian sky. Ever and anon, he springs from level talk or ponderous triviality into the most glorious heights of poetry (and we hear, as it were, a voice of more than mortal music reverberated from the mountains, and filling the valleys with sounds of melody sweeter than the fall of their own rivers. * * *

In spite of the heavy passages—in spite of the somewhat cumbrous gravity with which trivial matters are sometimes narrated or discussed—in spite of the absence of that graceful ease, and occasional humour, which Cowper's blank verse so eminently possesses, the poem of the *Prelude* has the strongest claims to the respectful admiration of the reflecting portion of the public. The finer passages have all the grandeur of the *Excursion*, with, as it seems to us, more vigour, and buoyancy, and fresh delight of composition. When the poet takes up a strain congenial to him, he seems to go on rejoicing in his strength, and pealing out tone after tone of rising grandeur and increasing melody. * * *

* * * When we turn over the book, we are struck more and more with passages which seem to come like streams of light upon the mountain-tops, and to reveal beautiful heights of the mind of man, which, without the aid of this great poet, we had never been able to see. * * * Though the work affords plenty of occasion for critical fault-finding, we yet feel satisfied that, such as it is, it will elevate even the fame of Wordsworth. Greater praise than this we cannot bestow.

† "The New Poem by Wordsworth," from the *Dublin University Magazine*, XXXVI (1850), 329–37.

From the *Examiner*†

* * *

Matters standing thus, it has not been without a melancholy sense of the uncertainty of human projects, and of the contrast between the sanguine enterprise and its silent evaporation (so often the "history of an individual mind"),[1] that we have perused this *Prelude* which no completed strain was destined to follow. Yet in the poem itself there is nothing to inspire depression. It is animated throughout with the hopeful confidence in the poet's own powers, so natural to the time of life at which it was composed; it evinces a power and soar of imagination unsurpassed in any of his writings; and its images and incidents have a freshness and distinctness which they not seldom lost, when they came to be elaborated, as many of them were, in his minor poems of a later date.

* * *

The great defect of Wordsworth, in our judgment, was want of sympathy with, and knowledge of, men. From his birth till his entry at college, he lived in a region where he met with none whose minds might awaken his sympathies, and where life was altogether un-eventful. On the other hand, that region abounded with the inert, striking, and most impressive objects of natural scenery. The elementary grandeur and beauty of external nature came thus to fill up his mind to the exclusion of human interests. To such a result his individual constitution powerfully contributed. The sensuous element was singularly deficient in his nature. He never seems to have passed through that erotic period out of which some poets have never emerged. A soaring, speculative imagination, and an impetuous, resistless self-will, were his distinguishing characteristics. From first to last he concentrated himself within himself; brooding over his own fancies and imaginations to the comparative disregard of the incidents and impressions which suggested them; and was little susceptible of ideas originating in other minds. We behold the result. He lives alone in a world of mountains, streams, and atmospheric phenomena, dealing with moral abstractions, and rarely encountered by even shadowy spectres of beings outwardly resembling himself. There is measureless grandeur and power in his moral speculations. There is intense reality in his pictures of external nature. But though his human characters are presented with great skill of metaphysical analysis, they have rarely life or animation. He

---

† "*The Prelude*," from the *Examiner*, No. 2217 (1850), pp. 478–80.
1. In his Preface to *The Excursion* (1814), Wordsworth referred to the unpublished *Prelude* as "the history of the Author's mind."

is always the prominent, often the exclusive, object of his own song.

* * *

The *Prelude* may take a permanent place as one of the most perfect of his compositions. It has much of the fearless felicity of youth; and its imagery has the sharp and vivid outline of ideas fresh from the brain. The subject—the development of his own great powers—raises him above that wilful dallying with trivialities which repels us in some of his other works. And there is real vitality in the theme, both from our anxiety to know the course of such a mind, and from the effect of an absorbing interest in himself excluding that languor which sometimes seized him in his efforts to impart or attribute interest to themes possessing little or none in themselves. Its mere narrative, though often very homely, and dealing in too many words, is often characterised also by elevated imagination, and always by eloquence. * * *

* * *

Polemical though they be, even the extracts we have thus given contain enough of the play of high imagination which pervades the poem to indicate its value in purely aesthetical respects. But it is in the record of his extra-academic life that the poet soars his freeest flight, in passages where we have a very echo of the emotions of an emancipated worshipper of nature flying back to his loved resorts. Apart from its poetic value, the book is a graphic and interesting portraiture of the struggles of an ingenuous and impetuous mind to arrive at a clear insight into its own interior constitution and external relations, and to secure the composure of self-knowledge and of equally adjusted aspirations. As a poem it is likely to lay fast and enduring hold on pure and aspiring intellects, and to strengthen the claim of Wordsworth to endure with his land's language.

HENRY CRABB ROBINSON†

I did not go down to Westmorland to attend the funeral. Indeed the interment took place on the Saturday, and I should have scarcely had time. But I find I was expected and therefore I regret my absence. But in the first letter the time was not mentioned and I therefore inferred that I was not expected.

The grief of friends ought to be absorbed in the contemplation of

† (1775–1867). Crabb Robinson's diary and correspondence contain anecdotes about many literary personages of the time, both in England and on the Continent.

the public loss, and yet the public of to-day will be the immediate gainers. There will be published forthwith THE POEM which perhaps for the earnest and contemplative few of the present and future generations will be the most precious of the great man's works. In 14 books Wordsworth has recorded the formation of his character. This was written when his mind was in all its strength.

(To Jacob Pattison, May 4, 1850)

FREDERICK DENISON MAURICE†

I am sure that you are right, Wordsworth's Prelude seems to me the dying utterance of the half century we have just passed through, the expression—the English expression at least—of all that self-building process in which, according to their different schemes and principles, Byron, Goethe, Wordsworth, the Evangelicals (Protestant and Romanist), were all engaged, which their novels, poems, experiences, prayers, were setting forth, in which God, under whatever name, or in whatever aspect He presented Himself to them, was still the agent only in fitting them to be world-wise, men of genius, artists, saints.

(To Charles Kingsley, 1851)

THOMAS BABINGTON MACAULAY*

I brought home, and read, the 'Prelude.' It is a poorer 'Excursion;' the same sort of faults and beauties; but the faults greater and the beauties fainter, both in themselves and because faults are always made more offensive, and beauties less pleasing, by repetition. The story is the old story. There are the old raptures about mountains and cataracts; the old flimsy philosophy about the effect of scenery on the mind; the old crazy, mystical metaphysics; the endless wildernesses of dull, flat, prosaic twaddle; and here and there fine descriptions and energetic declamations interspersed. The story of the French Revolution, and of its influence on the character of a young enthusiast, is told again at greater length, and with less force and pathos, than in the 'Excursion.' The poem is to the last degree Jacobinical,[1] indeed Socialist. I understand perfectly why Wordsworth did not choose to publish it in his life-time.

(Journal, July 28, 1850)

---

† Maurice (1805–72) was a liberal theologian who declared himself a Christian socialist; he was professor of English literature and history at King's College, London, 1840–53.

* Macaulay (1800–59), distinguished historian and man of letters.
1. The term Jacobin was applied indiscriminately to those in Britain who sympathized with the French Revolution.

HENRY WADSWORTH LONGFELLOW

We have finished Wordsworth's 'Prelude.' It has many lofty passages. It soars and sinks, and is by turns sublime and commonplace. It is Wordsworth as he was at the age of thirty-five or forty.

(Journal, August 21, 1850)

RALPH WALDO EMERSON

Wordsworth's "Prelude" is not quite solid enough in its texture; is rather a poetical pamphlet, though proceeding from a new and genuine experience. It is like Milton's *Areopagitica*,[1] an immortal pamphlet.

(Journals, February 27, 1858)

MATTHEW ARNOLD

* * *

Wordsworth has been in his grave for some thirty years, and certainly his lovers and admirers cannot flatter themselves that this great and steady light of glory as yet shines over him. He is not fully recognised at home; he is not recognised at all abroad. Yet I firmly believe that the poetical performance of Wordsworth is, after that of Shakspeare and Milton, of which all the world now recognises the worth, undoubtedly the most considerable in our language from the Elizabethan age to the present time. * * *

The *Excursion* and the *Prelude*, his poems of greatest bulk, are by no means Wordsworth's best work. His best work is in his shorter pieces, and many indeed are there of these which are of first-rate excellence. * * * Wordsworth has in constant possession, and at command, no style of this kind; but he had too poetic a nature, and had read the great poets too well, not to catch, as I have already remarked, something of it occasionally. We find it not only in his Miltonic lines; we find it in such a phrase as this, where the manner is his own, not Milton's—

> . . . the fierce confederate storm
> Of sorrow barricadoed evermore
> Within the walls of cities;[1]

---

1. Milton's great pamphlet (1644), arguing eloquently for freedom of speech and publication.
1. From the verse Prospectus to *The Recluse* which Wordsworth included in his preface to *The Excursion* (1814), lines 78–80.

although even here, perhaps, the power of style, which is undeniable, is more properly that of eloquent prose than the subtle heightening and change wrought by genuine poetic style. * * *

* * * And let us be on our guard, too, against the exhibitors and extollers of a "scientific system of thought" in Wordsworth's poetry. The poetry will never be seen aright while they thus exhibit it. The cause of its greatness is simple, and may be told quite simply. Wordsworth's poetry is great because of the extraordinary power with which Wordsworth feels the joy offered to us in nature, the joy offered to us in the simple primary affections and duties; and because of the extraordinary power with which, in case after case, he shows us this joy, and renders it so as to make us share it.

* * *

(From the Preface to *The Poems of Wordsworth*,
edited by Matthew Arnold [1879])

A. C. BRADLEY

* * * First, not a little of Wordsworths' poetry either approaches or actually enters the province of the sublime. His strongest natural inclination tended there. He himself speaks of his temperament as 'stern,' and tells us that

> to the very going out of youth
> [He] too exclusively esteemed *that* love,
> And sought *that* beauty, which, as Milton says,
> Hath terror in it.[1]

This disposition is easily traced in the imaginative impressions of his childhood as he describes them in the *Prelude*. His fixed habit of looking

> with feelings of fraternal love
> Upon the unassuming things that hold
> A silent station in this beauteous world,[2]

was only formed, it would seem, under his sister's influence, after his recovery from the crisis that followed the ruin of his towering hopes in the French Revolution. It was a part of his endeavour to find something of the distant ideal in life's familiar face. And though this attitude of sympathy and humility did become habitual, the first bent towards grandeur, austerity, sublimity, retained its force. * * * Wordsworth is indisputably the most sublime of our poets since Milton.

1. *The Prelude* (1850), XIV, 243–46.   2. Ibid., XIII, 45–47.

We may put the matter, secondly, thus. However much Wordsworth was the poet of small and humble things, and the poet who
saw his ideal realised, not in Utopia, but here and now before his
eyes, he was, quite as much, what some would call a mystic. He saw
everything in the light of 'the visionary power.'[3] He was, for himself,

> The transitory being that beheld
> This Vision.[4]

He apprehended all things, natural or human, as the expression of
something which, while manifested in them, immeasurably tran-
scends them. And nothing can be more intensely Wordsworthian
than the poems and passages most marked by this visionary power
and most directly issuing from this apprehension. The bearing of
these statements on Wordsworth's inclination to sublimity will be
obvious at a glance.

Now we may prefer the Wordsworth of the daffodils to the
Wordsworth of the yew-trees, and we may even believe the poet's
mysticism to be moonshine; but it is certain that to neglect or throw
into the shade this aspect of his poetry is neither to take Wordsworth as he really was nor to judge his poetry truly, since this
aspect appears in much of it that we cannot deny to be first-rate.
Yet there is, I think, and has been for some time, a tendency to this
mistake. It is exemplified in Arnold's Introduction and has been
increased by it, and it is visible in some degree even in Pater's essay.
Arnold wished to make Wordsworth more popular; and so he was
tempted to represent Wordsworth's poetry as much more simple and
unambitious than it really was, and as much more easily apprehended than it ever can be. * * *

* * * Pater says, for example, that Wordsworth is the poet of
nature, 'and of nature, after all, in her modesty. The English Lake
country has, of course, its grandeurs. But the peculiar function of
Wordsworth's genius, as carrying in it a power to open out the soul
of apparently little and familiar things, would have found its true
test had he become the poet of Surrey, say! and the prophet of its
life.'[5] This last sentence is, in one sense, doubtless true. The 'function' referred to could have been exercised in Surrey, and was
exercised in Dorset and Somerset, as well as in the Lake country.
And this function was a 'peculiar function of Wordsworth's genius.'
But that it was *the* peculiar function of his genius, or more peculiar
than that other function which forms our present subject, I venture
to deny; and for the full exercise of this latter function, it is hardly

---

3. Ibid., II, 311.
4. The Prospectus to *The Recluse*, lines
97–98.

5. Walter Pater, "Wordsworth" (1874),
in *Appreciations* (London, 1897), p. 48.

hazardous to assert, Wordsworth's childhood in a mountain district, and his subsequent residence there, were indispensable. This will be doubted for a moment, I believe, only by those readers (and they are not a few) who ignore the *Prelude* and the *Excursion*. But the *Prelude* and the *Excursion*, though there are dull pages in both, contain much of Wordsworth's best and most characteristic poetry. * * *

(From "Wordsworth," in *Oxford Lectures on Poetry* [1909])

Recent Critical Essays

JONATHAN WORDSWORTH

The Two-Part *Prelude* of 1799†

In most people's view there are two *Preludes*, the much revised official version, which was published by Wordsworth's executors immediately after his death in 1850, and the "early" or "1805" *Prelude* printed from two MSS. of 1805–6 by De Selincourt in 1926. But there is in fact a third, even earlier poem ("1799"), with its own distinctive qualities, and with very much the same authority as the text of 1805. Had De Selincourt printed it forty years ago it would long since have become established: as it is, it is virtually unknown.[1] And yet it is a work "Single and of determined bounds", preserved as is the version of 1805 in two faircopy manuscripts that were made because for the time at least Wordsworth regarded his task as complete.[2] In this form *The Prelude* has 956 lines, deals solely with the poet's childhood and adolescence, and very roughly corresponds to Books I and II of 1805 and 1850. There is an interesting, though perhaps not obvious, comparison to be drawn between the growth of *The Prelude* and that of *The Rape of the Lock*. The two-Part *Prelude* of 1799, like the *Rape* of 1712, is a short, self-contained, relatively unambitious poem that reflects very clearly the original impulse of composition. In 1805 it is submerged in a longer work, as was the *Rape* in 1714, becomes more pretentious, and in particular is given much fuller epic treatment. Finally, the text of 1850, like the *Rape* of 1717, presents a poem not radically changed, but tidied up from a moral point of view. The major difference is, of course, that while Pope is of all English poets the most skillful reviser, Wordsworth's revisions are normally—not always, but normally—for the worse; and this is true even at the period when in terms of original composition he is writing at his very best. The two-Canto *Rape of the Locke* is read only as the finished work in

† The lecture of which this is a revised and extended version was delivered at Cornell University on April 7, 1970, and printed as "The Growth of a Poet's Mind" in *The Cornell Library Journal*, XI (Spring 1970), 3–24. *Prelude* quotations have been adjusted to the texts presented in this volume.

1. Only J. R. MacGillivray, "The Three Forms of *The Prelude*" (*Essays in English Literature from the Renaissance to the Victorian Age, Presented to A.S.P. Woodhouse*, ed. Miller MacLure and F. W. Watt [Toronto, 1964]) had discussed *1799* in print before 1970, but John Finch was working on the poem at the time of his death in a fire at Cornell, April 1967, and in its original form this essay was much indebted to his unpublished doctoral thesis, "Wordsworth, Coleridge and *The Recluse*, 1798–1814."

2. I use the word "task" to gloss over the question as to whether in December 1799 Wordsworth regarded the two-Part *Prelude* as a finished poem. The evidence is inconclusive—see *1799* Introduction above—but MSS. V and U represent the completion of the original phase of composition, offering a work that is a thematic unit, and that seems admirably self-contained.

embryo: the two-Part *Prelude* will presently be recognized as great poetry in its own right, a poem of much smaller scope but also much more concentrated power than the thirteen-Book version of 1805.

Take for example 1799, I, 296–319, a passage that to readers of 1805 should be at once familiar and strange:

> I remember well,
> ('Tis of an early season that I speak,
> The twilight of rememberable life),
> While I was yet an urchin, one who scarce
> Could hold a bridle, with ambitious hopes
> I mounted, and we rode towards the hills.
> We were a pair of horsemen: honest James
> Was with me, my encourager and guide.
> We had not travelled long ere some mischance
> Disjoined me from my comrade, and, through fear
> Dismounting, down the rough and stony moor
> I led my horse, and stumbling on, at length
> Came to a bottom where in former times
> A man, the murderer of his wife, was hung
> In irons. Mouldered was the gibbet-mast;
> The bones were gone, the iron and the wood;
> Only a long green ridge of turf remained
> Whose shape was like a grave. I left the spot,
> And reascending the bare slope I saw
> A naked pool that lay beneath the hills,
> The beacon on the summit, and more near
> A girl who bore a pitcher on her head
> And seemed with difficult steps to force her way
> Against the blowing wind.

In 1799 these lines stand as they originally stood towards the end of Part I, together with the Drowned Man of Esthwaite Water (used later in Book V), the famous assertion "There are in our existence spots of time . . . ", and the Waiting for the Horses; in 1805 they have been transplanted, with no particular appropriateness, to Book XI. They have also been revised, weighted with new and cumbersome detail:

> The gibbet-mast was mouldered down, the bones
> And iron case were gone, but on the turf
> Hard by, soon after that fell deed was wrought,
> Some unknown hand had carved the murderer's name.
> The monumental writing was engraven
> In times long past, and still from year to year
> By superstition of the neighbourhood
> The grass is cleared away; and to this hour
> The letters are all fresh and visible.

> Faltering, and ignorant where I was, at length
> I chanced to espy those characters inscribed
> On the green sod: forthwith I left the spot . . .
>
> (1805, XI, 290–301)

"The monumental writing was engraven / In times long past . . ."
—Thomas Nicholson, the murderer in question, was hanged on
August 31, 1767, two years and seven months before Wordsworth's
birth; the urchin who "scarce / Could hold a bridle" is commonly
thought to have been five; so that the letters, even if carved *very*
"soon after that fell deed was wrought", were at most seven or eight
years old. Unless made of remarkably inferior wood, the gibbet
would not by then have fallen, much less "mouldered down." As is
so often true in *The Prelude,* despite circumstantial detail we are
dealing not with fact, but with poetry of the imagination.[3]

It is as imaginative writing that the version of the two-Part poem
is so very much superior. The addition of 1805 is not only garru-
lous, it is distracting, and oddly trivial in its associations. Wordsworth is seen playing up the murder-and-mystery ("fell deed,"
"unknown hand," "times long past") in a way that could be justified
only if it told us something about the child's state of mind. The
possibility that it is doing so recedes, however, as we move on into
poetry that has all the appearance of a versified guidebook entry:
"still from year to year by superstition of the neighbourhood the
grass is cleared away." The sense of expectation created at the
beginning of the passage has gone. In order to get back to the
frightened child stumbling down the moor, Wordsworth has now to
insert a clumsy reminder: "Faltering, and ignorant where I was, at
length / I chanced to espy. . . . " It is impossible to know what he
thought had been gained by the additional lines—perhaps someone
told him in 1804 about the letters engraved on the turf, and he
couldn't resist putting them in.[4] Certainly they have little to do with
the imaginative world of the woman on the hill whose garments are
vexed and tossed by the wind. The original lines, by contrast, are
beautifully homogeneous:

> down the rough and stony moor
> I led my horse, and stumbling on, at length
> Came to a bottom where in former times
> A man, the murderer of his wife, was hung
> In irons. Mouldered was the gibbet-mast;
> The bones were gone, the iron and the wood;
> Only a long green ridge of turf remained

3. See *1799,* I, 308*n,* above, for evidence
that Wordsworth was actually conflating
two quite different murder stories, one
belonging to Penrith, the other to Hawkshead.

4. There seems to have been no written
source for the story until the anonymous
History of Penrith, 1858; see *1805,* XI,
302*n,* above.

Whose shape was like a grave. I left the spot,
And reascending the bare slope I saw
A naked pool that lay beneath the hills,
The beacon on the summit, and more near
A girl who bore a pitcher on her head
And seemed with difficult steps to force her way
Against the blowing wind. It was in truth
An ordinary sight, but I should need
Colours and words that are unknown to man
To paint the visionary dreariness
Which, while I looked all round for my lost guide,
Did at that time invest the naked pool,
The beacon on the lonely eminence,
The woman and her garments vexed and tossed
By the strong wind.

(1799, I, 306–27)

I suppose it is the fussiness of the engraven letters that one most resents, and the fact that they delay the appearance of the inexplicably evocative figure who is to be the central focus of the landscape. But the 1805 addition in fact does more, and worse, than this. It obscures the very nature of the poetry that Wordsworth is writing —poetry not of fact and guidebook detail but of strange imaginative power, poetry in which what is *not* seen is as important as what is. "The bones were gone, the iron and the wood" is not only beautiful in its rhythm, but reduces the unseen horrors of the gallows— the gruesome deterrent of a corpse swinging and rotting in its iron cage—to the elemental level on which Wordsworth's imagination plays. Similarly, "the long green ridge of turf," perhaps actually a grave, perhaps just seeming one to the frightened child, is in either case a tranquil, reconciling, very Wordsworthian, end to the violence of the past. The poetry in this version is all of a piece. In 1805 one has to clear one's mind of the superstition, mysteriousness, cluttering detail, before responding to the vision of the girl with her pitcher on the hill. In the two-Part poem, one's mood has been prepared. One ascends the bare slope and meets almost without surprise the most purely imaginative of Wordsworth's solitaries.

The two-Part *Prelude* in fact offers in a simpler and more concentrated form much of what one thinks of as best in the thirteen-Book poem. It does not constitute an alternative to 1805, but in so far as Wordsworth's vision of childhood is the inspiration and sustaining force of all versions of *The Prelude*, 1799 has outstanding claims. Lacking, of course, are the experiences of Wordsworth's young manhood, the moment of consecration in Book IV, the Crossing of the Alps in Book VI (with the famous lines upon imagination and the Simplon Pass) and the climactic Ascent of Snowdon from

Book XIII, but almost all the childhood "spots of time" are to be found, and found in their original sequence. The presence of the additional "spots" gives the poetry extraordinary power—the fact that in Part I after the woodcock-snaring, birds-nesting, boat-stealing, and skating episodes of Book I, there are the Drowned Man, the woman with her garments vexed and tossed, and the Waiting for the Horses, still to come. But even more important is the effect of returning Wordsworth's famous definition to its original place.

As it stands in Book XI of 1805, the assertion "There are in our existence spots of time . . .", though of course highly impressive, is removed a very long way from the poetry of Book I with which it had originally been connected, and has to take a structural weight that it cannot at all easily bear. In 1799, by contrast, it is at the centre of Wordsworth's thinking—a support alike for his faith in the value of primal experience, and for the further definitions of Part II as he goes on to explore more fully the role of imagination. In its early form the passage is brief and to the point, half the length of the more pompous later version:

> There are in our existence spots of time
> Which with distinct preeminence retain
> A fructifying virtue, whence, depressed
> By trivial occupations and the round
> Of ordinary intercourse, our minds—
> Especially the imaginative power—
> Are nourished and invisibly repaired;
> Such moments chiefly seem to have their date
> In our first childhood.
>   (1799, I, 288–96)

An interesting comparison is set up by the echoes of *Tintern Abbey.* Wordsworth is concerned, as he had been six months earlier in July 1798, with moods in which "the heavy and the weary weight / Of all this unintelligible world / Is lightened," and lightened not by a present event, but by memories of the past. One can go further, and say that in both *Tintern Abbey* and the two-Part *Prelude* the memories as well as being restorative imply an imaginative creation, and that they are abnormally non-nostalgic. And, in terms of function, one can add that the poetry in both cases demonstrates, and exists to justify, the prevailing optimism of Wordsworth's view of life. Here the resemblances cease. In *Tintern Abbey* the restorative memories are of landscape, whereas the "spots of time," if they are about Nature at all, are about it in a far less obvious sense. But the main difference, of course, is that in the lines from the two-Part *Prelude* the pantheism of July 1798 has been replaced. Wordsworth, who six months before had derived his love of Nature, and his belief in her restorative influence, from "A motion and a spirit, that impels / All thinking things, all objects of all thought," is now seen taking up a purely humanist position. To understand what has happened is, I believe, to understand the greatness of the early *Prelude*—indeed, to a large extent, of the poem in all its forms.

For a start one has to go back to examine the impulse behind 1799, why it was that Wordsworth started writing. "Was is for *this*," he begins, unconscious for the moment that he has embarked on a major work:

> Was it for *this*
> That one, the fairest of all rivers, loved
> To blend his murmurs with my nurse's song . . .

> For *this* didst thou,
> O Derwent . . .

> fairest of all streams,
> Was it for *this* that I, a four years' child,
> A naked boy, among thy silent pools
> Made one long bathing of a summer's day . . .
> (1799, I, 1–3, 6–7, 16–19)

From these questions the two-Part *Prelude* evolves. It is Wordsworth's excuse for not getting on with the great philosophical work which Coleridge felt so confident that he could write. At the end of Part I, in a reflective passage that is addressed specifically to Coleridge, Wordsworth remarks:

> Meanwhile my hope has been that I might fetch
> Reproaches from my former years, whose power
> May spur me on, in manhood now mature,
> To honourable toil.
>
> (1799, I, 450–53)

In 1805 there is talk at this point of fetching "invigorating thoughts" as well, but in 1799 the emphasis is solely on reproach. Wordsworth is going back into his childhood to find out what is wrong, writing this poem to find out why he cannot write the one he should. Almost at once, however, it must have been apparent to him that as well as stimulating reproaches, his childhood memories could provide material that would actually replace the philosophy that Coleridge expected him to produce. In the long run this would be no help, but for the moment it offered a very congenial alternative.

The scheme of *The Recluse* (the poem that Wordsworth should have been writing) had been mapped out at Alfoxden in the spring of 1798, at the height of Wordsworth's belief in the One Life—a belief inspired by the Unitarian Coleridge—but by the end of the year, at Goslar, Wordsworth seems to be thinking in different terms. Had *The Recluse* been started at Alfoxden it would only have been a pantheist manifesto like *The Pedlar*:

> in all things
> He saw one life, and felt that it was joy.[5]

At Goslar there is just one instance of similar commitment, in a discarded draft of *MS. JJ* (MS. Drafts and Fragments I [a], 98–115, above); elsewhere the pantheism has been reduced to a literary, sub-classical spirit world—"polytheism" might be the better word:

> Ye powers of earth, ye genii of the springs,
> And ye that have your voices in the clouds,
> And ye that are familiars of the lakes
> And of the standing pools, I may not think
> A vulgar hope was yours when ye employed
> Such ministry . . .
> (1799, I, 186–91)

The "Godkins and Goddesslings"[6] are unfortunate, but they fade out very early in the poem, and one could argue that they convey Wordsworth's sense of having had a divinely favored childhood with an acceptable *lack* of credibility (we should not, after all, be happier if he said that God had led him to steal boats). In fact I think we read past them easily enough, aware at once of their clumsiness and their usefulness to the poet. When Wordsworth tells us of his belief that

> there are spirits which, when they would form
> A favored being, from his very dawn
> Of infancy do open out the clouds
> As at the touch of lightning, seeking him
> With gentle visitation . . .
> (1799, I, 69–73)

and others

> who use,
> Yet haply aiming at the self-same end,
> Severer interventions, ministry
> More palpable . . .
> (1799, I, 77–80)

we react not as to an expression of faith in supernatural powers, but as to a figurative way of saying that in his (for the period) very

5. Lines 217–18, quoted from Jonathan Wordsworth, *The Music of Humanity* (London and New York, 1969), 179.

6. The phrase is used by Coleridge of Greek polytheism in 1802 (Griggs, II, 865).

surprising view, it was the painful moments of a happy childhood that had been most formative.

But this is to make Wordsworth's relation to his earlier belief sound simpler than it was. He never repudiated the One Life, and when looking for material (as he habitually did) in his own unpublished verse, he was at all times willing to incorporate pantheist lines from 1798. The process goes on as late as *The Excursion* of 1814, where one comes across "There is an active principle alive / In all things", changed in tone but not in substance,[7] and it begins in Part II of the two-Part *Prelude*, written at Sockburn in autumn 1799. At this period Wordsworth not only incorporated a central passage from *The Pedlar* in order to portray his own state of mind aged seventeen—including the lines quoted above (with altered pronoun), "In all things / *I* saw one life, and felt that it was joy"—but also, more surprisingly, tried to write a companion piece in the same exalted vein. One cannot know what were his feelings as he did so—to what extent he was recording a positive conviction—but it is interesting that he seems almost at once to have decided that he had gone too far. In the original draft, preserved in *Peter Bell*, MS. 2, we hear of "Relapses from the one interior life,"

> In which all beings live with God, *themselves*
> *Are God*, existing in one mighty whole,
> As undistinguishable as the cloudless east
> At noon is from the cloudless west, when all
> The hemisphere is one cerulean blue.
>   (MS. Drafts and Fragments [2d], 16–20, above)

"Themselves / Are God", the extreme pantheist view is logical enough if one believes in a spirit that impels "all thinking things" as well as "all objects of all thought", and at the time of *Tintern Abbey* Wordsworth might well not have shied away from it—though he must have known how badly it frightened Joseph Priestley, and Coleridge, and many another descendant of Spinoza[8]—but now one can actually watch him taking fright. In MS. RV, where the bulk of the passage has been incorporated in an early version of Part II, the central lines have been modified to read:

> In which all beings live with God, *are lost*
> *In God and Nature*, in one mighty whole . . .

And in the duplicate faircopies of 1799, MSS. V and U, the sequence is cut altogether. One important fragment does however remain of Wordsworth's original draft from the *Peter Bell MS.*—a

---

7. As the opening of Book IX.
8. Benedictus de Spinoza (1632–77) held that God is immanent within the universe and was a lasting influence on Coleridge —as was Joseph Priestley (1733–1804), scientist and founder of modern Unitarianism.

passage of four lines that had been imbedded earlier in the poem in an address to Coleridge at II, 251–4:

> Thou, my friend, art one
> More deeply read in thy own thoughts, no slave
> *Of that false secondary power by which*
> *In weakness we create distinctions, then*
> *Believe our puny boundaries are things*
> *Which we perceive, and not which we have made.*

Wordsworth's observation is extremely sharp, but the passage is remarkable above all for its positioning. By implication it comes to refer to a tendency in the poet himself to categorize, impose distinctions, in contrast to the unified vision of Coleridge that is the subject of the following lines:

> To thee, unblinded by these outward shews,
> The unity of all has been revealed . . .
>   (1799, II, 255–56)

This admiring, slightly envious, reference to Coleridge's Unitarianism points up the difference between the two poets' commitment to the One Life. Coleridge believed in it, and passed it on to Wordsworth, as a form of Christianity; but Wordsworth took it over without its doctrinal implications. It came to him as confirmation of a harmony intuitively perceived. Coleridge was clear enough in theory that

> 'Tis the sublime of man,
> Our noontide Majesty, to know ourselves
> Parts and proportions of one wond'rous whole! . . .[9]

but in practice found it difficult to do anything of the kind:

> the universe itself—what but an immense heap of *little* things?
> . . . My mind feels as if it ached to behold & know something
> great—something *one & indivisible*—and it is only in the faith
> of this that rocks or waterfalls, mountains or caverns give me
> the sense of sublimity or majesty! . . .[1]

Wordsworth, by contrast, did think of rocks and waterfalls in terms of "the one & indivisible"—it was natural to him to do so. For a brief period in 1798 Coleridge gave this intuition a philosophical basis, fitted it to a system; but, for some reason that we cannot know, the system lost its hold. By the time of the two-Part *Prelude* Wordsworth has been thrown back on the intuition, is envious of Coleridge to whom "the unity of all" has been positively *revealed*, and is himself to be seen looking for a new and different means of

9. *Religious Musings*, 135–37.
1. Letter to John Thelwall, October 14, 1797; Griggs, I, 349.

reconciling the apparent disparateness of experience. Both the structure of his poem, and the structure of his thought, seem to require a supernatural frame of reference. Yet it is the fact of being without one that spurs him in Part I to write his greatest poetry, forces him to define in purely human terms why it is that certain memories of the past should have such importance in his mind. While in Part II, one sees for the first time the astonishing flirtation with the transcendental—use of transcendental implication not in its own right, but as a means of stressing the primacy of the human mind—that is characteristic of Wordsworth's definitions of the role of imagination, 1799–1804.

Again and again in the "spots of time" of Part I Wordsworth portrays, or evokes, moods that are very closely analogous to perception of the supernatural, but which never in fact cross the borderline. Sometimes it is almost a sleight of hand that is being practised:

> oh, at that time,
> While on the perilous ridge I hung alone,
> With what strange utterance did the loud dry wind
> Blow through my ears; the sky seemed not a sky
> Of earth, and with what motion moved the clouds!
> (1799, I, 62–66)

The force of the poetry persuades one to read the last line more as question than as exclamation, as if it were suggesting that the sky was indeed not a sky of earth, and the clouds were moved by some other-than-earthly power; yet one is simultaneously aware that no such transcendental claims are being made. The poetry is vitally dependent on this double awareness. It is the greatness of Wordsworth's writing that we respond to the low breathings of the Woodcock-snaring, the huge and mighty forms of the Boat-stealing, *both as child and as adult*—at once vividly aware *with* the child of the presence of the supernatural, and conscious that *in* the child this awareness is the product of guilt.

In effect Wordsworth is having his cake and eating it. Very recently he had believed it possible to make personal contact with the principle of being; now it seems that he no longer does, or no longer does with any great conviction. Like Thomas Hardy later, he is left "hoping it might be so." Just what Wordsworth experienced as a child we cannot tell; but it is a fair assumption that it was nothing beyond the guilt, fear, and other quite ordinary emotions that an adult perceives in the "spots of time." It is the need to replace his faith in the One Life that gives the "spots" their intensity, the fact that like Hardy, who would go to see the Christmas oxen kneel

> In the lonely barton by yonder coombe,
> Our childhood used to know . . .[2]

Wordsworth is yearning for a certainty in which he cannot rationally believe. Having lost the passionate conviction of *The Pedlar* and *Tintern Abbey* in which the universe had seemed to be one of blessedness and love, and Nature's "privilege" had been "to lead from joy to joy," he goes back to earlier periods in his life when, however painfully, he had seemed to approach the borders of another world.[3] No doubt these memories did hold for him a special importance, but it was the peculiar circumstances of his loss that enabled him to create from them at one brief moment in the winter of 1798–99 poetry that despite its particular detail has seemed to so many to have a universal relevance.

The earlier "spots" of the two-Part *Prelude* (those associated with Book I of the longer poem) evoke the peculiar quality of childhood, invite the reader to participate both as adult and as child in a re-creation of primal experience: the second group attempts to define how such experience is intensified within the mind, becomes a link in the chain of development, a portion of the child's, and of the adult's, identity. These later "spots" show in their original context a progression that may be assumed to be deliberate. One starts with the episode of the Drowned Man, which is highly important in its effect on the sequence as a whole, but in itself very simple. Wordsworth as a child of nine, newly arrived at Hawkshead Grammar School, is exploring Esthwaite Water—

> thy paths, thy shores
> And brooks, were like a dream of novelty
> To my half infant mind . . .

—and sees across the water a pile of clothes:

> Twilight was coming on, yet through the gloom
> I saw distinctly on the opposite shore,
> Beneath a tree and close by the lake side,
> A heap of garments, as if left by one
> Who there was bathing. Half an hour I watched
> And no one owned them; meanwhile the calm lake
> Grew dark with all the shadows on its breast,
> And now and then a leaping fish disturbed
> The breathless stillness. The succeeding day
> There came a company, and in their boat
> Sounded with iron hooks and with long poles.

2. *The Oxen*, 13–14. The quotation above is from the concluding line of this poem. [*Editors.*]

3. For an extended discussion of Wordsworth's concern with border states, and a much fuller treatment of the 1799 *Prelude*, see my forthcoming book, *William Wordsworth: The Borders of Vision*.

> At length the dead man, 'mid that beauteous scene
> Of trees and hills and water, bolt upright
> Rose with his ghastly face.
>
> (1799, I, 261–63, 266–79)

So much for the actual description, plain, beautifully visualized, making no claims for itself. In 1805, when exiled to the fifth (and most obviously hodge-podge) Book of the extended poem, the passage is followed by some fairly unconvincing assertions designed to tie it into the theme of education—the child is apparently not frightened, because he has read about such things in fairy tales. In 1799, however, there is a bridge passage of great importance that links the episode through into the discussion of "spots of time": "I might advert," it begins, rather pompously,

> To numerous accidents in flood or field,
> Quarry or moor, or 'mid the winter snows,
> Distresses and disasters, tragic facts
> Of rural history, that impressed my mind
> With images to which in following years
> Far other feelings were attached—with forms
> That yet exist with independent life,
> And, like their archetypes, know no decay.
>   There are in our existence spots of time . . .
>
> (1799, I, 279–88)

Thus in the two-Part *Prelude* one moves from the Drowned Man (whose ghastly face is allowed to be disquieting) through a discussion of the imaginative process that impresses such "tragic facts" upon the mind, to an affirmation of their restorative power, and on into the two more fully worked-out "spots" that reinforce it. It is not too much to say that the Drowned Man exerts his influence on the whole sequence, setting up an expectation of the sort of memories that are to be talked about, and preparing for the mood of "visionary dreariness" that is to be evoked. The episode is, however, very limited—I would suggest *deliberately* limited. What happens is vividly seen, vividly described, but still on the level of an event— something that could be experienced by others, though most impressive to the poet because of his "more than usual organic sensibility", and because of the solitary intensity of his waiting. The incident prepares the way for Wordsworth's definitions, and these in turn prepare for the "spots" in which experience becomes fully imaginative, takes on an independent life within the mind, and, in that context, achieves an archetypal permanence.

And so I come back to the woman with her garments vexed and tossed by the wind. I make no apology for being fascinated by this great piece of Wordsworthian poetry, and especially by the central figure. In a curious way the passage reminds one of *The Thorn.* The mound where Martha Ray may have buried her child becomes the "long green ridge of turf . . . Whose shape was like a grave"; the pond in which she may have drowned it becomes the "naked pool that lay beneath the hills"; Martha on her hilltop, known to "every wind that blows," surely lies behind the woman forcing her way "with difficult steps . . . against the blowing wind." Again the background is one of murder, but the horror and titillation of the earlier poem have gone. In *The Thorn* the narrator and his questioning force us to ask "Did it really happen?" "What is it all about?"—here no questions are raised. Martha is on the hill because she was jilted, because she is mad, because she is a murderess: the woman with her garments vexed and tossed simply exists. If we look for them we can see that she has affinities to Martha, and even in a different way to Margaret of *The Ruined Cottage;* but the wind that blows her clothing implies no suffering, the water she carries, no relationship. It is unthinkable, for instance, that she should befriend the child, put her pitcher down to give him a drink. Even the Leech Gatherer, part stone, part sea-beast as he is, may be approached; but not this most dream-like of Wordsworth's solitaries. Not that she is insubstantial—she is forcing her way with success against the wind—but she seems to stand outside the ordinary limitations of a physical world. One responds to her almost as an emanation of the child's mind, not merely acted upon, but produced by the "visionary dreariness" that is his mood.

If one turns to the Waiting for the Horses, which concludes the sequence, it is to find a still further development away from objective reality towards a poetry purely of the mind. Wordsworth has climbed a crag to keep watch for the horses that have been sent to take him and his two brothers home from school:

> 'Twas a day
> Stormy, and rough, and wild, and on the grass
> I sate, half-sheltered by a naked wall.
> Upon my right hand was a single sheep,
> A whistling hawthorn on my left, and there,
> Those two companions at my side, I watched
> With eyes intensely straining, as the mist
> Gave intermitting prospects of the wood
> And plain beneath.
>
> (1799, I, 341–49)

One wall, one sheep, one tree—the ingredients of Wordsworth's poetry can seldom have been less exciting; and yet we read on, waiting expectantly as the child himself is waiting. This time there is to be no Drowned Man bobbing up with his ghastly face, not even

the much less palpable presence of the woman on the hill. Wordsworth has moved on. With the Drowned Man, the beauty of the
poetry lies in the child's anticipation—

> meanwhile the calm lake
> Grew dark with all the shadows on its breast . . .
> (1799, I, 271–72)

—but something *does* happen, and we are invited to think that the
incident is intensified within the memory by the waiting. With the
woman on the hill we enter another, far more imaginative, world, in
which the distinction between perception and projection is blurred.
Wordsworth is talking now clearly about the mind, not the external
world; and yet the formula is still the same as in the crude earlier
"spots of time": heightened emotion leading to heightened response
and the fixing in the memory of an event not as it was, but as at the
time it seemed. In the Waiting for the Horses there is a further, very
surprising, extension. Out of the unpromising details described in
the passage quoted above, the mind *later* creates an important and
formative experience. To be more precise, Wordsworth's father dies;
his death seems to the child a punishment for the hopes that he had
felt as he waited to come home; and this guilt imbues the remembered scene with new vividness and power:

> And afterwards the wind and sleety rain,
> And all the business of the elements,
> The single sheep, and the one blasted tree,
> And the bleak music of that old stone wall,
> The noise of wood and water, and the mist
> Which on the line of each of those two roads
> Advanced in such indisputable shapes—
> All these were spectacles and sounds to which
> I often would repair, and thence would drink
> As at a fountain. And I do not doubt
> That in this later time, when storm and rain
> Beat on my roof at midnight, or by day
> When I am in the woods, unknown to me
> The workings of my spirit thence are brought.
> (1799, I, 361–74)

Readers of 1805 (and 1850) are probably aware of a slackening
in the poetry as Wordsworth moves from memories of intense,
solitary childhood experience in the first Book, to those of convivial
adolescence in the second. In 1799 the falling-off might be expected
to be clearer still—Part II is substantially similar to Book II, and
follows a more powerful opening section. But the two Parts of 1799
are a single unit, as the first two Books of 1805 are not. And the

"additional" lines of Part I are not merely good poetry, they are the basis of a continuing discussion, and essential to a full understanding of Part II. As Professor MacGillivray pointed out in his pioneering essay on "The Three Forms of *The Prelude*" (1964), 1799 is more tightly constructed than 1805, and has as its single theme the birth and growth of imagination. The study of developing consciousness in Part II is qualified (as the corresponding lines in Book II cannot be) by awareness of Wordsworth's theory of the mind as self-nourished by experience that is modified, re-created, over the years. At the same time, the great central section of Part II, the study of the child in relationship to his mother (1799, II, 267–310), comes into its own when it is seen to be a radical and necessary development of the thinking of Part I.

As Wordsworth began work on Part II, after an eight months' interval, he does seem to have intended a simple extension of his poem to take in the period of adolescence. The first two hundred lines he composed[4] are memorable for the beautiful yet undeveloped "spots of time" showing the boy's response to the song of the wren at Furness Abbey (1799, II, 98–139—revised, incidentally, for the worse in 1805) and to the flute-playing on Windermere (1799, II, 204–14). Wordsworth was not at this stage asking questions, he was recording—making permanent—moments of deep, yet relatively uncomplex emotion. But sooner or later the questions did have to be asked. To what was the boy responding? And what was the power within that enabled him to make such responses? At lines 239–42 Wordsworth was hastening on

> to tell
> How Nature, intervenient till this time
> And secondary, now at length was sought
> For her own sake.

But then he paused:

> who shall parcel out
> His intellect by geometric rules . . . ?

> Who that shall point as with a wand, and say
> "This portion of the river of my mind
> Came from yon fountain"?
>
> (lines 242–49)

It is at this point that we come on the envious reference to Coleridge as one to whom the unity of all has been *revealed*; Wordsworth is feeling the lack of a supporting transcendental frame of reference—feeling his way towards a definition of what he needs to, or can, believe. The polytheist spirits of Part I, with whatever degree

4. Lines 6–45 were inserted at a secondary stage.

of seriousness one takes them, must represent relatively late environmental influences. Now, in order to carry his poem forward, answer the basic question as to what may be found by those who seek Nature *for her own sake*, Wordsworth has first to move backwards. We return in lines 267–310 to "the infant babe," who alone can tell us what are the sources of the adult creative power already to be seen in the child of the "spots of time."

One might say crudely that this great passage—too long to quote in full—works on three levels. The first is that of Wordsworth's intuition that the child "gather[s] passion from his mother's eye," that her "feelings pass into his torpid life / Like an awakening breeze":

> Thus day by day
> Subjected to the discipline of love,
> His organs and recipient faculties
> Are quickened, are more vigorous; his mind spreads,
> Tenacious of the forms which it receives.
> In one beloved presence . . .
>
> And those sensations which have been derived
> From this beloved presence—there exists
> A virtue which irradiates and exalts
> All objects through all intercourse of sense.
> (1799, II, 273–75, 280–85, 287–90)

One is alerted to the second level, that of near-transcendental implication, by the echo in these last two lines of *Tintern Abbey*, 101–2:

> A motion and a spirit, that impels
> All thinking things, all objects of all thought . . .[5]

Objects of the external world are irradiated for the child by the presence of his mother, just as for the Wordsworth of 1798 they had been permeated by the One Life:

> I have felt
> A presence that disturbs me with the joy
> Of elevated thoughts; a sense sublime
> Of something far more deeply interfused . . .
> (*Tintern Abbey*, 94–97)

To confirm that there was at least an unconscious link in Wordsworth's mind, the word "interfused" (not elsewhere recorded until a *Prelude* revision of 1832) appears two lines further on in the Infant Babe:

> No outcast he, bewildered and depressed;
> Along his infant veins are interfused

5. The link was first pointed out by F. R. Leavis; see *1799*, II, 290n.

> The gravitation and the filial bond
> Of Nature that connect him with the world.
>
> (1799, II, 291–94)

Professor Onorato has suggested that Wordsworth's odd reference to the child as potentially an "outcast" reflects his own traumatic sense of desertion at the time of his mother's death,[6] and his case is strengthened by the original RV reading "abandoned" for "bewildered" in II, 291. Wordsworth's need was to feel that he belonged, that he was part of an integrated whole; in July 1798 the need could be satisfied by pantheist affirmation, in autumn 1799 there was no comparable certainty. And so we get a bond connecting the child to the world that is both straightforwardly human—"filial" by virtue of the child's relationship to his mother—and potentially transcendental, in that the mother has been replaced, and the child is now a son of Nature. An early single-line version of lines 274–75 shows just how close these two ways of thinking were for Wordsworth: "Such passion [the mother's love] is the awakening breeze of life."

A similar ambivalence—part retreat from, part reliance upon, the supernatural—is to be seen in the surprising qualities that Wordsworth attributes to the child:

> Emphatically such a being lives,
> An inmate of this *active* universe.
> From Nature largely he receives, nor so
> Is satisfied, but largely gives again;
> For feeling has to him imparted strength,
> And—powerful in all sentiments of grief,
> Of exultation, fear and joy—his mind,
> Even as an agent of the one great mind,
> Creates, creator and receiver both,
> Working but in alliance with the works
> Which it beholds.
>
> (1799, II, 295–305)

We have an "*active* universe"—the italics are present in all three MSS.—but not a universe activated by the One Life. The child is godlike in his powers, and acts as an agent of God, but he is not imbued with godhead. He receives, and because he is strong in feeling (initially his mother's love) he gives again; but he works merely in alliance with the external world, he does not share the same life force. Love remains the activating principle, but it is a local love—that of mother and child—enhanced by transcendental reference and implication, not the total sharing of 1798:

> Such, verily, is the first
> Poetic spirit of our human life—
> By uniform control of after years

---

6. See Richard J. Onorato, *The Character of the Poet* (Princeton, 1971), 69–70.

> In most abated and suppressed, in some
> Through every change of growth or of decay
> Preeminent till death.
>
> (1799, II, 305–10)

There had been hints towards a definition of imagination in Wordsworth's earlier poetry,[7] but in the Infant Babe one hears for the first
time the tones of his and Coleridge's more famous later pronounce-
ments. As "creator and receiver both," the child anticipates the
creative and perceptive "higher minds" of 1805, XIII:

> They from their native selves can send abroad
> Like transformation, for themselves create
> A like existence, and, whene'er it is
> Created for them, catch it by an instinct . . .
>
> (lines 93–96)

And one should not be afraid to say that he anticipates too the
primary imagination of *Biographia Literaria*—"the living Power and
prime Agent of all human Perception . . . a repetition in the finite
mind of the eternal act of creation in the infinite I AM."[8] In its
more ordinary, "secondary", aspects the imagination could be tied
down, but Wordsworth in his greatest years, and Coleridge at all
times, wished to make for it claims of a more exalted kind. Their
language is evocative, expressive of need and hope rather than certainty, because they are ascribing to the human mind a godlike
quality in which they only half dare to believe.

Among the last passages of 1799, two especially stand out—the
extraordinary statement in lines 417–25 that the boy's devotion to
Nature was based on qualities that he himself conferred:

> An auxiliar light
> Came from my mind, which on the setting sun
> Bestowed new splendour; the melodious birds,
> The gentle breezes, fountains that ran on
> Murmuring so sweetly in themselves, obeyed
> A like dominion, and the midnight storm
> Grew darker in the presence of my eye.
> Hence my obeisance, my devotion hence,
> And *hence* my transport.

And, more impressive still, the lines (actually written in 1798) that
express perhaps better than anything else in his poetry the urgency
of Wordsworth's personal quest:

> I deem not profitless these fleeting moods
> Of shadowy exaltation; not for this,
> That they are kindred to our purer mind

---

7. See, e.g., *Pedlar*, 30–43 and lines 105–
10 of the draft conclusion to *The Ruined
Cottage* (*Music of Humanity*, 174, 272).

8. *Biographia Literaria*, ed. George Watson (London and New York, 1956), p.
167.

And intellectual life, but that the soul—
Remembering how she felt, but what she felt
Remembering not—retains an obscure sense
Of possible sublimity, to which
With growing faculties she doth aspire,
With faculties still growing, feeling still
That whatsoever point they gain they still
Have something to pursue.

(1799, II, 361–71)

What other major poet can one *now* take seriously when he talks about the development of individual consciousness? There are times when Wordsworth fails to convince, or when he is blatantly writing for propagandist purposes, but in his greatest work—*The Ruined Cottage,* for instance, and *The Prelude* in all its forms—he shows an insight into the workings of the mind that is not to be found elsewhere in English poetry. In Keats's phrase, he thinks into the human heart. It is surely no bad thing to do.

M. H. ABRAMS

The Design of *The Prelude:* Wordsworth's Long Journey Home†

In the "Prospectus" to his intended masterwork, *The Recluse,* Wordsworth announces that his "high argument" will be the capacity of the mind of man, "When wedded to this goodly universe / In love and holy passion," to transform the world into a paradise which will be "A simple produce of the common day."[1] He goes on to pray to the "prophetic Spirit" that

if with this
I mix more lowly matter; with the thing
Contemplated, describe the Mind and Man
Contemplating; and who, and what he was—
The transitory Being that beheld
This Vision; when and where, and how he lived;—
Be not this labour useless.

In this way Wordsworth designated and justified the personal narrative which makes up the opening book of *The Recluse* he called *Home at Grasmere,* as well as the entire poem that his wife later

---

† From M. H. Abrams, *Natural Supernaturalism: Tradition and Revolution in Romantic Literature* (New York; W. W. Norton & Company, 1971). This essay incorporates a revised version of chapter 2, section 1, and chapter 5, section 2.

1. Wordsworth excerpted the verse passage that he called "a kind of Prospectus of the design and scope" of *The Recluse* from the conclusion to *Home at Grasmere* and printed it in his Preface to *The Excursion* (1814).

named *The Prelude*. Wordsworth described the latter work as a "tributary" and also "as a sort of portico to the Recluse, part of the same building."[2] The time taken to compose *The Prelude* straddled the writing of the Prospectus, and the completed *Prelude* was conceived as an integral part of the overall structure whose "design and scope" Wordsworth specified in that poetic manifesto. "The Poem on the growth of your own mind," as Coleridge recalled the plan in 1815, "was as the ground-plat and the Roots, out of which the Recluse was to have sprung up as the Tree"—two distinct works, but forming "one compleat Whole."[3] The role of *The Prelude*, as Wordsworth himself describes his grand design, is to recount the mental growth of a "transitory Being," culminating in his achievement of a "Vision," and in the recognition that his mission is to impart the circumstances and results of that vision in the enduring form of an unprecedented poem:

> Possessions have I that are solely mine,
> Something within which yet is shared by none . . .
> I would impart it, I would spread it wide,
> Immortal in the world which is to come.[4]

The Idea of The Prelude

In this era of constant and drastic experimentation with literary materials and forms, it is easy to overlook the radical novelty of *The Prelude* when it was completed in 1805. The poem amply justified Wordsworth's claim to have demonstrated original genius, which he defined as "the introduction of a new element into the intellectual universe" of which the "infallible sign is the widening the sphere of human sensibility."[5]

The Prelude is a fully developed poetic equivalent of two portentous innovations in prose fiction, of which the earliest examples had appeared in Germany only a decade or so before Wordsworth began writing his poem: the *Bildungsroman* (Wordsworth called *The Prelude* a poem on "the growth of my own mind") and the *Künstlerroman*[6] (Wordsworth also spoke of it as "a poem on my own poetical education," and it far surpassed all German examples in the detail with which his "history," as he said, was specifically "of a

2. To De Quincey, March 6, 1804, *Letters: The Early Years* (2nd ed.; Oxford, 1967), p. 454; to Beaumont, June 3, 1805, ibid., p. 594.
3. To Wordsworth, May 30, 1815, *Collected Letters* (Oxford, 1956–59) [Griggs], IV, 573.
4. *Home at Grasmere*, lines 686–91, preceding the Prospectus.
5. "Essay, Supplementary to the Preface of 1815."
6. *Bildungsroman*: a novel about the protagonist's development from infancy to maturity. *Künstlerroman*: a novel about the development of an artist.

Poet's mind").[7] The whole poem is written as a sustained address to Coleridge—"I speak bare truth / As if alone to thee in private talk" (X, 372–73); Coleridge, however, is an auditor *in absentia,* and the solitary author often supplements this form with an interior monologue, or else carries on an extended colloquy with the landscape in which the interlocutors are "my mind" and "the speaking face of earth and heaven" (V, 11–12). The construction of *The Prelude* is drastically achronological, starting not at the beginning, but at the end—during Wordsworth's walk to "the Vale that I had chosen" (I, 100), which telescopes the circumstances of two or more occasions but refers primarily to his walk to the Vale of Grasmere, that "hermitage" (I, 115) where he has taken up residence at that stage of his life with which the poem concludes.[8] During this walk an outer breeze, "the sweet breath of Heaven," evokes within the poet, "a corresponding mild creative breeze," a prophetic *spiritus* or inspiration which assures him of his poetic vocation and, though it is fitful, eventually leads to his undertaking *The Prelude* itself; in the course of the poem, at times of imaginative dryness, the revivifying wind recurs in the role of a poetic leitmotif.[9]

Wordsworth does not tell his life as a simple narrative in past time but as the present remembrance of things past, in which forms and sensations "throw back our life" (I, 660–61) and evoke the former self which coexists with the altered present self in a multiple awareness that Wordsworth calls "two consciousnesses." There is a wide "vacancy" between the I now and the I then,

> Which yet have such self-presence in my mind
> That, sometimes, when I think of them, I seem
> Two consciousnesses, conscious of myself
> And of some other Being.
>
> (II, 27–33)

The poet is aware of the near impossibility of disengaging "the naked recollection of that time" from the intrusions of "after-meditation" (III, 644–48). In a fine and subtle figure for the interdiffusion of the two consciousnesses (IV, 247–64), he describes himself as one bending from a drifting boat on a still water, perplexed to distinguish actual objects at the bottom of the lake from surface

---

7. *Letters: The Early Years,* p. 518; Isabella Fenwick note to "There Was a Boy"; and *The Prelude,* XIII, 408. (All references are to *The Prelude* of 1805, unless indicated by the date 1850.) [Quotations are drawn from *Oxford "Prelude"* —Editors.]
8. For convincing evidence that the chief prototype of the walk described in the "preamble" to *The Prelude* was Wordsworth's walk to Grasmere, see John Finch, "Wordsworth's Two-Handed Engine," *Bicentenary Wordsworth Studies,* ed. Jonathan Wordsworth (Ithaca, N.Y., 1970). But Wordsworth probably telescoped events from several walks in real life, to make the "preamble" to *The Prelude* a typological change of venue, signifying a new stage in his spiritual history.
9. E.g., VII, 1–56; XI, 1–12.

reflections of the surrounding scene, from the tricks and refractions of the water currents, and from his own intrusive but inescapable mirror image (that is, his present awareness). Thus "incumbent o'er the surface of past time" the poet, seeking the elements of continuity between his two disparate selves, conducts a persistent exploration of the nature and significance of memory, of his power to sustain freshness of sensation and his "first creative sensibility" against the deadening effect of habit and analysis, and of manifestations of the enduring and the eternal within the realm of change and time. Only intermittently does the narrative order coincide with the order of actual occurrence. Instead Wordsworth proceeds by sometimes bewildering ellipses, fusions, and as he says, "motions retrograde" in time (IX, 8).

Scholars have long been aware that it is perilous to rely on the factual validity of *The Prelude*, and in consequence Wordsworth has been charged with uncertainty, ineptitude, bad memory, or even bad faith. The poem has suffered because we know so much about the process of its composition between 1798 and 1805—its evolution from a constituent part to a "tail-piece" to a "portico" of *The Recluse*, and Wordsworth's late decision, in 1804, to add to the beginning and end of the poem the excluded middle: his experiences in London and in France. A work is to be judged, however, as a finished and free-standing product; and in *The Prelude* as it emerged after some seven years of working and reworking, the major alterations and dislocations of the events of Wordsworth's life are imposed deliberately, in order that the design inherent in that life, which has become apparent only to his mature awareness, may stand revealed as a principle which was invisibly operative from the beginning. A supervising idea, in other words, controls Wordsworth's account and shapes it into a structure in which the protagonist is put forward as one who has been elected to play a special role in a providential plot. As Wordsworth said in the opening passage, which represents him after he has reached maturity: in response to the quickening outer breeze

> to the open fields I told
> A prophecy: poetic numbers came
> Spontaneously, and cloth'd in priestly robe
> My spirit, thus singled out, as it might seem,
> For holy services.
>
> (I, 59–63)

Hence in this history of a poet's mind the poet is indeed the "transitory Being," William Wordsworth, but he is also the exemplary poet-prophet who has been singled out, in a time "of hopes o'erthrown . . . of dereliction and dismay" (II, 448–57), to bring mankind tidings

of comfort and joy; as Wordsworth put it in one version of the
Prospectus,

> that my verse may live and be
> Even as a light hung up in heaven to chear
> Mankind in times to come.

The spaciousness of his chosen form allows Wordsworth to in
troduce some of the clutter and contingency of ordinary life. In
accordance with his controlling idea, however, he selects for extended treatment only those experiences which are significant for his
evolution toward an inherent end, and organizes his life around an
event which he regards as the spiritual crisis not of himself only, but
of his generation: that shattering of the fierce loyalties and inordinate hopes for mankind which the liberal English—and European
—intellectuals had invested in the French Revolution.

> Not in my single self alone I found,
> But in the minds of all ingenuous Youth,
> Change and subversion from this hour.
>   (X, 232–34)

The Prelude, correspondingly, is ordered in three stages. There is a
process of unified mental development which, although at times
suspended, remains a continuum; this process is shattered by a crisis
of apathy and despair; but the mind then recovers an integrity
which, despite admitted losses, is represented as a level higher than
the initial unity, in that the mature mind possesses powers, together
with an added range, depth, and humanity, which are the products
of the critical experiences it has undergone. The discovery of this
fact resolves a central problem which has been implicit throughout
The Prelude—the problem of how to justify the human experience
of pain and loss and suffering; he is now able to recognize that his
life is "in the end / All gratulant if rightly understood" (XIII,
384–85).

The narrative is punctuated with recurrent illuminations, or
"spots of time," and is climaxed by two major revelations. The first
of these is Wordsworth's discovery of precisely what he has been
born to be and to do. At Cambridge he had reached a stage of life,
"an eminence," in which he had felt that he was "a chosen Son"
(III, 82 ff., 169), and on a walk home from a dance during a
summer dawn he had experienced an illumination that he should be,
"else sinning greatly, / A dedicated Spirit" (IV, 343–44); but for
what chosen, or to what dedicated, had not been specified. Now,
however, the recovery from the crisis of despair after his commitment to the French Revolution comprises the insight that his destiny is not one of engagement with what is blazoned "with the

pompous names / Of power and action" in "the stir / And tumult of
the world," but one of withdrawal from the world of action so that
he may meditate in solitude: his role in life requires not involve-
ment, but detachment.[1] And that role is to be one of the "Poets,
even as Prophets," each of whom is endowed with the power "to
perceive / Something unseen before," and so to write a new kind of
poetry in a new poetic style. "Of these, said I, shall be my Song; of
these . . . / Will I record the praises": the ordinary world of lowly,
suffering men and of commonplace or trivial things transformed
into "a new world . . . fit / To be transmitted," of dignity, love, and
heroic grandeur (XII, 220–379). Wordsworth's crisis, then, involved what we now call a crisis of identity, which was resolved in
the discovery of "my office upon earth" (X, 921). And since the
specification of this office entails the definition, in the twelfth book,
of the particular innovations in poetic subjects, style, and values
toward which his life had been implicitly oriented, *The Prelude* is
a poem which incorporates the discovery of its own *ars poetica*.[2]

His second revelation he achieves on a mountaintop. The occasion is the ascent of Mount Snowdon, which Wordsworth, in
accordance with his controlling idea, excerpts from its chronological position in his life in 1791, before the crucial experience of
France, and describes in the concluding book of *The Prelude*. As he
breaks through the cover of clouds the light of the moon "upon the
turf / Fell like a flash," and he sees the total scene as "the perfect
image of a mighty Mind" in its free and continuously creative
reciprocity with its milieu, "Willing to work and to be wrought
upon" and so to "create / A like existence" (XIII, 36–119). What
has been revealed to Wordsworth in this symbolic landscape is the
grand locus of *The Recluse* which he announced in the Prospectus,
"The Mind of Man— / My haunt, and the main region of my
song," as well as the "high argument" of that poem, the union
between the mind and the external world and the resulting "creation
. . . which they with blended might / Accomplish." The event which
Wordsworth selects for the climactic revelation in *The Prelude*,
then, is precisely the moment of the achievement of "this Vision" by
"the transitory Being" whose life he had, in the Prospectus, undertaken to describe as an integral part of *The Recluse*.

In the course of *The Prelude* Wordsworth repeatedly drops the
clue that his work has been designed to round back to its point of
departure. "Not with these began / Our Song, and not with these
our Song must end," he cried after the crisis of France, invoking the
"breezes and soft airs"[3] that had blown in the "glad preamble" to
his poem and, by evoking an inner "creative breeze," had then

---

1. *The Prelude*, XII, 44–76, 112–16. Cf. 2. Poetic art.
Home at Grasmere, lines 664–752.   3. XI, 1 ff. and VII, 1 ff.

assured him of his poetic vocation. As he nears the end of the song, he says that his self-discovery constitutes a religious conclusion ("The rapture of the Hallelujah sent ∕ From all that breathes and is") which is at the same time, as he had planned from the outset, an artistic beginning:

> And now, O Friend; this history is brought
> To its appointed close: the discipline
> And consummation of the Poet's mind.
>   . . . we have reach'd
> The time (which was our object from the first)
> When we may, not presumptuously, I hope,
> Suppose my powers so far confirmed, and such
> My knowledge, as to make me capable
> Of building up a work that should endure.
>   (XIII, 261–78)

That work, of course, is *The Recluse*, for which *The Prelude* was designed to serve as "portico . . . part of the same building." *The Prelude*, then, is an involuted poem which is about its own genesis —a prelude to itself. Its structural end is its own beginning; and its temporal beginning, as I have pointed out, is Wordsworth's entrance upon the stage of his life at which it ends. The conclusion goes on to specify the circular shape of the whole. Wordsworth there asks Coleridge to "Call back to mind ∕ The mood in which this Poem was begun." At that time,

>   I rose
> As if on wings, and saw beneath me stretch'd
> Vast prospect of the world which I had been
> And was; and hence this Song, which like a lark
> I have protracted. . . .
>   (XIII, 370–81)

This song, describing the prospect of his life which had been made visible to him at the opening of *The Prelude*, is *The Prelude* whose composition he is even now concluding.

The Circuitous Journey

It is time to notice that Wordsworth's account of unity achieved, lost, and regained is held together, as various critics have remarked, by the persistent image of a journey: like a number of works by his contemporaries, Wordsworth's "poem on my own poetical education" converts the wayfaring Christian of the Augustinian spiritual journey[4] into the self-formative traveler of the Romantic educa-

---

4. A reference to the subject of St. Augustine's autobiographical *Confessions*, written late in the fourth century A.D.

tional journey. The poem in fact opens, as Elizabeth Sewell has said, "with the poet in a prospect of wide landscape and open sky," on a literal walk which serves as "the great over-all poetic figure or trope of a journey which he is about to undertake."[5] In the course of this episode the aimless wanderer becomes "as a Pilgrim resolute" who takes "the road that pointed toward the chosen Vale," and at the end of the first book the road translates itself into the metaphorical way of his life's pilgrimage:

> Forthwith shall be brought down
> Through later years the story of my life.
> The road lies plain before me. . . .
> (1850; I, 91–93, 638–40)

The Prelude is replete with "the Wanderers of the Earth" (XII, 156), and after the period of childhood, its chief episodes are Wordsworth's own wanderings through the English countryside, the Alps, Italy, France, and Wales—literal journeys through actual places which modulate easily into symbolic landscapes traversed by a metaphorical wayfarer. This organizing figure works in two dimensions. In one of these, *The Prelude* represents the life which the poet narrates as a self-educative journey, "from stage to stage / Advancing," in which his early development had been "progress on the self-same path," the crisis following the French Revolution had been "a stride at once / Into another region," and the terminus is his achievement of maturity in "the discipline / And consummation of the Poet's mind."[6] In the second application, the poet repeatedly figures his own imaginative enterprise, the act of conceiving and composing *The Prelude* itself, as a perilous quest through the uncharted regions of his own mind.

At times the vehicle for this latter poetic journey is a voyage at sea, connoting the wanderings of Odysseus in his search for home:

> What avail'd,
> When Spells forbade the Voyager to land,
> The fragrance which did ever and anon
> Give notice of the Shore? . . .
> My business was upon the barren sea,
> My errand was to sail to other coasts.
> (XI, 48–56; see I, 35–38)

Elsewhere Wordsworth's implied parallel is to Dante, who "Nell mezzo del cammin di nostra vita"[7] had been granted a visionary journey, with a relay of guides, through hell and the earthly paradise to heaven:

---

5. *The Orphic Voice: Poetry and Natural History* (New Haven, 1960), pp. 338–39.
6. *The Prelude*, XI, 43–44; X, 239–42; XIII, 270–71.

7. "In the middle of the journey of our life"; the line occurs in the opening passage of Dante's *Divine Comedy*.

> A Traveller I am,
> And all my Tale is of myself; even so,
> So be it, if the pure in heart delight
> To follow me; and Thou, O honor'd Friend!
> Who in my thoughts art ever at my side,
> Uphold, as heretofore, my fainting steps.
>
> (III, 196–201)

At the beginning of the ninth book, "as a traveller, who has gained the brow / Of some aerial Down" and "is tempted to review / The region left behind him," Wordsworth turns back to his earlier youth, before he moves reluctantly on into the discordant "argument" that begins with his residence in France—"Oh, how much unlike the past!" (1850: IX, 1–22). The eleventh book, narrating the process of Wordsworth's recovery, opens in a parallel to Milton's description of his epic journey back from hell to the realms of light (XI, 1–7; see *Paradise Lost*, III, 13–20). And through all these regions the imagined presence of Coleridge serves both as auditor and guide, heartening the exhausted poet in his pilgrimage and quest:

> Thou wilt not languish here, O Friend, for whom
> I travel in these dim uncertain ways
> Thou wilt assist me as a Pilgrim gone
> In quest of highest truth.
>
> (XI, 390–93)

The last book of *The Prelude*, in symmetry with its first book, opens with a literal walk which translates itself into a metaphor for the climactic stage both of the journey of life and of the imaginative journey which is the poem itself. This time, however, the walk is not a movement along an open plain but the ascent of a mountain, the traditional place for definitive visions since Moses had climbed Mount Sinai. As in Hegel's contemporary *Phenomenology*[8] the spirit, at the climax of its educational journey, recognizes itself in its other, so Wordsworth's mind, confronting nature, discovers itself in its own perfected powers:

> A meditation rose in me that night
> Upon the lonely Mountain . . .
>   and it appear'd to me
> The perfect image of a mighty Mind.

In the earliest stage of its development Wordsworth's "Babe, / Nurs'd in his Mother's arms" had not only acquired "The gravitation and the filial bond . . . that connect him with the world," but had also, as "inmate of this *active* universe," established the beginnings of the reciprocative power by which

---

8. *Phenomenology of the Spirit* (1807) was the first important book by the German philosopher, G.W.F. Hegel.

> his mind . . .
> Creates, creator and receiver both,
> Working but in alliance with the works
> Which it beholds.—Such, verily, is the first
> Poetic spirit of our human life.
>
> (II, 265–76)

On Mount Snowdon, in an evident parallel and complement to this early passage, his mind recognizes, in that image of itself "which Nature thus / Thrusts forth upon the senses," the same power, which has now developed into "the fulness of its strength." As mist and moonlight transform the natural scene, so higher minds by a similiar "Power"

> can send abroad
> Like transformation, for themselves create
> A like existence, and, whene'er it is
> Created for them, catch it by an instinct . . .
> Willing to work and to be wrought upon

by the works which they behold. An essential alteration, however, is that the mature poetic mind, whose infant perception had been a state of undifferentiated consciousness, has acquired self-consciousness, and is able to sustain the sense of its own identity as an individuation-in-unison with the objects it perceives. In Wordsworth's terse rendering,

> hence the highest bliss
> That can be known is theirs, the consciousness
> Of whom they are habitually infused
> Through every image, and through every thought,
> And all impressions.
>
> (XIII, 84–111)

I have remarked that *The Prelude* has a circular organization. This circularity of its form, we now see, is correlative with the circularity of its subject matter. In the opening passage of *The Prelude* the narrator is confirmed in his vocation as a poet-prophet and, in response to an impulse from the autumnal wood, chooses as his goal "a known Vale, whither my feet should turn," in the assurance "of some work of glory there forthwith to be begun." "Keen as a Truant or a Fugitive, / But as a Pilgrim resolute," and also (in a complementary pedestrian metaphor) "like a home-bound labourer," he then pursued his way until a three days' walk "brought me to my hermitage" (1850; I, 71–80, 90–107). At the end of *The Prelude* Wordsworth, having taken up his "permanent abode" (XIII, 338) in this hermitage, calls "back to mind" the occasion of its beginning. But *The Prelude* has a complex function, for it is designed not only as a poem in itself, but also as a "portico" to *The Recluse*. The spiritual journey thus circles back at its conclusion to the literal journey with which it had originated; but this beginning at once turns over into the opening book of Wordsworth's "work of glory," *The Recluse* proper, which describes his way of life in the chosen vale.[9] Only now does he identify the aspect of the vale which had all along made it the goal of his tortuous literal, spiritual, and poetic journey. That goal, as in all the ancient genre of the circuitous pilgrimage of life, is home—*Home at Grasmere.*

The initial passage of *Home at Grasmere* makes it clear that the place to which the poet has returned is not his literal home but one which, on his first overview of the "Vale below" when he had chanced across it as "a roving School-boy," he had recognized to be his spiritual home. "Perfect was the Spot . . . stirring to the Spirit"; and he had immediately felt that "here / Must be his Home, this Valley be his World." Throughout his youth the vale had lingered in memory, "shedding upon joy / A brighter joy," and now the home of his imagining has become his actual home (the word reverberates through the opening passage):

> And now 'tis mine, perchance for life, dear Vale,
> Beloved Grasmere (let the Wandering Streams
> Take up, the cloud-capt hills repeat, the Name),
> One of thy lowly Dwellings is my Home.
>
> (1–59)

The place in which, "on Nature's invitation" (line 71), Wordsworth's literal and metaphoric wanderings have terminated is identified, after the venerable formula of the Christian quest, as a home which is also a recovered paradise. In his Pisgah-sight[1] of it as a schoolboy he had looked upon it as a "paradise before him" (line 14); and it remains, after he takes up his abode in it, an "earthly counterpart" of heaven (line 642), which he describes in terms echoing Milton's description of the Garden of Eden, and in which Wordsworth and Dorothy, "A solitary pair" (line 255) are somewhat incongruously the Adam and Eve. The journey to this ultimate stage has taken him through "the realities of life so cold," but this had been a fortunate fall into experience, for "the cost" of what he has lost from the earlier stage of his life is greatly outweighed by "what I keep, have gain'd / Shall gain," so that

> in my day of Childhood I was less
> The mind of Nature, less, take all in all,
> Whatever may be lost, than I am now.

---

9. As de Selincourt points out (*Wordsworth's Political Works* [*Oxford Wordsworth*], V. 365), the opening book of *The Recluse* "is in fact a continuation of his poetical autobiography from the place where *The Prelude* leaves off." This place, as we have seen, is also the place from which *The Prelude* has set out.
1. Pisgah was the mountain from the top of which Moses was granted a view of the promised land; Deuteronomy 34:1–4.

For him, man's ancient dream of felicity has been brought down
from a transcendent heaven and located in this very world—

> the distant thought
> Is fetch'd out of the heaven in which it was.
> The unappropriated bliss hath found
> An owner, and that owner I am he.
> The Lord of this enjoyment is on Earth
> And in my breast.[2]

Here he dwells, therefore, as a second Adam—more fortunate, indeed, than his predecessor, for he knows what it is to have lacked
the Eden he now possesses:

> The boon is absolute; surpassing grace
> To me hath been vouchsafed; among the bowers
> Of blissful Eden this was neither given,
> Nor could be given, possession of the good
> Which had been sighed for, ancient thought fulfilled
> And dear Imaginations realized
> Up to their highest measure, yea and more.[3]

As in comparable passages in Hölderlin and Novalis[4] (in Blake
the parallel is more with Beulah than with the New Jerusalem[5]), all
the natural scene becomes alive, human, and feminine, and encloses
the poet in an embrace of love:

> Embrace me then, ye Hills, and close me in. . . .
> But I would call thee beautiful, for mild
> And soft, and gay, and beautiful thou art,
> Dear Valley, having in thy face a smile
> Though peaceful, full of gladness.

> (lines 110–17)

And when the solitary pair had first entered this valley together in
the winter season, its elements had addressed them as fellow beings:

> "What would ye," said the shower,
> "Wild Wanderers, whither through my dark domain?"
> The sunbeam said, "be happy." When this Vale
> We entered, bright and solemn was the sky

---

2. Lines 60 ff., MS. variant, *Poetical
Works* [*Oxford Wordsworth*], V, 315–16.
3. Lines 103–9. As late as in a poem of
1811 Wordsworth parallels his "Departure
from the Vale of Grasmere" to that of a
tenant of "Elysian plains" or of "celestial Paradise," whom it might please to
absent himself from felicity long enough
to take a round trip to a lower realm:
"O pleasant transit, Grasmere! to re-
sign / Such happy fields, abodes so calm
as thine. * * * / Ne'er can the way be
irksome or forlorn / That winds into itself for sweet return" (*Poetical Works*
[*Oxford Wordsworth*], III, 64).
4. J.C.F. Hölderlin (1770–1843) and Novalis, pseudonym of Friedrich Leopold,
Freiherr von Hardenberg (1772–1801),
German romantic poets.
5. Blake's "Beulah" is the peaceable,
pastoral "State" of the human condition.
The New Jerusalem is the city that descends from heaven as the Bride of the
Lamb, Revelation 21:2.

> That faced us with a passionate welcoming,
> And led us to our threshold

—a threshold which in an earlier version of the text had been that of "a home / Within a home, which was to be" (lines 168–73).

The poet's spiritual home, however, is inescapably a paradise of this earth, for man in Grasmere Vale differs "but little from the Man elsewhere," exhibiting the vices of "selfishness, and envy, and revenge, . . . / Flattery and double-dealing, strife and wrong" (lines 347–57). But, he asks, is there not a strain of poetry that shall be "the acknowledged voice of life," and so speak "of solid good / And real evil" in a complex harmony that is of a higher order than the simple pastoral fantasy—

> More grateful, more harmonious than the breath
> The idle breath of softest pipe attuned
> To pastoral fancies?
>
> (lines 401–9)

For this poetry of real life he dismisses the escapist poetry of wish-fulfillment, "all Arcadian dreams / All golden fancies of the golden Age" engendered by man's "wish to part / With all remembrance of a jarring world" (lines 625–32). Confident of "an internal brightness," he is finally ready to assume "his office" as a mature artist, and to announce his poetic manifesto: In this "peaceful Vale . . . / A Voice shall speak, and what will be the Theme?" (lines 664–76, 751–53).

Home at Grasmere concludes with the answer to this question, in the verse passage that Wordsworth later excerpted to serve as the "Prospectus of the design and scope" of *The Recluse* and its "preparatory poem," *The Prelude.* This statement, we now recognize, in fact epitomizes, and proclaims as valid for other men, what the poet himself has learned during the arduous journey of his life that has now terminated in the earthly paradise of Grasmere Vale. Its scope, he tells us, will encompass the poetic narrative of that life itself, in the account of "the transitory Being" who had beheld the "Vision" which constitutes his poetic credential, and which it is his unique mission to impart. This vision is of "the Mind of Man," through which he will undertake a journey that must ascend higher than Milton's heaven and sink deeper than Milton's hell. Of this audacious poetic enterprise it will be the "high argument" that the human mind is capable of recreating the world of ordinary experience; and this new world, despite the inescapability of human evil and anguish—no less prevalent in the solitude of "fields and groves" than when "barricadoed . . . / Within the walls of cities"—is the equivalent in actual experience of the "mere fiction" of "groves Elysian, Fortunate Fields," and constitutes a sufficient paradise to which we have immediate access. Here we return to Wordsworth's central metaphor for an imaginative apocalypse that will restore paradise, derived from the marriage of the Lamb and the New Jerusalem that inaugurates "a new heaven and a new earth" in the biblical Apocalypse, but adapted to his own naturalistic premises of mind and its interaction with nature. Only let a man succeed in restoring his integrity, by consummating a marital union between his mind and "the external World" which, to the sensual in their "sleep of Death," has become a severed and alien reality, and he shall find "Paradise, and groves Elysian . . . / A simple produce of the common day." Precisely this, of course, is the subject, plot, and implicit argument of the story that Wordsworth has just finished telling in *The Prelude* and in its continuation, *Home at Grasmere*.

GEOFFREY H. HARTMAN

A Poet's Progress: Wordsworth and the *Via Naturaliter Negativa*†

The exact role that Nature played in Wordsworth's experience has not been defined beyond controversy. A number of readers have felt that his poetry honors and even worships Nature; and in this they have the support of Blake, a man so sensitive to any trace of "Natural Religion" that he blamed some verses of Wordsworth's for a bowel complaint which almost killed him.[1] Scholarship, luckily, tempers the affections, and the majority of scholarly readers have emphasized the poet's progression from Nature Worship or even Pantheism to a highly qualified form of natural religion, with increasing awareness of the "ennobling interchange" between mind and Nature and a late yielding of primacy to the activity of the mind or the idealizing power of Imagination. A very small group, finally—represented by occasional insights rather than by a sustained position—has pointed to the deeply paradoxical or problematic character of Wordsworth's dealings with Nature and suggested that what he calls Imagination may be *intrinsically* opposed to images culled or developed from Nature.[2] This last and rarest position seems to me quite close to the truth, yet I do not feel it conflicts totally with the more traditional readings, which stress the

† From *Modern Philology*, LIX (1962), pages 214–24. Several of the original footnotes have been shortened. The Latin phrase means "the naturally negative way."

1. See *Blake, Coleridge, Wordsworth, Lamb, etc., being Selections from the Remains of Henry Crabb Robinson*, ed. E. J. Morley (Manchester, 1932), pp. 5 and 15.

2. See, for example, Paul de Man, "Structure intentionnelle de l'Image romantique," *Revue Internationale de Philosophie*, no. 51 (1960), pp. 1–17.

poet's adherence to Nature. My purpose is to show, via three important episodes of *The Prelude*, that Wordsworth came to realize that Nature itself led him beyond Nature; and how and when the realization was achieved. The poet's sense of a reality in Nature is kept alive by the very fact that Nature itself weans his mind, and especially his poetic mind, from its early dependence on immediate sensuous stimuli. And since this movement of transcendence, or what mystics have often called the negative way, is shown by Wordsworth as inherent in life, and as achieved without violent or ascetic discipline, I have thought to name it a *via naturaliter negativa*.

I

The Prelude opens with a success immediately followed by a failure. Released from the "vast city" and anticipating a new freedom, the poet pours out a rush of fifty lines: "poetic numbers came / Spontaneously to clothe in priestly robe / A renovated spirit" (I, lines 51–53).[3] Here is the consecration, the promise of poetry as a sacrament, a gift efficacious beyond the moment. Why should a chance inspiration assume such significance? The reason is that Wordsworth was not used to make "A present joy the matter of a song"; yet here, apparently, is evidence that he may soon become self-creative, or need no more than a "gentle breeze" (the untraditional muse of the epic's opening) to produce a tempest of poetry. "Matins and vespers[4] of harmonious verse!" is the hope held out to him, and having punctually performed Matins the poet is content to slacken, to be gradually calmed by the clear autumn afternoon.

He meditates beneath a tree on a great poetic work soon to be begun. The sun sets, and city smoke is "ruralized" by distance. He starts to continue his journey, but now it is clearly time for vespers:

> It was a splendid evening, and my soul
> Once more made trial of her strength, nor lacked
> Aeolian visitations.
>
> (lines 94–96)

An outside splendor challenges the creative mind. Is the poet strong enough to answer it spontaneously, as if he needed only a suggestion, the first chord?

> but the harp
> Was soon defrauded, and the banded host
> Of harmony dispersed in straggling sounds,
> And lastly utter silence! "Be it so;
> Why think of anything but present good?"
>
> (lines 96–100)

3. Quotations, unless otherwise stated, are from the 1850 text of *The Prelude*, ed. E. de Selincourt (Oxford, 1928).

4. Morning and evening prayers. [*Editors.*]

Wordsworth once again sees present good, like present joy, strangely opposed to the quickening of verse. The poetic outburst which he had considered a religious thing ("punctual service high . . . holy services") is now disdained as profane and *servile*:

> So, like a home-bound labourer I pursued
> My way beneath the mellowing sun, that shed
> Mild influence; nor left in me one wish
> Again to bend the Sabbath of that time
> To a servile yoke.
>
> (lines 101–5)

His reversal of mood is surprisingly complete. One who, at the impassioned outset of his reflections, had been so sure of the freely creative, autonomous nature of his poetic soul that famous passages on the emancipated spirit—from *Paradise Lost* and *Exodus*[5]—swell the current of his verse, while he thinks to possess total freedom of choice,

> now free,
> Free as a bird to settle where I will

that same person now writes of himself, with a slight echo of Gray's *Elegy*:

> So, like a home-bound labourer I pursued
> My way. . . .

The meaning of the reversal is not immediately clear. It does not deject the poet; it endows him, on the contrary, with a Chaucerian kind of cheer and leisure:

> What need of many words?
> A pleasant loitering journey, through three days
> Continued, brought me to my hermitage.
> I spare to tell of what ensued, the life
> In common things—the endless store of things.
>
> (lines 105–9)

The form of the reversal is that of a return to Nature, at least to its rhythm. For the moment no haste remains, no tempest, no impatience of spirit. It is the mood of the hawthorn shade, of a portion of Wordsworth's Cambridge days, when he laughed with Chaucer and heard him, while birds sang, tell tales of love (III, lines 278–81).

In the exultant first lines of *The Prelude* Wordsworth had foreseen the spirit's power to become self-creative. Though fostered by

---

5. Emancipated—but through exile. See *Prelude*, I, lines 14 and 16–18. The significance of the frame of exile will become apparent. A reminiscence of Virgil, *Bucolics*, I, may also be present.

Nature it eventually outgrows its dependence, sings and storms at will (lines 33–38). The poet's anticipation of autonomy is probably less a matter of pride than of necessity: he will steal the initiative from Nature, so as to freely serve or sustain the natural world, should its hold on the affections slacken. His poetic power, though admittedly in Nature's gift, must perpetuate, like consecration, vital if transitory feelings. Without poetry the supreme moment is nothing.

> Dear Liberty! Yet what would it avail
> But for a gift that consecrates the joy?
> (lines 31–32)

The reversal teaches that this desire for immediate consecrations is a wrong form of worship. The world demands a devotion less external and wilful, a wise passiveness which the creative will may profane. The tempest "vexing its own creation" is replaced by a "mellowing sun, that shed / Mild influence." Nature keeps the initiative. The mind at its most free is still part of a deep mood of weathers.

Wordsworth's failure to consecrate, through verse, the splendid evening is only the last event in this reversal. It begins with the poet placing (so to say) the cart before the horse, Poetry before Nature: "To the open fields I told / A prophecy: poetic numbers came . . ." (lines 50 ff.). He never, of course, forgets the double agency of inward and outward which informs every act of poetry. So his heart's frost is said to be broken by both outer and inner winds (lines 38 ff.). Such reciprocity is at the heart of all his poems. Yet he continually anticipates a movement of transcendence: Nature proposes but the Poet disposes. Just as the breeze engendered in the mind a self-quickening tempest, so poetry, the voice from that tempest, reechoing in the mind whence it came, seems to increase there its perfection (lines 55 ff.). The origin of the whole moves farther and farther from its starting point in the external world. A *personal* agent replaces that of Nature: "I paced on . . . down I sate . . . slackening my thoughts by choice" (lines 60 ff.). There is a world of difference between this subtle bravado and the ascendancy of *impersonal* constructions in the final episode: "Be it so; Why think of anything but . . . What need of many words? . . . I pursued My way . . . A pleasant loitering journey . . . brought me to my hermitage."

This change, admittedly, is almost too fine for common language. Syntax becomes a major device but not a consistent one. In the 1850 text, while the poet muses in the green, shady place, certain neoclassical patterns, such as the noble passive combined with synecdoche, create an atmosphere in which personal and impersonal, active and passive, blend strongly:

> Many were the thoughts
> Encouraged and dismissed, till choice was made
> Of a known Vale, whither my feet should turn.
>
> > (lines 70–72)

Devices still more subtle come into play. In the passage immediately preceding, Wordsworth describes the quiet autumn afternoon:

> a day
> With silver clouds, and sunshine on the grass,
> And in the sheltered and the sheltering grove
> A perfect stillness.
>
> > (lines 67–70)

"Sheltered and sheltering"—typical Wordsworthian verbosity? The redundance, however, does suggest that whatever is happening here happens in more than one place; compare "silver clouds and sunshine on the grass." The locus doubles, redoubles: that two-fold agency which seems to center on the poet is active all around to the same incremental effect. The grove, sheltered, shelters in turn, and makes "A perfect stillness." The poet, in a sense, is only a single focus to something universally active. He muses on this intensifying stillness, and within him rises a picture, gazing on which with *grow-ing* love "a higher power than Fancy" enters to affirm his musings. The reciprocal and incremental movement, mentioned explicitly in lines 31 ff., occurs this time quite unself-consciously, clearly within the setting and through the general influences of Nature.

No wonder, then, that the city, which the poet still strove to shake off in the first lines, appears now not only distant but also "ruralized," taking on the colors of Nature, as inclosed by it as the poet's own thought. The reversal is finalized by the episode of the splendid sunset. Wordsworth not only cannot, he *need* not steal the initiative from Nature. Her locus is universal, not individual; she acts by expedients deeper than will or thought. Wordsworth's failure intensifies his sense of a principle of generosity in Nature. That initial cry of faith, "I cannot miss my way" (line 18), becomes true, but not because of his own power. The song loses its way.

Wordsworth's first experience is symptomatic of his creative difficulties. One impulse vexes the creative spirit into self-dependence, the other exhibits Nature as that spirit's highest guardian object. The poet is driven at the same time from and toward the external world by dynamic dissatisfaction. No sooner has he begun to enjoy his Chaucerian leisure than restiveness breaks in. The "pilgrim," despite "the life in common things—the endless store of things," cannot rest content with his hermitage's sabbath. Higher hopes, "airy phantasies," clamor for life (lines 114 ff.). The poet's account of his creative difficulties (lines 146–269) documents in full his vacillation between a natural and a more-than-natural theme, between a Romantic tale and one of "natural heroes," or "A tale from my own heart" and "some philosophic song"—but he adds, immediately swinging back to the humble, "Of Truth that cherishes our daily life." Is this indeterminacy the end at which Nature aims, this curious and never fully clarified restlessness the ultimate confession of his poetry?

It would be hard, in that case, to think of *The Prelude* as describing the "growth of a poet's mind"; for what the first part of Book I records is, primarily, Wordsworth's failure to be an epic poet, a poet in the tradition of Spenser and Milton. "Was it for this," he asks, that Nature spent all her care (lines 269 ff.)? The first six books of *The Prelude* trace every moment of that care. There is little doubt in Wordsworth that Nature intended him for a poet. Why else that continual prediction and fostering of the spirit's autonomy from childhood on? And yet, the very moment the spirit tries to seize autonomy, to quicken like Ezekiel's self-moved chariot,[6] Nature humbles it by an evidence of subtle supremacy, or Wordsworth humbles himself by shrinking from visionary subjects.

Wordsworth never achieves his philosophic song. *Prelude* and *Excursion* are no more than "ante-chapels" to the "gothic church" of his unfinished work. An unresolved antagonism between Poetry and Nature prevents him from being a sustained visionary poet in the manner of Spenser and Milton. It is a paradox, though not an unfruitful one, that Wordsworth should so scrupulously record Nature's workmanship, which prepares the soul for its independence from sense experience, yet refrain to use that independence out of respect to Nature. His greatest verse *takes its origin* in the memory of given experiences to which he is often pedantically faithful. He adheres, apparently against Nature, to natural fact. That is his secret, and our problem.

II

It might seem that the failure of poetic nerve recorded in *Prelude* I is simply a sign of Nature's triumph over the poet. He recognizes poetry is not prophecy or a sacramental gift. Though Wordsworth suffers a reversal, and the splendid evening shows his soul's weakness, such a conclusion is premature. Nature, for Wordsworth, is never an enemy but always a guide or guardian whose most adverse-seeming effects are still pedagogy. *Prelude* I is filled with examples of Nature's unpredictable, often fearful methods. Even if we do not appeal to further knowledge of his work, the poem's opening drama shows only that Wordsworth cannot write poetry about Nature as an immediate external object. That may appear to contradict what readers have valued most, his power to represent the natural world

6. The chariot is described in Ezekiel 1:15–21. [*Editors.*]

with childhood intensity, to give it back its soul, to awaken the mind (as Coleridge remarked) to the lethargy-shrouded loveliness of common things. There is, however, a distinction to be made between the immediacy of Nature and the immediacy of a poem dealing with Nature, though they are often so close that Matthew Arnold sees Nature herself guiding the pen in Wordsworth's hand.

Wordsworth's poetry places itself at a significant remove from the founding experience. This is not a naïve or purely personal fact. *The Prelude* never represents Nature simply as an immediate or ultimate object, even where the poet's recall is most vivid. Every incident involving Nature is propaedeutic and relates to that "dark Inscrutable workmanship" mentioned by *Prelude* I, lines 340 ff. I have suggested elsewhere how the fine skating scene of the first book (lines 425–463), though painted for its own sake, to capture the animal spirits of children spurred by a clear and frosty night, moves from vivid images of immediate life to an absolute calm which foreshadows a deeper yet also more hidden or mediate source of life.[7] This apparent action of Nature on itself, to convert the immediate or external into the quietly mediate, which then unfolds a new, less exhaustible source of life, is analogous to the action of the mind on itself which characterizes the poet in the 1800 Preface to *Lyrical Ballads*. Poetry, says Wordsworth, is the spontaneous overflow of powerful feelings, but qualifies at once: "It takes its origin from emotion recollected in tranquillity: the emotion is contemplated till, by a species of reaction the tranquillity gradually disappears, and an emotion, kindred to that which was before the subject of contemplation, is gradually produced, and does itself actually exist in the mind."

One process potentially results in poetry, the other in the mind making that poetry. The two have a similar, perhaps continuous structure. Both show the passing of immediacy into something more mediate or meditative, but also its revival as a new kind of immediacy. Now this, surely, is like the basic movement of the *Prelude*'s first episode. It begins with an outburst, a "passion" of words rising immediately from the poet like animal spirits from children, having no full external cause. Then as the moment of fervor spreads, the landscape reveals its secret pressures, blends with and overshadows the thoughts of the poet. A splendid image, finally, outspeaks the poet, just as Nature in I, lines 458 ff. foretells her ever calmer presence to the reflective child. Thus Nature is not an "object" but a presence and a power; a motion and a spirit; not something to be worshiped or consumed, an immediate or ultimate principle of life, but—and here it becomes most hard to find terms that preserve the

7. *The Unmediated Vision* (New Haven, Conn., 1954), pp. 17–20.

poet in the thinker—something whose immediacy, like that of a poem, is not separable from the work of perfect mediation. Wordsworth fails to celebrate his sunset because poetry is not an act of consecration and Nature not an immediate external object to be consecrated. When the external stimulus is too clearly present, the poet falls mute and corroborates Blake's strongest objection: "Natural Objects always did and now do weaken, deaden and obliterate Imagination in Me."[8]

A second, though chronologically earlier failure vis-à-vis the external world is related in *Prelude* VI. It occurs just before Wordsworth feels love for man begin to emerge out of his love for Nature. The poet, having finished his third year of studies at Cambridge (he is twenty years old), goes on a walking tour of France and Switzerland. It is the summer of 1790, the French Revolution has achieved its greatest success and acts as a subtle, though in the following books increasingly human, background to his concern with Nature. Setting out to cross the Alps by way of the Simplon Pass, Wordsworth and his friend are separated from their companions and try the ascent by themselves. After climbing some time and not overtaking anyone, they meet a peasant who tells them they must return to their starting point, and follow a stream down instead of further ascending, i.e., they had already crossed the Alps. Disappointed, "For still we had hopes that pointed to the clouds," they start downward beset by a "melancholy slackening," which, however, is soon dislodged (lines 557–591, 617 ff.).

This simple episode stands, however, within a larger, interdependent series of events. An unexpected revelation comes almost immediately (lines 624–40), while the whole is preceded by a parallel instance of disappointment with the natural world followed by a compensatory vision (lines 523 ff.). In addition to this temporal structure of blankness and revelation, of the soulless image and the sudden renewed immediacy, we find an amazing instance of a past event's transtemporal thrust. The poet, after telling the story of his disappointment, is suddenly, in the very moment of composition, overpowered by a feeling of glory to which he gives expression in rapturous and almost self-obscuring lines (lines 592 ff.). Not until the moment of composition, some fourteen years after the event,[9] does the full motive behind his blind upward climb and

8. Marginalia to Wordsworth's poems. Northrop Frye, *Selected Poetry and Prose of William Blake* (New York: Modern Library ed.), p. 455. I may venture the opinion that Wordsworth, at the beginning of *The Prelude*, goes back to Nature, not to increase his chances of sensation, but rather to emancipate his mind from immediate external excitements, the "gross and violent stimulants" (1800 *Preface to Lyrical Ballads*) of the city he leaves behind him.

9. That the rising up of Imagination probably occurred as Wordsworth was remembering his disappointment, rather than immediately after it (i.e., in 1804, not in 1790) was pointed out by W. G. Fraser in the *TLS* of April 4, 1929, no. 1,418, p. 276.

subsequent melancholy slackening strike home: and it strikes so hard that Wordsworth, for the first time in his narrative, gives to the unconditioned power revealed by the extinction of the immediate external motive (his desire to cross the Alps), as by the abyss of intervenient years, the explicit name *Imagination*:

> Imagination—here the Power so called
> Through sad incompetence of human speech,
> That awful Power rose from the mind's abyss
> Like an unfathered vapour that enwraps,
> At once, some lonely traveller. I was lost;
> Halted without an effort to break through;
> But to my conscious soul I now can say—
> "I recognize thy glory."
>
> (lines 592–99)

Thus Wordsworth's failure vis-à-vis Nature (or its failure vis-à-vis the Poet) is doubly redeemed. After descending, and passing through a gloomy strait (VI, lines 621 ff.), he encounters a magnificent view. And crossing, one might say, through the gloomy gulf of time, his disappointment becomes retrospectively a prophetic instance of that blindness to the external world which is the tragic, pervasive, and necessary condition of the mature poet. His failure taught him gently what now (1804) literally *blinds* him; the growing independence of Imagination from the immediate external world.

I cannot miss my way, the poet exults in the opening verses of the *Prelude*. And he cannot, as long as he respects the guidance of Nature, which leads him along a gradual *via negativa*, to make his soul more than "a mere pensioner / On outward forms" (VI, line 737). It is not easy, however, to "follow Nature." The path, in fact, becomes so circuitous that a poet follows Nature least when he thinks to follow her most. He must pass through the gloomy strait where the external image is lost yet suddenly revived with more than original immediacy. Thus a gentle breeze, in *Prelude* I, calls forth a tempest of verse, but a splendid evening wanes into silence. A magnificent hope, in *Prelude* VI, seems to die for lack of sensuous food, but years later the simple memory of failure calls up that hope in a magnificent tempest of verse. The poet is forced to discover the autonomy of his imagination, its independence from present joy, from strong outward stimuli—but this discovery, which means a transcendence of Nature, is brought on gradually, mercifully.

The poet does not sustain the encounter with Imagination. His direct cry is broken off, replaced by an impersonal construction, "—here the Power . . . ," and it is not Imagination but his "conscious soul" he addresses directly in the following lines. What, in any case, is a soul to do with its extreme recognition? It has glimpsed the height of its freedom. At the end of this passage Wordsworth returns to the idea that the soul is halted by the light of its discovery, as a traveler by a sudden bank of mist. But the intensifying simile this time suggests not only a divorce from but also, proleptically, a return to Nature on the part of the independent soul:

> Strong in herself and in beatitude
> That hides her, like the mighty flood of Nile
> Poured from his fount of Abyssinian clouds
> To fertilise the whole Egyptian plain.
> (lines 613–16)

III

We are now in a position to compare the structure of all the episodes. The first (I, lines 1 ff.) falls roughly into three parts: the spontaneous "tempest" of verse, the quietly active grove, and the splendid evening that ends too calmly. In the skating scene of Book I, the splendid silence of a winter evening, set off by the clear strokes of a clock, increases to a tumult of reciprocal sounds, which yield in turn to a vision of a silently sustaining power. In the one case we go from Poetry to Nature, in the other from Nature to a more deeply mediated conception of Nature. Thus, at the beginning of his narrative, Wordsworth prefers to plunge into *medias res*,[1] where the *res* is Poetry, or Nature only in so far as it has guided the poet to a height whence he must find his own way.

The major episode of Book VI, the encounter with Imagination, may also be regarded as falling into three parts. Its first term is neither Nature nor Poetry. It is, rather, Imagination in embryo—muted yet strengthened by Nature's inadequacies. Though the poet's memory of Nature's past intimacy reaches its height, her presences are no longer intimate. Blankness and utter dark vacillate before his eyes, relieved only occasionally by sights of "milder magnificence." At first the vine-clad hills of Burgundy, the valley of the Saône, and later of the Rhône, lead him and his friend gently on; but soon the quiet river, the church spires and bells, disappear, and they enter the solitary precincts of the Alps. Nature now appears in turn excessive or null; sublimity and profound calm, known from earliest childhood, revolve in their intensity, are too awe-ful or too calm. A human response is scarcely possible in the face of such "ungrateful" vicissitude.

Yet this is the very time of the active Imagination's birthpangs. "The poet's soul was with me," Wordsworth writes at the beginning

---

1. "The middle of things." A quotation from Horace, *The Art of Poetry*, in which Horace advises the poet to start his narrative in the midst of the action. [*Editors.*]

of the book, and later notes, in his curiously matter-of-fact, yet absolutely unrevealing fashion, that dejection itself would often lead him on to pleasurable thoughts. Still deeper than such dejection, a "stern mood, an under-thirst / Of vigour" (lines 558 ff.) makes itself felt and produces a special sort of sadness; and now, in order to throw light on the nature of that sadness, the "melancholy slackening" which ensues on the nature of the peasant's words, he tells the incident of his crossing the Alps.

The first part of the tryptich, then, illustrates a critical stage in the history of the poet's Imagination. The stern mood can only be Wordsworth's premonition of spiritual autonomy, of independence from the immediacy of sense experience, fostered in him by Nature since earliest childhood. We know with some precision how this mood manifests itself. In *Prelude* II, lines 312 ff., it is described as "an obscure sense / Of possible sublimity" for which the soul, remembering *how* it felt but not *what* it felt, continually aspires to find a new content. The element of obscurity, therefore, is inseparable from the soul's capacity of growth; it is obscurity that both feeds the soul and vexes it toward self-dependence. The divine yet natural pasturage becomes viewless; the soul cannot easily find the immediate external source from which it used to drink the visionary power; and, while dim memories of passionate commerce with external things drive it more than ever to the natural world, this world makes itself more than ever inscrutable.[2] The travelers' separation from their guides, then that of the road from the stream (lines 568 ff.), and finally their trouble with the peasant's words, that have to be "translated," all subtly express the soul's desire for a world "beyond." Yet only when poet, brook, and road are once again "fellow-travellers" (line 622), when Wordsworth holds on to Nature, does that reveal (a Proteus in the grasp of the hero) its prophecy.

With this we come to what was, originally, the second part of the adventure: the dislodgement of melancholy and the gloomy strait's "Characters of the great Apocalypse" (lines 617–40). In its temporal rather than narrative sequence, therefore, the episode has only two parts. The first term, the moment of natural immediacy, is omitted; we go straight to the second term, the inscrutability of an external image, which leads via the gloomy strait to an apocalyptic image. Yet, as if this pattern demanded a substitute third term, Wordsworth's tribute to "Imagination" severs the original temporal sequence and forestalls Nature's exhibition to the bodily eye with an ecstatic excursus on the inner eye.

In the 1805 *Prelude* the transition from the poet narrating the past, gazing like a traveler into the mind's abyss, to the poet gripped

---

2. Cf. the Great Ode; also *Prelude* I, lines 597 ff.

by something rising unexpectedly from that abyss, is still respected in cursory fashion (line 526); but the 1850 *Prelude*, as if the poet labored under a "strong confusion," solders past and present so well that the circuitous series of events seems immediately to evoke "Imagination." The apocalypse of the gloomy strait loses, in any case, the character of a *terminal* experience and appears as an anagogical device, now transcended. For the Imagination, at the time of writing, is called forth by the barely scrutable, not by the splendid image. This (momentary) displacement of emphasis is the more effective in that the style of lines 617 ff., and the very characters of the apocalypse, suggest that the hiding places of power cannot be localized in Nature.[3]

Thus the three parts (henceforth VI-*a*, VI-*b*, and VI-*c*) trace the mind's growth toward independence from the immediate external world. The measure of that independence is "Imagination," and to define what Wordsworth means by this word is to add a sad incompetence of the interpreter to that of the poet. But we see that the mind must pass through a stage where it experiences Imagination as a power separate from Nature, that the poet must come to think and feel by his own choice or from the structure of his own mind.[4]

VI-*a* (lines 557–91) shows the young poet still dependent on the immediacy of the external world. Imagination secretly frustrates that dependence, yet its victory dooms more than the external world. For its blindness toward Nature is accompanied by a blindness toward itself.

VI-*b* (lines 592–616) gives an example of thought or feeling that came from the poet's mind without immediate external excitement. There remains, of course, the memory of VI-*a*, and VI-*a* tells of an experience with an external, though no longer immediate, world. From the perspective of VI-*b*, however, that world is not even external. The poet recognizes that the power he has looked for in the world outside was really within and frustrating his search. The shock of recognition then feeds the very blindness toward the external world which produced that shock.

In VI-*c* (lines 617–40) the landscape is once more an immediate

---

3. Of the four sentences which comprise lines 617–40, the first three alternate the themes of eager and of restrained movement ("melancholy slackening . . . Downward we hurried fast . . . at a slow pace"); and the fourth sentence, without explicit transition, commencing in midverse (line 624), rises very gradually and firmly into a development of sixteen lines. These depend on a single verb, an unemphatic "were," held back till the beginning of line 636; the verb thus acts as a pivot that introduces, without shock or simply as the other side of the coin, the falling and interpretative movement. This structure, combined with a skilful interchange throughout of asyndetic and conjunctive phrases, always avoids the sentiment of abrupt illumination for that of a majestic swell fed by innumerable sustaining events, and thereby strengthens our feeling that the vision, though climactic, is neither terminal nor discontinuous.

4. Cf. Preface to *Lyrical Ballads* (1802): "[The poet] has acquired a greater readiness and power in expressing . . . especially those thoughts and feelings which, by his own choice, or from the structure of his own mind, arise in him without immediate external excitement. . . ."

external object of experience. The mind cannot separate in it what it most desired to see and what it sees bodily. It is a moment of apocalypse, in which the poet sees not as in a glass, darkly, but face to face. Thus, VI-*c* magnifies subtle details of VI-*a* and *seems* to actualize figurative details of VI-*b*.[5] The matter-of-fact interplay of quick and lingering movement, of up-and-down perplexities in the ascent (lines 562–85) reappears in larger letters; while the interchanges of light and darkness, of cloud and cloudlessness, of rising like a vapor from the abyss and pouring like a flood from heaven have entered the landscape almost bodily. The gloomy strait also participates in this actualization. It is revealed as the secret middle term which leads from the barely scrutable presence of Nature to its resurrected image. The travelers who move freely with or against the terrain, hurrying upward, pacing downward, perplexed at the crossing, are now led narrowly by the pass as if it were their rediscovered guide.

IV

The Prelude, as a history of a poet's mind, foresees the time when the "Characters of the great Apocalypse" will be intuited without the medium of Nature. The time approaches even as the poet writes and occasionally cuts across his narrative, the Imagination rising up, as in Book VI, "Before the eye and progress of my Song" (1805).[6] This expression, so rich when taken literally yet so conventional when taken as a simple figure, Wordsworth replaced in the 1850 version, but did not lose sight of. It suggests that the Imagination forestalled Nature, so that the very "eye" of the song, trained on a temporal sequence with the vision in the strait as its last term, was disrupted, obscured. The poet, in both versions, says that he was halted and could not or did not make any effort to "break through." If this has an intent more specific than to convey abstractly the Imagination's power—if, in other words, the effect the Imagination has tells us something specific about the power behind that effect—then the poet was momentarily forced to deny Nature the magnificence of self-representation it had shown in the gloomy strait and to attribute that instead to Imagination, whose interposition (VI-*b*) proves it to be a power more independent of time and place than Nature, and so a better type "Of first, and last, and midst, and without end" (line 640).

In VI-*b* something that happens during composition enters the poem as a new biographical event. Wordsworth has just described his disappointment (VI-*a*) and turns in anticipation to Nature's

---

5. VI-*b* was composed before VI-*c*, so that while the transference of images goes *structurally* from VI-*b* to VI-*c*, *chronologically* the order is reversed.

6. De Selincourt (op. cit. p. 542) calls this rightly a Shakespearean doublet, and refers to *King John* II, i, 208.

compensatory finale (VI-c). He is about to respect the original temporal sequence, "the eye and progress" of his song. But as he looks forward, in the moment of composition, from blankness toward revelation, a new insight cuts him off from the latter. The original disappointment is seen not as a test, or as a prelude to magnificence, but as a revelation in itself. It suddenly reveals a power that worked against Nature in order to be recognized. The song's progress comes to a halt because the poet is led beyond Nature. Unless the temporal, which is also the natural, order be respected by the poet, his song, at least as narrative, must cease. Here Imagination, not Nature (I, line 96), defeats Poetry.

This conclusion may be checked by comparing the versions of 1805 and 1850. The latter replaces "Before the eye and progress of my Song" with a more direct metaphorical transposition. Imagination is said to rise from the mind's abyss "Like an unfathered vapour that enwraps, / At once, some lonely traveller." The (literal) traveler of 1790 becomes the (mental) traveler at the moment of composition. And though one Shakespearean doublet has disappeared, another implicitly takes its place: does not Imagination rise from "the dark backward and abysm of time" (*The Tempest*, I, ii, 50)? The result, in any case, is a disorientation of time added to that of way; an apocalyptic moment in which past and future overtake the present; and the poet, cut off from Nature by Imagination, is, in an absolute sense, lonely.

The last stage of Book VI as a progress poem has been reached. The travelers of VI-a had already left behind their native land, the public rejoicing of France, rivers, hills, and spires; they have separated from their guide and, finally, from the unbridged mountain stream. Now Imagination separates the poet from all else, human companionship, the immediate scene, the remembered scene. The end of the natural *via negativa* is near. There is no more "eye and progress": the invisible progress of VI-a reveals itself now as a progress independent of visible ends, engendered by the desire for an "invisible world"—the substance of things hoped for, the evidence of things not seen. Wordsworth descants on the Pauline definition of faith:

> in such strength
> Of usurpation, when the light of sense
> Goes out, but with a flash that has revealed
> The invisible world, doth greatness make abode,
> There harbours; whether we be young or old,
> Our destiny, our being's heart and home,
> Is with infinitude, and only there;
> With hope it is, hope that can never die,
> Effort, and expectation, and desire,

And something evermore about to be

(lines 599–608)[7]

If there is any further possibility of progress for the enwrapped and rapt poet, it is that of song itself, no longer subordinate to the mimetic function, the experience faithfully traced to this height. The poet is a traveler in so far as he must respect Nature's past guidance and retrace his route. He did come, after all, to an important instance of bodily vision. The way is the song. But the song all the time strives to become the way. And when this happens, when the song seems to capture the initiative, in such supreme moments of poetry as VI-*b* or even VI-*c*, the way is lost. Nature's apocalypse shows "Winds thwarting winds, bewildered and forlorn," destroys the concept of the linear path, and also severs finally the "eye" from the "progress."[8]

In VI-*c*, however, Nature still stands over and against the poet; he is yet the observer, the eighteenth-century gentleman admiring new manifestations of the sublime, even if the "lo!" or "mark!" is suppressed. He moves haltingly, but he moves; and the style of the passage emphasizes continuities. Yet with the Imagination athwart there is no movement, no looking before and after. The song itself must be the way, though the way of a blinded man, who admits "I was lost." When he *speaks* once more to his conscious soul (line 598), he can only recognize that "infinitude" is not at the end of the path but in a crossing and a losing of the way, by which a power transcending all single ways guides the traveler to itself.

The poet's desire to cross the Alps may already imply a wish to overcome Nature. Yet the stern mood of VI-*a* (Imagination not yet recognized as a power distinct from Nature) helps the poet to gain more than this—its own—end. It gains the poet's end *imperceptibly* in order to defeat the very idea of an end as the motive power. The travelers' *melancholy* slackening, when they think the end attained, proves it was more than a specific end (here the crossing of the Alps) which moved them. And in VI-*c* Nature itself affirms this lesson. The travelers find a vision which both clarifies the idea by which they were moved and destroys it as the idea of an end— specifically the idea of Nature as an end. It is, rather, the idea of something "without end" and, specifically, *the idea of Nature itself teaching the travelers to transcend Nature*. The apocalypse is a picture of a self-thwarting march and countermarch of elements, a divine mockery of the concept of the Single Way. Nature seems to

7. The last line of this passage echoes and resolves Wordsworth's comment on Mt. Blanc. The latter is said to have "usurped upon a living thought / That never more could be" (VI, line 527 f.). The two verses, juxtaposed, sound the depth of the contrast between Nature and Imagination.

8. Cf. Geoffrey Hartman, *The Unmediated Vision* (New Haven, 1954), pp. 129–132.

have guided the travelers to a point where they see the power which causes it to move and be moving. This power, when distinct from Nature (as in VI-*b*), is called Imagination. But, when thus distinct, when unmediated, it blinds speech and extinguishes the light of the senses. The unfathered vapor, as it shrouds the poet's eye, also shrouds the eye of his song, whose tenor is Nature guiding and fostering the power of song.

Wordsworth has discovered the hidden guide which moved him by means of Nature as Beatrice moves Dante by means of Vergil.[9] It is not Nature as such but Nature indistinguishably blended with Imagination which compels the poet along a *via naturaliter negativa*. Yet, if VI-*b* prophesies against the world of sense experience, Wordsworth's affection and point of view remain unchanged. After a cloudburst of passionate verses he returns to the pedestrian attitude of 1790, when the external world and not imagination appeared as his guide ("Our journey we renewed, / Led by the stream," etc.).[1] For, with the exception of VI-*b*, Imagination never moves the poet directly, but always *sub specie naturae*. The childhood "visitings of imaginative power" depicted in Books I and XII also appeared in the guise or disguise of Nature. Wordsworth's journey as a poet can only continue with eyes, but the Imagination experienced as a power distinct from Nature opens his eyes by putting them out. Thus, Wordsworth does not adhere to Nature because of natural fact, but despite it and because of human and poetic fact. Imagination is not called an awe-ful power for nothing.

RICHARD J. ONORATO

The Prelude: Metaphors of Beginning and Where They Lead†

It is to the metaphors at the beginning of *The Prelude* that we must attend. Through them Wordsworth expresses beginnings, conscious and unconscious aspirations, and memories of much greater consequence than those suggested by the scholarly concern for date, place, and factual representation. His conscious artifice, his desire to recall and imagine, to remember and invent, the principal character of the poem, reveals at the same time the kind of preconscious

9. In *The Divine Comedy*, Dante's guide through Hell and Purgatory is the Roman epic poet, Virgil. Beatrice takes over to guide him through Paradise. [*Editors.*]
1. The "return to Nature" is anticipated by the last lines of VI-*b* (lines 613–16).

† From Richard J. Onorato, *The Character of the Poet: Wordsworth in "The Prelude"* (Princeton University Press, 1971), pages 100–115. The selection has been revised by the author.

association that Imagination forces upon Memory; and the apparent inaccuracy of memory perhaps attests to deeper memories. The extended thirteen-book *Prelude* is attempting a greater self-acceptance and requires the introduction at the outset of a character seeking that.[1] To begin with, then, here are the first 54 lines of Book I.

> Oh there is blessing in this gentle breeze
> That blows from the green fields and the clouds
> And from the sky: it beats against my cheek,
> And seems half conscious of the joy it gives.
> Oh welcome Messenger! O welcome Friend!
> A captive greets thee, coming from a house
> Of bondage, from yon City's walls set free,
> A prison where he hath been long immured.
> Now I am free, enfranchis'd and at large,
> May fix my habitation where I will.
> What dwelling shall receive me? In what Vale
> Shall be my harbour? Underneath what grove
> Shall I take up my home, and what sweet stream
> Shall with its murmur lull me to my rest?
> The earth is all before me: with a heart
> Joyous, nor scar'd at its own liberty,
> I look about, and should the guide I chuse
> Be nothing better than a wandering cloud,
> I cannot miss my way. I breathe again;
> Trances of thought and mountings of the mind
> Come fast upon me: it is shaken off,
> As by miraculous gift 'tis shaken off,
> That burthen of my own unnatural self,
> The heavy weight of many a weary day
> Not mine, and such as were not made for me.
> Long months of peace (if such bold word accord
> With any promises of human life),
> Long months of ease and undisturb'd delight
> Are mine in prospect; whither shall I turn

1. This "Preamble" (1805 ed., lines 1–54) does not occur in any MS. earlier than *MS. M*, written in March–April 1804. De Selincourt, accepting Garrod's suggestion that the date of composition was 1795, identifies the city (line 7) as Bristol and the goal of the journey as Racedown, to which Wordsworth had walked in September 1795. (See *The Prelude*, ed. de Selincourt and Darbishire, 1959, pp. 510–11). John Finch, however, argues convincingly that the date of composition was 1799 rather than 1795 and that, while the walk in the "Preamble" fuses, imaginatively, two or more experiences, the chosen "Vale" (lines 82, 100) is primarily Grasmere, the "hermitage" (line 115) is primarily Dove Cottage, and the "City" (lines 7, 98) is a symbolic one, representing a stage of life, a "bondage," from which Wordsworth has finally escaped. This footnote calls attention to a long-standing problem of interpretation among scholars of *The Prelude* and, at the same time, initiates a revision of part of the argument in *The Character of The Poet* in the light of recent scholarship. Advised of that revision, the reader is urged to see the excellent article on which it is based: John Finch, "Wordsworth's Two-Handed Engine," in *Bicentenary Wordsworth Studies in Memory of John Alban Finch*, ed. Jonathan Wordsworth (Ithaca and London, 1970), pp. 1–13.

By road or pathway or through open field,
Or shall a twig or any floating thing
Upon the river, point me out my course?
    Enough that I am free; for months to come
May dedicate myself to chosen tasks;
May quit the tiresome sea and dwell on shore,
If not a Settler on the soil, at least
To drink wild water, and to pluck green herbs,
And gather fruits fresh from their native bough.
Nay more, if I may trust myself, this hour
Hath brought a gift that consecrates my joy;
For I, methought, while the sweet breath of Heaven
Was blowing on my body, felt within
A corresponding mild creative breeze,
A vital breeze which travell'd gently on
O'er things which it had made, and is become
A tempest, a redundant energy
Vexing its own creation. 'Tis a power
That does not come unrecogniz'd, a storm,
Which, breaking up a long-continued frost
Brings with it vernal promises, the hope
Of active days, of dignity and thought,
Of prowess in an honorable field,
Pure passions, virtue, knowledge, and delight,
The holy life of music and verse.

$$(I, 1-54)^2$$

Wordsworth speaks metaphorically of a condition of bondage being left behind, and while in fact he is setting off for the country and leaving behind the city, he is using the actual occasion to distinguish figuratively between senses of himself that come at such moments. As in the traditional Christian allegorical reading of the historical books of the Bible, "coming from a house of bondage" (the Exodus) is to be understood as a metaphor for the soul finding its freedom. (In *Purgatorio*, Dante has the souls crossing from mortal life to the Mountain of Purgatory singing "In exitu Israel de Egyptu.")[3] Wordsworth is being deliberately Biblical here, his spirit willing to follow "a wandering cloud," confident of its way. He is speaking of spiritual freedom, and he makes clear, in language suggestive of spiritual possession ("Trances of thought and mountings of the mind / Come fast upon me") that he may become, momentarily, an oracle to himself in poetic utterance.

As we observed in our reading of "Tintern Abbey," what is being opposed here is not the relative merits of country life and city life,

---

2. All the quotations in this essay are from *The Prelude* of 1805 as printed in Oxford *"Prelude,"* unless indicated otherwise. [*Editors.*]

3. Dante, *Purgatorio*, II, 46. The quotation is from Psalm 114:1—"When Israel went out of Egypt." [*Editors.*]

but rather the psychic possibilities for which the one and the other stand. City life stands for the "burthen of my own unnatural self / The heavy weight of many a weary day / Not mine, and such as were not made for me"; and the language unmistakably suggests "Tintern Abbey," "the burthen of the mystery," the "heavy and the weary weight of all that unintelligible world," "the dreary intercourse of daily life." The country life, here as there, stands for what the Hermit stands for in "Tintern Abbey," which is why, I think, it occurs to Wordsworth to say "hermitage" soon afterwards. He distinguishes a real "me" which can withdraw from the life of the "unnatural self"—"unnatural" in so far as it has been "bound" to circumstance.

If we accept as fact that these lines were composed extemporaneously on the way to Grasmere in 1799, why after all does he pretend in these lines not to know where he is going?

> Now I am free, enfranchis'd and at large,
> May fix my habitation where I will.
> What dwelling shall receive me? in what Vale
> Shall be my harbour? Underneath what grove
> Shall I take up my home, and what sweet stream
> Shall with its murmur lull me to my rest?
>
> (I, 9–14)

Why so elaborate a metaphorical characterization of following his newly-free spirit—"a wandering cloud," "a twig or any floating thing / Upon the river shall point me out my course"—if he knows the actual direction well enough and even the roads he will take? Should we be concerned, as some scholars have been,[4] about the possible confusion in recollection between Racedown and Grasmere? Is it not, rather, that in his spontaneous attempt to imagine the destined habitat for his free and contented spirit, he is simply anticipating it imaginatively in the imagery associated with spiritual contentment? In doing so, he is preconsciously recalling the past—a grove, a home, a stream and a vale, something lost, now reconstituted as the spirit wishes it were.[5] If Grasmere is perfect, he was saying, it will look like that. Most likely, a few years earlier, while preparing to retire to Racedown to write, he had wished the same of Racedown in much the same way, and even of Alfoxden, where next he moved to be nearer Coleridge. But the one was near the sea and the other nothing like the Lake Country. Perhaps it was in Germany, where he lived for a while after Alfoxden and before Grasmere, that this wishful language started teasing his mind,

4. See *The Prelude*, edited by de Selincourt and Darbishire (Oxford, 1959), pp. 510–12, footnotes to lines 1–122 especially.

5. The ways in which Wordsworth's imagination engages preconscious suggestions and unconscious wishes are treated here.

evoked by the poetic reminiscences of his boyhood that he began
sketching out while there. How natural, then, the choice of Grasmere was for him and Dorothy, however disappointing that choice
was to Coleridge, and how appropriate his "glad Preamble," his
spontaneous attempt to say so while going there. To settle perma-
nently and write, he required what his spirit desiderated, the mountain and valley scene which was for him the setting of the "first
poetic impulse." Thus, the pleasant day in Grasmere, on which he
wrote the passage, is not confused in his memory with Racedown,
but it is simply the fulfillment of a wish he had once tried to express
spontaneously in terms of a longed for hermitage where his imagination would be free to create.

We have already begun to interpret the characteristics of that
landscape and its appeal, its way of figuring in past states of relat-
edness with the mother; but even without a previously adverted eye
no alert reader could miss the similarity between "and what
stream / Shall with its murmur lull me to my rest?" (I, 113–4) and
the stream that stands for the infant condition:

> Was it for this
> That one, the fairest of all Rivers, lov'd
> *To blend his murmurs* with my Nurse's song,
> And from his alder shades and rocky falls,
> And from his fords and shallows, sent a voice
> That flow'd along my dreams? for this, didst Thou,
> O Derwent! travelling over the green Plains
> Near my 'sweet Birthplace,' didst thou, beauteous
>   Stream,
> Make ceaseless music through the night and day
> Which with its steady cadence, tempering
> Our human waywardness, compos'd my thoughts
> To more than infant softness, giving me,
> Among the fretful dwellings of mankind,
> A knowledge, a dim earnest, of the calm
> That Nature breathes among the hills and groves.
> (I, 271–285; my italics)

As in "Tintern Abbey" where the beauteous forms of a river valley
held within the mind stand for a state of soul modelled on the
preconscious recollection of infancy and association with the
mother, so here does the spiritual preference for a journey to a hermitage make clear what is anticipated by the inspired spirit becoming
free of the "unnatural self" and imagining its goal at the moment of
setting off. If these lines were composed on the way to Grasmere in
1799, then we have as early as that an indication of the unconscious
intention to return through imagination to the past, for the journey
to contentment is a return.

This opening passage ends in as highly a metaphorical way as it begins:

> if I may trust myself, this hour
> Hath brought a gift that consecrates my joy;
> For I, methought, while the sweet breath of Heaven
> Was blowing on my body, felt within
> A corresponding mild creative breeze,
> A vital breeze which travell'd gently on
> O'er things which it had made, and is become
> A tempest, a redundant energy
> Vexing its own creation. 'Tis a power
> That does not come unrecogniz'd, a storm,
> Which, breaking up a long-continued frost
> Brings with it vernal promises, the hope
> Of active days, of dignity and thought,
> Of prowess in an honorable field,
> Pure passions, virtue, knowledge, and delight,
> The holy life of music and of verse.
>
> (I, 39–54)

An actual breeze felt as sensation on the body seems to be a heaven-sent sign for his poetry because of a more significant answering breeze felt within him—"A corresponding mild creative breeze." The potential of creativity, he finds, is no more easily controlled than it is easily realized, and hence it seems tempestuous; it either vexes what is being created (these spontaneous lines) or seems to have become vexed by them. Making poetry is self-conscious; in some way it vexes the contentment presumably sought. Wordsworth says at line 68 that he then gave "a respite to this passion" and settled into "a gentler happiness":

> On the ground I lay
> Passing through many thoughts, yet mainly such
> As to myself pertain'd. I made a choice
> Of one sweet Vale whither my steps should turn
> And saw, methought, the very house and fields
> Present before my eyes . . .
>
> (I, 79–84)

He is going to Grasmere; in contented musing, he anticipates that "sweet Vale." But the contentment and passivity described here may remind us of the affections leading us on in "Tintern Abbey," away from consciousness of self:

> Thus long I lay
> Chear'd by the genial pillow of the earth
> Beneath my head, sooth'd by a sense of touch
> From the warm ground, that balanced me, else lost

> Entirely, seeing nought, nought hearing, save
> When here and there, about the grove of Oaks
> Where was my bed, an acorn from the trees
> Fell audibly, and with a startling sound.
>
> (I, 87–94)

Then, self-consciousness returns to startle his vacancy and remind him subsequently of poetry, the "work of glory" he had put from mind.

In any case, there is conflict in poetic utterance at present; the mild creative breeze has become a tempest. But in his own way, through the recurrence of poetic figures, Wordsworth makes perfectly clear to us, if we will only utilize his characterizations fully, that at one time these very sensations of an inner breeze were felt by the Babe without conflict. They came from Nature through the mother, the essential reality of the world. It was she who fostered "the first poetic spirit of our human life"; he says of the Blest Babe:

> Such feelings pass into his torpid life
> Like an awakening breeze, and hence his mind
> Even [in the first trial of its powers]
> Is prompt and watchful, eager to combine
> In one appearance, all the elements
> And parts of the same object, else detach'd
> And loth to coalesce.
>
> (II, 244–250)

And it is to her absent and traumatically introjected reality that both the present poetic urge, the "mild creative breeze," and its tempestuous force as a disturbance within him attest.[6]

He tells us early in his story of "that spirit of religious love in which / I walked with Nature" when as a boy after his mother's death he was alone in life:

> But let this, at least
> Be not forgotten, that I still retain'd
> My first creative sensibility,
> That by the regular action of the world
> My soul was unsubdu'd . . .
>
> (II, 377–381)

The description that follows these lines is of a power held within, unmanageable but one's own; it seems to fit exactly the descriptions of the power associated with the mother that composes things beau-

---

6. See Freud, "On Narcissism," *The Complete Psychological Works*, edited by James Strachey and Anna Freud (London, 1953–), vol. XIV.

tifully and that power as it is subject to inner disturbance, "vexing its own creation":

> A plastic power
> Abode with me, a forming hand, at times
> Rebellious, acting in a devious mood,
> A local spirit of its own, at war
> With general tendency, but for the most
> Subservient strictly to the external things
> With which it commun'd. An auxiliar light
> Came from my mind which on the setting sun
> Bestow'd new splendor, the melodious birds,
> The gentle breezes, fountains that ran on,
> Murmuring so sweetly in themselves, obey'd
> A like dominion; and the midnight storm
> Grew darker in the presence of my eye.
> Hence my obeisance, my devotion hence,
> And hence my transport.
>
> (II, 381–395)

The "midnight storm," on which the poet remembers imposing his tempestuous imagination, was experienced in one of those many situations that the boy sought with fascination in solitude.

His fuller characterization of the necessary solitude supplies us with an amazing connection between the disturbances he experienced in it and the various imaginative senses of it he retained in memory:

> for I would walk alone,
> In storm and tempest, or in star-light nights
> Beneath the quiet Heavens; and, at that time,
> Have felt whate'er there is of power in sound
> To breathe an elevated mood, by form
> Or image unprofaned; and I would stand,
> Beneath some rock, listening to sounds that are
> The ghostly language of the ancient earth,
> Or make their dim abode in distant winds.
> Thence did I drink the visionary power.
> I deem not profitless those fleeting moods
> Of shadowy exultation: not for this,
> That they are kindred to our purer mind
> And intellectual life; but that the soul,
> Remembering how she felt, but what she felt
> Remembering not, retains an obscure sense
> Of possible sublimity, to which
> With growing faculties she doth aspire,
> With faculties still growing, feeling still
> That whatsoever point they gain, they still
> Have something to pursue.
>
> (II, 321–341)

On the one hand, he is simply saying that he heard the stormy wind in the darkness and felt exhilarated by it; on the other hand, he says imaginatively that he was listening to Nature's disembodied voice, "the ghostly language of the ancient earth," and feeling the longing of the soul to pursue something sublime by the further growth of faculties capable of such pursuit. In a characteristic way, he "*drinks*" in this "visionary power" from the experience of "sounds that are / The ghostly language of the ancient earth / Or make their dim abode in the distant winds." It is the visionary faculty that must grow—the ability to "see" the presence in Nature, the ability to hear Nature's language more clearly, and, one supposes, the ability to speak that language expressively as poetry. The supposition is correct. Later, in Book V, he will echo these very words in talking about Poetry and the "great Nature that exists in works / Of mighty poets. . . ."

> he who, in his youth
> A wanderer among the wood and fields,
> With living Nature hath been intimate,
> Not only in that raw unpractis'd time
> Is stirr'd to ecstasy, as others are,
> By glittering verse; but, he doth furthermore,
> In measure only dealt out to himself,
> Receive enduring touches of deep joy
> From the great Nature that exists in works
> Of mighty Poets. *Visionary Power*
> *Attends upon the motions of the winds*
> *Embodied in the mystery of words.*
> *There darkness makes abode, and all the host*
> *Of shadowy things do work their changes there,*[7]
> As in a mansion like their proper home:
> Even forms and substances are circumfus'd
> By that transparent veil with light divine;
> And through the turnings intricate of Verse,
> Present themselves as objects recognis'd,
> In flashes, and with a glory scarce their own.
>
> (V, 610–629; my italics)

But there remains some uncertainty about poetic expression, about what exactly may be seen in moments of "vision," that has to do with Wordsworth's sense of human language itself.

What is the darkness that makes abode in the mystery of words,

7. William Collins's "Ode on the Poetical Character" (1746) has the line "shad'wy tribes of mind," which seems to be in Wordsworth's mind here. Interestingly enough, Collins was celebrating the inimitability of Milton, whereas succeeding Milton was the subject often on Wordsworth's mind. Collins asks: "Where is the Bard, whose soul can now / Its high presuming Hopes avow? / Where he who thinks, with Rapture blind, / This hallow'd work for him design'd?" and he answers: "In vain— Such Bliss to One alone / Of all the Sons of Soul was known, / And Heav'n and fancy, kindred Pow'rs, / Have o'er-turn'd th'inspiring Bow'rs / Or curtain'd close the Scene from ev'ry future view."

and what are the shadowy things that work their changes there, if poetry is a "light divine" by which objects are seen with a flash, recognized and glorified? How does one get from the mystery and the darkness of words to the spiritual illumination caused by their use in poetry? The "Great Nature that exists in works of mighty poets" is said to be accessible in a special way to one who has been intimate with Nature, who has heard the "ghostly language of the ancient earth." Here, too, Wordsworth is emphasizing hearing rather than speaking. He has heard something in Nature "speak" to him in the windy darkness, and he is using that experience to characterize what he has "heard" in the peculiar utterance of poetry. Why, though, has he relocated his visionary sense of something "in" Nature's darkness and mystery in language itself, in the "mystery of words?"

Fortunately, Wordsworth has already told us something else about the experience of poetry:

> Dumb yearnings, hidden appetites are ours,
> And they must have their food: our childhood sits,
> Our simple childhood sits upon a throne
> That hath more power than all the elements.
> I guess not what this tells of Being past,
> Nor what it augurs of the life to come;
> But so it is; and in that dubious hour,
> That twilight when we first begin to see
> This dawning earth, to recognise, expect;
> And in the long probation that ensues,
> The time of trial, ere we learn to live
> In reconcilement with our stinted powers,
> To endure this state of meagre vassalage;
> Unwilling to forego, confess, submit,
> Uneasy and unsettled; yoke-fellows
> To custom, mettlesome, and not yet tam'd
> And humbled down, oh! then we feel, we feel
> We know when we have Friends. Ye dreamers, then,
> Forgers of lawless tales! we bless you then,
> Impostors, drivellers, dotards, as the ape
> Philosophy will call you: then we feel
> With what, and how great might ye are in league,
> Who make our wish our power, our thought a deed,
> An empire, a possession; Ye whom Time
> And Seasons serve; all Faculties; to whom
> Earth crouches, th' elements are potter's clay,
> Space like a Heaven fill'd up with Northern lights;
> Here, nowhere, there, and everywhere at once.
>
> (V, 530–557)

It becomes quite plain: infantile appetite, the capacity for almost unlimited sensation and fantasy comes in a period that is rich and dumb. We have observed how language, which seems at first to enable the infant to express his wants and which is imbued with the pleasurable sense of association with the mother, is ultimately utilitarian and reductive. So language gradually limits the wonder of experience, darkens the vision and recollection of pleasure. Only the experiences offered by poetry, which is partially elusive of the limits of ordinary human speech, are capable of evoking the infantile and fantastic sense of alternatives to reality, of a prior and superior existence, perhaps as soul, from which the sense of self and time are a gradual estrangement.

Wordsworth also says here, as in "The Immortality Ode" that we come "from our native continent / To earth and human life," which makes us imagine, whichever way we choose, a pre-existence to the "human life" of the self. The habituation to the world is through the mother: and, if we recall from Book II that Wordsworth uses language there too as a metaphor for the process, we must be struck by the consistency of his metaphorical sense of things:

> by intercourse of touch,
> I held mute dialogues with my Mother's heart.
> (II, 282–283)

But with this same metaphor of speech-without-words, representing the hearing or ingesting of primal lessons and earliest visions, he also describes the relationship between the mother-substitute, Nature, and the growing child:

> A Child, I held unconscious intercourse
> With the eternal Beauty, drinking in
> A pure organic pleasure from the lines
> Of curling mist, or from the level plain
> Of waters colour'd by the steady clouds.
> (I, 589–593)

> the earth
> And common face of Nature spake to me
> Rememberable things.
> (I, 614–616)

He remembers, too, that the pure pleasure of childish play seemed to absorb the beauty of the surroundings; and he says explicitly that in this way Nature "*Peopled* my mind with beauteous forms or grand / And made me love them . . . ,"[8] just as the ambience of the mother's love had once suffused the natural objects of the world for the infant with light, love, and wonder. (Notice, too, that "peopled" figuratively preserves in the beauteous forms of Nature a very human association.) And Wordsworth himself sur-

8. *The Prelude*, I, 573–574.

mises that Nature's way of doing this for the child is a further development of the mother-infant relationship:

> those first-born affinities that fit
> our new existence to existing things,
> And, in our dawn of being, constitute
> The bond of union betwixt life and joy.
>
> (I, 582–585)

The "ghostly language of the ancient earth" heard in solitude in the windy darkness is a projection into Nature of a preconscious sense of a lost relationship, of the dialogue that the infant had with the mother's heart. Nature metaphorically "speaking" to him in solitude, wind, and darkness makes him want to speak that "visionary" language which he tells us later is poetry. To speak of visionary things is to use the imagination to evoke, and perhaps subsequently recognize, lost objects of love and wonder, to reveal in special utterance their ghostly or shadowy existence in the mind, called elsewhere "those phantoms of conceit," "the many feelings that oppressed my heart."

Here, too, we should notice how "heart" is associated with the mother and death. "Mute dialogues with my mother's *heart*" calls to mind: "the heart / And hinge of all our learning and our loves . . ." and "our being's heart and home is with infinitude. . . ."[9] A revision made by Wordsworth in the Poetry passage from Book V suggests further that it is a knowledge of what has been lost in death that poetry might uncover and present ("as objects recognized in flashes") when the poet's ability to speak in a visionary way matches his sense of being spoken to. When he changes "the motions of the winds" to "the motions of the *viewless* winds," I think that he is also preconsciously recalling Claudio's speech from *Measure For Measure*, which supplies the context of the imagination attempting to deal with the fear of death as an incomprehensible journey:

> Ay, but to die, and go we know not where;
> To lie in cold obstruction and to rot;
> This sensible warm motion to become
> A kneaded clod, and the delighted spirit
> To bathe in fiery floods, or to reside
> In thrilling region of thick-ribbed ice;
> To be imprison'd in the viewless winds,
> And blown with restless violence round about
> The pendent world . . .
>
> (III, i, 118–126)

Death and darkness are associated with the "*ghostly* language of the ancient earth" and with the "viewless winds" of poetry. But illumi-

9. These lines are from *The Prelude*, II, 283; V, 257–258; VI, 604: 1850 version.

nating light and glory are also associated with poetry. We remember from Book II that the "one belov'd Presence," which so closely resembles the "Presence" in Nature of "Tintern Abbey," is one that "*irradiates* and exalts . . . all objects through all intercourse of sense"; and this, I think, suggests why poetry is also said to have a "light divine" which suffuses objects and presents them "in flashes," whereas there is a darkness inherent in language.

WILLIAM EMPSON

Sense in *The Prelude*†

One does not think of the poetry of Wordsworth, even the parts which expound his philosophy, as depending on a concentrated richness of single words. There are of course "key" words like Nature and Imagination, and these may in reality be very puzzling, but he seems to be making a sturdy effort to expound them in discursive language. The apparently flat little word *sense* has I think a more curious part to play. It comes into practically all the great passages of *Tintern Abbey* and *The Prelude* on the mind's relation to Nature. And so far from being expounded it might seem a kind of expletive that he associates with this line of thought, or a convenience of grammar for expressing it. Yet in fact, of course, whether or not Wordsworth is drawing on Hartley[1] or Coleridge, his whole position depends on some rather undeveloped theory about how the mind interprets what it gets from the senses. Nor does the word drop from him casually; in the great majority of uses he makes it prominent by putting it at the end of the line, and this tends to hold it slightly apart from the stock phrase it comes in, so that some wider meaning for it can be suggested.

Taking Mr. de Selincourt's edition for the 1805 manuscript, I found 35 uses of *sense* at the end of a line and 12 elsewhere; the (posthumous) 1850 text has 31 uses at the end of a line and 11 elsewhere. There are changes moving the word in both directions, but both texts put just under three-quarters of the uses of *sense* at the end of a line, and these I think include all the important uses. The figures are minima, because no doubt I missed some. I did not count any of the derivative words, even *senseless*. *Tintern Abbey* only uses the word three times, and makes "feeling" do much of the work; but the crucial stylistic inventions for Wordsworth's *sense* come in those three.

† From William Empson, *The Structure of Complex Words* (London: Chatto and Windus, 1951), pp. 289–305.
1. David Hartley, author of *Observations on Man* (1749), which undertook to derive all the operations of mind from the association of ideas that were contiguous in sense experience. [*Editors.*]

The most frequent version of it, as one might expect, is the form "a sense of . . ." which the N.E.D.[2] explains as "not by direct perception but more or less vaguely or instinctively". This was not a hundred years old, perhaps a good deal less. I shall quote a series of examples with *sense* at the end of the line to show how the effect adds up. The most famous example, from *Tintern Abbey*, has not yet got used to the position for *sense* but gets the corresponding *of* at the start of the next line.

> A sense sublime
> Of something far more deeply interfused . . .
> [*Tintern Abbey*, 95–96]

> While here I stand, not only with the sense
> Of present pleasure, but with pleasing thoughts
> That in this moment there is life and food
> For future years.
> [*Tintern Abbey*, 62–65]

For the surface meaning, *sense* is dragged in here very unnecessarily.

> my brain
> Worked with a dim and undetermined sense
> Of unknown modes of being.[3]

There is a suggestion here from the pause at the end of the line that he had not merely "a feeling of" these unknown modes but something like a new "sense" which was partly able to apprehend them— a new *kind* of sensing had appeared in his mind.

> [*the soul*] retains an obscure sense
> Of possible sublimity. . . .
> [II, 317–18]

> Place also by the side of this dark sense
> Of noble feeling, that those spiritual men,
> Even the great Newton's own ethereal self,
> Seemed humbled in these precincts thence to be
> The more endeared.
> [III, 268–72]

He is trying to do his best for Cambridge and give it *sense* at the end of a line; but the language is thin, indeed to put his *sense* and *feeling* together always acts as a dilution. But presumably it means "Wordsworth's sense that *they* had noble feelings", so that it would again imply a peculiar mode of knowledge. Most of the later examples of the form are comparatively trivial.

---

2. *A New English Dictionary*, later and now known as the *Oxford English Dictionary*. [*Editors*.]

3. *The Prelude*, I, 391–93. Unless indicated otherwise, all quotations are from *The Prelude* of 1850. [*Editors*.]

And though an aching and a barren sense
Of gay confusion still be uppermost . . .
                    [III, 627–28]

How arch his notices, how nice his sense
Of the ridiculous. . . .
                    [V, 310–11]

                This only let me add
From heart-experience, and in humblest sense
Of modesty . . .
                    [V, 584–86]

            [*from astronomy*] I drew
A pleasure quiet and profound, a sense
Of permanent and universal sway . . .
                    [VI, 129–31]

                    a sense
Of what in the Great City had been done . . .
                    [VIII, 625–26]

When every day brought with it some new sense
Of exquisite regard for common things.
                    [XIV, 261–62]

And, to end with something more worth attention,

                a voice
Labouring, a brain confounded, and a sense,
Death-like, of treacherous desertion, felt
In that last place of refuge—my own soul.
                    [X, 412–15]

I only noticed five cases where "a sense of" is used without *sense* being at the end of a line. They come fairly late in the poem and carry none of this weight (e.g. "sense of beauty" VIII, 74, "of right" IX, 388).

The word, of course, can also be used merely for one of the senses:

As we grow up, such thraldom of that sense
Seems hard to shun.
                    [XII, 150–51]

Here it is the sense of sight, or rather the pleasure in scenery, which tends to have too much power. The word is simple enough, but even here he is not merely thinking of reception of sense data.

Also, examples of *sense* meaning only "good judgement" or "common sense" undoubtedly occur:

> that were to lack
>   All sense . . .
>   [III, 367–68]

> To tell us what is passion, what is truth,
> What reason, what simplicity and sense.
>   [VI, 113–14]

> Words follow words, sense seems to follow sense.
>   [VII, 508]

In one place we even have a bad kind of *sense*:

> The tendency, too potent in itself,
> Of use and custom to bow down the soul
> Under a growing weight of vulgar sense . . .
>   [XIV, 157–59]

"Oppress it by the laws of vulgar sense" is the 1805 version. The idea I suppose is "what vulgar people call good sense, knowing the price of things, etc." It comes very late in the poem. In any case, all these are in a way negative uses; in the positive ones he makes "good sense" something larger than the ordinary idea of it. Even

> real feeling and just sense
>   [XIII, 172]

has a peculiar emphasis. In spite of his disadvantages, he reflects, he might have had a good effect on the French Revolution if he had tried, because any man might

> That with desires heroic and firm sense
>   [1805; X, 147]

had made a bold stand. In the 1850 version, this has become "strong in hope, and trained to noble aspirations"; Wordsworth perhaps felt that the reader could not be expected to know how much he had felt *sense* to imply. Even the phrase "common sense" makes an appearance in the 1805 version, but certainly looks bigger than usual. It is about the unfortunate child who has been educated from books:

> Forth bring him to the air of common sense
> And, fresh and shewy as it is, the Corpse
> Slips from us into powder.
>   [1805; V, 352–54]

While cutting this out of the 1850 version, Wordsworth put back "common sense" a little higher up, in a flat appeal to the reader which feels rather out of style. In any case, though the idea "com-

mon sense" occurs, an adjective will often be added to this version
of *sense* to make it carry higher claims:

> one whom circumstance
> Hath called upon to embody his deep sense
> In action, give it outwardly a shape,
> And that of benediction, to the world.
>
> [IX, 400–403]

Good judgement here becomes practically the Creative Imagination
applied to politics.

> He deemed that my pursuits and labours lay
> Apart from all that leads to wealth, or even
> A necessary maintenance insures,
> Without some hazard to the finer sense.
>
> [XIV, 364–67]

This rather pompous stuff is almost exactly the prosaic use of
"sensibility"; it is viewed as a special degree of "good judgement"
but hints vaguely at something more artistic. The passage is the
same in the 1805 version.

I think it is important that Wordsworth refuses to say "sensibility" in these poems at all, except once about babies (II, 270) and
once about the growing child who still has some of the claims of the
baby (II, 360). Babies are entitled to a "tender, delicate, easily
hurt" kind of sensibility, what "The Man of Feeling" had been
proud of, but not (in Wordsworth's view) adults. Excessive sensibility was, I suppose, connected in his mind with the modish affecta-
tions of the people who used Poetic Diction, and he would not have
liked his contemporary Marianne Dashwood,[4] but to make a direct
attack on the word might have been confusing. Cutting it out had
an unexpected but rather helpful consequence; it put a lot of extra
work on *sense* and thereby made the word more fluid.

There are points, indeed, where the language tells us plainly that
a new kind of *sense* is in question. To begin with a slighter case, he
suggests that poets

> Have each for his peculiar dower, a sense
> By which he is enabled to perceive
> Something unseen before
>
> [1805; XII, 303–5]

and perhaps this will show Wordsworth what used to happen at
Stonehenge. The 1850 edition reduces the suggestion of vanity in
this fancy by removing *sense* from the end of the line. Again we
have:

4. A character in Jane Austen's *Sense and Sensibility* (1811), noted for her excess
of feeling. [*Editors.*]

> Nor less do I remember to have felt
> Distinctly manifested at this time
> A dawning, even as of another sense,
> A human-heartedness about my love
> For objects hitherto the gladsome air
> Of my own private being, and no more.
>   [1805; IV, 222–27]

This seems to throw light on a use of the word twenty lines earlier:

> Yes, I had something of another eye
> And often, looking round, was moved to smiles,
> Such as a delicate work of humour breeds.
> I read, without design, the opinions, thoughts
> Of these plain-living People, in a sense
> Of love and knowledge.
>   [1805; IV, 200–205]

Such is the 1805 version; I give the line reference to the 1850 one for convenience (IV, 209–14). There it is altered to "now observed with clearer knowledge". Wordsworth, no doubt, felt that this use of *sense* would hardly be intelligible, and indeed it must mean that he read them with a new faculty of sensing. Unfortunately, he chose to get his pet word back into the text somehow, and it comes in the first line of the paragraph, very intelligibly, but with a disagreeable complacence:

> Yes, I had something of a subtler sense.

The passage about the Chartreuse, which was entirely rewritten, gives a more striking example of how he came to alter his idea of the word:

> be the house redeemed
> With its unworldly votaries, for the sake
> Of conquest over sense, hourly achieved
> Through faith and meditative reason.
>   [VI, 456–59]

The 1805 version has no example of *sense* meaning sensuality, and this I should think was deliberate. Even for the 1850 one, Wordsworth did not allow it to come at the end of a line. His own "conquest over sense" is something of an unwanted irony here.

More general examples of the same process are given by "The incumbent mystery of sense and soul" (XIV, 286) and "In sense conducting to ideal form" (XIV, 76), where he is introducing at least the hint of a dichotomy in the course of re-writing; *sense* appears to be the opposite of soul, and the "mystery" is that they can be connected at all. However, I do not want to make out that the re-writing shows an important change of opinion. In any case, there are signs that his use of the word had changed in the six years between ending Book VI and starting Book VII; all the impressive examples come before that. What is really in question, I think, is not any theory in Wordsworth's mind about the word but a manipulative feeling, of what he could make it do; a thing more familiar perhaps to poets than critics, and one which a poet easily forgets; the period during which Wordsworth could feel how to use this word was, I think, very brief. In general, I agree with a recent defender of the older man (M. E. Burton, *One Wordsworth*) who says that he did not try to hide his early political and religious opinions any further when he re-wrote, indeed, he sometimes enlarged upon a vaguely unorthodox idea such as the world-soul; he was merely "improving the style". But this improvement, which was mainly a process of packing the lines more fully, meant invoking Milton and his sense of the unrelaxing Will; whereas the whole point and delicacy of the first version was to represent a wavering and untrammelled natural growth. The improvement was, therefore, about the most destructive thing he could have done, far worse than changing the supposed opinions. Incidentally, I think there was also a good influence of Milton, already strong in the first version, which came from a very different side of that author's feeling about the world; it is remarkable surely that the first paragraph of *The Prelude*, describing how Wordsworth is now free to wander where he chooses and write as much as he likes, makes two distinct quotations from the throwing out from Paradise of Adam and Eve ("The earth is all before me" (I, 14), "Whither shall I turn?" (I, 26)). Indeed the repeated claims that it was somehow a good thing to have lost his first inspiration are a rather close parallel to Milton's baffling but very strong feelings about Paradise.

I have tried to review the general background of the uses, and must now approach the important ones.

> in such strength
> Of usurpation, when the light of sense
> Goes out, but with a flash that has revealed
> The invisible world, doth greatness make abode.
> [VI, 559–602]

Maybe this tidier version of the great passage is an improvement, but the 1805 one certainly demands attention:

> in such strength
> Of usurpation, in such visitings
> Of awful promise, when the light of sense
> Goes out in flashes that have shown to us
> The invisible world, doth Greatness make abode.

It is not long after the Chartreuse passage, and perhaps Wordsworth in making his changes remembered the ascetic view of *sense* he had put in for the monks. The removal of the sensuous world, in the new version, is the point of vision. But this idea was already present in the old one; the *invisible world* clearly means to suggest something like it. I am rather reluctant to insist on the ambiguity of the passage, because in general the style does not want any concentrated piece of trickery; Wordsworth is trying to state his position, even if he fails. But the trick he has stumbled upon here is as glorious as such a thing could be. *The light . . . goes out* can mean "light proceeds from the source" as well as "the source fails". By combining the two, Wordsworth induces his baffling *sense* to become a lighthouse occasionally flashing not on any spiritual world but on the dangerous and actual sea, which at other times is invisible merely because the captain is in darkness. I am not certain, to be sure, whether lighthouses already flashed in Wordsworth's time, and the essential image is the last bright flash of the guttering candle; this in itself allows mere sensation to carry mysterious and rarely seen powers. The ecstasy both destroys normal *sense* and fulfils it, and the world thus shown is both the same as and wholly different from the common one. The verbal ambiguity in the first version only drives home the paradox which he retained in the later one.

The most fundamental statement of this theory of the senses is made about the famous baby at the breast:

> For him, in one dear Presence, there exists
> A virtue which irradiates and exalts
> Objects through widest intercourse of sense.
> No outcast he, bewildered and depressed . . .
> For feeling has to him imparted power
> That through the growing faculties of sense
> Doth like an agent of the one great Mind
> Create, creator and receiver both,
> Working but in alliance with the works
> Which it beholds.
>
> [II, 238–60]

The 1805 version brings in *sensations* and *sentiment* but does not have *sense* twice:

> In one beloved presence, nay and more,
> In that most apprehensive habitude
> And those sensations which have been derived
> From this beloved Presence, there exists

"a virtue" and so on, and

> For feeling has to him imparted strength
> And powerful in all sentiments of grief,
> Of exultation, fear, and joy, his mind
> Even as an agent of the one great mind,

"creates" and so on. The earlier version is thus rather more pantheist, emphasises emotion more, and is perhaps less dependent on key words; the notion that feeling "returns as power" had come to seem a settled epigram to Wordsworth when he shortened the second part of this quotation, and in the same way it seemed an adequate theoretical coverage to say "faculties of sense" rather than list the child's emotions, which might suggest that he admired it (as the Chinese sage Laotze did) because it yelled so loudly. In the first part of the quotation the change makes the idea prettier and cruder; the original point was that the "sensation" of affection, and I suppose of resistance as well, towards the mother are what teach the "senses" of the child to grasp the world, a thing which must be done by an interchange like that between persons. *Sensations* here are not sensedata, and thereby free from the ambiguity of *sense*, but a more highly developed compound of emotion and knowledge even than *sense*, and therefore convenient for forcing us to understand it. Indeed, the 1805 version has no unambiguous term for sensedata, and I suppose would have denied the reality of the concept; in the 1850 version Wordsworth sometimes inserts "bodily" before *sense* to make a passage clearer (e.g. XIV, 88) but the earlier version hardly ever descends to this (once in 1805 XI, 272).

Obviously the meaning "good judgement" is given a very back seat when the word is used for such a theory. It need not be ignored or denied, but it is only a middling part of the range which has now to be covered by the word, and we are more interested in the two ends of the range. Using the word for the baby makes the process more complete. No doubt the baby does have to use good judgement, but its powers of mind are applied to such extraordinary things from our point of view, the building up of the idea of space for example, that we do not think of them as needing "good sense". The whole poetical and philosophical effect comes from a violent junction of sensedata to the divine imagination given by love, and the middle term is cut out.

The uses of the word so far, however striking, can be said to keep within its previous range. It appears that Wordsworth also invented a new form, "the sense" used absolutely, and the new form must be supposed to imply some new meaning. There are, to be sure, precedents for the form, but only with a context that makes the meaning an obvious one. The N.E.D. has "5" "pierced to the sense" (to the quick), "11b" "if they had had the sense to do it they could have . . .", and "1e" "the process of ink-making is noisome to the sense". Perhaps this last heading, defined as "that one of the senses indicated by the context", would cover Lucio's "wanton stings and motions of the sense",[5] which otherwise seems to be ignored. Pope

5. *Measure for Measure*, I, iv, 59. [*Editors.*]

has a use which feels more like those of Wordsworth, "darkness strikes the sense no less than light", but I take it he meant quite narrowly "the sense of sight". None of these would prevent the bare and blank use by Wordsworth from appearing a novelty. He has already got it in *Tintern Abbey*, and it is already tearing upon the tripod:

> well pleased to recognize
> In Nature and the language of the sense,
> The anchor of my purest thoughts, the nurse,
> The guide, the guardian of my heart, and soul
> Of all my moral being.
>   [*Tintern Abbey*, 107–11]

"The" does not refer back to any *sense* previously defined, but this very sentence is expressing his theory; it goes

> Therefore am I still
> A lover of the meadows and the woods . . .
>   of all the mighty world
> Of eye and ear—both what they half create,
> And what perceive; well pleased to recognize . . .

Thus one feels that "the sense" is a combination of "that sense" (the kind of *sense* just adumbrated) and "the senses" in general. The new grammar was really needed by the poetry; even Wordsworth could not have got away with saying that the language of *the senses* was the soul of all his moral being. "*Language*" does much of the work—the senses can no doubt "show" us profound things (like Professor Wittgenstein)[6] through the means by which they "tell" us every-day things; but the traditional idea of the weakness and corruptibility of the senses would have been bound to poke up its head. With the new grammar "the sense" can take over some of the defining work from "the language"; we may even take "the sense" as a peculiar power of imagination and its "language" as the mere sensedata from which we learn it. Either term could serve to ward off misunderstanding.

After this invention of the form he used it without any help from the context.

> Nor, sedulous as I have been to trace
> How Nature by extrinsic passion first
> Peopled the mind with forms sublime or fair,
> And made me love them, may I here omit
> How other pleasures have been mine, and joys
> Of subtler origin; how I have felt,

---

6. Ludwig Wittgenstein (1899–1951), eminent philosopher at Cambridge University, who analyzed acutely the meanings, or the uses, of words in our everyday language. [*Editors.*]

> Not seldom even in that tempestuous time,
> Those hallowed and pure motions of the sense
> Which seem, in their simplicity, to own
> An intellectual charm; that calm delight
> Which, if I err not, surely must belong
> To those first-born affinities that fit
> Our new existence to existing things,
> And, in our dawn of being, constitute
> The bond of union between life and joy.
>   Yes, I remember when the changeful earth
> And twice five summers on my mind had stamped
> The faces of the moving year, even then
> I held unconscious intercourse with beauty
> Old as creation, drinking in a pure
> Organic pleasure from the silver wreaths
> Of curling mist, or from the level plain
> Of waters coloured by impending clouds.
>
>   [I, 544–66]

The 1805 version is noticeably better in the last five lines, but there is no important difference elsewhere:

> A Child, I held unconscious intercourse
> With the eternal Beauty, drinking in
> A pure organic pleasure from the lines
> Of curling mist, or from the level plain
> Of waters coloured by the steady clouds.

The next paragraph says he would stand looking at the water

> . . . bringing with me no peculiar sense
> Of quietness or peace,

but "gathering . . . New pleasure, like a bee among the flowers".

Wordsworth, I think, realised that he had to use hidden devices so that he might talk as if he had never heard of the meaning "sensuality"; the chief function of *pure* here is to keep it out of view. But apart from this hidden denial of a meaning (a common and important process), which adds obscurity to the uses of the word, there is a curious blankness even about the meanings allowed. I have quoted at length here to show how the context before and after leads us in the two opposite directions. The second sentence, or paragraph, begins by saying that he remembers taking a pure organic pleasure in the scenery at this period (when he was ten). But the beginning of the first long sentence makes a careful distinction between his love for the scenery and the "joys of subtler origin"; and these are what he is claiming to remember. I am not saying that there is a real contradiction in this obscurity, only that it imposes a double meaning on "the sense". If the child were enjoying the scenery we would expect the term to mean or anyway to include "the senses", but our attention is first directed away from them so that it means some "inner sense", and *the* in the singular makes it look like the supreme sense of Imagination. But then the next sentence pushes it back to the sensations about the scenery again. I take it that the child felt a gush of well-being from far within, apparently without cause, but marking some profound adjustment to life; and Wordsworth goes on to say that he remembers attaching this feeling to the scenery. The effect is that, though Sensation and Imagination appear as the two extreme ends of the scale in view, so that one might expect them to be opposites, the word is so placed that it might equally well apply to either. And the middle of the scale, the idea of ordinary common sense, is cut out from these uses no less firmly than the idea of sensuality. That is, instead of falling into the usual fallacies about good sense, you are forced to keep the whole range of the word in view, and there is a claim that the whole range of the word has been included in one concept. At least, I do not see what else the claim can be; and I suppose most people would agree that the word is made to echo Wordsworth's doctrine somehow.

A conceivable meaning for *the sense* is the archaic "common sense", that which correlates the messages of the different external senses. It is "the senses regarded as unified", and that is already a kind of rudimentary power of interpreting them. It was not then so remote as to be quite unfamiliar to Wordsworth. On the other hand, the passage as a whole obviously means "My Imagination was already stirring", but which of the words means his imagination, if *the sense* does not? This may be an unreasonable process of thought, but it seems to describe the way we are driven to give the term an obscure but splendid claim. It must be remembered that, here as so often in the poem, the language is in any case extremely loose; the theoretical turns of phrase in the first paragraph lead us to expect the "bond of union" to be between the child and the external world—an epistemology is being given—but the peroration sweeps this aside to contemplate only "life and joy". No doubt the reason why this seems fine is that one accepts *life* as the child and *joy* as inherent in Mother Nature, but such extreme optimism is made plausible only by being left vague. In the same way *the sense* feels inherently vague; but this is no reason why we should not try to account for its behaviour.

In the "Statements in Words" chapter I gave as an example of the fourth type the use of *law* for "both human and divine law"; the law you are talking about will commonly appear to be one or the other, but you may imply that such laws as this one satisfy the conditions for both. In such a case, though the order of terms for the equation is indifferent, it will be fixed on any particular occasion. The

Wordsworthian use of *sense*, if I am right, is a much more thorough example of the process, not merely because the unifying concept required is much more obscure, but because in any one use of the equation you are not certain which term is meant to come first. However, I should claim that these two sorts of equation can be classed together for the purpose in hand, which is to consider what the different forms of interpretation can be.

Granting that the Wordsworth one is an equation of some sort, it is still not obvious how this equation could be translated into a sentence. "Sensation is Imagination" is a possible slogan, but both this and its inverse seem very open to misunderstanding without making the real point. "Sensation and Imagination are included in a larger class" is merely dull; besides, the important thing may well be that they overlap to form a narrower class. "Sensation and Imagination interlock" seems the best way to put it. But I think it is fair to say that Wordsworth had not got any translation ready; he was much better at adumbrating his doctrine through rhetorical devices than at writing it out in full.

To be sure, I do not mean to claim that the form always carries so much weight; for example it is used in the 1805 version to build a graceful piece of deliberate tedium, later omitted.

> On I went
> Tranquil, receiving in my own despite
> Amusement, as I slowly passed along,
> From such near objects as from time to time
> Perforce intruded on the listless sense
> Quiescent, and disposed to sympathy.
> [1805; IV, 375–80]

Even here it can be read as something like "imagination"; indeed, you might say that Wordsworth, rather pompously, is thinking of his imagination as a pet dog which never left his side. The example shows that the form was still connected in his mind with the actual process of receiving sensations. But, in contrast to that, another of these fairly trivial uses shows him treating it as a sort of technical term. During the French Revolution, he is saying, many young idealists and theorists felt that they must learn to deal with practical affairs:

> The play-fellows of fancy, who had made
> All powers of swiftness, subtlety, and strength
> Their ministers,—who in lordly wise had stirred
> Among the grandest objects of the sense,
> And dealt with whatsoever they found there
> As if they had within some lurking right
> To wield it . . .
> Were called upon to exercise their skill
> [XI, 126–39]

—in the real world. This is particularly baffling because *the sense* appears to be the despised Fancy. In ordinary English, that is, you would expect it to refer to a sense *of* a kind already mentioned, and a sense of fancy is the only plausible candidate. But it is considered ironical that these people thought they had a right to deal with whatever they *found there*, that is, in *the sense* or among its *grandest objects*. Of course, it may be said that fancy often deals with grand objects, only not practically enough. The irony of Wordsworth is always cumbrous, and he does not mean to express contempt for these people by it (the passage is hardly altered from 1805); nor therefore, you might argue, for their kind of fancy. I do not see how to disprove such an argument, but I believe that at this stage of the poem he regarded *the sense* as practically equivalent to "Imagination", so that it comes in as a natural opposite to Fancy (the irony against these people is due because they supposed that fancy would work where imagination is required). I think, indeed, that he would have been startled to find anyone identifying the two opposites for reasons of grammar. The interest of the example, supposing that this account is true, is that he was taking his new form as something well established.

I ought now to give some account of *feeling*. One might think that it was the opposite word to *sense*, rather as *wit* is in Pope; but Wordsworth does not oppose the two words, and the effect when he puts them together is one of verbosity rather than anything else. Both of them (and *sensation* too) are concerned with both knowledge and emotion; a feeling of impending doom is very like a sense of one. The choice between using one or the other is I think often made on rather obscure grounds of tact. "A sense of" impending doom claims that there is really something there to feel, though your interpretation of it may be wrong, whereas "a feeling of it" admits that you may be wholly mistaken. However, this contrast may be used in a rather contradictory way. If you want to say that you have come to a decision, though you realize the subject is complicated, you say you "feel", and whatever the other man says you can still have your feeling. To say you have a *sense* that your plan is the best would really be milder, though it makes a larger claim, because it is not wholly closed to argument. "When people begin to 'feel' ", Samuel Butler[7] noticed, "they are always taking what seems to them the more worldly course". It is because the subject is so complicated (not a thing you could claim to know about) that they are prepared to act in a way which might seem against their principles. This rather odd social development makes it hard to nail down a difference between the words in general. I

7. Samuel Butler (1835–1902), satirist and man of letters, author of the novel *The Way of All Flesh*. [*Editors*.]

should fancy that Wordsworth made more use of *feeling* in *Tintern Abbey* because he was writing with more direct conviction, though no doubt it is also true that he had not yet fixed his technical terms. But in any case it does not seem possible to exchange the words in his later work:

> So feeling comes in aid
> Of feeling, and diversity of strength
> Attends us, if but once we have been strong.
>   [XXI, 269–71]

The whole passage is a very fine one. But why could not Wordsworth use his technical terms here?

> A single operation of the sense
> Gives power, and diversity of strength . . .

Why, I wonder, does my invention look so ridiculous? No doubt it fails to meet the point about "diversity"; it seems a narrow piece of theorising. But also I think it feels out of the style because it makes *the sense* too definite; only some high idea of "the sense of imagination" will fit the requirements of the assertion, whereas Wordsworth always (even in "the grandest objects of the sense") left room for the alternative reading by which it meant the processes of sensing in general. Indeed, this double meaning was required by the theory which he used it to expound.

The reader may also have felt my little attempt ridiculous because he remembered the context, which is a particularly strange one. "I am lost" Wordsworth is just going to say; he uses *feeling* for a reason not really unlike that of Samuel Butler's people; and in any case he is actually talking about feelings rather than some act of imagination which would transcend them. He first describes the fear of the child losing its guide on the grim moor, and the "visionary dreariness" of the place, and then says that this place, when he came back "in the blessed hours Of early love, the loved one at my side", gave him ideas of "pleasure and youth's golden gleam".

> And think ye not with radiance more sublime
> For these remembrances, and for the power
> They had left behind? So feeling comes in aid . . .

It is not even clear that the child used *the sense*; the only strength he showed was to face and recognise the horror of the thing. And what kind of strength does Wordsworth now require, out walking with the bride rather coldly planned for? Apparently even a time of agony in his childhood was better than—more than that, it gave him strength to endure—the chief pleasure he could arrange for his middle age. Of course, he would have denied that he had meant this, but he is reporting experiences, without much distortion for the sake of theory, and it would be no use to try to simplify his opinions.

Mr. James Smith[8] has pointed out a similar jump in the famous passage on crossing the Alps, and it has the advantage for my purpose of falling into an "A is B" form. Critics have insinuated that the experience was a good deal "written up", judging by Wordsworth's travel diary; but if you examine the language of the poem it is sufficiently frank. On being told that he had crossed the Alps, he says, "Imagination"—

> That awful Power rose from the mind's abyss
> Like an unfathered vapour that enwraps,
> At once, some lonely traveller. I was lost;
> Halted without an effort to break through;
> But to my conscious soul I now can say
> "I recognise thy glory"; in such strength
> Of usurpation . . .
>
> [VI, 594–600]

—and "the light of sense goes out". The 1850 version says rather more clearly than the 1805 one ("and now recovering, to my soul I say") that he only recognised the Imagination afterwards; but they both say it. The next paragraph, indeed, calmly begins by saying that what this news caused at the time was "a melancholy slackening". But they hurry on down the gorge and see

> The immeasurable height
> Of woods decaying, never to be decayed . . .
> Winds thwarting winds, bewildered and forlorn . . .
> The rocks that muttered close upon our ears,
> Black drizzling crags that spake by the way-side
> As if a voice were in them; the sick sight
> And giddy prospect of the raving stream . . .

Nature is a ghastly threat in this fine description; he might well, as in his childhood, have clasped a tree to see if it was real. But what all this is *like*, when the long sentence arrives at its peroration, is "workings of one mind" (presumably God's or Nature's, so it is not merely *like*),

> Characters of the great Apocalypse,
> The types and symbols of Eternity,
> Of first, and last, and midst, and without end.

The actual horror and the eventual exultation are quite blankly identified by this form of grammar. Now, of course, the historical process of learning to enjoy mountains really was a matter of taking

---

8. "Wordsworth: A Preliminary Survey," *Scrutiny*, VII, 1 (1938), pp. 33–55 [*Editors*.]

this jump. I do not want to appear more prosy than Jane Austen on the subject. Her chief discussion of it comes in *Sense and Sensibility*, chapter xviii, and we find she is perfectly at home with horror; the man who says he likes scenery to be cheerful is suspected of trying to be singular, but on the whole, it is felt, he is only rebuking excess or sympathising with farmers—at bottom he likes horror all right, like any other person of taste. One need not say, as I understand Mr. James Smith to do, that owing to a narrow theory about Nature Wordsworth is forcing an obviously wrong interpretation onto his feelings here. The point of identifying these two very different states of feeling, as a matter of style, is to insist that they are profoundly connected; one of them grows out of the other, or something like that. No doubt some kind of pantheism is implied, because Wordsworth feels that Eternity is turbulent like the Alps and not calm like the Christian God. But the last line of the passage contradicts this idea by putting the calm back, and in any case the metaphysics would be a deduction only; what he sets out to do is to describe the whole development of his feelings about crossing the Alps, and he asserts it as a unity.

I have been wandering away here from the verbal approach and the word *sense*, and I needed to do so, because if my account of *sense* is to be convincing I need to show that a similar process is at work generally in the poem. The word, I maintain, means both the process of sensing and the supreme act of imagination, and unites them by a jump; the same kind of jump as that in the sentence about crossing the Alps, which identifies the horror caused by the immediate sensations with the exultation that developed from them. And in both cases, one might complain, what is jumped over is "good sense"; when Wordsworth has got his singing robes on he will not allow any mediating process to have occurred.

A sturdy Wordsworthian, I suppose, would answer that there really is a consistent theory expounded, and that my linguistic approach merely ignores it. But then the Hartley theory, which Mr. Herbert Read describes as "practically what would now be called Behaviourism", left much the same gap to be jumped. Perhaps I should quote some of his exposition of it (in his *Wordsworth*):

> According to Hartley's psychology, our passions or affections are no more than aggregates of simple ideas united by association; and simple ideas are ideas surviving sensations after the objects which caused them have been removed. First, sensations, "which arise from the impressions made by external objects upon the several parts of our bodies"; then simple ideas of sensation; finally, under the power of association, all the various faculties of the human mind, such as memory, imagination, understanding, affection, and will.[9]

9. Herbert Read, *Wordsworth* (London and Toronto, 1932), p. 149. [*Editors.*]

Indeed, there is at least one passage, in the rejected manuscript Y given in Mr. de Selincourt's edition, where Wordsworth positively asserts the connection of ideas which I claim to find buried in his use of *the sense*. After the child has grasped simple ideas, he says:

> And the world's native produce, as it meets
> The sense with less habitual strength of mind,
> Is pondered as a miracle,

he grows up wanting to believe myths and legends; but the wiser man after maturity will abandon them and return to the Nature which the child experienced,

> as it were
> Resolving into one great faculty
> Of being bodily eye and spiritual need[1]

and there is a very fine long passage about the strength which his thought can then attain. There is no unwillingness to expound the idea in this rejected and rather bold document; we are plainly told that the new faculty combines sensation and imagination. Perhaps I am taking a narrow and stupid view, but the idea seems to me to remain pretty unintelligible, however plainly and lengthily it is expressed; and at any rate most readers of the poetry, who have not read Hartley, must pick up the idea in the form which I have tried to describe. Besides, Wordsworth seems to have followed Coleridge in going to the opposite philosophical extreme, from Associationism to Idealism, without feeling that the change needed to be made obvious in these poetical expression of his theory. It does not seem unfair to say that he induced people to believe he had expounded a consistent philosophy through the firmness and assurance with which he used equations of Type IV; equations whose claim was false, because they did not really erect a third concept as they pretended to; and in saying this I do not mean to deny that the result makes very good poetry, and probably suggests important truths.

HERBERT LINDENBERGER

Images of Interaction in *The Prelude*†

1. *Wind and Water*

The distinctive thing about the images of *The Prelude* is that they provide the basic setting for the poem: water, islands, mountains,

1. Oxford *"Prelude,"* pp. 572–74, lines 56–154. [*Editors.*]
† From Herbert Lindenberger, *On Words-* *worth's "Prelude"* (Princeton University Press, 1963), chapter III (pages 69–98).

breezes, and growing things. When Wordsworth describes a stream he knew in childhood he can start out wholly on the level of literal description—the poem is, after all, an autobiography—and before the reader has gone much further the stream has become a metaphor for the workings of the imagination. It is difficult to distinguish between the literal and metaphorical level in Wordsworth, for the literal becomes figurative and then literal again. Distinctions between tenor and vehicle, crucial as they are to the understanding of Renaissance and metaphysical verse, are of little avail in this type of poetry. Wordsworth's use of imagery stands at an opposite extreme, one might say, from that of a Shakespearean play. When we speak of the imagery of sickness in *Hamlet* we think of a body of images which, however closely they seem to grow out of the play's action, can still, for purposes of discussion at least, be viewed as distinct from the plot. The characters are not physically sick in the literal sense: the images are essentially an imaginative extension of the dramatic situation that Shakespeare is probing. We could conceivably cut the metaphorical element out of *Hamlet* and still have a substantial, though certainly impoverished drama. But to rob *The Prelude* of its images is to rob it of its whole plot and continuity.

One might think of the imagery of *The Prelude* as a kind of *donnée*, something concretely observed by the poet, and something he must constantly return to as he narrates the events of his life; yet it is also something he thinks *through*, a mode of language which continually leads him away from itself to encompass larger areas of human experience. In the opening lines of the poem he starts with the simple fact of the breeze that blows upon him as he leaves London:

> Oh there is blessing in this gentle breeze
> That blows from the green fields and from the clouds
> And from the sky: it beats against my cheek,
> And seems half-conscious of the joy it gives.[1]

From the beginning the breeze seems both rooted in the sensory, observable world and at the same time ("half-conscious of the joy it gives") connected to higher powers. A few lines later the poet speaks of his own breathings:

> I breathe again;
> Trances of thought and mountings of the mind
> Come fast upon me,
>
> (I, 19–21)

and soon thereafter the two processes, the breathings within nature and within the poet, are brought together, and then connected with the creative process:

1. All quotations in this essay are from *Oxford "Prelude,"* 1805 text. [*Editors.*]

> For I, methought, while the sweet breath of Heaven
> Was blowing on my body, felt within
> A corresponding mild creative breeze,
> A vital breeze which travell'd gently on
> O'er things which it had made, and is become
> A tempest, a redundant energy
> Vexing its own creation. 'Tis a power
> That does not come unrecogniz'd, a storm,
> Which, breaking up a long-continued frost
> Brings with it vernal promises, the hope
> Of active days, of dignity and thought. . . .
>
> (41–51)

Although the field of reference has moved from the physical world
to the mental world of the poet, we are still reminded—in the
metaphor of the storm breaking up the frost—of the physical
origins of the figure. What started out as literal observation has
become metaphor, and in the course of this shift the image has
unobtrusively changed character from a "gentle breeze" to a storm:
the flexibility we noted in the rhetorical roles which the image
plays is accompanied by a corresponding flexibility of meaning.

The dominating images of *The Prelude* are wind and water,
images which by their very nature—their flowing, transforming
quality, their ability to interact with other natural elements, and
also their traditional associations—allow the poet free range between the observable world and the higher transcendental reality
which he wishes to make visible to us. Their chief function, one
might say, is to act as intermediaries between the two worlds. In the
incident about the stolen boat in Book I the water remains throughout a part of the observed scene:

> The moon was up, the Lake was shining clear
> Among the hoary mountains.
>
> . . . Not without the voice
> Of mountain-echoes did my Boat move on,
> Leaving behind her still on either side
> Small circles glittering idly in the moon,
> Until they melted all into one track
> Of sparkling light.
>
> (383–84; 389–94)

Yet as we follow the play of moonlight upon the water we feel
ourselves gradually being led into a deeper reality, something which,
at the end of the passage, will culminate in the vision of the "huge
and mighty Forms that do not live / Like living men . . ." (425–
26). Soon after this passage, directly after the apostrophe "Wisdom
and Spirit of the universe," we return to the literal image of water,
not only in its usual state, but in the form of mist:

In November days,
When vapours, rolling down the valleys, made
A lonely scene more lonesome; among woods
At noon, and 'mid the calm of summer nights,
When, by the margin of the trembling Lake,
Beneath the gloomy hills I homeward went
In solitude, such intercourse was mine;
'Twas mine among the fields both day and night
And by the waters all the summer long.

(443–51)

We have returned to the observable world, yet in the rolling of vapors and the trembling of waters the reader still feels himself in an atmosphere of vision. Only somewhat later does Wordsworth make explicit the water's role as intermediary:

Even then,
A Child, I held unconscious intercourse
With the eternal Beauty, drinking in
A pure organic pleasure from the lines
Of curling mist, or from the level plain
Of waters colour'd by the steady clouds.

(588–93)

But in the course of the poem we come to take the transcendental meanings of the wind and the water so for granted that we are immediately aware of their relevance even in a naturalistic description such as the following:

And in the shelter'd coppice where I sate,
Around me, from among the hazel leaves,
Now here, now there, stirr'd by the straggling wind,
Came intermittingly a breath-like sound,
A respiration short and quick, which oft,
Yea, might I say, again and yet again,
Mistaking for the panting of my Dog,
The off-and-on Companion of my walk,
I turn'd my head, to look if he were there.

(IV, 172–80)

The dog is something of a deflecting agent: it is as though Wordsworth is too reticent to remind us once more of the transcendental associations of the breeze, yet these associations have been so thoroughly established in the poem thus far that the reader is less easily fooled by the nature of the breeze than was the young Wordsworth.

One could speak of the wind and water as functioning on two separate levels: on the one hand, as we have seen, they are *literally* intermediaries between the visible and the invisible worlds, but they also have a rhetorical function, for they serve to prepare the reader for the great moments of vision. They are, one might say, a mode of transition both between the parts of the poet's universe and between the reader and the visionary experience which the poet is preparing him for. Thus, at the beginning of the ascent of Snowdon the stress is all on the low, thick mist:

> It was a Summer's night, a close warm night,
> Wan, dull and glaring, with a dripping mist
> Low-hung and thick that cover'd all the sky,
> Half threatening storm and rain.
> (XIII, 10–13)

Momentarily we feel our senses dulled, as though we must be cut off from familiar ways of thinking and feeling before we are ready for new ones. Above all, there is a quality of imminence (as well as immanence) about the scene, of something larger about to happen than merely the "half threatening storm and rain."

In their gentler aspects, as we have seen, the wind and water help bring together the divergent orders of Wordsworth's world, but in their harsher moments they serve yet another function—as manifestations of power and vitality in the universe. Thus, on the Simplon Pass we are shown

> The stationary blasts of water-falls,
> And every where along the hollow rent
> Winds thwarting winds, bewilder'd and forlorn,
> The torrents shooting from the clear blue sky,

culminating in the vision of

> Characters of the great Apocalypse,
> The types and symbols of Eternity,
> Of first and last, and midst, and without end.
> (VI, 558–61; 570–72)

Again in the vision on Snowdon, as the mist begins to lift we see

> A fracture in the vapour,
> A deep and gloomy breathing-place through which
> Mounted the roar of waters, torrents, streams
> Innumerable, roaring with one voice.

As in the passage on the Simplon, we are first shown the elements in all their immediacy; only then are we prepared for the explanation of their meaning:

> The universal spectacle throughout
> Was shaped for admiration and delight,
> Grand in itself alone, but in that breach
> Through which the homeless voice of waters rose,
> That dark deep thoroughfare had Nature lodg'd

The Soul, the Imagination of the Whole.
(XIII, 56–65)

Often, when the context does not permit Wordsworth to represent wind and water as part of the surrounding scene, he makes use of their symbolic value by introducing them on the figurative level. Thus, on seeing a blind beggar on the London streets, he reflects, "My mind did at this spectacle turn round / As with the might of waters . . ." (VII, 615–616). Here the whole previously established context exerts its pressure in the simile, while at the same time the Biblical phrase confirms our sense of the transcendental powers inherent in the water image.[2] In the following discursive passage, which attempts to generalize upon his experience in London, all the nature images which had hitherto appeared on the literal level become part of an extended simile:

> And not seldom
> Even individual remembrances,
> By working on the Shapes before my eyes,
> Became like vital functions of the soul;
> And out of what had been, what was, the place
> Was throng'd with impregnations, like those wilds
> In which my early feelings had been nurs'd,
> And naked valleys, full of caverns, rocks,
> And audible seclusions, dashing lakes,
> Echoes and Waterfalls, and pointed crags
> That into music touch the passing wind.
> (VIII, 786–96)

The simile is meant to do considerably more than illustrate the effect that the memory of London had on him. Not only has the memory process taken on visible and audible shape, but the powers that are unleashed in the natural setting return us to a more directly observable form of reality than the mental processes which he had been trying to depict. Indeed, the simile acts less to illustrate these processes than to turn us away from them and celebrate once more his native domain. Again, similarly to the Biblical overtones that emanated from the phrase "might of waters," the final line of this passage takes us out of the immediate context by a play on our associations: we think of the "Aeolian visitations" at the poem's opening, perhaps even more specifically of Coleridge's famous lines,

2. In these lines from Exodus the Lord's power is seen manifesting itself both in wind and water: "Thou didst blow with Thy wind, the sea covered them; / They sank as lead in the mighty waters" (15: 10). Biblical phrases, whether used on the literal level or as expressed metaphors are a central part of the Romantic world of images from Blake through Melville. Through his sense of the particular Biblical context—whether a prophetic outcry or a celebration of divine immanence in nature—the reader of Romantic literature is expected to transfer the Biblical meaning to the modern passage.

> And what if all of animated nature
> Be but organic Harps diversely fram'd,
> That tremble into thought, as o'er them sweeps
> Plastic and vast, one intellectual breeze,
> At once the Soul of each, and God of all?
>> ("The Eolian Harp")

Wordsworth's simile has not only drawn us back to physical nature, but through the implicit image of the harp, has extended the poem's range of reference once more to the mental realm.

The all-pervasiveness of the wind and the water in *The Prelude* is apparent throughout the very fabric of the language, as when we read of nature's power

> To breathe
> Grandeur upon the very humblest face
> Of human life.
>> (XII, 284–86)

In the lines:

> By simple strains
> Of feeling, the pure breath of real life,
> We were not left untouch'd,
>> (VI, 471–73)

the equating of "strains of feeling" with breath immediately links them to the vital impulse of the universe. The verb *spread*, with its implicit plastic qualities, often acts as a kind of conducting agent in the interaction process:

> Such a holy calm
> Did over*spread* my soul . . .
>> (II, 367–68)

> Man . . . daily *spreads* abroad
> His being with a strength that cannot fail.
>> (IV, 159–61)

In its most memorable instance it serves as a medium for a larger imaginative apprehension of the life that flows through all things: thus, after starting with the proposition

> I at this time
> Saw blessings *spread* around me like a sea,
>> (II, 413–14)

he lets the word, with its implicit metaphor, set into motion a childlike jubilation in the oneness of life:

> I was only then
> Contented when with bliss ineffable

I felt the sentiment of Being spread
O'er all that moves, and all that seemeth still,
O'er all, that, lost beyond the reach of thought
And human knowledge, to the human eye
Invisible, yet liveth to the heart,
O'er all that leaps, and runs, and shouts, and sings,
Or beats the gladsome air, o'er all that glides
Beneath the wave, yea, in the wave itself
And mighty depth of waters.
                                                  (II, 418–28)

By the end of the passage we have come full swing from the water
as metaphor to the water itself, though the Biblical echo in the final
line suggests a new and higher order of symbolic meaning.

Of the four formal epic similes in *The Prelude*, two take us back
to the water: one to a still lake (IV, 247–61), the second to a river
(IX, 1–7). Even the "characters" of the poem are related in one
way or another to the wind and water. Michel Beaupuy's peripatetic
discussions with the poet take place along the Loire (the water can
set the scene for political as well as visionary meditation), and
Beaupuy's death is reported—mistakenly—having occurred while he
was "fighting in supreme command / Upon the Borders of the unhappy Loire" (IX, 430–31). The poet pays tribute to Raisley
Calvert for having "clear'd a passage for me, and the stream /
Flowed in the bent of Nature" (XIII, 366–67). Dorothy assumes
the role of nature goddess—somewhat like the unhappy Lucy for
whom she may well have served as model—and gives the breath of
life back to Nature:

            Methought such charm
    Of sweetness did her presence breathe around
    That all the trees, and all the silent hills
    And every thing she look'd on, should have had
    An intimation how she bore herself
    Towards them and to all creatures.
                                                  (XI, 216–21)

Even when the wind and water do not function as a means toward
transcendental vision—and this is often so in later parts of the poem
—they remain part of the poet's habit of mind, a way through
which he can approach other, less boldly exploratory modes of
experience.

2. Islands

If the wind and the water serve to portray relationship—to link
the observable with the inner world, the powers of the human mind
with those within the physical universe—there is also a type of

image within *The Prelude* that portrays separation, the isolation of one element from another. Its most obvious manifestation is in the recurrence of islands within the poem. Like the wind and the water, the island is part of the natural setting of Wordsworth's background, and, in consequence, of the poem itself. When we read a passage like the following, we hardly think of the island as a conscious symbol:

> When summer came
> It was the pastime of our afternoons
> To beat along the plain of Windermere
> With rival oars, and the selected bourne
> Was now an Island musical with birds
> That sang for ever; now a Sister Isle
> Beneath the oaks' umbrageous covert, sown
> With lillies of the valley, like a field;
> And now a third small Island where remain'd
> An old stone Table, and a moulder'd Cave,
> A Hermit's history.
>
> (II, 56–65)

Wordsworth here is far more the objective observer than the conscious symbolist.[3] Yet note the order in which the islands are introduced: the first, joyous and paradise-like; the next shaded and subdued, as though suited to the contemplative mood, yet through its flowers still sharing somewhat in the joyous atmosphere of the first; the last wholly and uncompromisingly dedicated to contemplation and solitude.

The island (with its companion trope, the lone boat) is one of the great Romantic images, and to record its history from Saint-Pierre to Innisfree[4] is to encompass much of the essential history of Romanticism. Here I merely wish to suggest that Wordsworth's conception of islands is something more than the result of personal observation, that it is, in fact, rooted in a far larger context of thought. One remembers, for instance, the twin islands in the Lac de Bienne which Rousseau describes at the end of his *Confessions*; the

3. As an observer, however, his childhood memories of these islands on Windermere are considerably more romantic than the description he prepared for prospective tourists in his *Guide to the Lakes*: "The islands, dispersed among these lakes, are neither so numerous nor so beautiful as might be expected from the account that has been given of the manner in which the level areas of the vales are so frequently diversified by rocks, hills, and hillocks, scattered over them; nor are they ornamented (as are several of the lakes in Scotland and Ireland) by the remains of castles or other places of defence; nor with the still more interesting ruins of religious edifices. Every one must regret that scarcely a vestige is left of the Oratory, consecrated to the Virgin, which stood upon Chapel-Holm in Windermere. . . ." (*Prose Works of William Wordsworth*, edited by A. B. Grosart, London, 1876, II, 247).

4. Jean Jacques Rousseau describes his experiences on the island of Saint-Pierre in his *Confessions* (written 1764–70); William Butler Yeats (1865–1939) wrote "The Lake Isle of Innisfree." [*Editors*.]

first of these, the isle of Saint-Pierre, "has fields, meadows, orchards, woods, vineyards; and all this, thanks to the diversified and hilly nature of the ground, provides a most pleasing variety of landscape. . . . The western part . . . has been planted with a long avenue, broken in the middle by a large hall in which all the inhabitants of the neighbouring shores gather on Sundays during the grape harvest to dance and enjoy themselves. There is only one house on the island, where the receiver lives. But it is large and comfortable, and situated in a hollow which protects it from the wind."

With its joyous peasants, its benign vegetation, and its house protected from the elements, Rousseau's island is the perfect embodiment of the idyllic mode of life. But "five or six hundred yards to the south of the island is another, much smaller, which is uncultivated and uninhabited, and appears to have been broken away at some time from the larger one by storms. Its gravelly soil produces nothing but willows and persicaria; it has, however, one considerable eminence, which is grassy and very pleasant."[5]

The notion of contrasting islands—the one idyllic, the other harsh and unfriendly—goes back to Rousseau's favorite book, *Robinson Crusoe*, in which the two landscapes can be found on the same island. One need not seek romantic meanings in the setting of Defoe's classic; but from Rousseau onward the island—in both its *allegro* and *penseroso*[6] aspects—serves as the ideal scenic background for contemplation. "It seemed to me," Rousseau writes, "that on that island I should be further removed from men, safer from their insults, and more forgotten by them; freer, in a word, to surrender to the pleasures of idleness and the contemplative life."[7] And directly following these passages Rousseau launches into his famous exposition of the art of revery, which he practiced along the lake shore or while drifting in his boat, itself an even more appropriate setting for revery than the more solid, substantial island.

Wordsworthian revery generally takes a more austerely visionary form than the gentler delights celebrated by Rousseau. But Wordsworth sometimes approaches Rousseau's idyllic domain when he speaks of shores, boats, and islands, as in the following passage:

> But ere the fall
> Of night, when in our pinnace we return'd
> Over the dusky Lake, and to the beach
> Of some small Island steer'd our course with one,
> The Minstrel of our troop, and left him there,

5. *Confessions*, tr. J. M. Cohen (London, 1955), p. 588.
6. Italian: "cheerful" and "pensive, grave." [*Editors.*]
7. *Confessions*, p. 589.

And row'd off gently, while he blew his flute
Alone upon the rock; Oh! then the calm
And dead still water lay upon my mind
Even with a weight of pleasure, and the sky
Never before so beautiful, sank down
Into my heart, and held me like a dream.[8]

(II, 170–80)

It is worth noting that Wordsworth here projects himself in the form of two solitaries: in his own person in the boat, and as the other boy playing music on the rock. In something of the same way he often refers to hermits—as at the opening of "Tintern Abbey" or in the passage on the three islands quoted at the start of this section —while preparing to relate his own solitary musings. Just as Wordsworth's images move at will between the literal and figurative levels, so it is little more than an academic question whether his solitaries appear in the first or third person.[9] Indeed, one of his most memorable uses of the island image occurs on the figurative level, when he encounters one of his solitaries in the fog and depicts him as though on a floating island:

Along a narrow Valley and profound
I journey'd, when, aloft above my head,
Emerging from the silvery vapours, lo!
A Shepherd and his Dog! in open day:
Girt round with mists they stood and look'd about
From that enclosure small, inhabitants
Of an aerial Island floating on,
As seem'd with that Abode in which they were,
A little pendant area of grey rocks,
By the soft wind breath'd forward.

(VIII, 92–101)

Separated as they are from the solid world, shepherd and dog gather a visionary aura about themselves. Somewhat later, the lone shepherd appears in a more explicitly visionary setting:

8. The mode of interaction which Wordsworth experiences in this revery is paralleled in his discussion of islands in the *Guide to the Lakes*: "The water is also of crystalline purity; so that, if it were not for the reflections of the incumbent mountains by which it is darkened, a delusion might be felt, by a person resting quietly in a boat on the bosom of Winandermere or Derwent-water, similar to that which Carver so beautifully describes when he was floating alone in the middle of lake Erie or Ontario, and could almost have imagined that his boat was suspended in an element as pure as air, or rather that the air and water were one." (*Prose Works*, II, 248) Characteristically, Wordsworth's direct source is not a literary one, but a travel book, Jonathan Carver's *Travels through the Interior Parts of North America* (London, 1778). For the Carver passage, see C. N. Coe, *Wordsworth and the Literature of Travel* (New York, 1953), pp. 34–35.

9. One might note that Wordsworth presents himself in the third person in the passage "There was a Boy" (V, 389–422), while the dream of the Arab, shell and stone (V, 49–139), related in the third person in the 1805 *Prelude*, is in the first person in the revised version.

> Mine eyes have glanced upon him, few steps off,
> In size a giant, stalking through the fog,
> His Sheep like Greenland Bears; at other times
> When round some shady promontory turning,
> His Form hath flash'd upon me, glorified
> By the deep radiance of the setting sun:
> Or him have I descried in distant sky,
> A solitary object and sublime,
> Above all height! like an aerial Cross,
> As it is stationed on some spiry Rock
> Of the Chartreuse, for worship.
>
> (VII, 400–410)

One could speak of a tendency throughout *The Prelude* to isolate objects in order to connect them later at a deeper level: islands, whether real or figurative, are places which cut you off so that these connections may be made. In the last passage there is no specific mention of an island, yet the same principle is at work here as in the earlier example: when Wordsworth suddenly spies the shepherd and his flock in their isolation, not only does he view them in a unique visual perspective ("his Sheep like Greenland Bears"), but this very perspective creates the transition by which we are enabled to view the shepherd as a spiritual manifestation. In the same way, as we saw earlier, the fog that enclosed the poet in his ascent up Mt. Snowdon was essentially a way of cutting him off from the earthly sphere before he could attain his higher vision. Isolation becomes the means toward interaction. We can, in fact, speak of an image of vacancy, whereby the objects of the visible world are systematically eliminated before our eyes to prepare for the revelation of a new way of seeing things. We feel something of this, for instance, in the passage concluding the incident of the stolen boat:

> In my thoughts
> There was a darkness, call it solitude,
> Or blank desertion, no familiar shapes
> Of hourly objects, images of trees,
> Of sea or sky, no colours of green fields;
> But huge and mighty Forms that do not live
> Like living men mov'd slowly through my mind
> By day and were the trouble of my dreams.
>
> (I, 420–27)

The island is less a physical entity than a way of thinking and feeling; "huge and mighty Forms" cannot emerge until the conventional world—whose fading presence we still experience despite the negatives—is reduced to a chaos of emptiness. In far lengthier fashion than above, he creates an elaborate image of emptiness in order to prepare for the meeting with the discharged soldier at the end of Book IV:

> On I went
> Tranquil, receiving in my own despite
> Amusement, as I slowly pass'd along,
> From such near objects as from time to time,
> Perforce intruded on the listless sense
> Quiescent, and dispos'd to sympathy,
> With an exhausted mind, worn out by toil. . . .
> Above, before, behind,
> Around me, all was peace and solitude,
> I look'd not round, nor did the solitude
> Speak to my eye; but it was heard and felt.
>
> (IV, 375–81; 388–91)

Quietness, fatigue, a sense of total calmness about himself, when solitude becomes a tangible thing, "heard and felt"—these are the necessary conditions for the visionary mood. When the soldier later appears, the reader perceives him in all his ghostly grandeur, but only because he has gradually felt himself removed from the earthly sphere (one need only compare the difference in effect of the 1850 version, from which Wordsworth omitted the crucial preparatory passage). In a work like *The Prelude*, which constantly mediates between inner and outer worlds, emptiness becomes an image of transition, the vision itself a type of island. Wordsworth's designation of his visionary moments as "spots of time" (XI, 258) is, in fact, a geographical metaphor which suggests the island-like qualities of these moments. Indeed, in some early (though later rejected) jottings toward *The Prelude* he equates his childhood memories directly with islands:

> Those recollect(ed) hours that have the charm
> Of visionary things—
> islands in the unnavigable depth
> Of our departed time.[1]

3. Caverns and Mountains

There is still another image, even less articulated, through which Wordsworth records intimations of the inner world. We become aware of it, for instance, each time we encounter such words as *under-thirst, under-presence, under-soul*, all of them, De Selincourt tells us in his edition (p. 622), apparent coinages of Wordsworth's. Its most memorable use occurs in the vision on Snowdon,

---

1. *The Prelude*, edited by E. de Selincourt and H. Darbishire (Oxfod, 1959), p. 641.

> The perfect image of a mighty Mind,
> Of one that feeds upon infinity,
> That is exalted by an under-presence,
> The sense of God, or whatsoe'er is dim
> Or vast in its own being,
>
> (XIII, 69–73)

where it is one of several alternatives that take part in the poet's struggle toward definition. It is no more than an intimation, but as such it hints at a hidden, subterranean reality which itself is never further defined. Yet one senses a relationship between these *under* elements and those much-mentioned hiding-places and inner recesses within the human soul:

> Oh! mystery of Man, from what a depth
> Proceed thy honours!
> . . . The hiding-places of my power
> Seem open; I approach, and then they close.
>
> (XI, 329–30; 336–37)
>
> 'Tis thine,
> The prime and vital principle is thine
> In the recesses of thy nature. . . .
>
> (XIII, 193–95)

Behind these terms there stands what David Perkins, in his recent study of Romantic symbolism, calls "the image of the cavern or abyss." Perkins discerns a double function for this image in Wordsworth: first, as symbolic of "an inevitable, and fearful, isolation from any external medium through which the mind can be healthfully governed," and second, as suggestive of "fertility and creation."[2] Like all of Wordsworth's central images, the cavern can stand potentially for several things, even apparent opposites. But the cavern differs from the other images in one important respect: it occurs but inconspicuously in the literal narrative. Wordsworth lists it, for instance, among the spots where nature's "presences" dwell: "On caves and trees, upon the woods and hills" (I, 496). It plays a role in the episode of the stolen boat, where the "rocky cave" from which the poet steals the boat later becomes deified, in the course of the passage, into the "Cavern of the Willow tree" (I, 395, 414). And, in turn, it comes to suggest the dark recesses of the poet's mind from which issues that "dim and undetermin'd sense / Of unknown modes of being" (419–20). The image is also used occasionally in a totally figurative sense, as in the somewhat tedious epic simile which compares the opposing ways in which Wordsworth had come to evaluate his London experience with a traveller's ways of looking at a cave (VIII, 711–51); then, too, he speaks of

2. *The Quest for Permanence* (Cambridge, Mass., 1959), p. 24.

those "caverns . . . within my mind" (III, 246) which were left inviolate amid the social temptations of Cambridge. Ineed, a reading of *The Prelude* leaves one with far less memory of actual caverns than of such caverns of the mind—both the individual human mind and the universal mind. Unlike the wind, water, and mountains, which dominate the poem's scenic background, the cavern functions chiefly as a metaphor, in fact, a literally submerged metaphor, one which we sense but dimly through the unnamed (and unnamable) depths and under-agents which Wordsworth has such frequent occasion to invoke.

Yet there is one extension of the cavern image which, though it occurs only twice in *The Prelude*, leaves one of the most powerful impressions among any of the natural scenes of the poem. I refer here to the mountain chasm which plays such a central role in his experiences at the Simplon Pass and on Mt. Snowdon. One might note first that mountains *in themselves*—when they seem remote and solid entities, without direct contact with man or the natural elements—are of little interest to Wordsworth. His imagination is stimulated only if the human mind, in some way, is able to interact with them. Mont Blanc, for instance, turned out to be a disappointment, not only since the reality failed to live up to Wordsworth's anticipations, but because, in its imperious self-sufficiency, the mountain has something final and dead about it:

> That day we first
> Beheld the summit of Mont Blanc, and griev'd
> To have a soulless image on the eye
> Which had usurp'd upon a living thought
> That never more could be.
>
> (VI, 452–56)

Only after he turned away from the summit and looked downward at the "dumb cataracts and streams of ice" (458) were his imagination's cravings satisfied. The "perilous ridge" (I, 347) on which he hung alone while plundering birds' nests was meaningful not only in itself, but through its "half-inch fissures," its blasts of wind, and the perilousness of his own position. The "huge cliff" in the episode of the stolen boat achieves its memorable power through the darkness and the surrounding scenery of water and cave. The Simplon Pass made no impression in itself; in fact, he and his companion went by it thinking there were still higher reaches to attain. Only after they entered the gorge on the other side did they encounter an appropriately visionary setting: indeed, the winds, torrents, crags, and mists with which they are surrounded bring together—though in their most violent form—most of *The Prelude*'s prevailing images. The top of Snowdon, as I have suggested, is essentially an island in the mist; but even after the transition has been made and the everyday world cut off, Wordsworth cannot apprehend its inner meaning until he encounters "a fracture in the vapour" (it hardly matters whether it is a real mountain gorge or not):

> A deep and gloomy breathing-place through which
> Mounted the roar of waters, torrents, streams
> Innumerable, roaring with one voice.
> . . . But in that breach
> Through which the homeless voice of waters rose,
> That dark deep thoroughfare had Nature lodg'd
> The Soul, the Imagination of the whole.
>
> (XIII, 57–59; 62–65)

Thus, despite the obvious symbolic value that Wordsworth felt in elevation, and specifically in the physical act of ascent, one notes that his visionary experience on mountains was more centrally concerned with depths rather than heights, with the continually intensifying inwardness suggested by the interaction of water, air, and rock in the deeper regions of the earth.

4. Some Reflections on Wordsworth's Nature Imagery

Wordsworth's deliberate blurring of tenor and vehicle, his insistence on fusing the literal level of things with their larger symbolic meanings—these are more than rhetorical strategies, for they are, in fact, central to the meaning and intent of his major poetry. The following statement by Coleridge, made in a letter to William Sotheby in 1802, suggests a program which brings together the realm of rhetoric with that of metaphysics: "Nature has her proper interest; & he will know what it is, who believes & feels, that every Thing has a Life of it's own, & that we are all *one Life*. A Poet's *Heart* & *Intellect* should be *combined, intimately* combined & *unified*, with the great appearances in Nature—& not merely held in solution & loose mixture with them, in the shape of formal Similies. I do not mean to exclude these formal Similies—there are moods of mind, in which they are natural—pleasing moods of mind, & such as a Poet will often have, & sometimes express; but they are not his highest, & most appropriate moods."[3]

"*Combined, intimately* combined & *unified*" (the italics are of course Coleridge's)—the interaction of man and nature as a demonstration of the "one life" becomes the central motive of the poet. The older rhetorical system with its "formal Similies" and its separation of tenor and vehicle would obviously not suffice for the lofty task which Coleridge contemplated for the poet. As works written not in a "pleasing mood of mind," but in the poet's "highest, & most appropriate mood," Wordsworth's major poems, like the "Dejection Ode" which Coleridge had written a few months before the letter to Sotheby, had by necessity to speak a language which would demonstrate the unity of the poet's inner world and the external world of nature. The rhetorical method which Wordsworth developed to fulfill this task became, one might say, a reenactment of the process of interaction. In reading poetry which makes such a radical attempt to fuse inner and outer, the reader trained to approach poetic imagery according to the methods of Renaissance or even of twentieth-century poetry is likely to keep asking which particular realm—nature or the mind—Wordsworth is actually talking about. But the question is scarcely necessary or germane to his poetry, for Wordsworth usually speaks of both realms at once. The "huge and mighty Forms" which pursue the poet for days after the stolen-boat incident exist at once in his own mind, in the external landscape, and, for that matter, in the universal mind as well. In something of the same way the imagination which is revealed to him atop Mt. Snowdon is a faculty within the mind of an individual poet, a manifestation of the universal mind, and even a part of the mountain ("in that breach . . . had Nature lodg'd / The Soul, the Imagination of the whole"). A recently published early draft, in fact, has shown that certain of the lines used to characterize Mt. Snowdon—"The perfect image of a mighty Mind, / Of one that feeds upon infinity, / . . . or whatso'er is dim / Or vast in its own being" (XIII, 69–70, 72–73)—were originally intended to characterize the mind of the poet:

> But also such an one must have been used
> To feed his soul upon infinity
> To deal with whatsoe'er be dim or vast
> In his own nature. . . .[4]

I can think of no interpretative task so difficult as trying to define Wordsworth's concept of the imagination on the basis of the utterances found in his poetry; indeed, the essentially analytical process of definition is quite antithetical to Wordsworth's constant endeavors to synthesize his concepts and percepts into dazzlingly new rhetorical formations.

Yet, despite his efforts to wipe out distinctions between outer scene and inner thought, one discerns a special significance in the literal level of discourse in *The Prelude*. This literal level—the level of real lakes and real mountains, of the real boy Wordsworth—throughout the poem provides a transition to guide the reader from his accustomed way of looking at things to the transcendental reality

4. *The Prelude*, page 620.

which Wordsworth repeatedly celebrates. The real world functions rhetorically both as something to start from and something to fall back on between the often bewildering visionary assertions of his intenser moments. Dr. Leavis, in pitting Shelley against Wordsworth, has remarked, for instance, on the younger poet's "weak grasp on the actual"; he compares the opening of Shelley's "Mont Blanc":

> The everlasting universe of things
> Flows through the mind, and rolls its rapid waves,
> Now dark—now glittering—now reflecting gloom—
> Now lending splendour, where from secret springs
> The source of human thought its tribute brings
> Of waters . . .

with Wordsworth's lines on the Simplon:

> Black drizzling crags that spake by the way-side
> As if a voice were in them, the sick sight
> And giddy prospect of the raving stream,
> The unfetter'd clouds and region of the Heavens,
> Tumult and peace, the darkness and the light
> Were all like workings of one mind, the features
> Of the same face. . . .
>
> (VI, 563–69)

Leavis notes "the unobtrusiveness with which [in the Wordsworth passage] 'outer' turns into 'inner'. . . . What is characteristic of Wordsworth is to grasp surely (which, in the nature of the case, must be delicately and subtly) what he offers, whether this appears as belonging to the outer world—the world as perceived, or to inner experience." In Shelley, so Leavis goes on with his comparison, "the metaphorical and the actual, the real and imagined, the inner and the outer, could hardly be more unsortably and indistinguishably confused."[5] Despite E. R. Wasserman's recent efforts to show what Shelley was really doing in "Mont Blanc"—and Wasserman demonstrates exhaustively that there was real method in Shelley's frenzy[6] —next to Wordworth's lines, "Mont Blanc" remains a more distinctly private type of poetry, a significant enough visionary meditation, but of a less persuasively universal order of experience.

It has not perhaps been sufficiently remarked how Wordsworth's major images seem even on the literal level to suggest the directions for their symbolic expansion. Kenneth MacLean, writing of the water image in *The Prelude*, has noted the following properties of water which Wordsworth chose to build from: "[Water] has the power to move and sound; to freshen and make float; to wash and

---

5. *Revaluation*, pp. 206, 212–14.
6. *The Subtler Language* (Baltimore, 1959), pp. 195–240.

to cleanse; the power to reflect; to distort, to sparkle magically; the power to be free; and finally, the power to create that rhythm, which, however it comes to life, can moderate, soothe, and give pleasure."[7] One hardly need list the various potentialities that Wordsworth found in breezes, mountains, islands, caverns, and, above all, in the combination of these images. It is significant, in fact, that in those parts of the poem where he did not have the natural landscape to work from, his imagery assumes far more conventional forms than those I have described in this chapter. The passages on the French Revolution, for instance, are dominated by storm imagery:

> In both her clamorous Halls,
> The National Synod and the Jacobins
> I saw the revolutionary Power
> Toss like a Ship at anchor, rock'd by storms . . .
> (IX, 46–49)

But these storms function essentially as background imagery: like the dominant strain of imagery within a Shakespearean play, they help define and give dramatic coloring to the central situation, but they are always rhetorically, at least, distinguishable from the narrative which they are intended to embellish. Yet Wordsworth was also aware that beyond their natural proclivities, his major images also contained innumerable literary and cultural associations to which his readers would automatically respond. "A stranger to mountain imagery naturally on his first arrival looks out for sublimity in every object that admits of it; and is almost always disappointed," he wrote in his *Guide to the Lakes* (*Prose Works*, II, 291–92). Obviously he did not need to go to much trouble convincing his readers of the grandeur and fascination of natural scenery. Moreover, as Marjorie Nicolson and Ernest Tuveson have painstakingly shown in their recent books on the development of the "aesthetics of the infinite," poetry and aesthetic theory had been preparing readers to find religious meaning in sublime scenery—above all, in mountains and caverns—for a whole century before Wordsworth.[8] In the light of their researches, in fact, Wordsworth's attempt to locate visionary power in natural scenery seems less the beginning of a tradition—as conventional literary history would have it—than the culmination of a way of thinking for which the groundwork had been laid long before. Wordsworth's distinctive achievement, one ventures to say, was not so much in the attitudes he expressed toward scenery as in the language he succeeded in devising for the

7. "The Water Symbol in *The Prelude*," *University of Toronto Quarterly*, XVII (1948), 387.
8. Nicolson, *Mountain Gloom and Moun-* *tain Glory*, Ithaca, 1959, esp. pp. 271–369; Tuveson, *The Imagination as a Means of Grace*, Berkeley, 1960.

interaction of the mind with external nature. After the suppleness of "Tintern Abbey" and *The Prelude*, the language of the eighteenth-century "sublime" poems—I refer to the term which Josephine Miles has employed to describe a genre that extends across the century from Blackmore through Akenside to Blake[9]—could no longer seem appropriate to a living body of literature.

The eighteenth century anticipated Wordsworth not only in the grander types of scenery, but also in those that made less urgent claims on the infinite. If islands were associated with romantic reveries from Rousseau onward, throughout the century—chiefly through the impact of *Robinson Crusoe*—they had provided scenic background for the study of solitude. W. K. Wimsatt, in his incisive account of the nature of Romantic nature imagery, has suggested the stylistic evolution of this imagery by examining three sonnets—by Thomes Warton, William Lisle Bowles, and the early Coleridge, respectively—addressed to local streams.[1] A long genealogy extending back to the beginning of our civilization stands behind the "Aeolian visitations" with which *The Prelude* so ecstatically opens; but if archetypal critics like Maud Bodkin have stressed the traditionality of the divinely inspired breeze, M. H. Abrams has lately insisted on the distinctly Romantic manner in which Wordsworth and his contemporaries treated the wind motif.[2]

Wordsworth's attempt to build his major poems out of images he had himself observed was rooted not only in his love of nature, but even more specifically in the epistemology which had come down to him. Tuveson has reminded us, for instance, how the unity of image and idea, of outer and inner, follows naturally from Locke's espistemology: "From the nature of the mind as described by Locke, we could expect a new poetry to be highly visual in nature, for the faculty of sight came to monopolize the analysis of intellectual activity. Since ideas are images, since even complex ideas are multiple pictures, and since understanding itself is a form of perception, the visual and the intellectual would tend to become amalgamated."[3]

Tuveson is speaking here of post-Lockean poetry[4] in general—not only the eighteenth-century "sublime" poem and nature lyric, but the image-centered poetry of Romanticism and of our own century. Again, what makes Wordsworth's poetry unique is not the

9. *Eras and Modes in English Poetry* (Berkeley and Los Angeles, 1957), pp. 48–77.
1. "The Structure of Romantic Nature Imagery," *The Verbal Icon* (Lexington, Ky., 1954), pp. 103–16.
2. "The Correspondent Breeze: A Romantic Metaphor," in *English Romantic Poets: Modern Essays in Criticism*, ed.

Abrams (New York, 1960 [2nd ed. 1975]), esp. pp. 44–52.
3. *The Imagination as a Means of Grace*, pp. 72–73.
4. The reference is to John Locke's philosophy, in which knowledge is based on sense experience, in his *Essay Concerning Human Understanding* (1690). [*Editors.*]

fact that he combined the sense-impressions of nature with more complex ideas, but the peculiar method which he developed to draw the intellectual from the visual. His need to combine both these realms in his poetry—and Locke's espistemology, as Tuveson shows, provides the rationale for such amalgamation—is also what keeps Wordsworth from being what we commonly consider a "landscape" poet. The true landscape poet is one who, like John Clare or Edward Thomas,[5] keeps primarily to visual impressions and only incidentally, if at all, to the more complex ideas toward which these might lead. Indeed, the attempt of modern poets in the Hulme-Pound tradition[6] to build poems fully out of sense impressions and to keep the intellectualizing observer out of the poem seems in the present context an extreme and all too narrow application of Lockian epistemology to poetry. The modern poet pretends to represent the external world "as it is"—spontaneously perceived, unspoiled by the intrusion of abstract thought.

Wordsworth, on the other hand, represents the external world only in order to get beyond it; if he lets his intellectualizing self intrude, the intrusion seems to follow so naturally from the concretely perceived premise with which he started that the reader is scarcely aware he has crossed the border which commonly separates the simple idea from the complex, the empirical realm from the transcendental. In a terse statement that Wordsworth once made to his nephew, Christopher Wordsworth, he distinguished between the poetry that simply records sense-impressions and that which goes beyond them: "S——, in the work you mentioned to me, confounds *imagery* and *imagination*. Sensible objects really existing, and felt to exist, are *imagery*; and they may form the materials of a descriptive poem, where objects are delineated as they are. Imagination is a subjective term: it deals with objects not as they are, but as they appear to the mind of the poet" (*Prose Works*, III, 464). Unlike the modern imagist (and unlike many eighteenth-century descriptive poets), he did not attempt to give the impression that his "objects are delineated as they are": the center of his art was his explicit demonstration of what happened to objects as they interacted with the mind of the poet.

In the history of poetic imagery Wordsworth and his contemporaries occupy a position roughly half-way between the Renaissance mode, in which the image remains subservient to the demands of logic, and that peculiarly modern condition which—to employ a term used by Rainer Maria Rilke in hailing the achievement of one of his post-Symbolist contemporaries—is characterized by the "lib-

5. John Clare (1793–1864), poet of rural scenes and experiences; Edward Thomas (1878–1917), whose poems represent, with loving accuracy, the English countryside. [*Editors.*]

6. T. E. Hulme (1883–1917), author of essays on art and poetry, whose theories influenced the Imagist Movement in poetry, of which Ezra Pound (1885–1972) was one of the founders. [*Editors.*]

eration of the poetic figure."[7] Wimsatt, in his paper on nature imagery cited earlier, pinpoints the Romantic position in this way:

"If we think of a scale of structures having at one end logic, the completely reasoned and abstracted, and at the other some form of madness or surrealism, matter or impression unformed and undisciplined (the imitation of disorder by the idiom of disorder), we may see metaphysical and neoclassical poetry as near the extreme of logic (though by no means reduced to that status) and romantic poetry as a step toward the directness of sensory presentation (though by no means sunk into subrationality)."[8]

If our age has proved slow to acknowledge the characteristic Romantic achievement, we must remember that the critical system in which we have been taught to think was dedicated primarily to defending the two extremes—the metaphysical and the modern—on Wimsatt's scale. And in our zeal to uphold these extremes we have often misunderstood—and hastily rejected—that "half-way position" which *The Prelude* so eminently represents.

W. B. GALLIE

Is *The Prelude* a Philosophical Poem?[†]

Is *The Prelude* a philosophical poem?[1] It is, of course, many things besides: it is an autobiography; it contains profound reflections on psychology, education and politics; and there are passages of an almost purely lyrical character. Does it also contain *philosophical poetry*?

On this question, the critics of Wordsworth are divided. Coleridge and Raleigh answer Yes; Arnold, Bradley, Dr. Leavis,[2] from their different points of view, agree in answering No. I believe that the first answer is right, although it has usually been supported by the wrong reasons. I believe the second answer to be wrong, although many of the arguments that are supposed to lead to it are in themselves sound enough. Those who say that *The Prelude* is not a philosophical poem, usually mean that it does not offer a coherent system of philosophy—that it expresses an original outlook and a personal wisdom, but that the only systematic philosophy in it comes at second-hand from Hartley or Coleridge and contributes

7. *Briefe aus den Jahren 1914–1921*, ed. Ruth Sieber-Rilke and Carl Sieber (Leipzig, 1928), p. 126. The poet of whom he wrote was Georg Trakl.
8. *The Verbal Icon*, p. 116.
† From *Philosophy*, XXII (1947), pages 124–38.
1. Throughout this article I am much

indebted to the criticisms and suggestions of my friend, Karl Britton.
2. These eminent critics of Wordsworth are Walter Raleigh (1861–1922); Matthew Arnold (1822–88); A. C. Bradley (1851–1935); F. R. Leavis (1895–1978). [*Editors.*]

not at all to the poem. And this is largely true. But the mistake is, to identify philosophy with system, philosophizing with "a philosophy." This is a mistake that has been repudiated again and again by many of the greatest philosophers, from Socrates and Plato to Locke and Kant and others.

I shall argue that *The Prelude* achieves philosophical poetry, because in it Wordsworth grapples with philosophical problems— problems which arise out of the story of his own early life—which are actually forced upon him by the poem itself; and because he tries to answer these problems in a way which would be possible only in poetry.

I shall not try to show that the peculiar greatness of *The Prelude* lies in its philosophical achievement. On the contrary, I believe that its greatness lies, like that of all Wordsworth's successful poetry, in its passion, its humanity, its conscientious realism. But these very qualities led Wordsworth, whenever his thought reached a certain level of generality, to feel the inadequacies of certain of our categories—both metaphysical and moral—as commonly used. He had not the ingenuity to replace these categories by a new system. But the impact of his poetry made them shake, and he is a philosophical poet because he makes us feel them shake and because he himself well knew that they were shaking, and was able to make some suggestions as to the form that the new categories might take. It would be idle to claim that in the last task Wordsworth was uniformly successful. But success in philosophy is always a relative matter, and a philosopher may have done a great deal if he has made us think even a little differently, not by presenting new facts to our notice, but by inducing us to shift the emphasis and orientation of some of the basic notions we use in everyday life. And this much can, I think, be claimed for the philosophy of *The Prelude*.

This is the claim, I believe, which Coleridge and Raleigh made for Wordsworth. But they expressed it in terms which left them open to important criticisms from the other side. I shall try to state the claim in a different way and shall consider what I believe to be the philosophical element in *The Prelude* under the following heads: (1) How the central philosophical problem of *The Prelude* arises from its autobiographical theme; (2) The analogy by which Wordsworth develops his answer to the problem; (3) The originality of his answer; (4) The part played by poetry in achieving his answer; (5) Its verification and its applicability to other problems.

(1) *How does the central philosophical problem of* The Prelude *arise from its autobiographical theme?*

The Prelude, Wordsworth tells us, was intended as a stock-taking of his poetic powers, an interim task to aid him in selecting the subject of his main work as poet. His initial question was, quite

simply, how could he give of his best as a poet? Unable to answer
the question thus posed, he turns back in a kind of despair to some
of his earliest memories, and these by the intensity of delight and
wonder they awaken in him, renew his confidence and brace his
mind for further efforts. But Wordsworth finds something puzzling,
paradoxical even, in this experience.[3] His present renewed confidence in his powers lies in a "calm existence," a tranquility of mind
and steady direction of purpose which enable him to range, disinter-
estedly, gratefully, in the appropriate artistic sense conscientiously,
over the whole field of his experience. But the intense, spontaneous
responses of his childhood stood in complete contrast to this "calm
existence"; they were a succession of impressions, gathered acci-
dentally, enjoyed without reflection, by-products of the muscular
zest and petty selfish aims of childish consciousness. Further, his
recollections were made up of "discordant elements," a confusion of
delight in beauty, pride in energy, awe before the unknown terror,
pain. The contrast of past and present puzzled him and led him to a
second problem. There appeared to be two opposing elements in
poetic inspiration; on the one hand the spontaneous receptivity and
response characteristic of childhood and on the other hand the self-
mastery, the calm of mind, the conscientiousness of the mature
artist. How could these be brought together into a satisfying and
productive harmony? This is perhaps the central problem in every
artist's self-discipline, and it is one on which Wordsworth had some
profound and original things to say. But no sooner is it posed than
it is seen to be but one case of a wider problem, that of the active
happiness, responsive and responsible, of every good man. For this
ideal, no less than that of poetic activity, requires a discipline which
can reconcile and harmonize the discords of spontaneous impulse
and response. It is not of himself only or of other poets and artists
that Wordsworth writes,

> Ah, is there one who ever has been young,
> Nor needs a warning voice to tame the pride
> Of intellect and virtue's self esteem?
> One is there, though the wisest and the best
> Of all mankind, who covets not at times
> Union that cannot be—who would not give,
> If so he might, to duty and to truth
> The eagerness of infantine desire?
>
> [II, 19–26]

Such perfect union of spontaneity and discipline may be impossible,
but Wordsworth knew from his own experience—from his own
happiness quite as much as from his acievements as a poet—that in
his life something like it had taken place. This led him to look for

3. See *The Prelude*, I, 340–56. [All references to *The Prelude* are to the 1850 edition.—
Editors.]

the external, as well as the internal, conditions in his own life, which had made this possible. Inspired by his own glimpses, he asks:

> Why is this glorious creature to be found
> One in ten thousand only? What one is,
> Why should not millions be?
>
> [XIII, 87–89]

But, recalling the circumstances that had specially favoured his own happy development, he sees part of the reason:

> ... Were it otherwise,
> And we found evil fast as we find good
> In our first years, or think that it is found,
> How could the innocent heart bear up and live?
>
> [VIII, 308–11]

And this line of thought is supported by many darker musings on the actual lot of humanity, on the stultification of its powers under the tendency,

> Of use and custom to bow down the soul
> Under a growing weight of vulgar sense,
> And substitute a universe of death
> For that which moves with light and life informed,
> Actual, divine and true. . . .
>
> [XIV, 158–62]

and on the effects of poverty and labour in excess which

> From day to day pre-occupy the ground
> Of the affections and to Nature's self
> Oppose a deeper nature. . . .
>
> [XIII, 198–201]

This last sentence is of particular interest. In its curious antithesis between Nature with a capital and a "deeper nature" not so dignified we have one of Wordsworth's most striking attempts to effect that kind of shift in our categories which he believed was necessary for an adequate statement of the *possibility* of happiness. Nature with a capital is that "eternal nature" of which he writes in the letter to John Wilson:[4] to render men's feelings more consonant to "eternal nature" is the supreme moral function of poetry, and to live our lives in consonance with it is Wordsworth's conception of happiness. The other, "deeper nature," the universe of death, the use and custom that bow down the soul, are Wordsworth's version of

4. In *Literary Criticism of William Wordsworth*, edited by Paul M. Zall, University of Nebraska Press, 1966, p. 72. [*Editors.*]

the problem of evil. Now when philosophers face this problem they all too often give us answers which "dispose of it"—e.g. by showing how the amount or the prospects or the possibilities of happiness far outweigh in a final balance those of misery. Such a final balance is of course highly problematical. In *The Prelude*, with his thoughts guided by the thing he knew most about—his own job and duty as a poet—Wordsworth gives an answer of a more modest and useful kind. As a poet, his most pressing interest was not in the justification of his work, but in its method; and as a moralist drawing his wisdom from the discipline of his art, he was interested primarily not in any transcendental assurance of happiness (or justification of misery) but in the *way* of happiness (to use a religious phrase) or (if the phrase be preferred) the *art* of it. In particular, he wanted to discover what part, on the one hand, men can contribute from their own inward resources towards finding and holding that way ("to what point and how, the mind is lord and master")[5] and, on the other hand, what men must receive in aid, stimulation, infection, "grace" from sources outside themselves—from other human beings and from nature.

Here is the central philosophical problem of *The Prelude*:— Wordsworth's version of the problem of "the true end of man." His answer to it is at once normative and interpretative; it is an attempt to show the reality of certain "may-bes" in human experience with a view to convincing us that these are, in the ethical sense, "must-bes." The central "may-be" is the possibility of human happiness conceived in terms of a certain discipline or way. ("What one is, why may not millions be?") The central "must-be" is not issued in an imperative. Wordsworth had this much in common with Plato as a moralist, that he makes the essential moment of morality one of recognition—in Wordsworth's case the recognition "that from thy-self it comes, that thou must give, else never canst receive."[6] And he believed that to *show* this truth was the only way to make men better.

(2) *The analogy by which Wordsworth develops his answer*

Throughout *The Prelude* Wordsworth's thought moves freely between the three planes I have distinguished. He uses his own personal problem to raise the general problem of artistic self-discipline; and his insights into this second problem provide him with an analogy which he applies to the problems of moral happiness. But on each and all of these planes his thought never leaves the world of common day. His findings, even when relating to the subtleties of poetic creation, are expressed always in intelligible, too often in

---

5. *The Prelude*, XII, 221–22. [*Editors.*]   6. *The Prelude*, XII, 276–77.

banal, language. In general, the terms of his problem are familiar to ordinary reflection; and for verification of his conclusions Wordsworth can appeal to "that knowledge which all men carry about with them."[7] The only apparent exceptions to this rule are the celebrated descriptions of "visiting of imaginative power."[8] What relation, it may reasonably be asked, have these strange experiences to anything that conduces to the happiness of ordinary men? To this Wordsworth could have answered as follows. These "visitings of imaginative power" were the experiences of a poet, and were of a quite unusual intensity, depth and suggestive power. They were therefore untypical of ordinary experience. It may nevertheless be possible for the ordinary reader to have some inkling of what they were like; and Wordsworth supplies some very revealing details of their perceptual and motor backgrounds. And secondly, for his main purpose in *The Prelude*, Wordsworth is not so much concerned with the operation of imagination—the way it works on its object—as with the felt effects of its visitings and the moral power and influence they leave behind. Now, from this point of view, it matters little whether imaginative experience be original and creative, as with the poet, or received from others, as with the rest of us. It is not therefore necessary to enter here into a full account of Wordsworth's theory—or rather his various sketches of a theory—of the imagination as an original power. It is enough to notice that Wordsworth was interested in the imagination as a *revealing* power, rather than as a shaping and creative power. Its peculiar virtue (he suggests) does not lie precisely in what it reveals, but in the fact that the insights given are always incomplete and so leave us with a sense of "something to pursue," of "something evermore about to be," and a sense of how little "we know both of ourselves and of the universe."[9] Thus the chief moral effect of such visitations is to give our minds renewed appetite and vigour, to call up our powers for further exploration and verification.

So much by the way of defence of one part—and that the most easily misunderstood—of the analogy by which Wordsworth develops his answer to his main philosophical problem. But precisely what part do imaginative experiences play in achieving and maintaining that artistic self-discipline which will foster, control and reconcile the wayward, irresponsible element in inspiration? Wordsworth saw clearly that these two elements in his own inspiration required one another. But he also had very definite views as to the kinds of experiences and sentiments which, in his own case, had been most effective in bringing them together. These were, first, the sentiment

7. This phrase is taken from Wordsworth's Preface to the *Lyrical Ballads* of 1805. [*Literary Criticism*, edited by Paul Zall, p. 52—*Editors*.]
8. See, in particular, II, 294–322; VI, 592–640; VII, 619–49; XII, 208–335; XIV, 28–111.
9. *The Prelude*, II, 322; VI, 608; VII, 645–46. [*Editors*.]

of gratitude—a generalized gratitude towards the past which kept him constantly aware of the debt he owed and of the return due from him for the unusually lively sensibility, the enthusiasm, and the tenderness which it was his privilege as a poet to enjoy. Secondly, there were those rare, unpredictable "spots of time" in which imagination reveals "the hiding-places of man's power," challenges us to recognize "our destiny, our being's heart and home," convinces us "that whatsoever point we gain, we yet have something to pursue," and yet leaves us "as if admonished from another world."[1] The cultivation of the habit of gratitude and the habitual re-living in memory of such spots of time give us the essence of Wordsworth's poetic method; they are the factors which energize "recollection in tranquility." And they interpenetrate and re-enforce one another in various ways. Thus gratitude to the past not only gave rise to Wordsworth's admiration of the "mystery of man" as revealed in childhood,[2] it contributed a great deal to his imaginative interpretation of Nature as "leader-on," as inviter and educator, and it also helped him to see (as in the experience described at the close of Bk. XII) the first germs of the integrating activity of imagination in a moment of childish terror and in a child's "trite reflections of morality." But the two factors can best be understood by considering the distinct contribution which each makes. Thus the felt effects of imaginative visitations inspire the creative, ambitious side of the required self-discipline; they provide a challenge to further effort, a realization of the apparently infinite possibilities of human experience and of the sorry little we usually make of these. Gratitude, on the other hand, provides the conscientious aspect of artistic self-discipline, its filial sense of debt to the experienced past and to received tradition and its almost parental sense of responsibility for the spontaneous, wayward, in themselves vulnerable and even self-destructive elements of poetic inspiration.

Wordsworth showed unusual artistic wisdom in preferring his "cult of memory" to a more direct quest of inspiration. His cult of memory is only one form of artistic self-discipline; but its two principles of gratitude to the past and habitual re-living of imaginative visitations could be generalized, I think, to provide maxims relevant to most of the arts. Certainly, his cult of memory provided Wordsworth with the discipline *he* needed, and his originality as a moralist—the way he shakes and alters our general conception of morality—lies in his application of its two principles of gratitude and imagination to the whole moral life of man.

But before considering how Wordsworth deals with his wider problem, we must examine the part he ascribes to Nature in the achievement of his own poetic self-discipline. For he was to carry

1. Ibid., XII, 208, 279–80; VI, 604; II, 321–22; VII, 649. [*Editors.*] 2. XII, 272. [*Editors.*]

his conclusions on this point also into his wider moral philosophy. Let us put the question quite bluntly. What did Nature mean to Wordsworth? In many of his poems Nature stands simply for whatever he perceived and loved in the external, extra-human world. But when Wordsworth wrote of Nature in relation to the general problem of human happiness and morality he often meant something very different. He meant by it the fact that certain extra-human objects can give us that

> . . . prepossession, without which the soul
> Receives no knowledge that can bring forth good,
> No genuine insight ever comes to her.
> [VIII, 325–27]

Nature, so conceived, is a moral agency. Sometimes it seems as if Wordsworth is ready to identify Nature with a local tradition—the simple and rustic life of the Lakes. But this identification is premature and in many other passages it is clear that his notion has a far wider generality. Sometimes it seems as if Wordsworth were really speaking of the influence of actual human beings—parents, friends, teachers. But again, what is intended is not an identification but an analogy, and an analogy of which Wordsworth was particularly fond. It is significant that the famous passage on the mother's influence on her child ("Blest the infant Babe . . .")[3] occurs in the middle of a series of descriptions of how Nature surrounds the infant with invitations, encouragements, challenges and admonishments. And the similarity Wordsworth found between "Nature's gifts" and the effects of human love at its strongest and purest is by no means a far-fetched or sentimental one. For the response of a child (and not of a child only) to each of these, is seen in a disposition to look for further beauty, to move out into the world confidently and hopefully, to feel generously, to think and plan with courage. Both Nature and the mother enable the child to feel himself "an inmate of this active universe":

> For him, in one dear Presence, there exists
> A virtue which irradiates and exalts
> Objects through widest intercourse of sense.
> [II, 238–40]

It is in this passage that Wordsworth describes how the child "drinks in the feelings of his mother's eye"—as though there were a direct communication of feeling. Is it any more fanciful to claim that there is similar communication from external nature to the child? At all events, it is an obvious fact that we can come to love a

3. II, 232–65.

place because its beauties lead us to look for further beauties, to acknowledge those we see with gratitude, and to feel at home amongst them. In describing in great detail the moral effects of such experiences, Wordsworth was only retelling more fully what every poet, indeed every man of feeling, has known since humanity began.

Nature, then, for Wordsworth when he is philosophising, means the fact that the extra-human world can have an incalculable moral effect on man. What is original in Wordsworth's thought is the notion that human happiness at its best arises out of a peculiar co-operation of this external nature and man's own inner nature; out of Nature's gift and man's response.

(3) *The originality of Wordsworth's answer*

Wordsworth's conception of the availability of Nature's gifts provides in one respect an interesting parallel to the Christian doctrine of the availability of grace. On either doctrine man must give—must make an original, peculiarly human response—if he is to receive. The required response, on Wordsworth's theory, must be made in terms of gratitude and imagination; on the Christian theory in terms of repentance, obedience and love of God. A striking difference between the two theories is seen, however, when we pass from the availability of Nature's gifts or of grace to the accounts of how men actually receive them. Here Wordsworth might be described as a "naturalistic predestinarian." He felt himself specially *chosen* because Nature's gifts had been made available to him in quite an untypical way. And in so far as he thought of himself as a "dedicated spirit" this was because of a "bond" which he *himself* had not chosen to embrace. Still less does the infant choose to "drink in the feelings of his mother's eye" and thus experience "the filial bond of nature that connects him with the world." On Wordsworth's view the *moral person*, the subject to whom we can significantly apply moral predicates, the subject who can choose, is a result of that "prepossession" which is brought about by the *actual* impact of Nature's gifts on a human being. Unless they arise out of that prepossession, what we commonly think of as moral predicates are something else—legal predicates for instance. Morality for Wordsworth presupposes the *actual experience* of happiness; and this on the one hand is a natural occurrence since it derives from causes and conditions which are not in man's power to choose or control, and on the other hand is "Nature's Invitation"; for once these conditions have been realized, men can feel Nature as something to follow, to cultivate, as something demanding a self-giving in return, a moral response that is *genuine* because it has a self-accepted standard. These causes and conditions which are beyond man's power to choose or control Wordsworth finds partly in "ex-

ternal nature"—in the actual, sensible presence of beauty and
grandeur—and partly in that "prime and vital" principle which lies,
Wordsworth tells man,

> In the recesses of thy nature, far
> From any reach of outward fellowship,
> Else is not thine at all.
> [XIV, 216–18]

This is his version of "From him that hath not shall be taken away
even that which he seemeth to have." But on Wordsworth's view
"the prime and vital principle" is never called out at all in many
human beings, and that through no fault of their own; their lives,
from birth, are harnessed to "the mean and vulgar works of man."[4]
In others it is crushed out by the weight of custom and routine. It
is only those who have known true happiness who can be judged
morally.

Wordsworth's claim that moral categories apply only within certain conditions which are realized (we must suppose) comparatively
rarely in human life can be considered either a revolutionary or a
retrograde one. It appears to cancel that universality—that recognition of moral personality in every human life—which was the signal
contribution of Christian ethics. Wordsworth by contrast seems
nearer to the "aristocratic" realism—the blunt acceptance of fundamental moral differences between men—which we find in most
Greek philosophy. But Wordsworth's intention was, of course, the
exact opposite of this. His aim was to show (to apply a fine saying
of Meredith's)[5] how men are kept from having souls in *this* world.
Seen in this light his conception of Nature's gifts, which at first
seems so much narrower and more exclusive than the Christian
notion of grace, turns out perhaps to be a more just, generous,
compassionate and practical one. If there is anything harsh in
Wordsworth's moral attitude (at any rate as expressed in *The Prelude*) it lies in his refusal to identify his feelings with those of the
"lost," to slide from a recognition of the *fact* of suffering to some
kind of exaltation or justification of it. This was an issue Wordsworth had faced in life. Had he returned to France during the
terror, he tells us,

> Doubtless, I should have then made common cause
> With some who perished; haply perished too,
> A poor mistaken and bewildered offering—
> Should to the breast of Nature have gone back,
> With all my resolutions, all my hopes,

4. I, 408. [*Editors.*]
5. George Meredith (1828–1909), novelist and poet. [*Editors.*]

> A poet only to myself, to men
> Useless. . . .
>
> [X, 229–35]

A strangely original prophet of duty, Wordsworth set his face in the opposite direction—to explore and enjoy and make known to men (in language all men might understand) the way of happiness.

What then is Wordsworth's conception of happiness, and how do his two principles of gratitude and imagination contribute to it? In the first place (as I have suggested) he does not think of happiness as something to be achieved only with the full insight, the final revelation. He thinks of it as something essentially incomplete and yet at the same time self-justifying. It contains its own self-renewing inspiration and its own discipline and admonishments. Secondly, this happiness is to be found in the very world that is the world of all of us. It originates in the filial bond that connects us with this active universe: it arises out of that grand elementary principle of pleasure in which all creatures share.

Yet such happiness is not complacency, either moral or intellectual. It gives rise to the active compassion of The Wanderer who "could *afford* to suffer with those whom he saw suffer";[6] and it is the happiness of the man who wrote the Ode to Duty. Wordsworth, of course, does not put forward his "theory" of happiness systematically. But its effectivness as a moral principle can, I think, readily be seen in Wordsworth's applications of its two main components— gratitude and imagination. Gratitude, in itself a pleasurable emotion, provides, on Wordsworth's view, a constant nursing-ground for a good will; not only because it keeps us in mind of all that we owe in so far as we have become moral beings, but because it conduces both consciously and—perhaps with even greater effect—unconsciously to automatic habits of right moral action. Wordsworth wrote of his sister ("And yet I knew a Maid . . .") as one whose "*life* was gratitude."[7] But a life so conceived lacks something, lacks something morally—a bracing element which Wordsworth claimed only imagination can contribute to the moral life. Parts of this contribution we have already considered in connection with artistic self-discipline—the challenge to intellectual effort, the sense of an unlimited field awaiting human exploration, and a humbling recognition of how feebly we respond to this challenge and opportunity.

But the exercise of imagination has other more direct and obvious bearings on the moral life. For imagination alone can reveal, and when revealed keep constantly real in our minds,

> Those mysteries of being which have made,
> And shall continue evermore to make

6. *The Excursion,* I, 369–70. [*Editors.*]   7. *The Prelude,* XII, 151–73. [*Editors.*]

Of the whole human race one brotherhood.
[XII, 85–87]

In the same way only imagination can reveal those usually unsuspected beauties, harmonies—and we might add problems—in Nature which engage artists, poets, scientists, but which, when most strikingly manifested,

men least sensitive see, hear, perceive,
And cannot choose but feel: . . .
[XIV, 84–85]

In general Wordsworth would claim that imagination reveals man's highest good, incompletely in respect of its objects (for these are inexhaustible) but in its exercise as completely as we can conceive.

But does Wordsworth claim that gratitude and imagination together comprise his "way of happiness" and together give us a moral principle under which all other moral principles, sentiments, duties, can be subsumed? Or does he simply claim that they are moral principles of the first importance whose characteristic operations have generally been misunderstood or ignored? To judge from the summing up we find in Bk. XIV Wordsworth makes the former —wilder—claim. And this is, I think, a sheer mistake on his part; for, to take but one example, how can insight into fairness (surely an essential ingredient in morality) be subsumed under either gratitude or imagination? This mistake, however, which would be damaging to a "systematizing" thinker, is not really important in an original thinker who is trying to shift, or re-orientate, some of the basic categories of our thought. Had Wordsworth contented himself simply with emphasizing his two great principles, he would still, I claim, have made a revolutionary contribution both to morals and to the metaphysics of the mind.

(4) *The part played by poetry in Wordsworth's answer:*

Could not Wordsworth's conclusions as to happiness and morality have been reached by ordinary philosophic reflection? I do not know. What I do know, and what we can all see if we read *The Prelude* as it is written, as a whole and not as a series of reflective lyrics linked by skipable commentary, is that poetry—the actual occurrence of unmistakable, sometimes incomparable poetry—plays an all-important role at every stage of its argument. We have seen how Wordsworth *uses* poetry to raise his initial problem as to his own calling and duty as a poet. In illustrating his own poetic method (*The Prelude* illustrates rather than explains or defends his cult of memory) Wordsworth again makes use of poetry in a yet more obviously necessary way. Similarly, without the poems of gratitude with which *The Prelude* abounds it would be hard to grasp all that Wordsworth means by the word gratitude and almost impossible to understand how his feelings for Nature related to his feeling for traditional life. And is it conceivable that any abstract description of the lasting effects of "imaginative visitations" could compare with Wordsworth's account of what he "saw" in the Simplon Pass or with the passage on the imagination which precedes it? In applying the lessons of his own poetic self-discipline to the wider moral field, Wordsworth is, admittedly, often very prosy; but in describing his sister as one whose life was gratitude, and in his best accounts of the monstrous confusions of city life and of the individual dignities of men and households he gives us something which probably only poetry could give.

Once it is granted, therefore, that in intention (however inadequately conceived) and in effect (however incomplete) *The Prelude* is philosphical poetry, it is easy to see how its poetry helps to make, not simply to express, its philosophy. But I think that something more than this can be claimed for *The Prelude*. I would claim that it contains masterpieces of argument. The posing of its initial problem in Bk. I is an example. The central passage of the Retrospect (Bk. VIII, lines 293–339) is another. But quite the most remarkable is the conclusion of Bk. XII. What do these amazing paragraphs tell us? How does their argument proceed? Their formal structure could, I think, quite easily be traced out—and we should find some gaps in it. But we should find also, in some hundred and eighty lines of the most moving poetry ever written, a condensed statement of Wordsworth's view of how imaginative experience contributes to the foundation of morality. In the marshalling of arguments, the selection of terms, and in the judgement as to what consequences shall be drawn and what premises made explicit, it is an incomparable intellectual achievement. Can we see what factors in Wordsworth's poetic technique and vocabulary were of special assistance to him here? In broad outline, I think we can.

We may begin by considering how difficult it is to handle argument, especially abstract argument, in poetry. The poet lacks (or the exigencies of verse prevent him from using) many "logical words" which would help in delimiting his field of discourse and in summing up conclusions and condensing them for the next step forward, and so on. Because of this, Wordsworth is twice compelled to confess the inadequacy of his statements;

> I see by glimpses now . . .

> and I would give,
> While yet we may, so far as words can give. . . .
> [XII, 281–83]

And these confessions, while logically adding nothing to the argument, add a great deal to the intensity with which we are made to feel its hesitating, jerky, but superbly dramatic advance. For somewhat similar reasons Wordsworth has to resort to repetition. The beacon and the naked pool, for example, are referrred to three times in this passage; but they re-enter the argument each time with a distinguishable purpose and effect. They are first presented as features in a scene that was naturally fitted to call out imaginative experience; they are next considered as elements in a typical imaginative experience, and they are considered lastly as instances of, or carriers of, that power which such visitations leave behind. This repetition is not simply for illustrative purposes. The purpose of the passage is to make us feel the peculiarly integrating effect of every imaginative experience. The abstract words by which we try to describe or analyse this effect are, inevitably, very inadequate. They lack precision, and precision is wanted here. But by his trick of repetition Wordsworth makes his whole concern with the moorland scene work in our thought, and work at three different levels of generality; he makes us feel it on the move and catch it on the rebound. And in this way an apparent defect in the poet's vocabulary is turned into a surprising asset.

In arguments of this order Wordsworth's use of abstract words is unequalled by any other English poet. How often do not the nouns —nature, man, society, life, joy, power, base, object, influence, sense, thing, sight, and the adjectives—common, general, individual, ordinary, abstract, single, greatest, least, occur with a quite transfiguring wealth of meaning in *The Prelude!* Another aspect of this verbal mastery which contributes so much to Wordsworth's philosophical achievement is his use of verbs which possess both a practical (manipulative or motor) and a logical meaning: work, hang, unite, build, dispose, lead, follow, substitute, annul. Of course not all Wordsworth's uses of abstractions are equally happy. But an inspection of this part of Wordsworth's poetic armoury makes it hard to doubt that he possessed something of "the genius of a great philosophic poet."[8]

(5) *The verification of Wordsworth's answer and its applicability to problems*

How are the statements of an *original* moralist (i.e. one who attempts to shift our use of certain moral and metaphysical categories) to be tested and verified? I do not know; and although it seems to me perhaps the most important philosophical question that exists (as important for philosophy and for understanding what

8. S. T. Coleridge, *Table Talk* (London, 1917), entry under July 21, 1832. [*Editors.*]

philosophy is as for practical life) I do not know of a single contemporary philosopher who has seriously considered it or at least
has offered a helpful answer.

In this situation I shall consider only two points, which are certainly relevant to such verification although they by no means comprise it. First, then, an original moralist—a Plato, a Spinoza, a
Wordsworth, a Nietzsche, a Bergson, a Schweitzer—must express his
view *forcibly*; he must, as it were, screw our moral vision round in
the direction he wants us to look even if he does not persuade us
that we ought to keep looking in that direction. Wordsworth,
through his use of his own poetry, seems to me to succeed in this
first task better than any of the thinkers I have just mentioned,
Plato alone excepted. But, secondly, we must feel in any moralist
who asks us to re-orientate our whole moral outlook, that he is thus
far being "reasonable" in that, in Cartesian phrase, he has made the
widest possible reviews of all relevant moral issues and that his own
original view takes cognisance of these. It is in this respect that
Spinoza, Bergson, and Schweitzer are such impressively persuasive
moralists. They write as men of profound and masterful culture—
moral, artistic, intellectual. And here Wordsworth, by contrast, falls
short. He seems narrow and provincial. But it seems to me that it
was not Wordsworth's moral experience and sympathies that were
narrow, nor the range of his moral insights (glimpses), but his
powers of generalization and of re-applying generalized results.
Within his own chosen range Wordsworth's generalizing power was
both bold and exact, and his power of producing "individual forms
in which are embodied universal ideals and abstractions" perhaps
unrivalled. The trouble was that he did not apply his results widely
enough. But there are, I think, a number of moral and metaphysical
issues to which Wordsworth's conception of the true end of man
could be applied with immense benefit to-day: notably the problem
of evil, the problem of how moral ideals can become (and remain)
operative in political institutions, and the moral problems involved
in the acceptance of scientific standards of truth. Wordsworth, of
course, said some illuminating things on each of these issues, but his
thoughts on them never went far enough. It was not, as Dr. Leavis
has suggested, "lack of material"[9] which kept Wordsworth from
developing his philosophical poetry; it was the fact that his philosophical powers were determined by—and worked only when fed
by—his own personal poetic interests, compulsions, intuitions.

This defect is perhaps inevitable in a philosophical poet: but it is
matched in Wordsworth's case by an asset which is of more than
compensating value. The best philosophical poetry of *The Prelude*

9. See F. R. Leavis, "Wordsworth," in *Revaluation: Tradition and Development in English Poetry* (London, 1949), p. 163. [*Editors.*]

not only expresses philosophical thinking, but in an uniquely intimate way embodies it—creates the struggle of thought, raises its problems and antitheses, focusses the struggle of thought, and advances it to original conclusions. More than this, Wordsworth's characteristic method of thinking makes us aware of a corresponding defect in familiar philosophical methods when these are applied in morals or the metaphysics of the mind. For these methods almost inevitably fail to show us mind "on the move" or happiness and morality "in the making." In as much as it indicates a way of overcoming this defect *The Prelude* deserves, I think, the description which Coleridge applied (in anticipation) to *The Recluse* as a whole—"the *first* and *only* philosophical poem."[1]

1. See S. T. Coleridge to Wordsworth, May 30, 1815, in Griggs, IV, p. 574. [*Editors.*]

Bibliography of Works
Cited or Consulted

Abrams, M. H. "The Correspondent Breeze: A Romantic Metaphor," *English Romantic Poets*, ed. M. H. Abrams, 2nd ed. (New York, 1975), pp. 37–54.
———. *Natural Supernaturalism, Tradition and Revolution in Romantic Literature* (New York, 1971).
Akenside, Mark. *Poems* (London, 1772).
Arnold, Matthew. *Complete Prose Works*, ed. R. H. Super (10 vols., Michigan, 1960–74).
Aulard, A. *Histoire Politique de la Revolution* (Paris, 1901).
Bacon, Francis. *Works*, ed. J. Spedding, R. L. Ellis, and D. D. Heath (14 vols., London, 1857–74).
Barker, Felix, and Jackson, Peter. *Two Thousand Years of London* (London, 1974).
Barrow, John. *Travels in China* (London, 1804).
Bartram, William. *Travels Through North and South Carolina*, 2nd ed. (London, 1794).
Beattie, James. *The Minstrel*, Book I (London, 1771), Book II (London, 1774).
Beaumont, Sir Harry [Joseph Spence]. *Moralities* (London, 1753).
Berkeley, George. *An Essay Towards a New Theory of Vision*, revised ed. (London, 1732).
Burke, Edmund. *Reflections on the Revolution in France* (London, 1790).
Carlyle, Thomas. *Reminiscences*, ed. James Anthony Froude (New York, 1881).
Cervantes, Miguel de. *The History and Adventures of the Renowned Don Quixote*, trans. T. Smollet (2 vols., London, 1755).
Clarke, James. *A Survey of the Lakes of Cumberland, Westmorland and Lancashire* (London, 1787).
Coleridge, Samuel Taylor. *Poems*, selected and ed. John Beer, Everyman's Library, revised ed. (London, 1973).
———. *Poetical Works*, ed. E. H. Coleridge (2 vols., Oxford, 1912).
———. *Lectures 1795 on Politics and Religion*, ed. Lewis Patton and Peter Mann, *CC*, I (Princeton and London, 1971).
———. *The Watchman*, ed. Lewis Patton, *CC*, II (Princeton and London, 1970).
———. *The Friend*, ed. Barbara Rooke, *CC*, IV (2 vols., Princeton and London, 1969).
———. *Lay Sermons*, ed. R. J. White, *CC*, VI (Princeton and London, 1972).
———. *Biographia Literaria*, ed. George Watson, Everyman's Library (London, 1971).
———. *Shakespearean Criticism*, ed. T. M. Raysor (2 vols., London, 1933).
———. *Miscellaneous Criticism*, ed. T. M. Raysor (London, 1936).
———. *Notebooks*, ed. Kathleen Coburn (New York, 1957–).
———. *Letters*, ed. E. L. Griggs (6 vols., Oxford, 1956–71).
Columbus, Ferdinand. *Life and Actions of Christopher Columbus*, 1571; first English ed., *Collection of Voyages and Travels*, printed for A. and J. Churchill (4 vols., London, 1704), II, pp. 557–688.
Cottle, Joseph. *Malvern Hills* (Bristol, 1798).
Cowper, William. *Poetical Works*, ed. H. S. Milford, 4th ed., with corrections and additions by Norma Russell, Oxford Standard Authors (London, 1971).
Curtis, Jared R. *Wordsworth's Experiments with Tradition: The Lyric Poems of 1802* (Ithaca and London, 1971).
Dampier, William. *A New Voyage round the World* (London, 1697).
Darwin, Erasmus. *The Botanic Garden*, Part I, "The Economy of Vegetables" (London, 1791), Part II, "The Loves of the Plants" (London, 1789).
Day, Thomas. *The History of Sandford and Merton* (London, 1783–89).
De Quincey, Thomas. *Confessions of an English Opium Eater*, ed. Aileen Ward, Signet Classic (New York, Toronto, 1966).
———. *Recollections of the Lakes and the Lake Poets*, ed. David Wright, Penguin (London, 1970).

———. Collected Writings, new and enlarged ed., David Masson (14 vols., Edinburgh, 1889–90).

Edgeworth, Maria. The Parent's Assistant (3 vols., London, 1796).

Edgeworth, Maria, and Lovell, Richard. Practical Education (2 vols., London, 1798).

Encyclopaedia Britannica. 3d ed. (18 vols., Edinburgh, 1797).

Erdman, David. "Coleridge, Wordsworth, and the Wedgwood Fund," BNYPL, LX (1956), pp. 425–43, 487–507.

Finch, John Alban. "Wordsworth's Two-Handed Engine," Bicentenary Wordsworth Studies, ed. Jonathan Wordsworth (Ithaca and London, 1970), pp. 1–13.

Fink, Z. S. Early Wordsworthian Milieu (Oxford, 1958).

Gibbon, Edward. History of the Decline and Fall of the Roman Empire (6 vols., London, 1776–88).

Gill, Stephen. "The Two-Part Prelude of 1798–9," see Wordsworth, Jonathan.

Girtin, Thomas, and Loshak, David. The Art of Thomas Girtin (London, 1954).

Glas, George. History of the Discovery of the Canary Isles (London, 1764).

Godwin, William. An Enquiry Concerning Political Justice, 2d ed. (2 vols., London, 1796).

Gray, Thomas. Poems of Gray, Collins and Goldsmith, ed. Roger Lonsdale, Longman's Annotated English Poets (London, 1969).

Hakluyt, Richard. Principall Navigations, Voiages and Discoveries of the English Nation (London, 1589).

Hartley, David. Theory of the Human Mind, ed. Joseph Priestley (London, 1775).

Hartman, Geoffrey H. Wordsworth's Poetry, 1787–1814 (New Haven and London, 1964).

Havens, Raymond Dexter. The Mind of a Poet: A Study of Wordworth's Thought (2 vols., Baltimore, 1941).

Haydon, Benjamin Robert. Diary, ed. Willard Bissell Pope (5 vols., Cambridge, Mass., 1960–63).

Hazlitt, William. Works, ed. P. P. Howe (21 vols., London, 1930–34).

Johnson, Samuel. The History of Rasselas, Prince of Abissinia (London, 1759).

Jonson, Ben. Poems, ed. George Burke Johnston, Muses' Library (London, 1954).

Kilvert, Francis. Diary, ed. William Plomer (2 vols., London, 1938).

Lamb, Charles. Works of Charles and Mary Lamb, ed. F. V. Lucas (7 vols., London, 1903–5).

Landon, Carol. "Some Sidelights on The Prelude," Bicentenary Wordsworth Studies, ed. Jonathan Wordsworth (Ithaca and London, 1970), pp. 359–76.

Leavis, F. R. Revaluation: Tradition and Development in English Poetry (London, 1936).

Lefebvre, Georges. The French Revolution from Its Origins to 1793, trans. Elizabeth Moss Evanson (London and New York, 1962).

———. The French Revolution from 1793 to 1799, trans. John Hall Stewart and James Friguglietti (London and New York, 1964).

Legouis, Émile. The Early Life of William Wordsworth, 1770–1798, trans. J. W. Matthews (London, 1897).

———. William Wordsworth and Annette Vallon (London, 1922).

Lindenberger, Herbert. On Wordsworth's "Prelude" (Princeton, 1963).

Locke, John. Educational Writings, ed. James L. Axtell (Cambridge, 1968).

MacGillivray, J. R. "The Three Forms of The Prelude, 1798–1805," reprinted, Wordsworth, "The Prelude": A Casebook, ed. W. J. Harvey and Richard Gravil (London, 1972), pp. 99–115.

Mackintosh, James. Vindiciae Gallicae (London, 1791).

Madelin, Louis. The French Revolution, English ed. (London, 1916).

Mant, Richard [Anon.] The Simpliciad: A Satirico-didactic Poem (London, 1808).

Maxwell, James, ed. William Wordsworth, The Prelude, Penguin (London, 1971).

Milton, John. Poems, ed. John Carey and Alistair Fowler, Longman's Annotated English Poets (London, 1968).

Moorman, Mary. William Wordsworth: A Biography. The Early Years (Oxford, 1957), The Later Years (Oxford, 1965).

Newton, John [Anon.] An Authentic Narrative of Some Remarkable and Interesting Particulars in the Life of * * * * * * (London, 1764).

North, Sir Thomas. Plutarch's Lives of the Noble Grecians and Romanes, trans. from the French of J. Amyot (London, 1579).

Onorato, Richard J. The Character of the Poet: Wordsworth in "The Prelude" (Princeton, 1971).

Owen, W. J. B. "Tipu's Tiger," NQ, CCXV (1970), pp. 379–80.

————. "Annotating Wordsworth," *Editing Texts of the Romantic Period*, ed. John D. Baird (Toronto, 1972), pp. 49–71.
Park, Mungo. *Travels in the Interior Districts of Africa* (London, 1799).
Pennant, Thomas. *Tour of Scotland in 1772* (Chester, 1774).
Penrith, History of [Anon.] (Penrith, 1858).
Perrin, W. G. *British Flags: Their Early History and Development at Sea* (Cambridge, 1922).
Pope, Alexander, Twickenham Edition, ed. John Butt et al. (9 vols., London, 1961–67).
Purchas, Samuel. *Hakluytus Posthumus or Purchas His Pilgrimes* (4 vols., London, 1625; 20 vols. Hakluyt Society, Glasgow, 1905–7).
Reed, Mark L. *Wordsworth: The Chronology of the Early Years, 1770–1799* (Cambridge, Mass., 1967).
————. *Wordsworth: The Chronology of the Middle Years, 1800–1815* (Cambridge, Mass., 1975).
————. Reply to Michael C. Jaye, "John Carter and the Dating of MS. C of Wordsworth's *Prelude*" (*NQ*, CCXIII [1968], pp. 21–22), *NQ*, CCXIII, p. 468.
Robinson, Henry Crabb. *Books and their Writers*, ed. E. J. Morley (3 vols., London, 1938).
————. *Diary, Reminiscences and Correspondence of Henry Crabb Robinson*, ed. Thomas Sadler (3 vols., London, 1869).
————. *Correspondence of Henry Crabb Robinson with the Wordsworth Circle*, ed. E. J. Morley (2 vols., Oxford, 1927).
Rogers, Samuel. *Pleasures of Memory* (London, 1792).
Rousseau, Jean-Jacques. *Oeuvres Complètes*, ed. Bernard Gagnebin and Marcel Raymond (Paris, 1959–69).
Rudé, George. *Hanoverian London, 1714–1808* (London, 1971).
Sammes, Aylett. *Britannia Antiqua Illustrata* (London, 1676).
Schneider, Ben Ross, Jr. *Wordsworth's Cambridge Education* (Cambridge, 1957).
Shakespeare, William. *Complete Works*, ed. Peter Alexander (London and Glasgow, 1951).
Shaver, Chester L. "Wordsworth's Vaudracour and Wilkinson's *The Wanderer*," *RES*, n.s. XII (1961), pp. 55–57.
Six, Georges. *Dictionnaire Biographique des Généraux* (2 vols., Paris, 1934).
Smith, Adam. *An Inquiry into the Nature and Causes of the Wealth of Nations* (2 vols., London, 1776).
Smyser, Jane Worthington. "Wordsworth's dream of poetry and science," *PMLA*, LXXI (1956), pp. 269–75.
Southey, Robert, and Lovell, Robert. *Poems* (London, 1795).
Spenser, Edmund. *The Faerie Queen*, ed. J. C. Smith (2 vols., Oxford, 1909).
Stoddart, John. *Remarks on Local Scenery and Manners in Scotland* (2 vols., London, 1801).
Taylor, Henry. *Correspondence*, ed. Edward Dowden (London, 1888).
Thompson, E. P. "Disenchantment or Default? A Lay Sermon," *Power and Consciousness*, ed. Conor Cruise O'Brien and William Dean Vanech (London and New York, 1969), pp. 150–81.
Thomson, James. *Poetical Works*, ed. J. Logie Robinson, Oxford Standard Authors (Oxford, 1908).
Thompson, T. W. *Wordsworth's Hawkshead*, ed. Robert Woof (Oxford, 1970).
Ticknor, George. *Life, Letters and Journals* (2 vols., Boston, 1876).
Todd, F. M. *Politics and the Poet, A Study of Wordsworth* (London, 1957).
West, Thomas [Anon.] *The Antiquities of Furness* (London, 1774).
————. *Guide to the Lakes*, 3d ed., revised and enlarged (London, 1784).
Watson, James, ed. *A Choice Collection of Comic and Serious Scots Poems both Ancient and Modern* (Edinburgh, 1706–11).
Williams, Helen Maria. *Letters Written in France in the Summer of 1790* (London, 1790).
Wordsworth, Christopher. *Memoirs of William Wordsworth* (2 vols., London, 1851).
Wordsworth, Dora. *Letters*, ed. Howard P. Vincent (Chicago, 1944).
Wordsworth, Dorothy. *Journals*, ed. E. de Selincourt (2 vols., London, 1951).
————. *Journals*, Oxford Paperbacks, ed. Mary Moorman (London, Oxford, New York, 1971).
Wordsworth, John. *Letters*, ed. Carl H. Ketcham (Ithaca, 1969).
Wordsworth, Jonathan. *The Music of Humanity* (London and New York, 1969).
————. *Bicentenary Wordsworth Studies*, ed. (Ithaca and London, 1970).
————. "The Climbing of Snowdon," *Bicentenary Wordsworth Studies*, pp. 449–74.
————. "The Five-Book *Prelude* of Early Spring 1804," *JEGP*, LXXVI (1977), pp. 1–25.

Wordsworth, Jonathan, and Gill, Stephen. "The Two-Part *Prelude* of 1798–9," *JEGP*, LXXII (1973), pp. 503–25.

———. "Wordsworth's 'Borderers,' " *English Romantic Poets*, ed. M. H. Abrams, 2nd ed. (New York, 1975), pp. 170–87.

Wordsworth, William. *Salisbury Plain*, ed. Stephen Gill. *CW*, I (Ithaca, 1975).

———. *The Prelude*, 1798–1799, ed. Stephen Parrish. *CW*, II (Ithaca, 1977).

———. *Home at Grasmere*, ed. Beth Darlington. *CW*, III (Ithaca, 1977).

———. [*Night-Piece, Discharged Soldier*] Beth Darlington, "Two Early Texts," *Bicentenary Wordsworth Studies*, ed. Jonathan Wordsworth (Ithaca and London, 1970), pp. 425–48.

———. [*Ruined Cottage, Pedlar*] Jonathan Wordsworth, *The Music of Humanity* (London and New York, 1969).

———. *Lyrical Ballads*, ed. R. L. Brett and A. R. Jones (London, 1963).

———. [1802 lyrics] Jared R. Curtis, *Wordsworth's Experiments with Tradition* (Ithaca and London, 1971).

———. *The Prelude*, ed. Ernest de Selincourt, revised Helen Darbishire (Oxford, 1959).

———. *Poems in Two Volumes*, 1807, ed. Helen Darbishire, 2nd ed. (Oxford, 1952).

———. *Poetical Works*, ed. E. de Selincourt and Helen Darbishire (5 vols., Oxford, 1940–49).

———. *Prose Works*, ed. W.J.B. Owen and Jane Worthington Smyser (3 vols., Oxford, 1974).

———. *Prose Works*, ed. A. B. Grosart [Fenwick Notes] (3 vols., London, 1876).

———. *Letters of William and Dorothy Wordsworth*, ed. E. de Selincourt. *The Early Years, 1787–1805*, revised Chester L. Shaver (Oxford, 1967); *The Middle Years, 1806–11*, revised Mary Moorman (Oxford, 1969); *1812–20*, revised Mary Moorman and Alan Hill (Oxford, 1970); *The Later Years, 1821–50* (3 vols., Oxford, 1939).

Wright, A. R. *British Calendar Customs*, ed. T. E. Lones, Folklore Society (3 vols., London, 1936).

Young, Edward. *Night Thoughts* (London, 1750).

Selected Reading

Abrams, M. H. "The Correspondent Breeze: A Romantic Metaphor," *English Romantic Poets*, ed. M. H. Abrams, 2nd ed. (New York, 1975), pp. 37–54.
———. *Natural Supernaturalism, Tradition and Revolution in Romantic Literature* (New York, 1971).
———. *Wordsworth: A Collection of Critical Essays*, ed. M. H. Abrams (Englewood Cliffs, N.J., 1972).
Coleridge, Samuel Taylor. *Notebooks*, ed. Kathleen Coburn (New York, 1957–).
———. *Letters*, ed. E. L. Griggs (6 vols., Oxford, 1956–71).
Davie, D. "Syntax in the Blank Verse of Wordsworth's *Prelude*," *Articulate Energy* (London, 1955).
De Quincey, Thomas. *Recollections of the Lakes and the Lake Poets*, ed. David Wright, Penguin (London, 1970).
Erdman, David. "Coleridge, Wordsworth, and the Wedgwood Fund," *BNYPL*, LX (1956), pp. 425–43, 487–507.
Ferry, D. *The Limits of Mortality* (Middletown, Conn., 1959).
Finch, John Alban. "Wordsworth's Two-Handed Engine," *Bicentenary Wordsworth Studies*, ed. Jonathan Wordsworth (Ithaca and London, 1970), pp. 1–13.
Fink, Z. S. *Early Wordsworthian Milieu* (Oxford, 1958).
Hartman, Geoffrey H. *Wordsworth's Poetry, 1787–1814* (New Haven and London, 1964).
Harvey, W. J., and Gravil, R., eds. *Wordsworth: The Prelude* [Casebook Series] (London, 1972).
Havens, Raymond Dexter. *The Mind of a Poet* (2 vols., Baltimore, 1941).
Jones, J. *The Egotistical Sublime* (London, 1954).
Kroeber, K. "Wordsworth: The Personal Epic," *Romantic Narrative Art* (Madison, Wis., 1960).
Leavis, F. R. *Revaluation: Tradition and Development in English Poetry* (London, 1936).
Lefebvre, Georges. *The French Revolution from Its Origins to 1793*, trans. Elizabeth Moss Evanson (London and New York, 1962).
———. *The French Revolution from 1793 to 1799*, trans. John Hall Stewart and James Friguglietti (London and New York, 1964).
Legouis, Émile. *The Early Life of William Wordsworth, 1770–1798*, trans. J. W. Matthews (London, 1897).
Lindenberger, Herbert. *On Wordsworth's "Prelude"* (Princeton, 1963).
McConnell, Frank. *The Confessional Imagination: A Reading of Wordsworth's Prelude* (Baltimore, 1974).
MacGillivray, J. R. "The Three Forms of *The Prelude*, 1798–1805," reprinted, *Wordsworth, The Prelude*, ed. W. J. Harvey and Richard Gravil (London, 1972), pp. 99–115.
Maxwell, James, ed. William Wordsworth, *The Prelude*, Penguin (London 1971).
Moorman, Mary. *William Wordsworth: A Biography. The Early Years* (Oxford, 1957); *The Later Years* (Oxford, 1965).
Onorato, Richard J. *The Character of the Poet: Wordsworth in "The Prelude"* (Princeton, 1971).
Reed, Mark L. *Wordsworth: The Chronology of the Early Years, 1770–1799* (Cambridge, Mass., 1967).
———. *Wordsworth: The Chronology of the Middle Years, 1800–1815* (Cambridge, Mass., 1975).
Salvesen, C. *The Landscape of Memory* (London, 1965).
Schneider, Ben Ross, Jr. *Wordsworth's Cambridge Education* (Cambridge, 1957).
Thompson, E. P. "Disenchantment or Default? A Lay Sermon," *Power and Consciousness*, ed. Conor Cruise O'Brien and William Dean Vanech (London and New York, 1969), pp. 150–81.
Thompson, T. W. *Wordsworth's Hawkshead*, ed. Robert Woof (Oxford, 1970).
Todd, F. M. *Politics and the Poet, A Study of Wordsworth* (London, 1957).
Wordsworth, Dorothy. *Journals*, Oxford Paperbacks, ed. Mary Moorman (London, Oxford, New York, 1971).

Wordsworth, Jonathan. *The Music of Humanity* (London and New York, 1969).
―――. *Bicentenary Wordsworth Studies*, ed. (Ithaca and London, 1970).
―――. "The Climbing of Snowdon," *Bicentenary Wordsworth Studies*, pp. 449–74.
―――. "Wordsworth's 'Borderers,'" *English Romantic Poets*, ed. M. H. Abrams, 2nd ed. (New York, 1975), pp. 170–87.
―――. "The Five-Book *Prelude* of Early Spring 1804," *JEGP*, LXXVI (1977), pp. 1–25.
―――. and Gill, Stephen. "The Two-Part *Prelude* of 1798–9," *JEGP*, LXXII (1973), pp. 503–25.
Wordsworth, William. *Salisbury Plain*, ed. Stephen Gill. *CW*, I (Ithaca, 1975).
―――. *The Prelude, 1798–1799*, ed. Stephen Parrish. *CW*, II (Ithaca, 1977).
―――. *Home at Grasmere*, ed. Beth Darlington. *CW*, III (Ithaca, 1977).
―――. *Lyrical Ballads*, ed. R. L. Brett and A. R. Jones (London, 1963).
―――. [1802 lyrics] Jared R. Curtis, *Wordsworth's Experiments with Tradition* (Ithaca and London, 1971).
―――. *The Prelude*, ed. Ernest de Selincourt, revised Helen Darbishire (Oxford, 1959).
―――. *Poems in Two Volumes*, 1807, ed. Helen Darbishire, 2nd ed. (Oxford, 1952).
―――. *Poetical Works*, ed. E. de Selincourt and Helen Darbishire (5 vols., Oxford, 1940–49).
―――. *Prose Works*, ed. W.J.B. Owen and Jane Worthington Smyser (3 vols., Oxford, 1974).
―――. *Letters of William and Dorothy Wordsworth*, ed. E. de Selincourt. *The Early Years, 1787–1805*, revised Chester L. Shaver (Oxford, 1967); *The Middle Years, 1806–11*, revised Mary Moorman (Oxford, 1969); *1812–20*, revised Mary Moorman and Alan Hill (Oxford, 1970); *The Later Years, 1821–50* (3 vols., Oxford, 1939).